One World,
Many Cultures

One World, Many Cultures

Fourth Edition

◆

STUART HIRSCHBERG

Rutgers: The State University of New Jersey, Newark

TERRY HIRSCHBERG

New York   San Francisco   Boston
London   Toronto   Sydney   Tokyo   Singapore   Madrid
Mexico City   Munich   Paris   Cape Town   Hong Kong   Montreal

Vice President: Eben W. Ludlow
Editorial Assistant: Grace Trudo
Executive Marketing Manager: Lisa Kimball
Editorial Production Service: Marbern House
Manufacturing Buyer: Suzanne Lareau
Cover Administrator: Linda Knowles
Electronic Composition: Omegatype Typography, Inc.

Library of Congress Cataloging-in-Publication Data

One world, many cultures / [compiled by] Stuart Hirschberg, Terry
 Hirschberg.—4th ed.
      p. cm.
   Includes bibliographical references and indexes.
   ISBN 0-205-31841-X
      1. College readers.   2. Pluralism (Social sciences)—Problems, exercises,
etc.   3. Ethnic groups—Problems, exercises, etc.   4. English language—
Rhetoric.   5. Readers—Social sciences.   I. Hirschberg, Stuart.
II. Hirschberg, Terry

   PE1417.O57   2000
   808'.0427—dc21   99-045189

Printed in the United States of America
10   9   8   7   6   5   4   3   05   04   03   02   01

In memory of
Robert Kaplan—
Rutgers thanks you.

Contents

2   Coming of Age   91

3   How Culture Shapes Gender Roles   149

8 Customs, Rituals, and Sports   464

Preface

This fourth edition of *One World, Many Cultures* is a global, contemporary reader whose international and multicultural selections offer a new direction for freshman composition courses.

In eight thematic chapters, consisting of sixty readings (thirty-four of which are new to this edition) by internationally recognized writers from thirty-one countries, we explore cultural differences and displacement in relation to race, class, gender, region, and nation. *One World, Many Cultures* also reflects the emphasis on cultural studies and autobiography that has become an integral part of many college programs since the third edition.

The selections challenge readers to see similarities between their own experiences and the experiences of others in radically different cultural circumstances. Compelling and provocative writings by authors from the Caribbean, Africa, Asia, Europe, South America, and Central America reflect the cultural and ethnic heritage of many students.

The forty-four nonfiction selections include diaries, essays, interviews, autobiographies, prison memoirs, and speeches. These and the sixteen short stories encourage readers to perceive the relationship between a wide range of experiences in different cultures and the corresponding experiences of writers within the United States. The fourth edition of *One World, Many Cultures* continues to provide a rich sampling of accounts by writers who are native to the cultures that they describe, allowing the reader to hear authentic voices rather than filtered journalistic reports.

New to This Edition

Over half the selections are new to this edition. Many have never been previously anthologized.

Eight new short works of fiction, many of which have been recently published, represent a wide variety of cultural and ethnic backgrounds.

Kazuo Ishiguro	"Family Supper"
Saida Hagi-Dirie Herzi	"Against the Pleasure Principle"
Jerzy Kosinski	"The Miller's Tale"
Mahasweta Devi	"Giribala"
Machado de Assis	"A Canary's Ideas"
Liliana Heker	"The Stolen Party"

Milorad Pavić   "The Wedgwood Tea Set"
H. G. Wells   "The Country of the Blind"

Half the readings are by women writers.

Chapter Descriptions

The eight chapters move from the most personal sphere of family life, through adolescent turning points, questions of sexual identity, responsibilities of working, and conflicts of class and race, to the more encompassing dimensions of citizenship, emigration, and social customs.

Chapter 1, "The Family in Different Cultures," introduces families in India, Morocco, Japan, and China and, within the United States, an African American family and a Mexican American family, among others. These selections illustrate that the family, whether defined as a single-parent household, a nuclear family, or the extended family of an entire community, passes on the mores and values of a particular culture to the next generation.

Chapter 2, "Coming of Age," provides insights into both formal and informal rites of passage, initiation ceremonies, and moments of discovery in the lives of a Chinese American girl, a Polish American woman, a Somalian writer, a Maasai warrior and young boys in Ireland and war-torn Poland, and an adventurer in Borneo.

Chapter 3, "How Culture Shapes Gender Roles," explores the role of culture in shaping sexual identity. Readers can gain insight into how gender roles are culturally conditioned rather than biologically determined. The extent to which sex role expectations, both heterosexual and homosexual, differ from culture to culture can be seen in societies as diverse as those of Puerto Rico, Japan, Lebanon, Botswana, India, and the United States.

Chapter 4, "How Work Creates Identity," explores work as a universal human experience through which we define ourselves and others. The role of culture in shaping attitudes toward work can be seen in the different experiences of a female auto mechanic in Vermont and a Mexican American rock blaster. We can share the work experiences of a disillusioned Japanese corporate employee, an American housecleaner who joins a cleaning commune in Japan, a sex show performer in Bangkok, a popular martial arts film star in Hong Kong, an Indian novelist turned filmmaker, and a Brazilian, self-proclaimed ornithologist who becomes obsessed by his work.

Chapter 5, "Class and Caste," takes up the crucial and often unrecognized relationships between race, identity, and social class through readings that explore positions of power and powerlessness. Selections include Jo Goodwin Parker's poignant revelation of what it means to be poor in the southern United States and Mahdokht Kashkuli's story of a family in modern-day Iran who must place one of their children in an orphanage. The voices heard are those of men and women of many races in several nations, including Antonio, a teen-age contract killer in Colombia's drug capital, Medellín. Unusual perspectives on class issues are provided by Mary Crow Dog's account of her experiences in a government-run school for Native Americans, Viramma's account of her life as an "untouchable" in south India, Lee Stringer's recollection as an African American of being homeless in New York City, and Liliana Heker's bittersweet story of a maid's daughter in Argentina who must come to terms with her place in society.

Chapter 6, "The Individual in Society," looks at the resilience and courage of ordinary citizens pitted against civil war in the Balkans, and state tyranny in the China of Mao Tse-tung during the Cultural Revolution and in Italy during Nazi occupation. We hear the voices of writers of conscience and survivors of oppressive regimes in Chile, in Kenya during British colonial rule, in contemporary Pakistan, and in Cyprus during the liberation struggle against the British.

Chapter 7, "Strangers in a Strange Land," explores the condition of exiles, whether refugees, immigrants, or travelers, who are caught between two cultures but are at home in neither. The need of those who have left home to make sense of their lives in a new place is a theme explored by Claire Chow, Luis Alberto Urrea, Gloria Anzaldúa, Jesse W. Nash, Palden Gyatso, David R. Counts, and H. G. Wells.

Chapter 8, "Customs, Rituals, and Sports," focuses on the role that ritual, religion, and various social practices, such as sports, play in shaping social behavior. The decisive influence of cultural values is explored through an analysis of the unusual culinary practices of the Chinese, how the importance of good teeth differs between the United States and East Europe, the meaning of fiestas in Mexico, and the role of voodoo in Haitian society. We gain insight into the role that rituals and sports play in accounts of competitive stone-lifting in the Basque region, the place of revenge in Bedouin culture, and how a family in Botswana resorted to an outlawed tribal ritual to produce rain.

Editorial Apparatus

A fifteen-page introduction covers the important aspects of critical reading, keeping a journal, and responding to the text and includes a sample selection by Edward T. Hall ("Hidden Culture") for students to annotate. Chapter introductions discuss the theme of each chapter as related to the individual selections. Biographical sketches preceding each selection give background information on the writer's life and identify the cultural, historical, and personal context in which the selection was written. Relevant background information is provided for all countries before the selections.

The questions that follow each selection are designed to encourage readers to discover relationships between personal experiences and ideas in the text, to explore points of agreement and areas of conflict sparked by the viewpoints of the authors, and to provide ideas for further research and inquiry.

The first set of questions, "Evaluating the Text," asks readers to think critically about the content, meaning, and purpose of the selections and to evaluate the author's rhetorical strategy, voice projected in relationship to his or her audience, evidence cited, and underlying assumptions.

The questions in "Exploring Different Perspectives" focus on relationships between readings within each chapter that illuminate differences and similarities between cultures. These questions encourage readers to make connections between diverse cultures, to understand the writer's values and beliefs, to enter into the viewpoints of others, and to understand how culture shapes perception and a sense of self.

The questions in "Extending Viewpoints through Writing" invite readers to extend their thinking by seeing wider relationships between themselves and others through writing of many different kinds, including personal or expressive as well as expository and persuasive writing and more formal research papers.

Following each chapter, "Connecting Cultures" challenges readers to make connections and comparisons among selections within the chapter and throughout the book. These questions provide opportunities to consider additional cross-cultural perspectives on a single issue or to explore a particular topic in depth.

A rhetorical index, a geographical index, a pronunciation key to author's names, and a map of the world identifying the countries mentioned in the selections are included to allow the text to accommodate a variety of teaching approaches.

Instructor's Manual

An *Instructor's Manual* provides guidelines for using the text and teaching short works of fiction, supplemental bibliographies of books and periodicals, suggested answers to discussion questions in the text, relevant websites and films, and additional activities, which include optional discussion questions and, in some cases, suggested answers and classroom activities.

Acknowledgments

Once again, we want to acknowledge our appreciation for the encouragement and sound advice of our editor, Eben W. Ludlow, and our

gratitude to all those teachers of composition who offered their
thoughtful comments and gave this fourth edition the benefit of their
scholarship and teaching experience. We very much want to thank the
following reviewers who suggested changes for this edition: Michael
G. Franz, Grand Rapids Community College; Edith M. Baker, Bradley
University; Michele Geslin Small, Northland College; and C. Kay Cre-
celius, Mineral Area College.

For their dedication and skill, we owe much to Allyn and Bacon's
able staff. We are most grateful, once again, to Fred T. Courtright for his
outstanding work as permissions editor.

One World,
Many Cultures

◆

Introduction

◆

Critical Reading for Ideas and Organization

One of the most important skills to have in your repertoire is the ability to survey unfamiliar articles, essays, or excerpts and to come away with an accurate understanding of what the author wanted to communicate and how the material is organized. On the first and in subsequent readings of any of the selections in this text, especially the longer ones, pay particular attention to the title, look for introductory and concluding paragraphs (with special emphasis on the author's statement or restatement of central ideas), identify the headings and subheadings (and determine the relationship between these and the title), and identify any unusual terms necessary to fully understand the author's concepts.

As you work your way through an essay, you might look for cues to enable you to recognize the main parts of the argument or help you perceive the overall organization of the article. Once you find the main thesis, underline it. Then work your way through fairly rapidly, identifying the main ideas and the sequence in which they are presented. As you identify an important idea, ask yourself how this idea relates to the thesis statement you underlined or to the idea expressed in the title.

Finding a Thesis

Finding a thesis involves discovering the idea that serves as the focus of the essay. The thesis is often stated in the form of a single sentence that asserts the author's response to an issue that others might respond to in different ways. For example, the opening paragraphs of "The Little Emperors" presents Daniela Deane's assessment of an important aspect of contemporary Chinese society:

> The one-child campaign, a strict national directive that seeks to limit each Chinese couple to a single son or daughter, has other dramatic consequences: millions of abortions, fewer girls and a generation of spoiled children.

This thesis represents the writer's view of a subject or topic from a certain perspective. Here, Deane states a view of China's one-child policy that will serve as a focus for her essay. Writers often place the thesis in the first paragraph or group of paragraphs so that the readers will be able to perceive the relationship between the supporting evidence and this main idea.

As you read, you might wish to underline the topic sentence or main idea of each paragraph or section (since key ideas are often developed over the course of several paragraphs). Jot it down in your own words in the margins, identify supporting statements and evidence (such as examples, statistics, and the testimony of authorities), and try to discover how the author organizes the material to support the development of important ideas. To identify supporting material, look for any ideas more specific than the main idea that is used to support it. Also look for instances where the author uses examples, descriptions, statistics, quotations from authorities, comparisons, or graphs to make the main idea clearer or prove it to be true.

Pay particular attention to important transitional words, phrases, or paragraphs to better see the relationships among major sections of the selection. Noticing how certain words or phrases act as transitions to link paragraphs or sections together will dramatically improve your reading comprehension. Also look for section summaries, where the author draws together several preceding ideas.

Writers use certain words to signal the starting point of an argument. If you detect any of the following terms, look for the main idea they introduce:

> since, because, for, as, follows from, as shown by, inasmuch as, otherwise, as indicated by, the reason is that, for the reason that, may be inferred from, may be derived from, may be deduced from, in view of the fact that

An especially important category of words is that which includes signals that the author will be stating a conclusion. Words to look for are these:

> therefore, hence, thus, so, accordingly, in consequence, it follows that, we may infer, I conclude that, in conclusion, in summary, which shows that, which means that, and which entails, consequently, proves that, as a result, which implies that, which allows us to infer, points to the conclusion that

You may find it helpful to create a running dialogue with the author in the margins, posing and then trying to answer the basic questions *who, what, where, when,* and *why,* and to note observations on how the main idea of the article is related to the title. These notes can later be used to evaluate how effectively any specific section contributes to the overall line of thought.

Responding to What You Read

When reading an essay that seems to embody a certain value system, try to examine any assumptions or beliefs the writer expects the audience to share. How is this assumption related to the author's purpose? If you do not agree with these assumptions, has the writer provided sound reasons and evidence to persuade you to change your mind?

You might describe the author's tone or voice and try to assess how much it contributed to the essay. How effectively does the writer use authorities, statistics, or examples to support the claim? Does the author identify the assumptions or values on which his or her views are based? Are they ones with which you would agree or disagree? To what extent does the author use the emotional connotations of language to try to persuade his or her reader? Do you see anything unworkable or disadvantageous about the solutions offered as an answer to the problem the essay addresses? All these and many other ways of analyzing someone else's essay can be used to create your own. Here are some specific guidelines to help you.

When evaluating an essay, consider what the author's purpose was in writing it. Was it to inform, explain, solve a problem, make a recommendation, amuse, enlighten, or achieve some combination of these goals? How is the tone or voice the author projects toward the reader related to his or her purpose in writing the essay?

You may find it helpful to write short summaries after each major section to determine whether you understand what the writer is trying to communicate. These summaries can then serve as a basis for an analysis of how successfully the author employs reasons, examples, statistics, and expert testimony to support and develop his or her main points.

For example, if the essay you are analyzing cites authorities to support a claim, assess whether the authorities bring the most timely opinions to bear on the subject or display any obvious biases, and determine whether they are experts in that particular field. Watch for experts described as "often quoted" or "highly placed reliable sources" without accompanying names, credentials, or appropriate documentation. If the experts cited offer what purports to be a reliable interpretation of facts, consider whether the writer also quotes equally trustworthy experts who hold opposing views.

If statistics are cited to support a point, judge whether they derive from verifiable and trustworthy sources. Also, evaluate whether the author has interpreted them in ways that are beneficial to his or her case, whereas someone who held an opposing view could interpret them quite differently. If real-life examples are presented to support the author's opinions, determine whether they are representative or whether they are too atypical to be used as evidence. If the author relies on hypothetical examples or analogies to dramatize ideas that otherwise would be hard to grasp, judge whether these examples are too farfetched to back up the claims being made. If the essay depends on the stipulated definition of a term that might be defined in different ways, check whether the author provides clear reasons to indicate why one definition rather than another is preferable.

As you list observations about the various elements of the article you are analyzing, take a closer look at the underlying assumptions and see whether you can locate and distinguish between those assumptions that are explicitly stated and those that are implicit. Once the author's assumptions are identified, you can compare them with your own beliefs about the subject, determine whether these assumptions are commonly held, and make a judgment as to their validity. Would you readily agree with these assumptions? If not, has the author provided sound reasons and supporting evidence to persuade you to change your mind?

Marking as You Read

The most effective way to think about what you read is to make notes as you read. Making notes as you read forces you to go slowly and think carefully about each sentence. This process is sometimes called annotating the text, and all you need is a pen or a pencil. There are as many styles of annotating as there are readers, and you will discover your own favorite technique once you have done it a few times. Some readers prefer to underline major points or statements and jot down their reactions to them in the margin. Others prefer to summarize each paragraph or section to help them follow the author's line of thinking. Other readers circle key words or phrases necessary to understand the main ideas. Feel free to use your notes as a kind of conversation with the text. Ask questions. Express doubts. Mark unfamiliar words or phrases to look up later. If the paragraphs are not already numbered, you might wish to number them as you go to help you keep track of your responses. Try to distinguish the main ideas from supporting points and examples. Most importantly, go slowly and think about what you are reading. Try to discover whether the author makes a credible case for the conclusions he or she reaches. One last point: take a close look at the idea expressed in the title before and after you read the essay to see how it relates to the main idea.

Distinguishing between Fact and Opinion

As you read, distinguish between statements of fact and statements of opinion. Statements of fact relate information that is widely accepted and objectively verifiable; facts are used as evidence to support the claim made by the thesis. By contrast, an opinion is a personal interpretation of data or a belief or feeling that however strongly presented should not be mistaken by the reader for objective evidence. For example, consider the following claim by Edward T. Hall in "Hidden Culture":

> Each culture and each country has its own language of space, which is just as unique as the spoken language, frequently more so. In England, for example, there are no offices for the members of Parliament. In the United States, our congressmen and senators proliferate their offices and their office buildings and simply would not tolerate a no-office situation.

The only statement that could be verified or refuted on the basis of objective data is "In England...there are no offices for the members of Parliament." All the the other statements, *however persuasive they may seem,* are Hall's interpretations of a situation (multiple offices and office buildings for U.S. government officials) that might be interpreted quite differently by another observer. These statements should not be mistaken for statements of fact.

A reader who could not distinguish between facts and interpretations would be at a severe disadvantage in understanding Hall's essay. Part of the difficulty in separating fact from opinion stems from the difficulty of remaining objective about statements that match our own personal beliefs.

Take a few minutes to read and annotate the following essay. Feel free to "talk back" to the author. You can underline or circle key passages or key terms. You can make observations, raise questions, and express your reactions to what you read.

A SAMPLE ESSAY FOR STUDENT ANNOTATION

Edward T. Hall

Hidden Culture

———————◆———————

1   A few years ago, I became involved in a sequence of events in Japan that completely mystified me, and only later did I learn how an overt act seen from the vantage point of one's own culture can have an entirely different meaning when looked at in the context of the foreign culture. I had been staying at a hotel in downtown Tokyo that had European as well as Japanese-type rooms. The clientele included a few Europeans but was predominantly Japanese. I had been a guest for about ten days and was returning to my room in the middle of an afternoon. Asking for my key at the desk, I took the elevator to my floor. Entering the room, I immediately sensed that something was wrong. Out of place. Different. I was in the wrong room! Someone else's things were distributed around the head of the bed and the table. Somebody else's toilet articles (those of a Japanese male) were in the bathroom. My first thoughts were, "What if I am discovered here? How do I explain my presence to a Japanese who may not even speak English?"

2   I was close to panic as I realized how incredibly territorial we in the West are. I checked my key again. Yes, it really was mine. Clearly they had moved somebody else into my room. But where was my room now? And where were my belongings? Baffled and mystified, I took the elevator to the lobby. Why hadn't they told me at the desk, instead of letting me risk embarrassment and loss of face by being caught in somebody else's room? Why had they moved me in the first place? It was a nice room and, being sensitive to spaces and how they work, I was loath to give it up. After all, I had told them I would be in the hotel for almost a month. Why this business of moving me around like someone who has been squeezed in without a reservation? Nothing made sense.

3   At the desk I was told by the clerk, as he sucked in his breath in deference (and embarrassment?) that indeed they had moved me. My particular room had been reserved in advance by somebody else. I was given the key to my new room and discovered that all my personal ef-

fects were distributed around the new room almost as though I had done it myself. This produced a fleeting and strange feeling that maybe I wasn't myself. How could somebody else do all those hundred and one little things just the way I did?

Three days later, I was moved again, but this time I was prepared. 4
There was no shock, just the simple realization that I had been moved and that it would now be doubly difficult for friends who had my old room number to reach me. *Tant pis,* I was in Japan. One thing did puzzle me. Earlier, when I had stayed at Frank Lloyd Wright's Imperial Hotel for several weeks, nothing like this had ever happened. What was different? What had changed? Eventually I got used to being moved and would even ask on my return each day whether I was still in the same room.

Later, at Hakone, a seaside resort where I was visiting with friends, 5
the first thing that happened was that we were asked to disrobe. We were given *okatas,* and our clothes were taken from us by the maid. (For those who have not visited Japan, the okata is a cotton print kimono.) We later learned, when we ventured out in the streets, that it was possible to recognize other guests from our hotel because we had all been equipped with identical okatas. (Each hotel had its own characteristic, clearly recognizable pattern.) Also, I noted that it was polite to wave or nod to these strangers from the same hotel.

Following Hakone, we visited Kyoto, site of many famous temples 6
and palaces, and the ancient capital of Japan.

There we were fortunate enough to stay in a wonderful little coun- 7
try inn on the side of a hill overlooking the town. Kyoto is much more traditional and less industrialized than Tokyo. After we had been there about a week and had thoroughly settled into our new Japanese surroundings, we returned one night to be met at the door by an apologetic manager who was stammering something. I knew immediately that we had been moved, so I said, "You had to move us. Please don't let this bother you, because we understand. Just show us to our new rooms and it will be all right." Our interpreter explained as we started to go through the door that we weren't in that hotel any longer but had been moved to *another* hotel. What a blow! Again, without warning. We wondered what the new hotel would be like, and with our descent into the town our hearts sank further. Finally, when we could descend no more, the taxi took off into a part of the city we hadn't seen before. No Europeans here! The streets got narrower and narrower until we turned into a side street that could barely accommodate the tiny Japanese taxi into which we were squeezed. Clearly this was a hotel of another class. I found that, by then, I was getting a little paranoid, which is easy enough to do in a foreign land, and said to myself, "They must think we are very low-status people indeed to treat us this way."

8   As it turned out, the neighborhood, in fact the whole district, showed us an entirely different side of life from what we had seen before, much more interesting and authentic. True, we did have some communication problems, because no one was used to dealing with foreigners, but few of them were serious.

9   Yet, the whole matter of being moved like a piece of derelict luggage puzzled me. In the United States, the person who gets moved is often the lowest-ranking individual. This principle applies to all organizations, including the Army. Whether you can be moved or not is a function of your status, your performance, and your value to the organization. To move someone without telling him is almost worse than an insult, because it means he is below the point at which feelings matter. In these circumstances, moves can be unsettling and damaging to the ego. In addition, moves themselves are often accompanied by great anxiety, whether an entire organization or a small part of an organization moves. What makes people anxious is that the move usually presages organizational changes that have been coordinated with the move. Naturally, everyone wants to see how he comes out vis-à-vis everyone else. I have seen important men refuse to move into an office that was six inches smaller than someone else's of the same rank. While I have heard some American executives say they wouldn't employ such a person, the fact is that in actual practice, unless there is some compensating feature, the significance of space as a communication is so powerful that no employee in his right mind would allow his boss to give him a spatial demotion—unless of course he had already reached his crest and was on the way down.

10   These spatial messages are not simply conventions in the United States—unless you consider the size of your salary check a mere convention, or where your name appears on the masthead of a journal. Ranking is seldom a matter that people take lightly, particularly in a highly mobile society like that in the United States. Each culture and each country has its own language of space, which is just as unique as the spoken language, frequently more so. In England, for example, there are no offices for the members of Parliament. In the United States, our congressmen and senators proliferate their offices and their office buildings and simply would not tolerate a no-office situation. Constituents, associates, colleagues, and lobbyists would not respond properly. In England, status is internalized; it has its manifestations and markers—the upper-class received English accent, for example. We in the United States, a relatively new country, externalize status. The American in England has some trouble placing people in the social system, while the English can place each other quite accurately by reading ranking cues, but in general tend to look down on the importance that Americans attach to space. It is very easy and very natural to look at things from

one's own point of view and to read an event as though it were the same all over the world.

I knew that my emotions on being moved out of my room in Tokyo   11
were of the gut type and quite strong. There was nothing intellectual about my initial response. Although I am a professional observer of cultural patterns, I had no notion of the meaning attached to being moved from hotel to hotel in Kyoto. I was well aware of the strong significance of moving in my own culture, going back to the time when the new baby displaces older children, right up to the world of business, where a complex dance is performed every time the organization moves to new quarters.

What was happening to me in Japan as I rode up and down eleva-   12
tors with various keys gripped in my hand was that I was reacting with the cultural part of my brain—the old, mammalian brain. Although my new brain, my symbolic brain—the neocortex—was saying something else, my mammalian brain kept repeating, "You are being treated shabbily." My neocortex was trying to fathom what was happening. Needless to say, neither part of the brain had been programmed to provide me with the answer in Japanese culture. I did have to put up a strong fight with myself to keep from interpreting what was going on as though the Japanese were the same as I. This is the conventional and most common response and one that is often found even among anthropologists. Any time you hear someone say, "Why *they* are no different than the folks back home—they are just like I am," even though you may understand the reasons behind these remarks you also know that the speaker is living in a single-context world (his own) and is incapable of describing either his world or the foreign one.

The "they are just like the folks back home" syndrome is one of the   13
most persistent and widely held misconceptions of the Western world, if not the whole world. There is very little any outsider can do about this, because it expresses views that are very close to the core of the personality. Simply talking about "cultural differences" and how we must respect them is a hollow cliché. And in fact, intellectualizing isn't much more helpful either, at least at first. The logic of the man who won't move into an office that is six inches smaller than his rival's is *cultural* logic; it works at a lower, more basic level in the brain, a part of the brain that synthesizes but does not verbalize. The response is a total response that is difficult to explain to someone who doesn't already understand, because it is so dependent on context for correct interpretation. To do so, one must explain the entire system; otherwise, the man's behavior makes little sense. He may even appear to be acting childishly—which he most definitely is not.

It was my preoccupation with my own cultural mold that ex-   14
plained why I was puzzled for years about the significance of being

moved around in Japanese hotels. The answer finally came after further experiences in Japan and many discussions with Japanese friends. In Japan, one has to "belong" or he has no identity. When a man joins a company, he does just that—joins himself to the corporate body—and there is even a ceremony marking the occasion. Normally, he is hired for life, and the company plays a much more paternalistic role than in the United States. There are company songs, and the whole company meets frequently (usually at least once a week) for purposes of maintaining corporate identity and morale.

15   As a tourist (either European or Japanese) when you go on a tour, you *join* that tour and follow your guide everywhere as a group. She leads you with a little flag that she holds up for all to see. Such behavior strikes Americans as sheeplike; not so the Japanese. The reader may say that this pattern holds in Europe, because there people join Cook's tours and the American Express tours, which is true. Yet there is a big difference. I remember a very attractive young American woman who was traveling with the same group I was with in Japan. At first she was charmed and captivated, until she had spent several days visiting shrines and monuments. At this point, she observed that she could not take the regimentation of Japanese life. Clearly, she was picking up clues, such as the fact that our Japanese group, when it moved, marched in a phalanx rather than moving as a motley mob with stragglers. There was much more discipline in these sightseeing groups than the average Westerner is either used to or willing to accept.

16   It was my lack of understanding of the full impact of what it means to belong to a high-context culture that caused me to misread hotel behavior at Hakone. I should have known that I was in the grip of a pattern difference and that the significance of all guests being garbed in the same okata meant more than that an opportunistic management used the guests to advertise the hotel. The answer to my puzzle was revealed when a Japanese friend explained what it means to be a guest in a hotel. As soon as you register at the desk, you are no longer an outsider; instead, for the duration of your stay you are a member of a large, mobile family. *You belong.* The fact that I was moved was tangible evidence that I was being treated as a family member—a relationship in which one can afford to be "relaxed and informal and not stand on ceremony." This is very highly prized state in Japan, which offsets the official properness that is so common in public. Instead of putting me down, they were treating me as a member of the family. Needless to say, the large, luxury hotels that cater to Americans, like Wright's Imperial Hotel, have discovered that Americans do tenaciously stand on ceremony and want to be treated as they are at home in the States. Americans don't like to be moved around; it makes them anxious. Therefore, the Japanese in these establishments have learned not to treat them as family members.

Keeping a Reading Journal

The most effective way to keep track of your thoughts and impressions and to review what you have learned is to start a reading journal. The comments you record in your journal may express your reflections, observations, questions, and reactions to the essays you read. Normally, your journal would not contain lecture notes from class. A reading journal will allow you to keep a record of your progress during the term and can also reflect insights you gain during class discussions and questions you may want to ask, as well as unfamiliar words you intend to look up. Keeping a reading journal becomes a necessity if your composition course will require you to write a research paper that will be due at the end of the semester. Keep in mind that your journal is not something that will be corrected or graded, although some instructors may wish you to share your entries with the class.

TURNING ANNOTATIONS INTO JOURNAL ENTRIES

Although there is no set form for what a journal should look like, reading journals are most useful for converting your brief annotations into more complete entries that explore in depth your reactions to what you have read. Interestingly, the process of turning your annotations into journal entries will often produce surprising insights that will give you a new perspective. For example, a student who annotated Edward T. Hall's "Hidden Culture" converted them into the following journal entries:

- Hall's personal experiences in Japan made him realize that interpreting an action depends on what culture you're from.
- Hall assumes hotels should treat long-term guests with more respect than overnight guests. "Like someone who had been squeezed in without a reservation" shows Hall's feelings.
- What does having your clothes replaced with an okata—cotton robe—have to do with being moved from room to room in a hotel? The plot thickens!
- The hotel in Hakone encourages guests—all wearing the same robes—to greet each other outside the hotel in a friendly, not formal, manner.
- Hall says that in America, size of office = personal value and salary. Hall compared how space works in the United States in order to understand Japanese attitudes towards space.
- Thesis—"culturally defined attitudes toward space are different for each culture." Proves this by showing how unimportant space is to members of Parliament in England when compared

with the great importance office size has for U.S. congresspersons and senators.

- Hall is an anthropologist. He realizes his reactions are instinctual. Hall wants to refute the idea that people are the same all over the world. Says that which culture you are from determines your attitudes and behavior.
- He learns from Japanese friends that workers are hired for life and view their companies as family. Would this be for me? In Japan, group identity is all-important.
- Hall describes two tour groups, one Japanese and one American, as an example of Japanese acceptance of regimentation, whereas Americans go off on their own.
- The answer to the mystery of why he was being moved: moving him meant he was accepted as a member of the hotel family. They were treating him informally, as if he were Japanese: a compliment, not an insult. Informality is highly valued because the entire culture is based on the opposite—regimentation and conformity.

SUMMARIZING

Reading journals may also be used to record summaries of the essays you read. The value of summarizing is that it requires you to pay close attention to the reading in order to distinguish the main points from the supporting details. Summarizing tests your understanding of the material by requiring you to restate, concisely, the author's main ideas in your own words. First, create a list composed of sentences that express in your own words the essential idea of each paragraph, or each group of related paragraphs. Your previous underlining of topic sentences, main ideas, and key terms (as part of the process of critical reading) will help you follow the author's line of thought. Next, whittle down this list still further by eliminating repetitive ideas. Then formulate a thesis statement that expresses the main idea behind the article. Start your summary with this thesis statement, and combine your notes so that the summary flows together and reads easily.

Remember that summaries should be much shorter than the original text (whether the original is one page or twenty pages long) and should accurately reflect the central ideas of the article in as few words as possible. Try not to intrude your own opinions or critical evaluations into the summary. Besides requiring you to read the original piece more closely, summaries are necessary first steps in developing papers that synthesize materials from different sources. The test for a good summary, of course, is whether a person reading it without having read the original article would get an accurate, balanced, and complete account of the original material.

Writing an effective summary is easier if you first compose a rough summary, using no more than two complete sentences to summarize each of the paragraphs or group of paragraphs in the original article. A student's rough summary of Hall's essay might appear as follows. Numbers show which paragraphs are summarized from the article.

1–3 Hall describes how a seemingly inexplicable event that occurred while he was staying in a Tokyo hotel, frequented mostly by Japanese, led him to understand that the same action can have a completely different significance from another culture's perspective. Without telling him, the hotel management had moved his personal belongings to a new room and had given his room to another guest.

4 Three days later when Hall is again moved without warning, he is less startled but begins to wonder why this had never happened during his stay at Frank Lloyd Wright's Imperial Hotel in Tokyo.

5 At another hotel in Hakone, Hall is given an *okata*, a kind of cotton robe, to wear instead of his clothes and is encouraged to greet other guests wearing the same *okata* when he sees them outside the hotel.

6–7 At a third hotel, a country inn near Kyoto, Hall discovers that he has been moved again, this time to an entirely different hotel in what he initially perceives to be a less desirable section of town. Hall interprets this as an insult and becomes angry that the Japanese see him as someone who can be moved around without asking his permission.

8 The neighborhood he had initially seen as less desirable turns out to be much more interesting and authentic than the environs of hotels where tourists usually stay.

9 Hall relates his feelings of being treated shabbily ("like a piece of derelict luggage") to the principle that in the United States, the degree of one's power and status is shown by how much control one has over personal space, whether in the Army or in corporations, where being moved to a smaller office means one is considered less valuable to the company.

10–11 Hall speculates that the equation of control over space with power may pertain only to the United States, since in England, members of Parliament have no formal offices, while their counterparts in the United States—congressmen and senators—attach great importance to the size of their offices. Hall begins to realize that he has been unconsciously applying an American cultural perspective to actions that can be explained only in the context of Japanese culture.

12 Hall postulates the existence of an instinctive "cultural logic" that varies from culture to culture, and he concludes that it is necessary to understand the cultural context in which an action takes place in order to interpret it as people would in that culture.

13–14 Once Hall suspends his own culturally based assumption that one's self-esteem depends on control over personal space, he learns from conversations with Japanese friends that in Japan one has an identity only as part of a group. Japanese workers are considered as family by the companies that hire them for life.

15 The emphasis Japanese society places on conforming to a group is evident in the behavior of Japanese tourists, who move as a coordinated group and closely follow their guide, while American tourists refuse to accept such discipline.

16 Hall realizes that wearing an *okata* and being moved to different rooms and to another, more authentic, hotel means that he is being treated in an informal manner reserved for family members. What Hall had misperceived as an insult—being moved without notice—was really intended as an honor signifying he had been accepted and was not being treated as a stranger.

Based on this list, a student's formulation of a thesis statement expressing the essential idea of Hall's essay appears this way:

> Every society has a hidden culture that governs behavior that might seem inexplicable to an outsider.

The final summary should contain both this thesis and your restatement of the author's main ideas without adding any comments that express personal feelings or responses to the ideas presented. Keep in mind that the purpose of a summary or concise restatement of the author's ideas in your own words is to test your understanding of the material. The summary would normally be introduced by mentioning the author as well as the title of the article:

> Edward T. Hall, writing in "Hidden Culture," believes every society has a hidden culture that governs behavior that might seem inexplicable to an outsider. In Japan, Hall's initial reactions of anger to being moved to another room in a hotel in Tokyo, having his clothes replaced by a cotton kimono or *okata* in Hakone, and being relocated to a different hotel in Kyoto led him to search for the reasons behind such seemingly bizarre events. Although control over space in America is related to status, Hall realizes that in other cultures, like England, where members of Parliament have no offices, this is not the case. Hall discovers that, rather than being an insult, being treated informally meant he was considered to be a member of the hotel "family."

Although some features of the original essay might have been mentioned, such as the significance of office size in corporations in the United States, the student's summary of Hall's essay is still an effective one. The summary accurately and fairly expresses the main ideas in the original.

USING YOUR READING JOURNAL TO GENERATE IDEAS FOR WRITING

You can use all the material in your reading journal (annotations converted to journal entries, reflections, observations, questions, rough and final summaries) to relate your own ideas to the ideas of the person who wrote the essay you are reading. Here are several different kinds of strategies you can use as you analyze an essay in order to generate material for your own:

1. What is missing in the essay? Information that is not mentioned is often just as significant as information the writer chose to include. First, you must have already summarized the main points in the article. Then, make up another list of points that are not discussed, that is, missing information that you would have expected an article of this kind to have covered or touched on. Write down the possible reasons why this missing material has been omitted, censored, or downplayed. What possible purpose could the author have had? Look for vested interests or biases that could explain why information of a certain kind is missing.

2. You might analyze an essay in terms of what you already know and what you didn't know about the issue. To do this, simply make a list of what concepts were already familiar to you and a second list of information or concepts that were new to you. Then write down three to five questions you would like answered about this new information and make a list of possible sources you might consult.

3. You might consider whether the author presents a solution to a problem. List the short-term and long-term effects or consequences of the action the writer recommends. You might wish to evaluate the solution to see whether positive short-term benefits are offset by possible negative long-term consequences not mentioned by the author. This might provide you with a starting point for your own essay.

4. After clearly stating what the author's position on an issue is, try to imagine other people in that society or culture who would view the same issue from a different perspective. How would the concerns of these people be different from those of the writer? Try to think of as many different people, representing as many different perspectives, as you can. Now, try to think of a solution that would satisfy both the author and at least one other person who holds a different viewpoint. Try to imagine that you are an arbitrator negotiating an agreement. How would your recommendation require both parties to compromise and reach an agreement?

1

The Family in Different Cultures

◆

The family has been the most enduring basis of culture throughout the world and has provided a stabilizing force in all societies. The complex network of dependencies, relationships, and obligations may extend outward from parents and children to include grandparents, cousins, aunts and uncles, and more distantly related relatives. In other cultures, the entire community or tribe is seen as an extended family. The unique relationships developed among members of a family provide a universal basis for common experiences, emotions, perceptions, and expectations. At the same time, each family is different, with its own unique characteristic relationships and bonds. Family relationships continue to exert a profound influence on one's life long after childhood. In the context of the family, we first learn what it means to experience the emotions of love, hope, fear, anger, and contentment. The works in this chapter focus on parent–child relationships, explore the connections between grandparents and grandchildren, and depict the impact of cultural values on these relationships.

The structure of the family is subject to a wide range of economic and social influences in different cultures. For example, child-rearing in Morocco is a vastly different enterprise from what it is in America because of the enormous differences in economic circumstances and political systems. The variety of family structures depicted by writers of many different nationalities offers insight into how the concept of the family is modified according to the constraints, beliefs, and needs of particular societies.

For many families, the family history is inseparable from the stories told about a particular member of the family, which define the character of the family and its relationship to the surrounding society. These stories can be told for entertainment or education and often explain old loyalties and antagonisms. Some are written and some are part of an oral history related by one generation to the next. The complex portraits of family life offered in this chapter allow us to share, sympathize, and identify with writers from diverse cultures and more completely understand our own family experiences in the light of theirs.

Patricia Hampl re-creates the experience of having Sunday dinners at her Czechoslovakian grandmother's house. The African American writer Gayle Pemberton, in "Antidisestablishmentarianism," describes how her no-nonsense grandmother taught her to think for herself. Pat Mora, in "Remembering Lobo," recalls the integral part her aunt played in her Mexican American family's life. The current Maharani of Jaipur, Gayatri Devi, recalls the opulent splendor of her childhood home in "A Princess Remembers." Serena Nanda, in "Arranging a Marriage in India," describes her participation in the lengthy process of getting her friend's son married. Daniela Deane reports on the unanticipated results of China's mandatory one-child policy in "The Little Emperors." A father's boorish insensitivity undermines what was to have been a happy reunion between a son and his father in John Cheever's story "Reunion." Fatima Mernissi, in "Moonlit Nights of Laughter," relates how privacy was a rare commodity in the Moroccan harem where she was raised. The delicacy known as *fugu* fish symbolizes the deadly nature of the family relationships in Kazuo Ishiguro's story, "A Family Supper."

Patricia Hampl

Grandmother's Sunday Dinner

◆

Patricia Hampl was born in 1946 and grew up in St. Paul, Minnesota. She graduated from the University of Minnesota, where she currently teaches, and studied at the Iowa Writer's Workshop. Hampl has often written about her connection to her Czech heritage, a theme that emerges in her autobiographical essay "Grandmother's Sunday Dinner." This account is drawn from her book A Romantic Education *(1981).*

1　Food was the potent center of my grandmother's life. Maybe the immense amount of time it took to prepare meals during most of her life accounted for her passion. Or it may have been her years of work in various kitchens on the hill and later, in the house of Justice Butler: after all, she was a professional. Much later, when she was dead and I went to Prague, I came to feel the motto I knew her by best—*Come eat*—was not, after all, a personal statement, but a racial one, the *cri de coeur* of Middle Europe.

2　Often, on Sundays, the entire family gathered for dinner at her house. Dinner was 1 P.M. My grandmother would have preferred the meal to be at the old time of noon, but her children had moved their own Sunday dinner hour to the more fashionable (it was felt) 4 o'clock, so she compromised. Sunday breakfast was something my mother liked to do in a big way, so we arrived at my grandmother's hardly out of the reverie of waffles and orange rolls, before we were propped like rag dolls in front of a pork roast and sauerkraut, dumplings, hot buttered carrots, rye bread and rollikey, pickles and olives, apple pie and ice cream. And coffee.

3　Coffee was a food in that house, not a drink. I always begged for some because the magical man on the Hills Brothers can with his turban and long robe scattered with stars and his gold slippers with pointed toes, looked deeply happy as he drank from his bowl. The bowl itself reminded me of soup, Campbell's chicken noodle soup, my favorite food. The distinct adultness of coffee and the robed man with his deep-drinking pleasure made it clear why the grownups lingered so long at the table. The uncles smoked cigars then, and the aunts said, "Oh, those cigars."

My grandmother, when she served dinner, was a virtuoso hanging   4
on the edge of her own ecstatic performance. She seemed dissatisfied,
almost querulous until she had corralled everybody into their chairs
around the table, which she tried to do the minute they got into the
house. No cocktails, no hors d'oeuvres (pronounced, by some of the
family, "horse's ovaries"), just business. She was a little power crazed:
she had us and, by God, we were going to eat. She went about it like a
goose breeder forcing pellets down the gullets of those dumb birds.

She flew between her chair and the kitchen, always finding more   5
this, extra that. She'd given you the *wrong* chicken breast the first time
around; now she'd found the *right* one: eat it too, eat it fast, because after the chicken comes the rhubarb pie. Rhubarb pie with a thick slice of
cheddar cheese that it was imperative every single person eat.

We had to eat fast because something was always out there in the   6
kitchen panting and charging the gate, champing at the bit, some
mound of rice or a Jell-O fruit salad or vegetable casserole or pie was
out there, waiting to be let loose into the dining room.

She had the usual trite routines: the wheedlings, the silent pout   7
("What! You don't like my brussels sprouts? I thought you liked *my*
brussels sprouts," versus your wife's/sister's/mother's. "I made that
pie just for you," etc., etc.). But it was the way she tossed around the
old clichés and the overused routines, mixing them up and dealing
them out shamelessly, without irony, that made her a pro. She tended
to peck at her own dinner. Her plate, piled with food, was a kind of
stage prop, a mere bending to convention. She liked to eat, she was
even a greedy little stuffer, but not on these occasions. She was a woman possessed by an idea, given over wholly to some phantasmagoria of
food, a mirage of stuffing, a world where the endless chicken and the
infinite lemon pie were united at last at the shore of the oceanic soup
plate that her children and her children's children alone could drain
…if only they would try.

She was there to bolster morale, to lead the troops, to give the   8
sharp command should we falter on the way. The futility of saying no
was supreme, and no one ever tried it. How could a son-in-law, already
weakened near the point of imbecility by the once, twice, thrice charge
to the barricades of pork and mashed potato, be expected to gather his
feeble wit long enough to ignore the final call of his old commander
when she sounded the alarm: "Pie, Fred?"

Just when it seemed as if the food-crazed world she had created   9
was going to burst, that she had whipped and frothed us like a sack of
boiled potatoes under her masher, just then she pulled it all together in
one easeful stroke like the pro she was.

She stood in the kitchen doorway, her little round Napoleonic self   10
sheathed in a cotton flowered pinafore apron, the table draped in its

white lace cloth but spotted now with gravy and beet juice, the troops mumbling indistinctly as they waited at their posts for they knew not what. We looked up at her stupidly, weakly. She said nonchalantly, "Anyone want another piece of pie?" No, no more pie, somebody said. The rest of the rabble grunted along with him. She stood there with the coffeepot and laughed and said, "Good! Because there *isn't* any more pie."

11   No more pie. We'd eaten it all, we'd put away everything in that kitchen. We were exhausted and she, gambler hostess that she was (but it was her house she was playing), knew she could offer what didn't exist, knew us, knew what she'd wrought. There was a sense of her having won, won something. There were no divisions among us now, no adults, no children. Power left the second and third generations and returned to the source, the grandmother who reduced us to mutters by her art.

12   That wasn't the end of it. At 5 P.M. there was "lunch"—sandwiches and beer; the sandwiches were made from the left-overs (mysteriously renewable resources, those roasts). And at about 8 P.M. we were at the table again for coffee cake and coffee, the little man in his turban and his coffee ecstasy and his pointed shoes set on the kitchen table as my grandmother scooped out the coffee and dumped it into a big enamel pot with a crushed eggshell. By then everyone was alive and laughing again, the torpor gone. My grandfather had been inviting the men, one by one, into the kitchen during the afternoon where he silently (the austere version of memory—but he must have talked, must have said *something*) handed them jiggers of whiskey, and watched them put the shot down in one swallow. Then he handed them a beer, which they took out in the living room. I gathered that the *little* drink in the tiny glass shaped like a beer mug was some sort of antidote for the *big* drink of beer. He sat on the chair in the kitchen with a bottle of beer on the floor next to him and played his concertina, allowing society to form itself around him—while he lived he was the center—but not seeking it, not going into the living room. And not talking. He held to his music and the kindly, medicinal administration of whiskey.

13   By evening, it seemed we could eat endlessly, as if we'd had some successful inoculation at dinner and could handle anything. I stayed in the kitchen after they all reformed in the dining room at the table for coffee cake. I could hear them, but the little man in his starry yellow robe was on the table in the kitchen and I put my head down on the oil cloth very near the curled and delighted tips of his pointed shoes, and I slept. Whatever laughter there was, there was. But something sweet and starry was in the kitchen and I lay down beside it, my stomach full, warm, so safe I'll live the rest of my life off the fat of that vast family security.

✧ *Evaluating the Text*

1. What role did the Sunday dinners prepared by Hampl's grandmother play in Hampl's life? In what sense might this dinner serve as a ritual to maintain the distinct Czechoslovakian identity of Hampl's family in America?

2. How does the manner in which Hampl's grandmother prepared and served the meal make you aware of her personality and objectives?

3. Which of the metaphors or similes used by Hampl to describe her grandmother most effectively communicate the person that Hampl remembers? How would you characterize Hampl's style in terms of her tone, diction, and use of irony and humor?

✧ *Exploring Different Perspectives*

1. Compare Hampl's memories of her grandmother's Sunday dinners with the experiences described by Gayatri Devi in "A Princess Remembers" of being served dinner by her grandmother in Baroda, India.

2. Compare the respective roles that Hampl's grandmother and Gayle Pemberton's grandmother played in their lives (see "Antidisestablishmentarianism").

✧ *Extending Viewpoints through Writing*

1. To what extent are the kind of meals that Hampl enjoyed at her grandmother's more typical of a bygone era than the meals that families have together today?

2. Describe a memorable family dinner using vivid images to evoke the sounds, sights, tastes, smells, and emotions you experienced during the event. Did one person play the kind of role that Hampl's grandmother did? If so, describe him or her and tell what happened.

Gayle Pemberton

Antidisestablishmentarianism

◆——————

Gayle Pemberton is currently William R. Kenan Professor of the Human-
ities at Wesleyan University. Born in 1948, she spent her childhood in
Chicago and Ohio. She received a Ph.D. in English and American Litera-
ture at Harvard University and has taught at Smith, Reed, and Bowdoin
Colleges. The Hottest Water in Chicago: On Family, Race, Time, and
American Culture *(1992) is part memoir, part social analysis, and part*
literary criticism. Pemberton focuses on her experiences growing up as an
African-American female in mid-twentieth-century America. The title
derives from her father's experience in 1954 as an organizer with the Ur-
ban League who had the dubious honor of integrating a Chicago hotel. As
Pemberton recounts, it was a desperately dirty establishment for tran-
sients whose owner had shamelessly boasted of offering "the hottest water
in Chicago." The chapter from this book, "Antidisestablishmentarian-
ism," describes the influential role played by Pemberton's grandmother in
shaping her outlook.

1   Okay, so where's Gloria Lockerman? I want to know. Gloria Lockerman was partially responsible for ruining my life. I might never have
ended up teaching literature if it had not been for her. I don't want to
"call her out." I just want to know how things are, what she's doing.
Have things gone well, Gloria? How's the family? What's up?

2   Gloria Lockerman, in case you don't recall, won scads of money on
"The $64,000 Question." Gloria Lockerman was a young black child, like
me, but she could spell anything. Gloria Lockerman became my nemesis
with her ability, her a-n-t-i-d-i-s-e-s-t-a-b-l-i-s-h-m-e-n-t-a-r-i-a-n-i-s-m.

3   My parents, my sister, and I shared a house in Dayton, Ohio, with
my father's mother and her husband, my stepgrandfather, during the
middle fifties. Sharing is an overstatement. It was my grandmother's
house. Our nuclear group ate in a makeshift kitchen in the basement;
my sister and I shared a dormer bedroom, and my parents actually had
a room on the main floor of the house—several parts of which were off-
limits. These were the entire living room, anywhere within three feet of
Grandma's African violets, the windows and venetian blinds, anything
with a doily on it, the refrigerator, and the irises in the backyard.

4   It was an arrangement out of necessity, given the unimpressive
state of our combined fortunes, and it did not meet with anyone's satis-

faction. To make matters worse, we had blockbusted a neighborhood. So, for the first year, I integrated the local elementary school—a thankless and relatively inhuman experience. I remember one day taking the Sunday paper route for a boy up the block who was sick. It was a beautiful spring day, dewy, warm. I walked up the three steps to a particular house and placed the paper on the stoop. Suddenly, a full-grown man, perhaps sixty or so, appeared with a shotgun aimed at me and said that if he ever saw my nigger ass on his porch again he'd blow my head off. I know—typical American grandfather.

Grandma liked spirituals, preferably those sung by Mahalia Jackson. She was not a fan of gospel and I can only imagine what she'd say if she were around to hear what's passing for inspirational music these days. She also was fond of country singers, and any of the members of "The Lawrence Welk Show." ("That Jimmy. Oh, I love the way he sings. He's from Iowa.") She was from Iowa, Jimmy was from Iowa, my father was from Iowa. She was crazy about Jimmy Dean too, and Tennessee Ernie Ford, and "Gunsmoke." She could cook with the finest of them and I wish I could somehow recreate her Parkerhouse rolls, but I lack bread karma. Grandma liked flowers (she could make anything bloom) and she loved her son. 5

She disliked white people, black people in the aggregate and pretty much individually too, children—particularly female children—her daughter, her husband, my mother, Episcopalianism, Catholicism, Judaism, and Dinah Shore. She had a hot temper and a mean streak. She also suffered from several nagging ailments: high blood pressure, ulcers, an enlarged heart, ill-fitting dentures, arteriosclerosis, and arthritis— enough to make anyone hot tempered and mean, I'm sure. But to a third grader, such justifications and their subtleties were ultimately beyond me and insufficient, even though I believe I understood in part the relationship between pain and personality. Grandma scared the daylights out of me. I learned to control my nervous stomach enough to keep from getting sick daily. So Grandma plus school plus other family woes and my sister still predicting the end of the world every time the sirens went off—Grandma threatened to send her to a convent—made the experience as a whole something I'd rather forget, but because of the mythic proportions of family, can't. 6

I often think that it might have been better had I been older, perhaps twenty years older, when I knew Grandma. But I realize that she would have found much more wrong with me nearing thirty than she did when I was eight or nine. When I was a child, she could blame most of my faults on my mother. Grown, she would have had no recourse but to damn me to hell. 7

Ah, but she is on the gene. Grandma did everything fast. She cooked, washed, cleaned, moved—everything was at lightning speed. She passed this handicap on to me, and I have numerous bruises, cuts, 8 and burns to show for it. Watching me throw pots and pans around in the creation of a meal, my mother occasionally calls me by my grand-mother's first name. I smile back, click my teeth to imitate a slipping upper, and say something unpleasant about someone.

9   Tuesday nights were "The $64,000 Question" nights, just as Sun-days we watched Ed Sullivan and Saturdays were reserved for Lawrence Welk and "Gunsmoke." We would all gather around the tele-vision in what was a small, informal family section between the ver-boten real living room and the mahogany dining table and chairs, used only three or four times a year. I don't remember where I sat, but it wasn't on the floor since that wasn't allowed either.

10   As we watched these television programs, once or twice I sat brief-ly on Grandma's lap. She was the world's toughest critic. No one was considered worthy, apart from the above-mentioned. To her, So-and-So or Whosits could not sing, dance, tell a joke, read a line—nothing. In her hands "Ted Mack's Amateur Hour" would have lasted three min-utes. She was willing to forgive only very rarely—usually when some-one she liked gave a mediocre performance on one of her favorite shows.

11   I must admit that Grandma's style of teaching critical thinking worked as well as some others I've encountered. My father had a dif-ferent approach. Throughout my youth he would play the music of the thirties and forties. His passion was for Billie Holiday, with Ella Fitzgerald, Peggy Lee, Sarah Vaughan, and a few others thrown in for a touch of variety. He enjoyed music, and when he wanted to get some musical point across, he would talk about some nuance of style that re-vealed the distinction between what he called "really singing" and a failure. He would say, "Now, listen to that there. Did you catch it? Hear what she did with that note?" With Grandma it was more likely to be:

12   "Did you hear that?"

13   "What?" I might ask.

14   "That. What she just sang."

15   "Yes."

16   "Well, what do you think of it?"

17   "It's okay, I guess."

18   "Well, that was garbage. She can't sing a note. That stinks. She's a fool."

19   Message across. We all choose our own pedagogical techniques.

20   Game shows are, well, game shows. I turned on my television the other day, and as I clicked through channels looking for something to watch I stopped long enough to hear an announcer say that the guest contestant was going to do something or other in 1981. Reruns of game shows? Well, why not? What difference does it make if the whole point is to watch people squirm, twist, sweat, blare, weep, convulse to get their hands on money and gifts, even if they end up being just "parting gifts"?

(I won some of them myself once: a bottle of liquid Johnson's Wax, a box of Chunkies, a beach towel with the name of a diet soda on it, plus a coupon for a case of the stuff, and several boxes of Sugar Blobs—honey-coated peanut butter, marshmallow, and chocolate flavored crispies, dipped in strawberry flavoring for that special morning taste treat!)

Game shows in the fifties were different, more exciting. I thought the studio sets primitive even when I was watching them then. The clock on "Beat the Clock," the coat and crown on "Queen for a Day"—nothing like that mink on "The Big Payoff" that Bess Meyerson modeled—and that wire card flipper on "What's My Line" that John Charles Daly used—my, was it flimsy looking. The finest set of all, though, was on "The $64,000 Question." Hal March would stand outside the isolation booth, the door closing on the likes of Joyce Brothers, Catherine Kreitzer, and Gloria Lockerman, the music would play, and the clock would begin ticking down, like all game show clocks: *TOOT-toot-TOOT-toot-TOOT-toot-BUZZZZZZ.*   21

There were few opportunities to see black people on television in those days. I had watched "Amos 'n' Andy" when we lived in Chicago. But that show was a variation on a theme. Natives running around or jumping up and down or looking menacing in African adventure movies; shuffling, subservient, and clowning servants in local color movies (or any other sort); and "Amos 'n' Andy" were all the same thing: the perpetuation of a compelling, deadly, darkly humorous, and occasionally laughable idea. Nonfictional blacks on television were limited to Sammy Davis, Jr. as part of the Will Mastin Trio and afterward, or Peg Leg Bates on "The Ed Sullivan Show" on Sunday, or the entertainers who might show up on other variety shows, or Nat King Cole during his fifteen-minute program. Naturally, the appearance of Gloria Lockerman caused a mild sensation as we watched "The $64,000 Question," all assembled.   22

"Look at her," Grandma said.   23

I braced myself for the torrent of abuse that was about to be leveled at the poor girl.   24

"You ought to try to be like that," Grandma said.   25

"Huh?" I said.   26

"What did you say?"   27

"Yes, ma'am."   28

I was shocked, thrown into despair. I had done well in school, as well as could be hoped. I was modestly proud of my accomplishments, and given the price I was paying every day—and paying in silence, for I never brought my agonies at school home with me—I didn't need Gloria Lockerman thrown in my face. Gloria Lockerman, like me, on television, spelling. I was perennially an early-round knockout in spelling bees.   29

My sister understands all of this. Her own story is slightly different and she says she'll tell it all one day herself. She is a very good singer   30 and has a superb ear; with our critical training, what more would she need? Given other circumstances, she might have become a performer herself. When she was about eleven Leslie Uggams was on Arthur Godfrey's "Talent Scouts" and was soon to be tearing down the "Name That Tune" runway, ringing the bell and becoming moderately famous. No one ever held Leslie Uggams up to my sister for image conscious-ness-raising. But my sister suffered nevertheless. She could out-sing Leslie Uggams and probably run as fast; she knew the songs and didn't have nearly so strange a last name. But, there she was, going nowhere in the Middle West, and there was Leslie Uggams on her way to "Sing Along With Mitch." To this day, my sister mumbles if she happens to see Leslie Uggams on television—before she can get up to change the channel—or hears someone mention her name. I told her I saw Leslie Uggams in the flesh at a club in New York. She was sitting at a table, just like the rest of us, listening with pleasure to Barbara Cook. My sis-ter swore at me.

31   Grandma called her husband "Half-Wit." He was a thin, small-boned man who looked to me far more like an Indian chief than like a black man. He was from Iowa too, but that obviously did not account for enough in Grandma's eyes. He had a cracking tenor voice, a head full of dead straight black hair, reddish, dull brown skin, and large sad, dark brown eyes. His craggy face also reminded me of pictures I'd seen of Abraham Lincoln—but, like all political figures and American fore-fathers, Lincoln, to my family, was fair game for wisecracks, so that re-semblance did Grandpa no good either. And for reasons that have gone to the grave with both of them, he was the most thoroughly henpecked man I have ever heard of, not to mention seen.

32   Hence, domestic scenes had a quality of pathos and high humor as far as I was concerned. My sister and I called Grandpa "Half-Wit" when we were alone together, but that seemed to have only a slight ef-fect on our relations with him and our willingness to obey him—though I cannot recall any occasions calling for his authority. Grandma was Grandma, Half-Wit was Half-Wit—and we lived with the two of them. I have one particularly vivid memory of Grandma, an aficionada of the iron skillet, chasing him through the house waving it in the air, her narrow, arthritis-swollen wrist and twisted knuckles turning the heavy pan as if it were a lariat. He didn't get hurt; he was fleet of foot and made it out the back door before she caught him. My father's real father had been dead since the thirties and divorced from Grandma since the teens—so Half-Wit had been in place for quite some years and was still around to tell the story, if he had the nerve.

33   Grandma had a glass menagerie, the only one I've seen apart from performances of the Williams play. I don't think she had a unicorn, but she did have quite a few pieces. From a distance of no less than five feet

I used to squint at the glass forms, wondering what they meant to Grandma, who was herself delicate of form but a powerhouse of strength, speed, and temper. I also wondered how long it would take me to die if the glass met with some unintended accident caused by me. Real or imagined unpleasantries, both in the home and outside of it, helped develop in me a somewhat melancholic nature. And even before we had moved to Ohio I found myself laughing and crying at the same time.

In the earlier fifties, in Chicago, I was allowed to watch such pro-   34
grams as "The Ernie Kovacs Show," "Your Show of Shows," "The Jackie Gleason Show," "The Red Skelton Show," and, naturally, "I Love Lucy." I was continually dazzled by the skits and broad humor, but I was particularly taken with the silent sketches, my favorite comedians as mime artists: Skelton as Freddy the Freeloader, Caesar and Coca in a number of roles, thoroughly outrageous Kovacs acts backed by Gershwin's "Rialto Ripples." My father was a very funny man and a skillful mime. I could tell when he watched Gleason's Poor Soul that he identified mightily with what was on the screen. It had nothing to do with self-pity. My father had far less of it than other men I've met with high intelligence, financial and professional stress, and black faces in a white world. No, my father would even say that we were all poor souls; it was the human condition. His mimicking of the Gleason character—head down, shoulders tucked, stomach sagging, feet splayed—served as some kind of release. I would laugh and cry watching either of them.

But my absolute favorite was Martha Raye, who had a way of   35
milking the fine line between tragedy and comedy better than most. I thought her eyes showed a combination of riotous humor and terror. Her large mouth contorted in ways that seemed to express the same two emotions. Her face was a mask of profound sadness. She did for me what Sylvia Sidney did for James Baldwin. In *The Devil Finds Work*, Baldwin says, "Sylvia Sidney was the only American film actress who reminded me of a colored girl, or woman—which is to say that she was the only American film actress who reminded me of reality." The reality Raye conveyed to me was of how dreams could turn sour in split-seconds, and how underdogs, even when winning, often had to pay abominable prices. She also could sing a jazz song well, with her husky scat phrasing, in ways that were slightly different from those of my favorite singers, and almost as enjoyable.

There were no comedic or dramatic images of black women on the   36
screen—that is, apart from Sapphire and her mother on "Amos 'n' Andy." And knowing Grandma and Grandpa taught me, if nothing else suggested it, that what I saw of black life on television was a gross burlesque—played to the hilt with skill by black actors, but still lacking reality.

37   Black female singers who appeared on television were, like their music, sacrosanct, and I learned from their styles, lyrics, and improvisations, lessons about life that mime routines did not reveal. Still, it was Martha Raye, and occasionally Lucille Ball and Imogene Coca at their most absurd, that aligned me with my father and his Poor Soul, and primed me to both love and despise Grandma and to see that in life most expressions, thoughts, acts, and intentions reveal their opposite polarities simultaneously.

38   Grandma died in 1965. I was away, out of the country, and I missed her funeral—which was probably a good idea since I might have been tempted to strangle some close family friend who probably would have launched into a "tsk, tsk, tsk" monologue about long-suffering grandmothers and impudent children. But, in another way, I'm sorry I didn't make it. Her funeral might have provided some proper closure for me, might have prompted me to organize her effect on my life sooner than I did, reconciling the grandmother who so hoped I would be a boy that she was willing to catch a Constellation or a DC-3 to witness my first few hours, but instead opted to take the bus when she heard the sad news, with the grandmother who called me "Sally Slapcabbage" and wrote to me and my sister regularly, sending us the odd dollar or two, until her death.

39   I remember coming home from school, getting my jelly sandwich and wolfing it down, and watching "The Mickey Mouse Club," my favorite afternoon show, since there was no afternoon movie. I had noticed and had been offended by the lack of black children in the "Club," but the cartoons, particularly those with Donald Duck, were worth watching. On this particular episode—one of the regular guest act days—a group of young black children, perhaps nine or ten of them, came on and sang, with a touch of dancing, "Old MacDonald Had a Farm," in an up-tempo, jazzy version. In spite of the fact that usually these guest days produced some interesting child acts, I became angry with what I saw. I felt patronized, for myself and for them. Clearly a couple of them could out-sing and out-dance any Mouseketeer—something that wasn't worth giving a thought to—but this performance was gratuitous, asymmetrical, a nonsequitur, like Harpo Marx marching through the Negro section in *A Day at the Races,* blowing an imaginary horn and exciting the locals to much singing, swinging, and dancing to a charming ditty called "Who Dat Man?"

40   I must have mumbled something as I watched the group singing "Old MacDonald." Grandma, passing through, took a look at what was on the screen, and at me, turned off the television, took my hand, led me to her kitchen, and sat me down at the table where she and Half-Wit ate, poured me some milk, and without so much as a blink of her eye, said, "Pay no attention to that shit."

✧ Evaluating the Text

1. What impression do you get of the circumstances surrounding Pemberton's early life? How do they help explain why her grandmother was so influential in shaping her outlook on life?

2. How would you characterize the voice that you hear in Pemberton's essay? What personality traits does she possess as a writer? Why is it important to know that the narrator's family was the only black family in that neighborhood? What can you infer about her experiences at school?

3. In what ways was the media's presentation of African Americans in the 1950s stereotyped? How does this help explain Pemberton's grandmother's reaction to Gloria Lockerman?

✧ Exploring Different Perspectives

1. Compare and contrast the effects of living in an extended family as described by Pemberton with Fatima Mernissi's narrative, "Moonlit Nights of Laughter."

2. Compare the effects on Pemberton and Pat Mora (see "Remembering Lobo") of growing up with a free-thinking, independent female relative.

✧ Extending Viewpoints through Writing

1. To what extent did one of your grandparents or relatives exert a shaping influence on your outlook, personality, and expectations? Describe one or two key incidents that illustrate this.

2. In your view, what television shows either reflect or fail to reflect African American life in the United States today?

Pat Mora

Remembering Lobo

————————◆————————

*Pat Mora was born in El Paso, Texas, in 1942. She received a bachelor's degree in 1963 from Texas Western College and earned a master's degree from the University of Texas at El Paso in 1967. Her two collections of po-*ems, Chance *(1984) and* Waters *(1986), celebrate the southwest and the desert. Mora's third volume of poetry,* Communion *(1991), explores basic questions of Hispanic identity as she travels to Cuba, New York, and central India. Mora has written books for children, including* A Birthday Present for Tia *(1992) and* Pablo's Tree *(1993). Her commentaries are collected in* Nepantla: Essays from the Land in the Middle *(1993), in which "Remembering Lobo" first appeared. Evoking the image of her aunt, this essay addresses the theme of what it means to be a Chicana in American society and celebrates Mora's cultural identity.*

1   We called her *Lobo.* The word means "wolf" in Spanish, an odd name for a generous and loving aunt. Like all names it became synonymous with her, and to this day returns me to my childself. Although the name seemed perfectly natural to us and to our friends, it did cause frowns from strangers throughout the years. I particularly remember one hot afternoon when on a crowded streetcar between the border cities of El Paso and Juarez, I momentarily lost sight of her. "Lobo! Lobo!" I cried in panic. Annoyed faces peered at me, disappointed at such disrespect to a white-haired woman.

2   Actually the fault was hers. She lived with us for years, and when she arrived home from work in the evening, she'd knock on our front door and ask, "*¿Dónde están mis lobitos?*" "Where are my little wolves?"

3   Gradually she became our *lobo,* a spinster aunt who gathered the four of us around her, tying us to her for life by giving us all she had. Sometimes to tease her we would call her by her real name. "*¿Dónde está Ignacia?*" we would ask. Lobo would laugh and say, "She is a ghost."

4   To all of us in nuclear families today, the notion of an extended family under one roof seems archaic, complicated. We treasure our private space. I will always marvel at the generosity of my parents, who opened their door to both my grandmother and Lobo. No doubt I am drawn to the elderly because I grew up with two entirely different white-haired women who worried about me, tucked me in at night, made me tomato soup or hot *hierbabuena* (mint tea) when I was ill.

Lobo grew up in Mexico, the daughter of a circuit judge, my grand- 5
father. She was a wonderful storyteller and over and over told us about
the night her father, a widower, brought his grown daughters on a flat-
bed truck across the Rio Grande at the time of the Mexican Revolution.
All their possessions were left in Mexico. Lobo had not been wealthy, but
she had probably never expected to have to find a job and learn English.

When she lived with us, she worked in the linens section of a local 6
department store. Her area was called "piece goods and bedding."
Lobo never sewed, but she would talk about materials she sold, using
words I never completely understood, such as *pique* and *broadcloth*.
Sometimes I still whisper such words just to remind myself of her. I'll
always savor the way she would order "sweet milk" at restaurants. The
precision of a speaker new to the language.

Lobo saved her money to take us out to dinner and a movie, to take 7
us to Los Angeles in the summer, to buy us shiny black shoes for
Christmas. Though she never married and never bore children, Lobo
taught me much about one of our greatest challenges as human beings:
loving well. I don't think she ever discussed the subject with me, but
through the years she lived her love, and I was privileged to watch.

She died at ninety-four. She was no sweet, docile Mexican woman 8
dying with perfect resignation. Some of her last words before drifting
into semiconsciousness were loud words of annoyance at the incompe-
tence of nurses and doctors.

"*No sirven.*" "They're worthless," she'd say to me in Spanish. 9

"They don't know what they're doing. My throat is hurting and 10
they're taking X rays. Tell them to take care of my throat first."

I was busy striving for my cherished middle-class politeness. "Shh, 11
shh," I'd say. "They're doing the best they can."

"Well, it's not good enough," she'd say, sitting up in anger. 12

Lobo was a woman of fierce feelings, of strong opinions. She was a 13
woman who literally whistled while she worked. The best way to cheer
her when she'd visit my young children was to ask for her help. Ask
her to make a bed, fold laundry, set the table or dry dishes, and the
whistling would begin as she moved about her task. Like all of us, she
loved being needed. Understandable, then, that she muttered in annoyance when her body began to fail her. She was a woman who found
self-definition and joy in visibly showing her family her love for us by
bringing us hot *té de canela* (cinnamon tea) in the middle of the night to
ease a cough, by bringing us comics and candy whenever she returned
home. A life of giving.

One of my last memories of her is a visit I made to her on Novem- 14
ber 2, *El Día de los Muertos,* or All Souls' Day. She was sitting in her
rocking chair, smiling wistfully. The source of the smile may seem a bit
bizarre to a U.S. audience. She was fondly remembering past visits to
the local cemetery on this religious feast day.

15   "What a silly old woman I have become," she said. "Here I sit in my rocking chair all day on All Souls' Day, sitting when I should be out there. At the cemetery. Taking good care of *mis muertos,* my dead ones.

16   "What a time I used to have. I'd wake while it was still dark outside. I'd hear the first morning birds, and my fingers would almost itch to begin. By six I'd be having a hot bath, dressing carefully in black, wanting *mis muertos* to be proud of me, proud to have me looking respectable and proud to have their graves taken care of. I'd have my black coffee and plenty of toast. You know the way I like it. Well browned and well buttered. I wanted to be ready to work hard.

17   "The bus ride to the other side of town was a long one, but I'd say a rosary and plan my day. I'd hope that my perfume wasn't too strong and yet would remind others that I was a lady.

18   "The air at the cemetery gates was full of chrysanthemums: that strong, sharp, fall smell. I'd buy tin cans full of the gold and wine flowers. How I liked seeing aunts and uncles who were also there to care for the graves of their loved ones. We'd hug. Happy together.

19   "Then it was time to begin. The smell of chrysanthemums was like a whiff of pure energy. I'd pull the heavy hose and wash the gravestones over and over, listening to the water pelting away the desert sand. I always brought newspaper. I'd kneel on the few patches of grass, and I'd scrub and scrub, shining the gray stones, leaning back on my knees to rest for a bit and then scrubbing again. Finally a relative from nearby would say, '*Ya, ya, Nacha,*' and laugh. Enough. I'd stop, blink my eyes to return from my trance. Slightly dazed, I'd stand slowly, place a can of chrysanthemums before each grave.

20   "Sometimes I would just stand there in the desert sun and listen. I'd hear the quiet crying of people visiting new graves; I'd hear families exchanging gossip while they worked.

21   "One time I heard my aunt scolding her dead husband. She'd sweep his gravestone and say, '*¿Porqué?* Why did you do this, you thoughtless man? Why did you go and leave me like this? You know I don't like to be alone. Why did you stop living?' Such a sight to see my aunt with her proper black hat and her fine dress and her carefully polished shoes muttering away for all to hear.

22   "To stifle my laughter, I had to cover my mouth with my hands."

✧ *Evaluating the Text*

   1. How does Mora's account of her aunt emphasize attributes that make Lobo an apt name? What qualities does Mora's aunt possess that provide a valuable counterbalance to the narrator's own personality?

   2. What is the significance of the Mexican custom of visiting the cemetery on All Souls' Day?

3. Why is the shift from the narrator's account to Lobo's own words effective? Why do you think Mora structures her account in this fashion?

✦ Exploring Different Perspectives

1. Compare the influence of Gayle Pemberton's grandmother (see "Antidisestablishmentarianism") with that of Pat Mora's aunt.

2. How do questions of language use and communication play an important role in Pat Mora's account and in John Cheever's story "Reunion"?

✦ Extending Viewpoints through Writing

1. Create a one-page vignette about a relative whom you think of as unusual or striking in some way. Provide descriptive details and examples that will help the reader visualize this person.

2. In what way do you embody the coming together of two diverse ethnic and cultural traditions from your mother's and father's sides of the family? Tell what you know about the past histories of both sides of your family.

Gayatri Devi, with Santha Rama Rau

A Princess Remembers

◆

Gayatri Devi was born in 1919 in London and raised in West Bengal, India, as the daughter of the Maharajah of Cooch Behar and the Princess of Baroda. She married the Maharajah of Jaipur in 1940 and has had a distinguished career as a member of the Indian Parliament from 1962 to 1977. As the Maharani of Jaipur, she is the founder of the Gayatri Devi Girl's Public School in Rajasthan. The following chapter is drawn from her autobiography A Princess Remembers: The Memoirs of the Maharani of Jaipur *(1976), written with Santha Rama Rau, who is herself the author of eleven books, including* Home to India *(1945) and numerous magazine articles that have appeared in* The New Yorker, The New York Times Sunday Magazine, *and* Reader's Digest. *In this account, Devi re-creates the palatial splendor of her childhood home and reveals the close ties she had with her mother.*

India is a republic in southern Asia whose 800 million people make it the second most populous country in the world, after China. Although Indian civilization dates back more than 5,000 years, European traders discovered it only in the sixteenth century. By 1757, Britain had gained control of India from the maharajas (ruling princes). In 1919, Mohandas "Mahatma" (great souled) Gandhi, a lawyer who had worked for Indians in South Africa, launched the movement for India's independence from Britain, using techniques of passive resistance and civil disobedience. His dream was realized in 1947 with the dissolution of the British Raj. India was then partitioned into India and Pakistan with hopes of ending the civil war between Hindu and Muslim communities. Gandhi was assassinated the following year. In 1984, Prime Minister Indira Gandhi (no relation to Mohandas) was assassinated by Sikh members of her own bodyguard. She was succeeded by her son, Rajiv Gandhi, who resigned in 1989, and was assassinated himself less than two years later, during a bid for re-election. Congress party leader P. V. Narasimha Rao became prime minister in 1991. The destruction by Hindus of a Muslim mosque in 1992 led to riots and calls for government investigations. In July of 1997, K. R. Narayanan became the first Dalit (Untouchable) to be elected president. The nation celebrated its fiftieth anniversary of independence on August 14, 1997. Since then, tensions in Kashmir have increased.

During our childhood, our family often journeyed the two thousand   1
miles from our home, the palace in Cooch Behar State, tucked into the
north-east corner of India, right across the country to my grandparents'
palace in the state of Baroda, on the shores of the Arabian Sea. All five of
us children had watched with excited anticipation the packing of mountains of luggage. We seemed to be preparing for the most unlikely extremes of heat and cold, not to mention more predictable occasions such
as a state visit or a horse show. On the day of our departure the station
was a bedlam, what with all the luggage and staff that accompanied us
wherever we went. But by the time we arrived everything was checked
and on board, thanks to the efforts of our well-trained staff.

Nonetheless, my mother invariably had a deluge of instructions   2
and questions as soon as we arrived. Where was the dressing-case that
she wanted in her compartment? she would ask, in her slightly husky,
appealing voice. Well, then, unload the baggage and find it. What about
her *puja* box, which contained the incenses and powders necessary for
the performance of her morning prayers? Ah, there it was. Fortunately,
that meant that no one need hurry back to the palace to fetch it.

When she did actually leave, telegrams were sent in all directions: 3
PLEASE SEND MY GOLD TONGUE-SCRAPER, or, HAVE LEFT MY SPOON AND LITTLE
ONYX BELL BEHIND, or, IN THE LEFT-HAND CUPBOARD IN THE THIRD DRAWER
DOWN YOU'LL FIND MY GREEN SILK DRESSING-GOWN. Then came the supple-
mentaries: NOT THE DARK GREEN, THE LIGHT GREEN, or, IN THAT CASE LOOK
IN THE DRESSING-ROOM.

Anyway, once we got started, those week-long journeys were   4
among the most cherished memories of my childhood. As a child it
seemed to me that we occupied the whole train. We had at least three
four-berth first-class compartments. My mother, elder sister, and a
friend or relation occupied one; my younger sister, a governess, and
myself were in another; my two brothers and their companion with an
aide in another. Then the aides and secretaries would have a couple of
second-class compartments, while the maids, valets, and butlers travelled third class.

In the twenties, a train trip by even the most plain-living Indian was   5
reminiscent of a Bedouin migration, for everything in the way of bedding, food, and eating utensils had to be taken along. In those days most
Indian trains had no dining-cars and did not provide sheets, blankets,
pillows, or towels, although there were proper bathrooms where you
could take a shower. We always travelled with our personal servants to
cope with the daily necessities of living on the long journey to Baroda.

First there was the overnight trip from Cooch Behar to Calcutta,   6
and we broke our journey for a couple of days in our house there. Then
we set off again for the longest part of the trip. The cooks prepared
"tiffin-carriers," a number of pans, each holding different curries, rice,

lentils, curds, and sweets. The pans fitted into each other, and a metal brace held them all together so that you could carry in one hand a metal tower filled with food. But those tiffin-carriers were intended to supply us with only our first meal on the train. From then on we were in the hands of a chain of railway caterers. You could give your order to the railway man at one stop and know that instructions would be wired ahead to the next stop and that your meal would be served, on the thick railway crockery, as soon as the train came into the station. More often than not we hadn't finished before the train left the station— but that didn't matter. Another waiter would be ready to pick up empty containers, glasses, cutlery, and plates at any further stop that the train made.

7   For us children the excitement of travelling across India by train was not so much in the ingenious arrangements for meals and service as in the atmosphere of the station platforms themselves. As soon as the train pulled in to any station, our carriage windows were immediately besieged by vendors of sweets, fruit, hot tea, and—my favourites—by men selling the charming, funny, painted wooden toys that I have seen nowhere except on Indian station platforms: elephants with their trunks raised to trumpet, lacquered in grey and scarlet, caparisoned in gold with floral designs picked out in contrasting colours; horses decked out as though for a bridegroom; camels, cheetahs, tigers, and dozens of others, all stiff and delightful, with wide, painted eyes and endearing, coquettish smiles. I wanted them all, but my mother said, "Nonsense, nonsense! You children have too many toys as it is." But she could never resist bargaining, so she had a lovely time with the fruit-, flower-, and sweets-vendors, and afterwards our compartment was filled with clinging tropical scents from all her purchases. I don't really know whether she was as good a bargainer as she thought—she was, by nature, very generous—and the vendors always went away looking appropriately bereaved, although with a secret air of satisfaction.

8   In any case, it didn't matter. All of us had the fun of chasing each other about the platforms, and when the train stayed in a station for an hour or more, we ate in the railway dining-room, ordering what we used to call "railway curry," designed to offend no palate—no beef, forbidden to Hindus; no pork, forbidden to Muslims; so, inevitably, lamb or chicken curries and vegetables. Railway curry therefore pleased nobody. Long before the train was due to leave we were summoned by our aides or governess or tutor, telling us to hurry, not to dawdle over our meal in the station restaurant; the train was leaving in five minutes. Of course it didn't, and we soon learned to trust the railway personnel, who let us loiter till the last possible moment before bustling us back to our compartments.

9   Finally we would arrive in Baroda to be met at the station by a fleet of Baroda State cars and driven to Laxmi Vilas, the Baroda Palace and

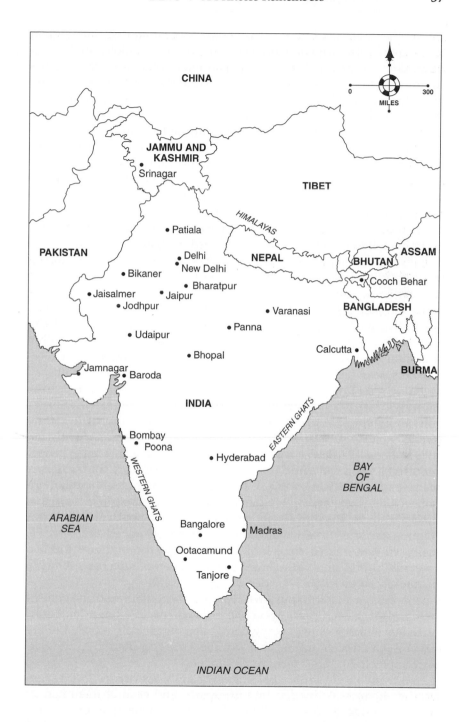

my mother's girlhood home. It is an enormous building, the work of the same architect who built our own palace in Cooch Behar in the mid-nineteenth century. In Baroda, he had adopted what I believe architects describe as the "Indo-Saracenic" style. Whatever one calls it, it is certainly imposing. Marble verandas with scalloped arches supported by groups of slender pillars bordered the building. Impressive façades were topped by onion-shaped domes. Outside the main entrance were palm trees standing like sentries along the edges of perfectly kept lawns that were watered daily. Tall and rather municipal-looking street lights with spherical bulbs illuminated the grand approach. And always on duty were the splendid household guards, dressed in white breeches with dark blue jackets and black top-boots. Because we were the grandchildren of the Maharaja, the ruler of the state, every time we went in or out of the front gate they played the Baroda anthem.

10   Inside, the palace was a strange blend of styles, partly Victorian, partly traditional Indian, with here and there a touch of antique English or French. There were courtyards with little pools surrounded by ferns and palms. Persian carpets flowed down interminable corridors. The halls were filled with displays of shields, swords, and armouries of spears. The sitting-rooms overflowed with French furniture, with photographs in silver frames, with ornaments and knickknacks on occasional tables. The palace also contained a gymnasium and a dispensary. Two doctors were permanently in residence, and one of them used to travel with my grandfather wherever he went.

11   Throughout the palace silent formality reigned, and there always seemed to be a number of anonymous, mysterious figures around—two or three sitting in every room. They must have had some proper place in the design of things, but we children never found out who they were or what they were doing. Waiting for an audience with our grandfather? Visiting from some other princely state? Guarding the many precious objects that were scattered throughout the palace? True to our training, we knew that we must pay our respects to our elders, so we may well have folded our hands in a *namaskar*, the traditional Indian greeting, or obeisance, to maidservants and companions as well as to distinguished guests.

12   In sharp contrast to our own decorous behaviour and the general standard of proper courtesy in the palace were the huge longtailed monkeys which roamed everywhere. They were easily aroused to anger and would often follow us down the passages, chattering and baring their teeth in a most terrifying manner.

13   As with all old Indian palaces and family residences, our grandparents' home was divided into two parts, and each of them had its separate entrance. This tradition of special zenana quarters for the women, and their keeping of purdah, literally "a curtain," to shield them from the eyes of any men other than their husband or the male

members of their immediate family, was introduced into India at the time of the Muslim invasions during the twelfth century. At first only Muslims kept these customs, but later, during the rule of the Mogul emperors of India, which lasted from the sixteenth century until the Indian Mutiny of 1857 when the British took over sovereign command, most of the princely states of India as well as the families of the nobles and the upper classes adopted a number of Muslim customs ranging from styles of architecture to a rich and varied cuisine. Among these borrowings was the tradition of keeping their womenfolk carefully segregated from the view of outside eyes.

In Baroda the full tradition of purdah no longer existed; both my grandparents were too liberal to allow it. Strict purdah would have required the women to stay entirely within the zenana quarters and, if they had any occasion to venture outside, to travel well chaperoned, only in curtained or shaded vehicles. But my grandparents treated the custom relatively loosely—women could go about fairly freely as long as they were chaperoned and had nothing to do with men outside their family circle. If, for instance, there was a cheetah hunt or a polo match, the ladies would all go together, separately from the men. They didn't have to be veiled; they just stayed on their side of the grounds and the men stayed on the opposite side. For us children, there were no restrictions at all. We wandered freely all over the palace, even to the billiard-room, which in Edwardian days was considered forbidden territory to any female.

My grandmother, a formidable lady, had grown up totally accepting the idea of purdah. Following the custom of her time and the tradition of her family, she had, through her early years, observed the strictest purdah, never appearing in public, and in private only before women, close male relatives, and her husband. When she was only fourteen, a marriage was arranged for her to the ruler of Baroda. Her family, like his, was Maratha, members of the Kshatriya caste, which included many warriors and rulers. Like other Indian communities, Marathas traditionally married among themselves. She was, besides, of the right noble background, and he, after the untimely death of his first wife, the Princess of Tanjore, wanted to marry again.

My grandfather, well ahead of his time in many of his attitudes and actions, hired tutors for my grandmother, first to teach her to read and write (she was illiterate when she was married), then to expand her education. Later still, he encouraged her to free herself from suffocating Indian traditions and to pursue a role in public life. It was owing to his liberal views that my grandmother emerged as an important leader in the women's movement in India. She became the president of the All-India Women's Conference, the largest women's organization in the world and one which concerns itself with women's rights as well as with the spread of education and the loosening of the constricting ties of orthodox Indian society on its women. She was not just a figure-head in this important office but a very effective spokeswoman for the emancipation of Indian women. Eventually she even wrote a book, now a standard reference work, on the position of Indian women in their society. After all, she could draw amply on her own experience, first as a sheltered, obedient daughter of a conservative family and later as a free and progressive wife.

17   But it wasn't for her—or for any of us, her three granddaughters or our mother—a total transformation. Within the family in the Baroda Palace she still retained much of the conventional manners and the severe sense of propriety of all upper-class Indian households. All of us always touched her feet as a sign of respect when we first arrived in Baroda, again before we left, and also on all ceremonial occasions. (This custom, still observed in most Hindu families, applied not only to our grandmother but to all close relatives who were our seniors, even brothers, sisters, and cousins who might be just a few months older.)

18   It was at public functions that my grandparents made it most clear that they had more or less dispensed with the rules of purdah, for they always appeared together. Although they still maintained separate kitchens and separate household staffs, my grandfather came to take his meals with the rest of us, and with whatever visitors happened to be staying in Baroda, in my grandmother's dining-room. There she served the most marvellous food in the Indian way, on *thals*, round silver trays loaded with small matching silver bowls containing quantities of rice pilau, meat, fish and vegetable curries, lentils, pickles, chutneys, and sweets. She was a great gourmet and the food from her kitchen was delicious, whether it was the Indian chef who was presiding or, when she was unsure of the tastes of foreign visitors, the cook for English food who was in charge. She spent endless time and trouble consulting with her cooks, planning menus to suit the different guests she invited. It was dangerous to be even faintly appreciative of any dish, for if you took a second helping, she noticed and thrust a third and a fourth upon you, saying, "Come on, come on, you know you like this." Her kitchen was particularly well known for the marvellous pickles it produced and for the huge, succulent prawns from the estuary. Only when there were a large number of outside guests, and on ceremonial occasions like my grandfather's Diamond Jubilee, were meals served from his kitchen and in the banqueting hall on his side of the palace.

19   On religious and ceremonial occasions, durbars were held in his great audience hall. These were very elaborate affairs, something like holding court. The nobility and other important families came formally to offer their allegiance to their rulers—usually a token of a single gold coin.

20   Often we went duck shooting, sometimes we watched the falconing, and then there were the special thrills of elephant fights and, better yet, the tense and gripping cheetah hunts, a speciality of Baroda, when

carefully trained cheetahs, hooded and chained, were taken out to the scrub land in shooting-brakes. There they were unhooded and let loose into a herd of black buck. With foot full down on the accelerator, one could just manage to keep pace with the astonishing speed of the animals during the chase.

My own favourite entertainment as a child came from the relatively tame performances of my grandfather's trained parrots. They used to ride tiny silver bicycles, drive little silver cars, walk tightropes, and enact a variety of dramatic scenes. I remember one in particular in which a parrot was run over by a car, examined by a parrot doctor, and finally carried off on a stretcher by parrot bearers. The grand climax of their performance was always a salute fired on a tiny silver cannon. It made the most amazing noise for a miniature weapon, and the parrots were the only ones to remain unperturbed.

While my grandmother approved of all these innocent diversions for the children, she wanted us to retain the traditional skills of Indian girls. She wanted us, for instance, to learn how to cook proper Maratha food. My sisters, Ila and Menaka, showed talent and profited by the lessons, while I never seemed able to grasp even the rudiments of cooking.

Because almost every princely Indian family put strong emphasis on sports—and also because we ourselves were sports-mad—we used to get up at daybreak and go riding. By the time we returned, my grandmother's side of the palace was already bustling with activity, with maids preparing for the day, women waiting for an audience, and countless arrangements being made. We used to go in to say our required "Good morning" to her before we went to our rooms to settle down to lessons with our tutors. The floors of her apartments were covered, in the traditional Indian fashion, with vast white cloths. We had to take off our shoes before entering, and everyone except my grandmother sat on the floor.

I remember her from those days as an admirable, remarkable, and somewhat terrifying woman. She must have been beautiful when she was young. Even to my childish eyes, at that time, she was still handsome and immensely dignified. She wasn't tall, though she gave the impression of height partly because her manner was so very regal. But she had a sour sense of humour.

My grandfather was an impressive though kindly figure in our lives, and I remember how his eyes were always laughing. We often took our morning ride with him on the four-mile bridle-path around the Baroda Palace grounds. It was difficult to keep up with him because he liked strenuous exercise and had his favourite horse specially trained to trot very fast.

When we returned to the palace he would leave us and spend the rest of the morning dealing with work that he lumped under the comprehensive heading of "matters of state." Though I didn't know the details at the time, the ruler of an Indian princely state had important functions to fulfil and was a real sovereign to his people. The British, as they gradually took over the major role in India during the nineteenth century, made varying agreements with the different princes defining the division of responsibilities, although much was also left to evolving custom. One major point of all the agreements was that the princes could have relations with foreign powers only through the British. Each of the more important states—and Baroda was one of the most important—had a British Resident who was the voice of the British Government of India. But the states had their own laws, their own courts of justice, their own taxes, and in many cases their own military forces, so that the people of each state looked towards the prince, and not towards anyone else, as the real governmental authority in their lives. My grandfather had, therefore, to confer with his ministers (who were responsible only to him) and to decide many things that affected the lives of millions of people.

27   I knew him, however, not as a statesman but as a man and a grandfather. One conversation with him lives clearly in my memory. I had gone to say good night to him. He was, as always at that time of day, at the billiard table. He stopped his game and said, in a friendly way, "Ah, I see you're off to bed. I hope you have a good sleep."

28   I explained to him that there was no question of sleep for some time to come as I had to think about all that had happened during the day.

29   "No, no," he said, gently but emphatically. "If you go to bed, you should sleep. If you are reading, you should read. If you are eating, you should eat. And if you are thinking, then you should think. Never mix the different activities. No good ever comes of it, and what's more, you can't enjoy—neither can you profit from—any of them."

30   Then, because he was playing billiards, he turned back to the table and gave the game his undivided attention once more. He lived by the clock all his life and did everything in strict order: up at sunrise, walk or ride, work until lunch, brief rest, work until tea, recreation, evening work, supper, reading. It had been the same for fifty years.

31   My grandfather was known as the Gaekwar of Baroda, Gaekwar being both a family name and a title. Most of the Indian princes had the hereditary titles of Maharaja ("Great King") or Raja (simply, "Ruler," or "King"), depending on the size, importance, and history of their states. I always knew that my grandfather was a special person but it was only years later, when I knew the full range of his background and accomplishments, that I realized what an extraordinary man he was.

32   He had spent the first twelve years of his life in a village about two hundred miles south of Baroda City. His father, a distant relative of the ruling family, was village headman and earned only a modest living from farming. However, when the previous ruler of Baroda was de-

posed by the British for misrule, someone from the family had to be chosen as a successor. My grandfather, along with one of his brothers and a cousin, was brought to the capital of the state and presented to the Dowager Maharani of Baroda, the widow of the deposed ruler's father. She was asked by the British to select one of the boys to be the new ruler, and her choice fell upon my grandfather.

Since he had been brought up in a village where a sound practical grasp of farming was considered the only necessary knowledge, he could neither read nor write, so the six years following his arrival at the palace were devoted exclusively to his education, and habits were instilled that lasted all his life. He always rose at six o'clock and went to bed at ten, and with the exception of two hours' riding (considered an essential princely skill), one hour of games of various kinds suitable to his rank, and breaks for meals, the entire day was devoted to work. He learned to read and write in four languages: Marathi, the language of his princely ancestors; Gujarati, the language of the bulk of the population in Baroda; Urdu, the language of his Muslim subjects, employing the Arabic script; and, of course, English. India was still the "brightest jewel" in the British imperial crown, so he had to study English history as well as Indian; beyond that, he received intensive tuition in arithmetic, geography, chemistry, political economy, philosophy, Sanskrit, and something that his tutor called "conversations on given subjects," which was, I suppose, designed to fill any gaps in the small-talk of royal social life.

It is astonishing, when I think back on it, that these two people, brought up in such a tradition-ridden atmosphere, married in the customary way by an arrangement between their elders, should have become leaders of change and reform, encouraging new and more liberal ideas in an orthodox society. My grandfather devoted his life to modernizing the state of Baroda, building schools, colleges, libraries, and an outstanding museum and providing an admirable and just administration. He took an enthusiastic interest in everything from commissioning a special translation of *Alice in Wonderland* into Marathi to working for Hindu women's emancipation, even to the point of introducing the revolutionary concept of divorce in Baroda. (My mother used to tease my grandmother, undaunted by her rectitude, about having a husband who was so warm an advocate of divorce. My grandmother tried to be dignified and huffy but was soon overcome by that wonderful silent laugh of hers, her face contorted, her body shaking like a jelly, and not a sound out of her mouth.)

My grandfather felt particularly strongly about the inequalities and abuses that had evolved in Indian society and were protected by the caste system. Hindus are born into one of four castes, which are, in descending order, the Brahmins (originally the scholars and priests), the Kshatriyas (warriors and often, as a result of skill in conquest or a reward for success, rulers and large landowners), Vaisyas (usually businessmen, traders, artisans), and Sudras (usually the peasants, though all peasants are not Sudras). In a separate group were those Hindus who were excluded from the ordinary social and religious privileges of Hinduism and were known as Untouchables. They performed the most menial tasks—sweeping streets, cleaning latrines—and thus were thought to carry pollution to caste Hindus.

36   Mahatma Gandhi, in the emotional battle for the acceptance of the Untouchables by Hindu society, acted as their champion, changing their name to Harijans (Loved Ones of God) and insisting that they be allowed access to temples from which they had always been excluded. Their legal battles were fought for them by one of the most brilliant men in Indian politics, Dr. Bhimrao Ramji Ambedkar, himself a Harijan. Dr. Ambedkar was one of my grandfather's special protégés, encouraged and educated by him when he was a penniless boy. After his long crusade for the advancement of his community, Dr. Ambedkar was appointed chairman of the committee that drafted the Constitution of free India.

37   My grandmother played a strong though less conspicuous part in the life of Baroda State. I can see her so plainly in the mornings, coping with her personal affairs—choosing saris, making up her mind about lengths of silk or cloth of gold that her maids held up, listening attentively to the cooks with menus for the day, giving orders to the tailor, asking about domestic details; in short, supervising the running of an enormous household—and still giving her alert attention to the grievances and complaints of any of her women subjects, whether it was the illness of a child or a dispute in a family about the inheritance of land.

38   This was all part of a maharani's duty, and so were the more ceremonial occasions, as when she presided over formal durbars in the women's apartments of the Baroda Palace. I especially remember the first one I saw, her birthday durbar. All the wives and womenfolk of the nobility and the great landowners were assembled in their richest clothes and jewellery to pay homage to my grandmother. She was seated on a *gaddi*, a cushioned throne, and wore a sari made of rose-pink cloth of gold, draped in the Maratha way with a pleated train between the legs.

39   Along with her dazzling sari, my grandmother wore all the traditional jewellery for this occasion, including heavy diamond anklets and a wealth of diamond rings on her fingers and toes. The noble ladies paid their respects to her with a formal folding of hands in a *namaskar* and offered her the traditional gold coin to signify their allegiance. At the end of the hall was a troupe of musicians and dancers from Tanjore in south India. Like many Indian princes, my grandfather maintained the troupe as palace retainers, and they always gave a performance of the classical south Indian dancing called *bharata natyam* at any impor-

tant palace occasion. At such festive times, the family all ate off gold *thals,* while everyone else ate off silver. (This distinction always used to embarrass me.)

My mother, Princess Indira Gaekwar of Baroda, was the only daughter of these two extraordinary people. Because of their advanced views on education, she was one of the first Indian princesses to go to school and to graduate from Baroda College. She also accompanied her parents on their trips to England. One of the earliest stories I know about her tells how she and her four brothers, all quite small and dressed identically in white pyjama trousers and brocade jackets, with gold-embroidered caps, were taken to Buckingham Palace to be presented to Queen Victoria. As they stood before her, the elderly Queen-Empress asked which one was the little girl. Five pairs of dark brown eyes stared back at her, and then, because they all enjoyed fooling grown-ups, one of the boys stepped forward. But they underestimated Queen Victoria, who, sensing that something was wrong, walked around to the back of the row of solemn children, and there a long black pigtail betrayed my mother.

It is difficult to describe my mother without slipping into unconvincing superlatives. She was, quite simply, the most beautiful and exciting woman any of us knew. Even now, when I have travelled widely and have met many famous beauties from all levels of society, she remains in my memory as an unparalleled combination of wit, warmth, and exquisite looks. She was photographed and painted many times, but while those pictures show the physical charm—the enormous eyes, the lovely modelling of her face, the slightly drooping mouth that made you want to make her smile, the tiny fragile figure—none of them captures the electric vitality that made her the focus of attention wherever she went. Her own passionate interest and concern for others made her both special and accessible to anybody. She was always called "Ma," not only by us but by friends and even by the peasants of Cooch Behar. As a child I was fascinated by her—what she said, what she did, what she wore. With her, nothing was ever dull and one felt that at any moment anything might happen.

She herself was oddly unaware of the impression she created, and this, I suppose, was due to her mother's fear, during her childhood, that she might become spoiled—an only daughter, adored by her father, loved and cherished by her brothers. If anyone commented favourably on my mother's looks, my grandmother would immediately counter the admiration with some deprecating comment like, "Her nose is too lumpy at the end—just look," or, "Her hair hasn't a trace of a curl to it."

My mother once told me that she had no idea that she was even passably good-looking until one day when her brothers were discussing some attractive girl they had met. Seeing their sister looking a bit dejected, one of them said, with true brotherly enthusiasm, "You know, you're not all that bad yourself."

44   For the first time she really *looked* at herself in the mirror and thought, Well, he may be right. I'm *not* all that bad.

✧ Evaluating the Text

1. What features of Devi's account give you the clearest idea of what her life was like in the privileged surroundings in which she was raised? What role do the different cultural customs reflected in her account play in Devi's life at the palace?

2. What kinds of things provided her with the most enjoyment? How was she educated and how was she made aware of the special responsibilities that she would have to assume as a member of royalty?

3. What impressions do you get of her grandparents and mother and their influence on her life?

✧ Exploring Different Perspectives

1. In what respects is Devi's childhood similar and dissimilar to that of Fatima Mernissi's (in a harem in Morocco) in terms of the self-enclosed worlds in which they were raised?

2. Which of the cultural values described by Gayatri Devi is still important in modern-day India, as evident in Serena Nanda's account "Arranging a Marriage in India"?

✧ Extending Viewpoints through Writing

1. Contained in the panoramic sweep of Devi's description are innumerable fascinating aspects of her everyday life that she touches on but does not explore in depth. Choose one of these and, after doing some research, write a short essay that explains its function in Indian culture.

2. What is the most exotic place you have ever visited? Describe the architecture, everyday rituals, and customs that will bring your reader into this world.

Serena Nanda

Arranging a Marriage in India

◆

Serena Nanda is professor of anthropology at John Jay College of Criminal Justice, City University of New York. Her fields of interest are visual anthropology, gender, and culture and law. She has carried out field studies in India, in tribal development, and on the social lives of women in urban India. Her published works include Cultural Anthropology, *third edition (1987),* American Cultural Pluralism and Law *(1990), and* Neither Man nor Woman: The Hijras of India *(1990), which won the Ruth Benedict Prize. In the following selection, which first appeared in* The Naked Anthropologist: Tales from Around the World, *edited by Philip R. DeVita (1992), Nanda looks at the cultural forces that have resulted in the practice of arranged marriages in Indian society.*

> *Sister and doctor brother-in-law invite correspondence from North Indian professionals only, for a beautiful, talented, sophisticated, intelligent sister, 5'3", slim, M.A. in textile design, father a senior civil officer. Would prefer immigrant doctors, between 26–29 years. Reply with full details and returnable photo.*
>
> *A well-settled uncle invites matrimonial correspondence from slim, fair, educated South Indian girl, for his nephew, 25 years, smart, M.B.A., green card holder, 5'6". Full particulars with returnable photo appreciated.*
>
> —Matrimonial Advertisements, *India Abroad*

In India, almost all marriages are arranged. Even among the educated middle classes in modern, urban India, marriage is as much a concern of the families as it is of the individuals. So customary is the practice of arranged marriage that there is a special name for a marriage which is not arranged: It is called a "love match." 1

On my first field trip to India, I met many young men and women whose parents were in the process of "getting them married." In many cases, the bride and groom would not meet each other before the marriage. At most they might meet for a brief conversation, and this meeting 2

*For information on India, see p. 34.

would take place only after their parents had decided that the match was suitable. Parents do not compel their children to marry a person who either marriage partner finds objectionable. But only after one match is refused will another be sought.

3   As a young American woman in India for the first time, I found this custom of arranged marriage oppressive. How could any intelligent young person agree to such a marriage without great reluctance? It was contrary to everything I believed about the importance of romantic love as the only basis of a happy marriage. It also clashed with my strongly held notions that the choice of such an intimate and permanent relationship could be made only by the individuals involved. Had anyone tried to arrange my marriage, I would have been defiant and rebellious!

4   At the first opportunity, I began, with more curiosity than tact, to question the young people I met on how they felt about this practice. Sita, one of my young informants, was a college graduate with a degree in political science. She had been waiting for over a year while her parents were arranging a match for her. I found it difficult to accept the docile manner in which this well-educated young woman awaited the outcome of a process that would result in her spending the rest of her life with a man she hardly knew, a virtual stranger, picked out by her parents.

5   "How can you go along with this?" I asked her, in frustration and distress. "Don't you care who you marry?"

6   "Of course I care," she answered. "This is why I must let my parents choose a boy for me. My marriage is too important to be arranged by such an inexperienced person as myself. In such matters, it is better to have my parents' guidance."

7   I had learned that young men and women in India do not date and have very little social life involving members of the opposite sex. Although I could not disagree with Sita's reasoning, I continued to pursue the subject.

8   "But how can you marry the first man you have ever met? Not only have you missed the fun of meeting a lot of different people, but you have not given yourself the chance to know who is the right man for you."

9   "Meeting with a lot of different people doesn't sound like any fun at all," Sita answered. "One hears that in America the girls are spending more time worrying about whether they will meet a man and get married. Here we have the chance to enjoy our life and let our parents do this work and worrying for us."

10   She had me there. The high anxiety of the competition to "be popular" with the opposite sex certainly was the most prominent feature of life as an American teenager in the late fifties. The endless worrying about the rules that governed our behavior and about our popularity ratings sapped both our self-esteem and our enjoyment of adolescence.

I reflected that absence of this competition in India most certainly may have contributed to the self-confidence and natural charm of so many of the young women I met.

And yet, the idea of marrying a perfect stranger, whom one did not   11
know and did not "love," so offended my American ideas of individualism and romanticism, that I persisted with my objections.

"I still can't imagine it," I said. "How can you agree to marry a man   12
you hardly know?"

"But of course he will be known. My parents would never arrange   13
a marriage for me without knowing all about the boy's family background. Naturally we will not rely only on what the family tells us. We will check the particulars out ourselves. No one will want their daughter to marry into a family that is not good. All these things we will know beforehand."

Impatiently, I responded, "Sita, I don't mean know the family, I   14
mean, know the man. How can you marry someone you don't know personally and don't love? How can you think of spending your life with someone you may not even like?"

"If he is a good man, why should I not like him?" she said. "With   15
you people, you know the boy so well before you marry, where will be the fun to get married? There will be no mystery and no romance. Here we have the whole of our married life to get to know and love our husband. This way is better, is it not?"

Her response made further sense, and I began to have second   16
thoughts on the matter. Indeed, during months of meeting many intelligent young Indian people, both male and female, who had the same ideas as Sita, I saw arranged marriages in a different light. I also saw the importance of the family in Indian life and realized that a couple who took their marriage into their own hands was taking a big risk, particularly if their families were irreconcilably opposed to the match. In a country where every important resource in life—a job, a house, a social circle—is gained through family connections, it seemed foolhardy to cut oneself off from a supportive social network and depend solely on one person for happiness and success.

Six years later I returned to India to again do fieldwork, this time   17
among the middle class in Bombay, a modern, sophisticated city. From the experience of my earlier visit, I decided to include a study of arranged marriages in my project. By this time I had met many Indian couples whose marriages had been arranged and who seemed very happy. Particularly in contrast to the fate of many of my married friends in the United States who were already in the process of divorce, the positive aspects of arranged marriages appeared to me to outweigh the negatives. In fact, I thought I might even participate in arranging a marriage myself. I had been fairly successful in the United States in

"fixing up" many of my friends, and I was confident that my match-making skills could be easily applied to this new situation, once I learned the basic rules. "After all," I thought, "how complicated can it be? People want pretty much the same things in a marriage whether it is in India or America."

18   An opportunity presented itself almost immediately. A friend from my previous Indian trip was in the process of arranging for the marriage of her eldest son. In India there is a perceived shortage of "good boys," and since my friend's family was eminently respectable and the boy himself personable, well educated, and nice looking, I was sure that by the end of my year's fieldwork, we would have found a match.

19   The basic rule seems to be that a family's reputation is most important. It is understood that matches would be arranged only within the same caste and general social class, although some crossing of sub-castes is permissible if the class positions of the bride's and groom's families are similar. Although dowry is now prohibited by law in India, extensive gift exchanges took place with every marriage. Even when the boy's family do not "make demands," every girl's family neverthe-less feels the obligation to give the traditional gifts, to the girl, to the boy, and to the boy's family. Particularly when the couple would be liv-ing in the joint family—that is, with the boy's parents and his married brothers and their families, as well as with unmarried siblings—which is still very common even among the urban, upper-middle class in In-dia, the girl's parents are anxious to establish smooth relations between their family and that of the boy. Offering the proper gifts, even when not called "dowry," is often an important factor in influencing the rela-tionship between the bride's and groom's families and perhaps, also, the treatment of the bride in her new home.

20   In a society where divorce is still a scandal and where, in fact, the divorce rate is exceedingly low, an arranged marriage is the beginning of a lifetime relationship not just between the bride and groom but be-tween their families as well. Thus, while a girl's looks are important, her character is even more so, for she is being judged as a prospective daughter-in-law as much as a prospective bride. Where she would be living in a joint family, as was the case with my friend, the girl's ability to get along harmoniously in a family is perhaps the single most impor-tant quality in assessing her suitability.

21   My friend is a highly esteemed wife, mother, and daughter-in-law. She is religious, soft-spoken, modest, and deferential. She rarely gos-sips and never quarrels, two qualities highly desirable in a woman. A family that has the reputation for gossip and conflict among its wom-enfolk will not find it easy to get good wives for their sons. Parents will not want to send their daughter to a house in which there is conflict.

22   My friend's family were originally from North India. They had lived in Bombay, where her husband owned a business, for forty years.

The family had delayed in seeking a match for their eldest son because he had been an Air Force pilot for several years, stationed in such remote places that it had seemed fruitless to try to find a girl who would be willing to accompany him. In their social class, a military career, despite its economic security, has little prestige and is considered a drawback in finding a suitable bride. Many families would not allow their daughters to marry a man in an occupation so potentially dangerous and which requires so much moving around.

The son had recently left the military and joined his father's business. Since he was a college graduate, modern, and well traveled, from such a good family, and, I thought, quite handsome, it seemed to me that he, or rather his family, was in a position to pick and choose. I said as much to my friend.   23

While she agreed that there were many advantages on their side, she also said, "We must keep in mind that my son is both short and dark; these are drawbacks in finding the right match." While the boy's height had not escaped my notice, "dark" seemed to me inaccurate; I would have called him "wheat" colored perhaps, and in any case, I did not realize that color would be a consideration. I discovered, however, that while a boy's skin color is a less important consideration than a girl's, it is still a factor.   24

An important source of contacts in trying to arrange her son's marriage was my friend's social club in Bombay. Many of the women had daughters of the right age, and some had already expressed an interest in my friend's son. I was most enthusiastic about the possibilities of one particular family who had five daughters, all of whom were pretty, demure, and well educated. Their mother had told my friend, "You can have your pick for your son, whichever one of my daughters appeals to you most."   25

I saw a match in sight. "Surely," I said to my friend, "we will find one there. Let's go visit and make our choice." But my friend held back; she did not seem to share my enthusiasm, for reasons I could not then fathom.   26

When I kept pressing for an explanation of her reluctance, she admitted, "See, Serena, here is the problem. The family has so many daughters, how will they be able to provide nicely for any of them? We are not making any demands, but still, with so many daughters to marry off, one wonders whether she will even be able to make a proper wedding. Since this is our eldest son, it's best if we marry him to a girl who is the only daughter, then the wedding will truly be a gala affair." I argued that surely the quality of the girls themselves made up for any deficiency in the elaborateness of the wedding. My friend admitted this point but still seemed reluctant to proceed.   27

"Is there something else," I asked her, "some factor I have missed?" "Well," she finally said, "there is one other thing. They have one   28 daughter already married and living in Bombay. The mother is always complaining to me that the girl's in-laws don't let her visit her own family often enough. So it makes me wonder, will she be that kind of mother who always wants her daughter at her own home? This will prevent the girl from adjusting to our house. It is not a good thing." And so, this family of five daughters was dropped as a possibility.

29   Somewhat disappointed, I nevertheless respected my friend's reasoning and geared up for the next prospect. This was also the daughter of a woman in my friend's social club. There was clear interest in this family and I could see why. The family's reputation was excellent; in fact, they came from a subcaste slightly higher than my friend's own. The girl, who was an only daughter, was pretty and well educated and had a brother studying in the United States. Yet, after expressing an interest to me in this family, all talk of them suddenly died down and the search began elsewhere.

30   "What happened to that girl as a prospect?" I asked one day. "You never mention her any more. She is so pretty and so educated, what did you find wrong?"

31   "She is too educated. We've decided against it. My husband's father saw the girl on the bus the other day and thought her forward. A girl who 'roams about' the city by herself is not the girl for our family." My disappointment this time was even greater, as I thought the son would have liked the girl very much. But then I thought, my friend is right, a girl who is going to live in a joint family cannot be too independent or she will make life miserable for everyone. I also learned that if the family of the girl has even a slightly higher social status than the family of the boy, the bride may think herself too good for them, and this too will cause problems. Later my friend admitted to me that this had been an important factor in her decision not to pursue the match.

32   The next candidate was the daughter of a client of my friend's husband. When the client learned that the family was looking for a match for their son, he said, "Look no further, we have a daughter." This man then invited my friends to dinner to see the girl. He had already seen their son at the office and decided that "he liked the boy." We all went together for tea, rather than dinner—it was less of a commitment—and while we were there, the girl's mother showed us around the house. The girl was studying for her exams and was briefly introduced to us.

33   After we left, I was anxious to hear my friend's opinion. While her husband liked the family very much and was impressed with his client's business accomplishments and reputation, the wife didn't like the girl's looks. "She is short, no doubt, which is an important plus point, but she is also fat and wears glasses." My friend obviously thought she could do better for her son and asked her husband to make his excuses to his client by saying that they had decided to postpone the boy's marriage indefinitely.

By this time almost six months had passed and I was becoming im-   34
patient. What I had thought would be an easy matter to arrange was
turning out to be quite complicated. I began to believe that between my
friend's desire for a girl who was modest enough to fit into her joint
family, yet attractive and educated enough to be an acceptable partner
for her son, she would not find anyone suitable. My friend laughed at
my impatience: "Don't be so much in a hurry," she said. "You Americans want everything done so quickly. You get married quickly and
then just as quickly get divorced. Here we take marriage more seriously. We must take all the factors into account. It is not enough for us
to learn by our mistakes. This is too serious a business. If a mistake is
made we have not only ruined the life of our son or daughter, but we
have spoiled the reputation of our family as well. And that will make it
much harder for their brothers and sisters to get married. So we must
be very careful."

What she said was true and I promised myself to be more patient,   35
though it was not easy. I had really hoped and expected that the match
would be made before my year in India was up. But it was not to be.
When I left India my friend seemed no further along in finding a suitable match for her son than when I had arrived.

Two years later, I returned to India and still my friend had not   36
found a girl for her son. By this time, he was close to thirty, and I think
she was a little worried. Since she knew I had friends all over India,
and I was going to be there for a year, she asked me to "help her in this
work" and keep an eye out for someone suitable. I was flattered that
my judgment was respected, but knowing now how complicated the
process was, I had lost my earlier confidence as a matchmaker. Nevertheless, I promised that I would try.

It was almost at the end of my year's stay in India that I met a fam-   37
ily with a marriageable daughter whom I felt might be a good possibility for my friend's son. The girl's father was related to a good friend of
mine and by coincidence came from the same village as my friend's
husband. This new family had a successful business in a medium-sized
city in central India and were from the same subcaste as my friend. The
daughter was pretty and chic; in fact, she had studied fashion design in
college. Her parents would not allow her to go off by herself to any of
the major cities in India where she could make a career, but they had
compromised with her wish to work by allowing her to run a small
dressmaking boutique from their home. In spite of her desire to have a
career, the daughter was both modest and home-loving and had had a
traditional, sheltered upbringing. She had only one other sister, already
married, and a brother who was in his father's business.

I mentioned the possibility of a match with my friend's son. The   38
girl's parents were most interested. Although their daughter was not
eager to marry just yet, the idea of living in Bombay—a sophisticated,

extremely fashion-conscious city where she could continue her education in clothing design—was a great inducement. I gave the girl's father my friend's address and suggested that when they went to Bombay on some business or whatever, they look up the boy's family.

39   Returning to Bombay on my way to New York, I told my friend of this newly discovered possibility. She seemed to feel there was potential but, in spite of my urging, would not make any moves herself. She rather preferred to wait for the girl's family to call upon them. I hoped something would come of this introduction, though by now I had learned to rein in my optimism.

40   A year later I received a letter from my friend. The family had indeed come to visit Bombay, and their daughter and my friend's daughter, who were near in age, had become very good friends. During that year, the two girls had frequently visited each other. I thought things looked promising.

41   Last week I received an invitation to a wedding: My friend's son and the girl were getting married. Since I had found the match, my presence was particularly requested at the wedding. I was thrilled. Success at last! As I prepared to leave for India, I began thinking, "Now, my friend's younger son, who do I know who has a nice girl for him...?"

EPILOGUE

This essay was written from the point of view of a family seeking a daughter-in-law. Arranged marriage looks somewhat different from the point of view of the bride and her family. Arranged marriage continues to be preferred, even among the more educated, westernized sections of the Indian population. Many young women from these families still go along, more or less willingly, with the practice and also with the specific choices of their families. Young women do get excited about the prospects of their marriage, but there is also ambivalence and increasing uncertainty as the bride contemplates leaving the comfort and familiarity of her own home where, as a "temporary guest," she had often been indulged, to live among strangers. Even in the best situation she will now come under the close scrutiny of her husband's family. How she dresses, how she behaves, how she gets along with others, where she goes, how she spends her time, her domestic abilities—all this and much more—will be observed and commented on by a whole new set of relations. Her interaction with her family of birth will be monitored and curtailed considerably. Not only will she leave their home, but with increasing geographic mobility she may also live very far from them, perhaps even on another continent. Too much expression of her fondness for her own family or her desire to visit them may be interpreted as an inability to adjust to her new family and may become a source of conflict. In an arranged marriage the burden of adjustment is clearly heavier for a woman than for a man. And this is in the best of situations.

In less happy circumstances, the bride may be a target of resentment and hostility from her husband's family, particularly her mother-in-law or her husband's unmarried sisters, for whom she is now a source of competition for the affection, loyalty, and economic resources of their son or brother. If she is psychologically or even physically abused, her options are limited, because returning to her parents' home or divorce is still very stigmatized. For most Indians, marriage and motherhood are still considered the only suitable roles for a woman, even for those who have careers, and few women can comfortably contemplate remaining unmarried. Most families still consider "marrying off" their daughter as a compelling religious duty and social necessity. This increases a bride's sense of obligation to make the marriage a success, at whatever cost to her own personal happiness.

The vulnerability of a new bride may also be intensified by the issue of dowry, which, although illegal, has become a more pressing issue in the consumer-conscious society of contemporary urban India. In many cases, if a groom's family is not satisfied with the amount of dowry that a bride brings to her marriage, the young bride will be constantly harassed to get her parents to give more. In extreme cases, the bride may even be murdered, and the murder disguised as an accident or suicide. This also offers the husband's family an opportunity to arrange another match for him, thus bringing in another dowry. This phenomenon, called dowry death, calls attention not just to the evils of dowry, but also to larger issues of the powerlessness of women.

✧ Evaluating the Text

1. From an Indian perspective, what are the advantages of an arranged marriage?

2. What considerations are taken into account in arranging a marriage in India?

3. What role does Nanda play in helping to find a suitable bride for her friend's son? How would you characterize Nanda's attitude toward arranged marriage and in what way does it change over the course of events?

✧ Exploring Different Perspectives

1. Compare and contrast the perspectives on life in India, then and now, as told by Gayatri Devi in "A Princess Remembers" and in Nanda's account. What values, if any, have remained the same?

2. Compare the expectations regarding the role of women in traditional cultures in the accounts by Nanda and Fatima Mernissi (see "Moonlit Nights of Laughter").

✧ Extending Viewpoints through Writing

1. Would you ever consider allowing your parents to arrange a marriage for you? If so, why would this be more advantageous or disadvantageous than finding someone for yourself?

2. What circumstances led your parents to get married? What considerations, in your opinion, played the most important role?

3. What did this essay add to your understanding of the pressures couples experience when getting married in India? To what extent are these pressures similar to or different from those experienced by couples in the United States?

Daniela Deane

The Little Emperors

◆————◆

Daniela Deane is a free-lance writer who contributes to the Washington Post *and* Newsweek. *She lives with her husband and two sons in Italy. "The Little Emperors," which first appeared in the* Los Angeles Times Magazine, *July 26, 1992, describes the consequences of China's population management program that encourages couples to marry late and have only one child. Faced with a staggering doubling of the population during Mao Zedong's (Tse-tung's) rule, China, the world's most populous country, with 1.16 billion people, has strictly enforced this one-child policy, and as of 1999 prenatal care became compulsory.*

The People's Republic of China is ruled by a government established in 1949 after the victory of Mao Zedong and his communist forces against the Nationalist forces of Chiang Kai-shek, who fled to Taiwan and set up a government in exile. Under Mao's leadership, industry was nationalized and a land reform program, based on collectivization, was introduced. China entered the Korean War against United Nations forces between 1950 and the Armistice of 1953. China's modern history has been characterized by cycles of liberalization followed by violent oppression. In 1957, reaction against the so-called let a hundred flowers bloom period led to a crackdown against intellectuals. In 1966, Mao launched the Cultural Revolution to purge the government and society of liberal elements. After Mao's death in 1976, a backlash led to the imprisoning of Mao's wife, Jiang Qing, and three colleagues (the "Gang of Four"). A period of liberalization once again followed, as Deng Xiao Ping came to power in 1977 and adopted more conciliatory economic, social, and political policies. The United States recognized the People's Republic of China as a valid government on January 1, 1979. The pattern re-emerged in June 1989, when government troops were sent into Tiananmen Square to crush the prodemocracy movement. Zhao Ziyang, who had shown sympathy toward the students, was ousted and replaced by hardliner Jing Zemin. The June events, in which thousands are reported to have died, led to a crackdown and execution of sympathizers throughout China, despite widespread international condemnation. A behind-the-scenes power struggle in 1992 by Deng Xiaoping has led to some economic market style reforms although political liberalization still is not allowed. In March 1998, Zhu Rongji was named to succeed Li Peng as premier.

Xu Ming sits on the worn sofa with his short, chubby arms and legs 1 splayed, forced open by fat and the layers of padded clothing worn in northern China to ward off the relentless chill. To reach the floor, the tubby 8-year-old rocks back and forth on his big bottom, inching forward slowly, eventually ending upright. Xu Ming finds it hard to move.

2   "He got fat when he was about 3," says his father, Xu Jianguo, holding the boy's bloated, dimpled hand. "We were living with my parents and they were very good to him. He's the only grandson. It's a tradition in China that boys are very loved. They love him very much, and so they feed him a lot. They give him everything he wants."

3   Xu Ming weighs 135 pounds, about twice what he should at his age. He's one of hundreds of children who have sought help in the past few years at the Beijing Children's Hospital, which recently began the first American-style fat farm for obese children in what was once the land of skin and bones.

4   "We used to get a lot of cases of malnutrition," says Dr. Ni Guichen, director of endocrinology at the hospital and founder of the weight reduction classes. "But in the last 10 years, the problem has become obese children. The number of fat children in China is growing very fast. The main reason is the one-child policy," she says, speaking in a drab waiting room. "Because parents can only have one child, the families take extra good care of that one child, which means feeding him too much."

5   Bulging waistlines are one result of China's tough campaign to curb its population. The one-child campaign, a strict national directive that seeks to limit each Chinese couple to a single son or daughter, has other dramatic consequences: millions of abortions, fewer girls and a generation of spoiled children.

6   The 10-day weight-reduction sessions—a combination of exercise, nutritional guidance and psychological counseling—are very popular. Hundreds of children—some so fat they can hardly walk—are turned away for each class.

7   According to Ni, about 5% of children in China's cities are obese, with two obese boys for every overweight girl, the traditional preference toward boys being reflected in the amount of attention lavished on the child. "Part of the course is also centered on the parents. We try to teach them how to bring their children up properly, not just by spoiling them," Ni says.

8   Ming's father is proud that his son, after two sessions at the fat farm, has managed to halve his intake of *jiaozi*, the stodgy meat-filled dumplings that are Ming's particular weakness, from 30 to 15 at a sitting. "Even if he's not full, that's all he gets," he says. "In the beginning, it was very difficult. He would put his arms around our necks and beg us for more food. We couldn't bear it, so we'd give him a little more."

9   Ming lost a few pounds but hasn't been able to keep the weight off. He's a bit slimmer now, but only because he's taller. "I want to lose

weight," says Ming, who spends his afternoons snacking at his grand-parents' house and his evenings plopped in front of the television set at home. "The kids make fun of me, they call me a fat pig. I hate the nick-names. In sports class, I can't do what the teacher says. I can run a little bit, but after a while I have to sit down. The teacher puts me at the front of the class where all the other kids can see me. They all laugh and make fun of me."

The many fat children visible on China's city streets are just the most   10
obvious example of 13 years of the country's one-child policy. In the vast countryside, the policy has meant shadowy lives as second-class citizens for thousands of girls, or, worse, death. It has made abortion a way of life and a couple's sexual intimacy the government's concern. Even women's menstrual cycles are monitored. Under the directive, couples literally have to line up for permission to procreate. Second children are some-times possible, but only on payment of a heavy fine.

The policy is an unparalleled intrusion into the private lives of a   11
nation's citizens, an experiment on a scale never attempted elsewhere in the world. But no expert will argue that China—by far the world's most populous country with 1.16 billion people—could continue with-out strict curbs on its population.

China's communist government adopted the one-child policy in   12
1979 in response to the staggering doubling of the country's population during Mao Tse-tung's rule. Mao, who died in 1976, was convinced that the country's masses were a strategic asset and vigorously encour-aged the Chinese to produce even-larger families.

But large families are now out for the Chinese—20% of the world's   13
population living on just 7% of the arable land. "China has to have a population policy," says Huang Baoshan, deputy director of the State Family Planning Commission. With the numbers ever growing, "how can we feed them, house them?"

Dinner time for one 5-year-old girl consists of granddad chasing   14
her through the house, bowl and spoon in hand, barking like a dog or mewing like a cat. If he performs authentically enough, she rewards him by accepting a mouthful of food. No problem, insists granddad, "it's good exercise for her."

An 11-year-old boy never gets up to go to the toilet during the   15
night. That's because his mother, summoned by a shout, gets up in-stead and positions a bottle under the covers for him. "We wouldn't want him to have to get up in the night," his mother says.

Another mother wanted her 16-year-old to eat some fruit, but the   16
teen-ager was engrossed in a video game. Not wanting him to get his fingers sticky or daring to interrupt, she peeled several grapes and popped one after another into his mouth. "Not so fast," he snapped. "Can't you see I have to spit out the seeds?"

17   Stories like these are routinely published in China's newspapers, evidence that the government-imposed birth-control policy has produced an emerging generation of spoiled, lazy, selfish, self-centered and overweight children. There are about 40 million only children in China. Dubbed the country's "Little Emperors," their behavior toward their elders is likened to that of the young emperor Pu Yi, who heaped indignities on his eunuch servants while making them cater to his whims, as chronicled in Bernardo Bertolucci's film *The Last Emperor.*

18   Many studies on China's only children have been done. One such study confirmed that only children generally are not well liked. The study, conducted by a team of Chinese psychologists, asked a group of 360 Chinese children, half who have siblings and half who don't, to rate each other's behavior. The only children were, without fail, the least popular, regardless of age or social background. Peers rated them more uncooperative and selfish than children with brothers and sisters. They bragged more, were less helpful in group activities and more apt to follow their own selfish interests. And they wouldn't share their toys.

19   The Chinese lay a lot of blame on what they call the "4-2-1" syndrome—four doting grandparents, two overindulgent parents, all pinning their hopes and ambitions on one child.

20   Besides stuffing them with food, Chinese parents have very high expectations of their one *bao bei*, or treasured object. Some have their still-in-strollers babies tested for IQ levels. Others try to teach toddlers Tang Dynasty poetry. Many shell out months of their hard-earned salaries for music lessons and instruments for children who have no talent or interest in playing. They fill their kids' lives with lessons in piano, English, gymnastics and typing.

21   The one-child parents, most of them from traditionally large Chinese families, grew up during the chaotic, 10-year Cultural Revolution, when many of the country's cultural treasures were destroyed and schools were closed for long periods of time. Because many of that generation spent years toiling in the fields rather than studying, they demand—and put all their hopes into—academic achievement for their children.

22   "We've already invested a lot of money in his intellectual development," Wang Zhouzhi told me in her Spartan home in a tiny village of Changping country outside Beijing, discussing her son, Chenqian, an only child. "I don't care how much money we spend on him. We've bought him an organ and we push him hard. Unfortunately, he's only a mediocre student," she says, looking toward the 10-year-old boy. Chenqian, dressed in a child-sized Chinese army uniform, ate 10 pieces of candy during the half-hour interview and repeatedly fired off his toy pistol, all without a word of reproach from his mother.

23   Would Chenqian have liked a sibling to play with? "No," he answers loudly, firing a rapid, jarring succession of shots. His mother

breaks in: "If he had a little brother or sister, he wouldn't get every-thing he wants. Of course he doesn't want one. With only one child, I give my full care and concern to him."

But how will these children, now entering their teen-age years and   24
moving quickly toward adulthood, become the collectivist-minded cit-izens China's hard-line communist leadership demands? Some think they never will. Ironically, it may be just these overindulged children who will change Chinese society. After growing up doing as they wished, ruling their immediate families, they're not likely to obey a central government that tells them to fall in line. This new generation of egotists, who haven't been taught to take even their parents into con-sideration, simply may not be able to think of the society as a whole—the basic principle of communism.

The need for family planning is obvious in the cities, where living   25
space is limited and the one-child policy is strictly enforced and largely successful. City dwellers are slowly beginning to accept the notion that smaller families are better for the country, although most would cer-tainly want two children if they could have them. However, in the countryside, where three of every four Chinese live—nearly 900 mil-lion people—the goal of limiting each couple to only one child has proved largely elusive.

In the hinterlands, the policy has become a confusing patchwork of   26
special cases and exceptions. Provincial authorities can decide which couples can have a second child. In the southern province of Guang-dong, China's richest, two children are allowed and many couples can afford to pay the fine to have even a third or fourth child. The amounts of the fines vary across the country, the highest in populous Sichuan province, where the fine for a second child can be as much as 25% of a family's income over four years. Special treatment has been given to China's cultural minorities such as the Mongolians and the Tibetans because of their low numbers. Many of them are permitted three or four children without penalty, although some Chinese social scientists have begun to question the privilege.

"It's really become a two-child policy in the countryside," says a   27
Western diplomat. "Because of the traditional views on labor supply, the traditional bias toward the male child, it's been impossible for them to enforce a one-child policy outside the cities. In the countryside, they're really trying to stop that third child."

Thirteen years of strict family planning have created one of the   28
great mysteries of the vast and remote Chinese countryside: Where have all the little girls gone? A Swedish study of sex ratios in China, published in 1990, and based on China's own census data, concluded that several million little girls are "missing"—up to half a million a year in the years 1985 to 1987—since the policy was introduced in late 1979.

29   In the study, and in demographic research worldwide, sex ratio at birth in humans is shown to be very stable, between 105 and 106 boys for every 100 girls. The imbalance is thought to be nature's way of compensating for the higher rates of miscarriage, stillbirth and infant mortality among boys.

30   In China, the ratio climbed consistently during the 1980s, and it now rests at more than 110 boys to 100 girls. "The imbalance is evident in some areas of the country," says Stirling Scruggs, director of the United Nations Population Fund in China. "I don't think the reason is widespread infanticide. They're adopting out girls to try for a boy, they're hiding their girls, they're not registering them. Throughout Chinese history, in times of famine, and now as well, people have been forced to make choices between boys and girls, and for many reasons, boys always win out."

31   With the dismantling of collectives, families must, once again, farm their own small plots and sons are considered necessary to do the work. Additionally, girls traditionally "marry out" of their families, transferring their filial responsibilities to their in-laws. Boys carry on the family name and are entrusted with the care of their parents as they age. In the absence of a social security system, having a son is the difference between starving and eating when one is old. To combat the problem, some innovative villages have begun issuing so-called girl insurance, an old-age insurance policy for couples who have given birth to a daughter and are prepared to stop at that.

32   "People are scared to death to be childless and penniless in their old age," says William Hinton, an American author of seven books chronicling modern China. "So if they don't have a son, they immediately try for another. When the woman is pregnant, they'll have a sex test to see if it's a boy or a girl. They'll abort a girl, or go in hiding with the girl, or pay the fine, or bribe the official or leave home. Anything. It's a game of wits."

33   Shen Shufen, a sturdy, round-faced peasant woman of 33, has two children—an 8-year-old girl and a 3-year-old boy—and lives in Sihe, a dusty, one-road, mud-brick village in the countryside outside Beijing. Her husband is a truck driver. "When we had our girl, we knew we had to have another child somehow. We saved for years to pay the fine. It was hard giving them that money, 3,000 yuan ($550 in U.S. dollars), in one night. That's what my husband makes in three years. I was so happy when our second child was a boy."

34   The government seems aware of the pressure its policies put on expectant parents, and the painful results, but has not shown any flexibility. For instance, Beijing in 1990 passed a law forbidding doctors to tell a couple the results of ultrasound tests that disclose the sex of their unborn child. The reason: Too many female embryos were being aborted.

And meanwhile, several hundred thousand women—called "guer-   35
rilla moms"—go into hiding every year to have their babies. They become part of China's 40-million-strong floating population that
wanders the country, mostly in search of work, sleeping under bridges
and in front of railway stations. Tens of thousands of female children
are simply abandoned in rural hospitals.

And although most experts say female infanticide is not wide-   36
spread, it does exist. "I found a dead baby girl," says Hinton. "We
stopped for lunch at this mountain ravine in Shaanxi province. We saw
her lying there, at the bottom of the creek bed. She was all bundled up,
with one arm sticking out. She had been there a while, you could tell,
because she had a little line of mold growing across her mouth and
nostrils."

Death comes in another form, too: neglect. "It's female neglect,   37
more than female infanticide, neglect to the point of death for little
girls," says Scruggs of the U.N. Population Fund. "If you have a sick
child, and it's a girl," he says, "you might buy only half the dose of
medicine she needs to get better."

Hundreds of thousands of unregistered little girls—called "black   38
children"—live on the edge of the law, unable to get food rations, im-
munizations or places in school. Many reports are grim. The government-run China News Service reported last year that the drowning of
baby girls had revived to such an extent in Guangxi province that at
least 1 million boys will be unable to find wives in 20 years. And partly
because of the gender imbalance, the feudalistic practice of selling
women has been revived.

The alarming growth of the flesh trade prompted authorities to en-   39
act a law in January that imposes jail sentences of up to 10 years and
heavy fines for people caught trafficking. The government also recently
began broadcasting a television dramatization to warn women against
the practice. The public-service message shows two women, told that
they would be given high-paying jobs, being lured to a suburban
home. Instead, they are locked in a small, dark room, and soon realize
that they have been sold.

Li Wangping is nervous. She keeps looking at the air vents at the   40
bottom of the office door, to see if anyone is walking by or, worse still,
standing there listening. She rubs her hands together over and over.
She speaks in a whisper. "I'm afraid to get into trouble talking to you,"
Li confides. She says nothing for a few minutes.

"After my son was born, I desperately wanted another baby," the   41
42-year-old woman finally begins. "I just wanted to have more children, you understand? Anyway, I got pregnant three times, because I
wasn't using any birth control. I didn't want to use any. So, I had to

have three abortions, one right after the other. I didn't want to at all. It was terrible killing the babies I wanted so much. But I had to."

42   By Chinese standards, Li (not her real name) has a lot to lose if she chooses to follow her maternal yearnings. As an office worker at government-owned CITIC, a successful and dynamic conglomerate, she has one of the best jobs in Beijing. Just being a city-dweller already puts her ahead of most of the population.

43   "One of my colleagues had just gotten fired for having a second child. I couldn't afford to be fired," continues Li, speaking in a meeting room at CITIC headquarters. "I had to keep everything secret from the family-planning official at CITIC, from everyone at the office. Of course, I'm supposed to be using birth control. I had to lie. It was hard lying, because I felt so bad about everything."

44   She rubs her hands furiously and moves toward the door, staring continuously at the air slats. "I have to go now. There's more to say, but I'm afraid to tell you. They could find me."

45   China's family-planning officials wield awesome powers, enforcing the policy through a combination of incentives and deterrents. For those who comply, there are job promotions and small cash awards. For those who resist, they suffer stiff fines and loss of job and status within the country's tightly knit and heavily regulated communities. The State Family Planning Commission is the government ministry entrusted with the tough task of curbing the growth of the world's most populous country, where 28 children are born every minute. It employs about 200,000 full-time officials and uses more than a million volunteers to check the fertility of hundreds of millions of Chinese women.

46   "Every village or enterprise has at least one family-planning official," says Zhang Xizhi, a birth-control official in Changping county outside Beijing. "Our main job is propaganda work to raise people's consciousness. We educate people and tell them their options for birth control. We go down to every household to talk to people. We encourage them to have only one child, to marry late, to have their child later."

47   China's population police frequently keep records of the menstrual cycles of women of childbearing age, on the type of birth control they use and the pending applications to have children. If they slip up, street committees—half-governmental, half-civilian organizations that have sprung up since the 1949 Communist takeover—take up the slack. The street committees, made up mostly of retired volunteers, act as the central government's ear to the ground, snooping, spying and reporting on citizens to the authorities.

48   When a couple wants to have a child—even their first, allotted one—they must apply to the family-planning office in their township or workplace, literally lining up to procreate. "If a woman gets preg-

nant without permission, she and her husband will get fined, even if it's their first," Zhang says. "It is fair to fine her, because she creates a burden on the whole society by jumping her place in line."

If a woman in Nanshao township, where Zhang works, becomes   49
pregnant with a second child, she must terminate her pregnancy unless she or her husband or their first child is disabled or if both parents are only children. Her local family-planning official will repeatedly visit her at home to pressure her to comply. "Sometimes I have to go to people's homes five or six times to explain everything to them over and over to get them to have an abortion," says Zhang Cuiqing, the family-planning official for Sihe village, where there are 2,900 married women of childbearing age, of which 2,700 use some sort of birth control. Of those, 570 are sterilized and 1,100 have IUDs. Zhang recites the figures proudly, adding, "If they refuse, they will be fined between 20,000 and 50,000 yuan (U.S. $3,700 to $9,500)." The average yearly wage in Sihe is 1,500 yuan ($285).

The lack of early sexual education and unreliable IUDs are combin-   50
ing to make abortion—which is free, as are condoms and IUDs—a cornerstone of the one-child policy. Local officials are told not to use force, but rather education and persuasion, to meet their targets. However, the desire to fulfill their quotas, coupled with pressure from their bosses in Beijing, can lead to abuses by overzealous officials.

"Some local family-planning officials are running amok, because of   51
the targets they have to reach," a Western health specialist says, "and there are a bunch of people willing to turn a blind eye to abuses because the target is so important."

The official *Shanghai Legal Daily* last year reported on a family-   52
planning committee in central Sichuan province that ordered the flogging of the husbands of 10 pregnant women who refused to have abortions. According to the newspaper, the family-planning workers marched the husbands one by one into an empty room, ordered them to strip and lie on the floor and then beat them with a stick, once for every day their wives were pregnant.

"In some places, yes, things do happen," concedes Huang of the   53
State Family Planning Commission. "Sometimes, family-planning officials do carry it too far."

The young woman lies still on the narrow table with her eyes shut   54
and her legs spread while the doctor quickly performs a suction abortion. A few moments, and the fetus is removed. The woman lets out a short, sharp yell. "OK, next," the doctor says.

She gets off the table and, holding a piece of cloth between her legs   55
to catch the blood and clutching her swollen womb, hobbles over to a bed and collapses. The next patient gets up and walks toward the

abortion table. No one notices a visitor watching. "It's very quick, it only takes about five minutes per abortion," says Dr. Huang Xiaomiao, chief physician at Beijing's Maternity Hospital. "No anesthetic. We don't use anesthetic for abortions or births here. Only for Cesarean sections, we use acupuncture."

56   Down the hall, 32-year-old Wu Guobin waits to be taken into the operating room to have her Fallopian tubes untied—a reversal of an earlier sterilization. "After my son was killed in an accident last year, the authorities in my province said I could try for another." In the bed next to Wu's, a dour-faced woman looks ready to cry. "She's getting sterilized," the nurse explains. "Her husband doesn't want her to, but her first child has mental problems."

57   Although it's a maternity hospital, the Family Planning Unit— where abortions, sterilizations, IUD insertions and the like are carried out—is the busiest department. "We do more abortions than births," says Dr. Fan Huimin, head of the unit. "Between 10 and 20 a day."

58   Abortions are a way of life in China, where about 10.5 million pregnancies are terminated each year. (In the United States, 1.6 million abortions are performed a year, but China's population is four to five times greater than the United States'.) One fetus is aborted for about every two children born and Chinese women often have several abortions. Usually, abortions are performed during the first trimester. But because some women resist, only to cave in under mental bullying further into their terms, abortions are also done in the later months of pregnancy, sometimes up till the eighth month.

59   Because of their population problem, the Chinese have become pioneers in contraceptive research. China will soon launch its own version of the controversial French abortion pill RU-486, which induces a miscarriage. They have perfected a non-scalpel procedure for male sterilization, with no suture required, allowing the man to "ride his bicycle home within five minutes." This year, the government plans to spend more than the $34 million it spent last year on contraception. The state will also buy some 961 million condoms to be distributed throughout the country, 11% more than in 1991.

60   But even with a family-planning policy that sends a chill down a Westerner's spine and touches every Chinese citizen's life, 64,000 babies are born every day in China and overpopulation continues to be a paramount national problem. Officials have warned that 24 million children will be born in 1992—a number just slightly less than the population of Canada. "The numbers are staggering," says Scruggs, the U.N. Population Fund official, noting that "170 million people will be added in the 1990s, which is the current population of England, France and Italy combined. There are places in China where the land can't feed that many more people as it is."

China estimates that it has prevented 200 million births since the   61
one-child policy was introduced. Women now are having an average of
2.4 children as compared to six in the late '60s. But the individual sacrifice demanded from every Chinese is immense.

Large billboards bombard the population with images of happy   62
families with only one child. The government is desperately trying to
convince the masses that producing only one child leads to a wealth-
ier, healthier and happier life. But foreigners in China tell a different
story, that the people aren't convinced. They tell of being routinely
approached—on the markets, on the streets, on the railway and asked
about the contraceptive policies of their countries. Expatriate women
in Beijing all tell stories of Chinese women enviously asking them
how many sons they have and how many children they plan to have.
They explain that they only have one child because the government
allows them only one.

"When I'm out with my three children on the weekend," says a   63
young American father who lives in Beijing, "people are always asking
me why am I allowed to have three children. You can feel when they
ask you that there is envy there. There's a natural disappointment
among the people. They just want to have more children. But there's a
resigned understanding, an acceptance that they just can't."

✧ Evaluating the Text

1. How has the one-child policy affected the ratio of the sexes of children? What Chinese cultural values and economic forces are responsible for the preference for boys?

2. How do the experiences of the parents help explain the kinds of expectations and hopes they have attached to their "little emperors"?

3. In your view, what will be the effects on Chinese society when this
   new generation of "little emperors" becomes adult? How does the way
   in which they have been raised create a potential conflict with the col-
   lectivist value system underlying Chinese society?

✧ Exploring Different Perspectives

1. Discuss the influences on family structure of growing up in communal
   societies like those in China and Morocco (see "Moonlit Nights of
   Laughter" by Fatima Mernissi).

2. Compare and contrast the effects on children in indulgent environments such as those described by Deane and by Gayatri Devi in "A
   Princess Remembers."

✧ Extending Viewpoints through Writing

1. What picture do you get of the extent to which the government in China intrudes into the everyday life of the Chinese citizen?

2. If you are an only child, to what extent have you been treated similarly to the only children in China? Have you wished that you had brothers and/or sisters? Why or why not? If you have siblings, would you have preferred to be an only child? Explain your reactions.

John Cheever

Reunion

◆

*John Cheever (1912–1982) was born in Quincy, Massachusetts. His parents
had planned for him to attend Harvard, but he was expelled at seventeen
from the Thayer Academy for smoking, which marked the end of his formal
education. Although he wrote five novels, he is best known for his deftly constructed short stories of suburban affluent America that frequently appeared
in* The New Yorker. *Collections of his work include* The Enormous Radio
(1953), The House Breaker of Shady Hill *(1958),* The Brigadier and
the Golf Widow *(1964), and* The Stories of John Cheever *(1978), which
won a Pulitzer Prize, and from which "Reunion" is reprinted.*

The last time I saw my father was in Grand Central Station. I was go- 1
ing from my grandmother's in the Adirondacks to a cottage on the Cape
that my mother had rented, and I wrote my father that I would be in
New York between trains for an hour and a half and asked if we could
have lunch together. His secretary wrote to say that he would meet me at
the information booth at noon, and at twelve o'clock sharp I saw him
coming through the crowd. He was a stranger to me—my mother divorced him three years ago, and I hadn't been with him since—but as
soon as I saw him I felt that he was my father, my flesh and blood, my future and my doom. I knew that when I was grown I would be something
like him; I would have to plan my campaigns within his limitations. He
was a big, good-looking man, and I was terribly happy to see him again.
He struck me on the back and shook my hand. "Hi, Charlie," he said.
"Hi, boy. I'd like to take you up to my club, but it's in the Sixties, and if
you have to catch an early train I guess we'd better get something to eat
around here." He put his arm around me, and I smelled my father the
way my mother sniffs a rose. It was a rich compound of whiskey, after-
shave lotion, shoe polish, woolens, and the rankness of a mature male. I
hoped that someone would see us together. I wished that we could be
photographed. I wanted some record of our having been together.

We went out of the station and up a side street to a restaurant. It was 2
still early, and the place was empty. The bartender was quarreling with a
delivery boy, and there was one very old waiter in a red coat down by the
kitchen door. We sat down, and my father hailed the waiter in a loud
voice. "*Kellner!*" he shouted. "*Garçon! Cameriere! You!*" His boisterousness
in the empty restaurant seemed out of place. "Could we have a little

service here!" he shouted. "Chop-chop." Then he clapped his hands. This caught the waiter's attention, and he shuffled over to our table.

3   "Were you clapping your hands at me?" he asked.

4   "Calm down, calm down, *sommelier,*" my father said. "If it isn't too much to ask of you—if it wouldn't be too much above and beyond the call of duty, we would like a couple of Beefeater Gibsons."

5   "I don't like to be clapped at," the waiter said.

6   "I should have brought my whistle," my father said. "I have a whistle that is audible only to the ears of old waiters. Now, take out your little pad and your little pencil and see if you can get this straight: two Beefeater Gibsons. Repeat after me: two Beefeater Gibsons."

7   "I think you'd better go somewhere else," the waiter said quietly.

8   "That," said my father, "is one of the most brilliant suggestions I have ever heard. Come on, Charlie, let's get the hell out of here."

9   I followed my father out of that restaurant into another. He was not so boisterous this time. Our drinks came, and he cross-questioned me about the baseball season. He then struck the edge of his empty glass with his knife and began shouting again. "*Garçon! Kellner! You!* Could we trouble you to bring us two more of the same."

10   "How old is the boy?" the waiter asked.

11   "That," my father said, "is none of your goddamned business."

12   "I'm sorry, sir," the waiter said, "but I won't serve the boy another drink."

13   "Well, I have some news for you," my father said. "I have some very interesting news for you. This doesn't happen to be the only restaurant in New York. They've opened another on the corner. Come on, Charlie."

14   He paid the bill, and I followed him out of that restaurant into another. Here the waiters wore pink jackets like hunting coats, and there was a lot of horse tack on the walls. We sat down, and my father began to shout again. "Master of the hounds! Tallyhoo and all that sort of thing. We'd like a little something in the way of a stirrup cup. Namely, two Bibson Geefeaters."

15   "Two Bibson Geefeaters?" the waiter asked, smiling.

16   "You know damned well what I want," my father said angrily. "I want two Beefeater Gibsons, and make it snappy. Things have changed in jolly old England. So my friend the duke tells me. Let's see what England can produce in the way of a cocktail."

17   "This isn't England," the waiter said.

18   "Don't argue with me," my father said. "Just do as you're told."

19   "I just thought you might like to know where you are," the waiter said.

20   "If there is one thing I cannot tolerate," my father said, "it is an impudent domestic. Come on, Charlie."

21   The fourth place we went to was Italian. "*Buon giorno,*" my father said. "*Per favore, possiamo avere due cocktail americani, forti, forti. Molto gin, poco vermut.*"

"I don't understand Italian," the waiter said.   22

"Oh, come off it," my father said. "You understand Italian, and you   23
know damned well you do. *Vogliamo due cocktail americani. Subito.*"

The waiter left us and spoke with the captain, who came over to   24
our table and said, "I'm sorry, sir, but this table is reserved."

"All right," my father said. "Get us another table."   25

"All the tables are reserved," the captain said.   26

"I get it," my father said. "You don't desire our patronage. Is that   27
it? Well, the hell with you. *Vada all' inferno.* Let's go, Charlie."

"I have to get my train," I said.   28

"I'm sorry, sonny," my father said. "I'm terribly sorry." He put his   29
arm around me and pressed me against him. "I'll walk you back to the
station. If there had only been time to go up to my club."

"That's all right, Daddy," I said.   30

"I'll get you a paper," he said. "I'll get you a paper to read on the   31
train."

Then he went up to a newsstand and said, "Kind sir, will you be   32
good enough to favor me with one of your goddamned, no-good, ten-
cent afternoon papers?" The clerk turned away from him and stared at
a magazine cover. "Is it asking too much, kind sir," my father said, "is
it asking too much for you to sell me one of your disgusting specimens
of yellow journalism?"

"I have to go, Daddy," I said. "It's late."   33

"Now, just wait a second, sonny," he said. "Just wait a second. I   34
want to get a rise out of this chap."

"Goodbye, Daddy," I said, and I went down the stairs and got my   35
train, and that was the last time I saw my father.

✧ Evaluating the Text

1. What clues tell the reader how much the anticipated meeting with his
   father means to the boy in the story?

2. How would you characterize the father's attitude toward those of
   other nationalities and lower social classes?

3. How does the sequence of episodes that takes place in the story make
   clear why the boy would wish never to see his father again?

✧ Exploring Different Perspectives

1. Both the son in Kazuo Ishiguro's story "Family Supper" and the boy in
   Cheever's story are estranged from their fathers. Compare the reasons
   for this in both works.

2. In your opinion, why does Pat Mora's aunt in "Remembering Lobo"
   make an ally of her niece against the world, whereas the father in
   Cheever's story alienates the son?

◇ *Extending Viewpoints through Writing*

1. Has the behavior of a relative or friend toward people of other nationalities or social classes ever caused you to feel shame or embarrassment as the boy does in Cheever's story? Describe the circumstances.

2. In your view, what significant role does alcoholism play in causing rifts between parents and children?

Fatima Mernissi

Moonlit Nights of Laughter

◆

Fatima Mernissi was born in Fez, Morocco. She is a distinguished scholar whose approach is one of a feminist sociologist. Mernissi currently teaches at the University of Mohammed V in Rabat, Morocco. Among her published works are Islam and Democracy: Fear of the Modern World *(1992) and* Dreams of Trespass: Tales of a Harem Girlhood *(1994), from which the following chapter is drawn. In it, Mernissi recalls her childhood as an inhabitant of a harem (from an Arabic word meaning "forbidden"), which she characterizes as a domain in which women—spouses and daughters—are almost completely isolated from the world. Yet, within this confinement, she describes how her strong-willed mother managed to create the rarest of all events, private family dinners.*

The kingdom of Morocco is situated in northwest Africa, bounded by the Atlantic Ocean on the west, the Mediterannean Sea on the north, Algeria to the southeast, and the western Sahara to the southwest. As a result of Arab conquest in the seventh century, most Moroccans are Muslims. Originally, the country was inhabited by Berber tribespeople, who today still form a large minority living mostly in the mountains. In 1912, most of Morocco became a French protectorate, and in 1956 it became an independent nation under a traditional monarchy. Fez, the city in Mernissi's account, is located in north-central Morocco and is noted for its Muslim art and handicrafts, particularly the brimless felt hat (the fez), which was formerly a characteristic item of dress in the Middle East. The city of nearly a million has more than 100 mosques.

On Yasmina's farm, we never knew when we would eat. Sometimes, Yasmina only remembered at the last minute that she had to feed me, and then she would convince me that a few olives and a piece of her good bread, which she had baked at dawn, would be enough. But dining in our harem in Fez was an entirely different story. We ate at strictly set hours and never between meals.

To eat in Fez, we had to sit at our prescribed places at one of the four communal tables. The first table was for the men, the second for the important women, and the third for the children and less important women, which made us happy, because that meant that Aunt Habiba could eat with us. The last table was reserved for the domestics and anyone who had come in late, regardless of age, rank, or sex. That table

73

was often overcrowded, and was the last chance to get anything to eat at all for those who had made the mistake of not being on time.

3   Eating at fixed hours was what Mother hated most about communal life. She would nag Father constantly about the possibility of breaking loose and taking our immediate family to live apart. The nationalists advocated the end of seclusion and the veil, but they did not say a word about a couple's right to split off from their larger family. In fact, most of the leaders still lived with their parents. The male nationalist movement supported the liberation of women, but had not come to grips with the idea of the elderly living by themselves, nor with couples splitting off into separate households. Neither idea seemed right, or elegant.

4   Mother especially disliked the idea of a fixed lunch hour. She always was the last to wake up, and liked to have a late, lavish breakfast which she prepared herself with a lot of flamboyant defiance, beneath the disapproving stare of Grandmother Lalla Mani. She would make herself scrambled eggs and *baghrir*, or fine crêpes, topped with pure honey and fresh butter, and, of course, plenty of tea. She usually ate at exactly eleven, just as Lalla Mani was about to begin her purification ritual for the noon prayer. And after that, two hours later at the communal table, Mother was often absolutely unable to eat lunch. Sometimes, she would skip it altogether, especially when she wanted to annoy Father, because to skip a meal was considered terribly rude and too openly individualistic.

5   Mother dreamed of living alone with Father and us kids. "Whoever heard of ten birds living together squashed into a single nest?" she would say. "It is not natural to live in a large group, unless your objective is to make people feel miserable." Although Father said that he was not really sure how the birds lived, he still sympathized with Mother, and felt torn between his duty towards the traditional family and his desire to make her happy. He felt guilty about breaking up the family solidarity, knowing only too well that big families in general, and harem life in particular, were fast becoming relics of the past. He even prophesied that in the next few decades, we would become like the Christians, who hardly ever visited their old parents. In fact, most of my uncles who had already broken away from the big house barely found the time to visit their mother, Lalla Mani, on Fridays after prayer anymore. "Their kids do not kiss hands either," ran the constant refrain. To make matters worse, until very recently, all my uncles had lived in our house, and had only split away when their wives' opposition to communal life had become unbearable. That is what gave Mother hope.

6   The first to leave the big family was Uncle Karim, Cousin Malika's father. His wife loved music and liked to sing while being accompanied by Uncle Karim, who played the lute beautifully. But he would rarely give in to his wife's desire to spend an evening singing in their salon,

because his older brother Uncle Ali thought it unbecoming for a man to sing or play a musical instrument. Finally, one day, Uncle Karim's wife just took her children and went back to her father's house, saying that she had no intention of living in the communal house ever again. Uncle Karim, a cheerful fellow who had himself often felt constrained by the discipline of harem life, saw an opportunity to leave and took it, excusing his actions by saying that he preferred to give in to his wife's wishes rather than forfeit his marriage. Not long after that, all my other uncles moved out, one after the other, until only Uncle Ali and Father were left. So Father's departure would have meant the death of our large family. "As long as [my] Mother lives," he often said, "I wouldn't betray the tradition."

Yet Father loved his wife so much that he felt miserable about not   7
giving in to her wishes and never stopped proposing compromises. One was to stock an entire cupboardful of food for her, in case she wanted to discreetly eat sometimes, apart from the rest of the family. For one of the problems in the communal house was that you could not just open a refrigerator when you were hungry and grab something to eat. In the first place, there were no refrigerators back then. More importantly, the entire idea behind the harem was that you lived according to the group's rhythm. You could not just eat when you felt like it. Lalla Radia, my uncle's wife, had the key to the pantry, and although she always asked after dinner what people wanted to eat the next day, you still had to eat whatever the group—after lengthy discussion—decided upon. If the group settled on couscous with chick-peas and raisins, then that is what you got. If you happened to hate chick-peas and raisins, you had no choice but to shut up and settle for a frugal dinner composed of a few olives and a great deal of discretion.

"What a waste of time," Mother would say. "These endless discus-   8
sions about meals! Arabs would be much better off if they let each individual decide what he or she wanted to swallow. Forcing everyone to share three meals a day just complicates things. And for what sacred purpose? None of course." From there, she would go on to say that her whole life was an absurdity, that nothing made sense, while Father would say that he could not just break away. If he did, tradition would vanish: "We live in difficult times, the country is occupied by foreign armies, our culture is threatened. All we have left is these traditions." This reasoning would drive Mother nuts: "Do you think that by sticking together in this big, absurd house, we will gain the strength we need to throw the foreign armies out? And what is more important anyway, tradition or people's happiness?" That would put an abrupt end to the conversation. Father would try to caress her hand but she would take it away. "This tradition is choking me," she would whisper, tears in her eyes.

So Father kept offering compromises. He not only arranged for   9
Mother to have her own food stock, but also brought her things he

knew she liked, such as dates, nuts, almonds, honey, flour, and fancy oils. She could make all the desserts and cookies she wanted, but she was not supposed to prepare a meat dish or a major meal. That would have meant the beginning of the end of the communal arrangement. Her flamboyantly prepared individual breakfasts were enough of a slap in the face to the rest of the family. Every once in a long while, Mother *did* get away with preparing a complete lunch or a dinner, but she had to not only be discreet about it but also give it some sort of exotic overtone. Her most common ploy was to camouflage the meal as a nighttime picnic on the terrace.

10   These occasional tête-à-tête dinners on the terrace during moonlit summer nights were another peace offering that Father made to help satisfy Mother's yearning for privacy. We would be transplanted to the terrace, like nomads, with mattresses, tables, trays, and my little brother's cradle, which would be set down right in the middle of everything. Mother would be absolutely out of her mind with joy. No one else from the courtyard dared to show up, because they understood all too well that Mother was fleeing from the crowd. What she most enjoyed was trying to get Father to depart from his conventional self-controlled pose. Before long, she would start acting foolishly, like a young girl, and soon, Father would chase her all around the terrace, when she challenged him. "You can't run anymore, you have grown too old! All you're good for now is to sit and watch your son's cradle." Father, who had been smiling up to that point, would look at her at first as if what she had just said had not affected him at all. But then his smile would vanish, and he would start chasing her all over the terrace, jumping over tea-trays and sofas. Sometimes both of them made up games which included my sister and Samir (who was the only one of the rest of the family allowed to attend our moonlit gatherings) and myself. More often, they completely forgot about the rest of the world, and we children would be sneezing all the next day because they had forgotten to put blankets on us when we had gone to sleep that night.

11   After these blissful evenings, Mother would be in an unusually soft and quiet mood for a whole week. Then she would tell me that whatever else I did with my life, I had to take her revenge. "I want my daughters' lives to be exciting," she would say, "very exciting and filled with one hundred percent happiness, nothing more, nothing less." I would raise my head, look at her earnestly, and ask what one hundred percent happiness meant, because I wanted her to know that I intended to do my best to achieve it. Happiness, she would explain, was when a person felt good, light, creative, content, loving and loved, and free. An unhappy person felt as if there were barriers crushing her desires and the talents she had inside. A happy woman was one who could exercise all kinds of rights, from the right to move to the right to create, compete, and challenge, and at the same time could feel loved for doing so. Part

of happiness was to be loved by a man who enjoyed your strength and was proud of your talents. Happiness was also about the right to privacy, the right to retreat from the company of others and plunge into contemplative solitude. Or to sit by yourself doing nothing for a whole day, and not give excuses or feel guilty about it either. Happiness was to be with loved ones, and yet still feel that you existed as a separate being, that you were not there just to make them happy. Happiness was when there was a balance between what you gave and what you took. I then asked her how much happiness she had in her life, just to get an idea, and she said that it varied according to the days. Some days she had only five percent; others, like the evenings we spent with Father on the terrace, she had full-blown one hundred percent happiness.

Aiming at one hundred percent happiness seemed a bit over-   12
whelming to me, as a young girl, especially since I could see how much Mother labored to sculpt her moments of happiness. How much time and energy she put into creating those wonderful moonlit evenings sitting close to Father, talking softly in his ear, her head on his shoulder! It seemed quite an accomplishment to me because she had to start working on him days ahead of time, and then she had to take care of all the logistics, like the cooking and the moving of the furniture. To invest so much stubborn effort just to achieve a few hours of happiness was impressive, and at least I knew it could be done. But how, I wondered, was I going to create such a high level of excitement for an entire lifetime? Well, if Mother thought it was possible, I should certainly give it a try.

"Times are going to get better for women now, my daughter," she   13
would say to me. "You and your sister will get a good education, and you'll walk freely in the streets and discover the world. I want you to become independent, independent and happy. I want you to shine like moons. I want your lives to be a cascade of serene delights. One hundred percent happiness. Nothing more, nothing less." But when I asked her for more details about how to create that happiness, Mother would grow very impatient. "You have to work at it. One develops the muscles for happiness, just like for walking and breathing."

So every morning, I would sit on our threshold, contemplating the   14
deserted courtyard and dreaming about my beautiful future, a cascade of serene delights. Hanging on to the romantic moonlit terrace evenings, challenging your beloved man to forget about his social duties, relax and act foolish and gaze at the stars while holding your hand, I thought, could be one way to go about developing muscles for happiness. Sculpting soft nights, when the sound of laughter blends with the spring breezes, could be another.

But those magical evenings were rare, or so they seemed. During   15
the days, life took a much more rigid and disciplined turn. Officially, there was no jumping around or foolishness allowed in the Mernissi household—all that was confined to clandestine times and spaces, such

as late afternoons in the courtyard when the men were out, or evenings on the deserted terraces.

✧ Evaluating the Text

1. What features of communal life in the harem did Mernissi's mother find most restrictive?

2. What compromises were invented to offset these limitations?

3. In light of Mernissi's mother's experiences in the harem, discuss the wishes or desires she projected onto her daughter. What do you think she meant by the phrase "one hundred percent happiness"?

✧ Exploring Different Perspectives

1. In what ways are both Gayle Pemberton's (see "Antidisestablishmentarianism") grandmother and Mernissi's mother critical of prevailing social values?

2. Compare and contrast the phenomena of the extended family in both Mernissi's and Pat Mora's (see "Remembering Lobo") narratives.

✧ Extending Viewpoints through Writing

1. Imagine living in a communal setting of the kind described by Mernissi? How do you think you would react to the lack of privacy at mealtimes and the need to arrange your schedule to conform to that of the group? What positive features might offset these disadvantages?

2. To what extent has privacy become an increasingly rare luxury in modern culture? In a short essay, explore the reasons for this.

Kazuo Ishiguro

A Family Supper

◆

Kazuo Ishiguro was born in Nagasaki, Japan in 1954 and moved to England in 1960 where he spent most of his life. As a young man, he had a variety of jobs, including being the grouse beater for the Queen Mother at Balmoral Castle in Aberdeen, Scotland. Because his parents had intended to return to Japan, they raised him as both Japanese and English, a bicultural emphasis that underlies "A Family Supper" (from Firebird 2, *1982). His novels include* A Pale View of Hills *(1982),* An Artist of the Floating World *(1986), and* The Remains of the Day *(1989), which won Britain's highest literary award, the Booker Prize, and was later made into a 1993 film starring Anthony Hopkins and Emma Thompson. His last published work was* The Unconsoled *(1995).*

Known historically as the "land of the rising sun," symbolized in the national flag, Japan is made up of four main islands off the coast of east Asia: Honshu (the largest, where the capital Tokyo and major cities are located), Hokkaido, Shikoku, and Kyushu. Two thirds of Japan's terrain is mountainous, including the most famous peak, Mount Fuji. Earth tremors are a frequent occurrence. Because Japan has few natural resources, and such a small percentage of land is suitable for cultivation, the country must import almost half its food supply and almost all raw materials required for industrial production. Despite this, Japan is one of the most productive industrial nations; its exports of automobiles, electronic equipment, televisions, textiles, chemicals, and machinery have made it an economic superpower. Education is free and compulsory to the age of fifteen, and Japan has an extraordinarily high literacy rate of 99 percent.

According to legend, Japan was founded by Emperor Jimmu in 660 B.C. and has had a line of emperors that continues into the present. The current emperor, Akihito, succeeded to the throne in 1989 following his father, Hirohito, who was emperor from 1926. Actual political control of the country from the twelfth to the late nineteenth century was held by feudal lords, called Shoguns. *In 1854, Commodore Matthew Perry reopened contact with Japan after the Shoguns had expelled all foreigners from the country in the seventeenth century. Subsequently, the Shoguns lost power to the emperor, and with the defeat of China in 1895 and victory over Russia in the Russo–Japanese War ending in 1905, Japan became a global power.*

In 1999 the Japanese Diet voted to recognize the rising-sun flag and the imperial hymn as the nation's offical flag and national anthem, a decision that caused concern because it evoked memories of Japan's imperial and militaristic past.

1   Fugu is a fish caught off the Pacific shores of Japan. The fish has held a special significance for me ever since my mother died after eating one. The poison resides in the sex glands of the fish, inside two fragile bags. These bags must be removed with caution when preparing the fish, for any clumsiness will result in the poison leaking into the veins. Regrettably, it is not easy to tell whether or not this operation has been carried out successfully. The proof is, as it were, in the eating.

2   Fugu poisoning is hideously painful and almost always fatal. If the fish has been eaten during the evening, the victim is usually overtaken by pain during his sleep. He rolls about in agony for a few hours and is dead by morning. The fish became extremely popular in Japan after the war. Until stricter regulations were imposed, it was all the rage to perform the hazardous gutting operation in one's own kitchen, then to invite neighbors and friends round for the feast.

3   At the time of my mother's death, I was living in California. My relationship with my parents had become somewhat strained around that period and consequently I did not learn of the circumstances of her death until I returned to Tokyo two years later. Apparently, my mother had always refused to eat fugu, but on this particular occasion she had made an exception, having been invited by an old school friend whom she was anxious not to offend. It was my father who supplied me with the details as we drove from the airport to his house in the Kamakura district. When we finally arrived, it was nearing the end of a sunny autumn day.

4   "Did you eat on the plane?" my father asked. We were sitting on the tatami floor of his tearoom.

5   "They gave me a light snack."

6   "You must be hungry. We'll eat as soon as Kikuko arrives."

7   My father was a formidable-looking man with a large stony jaw and furious black eyebrows. I think now, in retrospect, that he much resembled [Chinese Communist leader] Chou En-lai, although he would not have cherished such a comparison, being particularly proud of the pure samurai blood that ran in the family. His general presence was not one that encouraged relaxed conversation; neither were things helped much by his odd way of stating each remark as if it were the concluding one. In fact, as I sat opposite him that afternoon, a boyhood memory came back to me of the time he had struck me several times around the head for "chattering like an old woman." Inevitably, our conversation since my arrival at the airport had been punctuated by long pauses.

8   "I'm sorry to hear about the firm," I said when neither of us had spoken for some time. He nodded gravely.

9   "In fact, the story didn't end there," he said. "After the firm's collapse, Watanabe killed himself. He didn't wish to live with the disgrace."

"I see." 10

"We were partners for seventeen years. A man of principle and 11 honor. I respected him very much."

"Will you go into business again?" I asked. 12

"I am…in retirement. I'm too old to involve myself in new ventures 13 now. Business these days has become so different. Dealing with foreigners. Doing things their way. I don't understand how we've come to this. Neither did Watanabe." He sighed. "A fine man. A man of principle."

The tearoom looked out over the garden. From where I sat I could 14 make out the ancient well that as a child I had believed to be haunted. It was just visible now through the thick foliage. The sun had sunk low and much of the garden had fallen into shadow.

"I'm glad in any case that you've decided to come back," my father 15 said. "More than a short visit, I hope."

"I'm not sure what my plans will be." 16

"I, for one, am prepared to forget the past. Your mother, too, was al- 17 ways ready to welcome you back—upset as she was by your behavior."

"I appreciate your sympathy. As I say, I'm not sure what my plans 18 are."

"I've come to believe now that there were no evil intentions in your 19 mind," my father continued. "You were swayed by certain…influences. Like so many others."

"Perhaps we should forget it, as you suggest." 20

"As you will. More tea?" 21

Just then a girl's voice came echoing through the house. 22

"At last." My father rose to his feet. "Kikuko has arrived." 23

Despite our difference in years, my sister and I had always been 24 close. Seeing me again seemed to make her excessively excited, and for a while she did nothing but giggle nervously. But she calmed down somewhat when my father started to question her about Osaka and her university. She answered him with short, formal replies. She in turn asked me a few questions, but she seemed inhibited by the fear that her questions might lead to awkward topics. After a while, the conversation had become even sparser than prior to Kikuko's arrival. Then my father stood up, saying: "I must attend to the supper. Please excuse me for being burdened by such matters. Kikuko will look after you."

My sister relaxed quite visibly once he had left the room. Within a 25 few minutes, she was chatting freely about her friends in Osaka and about her classes at university. Then quite suddenly she decided we should walk in the garden and went striding out onto the veranda. We put on some straw sandals that had been left along the veranda rail and stepped out into the garden. The light in the garden had grown very dim.

"I've been dying for a smoke for the last half hour," she said, light- 26 ing a cigarette.

"Then why didn't you smoke?" 27

28   She made a furtive gesture back toward the house, then grinned mischievously.

29   "Oh, I see," I said.

30   "Guess what? I've got a boyfriend now."

31   "Oh, yes?"

32   "Except I'm wondering what to do. I haven't made up my mind yet."

33   "Quite understandable."

34   "You see, he's making plans to go to America. He wants me to go with him as soon as I finish studying."

35   "I see. And you want to go to America?"

36   "If we go, we're going to hitchhike," Kikuko waved a thumb in front of my face. "People say it's dangerous, but I've done it in Osaka and it's fine."

37   "I see. So what is it you're unsure about?"

38   We were following a narrow path that wound through the shrubs and finished by the old well. As we walked, Kikuko persisted in taking unnecessarily theatrical puffs on her cigarette.

39   "Well, I've got lots of friends now in Osaka. I like it there. I'm not sure I want to leave them all behind just yet. And Suichi...I like him, but I'm not sure I want to spend so much time with him, Do you understand?"

40   "Oh, perfectly."

41   She grinned again, then skipped on ahead of me until she had reached the well. "Do you remember," she said as I came walking up to her, "how you used to say this well was haunted?"

42   "Yes, I remember."

43   We both peered over the side.

44   "Mother always told me it was the old woman from the vegetable store you'd seen that night," she said. "But I never believed her and never came out here alone."

45   "Mother used to tell me that too. She even told me once the old woman had confessed to being the ghost. Apparently, she'd been taking a shortcut through our garden. I imagine she had some trouble clambering over these walls."

46   Kikuko gave a giggle. She then turned her back to the well, casting her gaze about the garden.

47   "Mother never really blamed you, you know," she said, in a new voice. I remained silent. "She always used to say to me how it was their fault, hers and Father's, for not bringing you up correctly. She used to tell me how much more careful they'd been with me, and that's why I was so good." She looked up and the mischievous grin had returned to her face. "Poor Mother," she said.

48   "Yes. Poor Mother."

49   "Are you going back to California?"

"I don't know. I'll have to see." 50

"What happened to…to her? To Vicki?" 51

"That's all finished with," I said. "There's nothing much left for me 52
now in California."

"Do you think I ought to go there?" 53

"Why not? I don't know. You'll probably like it." I glanced toward 54
the house. "Perhaps we'd better go in soon. Father might need a hand
with the supper."

But my sister was once more peering down into the well. "I can't 55
see any ghosts," she said. Her voice echoed a little.

"Is Father very upset about his firm collapsing?" 56

"Don't know. You never can tell with Father." Then suddenly she 57
straightened up and turned to me. "Did he tell you about old Watanabe? What he did?"

"I heard he committed suicide." 58

"Well, that wasn't all. He took his whole family with him. His wife 59
and his two little girls."

"Oh, yes?" 60

"Those two beautiful little girls. He turned on the gas while they 61
were all asleep. Then he cut his stomach with a meat knife."

"Yes, Father was just telling me how Watanabe was a man of prin- 62
ciple."

"Sick." My sister turned back to the well. 63

"Careful. You'll fall right in." 64

"I can't see any ghost," she said. "You were lying to me all that time." 65

"But I never said it lived down the well." 66

"Where is it then?" 67

We both looked around at the trees and shrubs. The daylight had al- 68
most gone. Eventually I pointed to a small clearing some ten yards away.

"Just there I saw it. Just there." 69

We stared at the spot. 70

"What did it look like?" 71

"I couldn't see very well. It was dark." 72

"But you must have seen something." 73

"It was an old woman. She was just standing there, watching me." 74

We kept staring at the spot as if mesmerized. 75

"She was wearing a white kimono," I said. "Some of her hair came 76
undone. It was blowing around a little."

Kikuko pushed her elbow against my arm. "Oh, be quiet. You're 77
trying to frighten me all over again." She trod on the remains of her cigarette, then for a brief moment stood regarding it with a perplexed expression. She kicked some pine needles over it, then once more
displayed her grin. "Let's see if supper's ready," she said.

We found my father in the kitchen. He gave us a quick glance, then 78
carried on with what he was doing.

79   "Father's become quite a chef since he's had to manage on his own," Kikuko said with a laugh.

80   He turned and looked at my sister coldly. "Hardly a skill I'm proud of," he said. "Kikuko, come here and help."

81   For some moments my sister did not move. Then she stepped forward and took an apron hanging from a drawer.

82   "Just these vegetables need cooking now," he said to her. "The rest just needs watching." Then he looked up and regarded me strangely for some seconds. "I expect you want to look around the house," he said eventually. He put down the chopsticks he had been holding. "It's a long time since you've seen it."

83   As we left the kitchen I glanced toward Kikuko, but her back was turned.

84   "She's a good girl," my father said.

85   I followed my father from room to room. I had forgotten how large the house was. A panel would slide open and another room would appear. But the rooms were all startlingly empty. In one of the rooms the lights did not come on, and we stared at the stark walls and tatami in the pale light that came from the windows.

86   "This house it too large for a man to live in alone," my father said. "I don't have much use for most of these rooms now."

87   But eventually my father opened the door to a room packed full of books and papers. There were flowers in vases and pictures on the walls. Then I noticed something on a low table in the corner of the room. I came nearer and saw it was a plastic model of a battleship, the kind constructed by children. It had been placed on some newspaper; scattered around it were assorted pieces of gray plastic.

88   My father gave a laugh. He came up to the table and picked up the model.

89   "Since the firm folded," he said, "I have a little more time on my hands." He laughed again, rather strangely. For a moment his face looked almost gentle. "A little more time."

90   "That seems odd," I said. "You were always so busy."

91   "Too busy, perhaps." He looked at me with a small smile. "Perhaps I should have been a more attentive father."

92   I laughed. He went on contemplating his battleship. Then he looked up. "I hadn't meant to tell you this, but perhaps it's best that I do. It's my belief that your mother's death was no accident. She had many worries. And some disappointments."

93   We both gazed at the plastic battleship.

94   "Surely," I said eventually, "my mother didn't expect me to live here forever."

95   "Obviously you don't see. You don't see how it is for some parents. Not only must they lose their children, they must lose them to things they don't understand." He spun the battleship in his fingers. "These little gunboats here could have been better glued, don't you think?"

"Perhaps. I think it looks fine."   96

"During the war I spent some time on a ship rather like this. But   97
my ambition was always the air force. I figured it like this: If your ship
was struck by the enemy, all you could do was struggle in the water
hoping for a lifeline. But in an airplane—well, there was always the final weapon." He put the model back onto the table. "I don't suppose
you believe in war."

"Not particularly."   98

He cast an eye around the room. "Supper should be ready by now,"   99
he said. "You must be hungry."

Supper was waiting in a dimly lit room next to the kitchen. The   100
only source of light was a big lantern that hung over the table, casting
the rest of the room in shadow. We bowed to each other before starting
the meal.

There was little conversation. When I made some polite comment   101
about the food, Kikuko giggled a little. Her earlier nervousness seemed
to have returned to her. My father did not speak for several minutes. Finally he said:

"It must feel strange for you, being back in Japan."   102

"Yes, it is a little strange."   103

"Already, perhaps, you regret leaving America."   104

"A little. Not so much. I didn't leave behind much. Just some   105
empty rooms."

"I see."   106

I glanced across the table. My father's face looked stony and for-   107
bidding in the half-light. We ate on in silence.

Then my eye caught something at the back of the room. At first I con- 108
tinued eating, then my hands became still. The others noticed and looked
at me. I went on gazing into the darkness past my father's shoulder.

"Who is that? In that photograph there?"   109

"Which photograph?" My father turned slightly, trying to follow   110
my gaze.

"The lowest one. The old woman in the white kimono."   111

My father put down his chopsticks. He looked first at the photo-   112
graph, then at me.

"Your mother." His voice had become very hard. "Can't you recog-   113
nize your own mother?"

"My mother. You see, it's dark. I can't see it very well."   114

No one spoke for a few seconds, then Kikuko rose to her feet. She   115
took the photograph down from the wall, came back to the table, and
gave it to me.

"She looks a lot older," I said.   116

"It was taken shortly before her death," said my father.   117

"It was dark. I couldn't see very well."   118

I looked up and noticed my father holding out a hand. I gave him   119
the photograph. He looked at it intently, then held it toward Kikuko.

Obediently, my sister rose to her feet once more and returned the picture to the wall.

120   There was a large pot left unopened at the center of the table. When Kikuko had seated herself again, my father reached forward and lifted the lid. A cloud of steam rose up and curled toward the lantern. He pushed the pot a little toward me.

121   "You must be hungry," he said. One side of his face had fallen into shadow.

122   "Thank you." I reached forward with my chopsticks. The steam was almost scalding. "What is it?"

123   "Fish."

124   "It smells very good."

125   In the soup were strips of fish that had curled almost into balls. I picked one out and brought it to my bowl.

126   "Help yourself. There's plenty."

127   "Thank you." I took a little more, then pushed the pot toward my father. I watched him take several pieces to his bowl. Then we both watched as Kikuko served herself.

128   My father bowed slightly. "You must be hungry," he said again. He took some fish to his mouth and started to eat. Then I, too, chose a piece and put it in my mouth. It felt soft, quite fleshy against my tongue.

129   The three of us ate in silence. Several minutes went by. My father lifted the lid and once more steam rose up. We all reached forward and helped ourselves.

130   "Here," I said to my father, "you have this last piece."

131   "Thank you."

132   When we had finished the meal, my father stretched out his arms and yawned with an air of satisfaction. "Kikuko," he said, "prepare a pot of tea, please."

133   My sister looked at him, then left the room without comment. My father stood up.

134   "Let's retire to the other room. It's rather warm in here."

135   I got to my feet and followed him into the tearoom. The large sliding windows had been left open, bringing in a breeze from the garden. For a while we sat in silence.

136   "Father," I said, finally.

137   "Yes?"

138   "Kikuko tells me Watanabe-san took his whole family with him."

139   My father lowered his eyes and nodded. For some moments he seemed deep in thought. "Watanabe was very devoted to his work," he said at last. "The collapse of the firm was a great blow to him. I fear it must have weakened his judgment."

140   "You think what he did…it was a mistake?"

141   "Why, of course. Do you see it otherwise?"

142   "No, no. Of course not."

"There are other things besides work," my father said.   143
"Yes."   144
We fell silent again. The sound of locusts came in from the garden.   145
I looked out into the darkness. The well was no longer visible.
"What do you think you will do now?" my father asked. "Will you   146
stay in Japan for a while?"
"To be honest, I hadn't thought that far ahead."   147
"If you wish to stay here, I mean here in this house, you would be   148
very welcome. That is, if you don't mind living with an old man."
"Thank you. I'll have to think about it."   149
I gazed out once more into the darkness.   150
"But of course," said my father, "this house is so dreary now. You'll   151
no doubt return to America before long."
"Perhaps. I don't know yet."   152
"No doubt you will."   153
For some time my father seemed to be studying the back of his   154
hands. Then he looked up and sighed.
"Kikuko is due to complete her studies next spring," he said. "Per-   155
haps she will want to come home then. She's a good girl."
"Perhaps she will."   156
"Things will improve then."   157
"Yes, I'm sure they will."   158
We fell silent once more, waiting for Kikuko to bring the tea.   159

✦ Evaluating the Text

1. Discuss the relationship between the lethal effects of the *fugu* fish, the suicide of Watanabe, the fact that he murdered his family, and the family supper described in the title. What possibilities do these juxtapositions create in the reader's mind?

2. There are a number of unsolved questions in this story, such as whether the narrator would return to the United States or move back to Japan to live with his family or whether the narrator's mother died accidentally or killed herself. At what points in the story does the imagery of the descriptions magnify ambiguity and create suspense?

3. To what extent does the narrator react to the assumption that would be typical for the Japanese—that a son would live with his family and provide for them? What part does this theme play in the story?

✦ Exploring Different Perspectives

1. Discuss the on-again, off-again relationships between the narrator and his father in this story and in John Cheever's story, "Reunion." To what extent do these relationships transcend the respective cultures?

2. Discuss how the *fugu* fish in Ishiguro's story and the dinner served by her grandmother in Patricia Hampl's account show how family relationships can be destructive or constructive. How does the food in each case symbolize the relationships of the family members?

✧ Extending Viewpoints through Writing

1. When the son in the story says "surely my mother didn't expect me to live here forever," Ishiguro states an idea that transcends cultures. In your opinion, is the father's expectation that both his children will live with him even after they are adults an unreasonable assumption? Why or why not?

2. What unsolved mysteries are part of your family folklore? To what extent do they overshadow family get-togethers?

Connecting Cultures

———————◆———————

Patricia Hampl, "Grandmother's Sunday Dinner"

How does food play a part in cementing social relationships in both Hampl's account and David R. Counts's narrative in "Too Many Bananas" in Chapter 7?

Gayle Pemberton, "Antidisestablishmentarianism"

In what ways do the grandmothers of Pemberton and Mary Crow Dog (see "Civilize Them with a Stick" in Chapter 5) offer advice and a historical perspective on racism in American culture?

Pat Mora, "Remembering Lobo"

In what way does the idea of work well done connect with a successful adaptation to American society for both Mora's aunt and Victor Villaseñor's father in "Rain of Gold" in Chapter 4?

Gayatri Devi, "A Princess Remembers"

Contrast the very different life experiences and perspectives offered by Devi and Viramma in "Pariah" in Chapter 5 at the extremes of society in India.

Serena Nanda, "Arranging a Marriage in India"

Compare and contrast the expectations for those getting married in India and in Japan (see Kyoko Mori's "Polite Lies" in Chapter 3).

Daniela Deane, "The Little Emperors"

Compare and contrast the child-rearing practices in China, as described by Deane, with those of the !Kung in Botswana (see Marjorie Shostak's "Memories of a !Kung Girlhood" in Chapter 3).

John Cheever, "Reunion"

Contrast the role that puncturing illusions and social class play in the stories by Cheever and Liliana Heker (see "The Stolen Party" in Chapter 5).

Fatima Mernissi, "Moonlit Nights of Laughter"

To what extent do Mernissi's account and Shirley Saad's short story "Amina" in Chapter 3 illustrate the restrictions mideastern Moslem cultures place on women?

Kazuo Ishiguro, "A Family Supper"

The son's identification with American cultural values brings him into conflict with his father's traditional Japanese outlook. How does this issue of self-definition enter into both this story and into the account by Claire Chow (see "Ethnicity and Identity: Creating a Sense of Self" in Chapter 7)?

2

Coming of Age

◆

In virtually every society, rites or ceremonies are used to signal adulthood. Many of these occasions are informal, but some are elaborate and dramatic. This chapter illustrates how such turning points are marked by these informal and formal rituals across a broad spectrum of cultures. The moments of insight may be the private psychological turning points or ceremonies that initiate the individual into adulthood within a community. These crucial moments when individuals move from childhood innocence to adult awareness often involve learning a particular society's rules governing what should or should not be done under different circumstances and the values, knowledge, and expectations as to how one should present oneself in a wide variety of situations.

Coming of age often occurs during adolescence when we explore the limits of what society will allow us to do. This is the time when rebellion and defiance against society's rules take place. We acquire societal norms through imitation, identification, and instruction into the behavior patterns that our society deems acceptable. From internalizing these values we get a sense of personal and social identity. This is often the time when we form our first voluntary associations or friendships and discover our capacity to trust and develop relationships, whether strong or fragile, that can lead to reward or disappointment.

In some cases, belonging to a group, association, fraternity, or sorority involves passing some initiation or test to gain acceptance. Because this chapter is rich in a wide variety of perspectives, it invites you to make discoveries about the turning points in your own life.

The essays and stories in this chapter focus on the psychological and cultural forces that shape the identity of those who are about to be initiated into their respective communities. From Ireland, we read the moving narrative of Christy Brown, who, after having been diagnosed as hopelessly retarded by cerebral palsy, describes his struggle in "The Letter 'A'," to communicate signs of intelligence by drawing the letter A with his left foot. The Chinese American writer Sucheng Chan describes with honesty and humor her struggle to confront her disabilities, in "You're Short, Besides!" The international French explorer

Douchan Gersi offers a hair-raising account appropriately titled "Initiated into an Iban Tribe of Headhunters," a firsthand narrative based on his experiences in modern-day Borneo. In the first autobiographical account ever written by a Maasai, Tepilit Ole Saitoti, in "The Initiation of a Maasai Warrior," describes the circumcision ceremony that served as his rite of passage into adulthood. A short story, "Against the Pleasure Principle," by the Somalian writer Saida Hagi-Dirie Herzi, assails the cultural prejudices that still encourage the practice of female circumcision. Raised as a Polish Catholic, Helen Fremont describes her search to confirm her suspicions that her family hid the fact that they were Jewish during World War II. In a chapter drawn from his widely-acclaimed novel, *The Painted Bird*, Jerzy Kosinski depicts the traumatic experiences of a young boy hiding from the Nazis.

Christy Brown

The Letter "A"

◆

Christy Brown (1932–1981) was born in Dublin, the tenth child in a family of twenty-two. Brown was diagnosed as having cerebral palsy and being hopelessly retarded. An intense personal struggle and the loving attention and faith of his mother resulted in a surprising degree of rehabilitation. Brown's autobiography, My Left Foot *(1954), describing his struggle to overcome his massive handicap, was the basis for the 1989 Academy Award-winning film. Brown is also the author of an internationally acclaimed novel,* Down All the Days *(1970). "The Letter 'A'," from his autobiography, describes the crucial moment when he first communicated signs of awareness and intelligence.*

The Republic of Ireland occupies all but the northeast corner of the island of Ireland, in the British Isles, and has a population of 3.5 million. Cork, founded in the seventh century, is the second-largest city in the Republic of Ireland. A treaty with Great Britain in 1922 partitioned Ireland into the Irish Free State and the six counties of Ulster in the northeast (whose population now numbers 1.5 million) and precipitated a civil war. The anti-treaty forces were identified with the Irish Republican Army (IRA), a nationalist organization that was defeated at the time but has continued to fight for the unification of Ireland. The ongoing conflict between Irish Roman Catholics and Ulster's Protestants stems from Henry VIII's attempt in 1541 to impose the Protestant Church of Ireland on the predominantly Catholic population. To this day, Ulster's Protestants and Catholics are divided over whether to remain under British rule or join the Republic of Ireland. In 1937, a new constitution was put forward, establishing the sovereign state of Ireland within the British Commonwealth. In 1949, the Republic of Ireland was proclaimed, and the country withdrew from the Commonwealth. Discussions with British authorities over the issue of returning Northern Ireland to Irish sovereignty have produced little progress. A high unemployment rate and a poor economy led to the collapse of Ireland's coalition government in 1992. A new coalition was formed under Albert Reynolds, who served as prime minister until 1994. Following his resignation, a new government was formed in April 1995, with John Bruton serving as prime minister until he was replaced by Bertie Aherne in 1997. Prospects for peace are uncertain in the new millenium.

1   I was born in the Rotunda Hospital,[1] on June 5th, 1932. There were nine children before me and twelve after me, so I myself belong to the middle group. Out of this total of twenty-two, seventeen lived, but four died in infancy, leaving thirteen still to hold the family fort.

2   Mine was a difficult birth, I am told. Both mother and son almost died. A whole army of relations queued up outside the hospital until the small hours of the morning, waiting for news and praying furiously that it would be good.

3   After my birth Mother was sent to recuperate for some weeks and I was kept in the hospital while she was away. I remained there for some time, without name, for I wasn't baptized until my mother was well enough to bring me to church.

4   It was Mother who first saw that there was something wrong with me. I was about four months old at the time. She noticed that my head had a habit of falling backward whenever she tried to feed me. She attempted to correct this by placing her hand on the back of my neck to keep it steady. But when she took it away, back it would drop again. That was the first warning sign. Then she became aware of other defects as I got older. She saw that my hands were clenched nearly all of the time and were inclined to twine behind my back; my mouth couldn't grasp the teat of the bottle because even at that early age my jaws would either lock together tightly, so that it was impossible for her to open them, or they would suddenly become limp and fall loose, dragging my whole mouth to one side. At six months I could not sit up without having a mountain of pillows around me. At twelve months it was the same.

5   Very worried by this, Mother told my father her fears, and they decided to seek medical advice without any further delay. I was a little over a year old when they began to take me to hospitals and clinics, convinced that there was something definitely wrong with me, something which they could not understand or name, but which was very real and disturbing.

6   Almost every doctor who saw and examined me labeled me a very interesting but also a hopeless case. Many told Mother very gently that I was mentally defective and would remain so. That was a hard blow to a young mother who had already reared five healthy children. The doctors were so very sure of themselves that Mother's faith in me seemed almost an impertinence. They assured her that nothing could be done for me.

7   She refused to accept this truth, the inevitable truth—as it then seemed—that I was beyond cure, beyond saving, even beyond hope. She could not and would not believe that I was an imbecile, as the doctors told her. She had nothing in the world to go by, not a scrap of evidence to support her conviction that, though my body was crippled,

[1]Rotunda Hospital, a hospital in Dublin, Ireland.

my mind was not. In spite of all the doctors and specialists told her, she would not agree. I don't believe she knew why—she just knew, without feeling the smallest shade of doubt.

Finding that the doctors could not help in any way beyond telling   8
her not to place her trust in me, or, in other words, to forget I was a human creature, rather to regard me as just something to be fed and washed and then put away again, Mother decided there and then to take matters into her own hands. I was *her* child, and therefore part of the family. No matter how dull and incapable I might grow up to be, she was determined to treat me on the same plane as the others, and not as the "queer one" in the back room who was never spoken of when there were visitors present.

That was a momentous decision as far as my future life was con-   9
cerned. It meant that I would always have my mother on my side to help me fight all the battles that were to come, and to inspire me with new strength when I was almost beaten. But it wasn't easy for her because now the relatives and friends had decided otherwise. They contended that I should be taken kindly, sympathetically, but not seriously. That would be a mistake. "For your own sake," they told her, "don't look to this boy as you would to the others; it would only break your heart in the end." Luckily for me, Mother and Father held out against the lot of them. But Mother wasn't content just to say that I was not an idiot: she set out to prove it, not because of any rigid sense of duty, but out of love. That is why she was so successful.

At this time she had the five other children to look after besides the   10
"difficult one," though as yet it was not by any means a full house. They were my brothers, Jim, Tony, and Paddy, and my two sisters, Lily and Mona, all of them very young, just a year or so between each of them, so that they were almost exactly like steps of stairs.

Four years rolled by and I was now five, and still as helpless as a   11
newly born baby. While my father was out at bricklaying, earning our bread and butter for us, Mother was slowly, patiently pulling down the wall, brick by brick, that seemed to thrust itself between me and the other children, slowly, patiently penetrating beyond the thick curtain that hung over my mind, separating it from theirs. It was hard, heartbreaking work, for often all she got from me in return was a vague smile and perhaps a faint gurgle. I could not speak or even mumble, nor could I sit up without support on my own, let alone take steps. But I wasn't inert or motionless. I seemed, indeed, to be convulsed with movement, wild, stiff, snakelike movement that never left me, except in sleep. My fingers twisted and twitched continually, my arms twined backwards and would often shoot out suddenly this way and that, and my head lolled and sagged sideways. I was a queer, crooked little fellow.

Mother tells me how one day she had been sitting with me for   12
hours in an upstairs bedroom, showing me pictures out of a great big

storybook that I had got from Santa Claus last Christmas and telling me the names of the different animals and flowers that were in them, trying without success to get me to repeat them. This had gone on for hours while she talked and laughed with me. Then at the end of it she leaned over me and said gently into my ear:

13 "Did you like it, Chris? Did you like the bears and the monkeys and all the lovely flowers? Nod your head for yes, like a good boy."

14 But I could make no sign that I had understood her. Her face was bent over mine hopefully. Suddenly, involuntarily, my queer hand reached up and grasped one of the dark curls that fell in a thick cluster about her neck. Gently she loosened the clenched fingers, though some dark strands were still clutched between them.

15 Then she turned away from my curious stare and left the room, crying. The door closed behind her. It all seemed hopeless. It looked as though there was some justification for my relatives' contention that I was an idiot and beyond help.

16 They now spoke of an institution.

17 "Never!" said my mother almost fiercely, when this was suggested to her. "I know my boy is not an idiot; it is his body that is shattered, not his mind. I'm sure of that."

18 Sure? Yet inwardly, she prayed God would give her some proof of her faith. She knew it was one thing to believe but quite another thing to prove.

19 I was now five, and still I showed no real sign of intelligence. I showed no apparent interest in things except with my toes—more especially those of my left foot. Although my natural habits were clean, I could not aid myself, but in this respect my father took care of me. I used to lie on my back all the time in the kitchen or, on bright warm days, out in the garden, a little bundle of crooked muscles and twisted nerves, surrounded by a family that loved me and hoped for me and that made me part of their own warmth and humanity. I was lonely, imprisoned in a world of my own, unable to communicate with others, cut off, separated from them as though a glass wall stood between my existence and theirs, thrusting me beyond the sphere of their lives and activities. I longed to run about and play with the rest, but I was unable to break loose from my bondage.

20 Then, suddenly, it happened! In a moment everything was changed, my future life molded into a definite shape, my mother's faith in me rewarded, and her secret fear changed into open triumph.

21 It happened so quickly, so simply after all the years of waiting and uncertainty, that I can see and feel the whole scene as if it had happened last week. It was the afternoon of a cold, gray December day. The streets outside glistened with snow, the white sparkling flakes stuck and melted on the windowpanes and hung on the boughs of the trees like molten silver. The wind howled dismally, whipping up little whirling columns of

snow that rose and fell at every fresh gust. And over all, the dull, murky sky stretched like a dark canopy, a vast infinity of grayness.

Inside, all the family were gathered round the big kitchen fire that 22 lit up the little room with a warm glow and made giant shadows dance on the walls and ceiling.

In a corner Mona and Paddy were sitting, huddled together, a few 23 torn school primers before them. They were writing down little sums onto an old chipped slate, using a bright piece of yellow chalk. I was close to them, propped up by a few pillows against the wall, watching.

It was the chalk that attracted me so much. It was a long, slender 24 stick of vivid yellow. I had never seen anything like it before, and it showed up so well against the black surface of the slate that I was fascinated by it as much as if it had been a stick of gold.

Suddenly, I wanted desperately to do what my sister was doing. 25 Then—without thinking or knowing exactly what I was doing, I reached out and took the stick of chalk out of my sister's hand—with my left foot.

I do not know why I used my left foot to do this. It is a puzzle to 26 many people as well as to myself, for, although I had displayed a curious interest in my toes at an early age, I had never attempted before this to use either of my feet in any way. They could have been as useless to me as were my hands. That day, however, my left foot, apparently by its own volition, reached out and very impolitely took the chalk out of my sister's hand.

I held it tightly between my toes, and, acting on an impulse, made 27 a wild sort of scribble with it on the slate. Next moment I stopped, a bit dazed, surprised, looking down at the stick of yellow chalk stuck between my toes, not knowing what to do with it next, hardly knowing how it got there. Then I looked up and became aware that everyone had stopped talking and was staring at me silently. Nobody stirred. Mona, her black curls framing her chubby little face, stared at me with great big eyes and open mouth. Across the open hearth, his face lit by flames, sat my father, leaning forward, hands outspread on his knees, his shoulders tense. I felt the sweat break out on my forehead.

My mother came in from the pantry with a steaming pot in her 28 hand. She stopped midway between the table and the fire, feeling the tension flowing through the room. She followed their stare and saw me in the corner. Her eyes looked from my face down to my foot, with the chalk gripped between my toes. She put down the pot.

Then she crossed over to me and knelt down beside me, as she had 29 done so many times before.

"I'll show you what to do with it, Chris," she said, very slowly and 30 in a queer, choked way, her face flushed as if with some inner excitement.

Taking another piece of chalk from Mona, she hesitated, then very 31 deliberately drew, on the floor in front of me, *the single letter "A."*

32   "Copy that," she said, looking steadily at me. "Copy it, Christy."

33   I couldn't.

34   I looked about me, looked around at the faces that were turned towards me, tense, excited faces that were at that moment frozen, immobile, eager, waiting for a miracle in their midst.

35   The stillness was profound. The room was full of flame and shadow that danced before my eyes and lulled my taut nerves into a sort of waking sleep. I could hear the sound of the water tap dripping in the pantry, the loud ticking of the clock on the mantel shelf, and the soft hiss and crackle of the logs on the open hearth.

36   I tried again. I put out my foot and made a wild jerking stab with the chalk which produced a very crooked line and nothing more. Mother held the slate steady for me.

37   "Try again, Chris," she whispered in my ear. "Again."

38   I did. I stiffened my body and put my left foot out again, for the third time. I drew one side of the letter. I drew half the other side. Then the stick of chalk broke and I was left with a stump. I wanted to fling it away and give up. Then I felt my mother's hand on my shoulder. I tried once more. Out went my foot. I shook, I sweated and strained every muscle. My hands were so tightly clenched that my fingernails bit into the flesh. I set my teeth so hard that I nearly pierced my lower lip. Everything in the room swam till the faces around me were mere patches of white. But—I drew it—*the letter "A."* There it was on the floor before me. Shaky, with awkward, wobbly sides and a very uneven center line. But it *was* the letter "A." I looked up. I saw my mother's face for a moment, tears on her cheeks. Then my father stooped and hoisted me onto his shoulder.

39   I had done it! It had started—the thing that was to give my mind its chance of expressing itself. True, I couldn't speak with my lips. But now I would speak through something more lasting than spoken words— written words.

40   That one letter, scrawled on the floor with a broken bit of yellow chalk gripped between my toes, was my road to a new world, my key to mental freedom. It was to provide a source of relaxation to the tense, taut thing that was I, which panted for expression behind a twisted mouth.

✧ *Evaluating the Text*

1. What unusual signs alerted Christy's mother that he might be physically impaired? What did her response to the doctors' diagnosis reveal about her as a person and her attitude toward Christy?

2. What did Christy's mother hope to achieve by showing him pictures of animals and flowers? How did her friends and relatives react to her decision to treat Christy as if he were capable of mental development?

How would Christy's day-to-day treatment have differed if his mother had not treated him as a member of the family?

3. Why does the narrative shift from Christy's mother's perspective to Christy's recollection of the day he was able to form the letter *A* with his left foot?

4. From the point of view of Christy's mother, father, and siblings, how did they know that his forming the letter *A* was a sign of intelligence and not merely an imitative gesture? How does the conclusion of this account suggest that this moment had deeper meaning for Christy than it did even for his family? What did this mean to him?

✧ Exploring Different Perspectives

1. In what way can Brown be considered to be just as courageous in meeting the challenge he faced as Tepilit Ole Saitoti was in exhibiting bravery during his initiation as a Maasai warrior (see "The Initiation of a Maasai Warrior")?

2. What similarities in coping with a disability can you discover in this account by Christy Brown and that of Sucheng Chan in "You're Short, Besides!"?

✧ Extending Viewpoints through Writing

1. On any given day, how do you think Christy would have been treated if his mother had not made the decision to treat him as a member of the family? Write two brief accounts analyzing why over a period of time the difference in the way he was treated might have been capable of producing the unexpected development Christy describes. Include in your account such everyday events as meals and visits from friends.

2. Rent a copy of the 1989 Academy Award-winning film *My Left Foot*, based on Christy Brown's autobiography of the same name, and discuss which treatment, film or written word, more effectively dramatized the issues at stake and the feelings of Christy and his family at the moment when he drew the letter *A*.

3. If you have ever been temporarily physically incapacitated or have a disability, write an essay that will help your audience understand your plight and the visible and subtle psychological aspects of discrimination that the disabled must endure every day.

Sucheng Chan

You're Short, Besides!

—————◆—————

Sucheng Chan graduated from Swarthmore College in 1963 and received an M.A. from the University of Hawaii in 1965. In 1973 she earned a Ph.D. from the University of California at Berkeley, where she subsequently taught for a decade. She is currently professor of history and chair of Asian-American studies at the University of California at Santa Barbara. Her works include Quiet Odyssey: A Pioneer Korean Woman in America *(1990) and the award-winning* The Asian Americans: An Interpretive History *(1991). "You're Short, Besides!" first appeared in* Making Waves: An Anthology of Writing By and About Asian-American Women *(1989). In recent years, she has served as the editor of numerous collections, including* Hmong Means Free: Life in Laos and America *(1994),* Major Problems in California History, *with Spencer C. Olin (1997), and* Claiming America: Constructing Chinese American Identities During the Exclusion Era, *with K. Scott Wong (1998).*

1   When asked to write about being a physically handicapped Asian American woman, I considered it an insult. After all, my accomplishments are many, yet I was not asked to write about any of them. Is being handicapped the most salient feature about me? The fact that it might be in the eyes of others made me decide to write the essay as requested. I realized that the way I think about myself may differ considerably from the way others perceive me. And maybe that's what being physically handicapped is all about.

2   I was stricken simultaneously with pneumonia and polio at the age of four. Uncertain whether I had polio of the lungs, seven of the eight doctors who attended me—all practitioners of Western medicine—told my parents they should not feel optimistic about my survival. A Chinese fortune teller my mother consulted also gave a grim prognosis, but for an entirely different reason: I had been stricken because my name was offensive to the gods. My grandmother had named me "grandchild of wisdom," a name that the fortune teller said was too presumptuous for a girl. So he advised my parents to change my name to "chaste virgin." All these pessimistic predictions notwithstanding, I hung onto life, if only by a thread. For three years, my body was periodically pierced with electric shocks as the muscles of my legs atrophied. Before my illness, I had been an active, rambunctious, precocious, and very curious

100

child. Being confined to bed was thus a mental agony as great as my physical pain. Living in war-torn China, I received little medical attention; physical therapy was unheard of. But I was determined to walk. So one day, when I was six or seven, I instructed my mother to set up two rows of chairs to face each other so that I could use them as I would parallel bars. I attempted to walk by holding my body up and moving it forward with my arms while dragging my legs along behind. Each time I fell, my mother gasped, but I badgered her until she let me try again. After four nonambulatory years, I finally walked once more by pressing my hands against my thighs so my knees wouldn't buckle.

My father had been away from home during most of those years   3 because of the war. When he returned, I had to confront the guilt he felt about my condition. In many East Asian cultures, there is a strong folk belief that a person's physical state in this life is a reflection of how morally or sinfully he or she lived in previous lives. Furthermore, because of the tendency to view the family as a single unit, it is believed that the fate of one member can be caused by the behavior of another. Some of my father's relatives told him that my illness had doubtless been caused by the wild carousing he did in his youth. A well-meaning but somewhat simple man, my father believed them.

Throughout my childhood, he sometimes apologized to me for   4 having to suffer retribution for his former bad behavior. This upset me; it was bad enough that I had to deal with the anguish of not being able to walk, but to have to assuage his guilt as well was a real burden! In other ways, my father was very good to me. He took me out often, carrying me on his shoulders or back, to give me fresh air and sunshine. He did this until I was too large and heavy for him to carry. And ever since I can remember, he has told me that I am pretty.

After getting over her anxieties about my constant falls, my mother   5 decided to send me to school. I had already learned to read some words of Chinese at the age of three by asking my parents to teach me the sounds and meaning of various characters in the daily newspaper. But between the ages of four and eight, I received no education since just staying alive was a full-time job. Much to her chagrin, my mother found no school in Shanghai, where we lived at the time, which would accept me as a student. Finally, as a last resort, she approached the American School, which agreed to enroll me only if my family kept an *amah* (a servant who takes care of children) by my side at all times. The tuition at the school was twenty U.S. dollars per month—a huge sum of money during those years of runaway inflation in China—and payable only in U.S. dollars. My family afforded the high cost of tuition and the expense of employing a full-time *amah* for less than a year.

We left China as the Communist forces swept across the country in   6 victory. We found an apartment in Hong Kong across the street from a school run by Seventh-Day Adventists. By that time I could walk a little, so the principal was persuaded to accept me. An *amah* now had to take care of me only during recess when my classmates might easily knock me over as they ran about the playground.

7   After a year and a half in Hong Kong, we moved to Malaysia, where my father's family had lived for four generations. There I learned to swim in the lovely warm waters of the tropics and fell in love with the sea. On land I was a cripple; in the ocean I could move with the grace of a fish. I liked the freedom of being in the water so much that many years later, when I was a graduate student in Hawaii, I became greatly enamored with a man just because he called me a "Polynesian water nymph."

8   As my overall health improved, my mother became less anxious about all aspects of my life. She did everything possible to enable me to lead as normal a life as possible. I remember how once some of her colleagues in the high school where she taught criticized her for letting me wear short skirts. They felt my legs should not be exposed to public view. My mother's response was, "All girls her age wear short skirts, so why shouldn't she?"

9   The years in Malaysia were the happiest of my childhood, even though I was constantly fending off children who ran after me calling, *"Baikah! Baikah!"* ("Cripple! Cripple!" in the Hokkien dialect commonly spoken in Malaysia). The taunts of children mattered little because I was a star pupil. I won one award after another for general scholarship as well as for art and public speaking. Whenever the school had important visitors my teacher always called on me to recite in front of the class.

10   A significant event that marked me indelibly occurred when I was twelve. That year my school held a music recital and I was one of the students chosen to play the piano. I managed to get up the steps to the stage without any problem, but as I walked across the stage, I fell. Out of the audience, a voice said loudly and clearly, "Ayah! A *baikah* shouldn't be allowed to perform in public." I got up before anyone could get on stage to help me and, with tears streaming uncontrollably down my face, I rushed to the piano and began to play. Beethoven's "Für Elise" had never been played so fiendishly fast before or since, but I managed to finish the whole piece. That I managed to do so made me feel really strong. I never again feared ridicule.

11   In later years I was reminded of this experience from time to time. During my fourth year as an assistant professor at the University of California at Berkeley, I won a distinguished teaching award. Some weeks later I ran into a former professor who congratulated me enthusiastically. But I said to him, "You know what? I became a distinguished teacher by *limping* across the stage of Dwinelle 155!" (Dwinelle 155 is a large, cold, classroom that most colleagues of mine hate to teach in.) I was rude not because I lacked graciousness but because this

man, who had told me that my dissertation was the finest piece of work he had read in fifteen years, had nevertheless advised me to eschew a teaching career.

"Why?" I asked.   12

"Your leg…" he responded.   13

"What about my leg?" I said, puzzled.   14

"Well, how would you feel standing in front of a large lecture class?"   15

"If it makes any difference, I want you to know I've won a number   16
of speech contests in my life, and I am not the least bit self-conscious
about speaking in front of large audiences…. Look, why don't you
write me a letter of recommendation to tell people how brilliant I am,
and let *me* worry about my leg!"

This incident is worth recounting only because it illustrates a di-   17
lemma that handicapped persons face frequently: those who care about
us sometimes get so protective that they unwittingly limit our growth.
This former professor of mine had been one of my greatest supporters
for two decades. Time after time, he had written glowing letters of recommendation on my behalf. He had spoken as he did because he
thought he had my best interest at heart; he thought that if I got a desk
job rather than one that required me to be a visible, public person, I
would be spared the misery of being stared at.

Americans, for the most part, do not believe as Asians do that   18
physically handicapped persons are morally flawed. But they are
equally inept at interacting with those of us who are not able-bodied.
Cultural differences in the perception and treatment of handicapped
people are most clearly expressed by adults. Children, regardless of
where they are, tend to be openly curious about people who do not
look "normal." Adults in Asia have no hesitation in asking visibly
handicapped people what is wrong with them, often expressing their
sympathy with looks of pity, whereas adults in the United States try
desperately to be polite by pretending not to notice.

One interesting response I often elicited from people in Asia but   19
have never encountered in America is the attempt to link my physical
condition to the state of my soul. Many a time while living and traveling
in Asia people would ask me what religion I belonged to. I would tell
them that my mother is a devout Buddhist, that my father was baptized
a Catholic but has never practiced Catholicism, and that I am an agnostic. Upon hearing this, people would try strenuously to convert me to
their religion so that whichever God they believed in could bless me. If I
would only attend this church or that temple regularly, they urged, I
would surely get cured. Catholics and Buddhists alike have pressed religious medallions into my palm, telling me if I would wear these, the
relevant deity or saint would make me well. Once while visiting the
tomb of Muhammad Ali Jinnah in Karachi, Pakistan, an old Muslim, after finishing his evening prayers, spotted me, gestured toward my legs,

raised his arms heavenward, and began a new round of prayers, apparently on my behalf.

20   In the United States adults who try to act "civilized" toward handicapped people by pretending they don't notice anything unusual sometimes end up ignoring handicapped people completely. In the first few months I lived in this country, I was struck by the fact that whenever children asked me what was the matter with my leg, their adult companions would hurriedly shush them up, furtively look at me, mumble apologies, and rush their children away. After a few months of such encounters, I decided it was my responsibility to educate these people. So I would say to the flustered adults, "It's okay, let the kid ask." Turning to the child, I would say, "When I was a little girl, no bigger than you are, I became sick with something called polio. The muscles of my leg shrank up and I couldn't walk very well. You're much luckier than I am because now you can get a vaccine to make sure you never get my disease. So don't cry when your mommy takes you to get a polio vaccine, okay?" Some adults and their little companions I talked to this way were glad to be rescued from embarrassment; others thought I was strange.

21   Americans have another way of covering up their uneasiness: they become jovially patronizing. Sometimes when people spot my crutch, they ask if I've had a skiing accident. When I answer that unfortunately it is something less glamorous than that they say, "I bet you *could* ski if you put your mind to it!" Alternately, at parties where people dance, men who ask me to dance with them get almost belligerent when I decline their invitation. They say, "Of course you can dance if you *want* to!" Some have given me pep talks about how if I would only develop the right mental attitude, I would have more fun in life.

22   Different cultural attitudes toward handicapped persons came out clearly during my wedding. My father-in-law, as solid a representative of middle America as could be found, had no qualms about objecting to the marriage on racial grounds, but he could bring himself to comment on my handicap only indirectly. He wondered why his son, who had dated numerous high school and college beauty queens, couldn't marry one of them instead of me. My mother-in-law, a devout Christian, did not share her husband's prejudices, but she worried aloud about whether I could have children. Some Chinese friends of my parents, on the other hand, said that I was lucky to have found such a noble man, one who would marry me despite my handicap. I, for my part, appeared in church in a white lace wedding dress I had designed and made myself—a miniskirt!

23   How Asian Americans treat me with respect to my handicap tells me a great deal about their degree of acculturation. Recent immigrants behave just like Asians in Asia; those who have been here longer or who grew up in the United States behave more like their white counterparts. I have not encountered any distinctly Asian American pattern

of response. What makes the experience of Asian American handicapped people unique is the duality of responses we elicit.

Regardless of racial or cultural background, most handicapped people have to learn to find a balance between the desire to attain physical independence and the need to take care of ourselves by not overtaxing our bodies. In my case, I've had to learn to accept the fact that leading an active life has its price. Between the ages of eight and eighteen, I walked without using crutches or braces but the effort caused my right leg to become badly misaligned. Soon after I came to the United States, I had a series of operations to straighten out the bones of my right leg; afterwards though my leg looked straighter and presumably better, I could no longer walk on my own. Initially my doctors fitted me with a brace, but I found wearing one cumbersome and soon gave it up. I could move around much more easily—and more important, faster—by using one crutch. One orthopedist after another warned me that using a single crutch was a bad practice. They were right. Over the years my spine developed a double-S curve and for the last twenty years I have suffered from severe, chronic back pains, which neither conventional physical therapy nor a lighter work load can eliminate. 24

The only thing that helps my backaches is a good massage, but the soothing effect lasts no more than a day or two. Massages are expensive, especially when one needs them three times a week. So I found a job that pays better, but at which I have to work longer hours, consequently increasing the physical strain on my body—a sort of vicious circle. When I was in my thirties, my doctors told me that if I kept leading the strenuous life I did, I would be in a wheelchair by the time I was forty. They were right on target; I bought myself a wheelchair when I was forty-one. But being the incorrigible character that I am, I use it only when I am *not* in a hurry! 25

It is a good thing, however, that I am too busy to think much about my handicap or my backaches because pain can physically debilitate as well as cause depression. And there are days when my spirits get rather low. What has helped me is realizing that being handicapped is akin to growing old at an accelerated rate. The contradiction I experience is that often my mind races along as though I'm only twenty while my body feels about sixty. But fifteen or twenty years hence, unlike my peers who will have to cope with aging for the first time, I shall be full of cheer because I will have already fought, and I hope won, that battle long ago. 26

Beyond learning how to be physically independent and, for some of us, living with chronic pain or other kinds of discomfort, the most difficult thing a handicapped person has to deal with, especially during puberty and early adulthood, is relating to potential sexual partners. Because American culture places so much emphasis on physical attractiveness, a person with a shriveled limb, or a tilt to the head, or the inability to speak clearly, experiences great uncertainty—indeed trauma—when 27 interacting with someone to whom he or she is attracted. My problem was that I was not only physically handicapped, small, and short, but worse, I also wore glasses and was smarter than all the boys I knew! Alas, an insurmountable combination. Yet somehow I have managed to have intimate relationships, all of them with extraordinary men. Not surprisingly, there have also been countless men who broke my heart—men who enjoyed my company "as a friend," but who never found the courage to date or make love with me, although I am sure my experience in this regard is no different from that of many able-bodied persons.

28   The day came when my backaches got in the way of having an active sex life. Surprisingly that development was liberating because I stopped worrying about being attractive to men. No matter how headstrong I had been, I, like most women of my generation, had had the desire to be alluring to men ingrained into me. And that longing had always worked like a brake on my behavior. When what men think of me ceased to be compelling, I gained greater freedom to be myself.

29   I've often wondered if I would have been a different person had I not been physically handicapped. I really don't know, though there is no question that being handicapped has marked me. But at the same time I usually do not *feel* handicapped—and consequently, I do not act handicapped. People are therefore less likely to treat me as a handicapped person. There is no doubt, however, that the lives of my parents, sister, husband, other family members, and some close friends have been affected by my physical condition. They have had to learn not to hide me away at home, not to feel embarrassed by how I look or react to people who say silly things to me, and not to resent me for the extra demands my condition makes on them. Perhaps the hardest thing for those who live with handicapped people is to know when and how to offer help. There are no guidelines applicable to all situations. My advice is, when in doubt, ask, but ask in a way that does not smack of pity or embarrassment. Most important, please don't talk to us as though we are children.

30   So, has being physically handicapped been a handicap? It all depends on one's attitude. Some years ago, I told a friend that I had once said to an affirmative action compliance officer (somewhat sardonically since I do not believe in the head count approach to affirmative action) that the institution which employs me is triply lucky because it can count me as non-white, female and handicapped. He responded, "Why don't you tell them to count you four times?... Remember, you're short, besides!"

✧ Evaluating the Text

1. What insight into cross-cultural perceptions of disabilities do you get from Chan's account? Specifically, how do Asian perceptions of disabilities differ from those in America?

2. To what extent did Chan have to overcome the well-meaning advice of family and friends and discount their perception of her diminished potential?

3. Chan has very strongly developed views, that is, she is an agnostic, doesn't believe in affirmative action, is uninhibited about sex, and has an unusual attitude toward the debilitating nature of her handicap. Which of her responses toward events made you aware of her unique personality?

✧ Exploring Different Perspectives

1. What personal attributes link Sucheng Chan with Christy Brown in confronting disabilities? (See "The Letter 'A.'")

2. How does the account by Sucheng Chan and the story by Saida Hagi-Dirie Herzi, "Against the Pleasure Principle," reveal stereotyped attitudes toward girls in the traditional cultures of China and Somalia?

✧ Extending Viewpoints through Writing

1. To what extent are attitudes toward disability conditioned by cultural forces?

2. Do you know anyone who has a sense of irony and detachment similar to Chan's toward a disability or ailment? Write a short account of how this attitude enables him or her to cope with circumstances that might devastate another person.

Douchan Gersi

Initiated into an Iban Tribe of Headhunters

◆ —————

Douchan Gersi is the producer of the National Geographic television series called Discovery. *He has traveled extensively throughout the Philippines, New Zealand, the Polynesian and Melanesian Islands, the Sahara Desert, Africa, New Guinea, and Peru. "Initiated into an Iban Tribe of Headhunters," from his book* Explorer *(1987), tells of the harrowing initiation process he underwent to become a member of the Iban Tribe in Borneo.*

Borneo, the third largest island in the Malay archipelago, is situated southwest of the Philippines and north of Java. The indigenous people of Borneo, or Dyaks, number over 1 million and occupy the sparsely populated interior, a region of dense jungles and rain forests. The northern portion of the island is Malaysian territory; the southern portion is part of the Republic of Indonesia. Gersi's account introduces us to the mode of life of the Iban, a people whose customs, including intertribal warfare and headhunting, have remained unchanged for centuries.

The hopeful man sees success where others see shadows and storm.
—O. S. Marden

1   Against Tawa's excellent advice I asked the chief if I could become a member of their clan. It took him a while before he could give me an answer, for he had to question the spirits of their ancestors and wait for their reply to appear through different omens: the flight of a blackbird, the auguries of a chick they sacrificed. A few days after the question, the answer came:

2   "Yes...but!"

3   The "but" was that I would have to undergo their initiation. Without knowing exactly what physical ordeal was in store, I accepted. I knew I had been through worse and survived. It was to begin in one week.

4   Late at night I was awakened by a girl slipping into my bed. She was sweet and already had a great knowledge of man's morphology. Like all the others who came and "visited" me this way every night, she was highly skilled in the arts of love. Among the Iban, only unmarried women offer sexual hospitality, and no one obliged these women to of-

fer me their favors. Sexual freedom ends at marriage. Unfaithfulness—
except during yearly fertility celebrations when everything, even incest
at times, is permitted—is punished as an offense against their matrimo-
nial laws.

As a sign of respect to family and the elders, sexual hospitality is   5
not openly practiced. The girls always came when my roommates were
asleep and left before they awoke. They were free to return or give their
place to their girlfriends.

The contrast between the violence of some Iban rituals and the   6
beauty of their art, their sociability, their kindness, and their personal
warmth has always fascinated me. I also witnessed that contrast
among a tribe of Papuans (who, besides being headhunters, practice
cannibalism) and among some African tribes. In fact, tribes devoted to
cannibalism and other human sacrifices are often among the most sociable of people, and their art, industry, and trading systems are more
advanced than other tribes that don't have these practices.

For my initiation, they had me lie down naked in a four-foot-deep   7
pit filled with giant carnivorous ants. Nothing held me there. At any
point I could easily have escaped, but the meaning of this rite of passage was not to kill me. The ritual was intended to test my courage and
my will, to symbolically kill me by the pain in order for me to be reborn
as a man of courage. I am not sure what their reactions would have
been if I had tried to get out of the pit before their signal, but it occurred
to me that although the ants might eat a little of my flesh, the Iban offered more dramatic potentials.

Since I wore, as Iban do, a long piece of cloth around my waist and   8
nothing more, I had the ants running all over my body. They were everywhere. The pain of the ants' bites was intense, so I tried to relax to
decrease the speed of my circulation and therefore the effects of the
poison. But I couldn't help trying to get them away from my face where
they were exploring every inch of my skin. I kept my eyes closed, in-
haling through my almost closed lips and exhaling through my nose to
chase them away from there.

I don't know how long I stayed in the pit, waiting with anguish for   9
the signal which would end my ordeal. As I tried to concentrate on my
relaxing, the sound of the beaten gongs and murmurs of the assistants
watching me from all around the pit started to disappear into a chaos
of pain and loud heartbeat.

Then suddenly I heard Tawa and the chief calling my name. I re-   10
moved once more the ants wandering on my eyelids before opening
my eyes and seeing my friends smiling to indicate that it was over. I got
out of the pit on my own, but I needed help to rid myself of the ants,
which were determined to eat all my skin. After the men washed my
body, the shaman applied an herbal mixture to ease the pain and

reduce the swellings. I would have quit and left the village then had I known that the "pit" experience was just the hors d'oeuvre.

11   The second part of the physical test started early the next morning. The chief explained the "game" to me. It was Hide and Go Seek Iban-style. I had to run without any supplies, weapons, or food, and for three days and three nights escape a group of young warriors who would leave the village a few hours after my departure and try to find me. If I were caught, my head would be used in a ceremony. The Iban would have done so without hate. It was simply the rule of their life. Birth and death. A death that always engenders new life.

12   When I asked, "What would happen if someone refused this part of the initiation?" the chief replied that such an idea wasn't possible. Once one had begun, there was no turning back. I knew the rules governing imitations among the cultures of tradition but never thought they would be applied to me. Whether or not I survived the initiation, I would be symbolically killed in order to be reborn among them. I had to die from my present time and identity into another life. I was aware that, among some cultures, initiatory ordeals are so arduous that young initiates sometimes really die. These are the risks if one wishes to enter into another world.

13   I was given time to get ready and the game began. I ran like hell without a plan or, it seemed to me, a prayer of surviving. Running along a path I had never taken, going I knew not where, I thought about every possible way I could escape from the young warriors. To hide somewhere. But where? Climb a tree and hide in it? Find a hole and squeeze in it? Bury myself under rocks and mud? But all of these seemed impossible. I had a presentiment they would find me anyway. So I ran straight ahead, my head going crazy by dint of searching for a way to safely survive the headhunters.

14   I would prefer staying longer with ants, I thought breathlessly. It was safer to stay among them for a whole day since they were just simple pain and fear compared to what I am about to undergo. I don't want to die.

15   For the first time I realized the real possibility of death—no longer in a romantic way, but rather at the hands of butchers.

16   Ten minutes after leaving the long house, I suddenly heard a call coming from somewhere around me. Still running, I looked all around trying to locate who was calling, and why. At the second call I stopped, cast my gaze about, and saw a woman's head peering out from the bushes. I recognized her as one of my pretty lovers. I hesitated, not knowing if she were part of the hunting party or a goddess come to save me. She called again. I thought, God, what to do? How will I escape from the warriors? As I stood there truly coming into contact with my impossible situation, I began to panic. She called again. With her fingers she showed me what the others would do if they caught me.

Her forefinger traced an invisible line from one side of her throat to the other. If someone was going to kill me, why not her? I joined her and found out she was in a lair. I realized I had entered the place where the tribe's women go to hide during their menstruation. This area is taboo for men. Each woman was her own refuge. Some have shelters made of branches, others deep covered holes hidden behind bushes with enough space to eat and sleep and wait until their time is past.

She invited me to make myself comfortable. That was quite diffi-   17
cult since it was just large enough for one person. But I had no choice. And after all, it was a paradise compared to what I would have undergone had I not by luck crossed this special ground.

Nervously and physically exhausted by my run and fear and de-   18
spair, I soon fell asleep. Around midnight I woke. She gave me rice and meat. We exchanged a few words. Then it was her turn to sleep.

The time I spent in the lair with my savior went fast. I tried to sleep   19
all day long, an escape from the concerns of my having broken a taboo. And I wondered what would happen to me if the headhunters were to learn where I spent the time of my physical initiation.

Then, when it was safe, I snuck back to the village…in triumph. I   20
arrived before the warriors, who congratulated and embraced me when they returned. I was a headhunter at last.

I spent the next two weeks quietly looking at the Iban through new   21
eyes. But strangely enough, instead of the initiation putting me closer to them, it had the opposite effect. I watched them more and more from an anthropological distance: my Iban brothers became an interesting clan whose life I witnessed but did not really share. And then suddenly I was bored and yearned for my own tribe. When Tawa had to go to an outpost to exchange pepper grains for other goods, I took a place aboard his canoe. Two days later I was in a small taxi-boat heading toward Sibu, the first leg in civilization on my voyage home.

I think of them often. I wonder about the man I tried to cure. I think   22
about Tawa and the girl who saved my life, and all the others sitting on the veranda. How long will my adopted village survive before being destroyed like all the others in the way of civilization? And what has become of those who marked my flesh with the joy of their lives and offered me the best of their souls? If they are slowly vanishing from my memories, I know that I am part of the stories they tell. I know that my life among them will be perpetuated until the farthest tomorrow. Now I am a story caught in a living legend of a timeless people.

✧ *Evaluating the Text*

1. What do the unusual sexual customs of hospitality bestowed upon outsiders suggest about the different cultural values of the Iban? Do these

customs suggest that the initiation would be harsher or milder than Gersi expected? Interpret this episode as it relates to the probable nature of Gersi's forthcoming initiation.

2. In a paragraph, explain the nature of the "hide and go seek" game that constituted the main test for a candidate. Explain why the use of the lighthearted term *game* is ironic in this context.

3. How does the reappearance of one of the girls who had earlier paid a nocturnal "visit" to Gersi result in his finding a safe hiding place? What does the nature of the hiding place reveal about the tribe's taboos?

4. Explain in what way the initiation resulted in Gersi feeling quite different than he had expected. That is, instead of feeling he was now part of the tribe, he actually felt more distant from them than he had felt before the initiation. To what factors do you attribute the unexpected sense of alienation? What did he discover about his own preconceptions during the initiation that stripped away certain romantic ideas he had about the Iban and the ability of any outsider to truly become a member of the tribe?

✧ *Exploring Different Perspectives*

1. Contrast how the experience Gersi describes is intended to empower the initiate with the quite opposite result produced by the operation described by Saida Hagi-Dirie Herzi in "Against the Pleasure Principle."

2. What similarities can you discover between Tepilit Ole Saitoti's experiences in "The Initiation of a Maasai Warrior" and those of Gersi? What might explain their very different reactions after being initiated?

✧ *Extending Viewpoints through Writing*

1. If you have ever been initiated into a fraternity or sorority or any other organization, compare the nature of Gersi's initiation with the one you experienced. In particular, try to identify particular stages in these initiations that mark the "death" of the outsider and the "rebirth" of the initiated member.

2. Examine any religious ritual, such as confirmation in the Catholic Church, and analyze it in terms of an initiation rite. For example, the ceremony of the Catholic Church by which one is confirmed as an adult member follows this pattern. A period of preparation is spent the year before confirmation. The ceremony has several stages, including confession, communion, and subsequent confirmation. Candidates

are routinely quizzed prior to communion about their knowledge of basic theology and must be sponsored by a member in good standing of the Catholic community. For example, what is the significance of the newly chosen confirmation name. What responsibilities and obligations do candidates incur who complete the confirmation ceremony?

3. What was your reaction to learning that the culture Gersi describes is one that exists today (in Borneo) two days away from taxi-boats and civilization? Would you ever consider undertaking a journey to such a place? Describe the most exotic place you want to visit, and explain why you would want to go there.

Tepilit Ole Saitoti

The Initiation of a Maasai Warrior

◆

Named for the language they speak—Maa, a distinct, but unwritten African tongue—the Maasai of Kenya and Tanzania, a tall, handsome, and proud people, still live much as they always have, herding cattle, sheep, and goats in and around the Great Rift Valley. This personal narrative is unique—the first autobiographical account written by a Maasai, which vividly documents the importance of the circumcision ceremony that serves as a rite of passage into warrior rank. Tepilit Ole Saitoti studied animal ecology in the United States and has returned to Kenya, where he is active in conservation projects. His experiences formed the basis for a National Geographic Society film, Man of Serengeti *(1971). This account first appeared in Saitoti's autobiography,* The Worlds of a Maasai Warrior *(1986).*

The United Republic of Tanzania was formed in 1964 by the union of Tanganyika and Zanzibar. It is bordered on the north by Kenya, Lake Victoria, and Uganda. Fossils discovered by British anthropologist Louis B. Leakey at Olduvai Gorge in northeastern Tanzania have been identified as the remains of a direct ancestor of the human species from 1.75 million years ago. Tanzania contains the famed Mount Kilimanjaro, which at 19,340 feet is the highest point in Africa. Tanzania also boasts the highest literacy rate in Africa. In May 1992 multiparty democracy was introduced into what had been a one-party state.

In 1999, bills were introduced that, if they become law, will return land to Maasai cattle-herding communities, secure their rights to land that they have inhabited for centuries, and gain them a fair share of the money raised from tourists. The Maasai are also trying to gain legal control over sacred sites to protect them from commercial exploitation.

1   "Tepilit, circumcision means a sharp knife cutting into the skin of the most sensitive part of your body. You must not budge; don't move a muscle or even blink. You can face only one direction until the operation is completed. The slightest movement on your part will mean you are a coward, incompetent and unworthy to be a Maasai man. Ours has always been a proud family, and we would like to keep it that way. We will not tolerate unnecessary embarrassment, so you had better be ready. If you are not, tell us now so that we will not proceed. Imagine yourself alone remaining uncircumcised like the water youth [white

114

people]. I hear they are not circumcised. Such a thing is not known in Maasailand; therefore, circumcision will have to take place even if it means holding you down until it is completed."

My father continued to speak and every one of us kept quiet. "The pain you will feel is symbolic. There is a deeper meaning in all this. Circumcision means a break between childhood and adulthood. For the first time in your life, you are regarded as a grownup, a complete man or woman. You will be expected to give and not just to receive. To protect the family always, not just to be protected yourself. And your wise judgment will for the first time be taken into consideration. No family affairs will be discussed without your being consulted. If you are ready for all these responsibilities, tell us now. Coming into manhood is not simply a matter of growth and maturity. It is a heavy load on your shoulders and especially a burden on the mind. Too much of this—I am done. I have said all I wanted to say. Fellows, if you have anything to add, go ahead and tell your brother, because I am through. I have spoken."

After a prolonged silence, one of my half-brothers said awkwardly, "Face it, man…it's painful. I won't lie about it, but it is not the end. We all went through it, after all. Only blood will flow, not milk." There was laughter and my father left.

My brother Lellia said, "Men, there are many things we must acquire and preparations we must make before the ceremony, and we will need the cooperation and help of all of you. Ostrich feathers for the crown and wax for the arrows must be collected."

"Are you *orkirekenyi?*" One of my brothers asked. I quickly replied no, and there was laughter. *Orkirekenyi* is a person who has transgressed sexually. For you must not have sexual intercourse with any circumcised woman before you yourself are circumcised. You must wait until you are circumcised. If you have not waited, you will be fined. Your father, mother, and the circumciser will take a cow from you as punishment.

Just before we departed, one of my closest friends said, "If you kick the knife, you will be in trouble." There was laughter. "By the way, if you have decided to kick the circumciser, do it well. Silence him once and for all." "Do it the way you kick a football in school." "That will fix him," another added, and we all laughed our heads off again as we departed.

The following month was a month of preparation. I and others collected wax, ostrich feathers, honey to be made into honey beer for the elders to drink on the day of circumcision, and all the other required articles.

Three days before the ceremony my head was shaved and I discarded all my belongings, such as my necklaces, garments, spear, and sword. I even had to shave my pubic hair. Circumcision in many ways is similar to Christian baptism. You must put all the sins you have committed during childhood behind and embark as a new person with a different outlook on a new life.

9   The circumciser came the following day and handed the ritual knives to me. He left drinking a calabash of beer. I stared at the knives uneasily. It was hard to accept that he was going to use them on my organ. I was to sharpen them and protect them from people of ill will who might try to blunt them, thus rendering them inefficient during the ritual and thereby bringing shame on our family. The knives threw a chill down my spine; I was not sure I was sharpening them properly, so I took them to my closest brother for him to check out, and he assured me that the knives were all right. I hid them well and waited.

10   Tension started building between me and my relatives, most of whom worried that I wouldn't make it through the ceremony valiantly. Some even snarled at me, which was their way of encouraging me. Others threw insults and abusive words my way. My sister Loiyan in particular was more troubled by the whole affair than anyone in the whole family. She had to assume my mother's role during the circumcision. Were I to fail my initiation, she would have to face the consequences. She would be spat upon and even beaten for representing the mother of an unworthy son. The same fate would befall my father, but he seemed unconcerned. He had this weird belief that because I was not particularly handsome, I must be brave. He kept saying, "God is not so bad as to have made him ugly and a coward at the same time."

11   Failure to be brave during circumcision would have other unfortunate consequences: the herd of cattle belonging to the family still in the compound would be beaten until they stampeded; the slaughtered oxen and honey beer prepared during the month before the ritual would go to waste; the initiate's food would be spat upon and he would have to eat it or else get a severe beating. Everyone would call him Olkasiodoi, the knife kicker.

12   Kicking the knife of the circumciser would not help you anyway. If you struggle and try to get away during the ritual, you will be held down until the operation is completed. Such failure of nerve would haunt you in the future. For example, no one will choose a person who kicked the knife for a position of leadership. However, there have been instances in which a person who failed to go through circumcision successfully became very brave afterwards because he was filled with anger over the incident; no one dares to scold him or remind him of it. His agemates, particularly the warriors, will act as if nothing had happened.

13   During the circumcision of a woman, on the other hand, she is allowed to cry as long as she does not hinder the operation. It is common to see a woman crying and kicking during circumcision. Warriors are usually summoned to help hold her down.

14   For women, circumcision means an end to the company of Maasai warriors. After they recuperate, they soon get married, and often to men twice their age.

The closer it came to the hour of truth, the more I was hated, particularly by those closest to me. I was deeply troubled by the withdrawal of all the support I needed. My annoyance turned into anger and resolve. I decided not to budge or blink, even if I were to see my intestines flowing before me. My resolve was hardened when newly circumcised warriors came to sing for me. Their songs were utterly insulting, intended to annoy me further. They tucked their wax arrows under my crotch and rubbed them on my nose. They repeatedly called me names.

By the end of the singing, I was fuming. Crying would have meant I was a coward. After midnight they left me alone and I went into the house and tried to sleep but could not. I was exhausted and numb but remained awake all night.

At dawn I was summoned once again by the newly circumcised warriors. They piled more and more insults on me. They sang their weird songs with even more vigor and excitement than before. The songs praised warriorhood and encouraged one to achieve it at all costs. The songs continued until the sun shone on the cattle horns clearly. I was summoned to the main cattle gate, in my hand a ritual cowhide from a cow that had been properly slaughtered during my naming ceremony. I went past Loiyan, who was milking a cow, and she muttered something. She was shaking all over. There was so much tension that people could hardly breathe.

I laid the hide down and a boy was ordered to pour ice-cold water, known as *engare entolu* (ax water), over my head. It dripped all over my naked body and I shook furiously. In a matter of seconds I was summoned to sit down. A large crowd of boys and men formed a semicircle in front of me; women are not allowed to watch male circumcision and vice versa. That was the last thing I saw clearly. As soon as I sat down, the circumciser appeared, his knives at the ready. He spread my legs and said, "One cut," a pronouncement necessary to prevent an initiate from claiming that he had been taken by surprise. He splashed a white liquid, a ceremonial paint called *enturoto*, across my face. Almost immediately I felt a spark of pain under my belly as the knife cut through my penis' foreskin. I happened to choose to look in the direction of the operation. I continued to observe the circumciser's fingers working mechanically. The pain became numbness and my lower body felt heavy, as if I were weighed down by a heavy burden. After fifteen minutes or so, a man who had been supporting from behind pointed at something, as if to assist the circumciser. I came to learn later that the circumciser's eyesight had been failing him and that my brothers had been mad at him because the operation had taken longer than was usually necessary. All the same, I remained pinned down until the operation was over. I heard a call for milk to wash the knives, which signaled the end, and soon the ceremony was over.

19   With words of praise, I was told to wake up, but I remained seated. I waited for the customary presents in appreciation of my bravery. My father gave me a cow and so did my brother Lellia. The man who had supported my back and my brother-in-law gave me a heifer. In all I had eight animals given to me. I was carried inside the house to my own bed to recuperate as activities intensified to celebrate my bravery.

20   I laid on my own bed and bled profusely. The blood must be retained within the bed, for according to Maasai tradition, it must not spill to the ground. I was drenched in my own blood. I stopped bleeding after about half an hour but soon was in intolerable pain. I was supposed to squeeze my organ and force blood to flow out of the wound, but no one had told me, so the blood coagulated and caused unbearable pain. The circumciser was brought to my aid and showed me what to do, and soon the pain subsided.

21   The following morning, I was escorted by a small boy to a nearby valley to walk and relax, allowing my wound to drain. This was common for everyone who had been circumcised, as well as for women who had just given birth. Having lost a lot of blood, I was extremely weak. I walked very slowly, but in spite of my caution I fainted. I tried to hang on to bushes and shrubs, but I fell, irritating my wound. I came out of unconsciousness quickly, and the boy who was escorting me never realized what had happened. I was so scared that I told him to lead me back home. I could have died without there being anyone around who could have helped me. From that day on, I was selective of my company while I was feeble.

22   In two weeks I was able to walk and was taken to join other newly circumcised boys far away from our settlement. By tradition Maasai initiates are required to decorate their headdresses with all kinds of colorful birds they have killed. On our way to the settlement, we hunted birds and teased girls by shooting them with our wax blunt arrows. We danced and ate and were well treated wherever we went. We were protected from the cold and rain during the healing period. We were not allowed to touch food, as we were regarded as unclean, so whenever we ate we had to use specially prepared sticks instead. We remained in this pampered state until our wounds healed and our headdresses were removed. Our heads were shaved, we discarded our black cloaks and bird headdresses and embarked as newly shaven warriors, Irkeleani.

23   As long as I live I will never forget the day my head was shaved and I emerged a man, a Maasai warrior. I felt a sense of control over my destiny so great that no words can accurately describe it. I now stood with confidence, pride, and happiness of being, for all around me I was desired and loved by beautiful, sensuous Maasai maidens. I could now interact with women and even have sex with them, which I had not been allowed before. I was now regarded as a responsible person.

In the old days, warriors were like gods, and women and men   24
wanted only to be the parent of a warrior. Everything else would be
taken care of as a result. When a poor family had a warrior, they ceased
to be poor. The warrior would go on raids and bring cattle back. The
warrior would defend the family against all odds. When a society respects the individual and displays confidence in him the way the Maasai do their warriors, the individual can grow to his fullest potential.
Whenever there was a task requiring physical strength or bravery, the
Maasai would call upon their warriors. They hardly ever fall short of
what is demanded of them and so are characterized by pride, confidence, and an extreme sense of freedom. But there is an old saying in
Maasai: "You are never a free man until your father dies." In other
words, your father is paramount while he is alive and you are obli-
gated to respect him. My father took advantage of this principle and
held a tight grip on all his warriors, including myself. He always
wanted to know where we all were at any given time. We fought
against his restrictions, but without success. I, being the youngest of
my father's five warriors, tried even harder to get loose repeatedly, but
each time I was punished severely.

Roaming the plains with other warriors in pursuit of girls and ad-   25
venture was a warrior's pastime. We would wander from one settlement to another, singing, wrestling, hunting, and just playing. Often I
was ready to risk my father's punishment for this wonderful freedom.

One clear day my father sent me to take sick children and one of his   26
wives to the dispensary in the Korongoro Highlands. We rode in the
L.S.B. Leakey lorry. We ascended the highlands and were soon
attended to in the local hospital. Near the conservation offices I met
several acquaintances, and one of them told me of an unusual circumcision that was about to take place in a day or two. All the local warriors and girls were preparing to attend it.

The highlands were a lush green from the seasonal rains and the   27
sky was a purple-blue with no clouds in sight. The land was overflowing with milk, and the warriors felt and looked their best, as they always did when there was plenty to eat and drink. Everyone was at
ease. The demands the community usually made on warriors during
the dry season when water was scarce and wells had to be dug were
now not necessary. Herds and flocks were entrusted to youths to look
after. The warriors had all the time for themselves. But my father was
so strict that even at times like these he still insisted on overworking us
in one way or another. He believed that by keeping us busy, he would
keep us out of trouble.

When I heard about the impending ceremony, I decided to remain   28
behind in the Korongoro Highlands and attend it now that the children
had been treated. I knew very well that I would have to make up a story

for my father upon my return, but I would worry about that later. I had left my spear at home when I boarded the bus, thinking that I would be coming back that very day. I felt lighter but now regretted having left it behind; I was so used to carrying it wherever I went. In gales of laughter resulting from our continuous teasing of each other, we made our way toward a distant kraal. We walked at a leisurely pace and reveled in the breeze. As usual we talked about the women we desired, among other things.

29   The following day we were joined by a long line of colorfully dressed girls and warriors from the kraal and the neighborhood where we had spent the night, and we left the highland and headed to Ingorienito to the rolling hills on the lower slopes to attend the circumcision ceremony. From there one could see Oldopai Gorge, where my parents lived, and the Inaapi hills in the middle of the Serengeti Plain.

30   Three girls and a boy were to be initiated on the same day, an unusual occasion. Four oxen were to be slaughtered, and many people would therefore attend. As we descended, we saw the kraal where the ceremony would take place. All those people dressed in red seemed from a distance like flamingos standing in a lake. We could see lines of other guests heading to the settlements. Warriors made gallant cries of happiness known as *enkiseer*. Our line of warriors and girls responded to their cries even more gallantly.

31   In serpentine fashion, we entered the gates of the settlement. Holding spears in our left hands, we warriors walked proudly, taking small steps, swaying like palm trees, impressing our girls, who walked parallel to us in another line, and of course the spectators, who gazed at us approvingly.

32   We stopped in the center of the kraal and waited to be greeted. Women and children welcomed us. We put our hands on the children's heads, which is how children are commonly saluted. After the greetings were completed, we started dancing.

33   Our singing echoed off the kraal fence and nearby trees. Another line of warriors came up the hill and entered the compound, also singing and moving slowly toward us. Our singing grew in intensity. Both lines of warriors moved parallel to each other, and our feet pounded the ground with style. We stamped vigorously, as if to tell the next line and the spectators that we were the best.

34   The singing continued until the hot sun was overhead. We recessed and ate food already prepared for us by other warriors. Roasted meat was for those who were to eat meat, and milk for the others. By our tradition, meat and milk must not be consumed at the same time, for this would be a betrayal of the animal. It was regarded as cruel to consume a product of the animal that could be obtained while it was alive, such as milk, and meat, which was only available after the animal had been killed.

After eating we resumed singing, and I spotted a tall, beautiful *esian-*   35
kiki (young maiden) of Masiaya whose family was one of the largest and
richest in our area. She stood very erect and seemed taller than the rest.

One of her breasts could be seen just above her dress, which was   36
knotted at the shoulder. While I was supposed to dance generally to
please all the spectators, I took it upon myself to please her especially. I
stared at and flirted with her, and she and I danced in unison at times.
We complemented each other very well.

During a break, I introduced myself to the *esiankiki* and told her I   37
would like to see her after the dance. "Won't you need a warrior to es-
cort you home later when the evening threatens?" I said. She replied,
"Perhaps, but the evening is still far away."

I waited patiently. When the dance ended, I saw her departing with   38
a group of other women her age. She gave me a sidelong glance, and I
took that to mean come later and not now. With so many others
around, I would not have been able to confer with her as I would have
liked anyway.

With another warrior, I wandered around the kraal killing time un-   39
til the herds returned from pasture. Before the sun dropped out of
sight, we departed. As the kraal of the *esiankiki* was in the lowlands, a
place called Enkoloa, we descended leisurely, our spears resting on our
shoulders.

We arrived at the woman's kraal and found that cows were now   40
being milked. One could hear the women trying to appease the cows
by singing to them. Singing calms cows down, making it easier to milk
them. There were no warriors in the whole kraal except for the two of
us. Girls went around into warriors' houses as usual and collected milk
for us. I was so eager to go and meet my *esiankiki* that I could hardly
wait for nightfall. The warriors' girls were trying hard to be sociable,
but my mind was not with them. I found them to be childish, loud,
bothersome, and boring.

As the only warriors present, we had to keep them company and   41
sing for them, at least for a while, as required by custom. I told the
other warrior to sing while I tried to figure out how to approach my *es-*
iankiki. Still a novice warrior, I was not experienced with women and
was in fact still afraid of them. I could flirt from a distance, of course.
But sitting down with a woman and trying to seduce her was another
matter. I had already tried twice to approach women soon after my circumcision and had failed. I got as far as the door of one woman's house
and felt my heart beating like a Congolese drum; breathing became difficult and I had to turn back. Another time I managed to get in the
house and succeeded in sitting on the bed, but then I started trembling
until the whole bed was shaking, and conversation became difficult. I
left the house and the woman, amazed and speechless, and never went
back to her again.

42   Tonight I promised myself I would be brave and would not make any silly, ridiculous moves. "I must be mature and not afraid," I kept reminding myself, as I remembered an incident involving one of my relatives when he was still very young and, like me, afraid of women. He went to a woman's house and sat on a stool for a whole hour; he was afraid to awaken her, as his heart was pounding and he was having difficulty breathing.

43   When he finally calmed down, he woke her up, and their conversation went something like this:

44   "Woman, wake up."

45   "Why should I?"

46   "To light the fire."

47   "For what?"

48   "So you can see me."

49   "I already know who you are. Why don't *you* light the fire, as you're nearer to it than me?"

50   "It's your house and it's only proper that you light it yourself."

51   "I don't feel like it."

52   "At least wake up so we can talk, as I have something to tell you."

53   "Say it."

54   "I need you."

55   "I do not need one-eyed types like yourself."

56   "One-eyed people are people too."

57   "That might be so, but they are not to my taste."

58   They continued talking for quite some time, and the more they spoke, the braver he became. He did not sleep with her that night, but later on he persisted until he won her over. I doubted whether I was as strong-willed as he, but the fact that he had met with success encouraged me. I told my warrior friend where to find me should he need me, and then I departed.

59   When I entered the house of my *esiankiki*, I called for the woman of the house, and as luck would have it, my lady responded. She was waiting for me. I felt better, and I proceeded to talk to her like a professional. After much talking back and forth, I joined her in bed.

60   The night was calm, tender, and loving, like most nights after initiation ceremonies as big as this one. There must have been a lot of courting and lovemaking.

61   Maasai women can be very hard to deal with sometimes. They can simply reject a man outright and refuse to change their minds. Some play hard to get, but in reality are testing the man to see whether he is worth their while. Once a friend of mine while still young was powerfully attracted to a woman nearly his mother's age. He put a bold move on her. At first the woman could not believe his intention, or rather was amazed by his courage. The name of the warrior was Ngengeiya, or Drizzle.

"Drizzle, what do you want?"   62
The warrior stared her right in the eye and said, "You."   63
"For what?"   64
"To make love to you."   65
"I am your mother's age."   66
"The choice was either her or you."   67

This remark took the woman by surprise. She had underestimated   68
the saying "There is no such thing as a young warrior." When you are a
warrior, you are expected to perform bravely in any situation. Your age
and size are immaterial.
"You mean you could really love me like a grownup man?"   69
"Try me, woman."   70
He moved in on her. Soon the woman started moaning with excite-   71
ment, calling out his name. "Honey Drizzle, Honey Drizzle, you *are* a
man." In a breathy, stammering voice, she said, "A real man."
Her attractiveness made Honey Drizzle ignore her relative old age.   72
The Maasai believe that if an older and a younger person have intercourse, it is the older person who stands to gain. For instance, it is believed that an older woman having an affair with a young man starts to
appear younger and healthier, while the young man grows older and
unhealthy.
The following day when the initiation rites had ended, I decided to   73
return home. I had offended my father by staying away from home
without his consent, so I prepared myself for whatever punishment he
might inflict on me. I walked home alone.

✧ Evaluating the Text

1. How is the candidate's life, reputation, and destiny dependent on the
   bravery he shows during the ceremony? What consequences would
   his family have to suffer if he were to flinch or shudder? What is the
   function of the relentless taunting by warriors and those who are
   newly circumcised prior to the ceremony?

2. What is Tepilit's attitude toward his father? What assumptions about a
   son's responsibilities account for how Tepilit's father treats him?

3. Several Maasai customs reveal the profound symbiotic relationship
   they have with nature and the animal world. For example, what is the
   rationale behind their practice of not eating milk and meat together?
   Why is Tepilit careful not to allow the blood from his wound to spill
   onto the ground as he lies on his bed bleeding from the surgery?

4. What responsibilities does Tepilit assume and what privileges is he allowed upon successful completion of the ceremony?

✧ Exploring Different Perspectives

1. Compare the very different objectives that circumcision is designed to achieve among the Maasai and in Somalia, as dramatized by Saida Hagi-Dirie Herzi in "Against the Pleasure Principle."

2. Compare the kinds of courage exhibited by Saitoti and Christy Brown in "The Letter 'A'" despite all that separates them.

✧ Extending Viewpoints through Writing

1. Every culture or society has some form of initiation that its members must undergo to become part of that society. In what way is the Maasai ritual Tepilit describes intended to deepen the bond between the community and the initiate in ways that are quite similar, allowing for cultural differences, to the Bar or Bat Mitzvah in Judaism and the confirmation ceremony in Christianity? In an essay, explore how any of these rites of passage affirm the culture, unite the candidate with his or her community, and ensure the continuation of traditions.

2. Despite obvious differences between the Maasai society and contemporary American culture, Tepilit's interactions with his friends and the opposite sex are quite typical of those of any teen-age boy. Write an essay exploring these similarities.

3. If you had to choose between being initiated as a warrior into the Maasai in East Africa or into the Marine Corps, which would you choose and why? Keep in mind the great differences in the length of time over which the initiation takes place, the respective penalties for not successfully completing the rite of passage, and the privileges and responsibilities that ensue from a successful completion.

Saida Hagi-Dirie Herzi

Against the Pleasure Principle

———————◆———————

Saida Hagi-Dirie Herzi is a Somalian writer whose story "Against the Pleasure Principle" first appeared in the Index on Censorship, *October 1990. The works in this publication are those that have been banned in the country of the writer and appear only because of the efforts and sponsorship of P.E.N., an international association of writers. Female genital mutilation, the subject of Herzi's story, is still widely practiced. By some estimates, 98 percent of females in Somalia have been subjected to it. The women in Somalian culture are subject to a number of other restrictions that indicate their low status in this overwhelmingly patriarchal society. Female children can only inherit half the amount of property to which their brothers are entitled and, according to the tradition of blood compensation, those found guilty of a woman's death are compelled to pay only half as much (50 camels) to the aggrieved family as they would if the victim were a man (100 camels).*

Located in East Africa, directly south of the Gulf of Aden and bordered on the east by the Indian Ocean and the west by Ethiopia and Kenya, Somalia is one of the poorest countries in the world with few natural resources. The Somali people trace their ancestry to Arabia and are almost exclusively Sunni Muslims. The structure of Somalian society is based on clans and subclans. Incessant conflict between political factions since 1988 and mass starvation (totaling perhaps 350,000 victims by 1992) brought about a peace-keeping effort by the United Nations, which subsequently failed to restore civil order. In August 1999, Kenya closed its border with Somalia to keep a dispute between various rival militia groups from spreading into Kenya.

1   Rahma was all excitement. Her husband had been awarded a scholarship to one of the Ivy League universities in the United States, and she was going with him. This meant that she was going to have her baby—the first—in the US. She would have the best medical care in the world.

2   But there was the problem of her mother. Her mother did not want her to go to the US. Rahma was not sure just what it was that her mother objected to but partly, no doubt, she was afraid she'd lose Rahma if she let her go. She had seen it happen with other girls who

went abroad: most of them did not come back at all and those who did came only to visit, not to stay. And they let it be known that they had thrown overboard the ways of their people and adopted the ways of the outside world—they painted their lips and their faces; they wore western dress; they went about the city laughing and singing outlandish songs; they spoke in foreign languages or threw in foreign words when they spoke the local language; and they generally acted as though they were superior to all those who stayed behind.

3   Her mother also seemed worried about Rahma having her baby in the US. Rahma had tried and tried again to reassure her that there was nothing to worry about: she would have the best medical attention. Problems, if any, would be more likely to arise at home than there. But it had made no difference. Her mother kept bombarding her with horror stories she had heard from Somali women coming back from the US—the dreadful things that happened to them when they went to US hospitals, above all when they had their babies there.

4   Like all women in her native setting, Rahma was circumcised, and, according to her mother, that would mean trouble for her when she was going to have a baby unless there was a midwife from her country to help her. Her mother was convinced that US doctors, who had no experience with circumcised women, would not know what to do.

5   Rahma had never given much thought to the fact that she had been only four years old when it happened, and nineteen years had passed since then. But she did remember.

6   It had not been her own feast of circumcision but that of her sister, who was nine then. She remembered the feeling of excitement that enveloped the whole house that morning. Lots of women were there; relatives were bringing gifts—sweets, cakes, various kinds of delicious drinks, trinkets. And her sister was the centre of attention. Rahma remembered feeling jealous, left out. Whatever it was they were going to do to her sister, she wanted to have it done too. She cried to have it done, cried and cried till the women around her mother relented and agreed to do it to her too. There was no room for fear in her mind: all she could think of was that she wanted to have done to her what they were going to do to her sister so that she too would get gifts, she too would be fussed over.

7   She remembered the preliminaries, being in the midst of a cluster of women, all relatives of hers. They laid her on her back on a small table. Two of the women, one to the left of her and the other to the right, gently but firmly held her down with one hand and with the other took hold of her legs and spread them wide. A third standing behind her held down her shoulders. Another washed her genitals with a mixture of *melmel* and *hildeed,* a traditional medicine. It felt pleasantly cool. Off to one side several women were playing tin drums. Rahma did not know that the intent of the drums was to drown the screams that would be coming from her throat in a moment.

The last thing she remembered was one of the women, a little knife   8
in one hand, bending over her. The next instant there was an explosion
of pain in her crotch, hot searing pain that made her scream like the
rabbit when the steel trap snapped its legs. But the din of the drums,
rising to a deafening crescendo, drowned her screams, and the women
who held her expertly subdued her young strength coiling into a
spring to get away. Then she must have passed out, for she remembered nothing further of the operation in which all the outer parts of
her small genitals were cut off, lips, clitoris and all, and the mutilated
opening stitched up with a thorn, leaving a passage the size of a grain
of sorghum.

When she regained consciousness, she was lying on her mat in her   9
sleeping corner, hot pain between her legs. The slightest movement so
aggravated the pain that tears would well up in her eyes. She remembered trying to lie perfectly still so as not to make the pain worse.

For some time after the operation she walked like a cripple: her   10
thighs had been tied together so that she could move her legs only from
the knees down, which meant taking only the tiniest of steps. People
could tell what had happened to her by the way she walked.

And she remembered how she dreaded passing water. She had to   11
do it sitting because she could not squat, and she had to do it with her
thighs closed tightly because of the bindings. To ease the pain of urine
pushing through the raw wound of the narrow opening, warm water
was poured over it while she urinated. Even so, it brought tears to her
eyes. In time the pain abated, but urinating had been associated with
discomfort for her ever since.

She remembered being told that she had needed only three thorn   12
stitches. Had she been older, it would have taken four, perhaps five,
stitches to sew her up properly. There are accepted standards for the
size of a girl's opening: an opening the size of a grain of rice is considered ideal; one as big as a grain of sorghum is acceptable. However,
should it turn out as big as a grain of maize, the poor girl would have
to go through the ordeal a second time. That's what had happened to
her sister; she herself had been luckier. When the women who inspected her opening broke out into the high-pitched *mash-harad* with which
women in her society signalled joy, or approval, Rahma knew that it
had turned out all right the first time.

Rahma's culture justified circumcision as a measure of hygiene, but   13
the real purpose of it, Rahma was sure, was to safeguard the woman's
virginity. Why else the insistence on an opening no larger than a grain
of sorghum, one barely big enough to permit the passing of urine and
of the menstrual blood? An opening as small as that was, if anything,
anti-hygienic. No, if the kind of circumcision that was practised in her
area had any purpose, it was to ensure that the hymen remained intact.
Her society made so much of virginity that no girl who lost it could

hope to achieve a decent marriage. There was no greater blow to a man's ego than to find out that the girl he married was not a virgin.

14   Rahma knew that, except for the first time, it was customary for women to deliver by themselves, standing up and holding on to a hanging rope. But the first time they needed assistance—someone to cut a passage large enough for the baby's passage. That was what so worried Rahma's mother. She did not think a US doctor could be trusted to make the right cut. Not having had any experience with circumcised women he would not know that the only way to cut was upward from the small opening left after circumcision. He might, especially if the baby's head was unusually big, cut upward *and* downward. How was he to know that a cut towards the rectum could, and probably would, mean trouble for all future deliveries? Nor would he know that it was best for the woman to be stitched up again right after the baby was born. It was, Rahma's mother insisted, dangerous for a circumcision passage to be left open.

15   When it became obvious that her words of warning did not have the desired effect on Rahma, her mother decided to play her last trump card—the *Kur*, a ritual feast put on, usually in the ninth month of a pregnancy, to ask God's blessing for the mother and the baby about to be born. Friends and relatives came to the feast to offer their good-luck wishes. It was her mother's intention to invite to the *Kur* two women who had had bad experiences with doctors in the US. They would talk about their experiences in the hope that Rahma would be swayed by them and not go away.

16   The *Kur* feast was held at her mother's place. When the ritual part of it was over and the well-wishers had offered their congratulations, some of the older women, who had obviously been put up to it by her mother, descended on Rahma trying to accomplish what her mother had failed to do—persuade her to put off going away at least until after the baby's birth.

17   It did not work. From the expression on Rahma's face that was only too obvious. So her mother signalled for the two special guests to do their part. The first, whose name was Hawa, had spent two years in the US as a student. She talked about the problems of a circumcised woman in a society that did not circumcise its women. "When people found out where I was from," she told her audience in a whisper, "they pestered me with questions about female circumcision. To avoid their questions, I told them that I had not been circumcised myself and therefore could not tell them anything about it. But that did not stop them from bugging me with more questions." The topic of circumcision, she told them, continued to be a source of embarrassment for as long as she was there.

18   Hawa then talked about her experience at the gynaecologist's office. She had put off seeing a gynaecologist as long as possible, but

when she could not put it off any longer, she looked for, and found, a woman doctor, thinking that she would feel comfortable with a woman. When the doctor started to examine her, Hawa had heard a gasp. The gasp was followed by a few stammering sounds that turned into a question. The doctor wanted to know whether she had got burned or scalded. When Hawa signalled by a shake of her head that she had done neither, the doctor asked her whether she had had an operation for cancer or something, in which the outer parts of her genitals had been amputated. Again Hawa denied anything, and to avoid further questions quickly added that the disfigurement which the doctor found so puzzling was the result of circumcision.

At that, Hawa's doctor went on with the examination without further questions. When she was finished, she turned to Hawa once more. "You had me confused there," she muttered, more to herself than to Hawa. "Don't hold my ignorance against me. I have heard and read about circumcision, but you are the first circumcised woman I have seen in my career. I neither knew that it was still practised nor did I have any idea it went so far."

"You know," she continued after a moment's pause, "I cannot for the world of me understand why your people have to do this to their women. Intercourse cannot be much fun for someone mutilated like that. Perhaps that's why they do it, to make sure the women won't get any pleasure out of sex. And what misery it must be for a woman sewn up like that to have a baby."

Hawa said she went away from the doctor's office thinking how right the doctor was about sex not being fun for circumcised women. She remembered the first time her husband made love to her, how horribly painful it had been. And it had continued to be painful for her even after she got used to it. She knew that for most of the women in her society sex was something to be endured not enjoyed. With all the sensitive parts of womanhood cut away, it was all but impossible for them to be sexually aroused and quite impossible for them to experience any of the pleasurable sensations that would redeem the act.

Hawa said she walked home feeling like a freak: what was left of her genitals must look pretty grim if the sight of it could make a doctor gasp. Why did her people do this to their women? Hundreds of millions of women the world over went through life the way God had created them, whole and unmutilated. Why could her people not leave well enough alone? It seemed to her, at least in this case, that man's attempts to improve on nature were a disaster.

The second woman, Dahabo, seemed to believe in circumcision as such. However, when a circumcised woman moved to a part of the world that did not practise circumcision problems were bound to arise. She too had lived in the US. She too had had her encounters with US doctors. She talked at length about her first such encounter. Like

Hawa's doctor, hers was a woman; unlike Hawa's hers was familiar with the idea of female circumcision. Nevertheless, Dahabo was her first case of a circumcised woman. Dahabo told her audience about the questioning she was subjected to by her doctor after the examination:

24   **Doctor:** Did you have any sort of anaesthesia when they circumcised you?

25   **Dahabo:** No, I did not, but I did not really feel any pain because I fainted and remained unconscious during the whole operation.

26   **Doctor:** Is circumcision still practised in your culture?

27   **Dahabo:** Yes, it is. I had it done to my five-year-old daughter before coming here.

28   **Doctor:** Any difference between your way and your daughter's way?

29   **Dahabo:** None whatsoever: the same women who circumcised me circumcised her.

30   At that point, Dahabo told her listeners, something happened that puzzled her: her doctor, eyes full of tears, broke into loud sobs, and she continued to sob while she opened the door to usher her patient out into the corridor. Dahabo said she had never understood what had made her doctor cry.

31   Rahma had no trouble understanding what it was that had moved the doctor to tears. She was close to tears herself as she left her mother's house to walk home. How much longer, she wondered, would the women of her culture have to endure this senseless mutilation? She knew that, though her people made believe circumcision was a religious obligation, it was really just an ugly custom that had been borrowed from the ancient Egyptians and had nothing to do with Islam. Islam recommends circumcision only for men.

32   The *Kur* did not achieve what her mother had hoped. Rahma was more determined than ever to accompany her husband to the US. True, there was still the problem of her mother; no doubt her mother meant well, no doubt she wanted the best for her, but Rahma had different ideas about that. She was, for instance, convinced that having her baby in the US was in the best interest of her and of the baby. She would like to have her mother's blessing for the move, but if that was not possible she would go without it. She had always hated circumcision. Now she hated it more than ever. No daughter of hers would ever be subjected to it.

✧ Evaluating the Text

1. What different cultural values and expectations come into conflict, regarding the propriety of female circumcision, in the story?

2. In what ways does the experience of the main character, Rahma, exemplify the different societal assumptions between America and Somalia about this practice?

3. Rahma's experiences and reactions are contrasted with those of two other women, Hawa, and Dahabo. What function do their accounts play in this story?

✧ Exploring Different Perspectives

1. To what extent is circumcision intended to physically and psychologically restrict girls in Somalian culture, whereas a comparable procedure is intended to confer authority on boys among the Maasai, as described by Tepilit Ole Saitoti in "The Initiation of a Maasai Warrior"? Discuss the different culturally defined values attached to circumcision as an initiatory ritual.

2. To what extent do the mothers in Herzi's story and in Helen Fremont's narrative "After Long Silence" try to conceal the truth from their daughters?

✧ Extending Viewpoints through Writing

1. Compare and contrast the value placed on female virginity in the culture that Herzi describes with contemporary American society. In your opinion, what factors explain the differences, and how do these differences reflect the different ways that women are viewed in these two cultures?

2. Is there any custom or practice that you would recommend be eliminated in contemporary society? Make a case supporting your choice.

Helen Fremont

After Long Silence

◆————————

Helen Fremont is a lawyer with the Massachusetts Public Defenders and teaches creative writing at Emerson College. Her fiction and essays have appeared in Prize Stories 1994: The O. Henry Awards, Ploughshares, The Harvard Review, *and other journals. In the following chapter from* After Long Silence *(1999), Fremont recounts her attempt to piece together clues that held the secret of who her parents really were. Were they, as they claimed, Polish Catholics who emigrated to America during World War II? Or were they Polish Jews who had constructed an elaborate fiction to survive the Holocaust at the price of their identity as Jews?*

1   When I was sixteen or seventeen, our family was invited to Susie Janiczek's wedding. Her parents were Auschwitz survivors and close friends of our parents'. They'd met in rural Michigan in 1953, when Dr. Janiczek helped my father set up his medical practice.

2   Dressed in our Sunday best, our family piled into my father's forest-green Chrysler New Yorker and followed the stream of big boxy American cars from the temple to the Sheraton hotel for the reception.

3   "My parents survived," Susie addressed the hundreds of Holocaust survivors in the ballroom, "and have given me this, a new life, new friends, the future." Flashbulbs snapped, and a hush fell over the room. "We have conquered the past," Susie added triumphantly to the nodding hairsprayed heads. "We have conquered Hitler! We will survive. We will flourish." She raised her white-gloved arms over her head, and the crowd cheered. A band of musicians in electric-blue tuxedos lifted their instruments from black cases behind her.

4   Lara and I and the handful of other American-born youngsters were paraded around and shown off by the older generation, who chattered among themselves in impenetrable Polish. Middle-aged ladies with layers of hair coloring and penciled eyebrows, sumptuously retouched lips, glossy fingernails in shades of berries. They clasped my hand with their diamond-studded fingers, smiled and assessed my figure, talking the whole time in Polish to my mother, who beamed with pride.

5   The men clustered together—solid black-and-white islands in the sea of colorful women. Unbuttoning their jackets, they smoked filterless cigarettes and drank champagne from slender flute glasses, their cheeks growing redder and redder.

I was used to seeing tattooed numbers on wrists and hearing Polish- 6
and German-peppered accents—many of my parents' closest friends
were survivors. I liked the way the wedding celebration was turning into
a joyous, arrogant in-your-face to history, to gas chambers and ghettos
and starvation and mass murders, as if it were my personal mission to
fly in the face of oppression. I was proof of the tenacity of my parents,
and I was fiercely proud of them. The only glaring gap in my understanding of the war against the Jews was my family's precise role in it.

It didn't bother me that Lara and I were the only non-Jews at that 7
wedding. We were the children of survivors in an ocean of survivors,
and it seemed the most natural thing in the world for us to celebrate—
religion didn't seem to enter into it. My mother explained the Jewish
traditions—the *chuppah,* the chairs, the broken champagne glass, so that
I understood what was happening. I never questioned how she knew so
much. I was used to my mother's complete fluency with the world.

It never occurred to me that someone in my family might actually 8
be Jewish, until a few years ago, when I was already in my thirties and
working as a public defender in Boston. One evening, at a Bar Association cocktail party, I was introduced to a statuesque high-heeled, slim-
hipped woman, the wife of a partner in a Boston firm. She told me she
was the daughter of a distinguished family of Philadelphia WASPS,
and only after she had married and had three children did she discover
that her mother was in fact Jewish. We exchanged family stories over a
glass of wine, and she threw back her head and laughed. "You're Jewish!" she said.

"No," I insisted, "Catholic. Polish Catholic." 9

"Then why were your parents in concentration camps?" Her eyes 10
gleamed a beautiful emerald-green, and she tried to suppress a smile.
She did not look the least bit Jewish. When she laughed, her yellow
hair seemed to break around her shoulders like waves on a beach.

"Lots of Poles were imprisoned during the war or taken by the 11
Germans," I explained. "They—"

"Of course," she interrupted, "but if they were Catholic they 12
wouldn't have had to escape and emigrate to the States. I bet your parents were Jewish. Or at least your mother."

It didn't take more than half a glass of wine for me to grow fond of 13
the idea. This would explain so much, I thought—all those mysteries of
childhood, my endless tiptoeing around a jigsaw-puzzle past in which
all the pieces were missing except my parents. As a child my questions
about our family had always elicited strange, winding soliloquies that
led to bedtime or, worse, dinner, the two most dreaded events of my day.
And when Lara and I had fought as children, my mother sometimes fell
to her knees, sobbing, "I should have died with my parents! I shouldn't

have lived! *Bosze, Bosze, Bosze.*" God, God, God. This was always a shoe-in to make Lara and me stop fighting and turn into perfect children before her eyes. But by the time Morn had called upon *Bosze,* she was beyond noticing us.

14   Perhaps, I now thought, all these mysteries could be explained: Maybe we were Jewish.

15   A few months later I ran the idea past Lara, who was living in San Diego and working as a psychiatrist. "I have this theory," I told her over the phone. "What if Mom and Dad were Jewish? Or maybe one of their parents was Jewish."

16   A long silence. "I really doubt it," she finally said.

17   "Well, I know it sounds crazy," I said quickly. "I mean, it's just this idea I have. But think about it. I mean, Mom escaped from Poland *dressed as an Italian soldier!* Why would she have to do that if she was Catholic? And why wouldn't *any* other relatives be alive? This would explain so much."

18   "I just can't see it," Lara said. "Why would they hide their religion now?"

19   I was disheartened by her lack of interest. "I know," I agreed, "it's pretty strange. But still...."

20   I couldn't let go of the idea. Believing we were Jewish offered me the possibility that my parents were still in hiding, that we were all in hiding, that all the underground emotional tunnels in our house were not just figments of my imagination.

21   But the more I thought about it, the less I could justify my suspicions. Lara had a point—why would my parents deny their Judaism here in America, fifty years later? Perhaps, I thought, we were Jewish, or partly Jewish, but my parents didn't even know *themselves* that they were Jewish.

22   I tried this idea out on them at Christmas a year later. Lara had flown in from San Diego for the holiday, and I had arrived from Boston after finishing a legal ethics report for my office. Before dinner I found my mother in the kitchen, hoisting the twenty-two-pound turkey to the counter.

23   "Hey, Mom," I said. She muscled the bird onto the cutting board. Her forearms were covered with little notchlike burns from years of cooking.

24   "Want some help?" I asked. I knew she never accepted help with anything.

25   "No, no," she said.

26   "So here's my theory, okay?"

27   She rustled through the drawer for a serving spoon.

28   "Maybe your mother was Catholic, and your father was Jewish, okay? Something like that. Big taboo. So when they married, your grandparents went through the roof, and that's why you don't know

anything about them. Huge mega-rift in the family. And you wouldn't even have known about it."

My mother was hacking up the turkey now, twisting its legs with her bare hands. The bone and cartilage broke, and steam poured from the leg sockets.

"So what do you think?" I prodded her.

She shrugged and took a butcher's knife to the wings, then started on the breast. Juice streamed down the sides of the turkey and gurgled in the pan. Her eyes narrowed, examining the turkey's exposed pink breast. "I don't know," she said. "Why do you think so?"

"I'm just guessing," I said. "But it would make sense. It would make sense if someone in your family was Jewish."

Thin slices of meat curled off the knife blade and onto her palm. She placed them on four waiting plates of white china.

"I doubt it," she said, pushing her bifocals back up her nose. "But I don't know. The Germans would have known about that, I wouldn't."

Her checks gleamed under the bright kitchen lights, and slight folds of skin gathered under her chin. She'd grown self-conscious about this lately and had taken to wearing turtlenecks.

"Put some broccoli on here," she said, pointing with the knife to a steaming pot. "And some of these baby potatoes." She swung the pot of boiled potatoes from the burner toward me in a swift, fluid motion: Mikhail Baryshnikov in oven mitts. It was hard to believe she was in her mid-seventies.

"That one's for Dad," she said, pointing to the plate in my left hand. "Now, take that in before it gets cold."

It's crazy, I told myself—these wild guesses of Jewish roots—as if I were casting about for some adventure to beef up my ordinary American existence. I carried the plates into the dining room, and our family sat down to dinner.

My mother brought in the last plate and passed the salt and pepper. "But what is it with you girls," she said, puzzled and slightly annoyed. "What is it with all this Jewish business?" She turned from me to Lara. "All I hear now for months from you is about the past, our family, and so on. What is it all about?"

I glanced across the table at my sister, but she avoided my eyes. She was researching our family history for her fellowship in child psychiatry, and now I wondered whether she, too, was beginning to think we were Jewish.

"I don't know," I said, "but I have the feeling that I'm Jewish. I don't know why, exactly."

My mother stabbed a piece of turkey with her fork and smothered it with dressing.

"Like that time," I said, "I went to visit Rachel after my first year of law school."

44   Rachel's mother was a Jewish Holocaust survivor. I'd spent a weekend at their house twelve years earlier. "Remember what I told you when I came back? That it was just like being at home. With her father listening to a violin concerto in the other room, and the living room filled with books, and all her mother's plants in the windows. And we sat at the kitchen counter, Rachel and her mother and I, and sipped coffee and talked and talked—and for a moment I thought I was with you and Dad—it was just so much like *home*. I can't explain it—but I remember I told you about it—there was a deep resonance somehow."

45   My mother snorted with disgust.

46   "It's not as if we discuss religion or anything," I said quickly, "but it just so happens that most of my closest friends are Jews. I can't help noticing it." My mother was chasing a bit of cranberry relish around her plate with a piece of roll. When she finally captured it, she chewed thoughtfully. "And most people assume I'm Jewish," I added. "It's always a surprise to them when I tell them I'm not." I named some of my closest friends in recent years: Kari and Allen, Sue Klein, Annie and David.

47   "Oh, I suppose next you're going to tell me that Jean Sacks is Jewish," my mother spat out.

48   I wasn't prepared for the hostility in her voice. Jean Sacks was my boss. African-American.

49   "I'm not saying my *only* friends are Jewish," I said quietly. "It's just that—"

50   "What about Paula?" my mother said, glaring at me. "She's not Jewish!"

51   "Yes," I agreed, adding irrelevantly, "but she married a Jew."

52   As soon as I said this I winced. I was undermining my own argument by descending to a finger count of the number of my friends who were Jewish and Gentile. Instead, to my surprise, it gave my mother pause.

53   "Yes, that's true," my mother said thoughtfully, pondering the fact of Paula's marriage to a Jew, as if this somehow compromised Paula's non-Jewish identity. "You're right about that." Amazingly, this seemed to carry great weight with my mother. She thought about it awhile and remained quiet.

54   Oh, I thought, what a ridiculous argument.

55   We finished our turkey in silence, and my mother returned to the kitchen and brought out the salad.

56   She placed the bowl on the table, a bit too abruptly, and it teetered before righting itself. The serving utensils jumped against the wooden sides of the bowl with a dull clatter. "What difference does it make!?" my mother suddenly exclaimed. "What difference does it make?" She was shaking with anger. I stared at her, dumbfounded.

"What difference does it make whether you're Jewish or Catholic   57
or Protestant or Buddhist?!" she screamed. "Who cares?"

I felt my eyes widen. Across from me, thin flames from our dinner   58
candles gleamed in the framed Emilio Greco sketches on the wall. There
was a story behind those drawings, but I didn't understand it yet. I
looked at my mother, unable to speak. "I care," I said finally, "*I* care."

"Then I've failed as a mother!" she cried. "I've failed! I brought you   59
up to be tolerant, not to size everyone up by their religion or color, or—"
Her voice broke, and she exploded with emotion, tears streaming.

"I *am* tolerant," I tried to reassure her, suddenly aware of how ri-   60
diculous this sounded. My father and sister waited to see how I could
dig myself out of this. Dinners in our family are often a kind of specta-
tor sport.

"Oh, look—I'm sorry, Mom," I said. "I didn't mean to upset you.   61
Really, I'm sorry." I was stunned by her reaction. I vowed never to raise
the subject again.

The following evening my mother showed Lara and me a postcard   62
written by Dad's mother in 1943, shortly before she was killed. We'd
never seen this card before. Zosia had brought it with her on a recent
visit.

The postcard was addressed to Zosia in Rome, and dated April 29,   63
1943. It was postmarked *Galicia*. A twelve-pfennig German postage
stamp clung to the right-hand corner—Hitler's face. His right profile,
with a bright ear against dark hair, a stern expression on his lips. His
hair combed over the left forehead, his mustache short, his cheeks haggard. Below this stamp was Zosia's Rome address, written in calligra-
phy with blue ink by Dad's mother. I picture her now, putting pen to
paper, and I see my father—the steel-blue eyes, the slight smile, the
pride with which he carves letters like rhapsodies of pen and ink.

The return address on the postcard was filled out by Dad's Ukrai-   64
nian music teacher: *Anya Karelewicz, Musiklehrerin, in Buczacz, Galizien,
Frankengasse Nr 15.* Beneath her address were various stamps and sig-
natures of censors, as well as the stamp of the Italian censor: *Commis-
sione Provinciale di Censura.* On the reverse side the message, first
written in the elegant handwriting of my grandmother Helen, and then
an additional few lines added by Anya.

Kochana Pani! my grandmother writes.   65

Dear Madam:

On the 28th of this month, I received the greetings sent to me along
with the news from you indicating that you are in good health and
think of us. So I take this opportunity to convey to you all my sincerest
greetings. You must have passed Easter happily...but I am not complaining since the holiday went pleasantly and quietly here. Now here,
too, it is getting warmer and we expect a warm spring.

> If it does not cause any great inconvenience, I would appreciate a
> rosary or a similar item consecrated by the church in Rome. Even with-
> out it I have you in my prayers and wish you good health.
>
> I kiss you all.

66   Beneath, scribbled in blue ink, are a few words from Dad's music
teacher:

> I, too, include my best wishes and again beg for news. Have you heard
> anything about Kovik?
>
> Anya K

67   The next night, back in Boston, I couldn't sleep. At midnight it finally dawned on me. The postcard was proof: My grandmother was
Jewish. My grandmother, a woman named Helen Buchman under the
Nazi occupation, was writing a postcard that would be read and
stamped by the censor, writing for a shred of hope, the trappings of a
Catholic cover. She must have been desperate by then. I didn't begin to
know the whole story. But the card, for all its Catholic dressing, was the
clearest proof we had that she was Jewish. I called Lara up.

68   "Lara," I said, "you know that postcard? Dad's Mom was Jewish. I
know it. And you know what? She didn't die in a bomb as Mom and
Dad always said. She was killed at Auschwitz. Or on the way to Auschwitz. Or somewhere. She was killed by the Nazis, I'm sure of it. If
you write to the Red Cross, I bet you anything she was killed in Auschwitz, not in her hometown. That's why Dad never found her grave.
She wasn't bombed in Buczacz."

69   I was right, and I was wrong. All I knew was Auschwitz. I had a lot
to learn.

✧ Evaluating the Text

1. What different events led Fremont to suspect that, rather than being
   Polish Catholic, her parents were actually Jewish? How would you
   characterize the kind of hold that this possibility had on Fremont's
   imagination? Why was it important for her to find out the truth?

2. Fremont's relationship with her mother is very complex, with Fremont
   prodding and her mother resisting her daughter's attempts to discover
   the truth. What is at stake for Fremont's mother in continuing the fiction now that they are living in America?

3. How would the possibility of having Jewish ancestors, if true, require
   Fremont to think of herself in an entirely different way?

✧ *Exploring Different Perspectives*

1. The reality of the Holocaust in Eastern Europe frames both Fremont's narrative and Jerzy Kosinski's story "The Miller's Tale." In what ways does this enter both works?

2. How do both Fremont and Sucheng Chan (see "You're Short, Besides!") redefine themselves by breaking away from old-world prejudices?

✧ *Extending Viewpoints through Writing*

1. What works on the Holocaust have you read or seen that give you a frame of reference in which to understand what both sides of the conflict between Fremont and her mother entailed? In a short essay, discuss what is at stake for each.

2. Describe any old-world prejudices from which you have tried to separate yourself. To what extent did this make you feel more American than you might have?

Jerzy Kosinski

The Miller's Tale

◆

Jerzy Kosinski (1933–1991) was born in Lodz, Poland. When the Nazis occupied Poland in 1939, he was sent by his parents to live in the country-side, where his nightmarish experiences later formed the basis for his clas-sic of Holocaust fiction, The Painted Bird *(1965). After receiving degrees in sociology and history, he emigrated to the United States and published two nonfiction books,* The Future Is Ours, Comrade *(1960) and* No Third Path *(1962) under the pseudonym Joseph Novak. In 1973, he was elected president of the American Center of PEN, an international writ-er's association. A prolific writer, Kosinski's second novel,* Steps *(1968), received the National Book Award. In 1970, he received the award from the American Academy of Arts and Letters for Literature. Other novels include* The Devil Tree *(1973),* Cockpit *(1975),* Pinball *(1982), and* The Hermit of 69th Street *(1988). His 1971 novella,* Being There, *was made into the Academy Award-winning 1979 film. Burdened by an in-creasingly serious heart condition, Kosinski committed suicide in 1991. Chapter 4 of* The Painted Bird, *"The Miller's Tale," depicts how a boy known only as "the gypsy" reacts to his first experience of seeing the ef-fects of jealousy and revenge in the lives of the East European peasants with whom he has found temporary shelter.*

The invasion of Poland by Germany in 1939 precipitated World War II, during which 6 million Poles, including 3 million Jews, died from starvation, disease, massacres, and executions in concentration camps such as Auschwitz and Treblinka. After the war, Poland was taken over by the Soviet Union and in 1952 became a People's Republic ruled without the overt repression seen in Hungary and Romania. Diminishing antago-nism between the Communist Party and the Roman Catholic Church dur-ing the 1970s paved the way for Pope John Paul II's 1979 visit to his homeland. An independent labor union known as Solidarity, led by Lech Walesa, emerged in the 1980s, demanding greater worker control in Pol-ish industry. After a long struggle—during which Solidarity was banned, marshal law imposed, and its members arrested—the deteriorating Polish economy, and Gorbachev's hands-off attitude, compelled the government to end marshal law in 1984, lift the ban on Solidarity in 1986, and an-nounce, in 1989, the first semidemocratic elections in Poland's history. The overwhelming victory of Solidarity candidates led to the appointment of Tadeusz Mazowiecki, a close associate of Walesa's, as premier, and marked the end of forty years of Communist Party domination in Poland.

The struggle for a stable economy continued with calls for Western investment in Poland during the period of transition.

I was now living at the miller's, whom the villagers had nick- 1
named Jealous. He was more taciturn than was usual in the area. Even
when neighbors came to pay him a visit, he would just sit, taking an occasional sip of vodka, and drawling out a word once in a while, lost in
thought or staring at a dried-up fly stuck to the wall.

He abandoned his reverie only when his wife entered the room. 2
Equally quiet and reticent, she would always sit down behind her husband, modestly dropping her gaze when men entered the room and
furtively glanced at her.

I slept in the attic directly above their bedroom. At night I was 3
awakened by their quarrels. The miller suspected his wife of flirting
and lasciviously displaying her body in the fields and in the mill before
a young plowboy. His wife did not deny this, but sat passive and still.
Sometimes the quarrel did not end. The enraged miller lit candles in
the room, put on his boots, and beat his wife. I would cling to a crack in
the floorboards and watch the miller lashing his naked wife with a
horsewhip. The woman cowered behind a feather quilt tugged off the
bed, but the man pulled it away, flung it on the floor, and standing over
her with his legs spread wide continued to lash her plump body with
the whip. After every stroke, red blood-swollen lines would appear on
her tender skin.

The miller was merciless. With a grand sweep of the arm he looped 4
the leather thong of the whip over her buttocks and thighs, slashed her
breasts and neck, scourged her shoulders and shins. The woman weakened and lay whining like a puppy. Then she crawled toward her husband's legs, begging forgiveness.

Finally the miller threw down the whip and, after blowing out the 5
candle, went to bed. The woman remained groaning. The following
day she would cover her wounds, move with difficulty, and wipe away
her tears with bruised, cut palms.

There was another inhabitant of the hut: a well-fed tabby cat. One 6
day she was seized by a frenzy. Instead of mewing she emitted half-
smothered squeals. She slid along the walls as sinuously as a snake,
swung her pulsating flanks, and clawed at the skirts of the miller's
wife. She growled in a strange voice and moaned, her raucous shrieks
making everyone restless. At dusk the tabby whined insanely, her tail
beating her flanks, her nose thrusting.

The miller locked the inflamed female in the cellar and went to his 7
mill, telling his wife that he would bring the plowboy home for supper.
Without a word the woman set about preparing the food and table.

The plowboy was an orphan. It was his first season of work at the 8
miller's farm. He was a tall, placid youth with flaxen hair which he

habitually pushed back from his sweating brow. The miller knew that the villagers gossiped about his wife and the boy. It was said that she changed when she gazed into the boy's blue eyes. Heedless of the risk of being noticed by her husband, she impulsively hiked her skirt high above her knees with one hand, and with the other pushed down the bodice of her dress to display her breasts, all the time staring into the boy's eyes.

9   The miller returned with the young man, carrying in a sack slung over his shoulder, a tomcat borrowed from a neighbor. The tomcat had a head as large as a turnip and a long, strong tail. The tabby was howling lustingly in the cellar. When the miller released her, she sprang to the center of the room. The two cats began to circle one another mistrustfully, panting, coming nearer and nearer.

10   The miller's wife served supper. They ate silently. The miller sat at the middle of the table, his wife on one side and the plowboy on the other. I ate my portion squatting by the oven. I admired the appetites of the two men: huge chunks of meat and bread, washed down with gulps of vodka, disappeared in their throats like hazelnuts.

11   The woman was the only one who chewed her food slowly. When she bowed her head low over the bowl the plowboy would dart a glance faster than lightning at her bulging bodice.

12   In the center of the room the tabby suddenly arched her body, bared her teeth and claws, and pounced on the tomcat. He halted, stretched his back, and sputtered saliva straight into her inflamed eyes. The female circled him, leaped toward him, recoiled, and then struck him in the muzzle. Now the tomcat stalked around her cautiously, sniffing her intoxicating odor. He arched his tail and tried to come at her from the rear. But the female would not let him; she flattened her body on the floor and turned like a millstone, striking his nose with her stiff, outstretched paws.

13   Fascinated, the miller and the other two stared silently while eating. The woman sat with a flushed face; even her neck was reddening. The plowboy raised his eyes, only to drop them at once. Sweat ran down through his short hair and he continually pushed it away from his hot brow. Only the miller sat calmly eating, watching the cats, and glancing casually at his wife and guest.

14   The tomcat suddenly came to a decision. His movements became lighter. He advanced. She moved playfully as if to draw back, but the male leapt high and flopped onto her with all fours. He sank his teeth in her neck and intently, tautly, plunged directly into her without any squirming. When satiated and exhausted, he relaxed. The tabby, nailed to the floor, screamed shrilly and sprang out from under him. She jumped onto the cooled oven and tossed about on it like a fish, looping her paws over her neck, rubbing her head against the warm wall.

15   The miller's wife and the plowboy ceased eating. They stared at each other, gaping over their food-filled mouths. The woman breathed

heavily, placed her hands under her breasts and squeezed them, clearly unaware of herself. The plowboy looked alternately at the cats and at her, licked his dry lips, and got down his food with difficulty.

The miller swallowed the last of his meal, leaned his head back, and abruptly gulped down his glass of vodka. Though drunk, he got up, and grasping his iron spoon and tapping it, he approached the plowboy. The youth sat bewildered. The woman hitched up her skirt and began puttering at the fire. 16

The miller bent over the plowboy and whispered something in his reddened ear. The youth jumped up as if pricked with a knife and began to deny something. The miller asked loudly now whether the boy lusted after his wife. The plowboy blushed but did not answer. The miller's wife turned away and continued to clean the pots. 17

The miller pointed at the strolling tomcat and again whispered something to the youth. The latter, with an effort, rose from the table, intending to leave the room. The miller came forward overturning his stool and, before the youth realized it, suddenly pushed him against the wall, pressed one arm against his throat, and drove a knee into his stomach. The boy could not move. Terror stricken, panting loudly, he babbled something. 18

The woman dashed toward her husband, imploring and wailing. The awakened tabby cat lying on the oven looked down on the spectacle, while the frightened tomcat leapt onto the table. 19

With a single kick the miller got the woman out of his way. And with a rapid movement such as women use to gouge out the rotten spots while peeling potatoes, he plunged the spoon into one of the boy's eyes and twisted it. 20

The eye sprang out of his face like a yolk from a broken egg and rolled down the miller's hand onto the floor. The plowboy howled and shrieked, but the miller's hold kept him pinned against the wall. Then the blood-covered spoon plunged into the other eye, which sprang out even faster. For a moment the eye rested on the boy's cheek as if uncertain what to do next; then it finally tumbled down his shirt onto the floor. 21

It all had happened in a moment. I could not believe what I had seen. Something like a glimmer of hope crossed my mind that the gouged eyes could be put back where they belonged. The miller's wife was screaming wildly. She rushed to the adjoining room and woke up her children, who also started crying in terror. The plowboy screamed and then grew silent covering his face with his hands. Rivulets of blood seeped through his fingers down his arms, dripping slowly on his shirt and trousers. 22

The miller, still enraged, pushed him toward the window as though unaware that the youth was blind. The boy stumbled, cried out, and nearly knocked over a table. The miller grabbed him by the shoulders, opened the door with his foot, and kicked him out. The boy yelled 23 again, stumbled through the doorway, and fell down in the yard. The dogs started barking, though they did not know what had happened:

24   The eyeballs lay on the floor. I walked around them, catching their steady stare. The cats timidly moved out into the middle of the room and began to play with the eyes as if they were balls of thread. Their own pupils narrowed to slits from the light of the oil lamp. The cats rolled the eyes around, sniffed them, licked them, and passed them to one another gently with their padded paws. Now it seemed that the eyes were staring at me from every corner of the room, as though they had acquired a new life and motion of their own.

25   I watched them with fascination. If the miller had not been there I myself would have taken them. Surely they could still see. I would keep them in my pocket and take them out when needed, placing them over my own. Then I would see twice as much, maybe even more. Perhaps I could attach them to the back of my head and they would tell me, though I was not quite certain how, what went on behind me. Better still, I could leave the eyes somewhere and they would tell me later what happened during my absence.

26   Maybe the eyes had no intention of serving anyone. They could easily escape from the cats and roll out of the door. They could wander over the fields, lakes, and woods, viewing everything about them, free as birds released from a trap. They would no longer die, since they were free, and being small they could easily hide in various places and watch people in secret. Excited, I decided to close the door quietly and capture the eyes.

27   The miller, evidently annoyed by the cats' play, kicked the animals away and squashed the eyeballs with his heavy boots. Something popped under his thick sole. A marvelous mirror, which could reflect the whole world, was broken. There remained on the floor only a crushed bit of jelly. I felt a terrible sense of loss.

28   The miller, paying no attention to me, seated himself on the bench and swayed slowly as he fell asleep. I stood up cautiously, lifted the bloodied spoon from the floor and began to gather the dishes. It was my duty to keep the room neat and the floor swept. As I cleaned I kept away from the crushed eyes, uncertain what to do with them. Finally I looked away and quickly swept the ooze into the pail and threw it in the oven.

29   In the morning I awoke early. Underneath me I heard the miller and his wife snoring. Carefully I packed a sack of food, loaded the comet[1] with hot embers and, bribing the dog in the yard with a piece of sausage, fled from the hut.

---

[1]*Comet:* a small portable stove consisting of a one-quart preserve can opened at one end with a lot of small nail holes punched in the sides attached to a three-foot loop of wire hooked to the top as a handle, served as a source of heat and as a weapon when filled with tinder (described in Ch. 3 of *The Painted Bird*).

At the mill wall, next to the barn, lay the plowboy. At first I meant to   30
pass him by quickly, but I stopped when I realized that he was sightless.
He was still stunned. He covered his face with his hands, he moaned
and sobbed. There was caked blood on his face, hands, and shirt. I
wanted to say something, but I was afraid that he would ask me about
his eyes and then I would have to tell him to forget about them, since
the miller had stamped them into pulp. I was terribly sorry for him.

I wondered whether the loss of one's sight would deprive a person   31
also of the memory of everything that he had seen before. If so, the man
would no longer be able to see even in his dreams. If not, if only the
eyeless could still see through their memory, it would not be too bad.
The world seemed to be pretty much the same everywhere, and even
though people differed from one another, just as animals and trees did,
one should know fairly well what they looked like after seeing them for
years. I had lived only seven years, but I remembered a lot of things.
When I closed my eyes, many details came back still more vividly. Who
knows, perhaps without his eyes the plowboy would start seeing an
entirely new, more fascinating world.

I heard some sound from the village. Afraid that the miller might   32
wake up, I went on my way, touching my eyes from time to time. I
walked more cautiously now, for I knew that eyeballs did not have
strong roots. When one bent down they hung like apples from a tree
and could easily drop out. I resolved to jump across fences with my
head held up; but on my first try I stumbled and fell down. I lifted my
fingers fearfully to my eyes to see whether they were still there. After
carefully checking that they opened and closed properly, I noticed with
delight the partridges and thrushes in flight. They flew very fast but
my sight could follow them and even overtake them as they soared under the clouds, becoming smaller than raindrops. I made a promise to
myself to remember everything I saw; if someone should pluck out my
eyes, then I would retain the memory of all that I had seen for as long
as I lived.

✧ Evaluating the Text

1. How would you characterize the boy from whose perspective the
   story is told? How has he been changed by seeing the effects of violence, sexuality, and jealousy? How does the boy's insight signal a
   turning point in his transformation from innocence to self-awareness?

2. The bizarre, violent, and traumatic events related in this tale are described objectively without any accompanying emotional reactions. In
   your opinion, why does Kosinski adopt this approach? Of what advantage is it to foreshadow the experiences of the miller and his wife
   with the behavior of the tomcat?

3. As contrasted with the boy's innocence, what does he learn about the effects of jealousy and revenge on human behavior? Why does the boy come to value memory as a result of the events he witnesses?

✧ Exploring Different Perspectives

1. As the thinly fictionalized story of a Jewish boy who becomes separated from his parents and must fend for himself in Poland during World War II, what additional dimension does this story add to Helen Fremont's account "After Long Silence"?

2. Compare Kosinski's story with Douchan Gersi's account, "Initiated into an Iban Tribe of Headhunters," in terms of what the narrators learn about the art of survival.

✧ Extending Viewpoints through Writing

1. How would the same events in the story appear from the perspective of one of the other characters? Rewrite this narrative as seen through the eyes of any one of the other characters, including the cat's.

2. How does Kosinski's handling of a naive character coming to terms with the existence of evil compare with other literary treatments of this theme, such as Herman Melville's *Billy Budd* (1924) or Charles Dickens's *David Copperfield* (1850)? For further research on the author, a good website is the *Resources Page for Jerzy Kosinski*. Other works by Kosinski that explore the themes in this story are: *Steps* (1968) and *The Devil Tree* (1973).

Connecting Cultures

◆

Christy Brown, "The Letter 'A'"

How do the attitudes toward disabilities differ in Brown's account and Lennard J. Davis's analysis (see "Visualizing the Disabled Body" in Chapter 3)?

Sucheng Chan, "You're Short, Besides!"

What contrasting attitudes toward disabilities emerge from Chan's account and Lennard J. Davis's analysis (see "Visualizing the Disabled Body" in Chapter 3)?

Douchan Gersi, "Initiated into an Iban Tribe of Headhunters"

The initiation ritual to which Gersi is subjected is similar in some respects to that of the near-death rituals practiced in Haiti by the voudon priests, albeit for very different objectives. Compare and contrast Gersi's account and Gino Del Guercio's analysis in "The Secrets of Haiti's Living Dead" in Chapter 8.

Tepilit Ole Saitoti, "The Initiation of a Maasai Warrior"

Discuss facing danger and injury in order to gain peer acceptance as a theme in both Saitoti's account and in Jackie Chan's "A Dirty Job" in Chapter 4.

Saida Hagi-Dirie Herzi, "Against the Pleasure Principle"

In what ways do Rahma's mother in Herzi's story and the mother in Fatima Mernissi's account (see "Moonlit Nights of Laughter" in Chapter 1) differ in the expectations they hold for their daughters?

Helen Fremont, "After Long Silence"

Compare and contrast Fremont's account with that of Natalia Ginzburg, an Italian Jew, who lived through the Holocaust (see "The Son of Man" in Chapter 6).

Jerzy Kosinski, "The Miller's Tale"

Discuss the loss of innocence as a theme in Kosinski's story and in Gloria Anzaldúa's story "Cervicide" in Chapter 7.

3

How Culture Shapes Gender Roles

◆

Culture plays an enormous part in shaping the expectations that we attach to sex roles. This process, sometimes called *socialization,* determines how each of us assimilates our culture's ideas of what it means to act as a male or female. We tend to acquire a sense of our own sexual identity in conjunction with societal expectations. Yet these expectations differ strikingly from culture to culture. For example, in male-dominated Islamic Middle Eastern societies, the gender roles and relationships between men and women are very different from those in modern industrial societies.

The characteristics that define gender roles have varied widely throughout history in such diverse cultures as those in Europe, the Orient, the Mideast, and the Americas. The responsibilities and obligations that collectively define what it means to be a woman or a man in different societies have changed dramatically in these societies, which have themselves changed in recent times. The movement toward equality between the sexes—a transformation that has been only partially realized—has allowed women to assume positions of leadership and perform tasks in the workplace, the professions, and society that were traditionally reserved for men. The works in this chapter address the changing cultural expectations attached to being a man or a woman, as well as the psychological and social stresses produced by these changes in redrawing the boundaries of gender roles, marriage, and parenthood.

How you see yourself is determined in large part by the social meanings attached to specific behavior for men and women in your culture, beginning with the fairy tales told to children, extending through the conceptions of masculinity and femininity promulgated by the media, and including opportunities available in the workplace.

149

The authors in this chapter provide insight into the way in which we acquire specific sexual identities, because of the cultural expectations, pressures, and values that shape the choices we make. How we feel about ourselves and our life experiences reveals the powerful role that gender stereotypes play in shaping our personal development. Some writers in this chapter speak out against the constricting effects of these rigid cultural expectations that enforce inflexible images of masculine and feminine behavior. Such restrictive stereotypes legitimize and perpetuate gender inequality.

Kim Chernin, in "The Flesh and the Devil," perceptively analyzes the cultural pressures that compel women to starve themselves to be thin. Judith Ortiz Cofer, in "The Myth of the Latin Woman," describes how different cultural expectations in her native Puerto Rico and the United States led her to be stereotyped as a "hot-blooded Latina." In "Visualizing the Disabled Body," Lennard J. Davis looks at the paradoxical double standard applied to physical imperfection in works of art and in human beings who are disabled. Paul Monette, in "Borrowed Time: An AIDS Memoir," retraces the origin of AIDS and describes its devastating effect in his own life. Marjorie Shostak relates an account by Nisa, of the !Kung tribe in Botswana, who describes the stages she went through before accepting her role as a woman, in "Memories of a !Kung Girlhood." The Lebanese writer, Shirley Saad, in "Amina," tells the story of a woman who has given birth to only girls and fears that her husband will take another wife in order to have a son. In "Polite Lies," Kyoko Mori describes how the limitations placed on women in Japanese society became painfully apparent to her when she returned for a visit. A thought-provoking story, "Giribala," by Mahasweta Devi, describes the social forces in Bengal, India, that permit a father to sell his daughters into prostitution.

Kim Chernin

The Flesh and the Devil

———————◆———————

Kim Chernin, born in 1940, is a freelance writer, editor, and self-described "feminist humanist." "The Flesh and the Devil" is a chapter from The Obsession: Reflections on the Tyranny of Slenderness *(1981). In this essay, Chernin draws on her personal experiences as well as surveys, research studies, and life stories of friends to support her incisive analysis of the extent to which cultural stereotypes dominate women's lives. Chernin's recent works include her controversial memoir,* My Life as a Boy *(1997) and a collection of narratives that she edited,* The Woman Who Gave Birth to Her Mother: Seven Stages of Change in Women's Lives *(1998).*

We know that every woman wants to be thin. Our images of womanhood are almost synonymous with thinness.

—Susie Orbach

...I must now be able to look at my ideal, this ideal of being thin, of being without a body, and to realize: "it is a fiction."

—Ellen West

When the body is hiding the complex, it then becomes our most immediate access to the problem.

—Marian Woodman

The locker room of the tennis club. Several exercise benches, two old-fashioned hair dryers, a mechanical bicycle, a treadmill, a reducing machine, a mirror, and a scale. 1

A tall woman enters, removes her towel; she throws it across a bench, faces herself squarely in the mirror, climbs on the scale, looks down. 2

A silence. 3

"I knew it," she mutters, turning to me. "I knew it." 4

And I think, before I answer, just how much I admire her, for this courage beyond my own, this daring to weigh herself daily in this way. And I sympathize. I know what she must be feeling. Not quite candidly, I say: "Up or down?" I am hoping to suggest that there might be people and cultures where gaining weight might not be considered a disaster. Places where women, stepping on scales, might be horrified to notice that they had reduced themselves. A mythical, almost unimaginable land. 5

151

6　　"Two pounds," she says, ignoring my hint. "Two pounds." And then she turns, grabs the towel and swings out at her image in the mirror, smashing it violently, the towel spattering water over the glass. "Fat pig," she shouts at her image in the glass. "You fat, fat pig...."

7　　Later, I go to talk with this woman. Her name is Rachel and she becomes, as my work progresses, one of the choral voices that shape its vision.

8　　Two girls come into the exercise room. They are perhaps ten or eleven years old, at that elongated stage when the skeletal structure seems to be winning its war against flesh. And these two are particularly skinny. They sit beneath the hair dryers for a moment, kicking their legs on the faded green upholstery; they run a few steps on the eternal treadmill, they wrap the rubber belt of the reducing machine around themselves and jiggle for a moment before it falls off. And then they go to the scale.

9　　The taller one steps up, glances at herself in the mirror, looks down at the scale. She sighs, shaking her head. I see at once that this girl is imitating someone. The sigh, the headshake are theatrical, beyond her years. And so, too, is the little drama enacting itself in front of me. The other girl leans forward, eager to see for herself the troubling message imprinted upon the scale. But the older girl throws her hand over the secret. It is not to be revealed. And now the younger one, accepting this, steps up to confront the ultimate judgment. "Oh God," she says, this growing girl. "Oh God," with only a shade of imitation in her voice: "Would you believe it? I've gained five pounds."

10　　These girls, too, become a part of my work. They enter, they perform their little scene again and again; it extends beyond them and in it I am finally able to behold something that would have remained hidden—for it does not express itself directly, although we feel its pressure—almost every day of our lives. Something, unnamed as yet, struggling against our emergence into femininity. This is my first glimpse of it, out there. And the vision ripens.

11　　I return to the sauna. Two women I have seen regularly at the club are sitting on the bench above me. One of them is very beautiful, the sort of woman Renoir would have admired. The other, who is probably in her late sixties, looks, in the twilight of this sweltering room, very much an adolescent. I have noticed her before, with her tan face, her white hair, her fashionable clothes, her slender hips and jaunty walk. But the effect has not been soothing. A woman of advancing age who looks like a boy.

12　　"I've heard about that illness, anorexia nervosa," the plump one is saying, "and I keep looking around for someone who has it. I want to go sit next to her. I think to myself, maybe I'll catch it...."

13　　"Well," the other woman says to her, "I've felt the same way myself. One of my cousins used to throw food under the table when no one was looking. Finally, she got so thin they had to take her to the hospital.... I always admired her."

What am I to understand from these stories? The woman in the   14
locker room who swings out at her image in the mirror, the little girls
who are afraid of the coming of adolescence to their bodies, the woman
who admires the slenderness of the anorexic girl. Is it possible to miss
the dislike these women feel for their bodies?

And yet, an instant's reflection tells us that this dislike for the body   15
is not a biological fact of our condition as women—we do not come
upon it by nature, we are not born to it, it does not arise for us because
of anything predetermined in our sex. We know that once we loved the
body, delighting in it the way children will, reaching out to touch our
toes and count over our fingers, repeating the game endlessly as we
come to knowledge of this body in which we will live out our lives. No
part of the body exempt from our curiosity, nothing yet forbidden, we
know an equal fascination with the feces we eliminate from ourselves,
as with the ear we discover one day and the knees that have become
bruised and scraped with falling and that warm, moist place between
the legs from which feelings of indescribable bliss arise.

From that state to the condition of the woman in the locker room is   16
a journey from innocence to despair, from the infant's naive pleasure in
the body, to the woman's anguished confrontation with herself. In this
journey we can read our struggle with natural existence—the loss of
the body as a source of pleasure. But the most striking thing about this
alienation from the body is the fact that we take it for granted. Few of
us ask to be redeemed from this struggle against the flesh by overcoming our antagonism toward the body. We do not rush about looking for
someone who can tell us how to enjoy the fact that our appetite is large,
or how we might delight in the curves and fullness of our own natural
shape. We hope instead to be able to reduce the body, to limit the urges
and desires it feels, to remove the body from nature. Indeed, the suffering we experience through our obsession with the body arises precisely
from the hopeless and impossible nature of this goal.

Cheryl Prewitt, the 1980 winner of the Miss America contest, is a   17
twenty-two-year-old woman, "slender, bright-eyed, and attractive."[1] If
there were a single woman alive in America today who might feel comfortable about the size and shape of her body, surely we would expect
her to be Ms. Prewitt? And yet, in order to make her body suitable for
the swimsuit event of the beauty contest she has just won, Cheryl Prewitt "put herself through a grueling regimen, jogging long distances
down back-country roads, pedaling for hours on her stationary bicycle." The bicycle is still kept in the living room of her parents' house so
that she can take part in conversation while she works out. This body
she has created, after an arduous struggle against nature, in conformity

[1]Sally Hegelson, *TWA Ambassador,* July 1980.

with her culture's ideal standard for a woman, cannot now be left to its own desires. It must be perpetually shaped, monitored, and watched. If you were to visit her at home in Ackerman, Mississippi, you might well find her riding her stationary bicycle in her parents' living room, "working off the calories from a large slice of homemade coconut cake she has just had for a snack."

18   And so we imagine a woman who will never be Miss America, a next-door neighbor, a woman down the street, waking in the morning and setting out for her regular routine of exercise. The eagerness with which she jumps up at six o'clock and races for her jogging shoes and embarks upon the cold and arduous toiling up the hill road that runs past her house. And yes, she feels certain that her zeal to take off another pound, tighten another inch of softening flesh, places her in the school of those ancient wise men who formulated that vision of harmony between mind and body. "A healthy mind in a healthy body," she repeats to herself and imagines that it is love of the body which inspires her this early morning. But now she lets her mind wander and encounter her obsession. First it had been those hips, and she could feel them jogging along there with their own rhythm as she jogged. It was they that had needed reducing. Then, when the hips came down it was the thighs, hidden when she was clothed but revealing themselves every time she went to the sauna, and threatening great suffering now that summer drew near. Later, it was the flesh under the arms—this proved singularly resistant to tautness even after the rest of the body had become gaunt. And finally it was the ankles. But then, was there no end to it? What had begun as a vision of harmony between mind and body, a sense of well-being, physical fitness, and glowing health, had become now demonic, driving her always to further exploits, running farther, denying herself more food, losing more weight, always goaded on by the idea that the body's perfection lay just beyond her present achievement. And then, when she began to observe this driven quality in herself, she also began to notice what she had been thinking about her body. For she would write down in her notebook, without being aware of the violence in what she wrote: "I don't care how long it takes. One day I'm going to get my body to obey me. I'm going to make it lean and tight and hard. I'll succeed in this, even if it kills me."

19   But what a vicious attitude this is, she realizes one day, toward a body she professes to love. Was it love or hatred of the flesh that inspired her now to awaken even before it was light, and to go out on the coldest morning, running with bare arms and bare legs, busily fantasizing what she would make of her body? Love or hatred?

20   "You know perfectly well we hate our bodies," says Rachel, who calls herself the pig. She grabs the flesh of her stomach between her hands. "Who could love this?"

21   There is an appealing honesty in this despair, an articulation of what is virtually a universal attitude among women in our culture to-

day. Few women who diet realize that they are confessing to a dislike for the body when they weigh and measure their flesh, subject it to rigorous fasts or strenuous regimens of exercise. And yet, over and over again, as I spoke to women about their bodies, this antagonism became apparent. One woman disliked her thighs, another her stomach, a third the loose flesh under her arms. Many would grab their skin and squeeze it as we talked, with that grimace of distaste language cannot translate into itself. One woman said to me: "Little by little I began to be aware that the pounds I was trying to 'melt away' were my own flesh. Would you believe it? It never occurred to me before. These 'ugly pounds' which filled me with so much hatred were my body."

The sound of this dawning consciousness can be heard now and again among the voices I have recorded in my notebook, heralding what may be a growing awareness of how bitterly the women of this culture are alienated from their bodies. Thus, another woman said to me: "It's true, I never used to like my body." We had been looking at pictures of women from the nineteenth century; they were large women, with full hips and thighs. "What do you think of them?" I said. "They're like me," she answered, and then began to laugh. "Soft, sensual, and inviting."

The description is accurate; the women in the pictures, and the woman looking at them, share a quality of voluptuousness that is no longer admired by our culture:

> When I look at myself in the mirror I see that there's nothing wrong with me—now! Sometimes I even think I'm beautiful. I don't know why this began to change. It might have been when I started going to the YWCA. It was the first time I saw so many women naked. I realized it was the fuller bodies that were more beautiful. The thin women, who looked so good in clothes, seemed old and worn out. Their bodies were gaunt. But the bodies of the larger women had a certain natural mystery, very different from the false illusion of clothes. And I thought, I'm like them; I'm a big woman like they are and perhaps my body is beautiful. I had always been trying to make my body have the right shape so that I could fit into clothes. But then I started to look at myself in the mirror. Before that I had always looked at parts of myself. The hips were too flabby, the thighs were too fat. Now I began to see myself as a whole. I stopped hearing my mother's voice, asking me if I was going to go on a diet. I just looked at what was really there instead of what should have been there. What was wrong with it? I asked myself. And little by little I stopped disliking my body.[2]

This is the starting point. It is from this new way of looking at an old problem that liberation will come. The very simple idea that an obses-

22

23

---

[2]Private communication.

sion with weight reflects a dislike and uneasiness for the body can have a profound effect upon a woman's life.

> I always thought I was too fat. I never liked my body. I kept trying to lose weight. I just tortured myself. But if I see pictures of myself from a year or two ago I discover now that I looked just fine.
>
> I remember recently going out to buy Häagen Dazs ice cream. I had decided I was going to give myself something I really wanted to eat. I had to walk all the way down to the World Trade Center. But on my way there I began to feel terribly fat. I felt that I was being punished by being fat. I had lost the beautiful self I had made by becoming thinner. I could hear these voices saying to me: "You're fat, you're ugly, who do you think you are, don't you know you'll never be happy?" I had always heard these voices in my mind but now when they would come into consciousness I would tell them to shut up. I saw two men on the street. I was eating the Häagen Dazs ice cream. I thought I heard one of them say "heavy." I thought they were saying: "She's so fat." But I knew that I had to live through these feelings if I was ever to eat what I liked. I just couldn't go on tormenting myself any more about the size of my body.
>
> One day, shortly after this, I walked into my house. I noticed the scales, standing under the sink in the bathroom. Suddenly, I hated them. I was filled with grief for having tortured myself for so many years. They looked like shackles. I didn't want to have anything more to do with them. I called my boyfriend and offered him the scales. Then, I went into the kitchen. I looked at my shelves. I saw diet books there. I was filled with rage and hatred of them. I hurled them all into a box and got rid of them. Then I looked into the ice box. There was a bottle of Weight Watchers dressing. I hurled it into the garbage and watched it shatter and drip down the plastic bag. Little by little, I started to feel better about myself. At first I didn't eat less, I just worried less about my eating. I allowed myself to eat whatever I wanted. I began to give away the clothes I couldn't fit into. It turned out that they weren't right for me anyway. I had bought them with the idea of what my body should look like. Now I buy clothes because I like the way they look on me. If something doesn't fit it doesn't fit. I'm not trying to make myself into something I'm not. I weigh more than I once considered my ideal. But I don't seem fat to myself. Now, I can honestly say that I like my body.[3]

24   Some weeks ago, at a dinner party, a woman who had recently gained weight began to talk about her body.

25   "I was once very thin," she said, "but I didn't feel comfortable in my body. I fit into all the right clothes. But somehow I just couldn't find myself any longer."

26   I looked over at her expectantly; she was a voluptuous woman, who had recently given birth to her first child.

---

[3]Private communication.

"But now," she said as she got to her feet, "now, if I walk or jog or   27
dance, I feel my flesh jiggling along with me." She began to shake her
shoulders and move her hips, her eyes wide as she hopped about in
front of the coffee table. "You see what I mean?" she shouted over to
me. "I love it."

This image of a woman dancing came with me when I sat down to   28
write. I remembered her expression. There was in it something secretive, I thought, something knowing and pleased—the look of a woman
who has made peace with her body. Then I recalled the faces of women
who had recently lost weight. The haggard look, the lines of strain
around the mouth, the neck too lean, the tendons visible, the head too
large for the emaciated body. I began to reason:

There must be, I said, for every woman a correct weight, which   29
cannot be discovered with reference to a weight chart or to any statisti-
cal norm. For the size of the body is a matter of highly subjective individual preferences and natural endowments. If we should evolve an
aesthetic for women that was appropriate to women it would reflect
this diversity, would conceive, indeed celebrate and even love, slenderness in a woman intended by nature to be slim, and love the rounded
cheeks of another, the plump arms, broad shoulders, narrow hips, full
thighs, rounded ass, straight back, narrow shoulders or slender arms,
of a woman made that way according to her nature, walking with head
high in pride of her body, however it happened to be shaped. And then
Miss America, and the woman jogging in the morning, and the woman
swinging out at her image in the mirror might say, with Susan Griffin
in *Woman and Nature:*

> And we are various, and amazing in our variety, and our differences
> multiply, so that edge after edge of the endlessness of possibility is
> exposed...none of us beautiful when separate but all exquisite as we
> stand, each moment heeded in this cycle, no detail unlovely....[4]

✧ Evaluating the Text

1. How do the kinds and range of examples Kim Chernin presents serve
   as evidence for her thesis?

2. According to Chernin, what kind of role do cultural values play in de-
   termining how women see themselves? What is her attitude toward
   these values?

3. What alternative value system does Chernin present to replace the prevailing cultural norms?

[4]Susan Griffin, *Woman and Nature: The Roaring inside Her,* New York, 1978.

❖ Exploring Different Perspectives

1. How do Kim Chernin and Lennard J. Davis (see "Visualizing the Disabled Body") address the issue of the stereotyping of the female body image in western cultures?

2. How do Kim Chernin and Judith Ortiz Cofer (see "The Myth of the Latin Woman") deal with the psychological effects of stereotyping based on appearance?

❖ Extending Viewpoints through Writing

1. To what extent has your own self-image been determined by prevailing cultural expectations of the kind described by Chernin? What parts of your body or aspects of your appearance would you change and why?

2. Analyze some of the cultural messages in ads or other media that communicate socially desirable values having to do with how you look. To what extent do these messages conflict with your own values regarding appearance?

Judith Ortiz Cofer

The Myth of the Latin Woman

◆

Judith Ortiz Cofer, a poet and novelist, was born in 1952 in Hormigueros, Puerto Rico. After her father, a career navy officer, retired, the family settled in Georgia where Cofer attended Augusta College. During college she married and, with her husband and daughter, moved to Florida where she finished a master's degree in English at Florida Atlantic University. A fellowship allowed her to pursue graduate work at Oxford University, after which she returned to Florida and began teaching English and writing poetry. Her first volume of poetry, Peregrina *(1985), won the Riverstone International Poetry Competition and was followed by two more poetry collections,* Reaching for the Mainland *(1987) and* Terms of Survival *(1988). Her first novel,* The Line of the Sun *(1989), was listed as one of 1989's "twenty-five books to remember" by the New York City Public Library System. Her recent works include a collection of short stories,* An Island Like You: Stories of the Barrio *(1995), and* The Year of Our Revolution *(1998). Cofer is a Professor of English and Creative Writing at the University of Georgia. In the following essay, drawn from her collection* The Latin Deli: Prose and Poetry *(1993), Cofer explores the destructive effects of the Latina stereotype.*

On a bus trip to London from Oxford University where I was earning some graduate credits one summer, a young man, obviously fresh from a pub, spotted me and as if struck by inspiration went down on his knees in the aisle. With both hands over his heart he broke into an Irish tenor's rendition of "Maria" from *West Side Story*. My politely amused fellow passengers gave his lovely voice the round of gentle applause it deserved. Though I was not quite as amused, I managed my version of an English smile: no show of teeth, no extreme contortions of the facial muscles—I was at this time of my life practicing reserve and cool. Oh, that British control, how I coveted it. But "Maria" had followed me to London, reminding me of a prime fact of my life: you can leave the island, master the English language, and travel as far as you can, but if you are a Latina, especially one like me who so obviously belongs to Rita Moreno's gene pool, the island travels with you.

This is sometimes a very good thing—it may win you that extra minute of someone's attention. But with some people, the same things can make *you* an island—not a tropical paradise but an Alcatraz, a place nobody wants to visit. As a Puerto Rican girl living in the United States

159

and wanting like most children to "belong," I resented the stereotype that my Hispanic appearance called forth from many people I met.

3   Growing up in a large urban center in New Jersey during the 1960s, I suffered from what I think of as "cultural schizophrenia." Our life was designed by my parents as a microcosm of their *casas* on the island. We spoke in Spanish, ate Puerto Rican food bought at the *bodega,* and practiced strict Catholicism at a church that allotted us a one-hour slot each week for mass, performed in Spanish by a Chinese priest trained as a missionary for Latin America.

4   As a girl I was kept under strict surveillance by my parents, since my virtue and modesty were, by their cultural equation, the same as their honor. As a teenager I was lectured constantly on how to behave as a proper *senorita.* But it was a conflicting message I received, since the Puerto Rican mothers also encouraged their daughters to look and act like women and to dress in clothes our Anglo friends and their mothers found too "mature" and flashy. The difference was, and is, cultural; yet I often felt humiliated when I appeared at an American friend's party wearing a dress more suitable to a semi-formal than to a playroom birthday celebration. At Puerto Rican festivities, neither the music nor the colors we wore could be too loud.

5   I remember Career Day in our high school, when teachers told us to come dressed as if for a job interview. It quickly became obvious that to the Puerto Rican girls "dressing up" meant wearing their mothers' ornate jewelry and clothing, more appropriate (by mainstream standards) for the company Christmas party than as daily office attire. That morning I had agonized in front of my closet, trying to figure out what a "career girl" would wear. I knew how to dress for school (at the Catholic school I attended, we all wore uniforms), I knew how to dress for Sunday mass, and I knew what dresses to wear for parties at my relatives' homes. Though I do not recall the precise details of my Career Day outfit, it must have been a composite of these choices. But I remember a comment my friend (an Italian American) made in later years that coalesced my impressions of that day. She said that at the business school she was attending, the Puerto Rican girls always stood out for wearing "everything at once." She meant, of course, too much jewelry, too many accessories. On that day at school we were simply made the negative models by the nuns, who were themselves not credible fashion experts to any of us. But it was painfully obvious to me that to the others, in their tailored skirts and silk blouses, we must have seemed "hopeless" and "vulgar." Though I now know that most adolescents feel out of step much of the time, I also know that for the Puerto Rican girls of my generation that sense was intensified. The way our teachers and classmates looked at us that day in school was just a taste of the cultural clash that awaited us in the real world, where prospective employers and men on the street would often misinterpret our tight skirts and jingling bracelets as a "come-on."

Mixed cultural signals have perpetuated certain stereotypes—for   6
example, that of the Hispanic woman as the "hot tamale" or sexual fire-
brand. It is a one-dimensional view that the media have found easy to
promote. In their special vocabulary, advertisers have designated "sizzling" and "smoldering" as the adjectives of choice for describing not
only the foods but also the women of Latin America. From conversations in my house I recall hearing about the harassment that Puerto
Rican women endured in factories where the "boss-men" talked to
them as if sexual innuendo was all they understood, and worse, often
gave them the choice of submitting to their advances or being fired.

It is custom, however, not chromosomes, that leads us to choose   7
scarlet over pale pink. As young girls, it was our mothers who influenced our decisions about clothes and colors—mothers who had
grown up on a tropical island where the natural environment was a riot
of primary colors, where showing your skin was one way to keep cool
as well as to look sexy. Most important of all, on the island, women perhaps felt freer to dress and move more provocatively since, in most cases, they were protected by the traditions, mores, and laws of a
Spanish/Catholic system of morality and machismo whose main rule
was: *You may look at my sister, but if you touch her I will kill you.* The extended family and church structure could provide a young woman
with a circle of safety in her small pueblo on the island; if a man
"wronged" a girl, everyone would close in to save her family honor.

My mother has told me about dressing in her best party clothes on   8
Saturday nights and going to the town's plaza to promenade with her
girlfriends in front of the boys they liked. The males were thus given
an opportunity to admire the women and to express their admiration in
the form of *piropos:* erotically charged street poems they composed on
the spot. (I have myself been subjected to a few *piropos* while visiting the
island, and they can be outrageous, although custom dictates that they
must never cross into obscenity.) This ritual, as I understand it, also entails a show of studied indifference on the woman's part; if she is "decent," she must not acknowledge the man's impassioned words. So I do
understand how things can be lost in translation. When a Puerto Rican
girl dressed in her idea of what is attractive meets a man from the mainstream culture who has been trained to react to certain types of clothing
as a sexual signal, a clash is likely to take place. I remember the boy who
took me to my first formal dance leaning over to plant a sloppy, over-ea-
ger kiss painfully on my mouth; when I didn't respond with sufficient
passion, he remarked resentfully: "I thought you Latin girls were supposed to mature early," as if I were expected to *ripen* like a fruit or vegetable, not just grow into womanhood like other girls.

It is surprising to my professional friends that even today some peo-   9
ple, including those who should know better, still put others "in their
place." It happened to me most recently during a stay at a classy metro-
politan hotel favored by young professional couples for weddings. Late

one evening after the theater, as I walked toward my room with a colleague (a woman with whom I was coordinating an arts program), a middle-aged man in a tuxedo, with a young girl in satin and lace on his arm, stepped directly into our path. With his champagne glass extended toward me, he exclaimed "Evita!"[1]

10   Our way blocked, my companion and I listened as the man half-recited, half-bellowed "Don't Cry for Me, Argentina." When he finished, the young girl said: "How about a round of applause for my daddy?" We complied, hoping this would bring the silly spectacle to a close. I was becoming aware that our little group was attracting the attention of the other guests. "Daddy" must have perceived this too, and he once more barred the way as we tried to walk past him. He began to shout-sing a ditty to the tune of "La Bamba"—except the lyrics were about a girl named Maria whose exploits rhymed with her name and gonorrhea. The girl kept saying "Oh, Daddy" and looking at me with pleading eyes. She wanted me to laugh along with the others. My companion and I stood silently waiting for the man to end his offensive song. When he finished, I looked not at him but at his daughter. I advised her calmly never to ask her father what he had done in the army. Then I walked between them and to my room. My friend complimented me on my cool handling of the situation, but I confessed that I had really wanted to push the jerk into the swimming pool. This same man—probably a corporate executive, well-educated, even worldly by most standards—would not have been likely to regale an Anglo woman with a dirty song in public. He might have checked his impulse by assuming that she could be somebody's wife or mother, or at least *somebody* who might take offense. But, to him, I was just an Evita or a Maria: merely a character in his cartoon-populated universe.

11   Another facet of the myth of the Latin woman in the United States is the menial, the domestic—Maria the housemaid or countergirl. It's true that work as domestics, as waitresses, and in factories is all that's available to women with little English and few skills. But the myth of the Hispanic menial—the funny maid, mispronouncing words and cooking up a spicy storm in a shiny California kitchen—has been perpetuated by the media in the same way that "Mammy" from *Gone with the Wind* became America's idea of the black woman for generations. Since I do not wear my diplomas around my neck for all to see, I have on occasion been sent to that "kitchen" where some think I obviously belong.

12   One incident has stayed with me, though I recognize it as a minor offense. My first public poetry reading took place in Miami, at a restaurant where a luncheon was being held before the event. I was nervous and excited as I walked in with notebook in hand. An older woman

---

[1]A musical about Eva Duarte de Peron, the former first lady of Argentina.

motioned me to her table, and thinking (foolish me) that she wanted me to autograph a copy of my newly published slender volume of verse, I went over. She ordered a cup of coffee from me, assuming that I was the waitress. (Easy enough to mistake my poems for menus, I suppose.) I know it wasn't an intentional act of cruelty. Yet of all the good things that happened later, I remember that scene most clearly, because it reminded me of what I had to overcome before anyone would take me seriously. In retrospect I understand that my anger gave my reading fire. In fact, I have almost always taken any doubt in my abilities as a challenge, the result most often being the satisfaction of winning a convert, of seeing the cold, appraising eyes warm to my words, the body language change, the smile that indicates I have opened some avenue for communication. So that day as I read, I looked directly at that woman. Her lowered eyes told me she was embarrassed at her faux pas, and when I willed her to look up at me, she graciously allowed me to punish her with my full attention. We shook hands at the end of the reading and I never saw her again. She has probably forgotten the entire incident, but maybe not.

Yet I am one of the lucky ones. There are thousands of Latinas 13 without the privilege of an education or the entrees into society that I have. For them life is a constant struggle against the misconceptions perpetuated by the myth of the Latina. My goal is to try to replace the old stereotypes with a much more interesting set of realities. Every time I give a reading, I hope the stories I tell, the dreams and fears I examine in my work, can achieve some universal truth that will get my audience past the particulars of my skin color, my accent, or my clothes.

I once wrote a poem in which I called all Latinas "God's brown 14 daughters." This poem is really a prayer of sorts, offered upward, but also, through the human-to-human channel of art, outward. It is a prayer for communication and for respect. In it, Latin women pray "in Spanish to an Anglo God/ with a Jewish heritage," and they are "fervently hoping/ that if not omnipotent,/ at least He be bilingual."

✧ Evaluating the Text

1. What characteristics define, from Cofer's perspective, the "Maria" stereotype in terms of style, clothes, and behavior? How has this stereotype been a source of harassment for Cofer?

2. How has the desire to destroy this stereotype and its underlying attitudes motivated Cofer to write the kinds of works she has?

3. How does Cofer use her personal experiences as a springboard to understanding sexual stereotyping of Latinas?

✧ Exploring Different Perspectives

1. How do both Judith Ortiz Cofer and Paul Monette (see "Borrowed Time: An AIDS Memoir") seek to replace sexual stereotypes with realistic portraits?

2. In what way do conflicting societal expectations determine how a woman's appearance signifies how she is perceived, as analyzed by Judith Ortiz Cofer and by Lennard J. Davis (see "Visualizing the Disabled Body")?

✧ Extending Viewpoints through Writing

1. Have you ever been in a situation where someone who is unaware of your ethnic, racial, or religious background disparaged the group to which you belong? What did you do?

2. Create a character sketch of a male chauvinist.

Lennard J. Davis

Visualizing the Disabled Body

◆

Lennard J. Davis is Professor of English and Director of Graduate Studies at Binghamton University in Binghamton, New York. He has written on disability for the Nation. *His previous books include* Factual Fictions: The Origins of the English Novel *(1983),* Resisting Novels: Etiology and Fiction *(1987), and* The Disabilities Study Reader *(1997). Although not hearing impaired himself, Davis was born to deaf parents and uttered his first word in sign language. Upon his father's death, Davis discovered the letters his parents wrote to each other during their courtship. He edited* Shall I Say a Kiss?: The Courtship Letters of a Deaf Couple, 1936–1938 *(1999), a unique window into the lives of a working-class, Jewish, British deaf couple prior to World War II. "Visualizing the Disabled Body" is drawn from* Enforcing Normalcy: Disability, Deafness, and the Body *(1995).*

> *A human being who is first of all an invalid is* all *body, therein lies his inhumanity and his debasement. In most cases he is little better than a carcass—.*
>
> —Thomas Mann, *The Magic Mountain*

> *...the female is as it were a deformed male.*
>
> —Aristotle, *Generation of Animals*

> *When I begin to wish I were crippled—even though I am perfectly healthy—or rather that I would have been better off crippled, that is the first step towards* butoh.
>
> —Tatsumi Hijikata, co-founder of the Japanese performance art/dance form *butoh*

She has no arms or hands, although the stump of her upper right arm extends just to her breast. Her left foot has been severed, and her face is badly scarred, with her nose torn at the tip, and her lower lip gouged out. Fortunately, her facial mutilations have been treated and are barely visible, except for minor scarring visible only up close. The big toe of her right foot has been cut off, and her torso is covered with scars, including a particularly large one between her shoulder blades, one that covers her shoulder, and one covering the tip of her breast where her left nipple was torn out.

165

2   Yet she is considered one of the most beautiful female figures in the world. When the romantic poet Heinrich Heine saw her he called her "Notre-Dame de la Beauté."

3   He was referring to the Venus de Milo.

4   Consider too Pam Herbert, a quadriplegic with muscular dystrophy, writing her memoir by pressing her tongue on a computer keyboard, who describes herself at twenty-eight years old:

> I weigh about 130 pounds; I'm about four feet tall. It's pretty hard to get an accurate measurement on me because both of my knees are permanently bent and my spine is curved, so 4' is an estimate. I wear size two tennis shoes and strong glasses; my hair is dishwater blonde and shoulder length. (S. E. Browne et al., eds, 1985. *With the Power of Each Breath: A Disabled Woman's Anthology.* Pittsburgh: Cleis Press, p. 147.)

5   In this memoir, she describes her wedding night:

> We got to the room and Mark laid me down on the bed because I was so tired from sitting all day. Anyway, I hadn't gone to the bathroom all day so Mark had to catheterize me. I had been having trouble going to the bathroom for many years, so it was nothing new to Mark, he had done it lots of times before.
>
> It was time for the biggest moment of my life, making love. Of course, I was a little nervous and scared. Mark was very gentle with me. He started undressing me and kissing me. We tried making love in the normal fashion with Mark on top and me on the bottom. Well, that position didn't work at all, so then we tried laying on our sides coming in from behind. That was a little better. Anyway, we went to sleep that night a little discouraged because we didn't have a very good lovemaking session. You would have thought that it would be great, but sometimes things don't always go the way we want them to. We didn't get the hang of making love for about two months. It hurt for a long time. (ibid., 155)

6   I take the liberty of bringing these two women's bodies together. Both have disabilities. The statue is considered the ideal of Western beauty and eroticism, although it is armless and disfigured. The living woman might be considered by many "normal" people to be physically repulsive, and certainly without erotic allure. The question I wish to ask is why does the impairment of the Venus de Milo in no way prevent "normal" people from considering her beauty, while Pam Herbert's disability becomes the focal point for horror and pity?

7   In asking this question, I am really raising a complex issue. On a social level, the question has to do with how people with disabilities are seen and why, by and large, they are de-eroticized. If, as I mentioned earlier, disability is a cultural phenomenon rooted in the senses, one needs to inquire how a disability occupies a field of vision, of touch, of

hearing; and how that disruption or distress in the sensory field translates into psycho-dynamic representations. This is more a question about the nature of the subject than about the qualities of the object, more about the observer than the observed. The "problem" of the disabled has been put at the feet of people with disabilities for too long.

Normalcy, rather than being a degree zero of existence, is more accurately a location of bio-power, as Foucault would use the term. The "normal" person (clinging to that title) has a network of traditional ableist assumptions and social supports that empowers the gaze and interaction. The person with disabilities, until fairly recently, had only his or her own individual force or will. Classically, the encounter has been, and remains, an uneven one. Anne Finger describes it in strikingly visual terms by relating an imagined meeting between Rosa Luxemburg and Antonio Gramsci, each of whom was a person with disabilities, although Rosa is given the temporary power of the abled gaze:

> We can measure Rosa's startled reaction as she glimpses him the misshapen dwarf limping towards her in a second-hand black suit so worn that the cuffs are frayed and the fabric is turning green with age, her eye immediately drawn to this disruption in the visual field; the unconscious flinch; the realization that she is staring at him, and the too-rapid turning away of the head. And then, the moment after, the consciousness that the quick aversion of the gaze was as much of an insult as the stare, so she turns her head back but tries to make her focus general, not a sharp gape. Comrade Rosa, would you have felt a slight flicker of embarrassment? shame? revulsion? dread? of a feeling that can have no name?

In this encounter what is suppressed, at least in this moment, is the fact that Rosa Luxemburg herself is physically impaired (she walked with a limp for her whole life). The emphasis then shifts from the cultural norm to the deviation; Luxemburg, now the gazing subject, places herself in the empowered position of the norm, even if that position is not warranted.

Disability, in this and other encounters, is a disruption in the visual, auditory, or perceptual field as it relates to the power of the gaze. As such, the disruption, the rebellion of the visual, must be regulated, rationalized, contained. Why the modern binary—normal/abnormal— must be maintained is a complex question. But we can begin by accounting for the desire to split bodies into two immutable categories: whole and incomplete, abled and disabled, normal and abnormal, functional and dysfunctional.

In the most general sense, cultures perform an act of splitting (*Spaltung*, to use Freud's term). These violent cleavages of consciousness are as primitive as our thought processes can be. The young infant splits the good parent from the bad parent—although the parent is the same entity. When the child is satisfied by the parent, the parent is the good parent; when the child is not satisfied, the parent is bad. As a child grows out of the earliest phases of infancy, she learns to combine those split images into a single parent who is sometimes good and sometimes not. The residue of *Spaltung* remains in our inner life, personal and collective, to produce monsters and evil stepmothers as well as noble princes and fairy godmothers.

11   In this same primitive vein, culture tends to split bodies into good and bad parts. Some cultural norms are considered good and others bad. Everyone is familiar with the "bad body": too short or tall, too fat or thin, not masculine or feminine enough, not enough or too much hair on the head or other parts of the body, penis or breasts too small or (excepting the penis) too big. Furthermore, each individual assigns good and bad labels to body parts—good: hair, face, lips, eyes, hands; bad: sexual organs, excretory organs, underarms.

12   The psychological explanation may provide a reason why it is imperative for society at large to engage in *Spaltung*. The divisions whole/incomplete, able/disabled neatly cover up the frightening writing on the wall that reminds the hallucinated whole being that its wholeness is in fact a hallucination, a developmental fiction. *Spaltung* creates the absolute categories of abled and disabled, with concomitant defenses against the repressed fragmented body.

13   But a psychological explanation alone is finally insufficient. Historical specificity makes us understand that disability is a social process with an origin. So, why certain disabilities are labeled negatively while others have a less negative connotation is a question tied to complex social forces. It is fair to say, in general, that disabilities would be most dysfunctional in postindustrial countries, where the ability to perambulate or manipulate is so concretely tied to productivity, which in itself is tied to production. The body of the average worker, as we have seen, becomes the new measure of man and woman. Michael Oliver, citing Ryan and Thomas (1980), notes:

> With the rise of the factory…[during industrialization] many more disabled people were excluded from the production process for "The speed of factory work, the enforced discipline, the time-keeping and production norms—all these were a highly unfavourable change from the slower, more self-determined and flexible methods of work into which many handicapped people had been integrated." (1990, 27)

Both industrial production and the concomitant standardization of the human body have had a profound impact on how we split up bodies.

14   We tend to group impairments into the categories either of "disabling" (bad) or just "limiting" (good). For example, wearing a hearing aid is seen as much more disabling than wearing glasses, although both

serve to amplify a deficient sense. But loss of hearing is associated with aging in a way that nearsightedness is not. Breast removal is seen as an impairment of femininity and sexuality, whereas the removal of a fore-skin is not seen as a diminution of masculinity. The coding of body parts and the importance attached to their selective function or dys-function is part of a much larger system of signs and meanings in soci-ety, and is constructed as such.

"Splitting" may help us to understand one way in which disability   15
is seen as part of a system in which value is attributed to body parts. The disabling of the body part or function is then part of a removal of value. The gradations of value are socially determined, but what is striking is the way that rather than being incremental or graduated, the assign-ment of the term "disabled," and the consequent devaluation are total. That is, the concept of disabled seems to be an absolute rather than a gradient one. One is either disabled or not. Value is tied to the ability to earn money. If one's body is productive, it is not disabled. People with disabilities continue to earn less than "normal" people and, even after the passage of the Americans with Disabilities Act, 69 percent of Amer-icans with disabilities were unemployed (*New York Times,* 27 October 1994, A:22). Women and men with disabilites are seen as less attractive, less able to marry and be involved in domestic production.

The ideology of the assigning of value to the body goes back to   16
preindustrial times. Myths of beauty and ugliness have laid the foun-dations for normalcy. In particular, the Venus myth is one that is dialec-tically linked to another. This embodiment of beauty and desire is tied to the story of the embodiment of ugliness and repulsion. So the appro-priate mythological character to compare the armless Venus with is Medusa. Medusa was once a beautiful sea goddess who, because she had sexual intercourse with Poseidon at one of Athene's temples, was turned by Athene into a winged monster with glaring eyes, huge teeth, protruding tongue, brazen claws, and writhing snakes for hair. Her hideous appearance has the power to turn people into stone, and Athene eventually completes her revenge by having Perseus kill Me-dusa. He finds Medusa by stealing the one eye and one tooth shared by the Graiae until they agree to help him. Perseus then kills Medusa by decapitating her while looking into his brightly polished shield, which neutralizes the power of her appearance; he then puts her head into a magic wallet that shields onlookers from its effects. When Athene re-ceives the booty, she uses Medusa's head and skin to fashion her own shield.

In the Venus tradition, Medusa is a poignant double. She is the nec-   17
essary counter in the dialectic of beauty and ugliness, desire and repul-sion, wholeness and fragmentation. Medusa is the disabled woman to Venus's perfect body. The story is a kind of allegory of a "normal" per-son's intersection with the disabled body. This intersection is marked by

the power of the visual. The "normal" person sees the disabled person and is turned to stone, in some sense, by the visual interaction. In this moment, the normal person suddenly feels self-conscious, rigid, unable to look but equally drawn to look. The visual field becomes problematic, dangerous, treacherous. The disability becomes a power derived from its otherness, its monstrosity, in the eyes of the "normal" person. The disability must be decapitated and then contained in a variety of magic wallets. Rationality, for which Athene stands, is one of the devices for containing, controlling, and reforming the disabled body so that it no longer has the power to terrorize. And the issue of mutilation comes up as well because the disabled body is always the reminder of the whole body about to come apart at the seams. It provides a vision of, a caution about, the body as a construct held together willfully, always threatening to become its individual parts—cells, organs, limbs, perceptions—like the fragmented, shared eye and tooth that Perseus ransoms back to the Graiae.

18   I have been concentrating on the physical body, but it is worth considering for a moment the issue of madness. While mental illness is by definition not related to the intactness of the body, nevertheless, it shows up as a disruption in the visual field. We "see" that someone is insane by her physical behavior, communication, and so on. Yet the fear is that the mind is fragmenting, breaking up, falling apart, losing itself—all terms we associate with becoming mad. With the considerable information we have about the biological roots of mental illness, we begin to see the disease again as a breaking up of "normal" body chemistry: amino acid production gone awry, depleted levels of certain polypeptide chains or hormones. Language production can become fragmentary, broken, in schizophrenic speech production. David Rothman points out that in eighteenth- and nineteenth-century America, insanity was seen as being caused by the fragmented nature of "modern" life—particularly the pressures brought to bear on people by a society in which economic boundaries were disappearing. This fragmenting of society produced a fragmentation of the individual person. So the asylums that sprung up during this period recommended a cure that involved a removal from the urban, alienated, fragmented environment to rural hospitals in which order and precision could be restored. "A precise schedule and regular work became the two characteristics of the best private and public institutions.... The structure of the mental hospital would counteract the debilitating influences of the community" (Rothman 1971, 144). As Rothman notes, "Precision, certainty, regularity, order" were the words that were seen as embodying the essence of cure (ibid., 145). The mind would be restored to "wholeness" by restoring the body through manual labor. However, needless to add, one had to have a whole body to have a whole mind. The general metaphor

here continues to be a notion of wholeness, order, clean boundaries, as opposed to fragmentations, disordered bodies, messy boundaries.

If people with disabilities are considered anything, they are or have been considered creatures of disorder—monsters, monstrous. Leslie Fieldler has taken some pains to show this in his book *Freaks*. If we look at Mary Shelley's *Frankenstein,* we find some of the themes we have been discussing emerge in novelistic form. First, we might want to note that we have no name for the creation of Dr Frankenstein other than "monster." (This linguistic lapsus is usually made up for in popular culture by referring to the creature itself as "Frankenstein," a terminology that confuses the creator with the created.) In reading the novel, or speaking about it, we can only call the creature "the monster." This linguistic limitation is worth noting because it encourages the reader to consider the creature a monster rather than a person with disabilities. [19]

We do not often think of the monster in Mary Shelley's work as disabled, but what else is he? The characteristic of his disability is a difference in appearance. He is more than anything a disruption in the visual field. There is nothing else different about him—he can see, hear, talk, think, ambulate, and so on. It is worth noting that in popular culture, largely through the early film versions of the novel, the monster is inarticulate, somewhat mentally slow, and walks with a kind of physical impairment. In addition, the film versions add Ygor, the hunchbacked criminal who echoes the monster's disability in his own. Even in the recent film version by Kenneth Branagh, the creature walks with a limp and speaks with an impediment. One cannot dismiss this filtering of the creature through the lens of multiple disability. In order for the audience to fear and loathe the creature, he must be made to transcend the pathos of a single disability. Of course, it would be unseemly for a village to chase and torment a paraplegic or a person with acromegaly. Disabled people are to be pitied and ostracized; monsters are to be destroyed; audiences must not confuse the two. [20]

In the novel, it is clear that Dr Frankenstein cannot abide his creation for only one reason—its hideous appearance. Indeed, the creature's only positive human contact is with the blind old man De Lacey, who cannot see the unsightly features. When De Lacey's family catches a glimpse of the creature, the women faint or run, and the men beat and pursue him. His body is a zone of repulsion; the reaction he evokes is fear and loathing. The question one wants to ask is why does a physical difference produce such a profound response? [21]

The answer, I believe, is twofold. First, what is really hideous about the creature is not so much his physiognomy as what that appearance suggests. The *corps morcelé* makes its appearance immediately in the construction of the monster. Ironically, Dr Frankenstein adapts Zeuxis's notion of taking ideal parts from individuals to create the ideal whole body. [22]

As he says, "I collected bones from charnel houses.... The dissecting room and the slaughter-house furnished many of my materials" (Shelley 1990, 54–5). From these fragments, seen as loathsome and disgusting, Frankenstein assembles what he wishes to create—a perfect human. It is instructive in this regard to distinguish the Boris Karloff incarnation of the creature—with the bolt through his neck—or Branagh's grotesquely sewn creature, from the image that Mary Shelley would have us imagine. Dr Frankenstein tells us:

> His limbs were in proportion, and I had selected his features as beautiful. Beautiful!—Great God! His yellow skin scarcely covered the work of muscles and arteries beneath; his hair was of a lustrous black and flowing; his teeth of a pearly whiteness; but these luxuriances only formed a more horrid contrast with his watery eyes, that seemed almost of the same colour as the dun white sockets in which they were set, his shrivelled complexion and straight black lips. (ibid., 57)

23   What then constitutes the horror? If we add up the details, what we see is a well-proportioned man with long black hair, pearly white teeth, whose skin is somewhat deformed—resulting in jaundice and perhaps a tightness or thinness of the skin, a lack of circulation perhaps causing shriveling, watery eyes and darkened lips. This hardly seems to constitute horror rather than, say, pathos.

24   What is found to be truly horrifying about Frankenstein's creature is its composite quality, which is too evocative of the fragmented body. Frankenstein's reaction to this living *corps morcelé* is repulsion: "the beauty of the dream vanished, and breathless horror and disgust filled my heart" (ibid., 57). Frankenstein attempted to create a unified nude, an object of beauty and harmony—a Venus, in effect. He ended up with a Medusa whose existence reveals the inhering and enduring nature of the archaic endlessly fragmented body, endlessly repressed but endlessly reappearing.

✧ Evaluating the Text

1. How does the contrast between the Venus de Milo and Pam Herbert draw attention to the paradox governing cultural perceptions of people with disabilities?

2. How does the phenomenon known as "splitting" help explain the stereotyped perception of people with disabilities?

3. What broadening effect does Davis's discussion have by including Mary Shelley's *Frankenstein* and issues of mythology and madness?

4. How does each of the examples tie in with Davis's theory that "disability is a cultural phenomenon rooted in the senses"?

✧ *Exploring Different Perspectives*

1. How are Lennard J. Davis's and Judith Ortiz Cofer's analyses based on messages communicated through the perception of physical appearance?

2. Compare the effects of the tyranny of absolute categories of what is normal and abnormal in the analyses by Davis and Kim Chernin (see "The Flesh and the Devil").

✧ *Extending Viewpoints through Writing*

1. Recently, the terms "differently abled" or "person with disabilities" have been preferred to the term "disabled person." Earlier, the term "disabled" was used to replace "handicapped." To what extent did Davis's analysis make you realize how the category of disability is a relative rather than an absolute term? For example, what if one were to include dyslexia, myopia, learning impairments, arthritis, or obesity? Discuss how attempts to control these terms reflect a desire to control public perceptions of these states.

2. Select a film you have seen in recent years and discuss the treatment of the central character in terms of the filmmaker's depiction of the "disabled." For example, Disney's 1996 release of *The Hunchback of Notre Dame, Forrest Gump, Rain Man, Mask, Nell, Immortal Beloved,* or *Lorenzo's Oil.* In your opinion, why are films depicting the disabled so popular?

Paul Monette

Borrowed Time: An AIDS Memoir

◆

Paul Monette was a distinguished writer of poetry, novels, and autobiographical volumes. He was born in 1945, attended Yale University, and first received critical attention in 1975 with the publication of his poetry collection, The Carpenter at the Asylum. *His novels include* Taking Care of Mrs. Carroll *(1978),* The Gold Diggers *(1979),* The Long Shot *(1981),* Lightfall *(1982),* Afterlife *(1990), and* Halfway Home *(1991). Following the death from AIDS of his longtime lover, Roger Horwitz, Monette addressed the tragedy in a collection of poems,* Love Alone: Eighteen Elegies for Rog *(1988), and wrote an acclaimed prose account,* Borrowed Time: An AIDS Memoir *(from which the following selection is taken) that received a National Book Critics Circle Award nomination for the best autobiography in 1988. Monette also wrote* Becoming a Man: Half a Life Story *(1992), in which he recounts the difficulties he had experienced in coming to term with his homosexuality.*

Monette was diagnosed as being HIV-positive in 1988 and died in 1995.

1   I don't know if I will live to finish this. Doubtless there's a streak of self-importance in such an assertion, but who's counting? Maybe it's just that I've watched too many sicken in a month and die by Christmas, so that a fatal sort of realism comforts me more than magic. All I know is this: The virus ticks in me. And it doesn't care a whit about our categories—when is full-blown, what's AIDS-related, what is just sick and tired? No one has solved the puzzle of its timing. I take my drug from Tijuana twice a day. The very friends who tell me how vigorous I look, how well I seem, are the first to assure me of the imminent medical breakthrough. What they don't seem to understand is, I used up all my optimism keeping my friend alive. Now that he's gone, the cup of my own health is neither half full nor half empty. Just half.

2   Equally difficult, of course, is knowing where to start. The world around me is defined now by its endings and its closures—the date on the grave that follows the hyphen. Roger Horwitz, my beloved friend, died of complications of AIDS on October 22, 1986, nineteen months and ten days after his diagnosis. That is the only real date anymore, casting its ice shadow over all the secular holidays lovers mark their

calendars by. Until that long night in October, it didn't seem possible that any day could supplant the brute equinox of March 12—the day of Roger's diagnosis in 1985, the day we began to live on the moon.

The fact is, no one knows where to start with AIDS. Now, in the sev-   3
enth year of the calamity, my friends in L.A. can hardly recall what it felt like any longer, the time before the sickness. Yet we all watched the toll mount in New York, then in San Francisco, for years before it ever touched us here. It comes like a slowly dawning horror. At first you are equipped with a hundred different amulets to keep it far away. Then someone you know goes into the hospital, and suddenly you are at high noon in full battle gear. They have neglected to tell you that you will be issued no weapons of any sort. So you cobble together a weapon out of anything that lies at hand, like a prisoner honing a spoon handle into a stiletto. You fight tough, you fight dirty, but you cannot fight dirtier than it.

I remember a Saturday in February 1982, driving Route 10 to Palm   4
Springs with Roger to visit his parents for the weekend. While Roger drove, I read aloud an article from *The Advocate:* "Is Sex Making Us Sick?" There was the slightest edge of irony in the query, an urban cool that seems almost bucolic now in its innocence. But the article didn't mince words. It was the first in-depth reporting I'd read that laid out the shadowy nonfacts of what till then had been the most fragmented of rumors. The first cases were reported to the Centers for Disease Control (CDC) only six months before, but they weren't in the newspapers, not in L.A. I note in my diary in December '81 ambiguous reports of a "gay cancer," but I know I didn't have the slightest picture of the thing. Cancer of the *what?* I would have asked, if anyone had known anything.

I remember exactly what was going through my mind while I was   5
reading, though I can't now recall the details of the piece. I was thinking: How is this not me? Trying to find a pattern I was exempt from. It was a brand of denial I would watch grow exponentially during the next few years, but at the time I was simply relieved. Because the article appeared to be saying that there was a grim progression toward this undefined catastrophe, a set of preconditions—chronic hepatitis, repeated bouts of syphilis, exotic parasites. No wonder my first baseline response was to feel safe. It was *them*—by which I meant the fast-lane Fire Island crowd, the Sutro Baths, the world of High Eros.

Not us.   6

I grabbed for that relief because we'd been through a rough patch   7
the previous autumn. Till then Roger had always enjoyed a sort of no-nonsense good health: not an abuser of anything, with a constitutional aversion to hypochondria, and not wed to his mirror save for a minor alarm as to the growing dimensions of his bald spot. In the seven years we'd been together I scarcely remember him having a cold or taking an aspirin. Yet in October '81 he had struggled with a peculiar bout of intestinal flu. Nothing special showed up in any of the blood tests, but over a

period of weeks he experienced persistent symptoms that didn't neatly connect: pains in his legs, diarrhea, general malaise. I hadn't been feeling notably bad myself, but on the other hand I was a textbook hypochondriac, and I figured if Rog was harboring some kind of bug, so was I.

8   The two of us finally went to a gay doctor in the Valley for a further set of blood tests. It's a curious phenomenon among gay middle-class men that anything faintly venereal had better be taken to a doctor who's "on the bus." Is it a sense of fellow feeling perhaps, or a way of avoiding embarrassment? Do we really believe that only a doctor who's *our* kind can heal us of the afflictions that attach somehow to our secret hearts? There is so much magic to medicine. Of course we didn't know then that those few physicians with a large gay clientele were about to be swamped beyond all capacity to cope.

9   The tests came back positive for amoebiasis. Roger and I began the highly toxic treatment to kill the amoeba, involving two separate drugs and what seems in memory thirty pills a day for six weeks, till the middle of January. It was the first time I'd ever experienced the phenomenon of the cure making you sicker. By the end of treatment we were both weak and had lost weight, and for a couple of months afterward were susceptible to colds and minor infections.

10   It was only after the treatment was over that a friend of ours, diagnosed with amoebas by the same doctor, took his slide to the lab at UCLA for a second opinion. And that was my first encounter with lab error. The doctor at UCLA explained that the slide had been misread; the squiggles that looked like amoebas were in fact benign. The doctor shook his head and grumbled about "these guys who do their own lab work." Roger then retrieved his slide, took it over to UCLA and was told the same: no amoebas. We had just spent six weeks methodically ingesting poison for no reason at all.

11   So it wasn't the *Advocate* story that sent up the red flag for us. We'd been shaken by the amoeba business, and from that point on we operated at a new level of sexual caution. What is now called safe sex did not use to be so clearly defined. The concept didn't exist. But it was quickly becoming apparent, even then, that we couldn't wait for somebody else to define the parameters. Thus every gay man I know has had to come to a point of personal definition by way of avoiding the chaos of sexually transmitted diseases, or STD as we call them in the trade. There was obviously no one moment of conscious decision, a bolt of clarity on the shimmering freeway west of San Bernardino, but I think of that day when I think of the sea change. The party was going to have to stop. The evidence was too ominous: *We were making ourselves sick.*

12   Not that Roger and I were the life of the party. Roger especially didn't march to the different drum of *so many men, so little time,* the motto and anthem of the sunstruck summers of the mid-to-late seventies. He'd managed not to carry away from his adolescence the mark of too much repression, or indeed the yearning to make up for lost time. In

ten years he had perhaps half a dozen contacts outside the main frame of our relationship, mostly when he was out of town on business. He was comfortable with relative monogamy, even at a time when certain quarters of the gay world found the whole idea trivial and bourgeois. I realize that in the world of the heterosexual there is a generalized lip service paid to exclusive monogamy, a notion most vividly honored in the breach. I leave the matter of morality to those with the gift of tongues; it was difficult enough for us to fashion a sexual ethics just for us. In any case, I was the one in the relationship who suffered from lost time. I was the one who would go after a sexual encounter as if it were an ice cream cone—casual, quick, good-bye.

But as I say, who's counting? I only want to make it plain to start   13
with that we got very alert and very careful as far back as the winter of '82. That gut need for safety took hold and lingered, even as we got better again and strong. Thus I'm not entirely sure what I thought on another afternoon a year and a half later, when a friend of ours back from New York reported a conversation he'd had with a research man from Sloan–Kettering.

"He thinks all it takes is one exposure," Charlie said, this after   14
months of articles about the significance of repeated exposure. More tenaciously than ever, we all wanted to believe the whole deepening tragedy was centered on those at the sexual frontiers who were fucking their brains out. The rest of us were fashioning our own little Puritan forts, as we struggled to convince ourselves that a clean slate would hold the nightmare at bay.

Yet with caution as our watchword starting in February of '82,   15
Roger was diagnosed with AIDS three years later. So the turning over of new leaves was not to be on everybody's side. A lot of us were already ticking and didn't even know. The magic circle my generation is trying to stay within the borders of is only as real as the random past. Perhaps the young can live in the magic circle, but only if those of us who are ticking will tell our story. Otherwise it goes on being *us* and *them* forever, built like a wall higher and higher, till you no longer think to wonder if you are walling it out or in.

✧ *Evaluating the Text*

1. How did coming to terms with the reality of AIDS compel Monette to reassess many of the assumptions taken for granted about the homosexual life-style?

2. To what extent does Monette's personal chronicle reflect the kind of changes that were simultaneously taking place in the nation?

3. In your opinion, why has Monette chosen to share the story of his life with Roger? How would you characterize the tone he projects?

❖ Exploring Different Perspectives

1. In what sense do both Monette and Lennard J. Davis (see "Visualizing the Disabled Body") offer constructive insights into the psychology of stereotyping?

2. The ways in which sexual mythologies are constructed about different groups are illustrated in both Monette's and Judith Ortiz Cofer's accounts (see "The Myth of the Latin Woman"). What function do these mythologies serve and how does each author attempt to deconstruct them?

❖ Extending Viewpoints through Writing

1. Rent either or both *And The Band Played On* (1993) and *Philadelphia* (1994), and write a short essay on how films such as these shape public perceptions toward those with AIDS.

2. Do some research on the Internet on the AIDS Quilt Project and write an analysis of the impact of this project both here and abroad.

Marjorie Shostak

Memories of a !Kung Girlhood

◆

Marjorie Shostak initially spent two years, from 1969 to 1971, living and working among the !Kung San of Botswana, as a research assistant on the Harvard Kalahari Desert Project. The !Kung or !Kung bushman live in southwestern Africa in isolated areas of Botswana (where they make up only 3 percent of the population), Angola, and Namibia. The ! is meant to represent a clicking sound in their language made by the tongue breaking air pockets in different parts of the mouth. Anthropologists have studied this nomadic community with great interest because they are one of the few peoples who live by hunting and gathering rather than by some form of agriculture. After gaining fluency in the language of the !Kung, Shostak returned to Botswana in 1975 for six months to complete the life histories of several women in the tribe. The results of her fieldwork first appeared in Kalahari Hunter–Gatherers: Studies of the !Kung San and Their Neighbors, *edited by Richard B. Lee and Irven De Vore (1976), and later in* Human Nature, *as "Memories of a !Kung Girlhood" (1978). Shostak's research also served as the basis for the 1983 book* Nisa: The Life and Words of a !Kung Woman. *In "Memories of a !Kung Girlhood," we hear the remembrances of Nisa, recalling her childhood and marriage. This book became a surprise best seller.*

After her death in 1996, the Marjorie Shostak Scholarship Fund was established at the University of Texas at Austin to aid students in Namibia and Botswana.

Located in South-Central Africa, Botswana became independent from British rule in 1966. Because of its landlocked location, Botswana continues to be economically dependent on South Africa and Zimbabwe, which controls railroad routes through Botswana. Religious practices are equally divided between Christianity and traditional tribal beliefs.

I remember when my mother was pregnant with Kumsa. I was still 1
small (about four years old) and I asked, "Mommy, that baby inside you...when that baby is born, will it come out from your bellybutton?" She said, "No, it won't come out from there. When you give birth, a baby comes from here." And she pointed to her genitals.

When she gave birth to Kumsa, I wanted the milk she had in her 2
breasts, and when she nursed him, my eyes watched as the milk spilled out. I cried all night...cried and cried.

3   Once when my mother was with him and they were lying down asleep, I took him away from her and put him down on the other side of the hut. Then I lay down beside her. While she slept I squeezed some milk and started to nurse, and nursed and nursed and nursed. Maybe she thought it was him. When she woke and saw me she cried, "Where …tell me…what did you do with Kumsa? Where is he?"

4   I told her he was lying down inside the hut. She grabbed me and pushed me hard away from her. I lay there and cried. She took Kumsa, put him down beside her, and insulted me by cursing my genitals.

5   "Are you crazy? Nisa-Big Genitals, what's the matter with you? What craziness grabbed you that you took a baby, dropped him somewhere else, and then lay down beside me and nursed? I thought it was Kumsa."

6   When my father came home, she told him, "Do you see what kind of mind your daughter has? Hit her! She almost killed Kumsa. This little baby, this little thing here, she took from my side and dropped him somewhere else. I was lying here holding him and fell asleep. She came and took him away, left him by himself, then lay down where he had been and nursed. Now, hit her!"

7   I said, "You're lying! Me…Daddy, I didn't nurse. Really I didn't. I don't even want her milk anymore."

8   He said, "If I ever hear of this again, I'll hit you. Now, don't ever do that again!"

9   I said, "Yes, he's my little brother, isn't he? My little baby brother and I *love* him. I won't do that again. He can nurse all by himself. Daddy, even if you're not here, I won't try to steal Mommy's breasts. They belong to my brother."

10   We lived and lived, and as I kept growing, I started to carry Kumsa around on my shoulders. My heart was happy and I started to love him. I carried him everywhere. I would play with him for a while, and whenever he started to cry, I'd take him over to mother to nurse. Then I'd take him back with me and we'd play together again.

11   That was when Kumsa was still little. But once he was older and started to talk and then to run around, that's when we were mean to each other all the time. Sometimes we hit each other. Other times I grabbed him and bit him and said, "Ooooh…what is this thing that has such a horrible face and no brains and is so mean? Why is it so mean to me when I'm not doing anything to it?" Then he said, "I'm going to *hit* you!" And I said, "You're just a *baby!* I, *I* am the one who's going to hit *you*. Why are you so miserable to me?" I insulted him and he insulted me and then I insulted him back. We just stayed together and played like that.

12   Once, when our father came back carrying meat, we both called out, "Ho, ho. Daddy! Ho, ho, Daddy!" But when I heard him say, "Daddy, Daddy," I yelled, "Why are you greeting my father? He's *my* father, isn't he? You can only say, 'Oh, hello Father.'" But he called out,

ABOUT THE !KUNG

Nisa is a 50-year-old !Kung woman, one of an estimated 13,000 !Kung San living on the northern fringe of the Kalahari Desert in southern Africa. Much of her life—as daughter, sister, wife, mother, and lover—has been spent in the semi-nomadic pursuit of food and water in the arid savanna.

Like many !Kung, Nisa is a practiced storyteller. The !Kung have no written language with which to record their experiences, and people sit around their fires for hours recounting recent events and those long past. Voices rise and fall, hands move in dramatic gestures, and bird and animal sounds are imitated as stories are told and retold, usually with much exaggeration.

I collected stories of Nisa's life as part of my anthropological effort to record the lives of !Kung women in their own words. Nisa enjoyed working with the machine that "grabs your voice" and the interviews with her produced 25 hours of tape and 425 pages of transcription. The excerpts included here are faithful to her narrative except where awkward or discontinuous passages have been modified or deleted, and where long passages have been shortened.

Although most of Nisa's memories are typical of !Kung life, her early memories, like those of most people, are probably idiosyncratic mixtures of fact and fantasy. Her memories of being hit for taking food are probably not accurate. The !Kung tend to be lenient and indulgent with their children, and researchers have rarely observed any physical punishment or the withholding of food.

Strong feelings of sibling rivalry, like those that Nisa describes, are common. !Kung women wean their children as soon as they find they are pregnant again because they believe the milk belongs to the fetus. Children are not usually weaned until they are three or four years old, which tends to make them resent their younger siblings. Nisa's complaints about being given too little food probably stem from her jealousy of her little brother.

Despite the lack of privacy, !Kung parents are generally discreet in their sexual activity. As children become aware of it, they engage each other in sexual play. Parents say they do not approve of this play but do little to stop it.

Many !Kung girls first marry in their early teens, but these relationships are not consummated until the girls begin menstruating around the age of 16. Early marriages are relatively unstable. Nisa was betrothed twice before marrying Tashay.

The exclamation point at the beginning of !Kung represents one of the many click sounds in the !Kung language. Clicks are made by the tongue breaking air pockets in different parts of the mouth; but the notation for clicks has been eliminated from the translation in all cases except for the name of the !Kung people. Nisa, for instance, should be written as N≠isa.

Marjorie Shostak

"Ho, ho…Daddy!" I said, "Be quiet! Only *I* will greet him. Is he your father? I'm going to hit you!"

13   We fought and argued until Mother finally stopped us. Then we just sat around while she cooked the meat.

14   This was also when I used to take food. It happened over all kinds of food—sweet *nin* berries or *klaru* bulbs…other times it was mongongo nuts. Sometimes before my mother left to go gathering, she'd leave food inside a leather pouch and hang it high on one of the branches inside the hut.

15   But as soon as she was gone, I'd take some of whatever food was left in the bag. If it was *klaru*, I'd find the biggest bulbs and take them. I'd hang the bag back on the branch and go sit somewhere to eat them.

16   One time I sat down in the shade of a tree while my parents gathered food nearby. As soon as they had moved away from me, I climbed the tree where they had left a pouch hanging, full of *klaru*, and took the bulbs.

17   I had my own little pouch, the one my father had made me, and I took the bulbs and put them in the pouch. Then I climbed down and sat waiting for my parents to return.

18   They came back. "Nisa, you ate the *klaru!*" What do you have to say for yourself?" I said, "Uhn uh, I didn't eat them."

19   I started to cry. Mother hit me and yelled, "Don't take things. You can't seem to understand! I tell you but you don't listen. Don't your ears hear when I talk to you?"

20   I said, "Uhn uh. Mommy's been making me feel bad for too long now. She keeps saying I steal things and hits me so that my skin hurts. I'm going to stay with Grandma!"

21   But when I went to my grandmother, she said, "No, I can't take care of you now. If I try you will be hungry. I am old and just go gathering one day at a time. In the morning I just rest. We would sit together and hunger would kill you. Now go back and sit beside your mother and father."

22   I said, "No, Daddy will hit me. Mommy will hit me. I want to stay with you."

23   So I stayed with her. Then one day she said, "I'm going to bring you back to your mother and father." She took me to them, saying, "Today I'm giving Nisa back to you. But isn't there someone here who will take good care of her? You don't just hit a child like this one. She likes food and likes to eat. All of you are lazy and you've just left her so she hasn't grown well. You've killed this child with hunger. Look at her now, how small she still is."

24   Oh, but my heart was happy! Grandmother was scolding Mother! I had so much happiness in my heart that I laughed and laughed. But then, when Grandmother went home and left me there, I cried and cried.

My father started to yell at me. He didn't hit me. His anger usually   25
came out only from his mouth. "You're so senseless! Don't you realize
that after you left, everything felt less important? We wanted you to be
with us. Yes, even your mother wanted you and missed you. Today, everything will be all right when you stay with us. Your mother will take
you where she goes; the two of you will do things together and go
gathering together."

Then when my father dug *klaru* bulbs, I ate them, and when he dug   26
chon bulbs, I ate them. I ate everything they gave me, and I wasn't
yelled at any more.

Mother and I often went to the bush together. The two of us would   27
walk until we arrived at a place where she collected food. She'd set me
down in the shade of a tree and dig roots or gather nuts nearby.

Once I left the tree and went to play in the shade of another tree. I   28
saw a tiny steenbok, one that had just been born, hidden in the grass and
among the leaves. It was lying there, its little eyes just looking out at me.

I thought, "What should I do?" I shouted, *"Mommy!"* I just stood   29
there and it just lay there looking at me.

Suddenly I knew what to do—I ran at it, trying to grab it. But it   30
jumped up and ran away and I started to chase it. It was running and I
was running and it was crying as it ran. Finally, I got very close and put
my foot in its way, and it fell down. I grabbed its legs and started to
carry it back. It was crying, "Ehn…ehn…ehn…."

Its mother had been close by and when she heard it call, she came   31
running. As soon as I saw her, I started to run again. I wouldn't give it
back to its mother!

I called out, "Mommy! Come! Help me with this steenbok! Mom-   32
my! The steenbok's mother is coming for me! Run! Come! Take this
steenbok from me."

But soon the mother steenbok was no longer following, so I took   33
the baby, held its feet together, and banged it hard against the sand until I killed it. It was no longer crying; it was dead. I felt wonderfully
happy. My mother came running and I gave it to her to carry.

The two of us spent the rest of the day walking in the bush. While   34
my mother was gathering, I sat in the shade of a tree, waiting and playing with the dead steenbok. I picked it up. I tried to make it sit up, to
open its eyes. I looked at them. After mother had dug enough *sha* roots,
we left and returned home.

My father had been out hunting that day and had shot a large   35
steenbok with his arrows. He had skinned it and brought it back hanging on a branch.

"Ho, ho. Daddy killed a steenbok!" I said, "Mommy! Daddy! I'm   36
not going to let anyone have any of *my* steenbok. Now *don't* give it to
anyone else. After you cook it, just my little brother and I will eat it, just
the two of us."

37   I remember another time when we were traveling from one place to another and the sun was burning. It was the hot, dry season and there was no water anywhere. The sun was burning! Kumsa had already been born and I was still small.

38   After we had been walking a long time, my older brother Dau spotted a beehive. We stopped while he and my father chopped open the tree. All of us helped take out the honey. I filled my own little container until it was completely full.

39   We stayed there, eating the honey, and I found myself getting very thirsty. Then we left and continued to walk, I carrying my honey and my digging stick. Soon the heat began killing us and we were all dying of thirst. I started to cry because I wanted water so badly.

40   After a while, we stopped and sat down in the shade of a baobab tree. There was still no water anywhere. We just sat in the shade like that.

41   Finally my father said, "Dau, the rest of the family will stay here under this baobab. But you, take the water containers and get us some water. There's a well not too far away."

42   Dau collected the empty ostrich eggshell containers and the large clay pot and left. I lay there, already dead from thirst and thought, "If I stay with Mommy and Daddy, I'll surely die of thirst. Why don't I follow my big brother and go drink water with him?"

43   With that I jumped up and ran after him, crying out, calling to him, following his tracks. But he didn't hear me. I kept running…crying and calling out.

44   Finally, he heard something and turned to see. There I was, "Oh, no!" he said. "Nisa's followed me. What can I do with her now that she's here?" He just stood there and waited for me to catch up. He picked me up and carried me high up on his shoulder, and along we went. He really liked me!

45   The two of us went on together. We walked and walked and walked and walked. Finally, we reached the well. I ran to the water and drank, and soon my heart was happy again. We filled the water containers, put them in a twine mesh sack, and my brother carried it on his back. Then he took me and put me on his shoulder again.

46   We walked the long way back until we arrived at the baobab where our parents were sitting. They drank the water. Then they said, "How well our children have done, bringing us this water! We are alive once again!"

47   We just stayed in the shade of the baobab. Later we left and traveled to another water hole where we settled for a while. My heart was happy…eating honey and just living.

48   We lived there, and after some time passed, we saw the first rain clouds. One came near but just hung in the sky. More rain clouds came over and they too just stood there. Then the rain started to spill itself and it came pouring down.

The rainy season had finally come. The sun rose and set, and the rain spilled itself and fell and kept falling. It fell without ceasing. Soon the water pans were full. And my heart! My heart within me was happy and we lived and ate meat and mongongo nuts. There was more meat and it was all delicious.   49

And there were caterpillars to eat, those little things that crawl along going "mmm…mmmmm…mmmmm…." People dug roots and collected nuts and berries and brought home more and more food. There was plenty to eat, and people kept bringing meat back on sticks and hanging it in the trees.   50

My heart was bursting. I ate lots of food and my tail was wagging, always wagging about like a little dog. I'd laugh with my little tail, laugh with a little donkey's laugh, a tiny thing that is. I'd throw my tail one way and the other, shouting, "Today I'm going to eat caterpillars …*cat-er-pillars!*" Some people gave me meat broth to drink, and others prepared the skins of caterpillars and roasted them for me to eat, and I ate and ate and ate. Then I went to sleep.   51

But that night, after everyone was dead asleep, I peed right in my sleeping place. In the morning, when everyone got up, I just lay there. The sun rose and had set itself high in the sky, and I was still lying there. I was afraid of people shaming me. Mother said, "Why is Nisa acting like this and refusing to leave her blankets when the sun is sitting up in the sky? Oh…she has probably wet herself!"   52

When I did get up, my heart felt miserable. I thought, "I've peed on myself and now everyone's going to laugh at me." I asked one of my friends, "How come, after I ate all those caterpillars, when I went to sleep I peed in my bed?" Then I thought, "Tonight, when this day is over, I'm going to lie down separate from the others. If I pee in my bed again, won't mother and father hit me?"   53

When a child sleeps beside her mother, in front, and her father sleeps behind and makes love to her mother, the child watches. Her parents don't fear her, a small child, because even if the child sees, even if she hears, she is unaware of what it is her parents are doing. She is still young and without sense. Perhaps this is the way the child learns. The child is still senseless, without intelligence, and just watches.   54

If the child is a little boy, when he plays with other children, he plays sex with them and teaches it to himself, just like a baby rooster teaches itself. The little girls also learn it by themselves.   55

Little boys are the first ones to know its sweetness. Yes, a young girl, while she is still a child, her thoughts don't know it. A boy has a penis, and maybe, while he is still inside his mother's belly, he already knows about sex.   56

When you are a child you play at nothing things. You build little huts and play. Then you come back to the village and continue to play. If people bother you, you get up and play somewhere else.   57

58   Once we left a pool of rain water where we had been playing and went to the little huts we had made. We stayed there and played at being hunters. We went out tracking animals, and when we saw one, we struck it with our make-believe arrows. We took some leaves and hung them over a stick and pretended it was meat. Then we carried it back to our village. When we got back, we stayed there and ate the meat and then the meat was gone. We went out again, found another animal, and killed it.

59   Sometimes the boys asked if we wanted to play a game with our genitals and the girls said no. We said we didn't want to play that game, but would like to play other games. The boys told us that playing sex was what playing was all about. That's the way we grew up.

60   When adults talked to me I listened. Once they told me that when a young woman grows up, she takes a husband. When they first talked to me about it, I said: "What? What kind of thing am I that I should take a husband? Me, when I grow up, I won't marry. I'll just lie by myself. If I married a man, what would I think I would be doing it for?"

61   My father said: "Nisa, I am old. I am your father and I am old; your mother's old, too. When you get married, you will gather food and give it to your husband to eat. He also will do things for you and give you things you can wear. But if you refuse to take a husband, who will give you food to eat? Who will give you things to have? Who will give you things to wear?"

62   I said to my father and mother, "No. There's no question in my mind—I refuse a husband. I won't take one. Why should I? As I am now, I am still a child and won't marry."

63   Then I said to Mother, "Why don't you marry the man you want for me and sit him down beside Father? Then you'll have two husbands."

64   Mother said: "Stop talking nonsense. I'm not going to marry him; you'll marry him. A husband is what I want to give you. Yet you say I should marry him. Why are you playing with me with this talk?"

65   We just continued to live after that, kept on living and more time passed. One time we went to the village where Old Kantla and his son Tashay were living. My friend Nhuka and I had gone to the water well to get water, and Tashay and his family were there, having just come back from the bush. When Tashay saw me, he decided he wanted to marry me. He called Nhuka over and said, "Nhuka, that young woman, that beautiful young woman…what is her name?"

66   Nhuka told him my name was Nisa, and he said, "That young woman…I'm going to tell Mother and Father about her. I'm going to ask them if I can marry her."

67   The next evening there was a dance at our village, and Tashay and his parents came. We sang and danced into the night. Later his father said, "We have come here, and now that the dancing is finished, I want

to speak to you. Give me your child, the child you gave birth to. Give her to me, and I will give her to my son. Yesterday, while we were at the well, he saw your child. When he returned he told me in the name of what he felt that I should come and ask for her today so I could give her to him."

My mother said, "Yes...but I didn't give birth to a woman, I bore a   68
child. She doesn't think about marriage, she just doesn't think about the inside of her marriage hut."

Then my father said, "Yes, I also conceived that child, and it is true: 69
She just doesn't think about marriage. When she marries a man, she leaves him and marries another man and leaves him and gets up and marries another man and leaves him. She refuses men completely. There are two men whom she has already refused. So when I look at Nisa today, I say she is not a woman."

Then Tashay's father said, "Yes, I have listened to what you have   70
said. That, of course, is the way of a child; it is a child's custom to do that. She gets married many times until one day she likes one man. Then they stay together. That is a child's way."

They talked about the marriage and agreed to it. In the morning   71
Tashay's parents went back to their camp, and we went to sleep. When the morning was late in the sky, his relatives came back. They stayed around and his parents told my aunt and my mother that they should all start building the marriage hut. They began building it together, and everyone was talking and talking. There were a lot of people there. Then all the young men went and brought Tashay to the hut. They stayed around together near the fire. I was at Mother's hut. They told two of my friends to get me. But I said to myself, "Ooooh...I'll just run away."

When they came, they couldn't find me. I was already out in the   72
bush, and I just sat there by the base of a tree. Soon I heard Nhuka call out, "Nisa...Nisa...my friend...there are things there that will bite and kill you. Now leave there and come back here."

They came and brought me back. Then they laid me down inside   73
the hut. I cried and cried, and people told me: "A man is not something that kills you; he is someone who marries you, and becomes like your father or your older brother. He kills animals and gives you things to eat. Even tomorrow he would do that. But because you are crying, when he kills an animal, he will eat it himself and won't give you any. Beads, too. He will get some beads, but he won't give them to you. Why are you afraid of your husband and why are you crying?"

I listened and was quiet. Later Tashay lay down by the mouth of   74
the hut, near the fire, and I was inside. He came in only after he thought I was asleep. Then he lay down and slept. I woke while it was still dark and thought, "How am I going to jump over him? How can I get out and go to Mother's hut?" Then I thought, "This person has married

me…yes." And, I just lay there. Soon the rain came and beat down and it fell until dawn broke.

75   In the morning, he got up first and sat by the fire. I was frightened. I was so afraid of him, I just lay there and waited for him to go away before I got up.

76   We lived together a long time and began to learn to like one another before he slept with me. The first time I didn't refuse. I agreed just a little and he lay with me. But the next morning my insides hurt. I took some leaves and wound them around my waist, but it continued to hurt. Later that day I went with the women to gather mongongo nuts. The whole time I thought "Ooooh…what has he done to my insides that they feel this way."

77   That evening we lay down again. But this time I took a leather strap, held my skin apron tightly against me, tied up my genitals with it, and then tied the strap to the hut's frame. I didn't want him to take me again. The two of us lay there and after a while he started to touch me. When he reached my stomach, he felt the leather strap. He felt around to see what it was. He said, "What is this woman doing? Yesterday she lay with me so nicely when I came to her. Why has she tied up her genitals this way?"

78   He sat me up and said, "Nisa…Nisa…what happened? Why are you doing this?" I didn't answer him.

79   "What are you so afraid of that you tied your genitals?"

80   I said, "I'm not afraid of anything."

81   He said, "No, now tell me what you are afraid of. In the name of what you did, I am asking you."

82   I said, "I refuse because yesterday when you touched me my insides hurt."

83   He said, "Do you see me as someone who kills people? Am I going to eat you? I am not going to kill you. I have married you and I want to make love to you. Have you seen any man who has married a woman and who just lives with her and doesn't have sex with her?"

84   I said, "No, I still refuse it! I refuse sex. Yesterday my insides hurt, that's why."

85   He said, "Mmm. Today you will lie there by yourself. But tomorrow I will take you."

86   The next day I said to him, "Today I'm going to lie here, and if you take me by force, you will have me. You will have me because today I'm just going to lie here. You are obviously looking for some 'food,' but I don't know if the food I have is food at all, because even if you have some, you won't be full."

87   I just lay there and he did his work.

88   We lived and lived, and soon I started to like him. After that I was a grown person and said to myself, "Yes, without doubt, a man sleeps with you. I thought maybe he didn't."

We lived on, and then I loved him and he loved me, and I kept on   89
loving him. When he wanted me I didn't refuse and he just slept with
me. I thought, "Why have I been so concerned about my genitals? They
are after all, not so important. So why was I refusing them?"

I thought that and gave myself to him and gave and gave. We lay   90
with one another, and my breasts had grown very large. I had become
a woman.

FOR FURTHER INFORMATION

Lee, Richard B., and Irven De Vore, eds. *Kalahari Hunter–Gatherers: Studies of the !Kung San and Their Neighbors.* Harvard University Press, 1976.
Lee, Richard B., and Irven De Vore, eds. *Man the Hunter.* Aldine, 1968.
Marshall, Lorna. *The !Kung of Nyae Nyae.* Harvard University Press, 1976.
Shostak, Marjorie. "Life before Horticulture: An African Gathering and Hunting Society." *Horticulture,* Vol. 55, No. 2, 1977.

✧ *Evaluating the Text*

1. How would you characterize Nisa's relationships with family members? How does she interact with her mother, father, older brother, baby brother, and grandmother? What explains the changes in her attitude toward her baby brother as she grows up?

2. What does the episode in which she describes killing the baby steenbok reveal about her inner conflict about becoming an adult?

3. Describe the circumstances that lead to Nisa's marriage to Tashay. What change in attitude must she undergo before the marriage takes place? What can you infer about the kinds of problems she faces in adapting to the role of a married woman in !Kung society? Keep in mind that she has left several prospective husbands before Tashay.

✧ *Exploring Different Perspectives*

1. Discuss how both Shostak's account and Kim Chernin's article (see "The Flesh and the Devil") point out interesting paradoxes between societies where food plays a central role.

2. Compare the cultural values and expectations connected with marriage among the !Kung with those of the Japanese as described by Kyoko Mori in "Polite Lies."

✧ *Extending Viewpoints through Writing*

1. What unexpected similarities can you discover between the !Kung and contemporary American society in terms of disciplining children, the

role played by grandparents (including their concern that their grandchildren are too thin), sibling rivalry, bed-wetting, playing sexual
games, and finding husbands for daughters who are fussy?

2. Nisa's narrative was originally elicited as answers to questions she
was asked over a period of time by Shostak. How do recurring motifs
in this account suggest the kinds of questions Shostak asked Nisa?
What conclusions might you draw about the relationship between
Nisa and Shostak from the answers that Nisa gave?

Shirley Saad

Amina

◆

Shirley Saad was born in Cairo in 1947 to a Lebanese father and a Polish-Rumanian mother. Saad was educated at St. Clare's College by Irish nuns and spoke English, French, and Italian until the 1952 revolution when Gamal Abdel Nasser gained power, after which the study of Arabic became mandatory in the schools. In 1961 her family moved to Lebanon. Largely self-taught, Saad was influenced by reading the novels of Hanan al-Shaykh and, while she lived in Abu Dhabi, started writing stories about restrictions imposed on women in the Arabic world. "Amina" sympathizes with the plight of a woman who has just given birth to a child and is apprehensive that her husband will take another wife if the child is not a son.

Located on the Mediterranean Sea, Lebanon is a republic in the Middle East bordered to the north and east by Syria and to the south by Israel. The site of the ancient maritime city-state Phoenicia, the region fell to successive Middle Eastern powers. Christianity was introduced under the Roman Empire in the first century and persisted even after the coming of Islam with the Arab conquest in the seventh century. Since independence in 1945, Lebanon has been plagued by civil strife between the Palestine Liberation Organization (PLO), Syrian, and Israeli forces, as well as indigenous Christian and Muslim factions. However, under a peace accord reached in 1990, militias representing these different factions withdrew from the capital, Beirut, and the Lebanese Army established control. With the fifteen-year civil war behind them, the Lebanese have begun the process of rebuilding the country's infrastructure. In July 1997, the United States lifted a ten-year ban on travel to Lebanon by United States citizens.

Amina opened her eyes and for a moment wondered where she 1
was. Then she remembered and a moan escaped her lips. The English nurse hurried over and bent down, "Don't you worry now," she said. "You'll be fine and the baby is all right."

Amina asked, not daring to hope, "Is it a boy or a girl?" 2

"A girl," replied the nurse cheerfully. "A beautiful, bouncing, four 3
kilograms girl. *Mabruk*, congratulations."

"*Allah yi barek fi omrek*," murmured Amina as she sank back on her 4
pillows. Another girl!

What a catastrophe. What would happen to her now? She had 5
brought four girls into the world, four girls in six years of marriage. She felt tears running down her cheeks, and remembered how happy and

191

proud she had been when her mother told her that she was engaged to be married.

6   She had seen Hamid twice, once at her cousin's house when he arrived unexpectedly. The girls all scattered to their quarters to put on their masks and veils. The next time, he came with his father to ask for her hand in marriage. The houseboy serving the coffee told the Indian housegirl who in turn, ran and told her mistress. So, she had gone to peek through the partition between the men's and women's *majlis.* She saw Hamid and his father sipping coffee and being congratulated by all the men in the family. They embraced and rubbed noses, big smiles on everyone's faces.

7   Amina remembered her wedding, the noise and the bustle, her hennaed hands and feet, the whispers among the older women which frightened her and the anticipation. Finally, she found herself alone with this stranger, who had turned out to be very kind and gentle and considerate.

8   Well, there would be no henna and celebration for this girl. God, why couldn't she have a boy? Just one, that's all she wanted, just one little baby boy.

9   She wished the midwife hadn't told her when she had that miscarriage that it had been a boy. The only one in six years, and she had to go and lose it. It was her fault too. She had no business climbing a ladder at five months. She slipped and fell and the doctors kept her in the hospital for a week, then told her she was all right and could go home. But there was no movement, no life, so she went back to the hospital and after two weeks of tests and X-rays and hope and despair, they finally decided the baby was dead.

10   After that, she had two more girls, and now the fourth.

11   Would Hamid divorce her? Would he take a second wife? His older brother had been pressing for two years now, urging him to take a second wife. Hamid loved Amina and his daughters, but he was human. He did have all that money and the social and political position and no boy to leave it to.

12   Her mother came in, then her sisters-in-law. Each one kissed her and said *"Mabruk,"* but she could tell they were not really happy. Her mother was especially fearful for her daughter's future and felt that some of the disgrace fell on her and the family too. The sisters-in-law were secretly jubilant, because they had boys. Hamid's social status and half his fortune would revert to their own sons if he never had any boys of his own. Of course, he was still young and he and Amina might try again. But for the moment the in-laws left reassured and falsely commiserated with Amina on her bad luck.

13   "It is God's will," they murmured, smiling under their masks. Their mouths were sad, but Amina could see the twinkle in their eyes. "God's will be done."

Friends started coming into the room. They kissed Amina and said   14
"Mabruk," then sat on the floor, cross-legged. Arranging their robes
around them, they sipped coffee from little thimble cups, eating fruits
and sweets.

Her cousin Huda came too. She wore a long, velvet dress, embroi-   15
dered on the sides and bodice, loose and flowing, to conceal her belly.
She was in her sixth month and looked radiantly serene. She sat on the
carpet and sipped her coffee.

Amina thought bitterly, "She already has two daughters and three   16
sons. What does she need another baby for? She's not so young any
more."

As if she had read her thoughts, Huda said, "This is my last baby. It   17
will be the baby for my old age. The others are married or away at
school all day. An empty house is a sad house. You need many sons
and daughters to keep your husband happy. You are still young, Amina. God has given you four daughters, maybe the next four will be
boys. God's will be done."

"As God wills it, so be it," murmured the other ladies smugly.   18

Hamid came in and the ladies all stood up, saluted him deferen-   19
tially, and hastily went into the next room. The maid served them
more coffee. Hamid looked at his wife, tried to smile and searched for
something nice to say. He thought she must be tired, disappointed,
ashamed of having failed him one more time and afraid of being
repudiated.

He sat down near the bed and said, "Well, mother of my children,   20
we will just have to try again, won't we?"

Amina burst into tears of sorrow, shame and relief.   21

"Don't cry," he said, distressed. "The important thing is that you   22
and the girls are in good health," smiling. "As long as we are young,
we will try again, eh?"

Amina blushed under her mask and pulled her veil around her   23
face. He patted her hand, got up, and left the room.

The ladies came rushing back in, like a flock of crows, eager for the   24
news, good or bad.

Amina's mother said solicitously, "What did he say, my daughter?"   25

"He said better luck next time, Mother!"   26

The mother let out a sigh of relief. They had another year's re-   27
prieve. The women congratulated Amina and left to spread the news.

Amina sank back on to her pillows and drifted off to sleep.   28

✧ *Evaluating the Text*

1. What insight do you gain into the kind of societal and personal pressures Amina is under from the reactions of her mother and in-laws?

2. How is the story shaped to build up suspense first as to the sex of the child and, second, as to how her husband will react to this news? What does Amina's husband's reaction reveal about him and his feelings for her?

3. How would you characterize the author's attitude toward the events she describes?

✧ Exploring Different Perspectives

1. Despite the apparent differences in the cultures of Lebanon and Japan, what similarities in marital expectations for women can you discover between Saad's story and Kyoko Mori's account "Polite Lies."

2. In what ways are the stories by Saad and Mahasweta Devi ("Giribala") structured to build suspense as to what the husband, in one case, and the wife, in the other, will ultimately decide to do?

✧ Extending Viewpoints through Writing

1. What recent developments (for example, ultrasound clinics in India and genetic screening in the United States) illustrate the pressure on women to produce sons? Contrast this with the recent trend in Japan where families want daughters.

2. Do you consider having children important to your future? Why or why not? What do you think the structure of the family will look like in the future?

Kyoko Mori

Polite Lies

◆──────────

Kyoko Mori was born in 1957 in Japan and emigrated to the United States when she was twenty. She is currently a teacher of creative writing at St. Norbert's College in Green Bay, Wisconsin. She has written two volumes of fiction for young adults, Shizuko's Daughter *(1993) and* One Bird *(1995). Her acclaimed memoir,* The Dream of Water *(1995), delves into her traumatic experiences as a child in Japan; her mother committed suicide and her father was emotionally abusive. The following section is from her 1997 book,* Polite Lies: On Being a Woman Caught between Cultures, *a work that insightfully discusses the differences in marriage and other cultural customs between America and Japan.*

If marriage is like a job in Japan, it is a job that most Japanese women are desperate to get. For a Japanese woman, to be unmarried carries the same sort of stigma that being unemployed holds for Americans—especially for American men. People think that you are not contributing enough to society or making the right kind of progress through life: you are not fulfilling the role you were born for. 1

I am painfully aware of this stigma every time I go to Japan. During my last visit, I went to see an old high school friend, Hiroko. We had tea at her house and talked about other school friends. 2

"Did you know that Nobuko has gotten married?" Hiroko asked me. 3

I was surprised to hear the news. On a previous visit I had learned that Nobuko was regional manager for the Japanese branch of Hilton hotels. Always traveling to Europe on business, she loved her job and was perfectly content to live with her parents in their big house in Ashiya. 4

"About a year ago," Hiroko continued. "Nobuko decided to get married." 5

"To whom?" I asked, expecting to hear about some exotic and dramatic romance, possibly with a foreigner. (I already knew that Japanese men usually don't have big romances with the nice Japanese women they marry.) 6

"She had no one in mind," Hiroko said. "But she quit her job so she could put all her efforts into finding a suitable husband. She and her mother looked at stacks and stacks of résumés from older men looking for a wife." 7

*For information on Japan, see p. 79.

8   Hiroko was saying that Nobuko had gone through an *omiai*, or marriage-arranging process: when someone is looking for a husband or a wife, her or his family consults other families to get the names of suitable people. Folders of information—résumés, photographs, birth certificates—are exchanged. Once a match is made, the families set up a group meeting at a public place like a restaurant or a hotel lobby. The man and the woman meet in the presence of their parents and even some of their siblings. If they like each other and the other members of the families have no objection, the couple begins to date so they can get to know each other a little before getting married. The marriage generally takes place within a few months.

9   "Nobuko and her mother didn't find anyone by asking their family friends, so they consulted an *omiai*-arranging service," Hiroko told me. "They must have looked at hundreds of résumés. They were looking for a well-to-do older man in Kobe or Osaka."

10   "What do you mean, older?" I asked. Nobuko would have been thirty-three at the time.

11   "Late forties, fifties, sixties," Hiroko explained. "There aren't many men younger than forty-five who are widowers."

12   "But there must have been some men our age who were single because they'd never married," I pointed out.

13   "Sure, but those men have never been married because they have health problems, or they aren't the settling-down type, or their mothers are too domineering. Men like those don't make a lot of money, and they don't make good husbands. Nobuko and her mother were looking for reliable men who had been married once and then widowed. She didn't quit her job only to marry a playboy, a mommy's boy, or an invalid."

14   I picked up my teacup and tried to drink, but I felt sick. Hiroko made it sound as if our friend had to look for a job in a bad market.

15   "Anyway," Hiroko said, brightening, "Nobuko got lucky. She found a business executive of a trading company whose wife had passed away a couple of years ago. He was younger than most—in his late forties—and both of his kids were already in college, so she doesn't have to raise someone else's kids. It was by far the best situation."

16   "Have you met her husband?" I asked.

17   "No," Hiroko sighed. "My husband and I were still in Chicago when they got married. Soon afterward, Nobuko's husband got transferred to New York, so they moved there. I didn't get a chance to meet him or to say goodbye to Nobuko."

18   "Have you heard from her, though? Is she happy?" I asked.

19   Hiroko didn't answer right away, so I knew that meant some form of no.

20   "At least she'll get to use her English," I offered. I didn't know what else to say. Nobuko speaks English, German, and French, as well as Japanese.

"I know," Hiroko said. "That's one of the reasons the man wanted to   21
marry her. Even when he was stationed in Osaka, he worked mostly
with Americans and Europeans. Foreign businessmen like to socialize at
people's homes. Being a widower was a real disadvantage to him. He
wanted to marry someone who could carry on conversations with his
guests, not just serve drinks and food and disappear into the kitchen.
Nobuko was a good choice. She's smart. She can talk about anything."

I felt depressed to think of our friend quitting her job to become a   22
multilingual hostess. "Why did she want to get married anyway?" I
asked. That was the part I didn't understand: she had wanted to get
married even though she had no one in mind. It wasn't as though she
had met and fallen madly in love with someone and sacrificed her job
to be with him. At least that would have made sense—she would have
been driven by something compelling, if destructive. Although I would
never choose reckless love that demands a big sacrifice, I understand
its appeal for other people. That kind of love is like religion. Once you
can accept the apparently irrational premise—that someone was crucified and then resurrected to atone for your sins, or that you and your
lover were destined to be together and only he can make you happy—
then everything else follows in an almost logical fashion. You can pre-
dict, accept, and even enjoy the consequences, the way skydivers must
love the freefall that is the inevitable and desired consequence of their
leap. Nobuko's actions were different. Her choice seemed both calcu-
lated and reckless, for no good reason.

Hiroko didn't really answer my question. She just said, "Nobuko   23
had to hurry because it was the last chance for her to be married. Time
was running out."

"Why? You said that she was only looking to be a second wife to   24
someone older. A second wife almost never has her own kids. She
could have waited ten, fifteen years to be an old man's wife."

"Oh, come on," Hiroko said. "Nobody marries a woman over forty,   25
even if he doesn't plan to have a child with her. Nobuko didn't have
that much time."

I stared at my cup of cold tea, feeling suddenly too angry to speak.   26
It was so unfair for a sixty-five-year-old man to say that a forty-one-
year-old woman was "too old" to be his wife. *How can Hiroko accept this
prejudice so easily?* I wondered. When I looked up, she shrugged her
shoulders and made a sour face, a gesture of resignation. "All right," I
said, trying to calm down and get back to my original question. "So
let's say she was getting too old and didn't have much time. But I still
don't understand. Why did she want to get married at all? I thought
she was happy working for Hilton."

Hiroko shook her head. "It was a good job, I'm sure," she said. "But   27
Nobuko worked so hard every day. All she did was work—even her
travels were for work. That must have been such an empty feeling—to
have nothing but your work."

28   It must be an empty feeling, equally, to be married to someone who wants a perfect wife to advance his career, but I could not point that out because that statement might apply to Hiroko, too. Hiroko had quit her job at an airline a few years back when her husband was chosen by his company to study for an M.B.A. in Chicago. To go with him and take care of him, she had to give up her job. He didn't speak much English. Hiroko is bilingual. He couldn't have lived in Chicago or done his homework in English without her help. Hiroko, too, was a perfect wife for her husband's career.

29   To be that perfect wife, she had given up a lot. Now that they were back in Japan, she was having a hard time finding a job: when she applied for jobs, she was told that she was qualified but too old. One employer even asked her if she had a friend with similar qualifications who was ten years younger. In Japan, where companies can openly discriminate against people on the basis of gender and age, Hiroko's chance of getting a good job didn't look great. Under those circumstances, she must want to believe, all the more, that marriage is more fulfilling than a job. It wasn't my place to contradict her and make her feel bad about herself and Nobuko. But I didn't think either of them was happy. Hiroko said nothing about her husband except that when they traveled together, they sometimes ran out of things to say to each other. That didn't sound promising at all. Hiroko was not an exception—all our friends from school talk in the same way about their husbands. They are intelligent and outspoken women, not at all the kind of people who expect little from life. Why do they put up with getting nothing from their husbands?

30   My friends and I—"nice" Japanese girls—had been taught that whatever we did for ourselves was "empty," while what we did to take care of other people, especially a husband or children, was "fulfilling." We grew up watching our mothers working hard as housekeepers, silent hostesses, and errand-women for our fathers, who never thanked their wives except by a begrudging nod or barely audible grunt. We never saw our parents hug, never heard our fathers compliment our mothers on anything. Maybe we were too used to seeing our mothers making sacrifices for nothing. Women our age don't expect any more from their marriages than our mothers did.

31   In my generation, as well as in my mother's or grandmothers', Japanese marriages don't provide women with "happiness." None of my Japanese friends have ever talked about the great conversations they have with their husbands, the emotional support they get from them in times of trouble, or even the fun they have together on trips. People in Japan often say that the marriages of Americans—which are based on sexual attraction, love, and romance—can only lead to divorce because sexual attraction and love can fade away so easily. Japanese arranged marriages are more stable, they argue, since these matches are based on suitability. Maybe it's true that romance often brings together people

who are not so compatible with each other—half of my American friends are divorced. But those who stay together do so by choice, trying to work out their differences because they love each other. I cannot imagine how a traditional Japanese couple starting out with nothing but "suitability" can feel the same motivation to be happy together when they turn out to be incompatible—which must happen to many couples since their "suitability" is based on family background, not personalities. I can only conclude that they stay together because stability is more important than the happiness of either party.

Whenever I talk to Japanese women, I wonder if personal happiness   32
is an American concept. The concept of happiness as an emotional "high" or personal "fulfillment" seems foreign to my Japanese friends. To them, happiness means stability and family harmony, living day to day and feeling useful and valued rather than despised as a selfish person. Though all my friends come from upper-middle-class families, most Japanese women, regardless of class or education, seem to share the same sense of happiness-as-stability-and-hard-work-for-others. The only women who are allowed to have "fun" in a more American sense—doing things that aren't useful but enjoyable—are widows, women who have put in their time at the duty of marriage. These are women who are assumed to be too old for sex, love, or romance, and their "fun" usually involves spending time with old friends who are also widows. Finally free from men, these women can find happiness in one another's company.

A few days after I visited my friend Hiroko, I went to see Mrs. Kuzuha, a woman who had been a good friend of my mother's. Our two   33
families had been neighbors in the early sixties, when we lived in the company-owned apartment complex before moving into houses of our own. Even after our move Mrs. Kuzuha and my mother spent a lot of time together; my brother and I played with the two Kuzuha boys, the younger of whom was my age. Until my mother's death, we were like an extended family with two mothers and four kids.

Mrs. Kuzuha made me dinner at her house up on a hill in Ashiya,   34
where she lives alone. Her husband had died two years before from cancer. The boys had gotten married and moved to Kyoto and Tokyo.

"When my husband died," Mrs. Kuzuha told me at dinner, "I was   35
sad, of course. He was a good person for the most part, though all men are selfish from time to time." She nodded in a discreet way and went on. "I don't resent him now for anything he did, and I was sorry for him during his illness. But it's good to be on my own now. I want to enjoy myself and be happy in my old age. I'm grateful to him for working so hard and leaving me comfortable."

She told me her daily routine. Every morning, she awoke at five   36
and listened to the English conversation program on the radio. Lying in bed, she would repeat the sentences after the announcer. She wanted to

improve her English because she and her friends often go to Europe on cruises. After getting up and having breakfast, she drove to the gym to exercise. She was in a Ping-Pong league.

37   "It isn't a league just for old people," she bragged, laughing. "There are men and women in their forties or even thirties. I have a pretty good serve. Once at a ski resort, I played with some college kids and won."

38   A few times a week, she also took karaoke-singing lessons. This was the first time I had ever even heard of lessons for karaoke.

39   "Oh, it's very popular," Mrs. Kuzuha said. "Singing is good for both the body and the spirit. It clears your head and makes you feel more cheerful. To sing, you have to stand up straight and take a deep breath. It's hard to feel depressed or lonely while standing up like that." She demonstrated by straightening her back.

40   We were having a typical Japanese dinner, at which the hostess gets up every few minutes to make more food. Mrs. Kuzuha had first prepared stir-fried vegetables and tofu. Halfway through that course, she got up to cook a Japanese-style omelette for me; then it was time to put together a green salad, to cut up some fruit, to make coffee, to offer me a slice of cheesecake. Offering food is how a Japanese woman shows her love. Mrs. Kuzuha was waiting on me as she had waited on her family all her life, while talking about how much she enjoyed being on her own.

41   "I only regret that your mother didn't live long enough to enjoy her old age," she told me. "Our husbands died within a year of each other. We could have been widows together. It would have been so nice to travel with her."

42   Being a Japanese widow is like being honorably retired. It is the only way a woman can be independent without being considered selfish.

✧ Evaluating the Text

1. How do Mori's encounters with her old high school friend, Hiroko, make Mori realize the stringent social pressures that govern women's lives in Japan?

2. Mori's narrative chronicles the ways in which the Japanese concept of the "perfect wife" dominates women's lives. Describe the conflict she experiences between this idea and the value that Americans place on personal happiness.

3. To what extent is the cumulative effect of this narrative connected with Mori's realization of how Americanized she has become?

✧ Exploring Different Perspectives

1. Compare and contrast the very different cultural pressures that tyrannize women in America and Japan in the accounts by Mori and Kim Chernin in "The Flesh and the Devil."

2. Compare the role of the "perfect wife" in the cultures of Japan and Lebanon as depicted in Mori's account and Shirley Saad's story "Amina."

✧ Extending Viewpoints through Writing

1. Mori writes as if none of the Japanese values regarding marriage operate in the United States. Discuss those American expectations that are quite close to the Japanese.

2. Did you ever have a conversation with an old friend from high school, whom you had not seen for a while, that gave you insight into cultural values that you had come to reject? Describe your experiences.

Mahasweta Devi

Giribala

———————◆———————

Mahasweta Devi was born in East Bengal in 1926, moved to West Bengal as an adolescent, and studied at Visva-Bharati and Calcutta universities where she received a master's degree in English. From a family with widespread literary and political influence, Devi joined the Gananatya, a group of highly accomplished, keenly political actors and writers who took the revolutionary step of bringing theater, on themes of burning interest in rural Bengal, to villages. Subsequently, she became a writer and journalist while holding a job as a college teacher in Calcutta. Over a period of years she has studied and lived among the tribal and outcast communities in southwest Bengal and southeast Bihar. Her stories, collected in Agnigarbha *(Womb of Fire) (1978) and in* Imaginary Maps *(1994), focus on the semilandless tribals and untouchables who are effectively denied rights guaranteed by the constitution, including a legal minimum wage. Her unique style of narrative realism reflects this emphasis on observations drawn from actual situations, persons, dialects, and idioms. "Giribala," translated into English from Bengali by Bardhan Kalpana, was first published in the magazine* Prasad *(Autumn 1982), a journal Devi created as a kind of people's magazine, which she still edits. Like her other stories, "Giribala" reflects carefully researched information Devi gathered directly from the lives of the rural underclass. This story tells the shocking tale of a woman whose husband sells their young daughters into prostitution.*

In 1997, Devi won the Magsaysay award, considered to be the Asian equivalent of the Nobel prize, and donated the cash prize of $50,000 to a tribal welfare society.

1   Giribala[1] was born in a village called Talsana, in the Kandi subdivision of Murshidabad district.[2] Nobody ever imagined that she could think on her own, let alone act on her own thought. This Giribala, like so many others, was neither beautiful nor ugly, just an average-looking girl. But she had lovely eyes, eyes that somehow made her appearance striking.

2   In their caste, it was still customary to pay a bride-price. Aulchand gave Giri's father eighty rupees[3] and a heifer before he married her. Gi-

*For information on India, see p. 34.
[1]Literally, "mountain girl."
[2]In the United Province, near New Delhi.
[3]Approximately $20.

ri's father, in turn, gave his daughter four tolas[4] of silver, pots and pans, sleeping mats, and a cartload of mature bamboo that came from the bamboo dumps that formed the main wealth of Giri's father. Aulchand had told him that only because his hut had burned down did he need the bamboo to rebuild it. This was also the reason he gave for having to leave her with them for a few days—so that he could go to build a home for them.

Aulchand thus married Giri, and left. He did not come back soon. 3

Shortly after the marriage, Bangshi Dhamali,[5] who worked at the 4
sub-post office in Nishinda, happened to visit the village. Bangshi enjoyed much prestige in the seven villages in the Nishinda area, largely due to his side business of procuring patients for the private practice of the doctor who was posted at the only hospital in the area. That way, the doctor supplemented his hospital salary by getting paid by the patients thus diverted from the hospital, and Bangshi supplemented his salary of 145 rupees from the sub-post office with the commission he got for procuring those patients. Bangshi's prestige went up further after he started using the medical terms he had picked up from being around the doctor.

For some reason that nobody quite recalled, Bangshi addressed 5
Giri's father as uncle. When Bangshi showed up on one of his patient-procuring trips, he looked up Giri's father and remarked disapprovingly about what he had just learned from his trip to another village, that he had given his only daughter in marriage to Aulchand, of all people.

"Yes. The proposal came along, and I thought he was all right." 6

"Obviously, you thought so. How much did he pay?" 7

"Four times twenty and one." 8

"I hope you're ready to face the consequences of what you've 9
done."

"What consequences?" 10

"What can I say? You know that I'm a government servant myself 11
and the right-hand man of the government doctor. Don't you think you should have consulted me first? I'm not saying that he's a bad sort, and I will not deny there was a time when I smoked *ganja*[6] with him. But I know what you don't know—the money he gave you as bride-price was not his. It's Channan's. You see, Channan's marriage had been arranged in Kalhat village. And Aulchand, as Channan's uncle, was trusted with the money to deliver as bride-price on behalf of Channan. He didn't deliver it there."

"What?" 12

"Channan's mother sat crying when she learned that Aulchand, 13
who had been living under their roof for so long, could cheat them like

[4]One tola = .40 ounce.
[5]Literally, "mischievous."
[6]Marijuana cigarettes, also known as "pip."

that. Finally, Channan managed to get married by borrowing from several acquaintances who were moved by his plight."

14   "He has no place of his own? No land for a home to stand on?"

15   "Nothing of the sort."

16   "But he took a cartload of my bamboo to rebuild the hut on his land!"

17   "I was going to tell you about that too. He sold that bamboo to Channan's aunt for a hundred rupees and hurried off to the Banpur fair."

18   Giri's father was stunned. He sat with his head buried in his hands. Bangshi went on telling him about other similar tricks Aulchand had been pulling. Before taking leave, he finally said, perhaps out of mercy for the overwhelmed man, "He's not a bad one really. Just doesn't have any land, any place to live. Keeps traveling from one fair to another, with some singing party or other. That's all. Otherwise, he's not a bad sort."

19   Giri's father wondered aloud, "But Mohan never told me any of these things! He's the one who brought the proposal to me!"

20   "How could he, when he's Aulchand's right hand in these matters?"

21   When Giri's mother heard all this from Giri's father, she was livid. She vowed to have her daughter married again and never to send her to live with the cheat, the thief.

22   But when after almost a year Aulchand came back, he came prepared to stop their mouths from saying what they wanted to say. He brought a large taro root, a new sari for his bride, a squat stool of jackfruit wood for his mother-in-law, and four new jute sacks for his father-in-law. Giri's mother still managed to tell him the things they had found out from Bangshi. Aulchand calmly smiled a generous, forgiving smile, saying, "One couldn't get through life if one believed everything that Bangshi-*dada* said.[7] Your daughter is now going to live in a brick house, not a mere mud hut. That's true, not false."

23   So, Giri's mother started to dress her only daughter to go to live with her husband. She took time to comb her hair into a nice bun, while weeping and lamenting, partly to herself and partly to her daughter, "This man is like a hundred-rooted weed in the yard. Bound to come back every time it's been pulled out. What he just told us are all lies, I know that. But with what smooth confidence he said those lies!"

24   Giri listened silently. She knew that although the groom had to pay a bride-price in their community, still a girl was only a girl. She had heard so many times the old saying: "A daughter born, To husband or death, She's already gone." She realized that her life in her own home and village was over, and her life of suffering was going to begin. Silently she

---

[7]*Dada*, meaning elder brother, is also used to refer politely to or to address a friend or acquaintance older than oneself, but not old enough to be referred to or addressed as uncle. [Author's note.]

wept for a while, as her mother tended to grooming her. Then she blew her nose, wiped her eyes, and asked her mother to remember to bring her home at the time of Durga puja[8] and to feed the red-brown cow that was her charge, adding that she had chopped some hay for the cow, and to water her young *jaba* tree that was going to flower someday.

Giribala, at the age of fourteen, then started off to make her home 25 with her husband. Her mother put into a bundle the pots and pans that she would be needing. Watching her doing that, Aulchand remarked, "Put in some rice and lentils too. I've got a job at the house of the *babu*. Must report to work the moment I get back. There'll be no time to buy provisions until after a few days."

Giribala picked up the bundle of rice, lentils, and cooking oil and 26 left her village, walking a few steps behind him. He walked ahead, and from time to time asked her to walk faster, as the afternoon was starting to fade. He took her to another village in Nishinda, to a large brick house with a large garden of fruit trees of all kinds. In the far corner of the garden was a crumbling hovel meant for the watchman. He took her to it. There was no door in the door opening. As if answering her thought, Aulchand said, "I'll fix the door soon. But you must admit the room is nice. And the pond is quite near. Now go on, pick up some twigs and start the rice."

"It's dark out there! Do you have a kerosene lamp?" 27

"Don't ask me for a kerosene lamp, or this and that. Just do what 28 you can."

A maid from the babu's household turned up and saved Giri. She 29 brought a kerosene lamp from the house and showed Giri to the pond, complaining about Aulchand and cautioning her about him. "What kind of heartless parents would give a tender young girl to a no-good ganja addict? How can he feed you? He has nothing. Gets a pittance taking care of the babu's cattle and doing odd jobs. Who knows how he manages to feed himself, doing whatever else he does! If you've been brought up on rice, my dear, you'd be wise enough to go back home to-morrow to leave behind the bits of silver that you have got on you."

But Giri did not go back home the next day for safekeeping her silver 30 ornaments. Instead, in the morning she was found busy plastering with mud paste the exposed, uneven bricks of the wall of the crumbling room. Aulchand managed to get an old sheet of tin from the babu and nailed it to a few pieces of wood to make it stand; then he propped it up as a door for the room. Giri promptly got herself employed in the babu household for meals as her wage. After a few months, Aulchand remarked about how she had managed to domesticate a vagabond like him, who grew up without parents, never stayed home, and always floated around.

[8]Rituals designed to worship a household goddess of good fortune.

31   Giri replied, "Go, beg the babus for a bit of the land. Build your own home."

32   "Why will they give me land?"

33   "They will if you plead for the new life that's on its way. Ask them if a baby doesn't deserve to be born under a roof of its own. Even beggars and roving street singers have some kind of home."

34   "You're right. I too feel sad about not having a home of my own. Never felt that way before, though."

35   The only dream they shared was a home of their own.

36   However, their firstborn, a daughter they named Belarani,[9] was born in the crumbling hovel with the tin door. Before the baby was even a month old, Giri returned to her work in the babu household, and, as if to make up for her short absence from work, she took the heavy sheets, the flatweave rugs, and the mosquito nets to the pond to wash them clean. The lady of the house remarked on how she put her heart into the work and how clean her work was!

37   Feeling very magnanimous, the lady then gave Giri some of her children's old clothes, and once in a while she asked Giri to take a few minutes' break from work to feed the baby.

38   Belarani was followed by another daughter, Poribala, and a son, Rajib, all born in the watchman's hovel at the interval of a year and a half to two years. After the birth of her fourth child, a daughter she named Maruni,[10] she asked the doctor at the hospital, where she went for this birth, to sterilize her.

39   By then Aulchand had finally managed to get the babu's permission to use a little area of his estate to build a home for his family. He had even raised a makeshift shack on it. Now he was periodically going away for other kinds of work assigned to him.

40   He was furious to learn that Giri had herself sterilized, so furious that he beat her up for the first time. "Why did you do it? Tell me, why?"

41   Giri kept silent and took the beating. Aulchand grabbed her by the hair and punched her a good many times. Silently she took it all. After he had stopped beating because he was tired and his anger temporarily spent, she calmly informed him that the Panchayat[11] was going to hire people for the road building and pay the wages in wheat.

42   "Why don't you see your father and get some bamboo instead?"

43   "What for?"

---

[9]Literally, "pretty queen."

[10]Literally meaning a girl likely to die; the name is perhaps intended to repel death, following the belief that death takes first the lives people want to cling to most. [Author's note.]

[11]Governing body of the local village, usually made up of five officials ("pancha" means "five").

"Because you're the one who has been wanting a home. I could   44
build a good one with some bamboo from your father."

"We'll both work on the Panchayat road and have our home. We'll   45
save some money by working harder."

"If only we could mortgage or sell your silver trinkets,…"   46

Giribala did not say anything to his sly remark; she just stared at   47
him. Aulchand had to lower his eyes before her silent stare. Giri had
put her silver jewelry inside the hollow of a piece of bamboo, stuffed it
up and kept it in the custody of the lady of the house she worked for.
Belarani too started working there, when she was seven years old, doing a thousand odd errands to earn her meals. Bela was now ten, and
growing like a weed in the rainy season. Giri would need the silver to
get her married someday soon. All she had for that purpose was the bit
of silver from her parents and the twenty-two rupees she managed to
save from her years of hard work, secretly deposited with the mistress
of the house, away from Aulchand's reach.

"I'm not going to sell my silver for a home. My father gave all he   48
could for that, a whole cartload of bamboo, one hundred and sixty-two
full stems, worth a thousand rupees at that time even in the markets of
Nishinda."

"The same old story comes up again!" Aulchand was exasperated.   49

"Don't you want to see your own daughter married someday?"   50

"Having a daughter only means having to raise a slave for others.   51
Mohan had read my palm and predicted a son in the fifth pregnancy.
But, no, you had to make yourself sterile, so you could turn into a
whore."

Giri grabbed the curved kitchen knife and hissed at him, "If ever I   52
hear you say those evil things about me, I'll cut off the heads of the children and then my own head with this."

Aulchand quickly stopped himself, "Forget I said it. I won't, ever   53
again."

For a few days after that he seemed to behave himself. He was sort   54
of timid, chastised. But soon, probably in some way connected with the
grudge of being chastised by her, the vile worm inside his brain started
to stir again; once again Mohan, his trick master, was his prompter.

Mohan had turned up in the midst of the busy days they were   55
spending in the construction of a bus road that was going to connect
Nishinda with Krishnachawk.[12] Giri and Aulchand were both working
there and getting as wages the wheat for their daily meals. Mohan too
joined them to work there, and he sold his wheat to buy some rice, a
pumpkin, and occasionally some fish to go with the wheat bread. He
had remained the same vagabond that he always was, only his talking

---

[12]A major junction.

had become more sophisticated with a bohemian style picked up from his wanderings to cities and distant villages. He slept in the little porch facing the room occupied by Giri and her family.

56   Sitting there in the evenings, he expressed pity for Aulchand, "Tch! Tch! You seem to have got your boat stuck in the mud, my friend. Have you forgotten all about the life we used to have?"

57   Giri snapped at him, "You can't sit here doing your smart talking, which can only bring us ruin."

58   "My friend had such a good singing voice!"

59   "Perhaps he had that. Maybe there was money in it too. But that money would never have reached his home and fed his children."

60   Mohan started another topic one evening. He said that there was a great shortage of marriage-age girls in Bihar,[13] so that the Biharis with money were coming down for Bengali brides and paying a bundle for that! He mentioned that Sahadeb Bauri, a fellow he knew, a low-caste fellow like themselves, received five hundred rupees for having his daughter married to one of those bride-searching Biharis.

61   "Where is that place?" Aulchand's curiosity was roused.

62   "You wouldn't know, my friend, even if I explained where it is. Let me just say that it's very far and the people there don't speak Bengali."

63   "They paid him five hundred rupees?" Aulchand was hooked in.

64   "Yes, they did."

65   The topic was interrupted at that point by the noise that rose when people suddenly noticed that the cowshed of Kali-babu,[14] the Panchayat big shot, was on fire. Everybody ran in that direction to throw bucketfuls of water at it.

66   Giri forgot about the topic thus interrupted. But Aulchand did not.

67   Something must have blocked Giri's usual astuteness because she suspected nothing from the subsequent changes in her husband's tone.

68   For example, one day he said, "Who wants your silver? I'll get my daughter married and also my shack replaced with bricks and tin. My daughter looks lovelier every day from the meals in the babu home!"

69   Giri's mind sensed nothing at all to be alerted to. She only asked, "Are you looking for a groom for her?"

70   "I don't have to look. My daughter's marriage will just happen."

71   Giri did not give much thought to this strange answer either. She merely remarked that the sagging roof needed to be propped up soon.

72   Perhaps too preoccupied with the thought of how to get the roof propped up, Giri decided to seek her father's help and also to see her parents for just a couple of days. Holding Maruni to her chest and Rajib and Pori by the hand, she took leave of Belarani, who cried and cried because she was not being taken along to visit her grandparents. Giri,

[13]A state near Bengal.
[14]Kali means dark complexion; literally, "black."

also crying, gave her eight annas to buy sweets to eat, telling her that she could go another time because both of them could not take off at the same time from their work at the babu's place, even if for only four days, including the two days in walking to and from there.

She had no idea that she was never to see Bela again. If she had, she   73
would not only have taken her along, but she would also have held her tied to her bosom, she would not have let her out of her sight for a minute. She was Giri's beloved firstborn, even though Giri had to put her to work at the babu household ever since she was only seven; that was the only way she could have her fed and clothed. Giri had no idea when she started for her parents' village, leaving Bela with a kiss on her forehead.

"A daughter born, To husband or death, She's already gone." That   74
must be why seeing the daughter makes the mother's heart sing! Her father had been very busy trying to sell his bamboo and acquiring two *bighas*[15] of land meanwhile. He was apologetic about not being able in all this time to bring her over for a visit, and he asked her to stay on a few more days once she had made the effort to come on her own. Her mother started making puffed rice and digging up the taro root she had been saving for just such a special occasion. While her hands worked making things for them to eat, she lamented about what the marriage had done to her daughter, how it had tarnished her bright complexion, ruined her abundant hair, and made her collarbones stick out. She kept asking her to stay a few more days, resting and eating to repair the years of damage. Giri's little brother begged her to stay for a month.

For a few days, after many years, Giri found rest and care and heap-   75
ing servings of food. Her father readily agreed to give her the bamboo, saying how much he wanted his daughter to live well, in a manner he could be proud of. Giri could easily have used a few tears and got some other things from her father. Her mother asked her to weep and get a maund[16] of rice too while he was in the giving mood. But Giri did not do that. Giri was not going to ask for anything from her loved ones unless she absolutely had to. She walked over to the corner of the yard, to look at the hibiscus she had planted when she was a child. She watched with admiration its crimson flowers and the clean mud-plastered yard and the new tiles on the roof. She also wondered if her son Rajib could stay there and go to the school her brother went to. But she mentioned nothing to her parents about this sudden idea that felt like a dream.

She just took her children to the pond, and, with the bar of soap she   76
had bought on the way, she scrubbed them and herself clean. She

---

[15]One *bigha* is roughly one-third of an acre. [Author's note.]
[16]Equal to approximately 85 pounds.

washed her hair too. Then she went to visit the neighbors. She was feeling lighthearted, as if she were in heaven, without the worries of her life. Her mother sent her brother to catch a fish from the canal, the new irrigation canal that had changed the face of the area since she last saw it. It helped to raise crops and catch fish throughout the year. Giri felt an unfamiliar wind of fulfillment and pleasure blowing in her mind. There was not the slightest hint of foreboding.

77   Bangshi Dhamali happened to be in the village that day, and he too remarked on how Giri's health and appearance had deteriorated since she went to live with that no-good husband of hers. He said that if only Aulchand were a responsible father and could look after the older kids, she could have gone to work in the house of the doctor who was now living in Bahrampur town, and after some time she could take all the children over there and have them all working for food and clothing.

78   Giri regarded his suggestion with a smile, and asked him instead, "Tell me, dad, how is it that when so many destitute people are getting little plots of land from the government, Rajib's father can't?"

79   "Has he ever come to see me about it? Ever sought my advice on anything? I'm in government service myself, and the right-hand man of the hospital doctor as well. I could easily have gotten him a plot of land."

80   "I'm going to send him to you as soon as I get back."

81   It felt like a pleasant dream to Giri, that they could have a piece of land of their own for a home of their own. She knew that her husband was a pathetic vagabond. Still, she felt a rush of compassion for him. A man without his own home, his own land. How could such a man help being diffident and demoralized?

82   "Are you sure, Bangshi-dada? Shall I send him to you then?"

83   "Look at your own father. See how well he's managed things. He's now almost a part of the Panchayat. I don't know what's the matter with uncle, though. He could have seen to it that Aulchand got a bit of the land being distributed. I once told him as much, and he insulted me in the marketplace, snapped at me that Aulchand should be learning to use his own initiative."

84   Giri decided to ignore the tendentious remark and keep on pressing Bangshi instead, "Please, Bangshi-dada, you tell me what to do. You know how impractical that man is. The room he's put up in all these years doesn't even have a good thatch roof. The moon shines into it all night and the sun all day. I'm hoping to get Bela married someday soon. Where am I going to seat the groom's party? And, dada, would you look for a good boy for my daughter?"

85   "There is a good boy available. Obviously, you don't know that. He's the son of my own cousin. Just started a grocery store of his own."

86   Giri was excited to learn that, and even Rajib's face lit up as he said that he could then go to work as a helper in his brother-in-law's shop

and could bring home salt and oil on credit. Giri scolded him for taking after his father, wanting to live on credit rather than by work.

Giri ended up staying six days with her parents instead of two. She 87 was about to take leave, wearing a sari without holes that her mother gave her, a bundle of rice on her head, and cheap new shirts and pants on her children. Just then, like the straw suddenly blown in, indicating the still unseen storm, Bangshi Dhamali came in a rush to see her father.

"I don't want to say if it is bad news or good news, uncle, but what 88 I just heard is incredible. Aulchand had told Bela that he was going to take her to see her grandparents. Then with the help of Mohan, he took her to Kandi town, and there he got the scared twelve-year-old, the timid girl who had known only her mother, married to some strange man from Bihar. There were five girls like Bela taken there to be married to five unknown blokes. The addresses they left are all false. This kind of business is on the rise. Aulchand got four hundred rupees in cash. The last thing he was seen doing was, back from drinking with Mohan, crying and slobbering, 'Bela! Bela!' while Kali-babu of the village Panchayat was shouting at him."

The sky seemed to come crashing down on Giribala's head. She 89 howled with pain and terror. Her father got some people together and went along with her, vowing to get the girl back, to break the hands of the girl's father, making him a cripple, and to finish Mohan for good.

They could not find Mohan. Just Aulchand. On seeing them, he kept 90 doing several things in quick succession. He vigorously twisted his own ears and nose to show repentance, he wept, perhaps with real grief, and from time to time he sat up straight, asserting that because Bela was his daughter it was nobody else's business how he got her married off.

They searched the surrounding villages as far as they could. Giri 91 took out the silver she had deposited with the mistress of the house and went to the master, crying and begging him to inform the police and get a paid announcement made over the radio about the lost girl. She also accused them, as mildly as she could in her state of mind, for letting the girl go with her father, knowing as they did the lout that he was.

The master of the house persuaded Giri's father not to seek police 92 help because that would only mean a lot of trouble and expense. The terrible thing had happened after all; Bela had become one more victim of this new business of procuring girls on the pretext of marriage. The police were not going to do much for this single case; they would most probably say that the father did it after all. Poor Bela had this written on her forehead!

Finally, that was the line everybody used to console Giri. The mas- 93 ter of the house in which she and Bela worked day and night, the neighbors gathered there, even Giri's father ended up saying that— about the writing on the forehead that nobody could change. If the daughter was to remain hers, that would have been nice, they said in consolation, but she was only a daughter, not a son. And they repeated the age-old saying: "A daughter born, To husband or death, She's already gone."

94   Her father sighed and said with philosophical resignation, "It's as if the girl sacrificed her life to provide her father with money for a house."

95   Giri, crazed with grief, still brought herself to respond in the implied context of trivial bickering, "Don't send him any bamboo, father. Let the demon do whatever he can on his own."

96   "It's useless going to the police in such matters," everybody said.

97   Giri sat silently with her eyes closed, leaning against the wall. Even in her bitter grief, the realization flashed through her mind that nobody was willing to worry about a girl child for very long. Perhaps she should not either. She too was a small girl once, and her father too gave her away to a subhuman husband without making sufficient inquiries.

98   Aulchand sensed that the temperature in the environment was dropping. He started talking defiantly and defending himself to her father by blaming Giri and answering her remark about him. "Don't overlook your daughter's fault. How promptly she brought out her silver chain to get her daughter back! If she had brought it out earlier, then there would have been a home for us and no need to sell my daughter. Besides, embarrassed as I am to tell you this, she had the operation to get cleaned out, saying, 'What good was it having more children when we can't feed the ones we've got?' Well, I've shown what good it can be, even if we got more daughters. So much money for a daughter!"

99   At this, Giri started hitting her own head against the wall so violently that she seemed to have suddenly gone insane with grief and anger. They had to grapple with her to restrain her from breaking her head.

100   Slowly the agitation died down. The babu's aunt gave Giri a choice nugget of her wisdom to comfort her. "A daughter, until she is married, is her father's property. It's useless for a mother to think she has any say."

101   Giri did not cry any more after that night.

102   Grimly, she took Pori to the babu's house, to stay there and work in place of Bela, and told her that she would kill her if she ever went anywhere with her father. In grim silence, she went through her days of work and even more work. When Aulchand tried to say anything to her, she did not answer; she just stared at him. It scared Aulchand. The only time she spoke to him was to ask, "Did you really do it only because you wanted to build your home?"

103   "Yes. Believe me."

104   "Ask Mohan to find out where they give the children they buy full meals to eat. Then go and sell the other three there. You can have a brick and concrete house. Mohan must know it."

105   "How can you say such a dreadful thing, you merciless woman? Asking me to sell the children. Is that why you got sterilized? And why didn't you take the bamboo that your father offered?"

Giri left the room and lay down in the porch to spend the night there. Aulchand whined and complained for a while. Soon he fell asleep.   106

Time did the ultimate, imperceptible talking! Slowly Giri seemed to accept it. Aulchand bought some panels of woven split-bamboo for the walls. The roof still remained covered with leaves. Rajib took the work of tending the babu's cattle. Maruni, the baby, grew into a child, playing by herself in the yard. The hardest thing for Giri now was to look at Pori because she looked so much like Bela, with Bela's smile, Bela's way of watching things with her head tilted to one side. The mistress of the house was full of similar praise for her work and her gentle manners.   107

Little Pori poured her heart into the work at the babu household, as if it were far more than a means to the meals her parents couldn't provide, as if it were her vocation, her escape. Perhaps the work was the disguise for her silent engagement in constant, troubling thoughts. Why else would she sweep all the rooms and corridors ten times a day, when nobody had asked her to? Why did she carry those jute sacks for paddy storage to the pond to wash them diligently? Why else would she spend endless hours coating the huge unpaved yard with a rag dipped in mud-dung paste until it looked absolutely smooth from end to end?   108

When Pori came home in the evening, worn out from the day's constant work, Giri, herself drained from daylong work, would feed her some puffed rice or chickpea flour that she might happen to have at home. Then she would go and spend most of the evening roaming alone through the huge garden of the babus, absently picking up dry twigs and leaves for the stove and listening to the rustle of leaves, the scurrying of squirrels in the dark. The night wind soothed her raging despair, as it blew her matted hair, uncombed for how long she did not remember.   109

The gentle face of her firstborn would then appear before her eyes, and she would hear the sound of her small voice, making some little plea on some little occasion. "Ma, let me stay home today and watch you make the puffed rice. If they send for me, you can tell them that Bela would do all the work tomorrow, but she can't go today. Would you, Ma, please?"   110

Even when grown up, with three younger ones after her, she loved to sleep nestled next to her mother. Once her foot was badly cut and bruised. The squat stool that the babu's aunt sat on for her oil massage had slipped and hit her foot. She bore the pain for days, until applying the warm oil from a lamp healed it. Whenever Giri had a fever, Bela somehow found some time in between her endless chores at the babu household to come to cook the rice and run back to work.   111

> Bela, Belarani, Beli—
> Her I won't abandon.
> Yet my daughter named Beli,
> To husband or death she's gone!

112   Where could she be now? How far from here? In which strange land? Giri roamed the nights through the trees, and she muttered absently, "Wherever you are, my daughter, stay alive! Don't be dead! If only I knew where you were, I'd go there somehow, even if I had to learn to fly like birds or insects. But I don't know where you were taken. I wrote you a letter, with the babu's help, to the address they left. You couldn't have got it, daughter, because it's a false address."

113   Absently Giri would come back with the twigs, cook the rice, feed Maruni, eat herself, and lie down with her children, leaving Aulchand's rice in the pot.

114   The days without work she stayed home, just sitting in the porch. The days she found work, she went far—by the bus that now plied along the road they had worked on a few years ago, the bus that now took only an hour and a half to reach Kandi town. There, daily-wage work was going on, digging feeder channels from the main canal. The babu's son was a labor contractor there. He also had the permit for running a bus. Giri took that bus to work.

115   There, one day she came across Bangshi Dhamali. He was sincere when he said that he had difficulty recognizing her. "You've ruined your health and appearance. Must be the grief for that daughter. But what good is grieving going to do after all?"

116   "Not just that. I'm now worried about Pori. She's almost ten."

117   "Really! She was born only the other day, the year the doctor built his house, and electricity came to Nishinda. Pori was born in that year."

118   "Yes! If only I had listened to what you said to me about going to work at the doctor's house and taken the children to town! My son now tends the babu's cattle. If I had gone then, they could all be in school now!"

119   "Don't know about your children being able to go to school. But I do know that the town is now flooded with jobs. You could put all your children to work at least for daily meals."

120   Giri was aware that her thinking of sending her children to school annoyed Bangshi. She yielded, "Anyway, Bangshi-dada. What good is it being able to read a few pages if they've to live on manual labor anyway? What I was really going to ask you is to look for a boy for my Pori."

121   "I'll tell Aulchand when I come to know of one."

122   "No. No. Make sure that you tell me."

123   "Why are you still so angry with him? He certainly made a mistake. Can't it be forgiven? Negotiating a daughter's wedding can't be done with the mother. It makes the groom's side think there's something wrong in the family. When it comes to your son's wedding, the bride's side would talk to you. It's different with the daughter."

124   "At least let me know about it all, before making a commitment."

125   "I'll see what I can do. I happen to know a rickshaw plier in Krishnachawk. Not very young, though. About twenty-five, I think."

"That's all right. After what happened to Bela, the groom's age is   126
not my main concern."

"Your girl will be able to live in Krishnachawk. But the boy has no   127
land, he lives by plying a rented rickshaw, which leaves him with
barely five rupees a day. Makes a little extra by rolling bidis[17] at night.
Doesn't have a home yet. He wants to get married because there's nobody to cook for him and look after him at the end of the day."

"You try for him. If it works out, I'd have her wedding this winter."   128

The total despondency in her mind since losing Bela suddenly   129
moved a little to let in a glimmer of hope for Pori. She went on hopefully, saying, "I'll give her everything I've got. After that, I'll have just
Maruni to worry about. But she's still a baby. I'll have time to think. Let
me tell you Bangshi-dada, and I'm saying this not because she's my
daughter, my Pori looks so lovely at ten. Perhaps the meals at the babu
house did it. Come dada, have some tea inside the shop."

Bangshi sipped the tea Giri bought him and informed her that her   130
father was doing very well for himself, adding to his land and his stores
of paddy, and remarked what a pity it was that he didn't help her much!

"It may not sound nice, sister. But the truth is that blood relation is   131
no longer the main thing these days. Uncle now mixes with his equals,
those who are getting ahead like himself, not with those gone to the
dogs, like your man, even if you happen to be his daughter."

Giri just sighed, and quietly paid for the tea with most of the few   132
coins tied in one end of the sari and tucked in her waist. Before taking
leave, she earnestly reminded Bangshi about her request for finding a
good husband for Pori.

Bangshi did remember. When he happened to see Aulchand shortly   133
after that, he mentioned the rickshaw plier. Aulchand perked up, saying
that he too was after a boy who plied a rickshaw, though his did it in
Bahrampur, a bit further away but a much bigger place than Krishnachawk. The boy had a fancy beard, mustache, and hair, and he talked
so smart and looked so impressive in some dead Englishman's pants
and jacket he had bought for himself at the second-hand market. Aulchand asked Bangshi not to bother himself anymore about the rickshaw
plier he had in mind.

Next time Giri saw Bangshi, she asked him if he had made contact   134
with the rickshaw plier in Krishnachawk. He said that he had talked
with Aulchand about it meanwhile and that she need not worry about it.

Aulchand then went looking for Mohan, his guide in worldly mat-   135
ters. And why not? There was not a place Mohan hadn't been to, all the
nearby small towns in West Bengal that Aulchand had only heard of: La-
lbagh, Dhulian, Jangipur, Jiaganj, Farakka. In fact, Aulchand didn't even

---

[17]Tobacco cigarettes rolled with leaves.

know that Mohan was now in a business flung much further, procuring girls for whorehouses in the big cities, where the newly rich businessmen and contractors went to satisfy their newfound appetite for the childlike, underdeveloped bodies of Bengali pubescent girls. Fed well for a few months, they bloomed so deliciously that they yielded back within a couple of years the price paid to procure them.

136   But it was very important to put up a show of marriage to procure them. It was no longer possible to get away with just paying some money for the girl. Any such straight procurer was now sure to get a mass beating from the Bengali villagers. Hence, the need for stories about a shortage of marriage-age girls in Bihar and now the need for something even more clever. The weddings now had to look real, with a priest and all that. Then there would have to be some talk about the rituals that must be performed at the groom's place according to their local customs to complete the marriage, and so with the family's permission they must get back right away.

137   The "grooms from Bihar looking for brides in Bengal" story had circulated long enough. Newer tactics became necessary. The local matchmakers, who got a cut in each deal, were no longer informed enough about what was going on, but they sensed that it held some kind of trouble for their occupation. They decided not to worry too much about exactly how the cheating was done. They just took the position that they were doing what the girl's parents asked them to do—to make contact with potential grooms. They played down their traditional role as the source of information about the groom's family and background.

138   The girls' families too decided to go ahead despite the nonperformance of their usual source of information. Their reason for not talking and investigating enough was that the high bride-price they were offered and the little dowry they were asked to pay might then be revealed, and, because there was no dearth of envious people, someone might undo the arrangement. In some cases, they thought that they had no choice but an out-of-state groom because even in their low-caste communities, in which bride-price was customary, the Bengali grooms wanted several thousands of rupees in watches, radios, bicycles, and so on.

139   Since the incident of Bela, Kali-babu of the Panchayat refused to hire Aulchand on the road project or any other construction under the Panchayat. Aulchand found himself a bit out of touch, but, with plenty of free time, he went away for a few days trying to locate Mohan.

140   Mohan, meanwhile, was doing exceedingly well considering that he never got past the fourth grade in school. He had set up another business like a net around the block development office of Nishinda, to catch the peasants who came there for subsidized fertilizers and loans, part of which they somehow managed to lose to Mohan before they could get back to their village. Mohan was an extremely busy man these days.

He firmly shook his head at Aulchand's request, saying, "Count   141
me out. Mohan Mandal has done enough of helping others. To help a
father get his daughter married is supposed to be a virtue. You got the
money. What did I get? The other side at least paid me forty rupees in
broker's fee. And you? You used your money all on bamboo wallpan-
els. Besides, I'm afraid of your wife."

"She's the one who wants a rickshaw plier in a nearby town."   142

"Really?"   143

"Yes. But listen. You stay out of the thing and just put me in touch   144
with a rickshaw plier boy in a big town like Bahrampur. My daughter
will be able to live there; we'll go there to visit them. I'd like nothing
better. Bela's mother too might be pleased with me."

"You want to make up with your wife this way, right?"   145

"I'd like to. The woman doesn't think of me as a human being. I   146
want to show her that I can get my daughter married well without anyone's help. Only you can supply me that invisible help."

Mohan laughed and said, "All right. But I'll not get involved. I'll   147
just make the contact, that's all. What if the big-town son-in-law has a
long list of demands?"

"I'll have to borrow."   148

"I see. Go home now. I'll see what I can do."   149

Mohan gave it some thought. He must be more careful this time.   150
He must keep the "groom from Bihar" setup hidden one step away and
have a rickshaw plier boy in front, the one who will do the marrying
and then pass her on. Aulchand's plea thus gave birth to a new idea in
Mohan's head, but first he had to find a rickshaw plier boy. Who could
play the part? He must go to town and check with some of his contacts.

Talking about Pori's marriage did reduce the distance between Gir-   151
ibala and Aulchand. Finally, one day Mohan informed Aulchand that
he had the right match. "How much does he want?" Aulchand asked.

"He's already got a watch and a radio. He plies a cycle-rickshaw, so   152
he wants no bicycle. Just the clothes for bride and groom, bed, shoes,
umbrella, stuff like that. Quite a bargain, really."

"How much will he pay in bride-price?"   153

"One hundred rupees."   154

"Does he have a home for my daughter to live in?"   155

"He has a rented room. But he owns the cycle-rickshaw."   156

Aulchand and Giri were happy. When the future groom came to   157
see the bride, Giri peeked from behind the door, studying him intently.
Big, well-built body, well-developed beard and mustache. He said that
his name was Manohar Dhamali. In Bahrampur, there was indeed a
rickshaw plier named Manohar Dhamali. But this man's real name was
Panu. He had just been acquitted from a robbery charge, due to insufficient evidence. Aulchand didn't know about this part. After getting out
of jail, Panu had just married a girl like Poribala in Jalangi, another in

Farakka, and delivered them to the "groom from Bihar" gang. He was commissioned to do five for five-hundred rupees. Not much for his efforts, he thought, but not bad with his options at the moment. Panu had plans to move further away, to Shiliguri, to try new pastures as soon as this batch was over and he had some money in hand.

158   At the time of Bela's marriage, no relative was there, not even Giribala. This time, Giri's parents came. Women blew conch shells and ululated happily to solemnize each ritual. Giri, her face shining with sweat and excited oil glands, cooked rice and meat curry for the guests. She brought her silver ornaments from the housemistress and put them on Pori, who was dressed in a new sari that Giri's mother had brought. Her father had brought a sackful of rice for the feast. The babu family contributed fifty rupees. The groom came by bus in the company of five others. Pori looked even more like Bela. She was so lovely in the glow on her skin left from the turmeric rub and in the red *alta*[18] edging her small feet.

159   Next day, with the groom she took the bus and left for the town.

160   That was the last time Giri saw Pori's face. The day after, Aulchand went to the town with Rajib and Giri's young brother to visit the newly married couple, as the custom required. The night advanced, but they did not return. Very, very late in the night, Giri heard the sound of footsteps of people coming in, but silently. Giri knew at once. She opened the door, and saw Bangshi Dhamali holding Rajib's hand. Rajib cried out, "Ma!" Giri knew the terrible thing had happened again. Silently she looked on them. Giri's brother told her. There wasn't much to tell. They did find a Manohar Dhamali in the town, but he was a middle-aged man. They asked the people around and were told that it must be another of Panu's acts. He was going around doing a lot of marrying. He seemed to be linked with some kind of gang.

161   Giri interrupted to ask Bangshi, "And Mohan is not behind this?"

162   "He's the mastermind behind this new play."

163   "And where's Rajib's father? Why isn't he with you?"

164   "He ran to catch Mohan when he heard that Mohan got five to seven hundred rupees from it. He left shouting incoherently, 'I want my daughter. I want my money.'"

165   Giri's little porch was again crowded with sympathetic, agitated people, some of them suggesting that they find Mohan and beat him up, others wanting to go to the police station, but all of them doing just a lot of talking. "Are we living in a lawless land?" Lots of words, lots of noise.

166   Close to dawn, Aulchand came home. Overwhelmed by the events, he had finally gone to get drunk and he was talking and bragging, "I found out where he got the money from. Mohan can't escape Aulchand-

[18]Colored design traditionally worn before a marriage.

sardar.[19] I twisted his neck until he coughed up my share of the money. Why shouldn't I get the money? The daughter is mine, and he'll be the one to take the money from putting her in a phony marriage? Where's Pori's mother? Foolish woman, you shouldn't have done that operation. The more daughters we have, the more money we can have. Now I'm going to have that home of ours done. Oh-ho-ho, my little Pori!"

Aulchand cried and wept and very soon he fell asleep on the porch. Giribala called up all her strength to quietly ask the crowd to go home. After they left, Giri sat by herself for a long time, trying to think what she should do now. She wanted to be dead. Should she jump into the canal? Last night, she heard some people talking, correctly perhaps, that the same fate may be waiting for Maruni too. 167

"Making business out of people's need to see their daughters married. Giri, this time you must take it to the police with the help of the babu. Don't let them get away with it. Go to the police, go to court." 168

Giri had looked on, placing her strikingly large eyes on their faces, then shaking her head. She would try nothing! Aulchand got his money at his daughter's expense. Let him try. Giri firmly shook her head. 169

Bangshi had remarked before leaving, "God must have willed that the walls come from one daughter and the roof from the other." 170

Giri had silently gazed at his face too with her striking eyes. 171

After some time, Aulchand was crying and doing the straw roof at the same time. The more tears he shed, the more dry-eyed Giri became. 172

The babu's elderly aunt tried to console her with her philosophy of clichés, "Not easy to be a daughter's mother. They say that a daughter born is already gone, either to husband or to death. That's what happened to you. Don't I know why you aren't crying? They say that one cries from a little loss, but turns into stone with too much loss. Start working again. One gets used to everything except hunger." 173

Giri silently gazed at her too, as she heard the familiar words coming out of her mouth. Then she requested her to go and tell the babu's wife that Giri wanted to withdraw her deposited money immediately. She went to collect the money. She put it in a knot in her sari and tucked the knot in her waist. 174

She came back and stood by the porch, looking at the home Aulchand was building. Nice room. The split-bamboo woven panels of the wall were neatly plastered with mud and were now being topped with a new straw roof. She had always dreamed of a room like this. Perhaps that was wanting too much. That was why Beli and Pori had to become prostitutes—yes, prostitutes. No matter what euphemism is used, nobody ever sets up home for a girl bought with money. 175

[19]Literally, "chief"; in the context, a form of self-praise.

176   Nice room. Giri thought she caught a flitting glimpse of Aulchand eyeing little Maruni while tying up the ends of the straw he had laid on the roof. Giri silently held those striking eyes of hers steadily on Aulchand's face for some time, longer than she had ever done before. And Aulchand thought that no matter how great her grief was, she must be impressed with the way their home was turning out after all.

177   The next morning brought the biggest surprise to all. Before sunrise, Giribala had left home, with Maruni on her hip and Rajib's hand held in hers. She had walked down to the big road and caught the early morning bus to the town. Later on, it also became known that at the Nishinda stop she had left a message for Pori's father with Bangshi Dhamali. The message was that Giri wanted Aulchand to live in his new room happily forever. But Giri was going away from his home to work in other people's homes in order to feed and raise her remaining children. And if he ever came to the town looking for her, she would put her neck on the rail line before a speeding train.

178   People were so amazed, even stunned by this that they were left speechless. What happened to Bela and Pori was happening to many others these days. But leaving one's husband was quite another matter. What kind of woman would leave her husband of many years just like that? Now, they all felt certain that the really bad one was not Aulchand, but Giribala. And arriving at this conclusion seemed to produce some kind of relief for their troubled minds.

179   And Giribala? Walking down the unfamiliar roads and holding Maruni on her hip and Rajib by the hand, Giribala only regretted that she had not done this before. If she had left earlier, then Beli would not have been lost, then Pori would not have been lost. If only she had had this courage earlier, her two daughters might have been saved.

180   As this thought grew insistent and hammered inside her brain, hot tears flooded her face and blurred her vision. But she did not stop even to wipe her tears. She just kept walking.

✧ Evaluating the Text

1. Under what circumstances did Aulchand marry Giribala? How does the reality of Giribala's married life contrast with the promises Aulchand made to her and her parents? In what respects has he deceived them?

2. How would you characterize the relationship between Aulchand and his right-hand man, Mohan? Who in your opinion is more to blame for what happens? Explains your reasons.

3. What circumstances lead Aulchand to sell their young daughter, Bela? How does Bela's fate echo that of her mother, Giribala?

4. What measures does Giribala take to prevent Pori, their other young daughter, from suffering the same fate as Bela? Why do her efforts come to nought?

✧ *Exploring Different Perspectives*

1. How do the forces related to caste, gender and culture contribute to shaping each society's concept of the family in Bengal and in Lebanon as depicted in Shirley Saad's story, "Amina"?

2. Compare the sets of circumstances that lead to arranged marriages in Devi's story and in Marjorie Shostak's account, "Memories of a !Kung Girlhood."

✧ *Extending Viewpoints through Writing*

1. What insights does the story provide into how the caste system and cultural traditions, such as the bride-price, function in the social context of Bengali culture?

2. To what extent is the effectiveness of Devi's story a result of the matter-of-fact, objective tone she employs in describing such shocking events? Devi is active in promoting social reform for women in Bengal and throughout India, and her works are written in part to bring about these reforms. How might "Giribala" have this effect?

Connecting Cultures

◆

Kim Chernin, "The Flesh and the Devil"

Discuss the cultural pressures on personal appearance as described by Kim Chernin and Slavenka Drakulíc in "On Bad Teeth" in Chapter 8.

Judith Ortiz Cofer, "The Myth of the Latin Woman"

Compare and contrast the male and female stereotyping of Hispanics in Cofer's narrative and Victor Villaseñor's account in "Rain of Gold" in Chapter 4.

Lennard J. Davis, "Visualizing the Disabled Body"

What differing attitudes toward disabilities emerge from Davis's analysis and Sucheng Chan's account (see "You're Short, Besides!" in Chapter 2)?

Paul Monette, "Borrowed Time: An AIDS Memoir"

Compare the perspectives on homosexuality in Monette's account and that of Luis Sepulveda's in "Daisy" in Chapter 6.

Marjorie Shostak, "Memories of a !Kung Girlhood"

Compare the cultural values and expectations that precede marriage among the !Kung with those described by Serena Nanda in "Arranging a Marriage in India" in Chapter 1. What role do families play in the negotiations for marriage in these two societies?

Shirley Saad, "Amina"

In what ways do children serve as scapegoats in the stories by Saad and Bessie Head (see "Looking for a Rain God" in Chapter 8)?

Kyoko Mori, "Polite Lies"

Compare the Japanese tradition of *omiai* as Mori describes it with Serena Nanda's analysis in "Arranging a Marriage in India" in Chapter 1 in terms of the function that the respective practices serve in each society.

Mahasweta Devi, "Giribala"

How have cultural prejudices against girls resulted in their economic exploitation and their being treated as second-class citizens in China (see Daniela Deane's "The Little Emperors" in Chapter 1) and in Bengal as depicted by Devi?

4

How Work Creates Identity

———————◆———————

The way we identify ourselves in terms of the work we do is far-reaching. Frequently, the first question we ask when we meet someone is "What do you do?" Through work we define ourselves and others; yet cultural values also play a part in influencing how we feel about the work we do.

In addition to providing a means to live, work has an important psychological meaning in all cultures. Some societies value work more than leisure; in other cultures, the reverse is true and work is viewed as something you do just to provide the necessities of life. In the United States, the work you perform is intertwined with a sense of identity and self-esteem.

Work in most societies involves the exchange of goods and services. In tribal cultures, as distinct from highly industrialized cultures, there is little job specialization, although age and gender determine the tasks that one performs. Economics may range from the barter system, in which goods are traded, to more complex market economies based on the reciprocal exchange of goods and services for money.

The attitude that people have toward the work they do varies within and among cultures. For example, think of the momentous change in attitude toward the work that women do in terms of equal opportunity and equal pay.

Lesley Hazleton, in "Confessions of a Fast Woman," describes the challenges and rewards of being an auto mechanic. The Thai writer Kon Krailet dramatizes the anguish of a young man in Bangkok who must conceal his profession from his family in the poignant story "In the Mirror." Victor Villaseñor, in "Rain of Gold," re-creates the moment when his father, a Mexican worker on his first day blasting rocks in a mine, had to prove himself. In Japan, Tomoyuki Iwashita, in "Why I Quit the Company," explains how the seeming security of lifetime employment does not offset sacrificing one's life for the corporation. From the United

States, a professional house cleaner, Louise Rafkin, in "A Yen for Cleaning," describes her unusual experiences in a cleaning commune in Japan. Jackie Chan, the actor known for his daredevil stunts, takes us behind the scenes on a Hong Kong film set in "A Dirty Job." Indian writer R. K. Narayan describes, in "Misguided 'Guide,'" the comedy of errors that resulted from trying to make a film from one of his novels. From Brazil, Machado de Assis spins a thought-provoking tale, "A Canary's Ideas," about the consequences when one's avocation becomes an obsession.

Lesley Hazleton

Confessions of a Fast Woman

———————◆———————

Lesley Hazleton was born in 1945 in Reading, England, received a B.A. in 1966 from Manchester University, and an M.A. in 1971 from the Hebrew University in Jerusalem. She immigrated to the United States in 1979. She has worked as a feature writer for the Jerusalem Post, 1968–1973, and as a reporter for Time–Life, Inc., Jerusalem, 1973–1976. She has been a distinguished writer in residence at Pacific Lutheran University, Tacoma, Washington, 1986, and has taught creative nonfiction writing at Pennsylvania State University, University Park, 1989. Her writings include Israeli Women *(1978),* Where Mountains Roar: A Personal Report from the Sinai and Negev Desert *(1980). Hazleton's dramatic reporting from the Middle East has been published in the award-winning* Jerusalem, Jerusalem *(1986). She has also written* England, Bloody England *(1989) and* Confessions of a Fast Woman *(1992). Since 1989, she has written the car column for* Lear's *magazine and has also written about cars and driving for* The New York Times, Connoisseur, Penthouse, *and* Newsday. *"Confessions of a Fast Woman," from her 1992 book of that name, tells how her lifelong passion for racing survived a stint working as an auto mechanic in upstate Vermont. Hazleton's sprightly comments on automotive matters can be found in the* Detroit Free Press.

1   I loved working at the sink. Harvey thought this was perverse of me. He was probably right. It was one of the dirtiest jobs in the shop.

2   The sink was a neatly self-enclosed system: a steel tub set atop a barrel containing parts cleaner, a small pump sucking the cleaner up from the barrel into a tube with a thick steel brush at the end, and a filter to clean the used fluid before it drained back into the barrel to be used again.

3   Working there, I'd stand with my back to everything else in the shop, concentrated entirely on the mass of gunked parts before me. The gunk was thick, black. The parts were so filthy they seemed almost anonymous, just so many interchangeable relics of the mechanical age. Even thinking of cleaning them at first seemed pointless.

4   But leave something to soak in that sink for a while, then come back to it and start scrubbing, and a kind of magic happened. What had been anonymous began to reveal form and personality. Vague shapes achieved particularity.

Black paled, gleamed here and there, turned slowly to silver. An 5
ancient alchemy took place right under my hands as I hosed and
scrubbed. Years of baked grease and oil and road dirt gave way to the
corrosiveness of the parts cleaner, and as I worked, it seemed that here,
under my very hands, I was rediscovering the original form, the bright
gleaming essence of each part. Old melted gaskets disappeared under
the brush. Flywheel teeth became sharp and effective. Clutch plates became intricate pieces of sculpture. I had a distinct sense of creating each
part anew, of restoring its form and function.

And all the time, of course, I was breathing in the fumes of the 6
parts cleaner, so that I am still not sure if the work itself was really that
satisfying, or if I was simply so high that it seemed that way.

All the cleaners began to smell good—a seductive, chemical smell 7
that seemed to enter my head, clear my sinuses, clean up all the syn-
apses of my brain. There was the 5-56, so much like dry-cleaning fluid
that I sometimes thought if I just stood in the path of its fumes, it would
clean the clothes right on me. Oddly, I'd always hated that smell before.
Then there was the Carb Clean, for gummed-up carbs; the Brakleen
brakes cleaner, each can with a thin red straw laid horizontally across
its black cap like the headgear of a Japanese geisha; and the Gunk—a
registered trademark name for heavy-duty engine cleaner.

I had no idea just how addictive the fumes were until a few weeks 8
into my apprenticeship, on our Monday off. I was driving past another
repair shop that was open on Mondays. The windows of my car were
wide open, and as I went by, I recognized the smells of parts cleaner,
gasoline, lubricants—all the acids and oils with which I now worked
five days a week. I slowed way down, breathed in deep, and was suf-
fused with an immense sense of well-being.

After a month, the shop and the smells and the work were in my 9
dreams. They were good dreams, but I'd wake with the fumes still in
my nostrils, wondering how smells from a dream could spill over into
the first moments of waking. Was the sense of smell independent of reality? Was my brain so addicted that it could create the smell by itself,
without any external stimulus?

No matter how seductive the fumes, however, there was no doubt 10
as to the corrosiveness of the parts cleaner: it turned my tanned hands
a whitish hue and made the skin parchment dry. I began to use rubber
gloves when working at the sink, but even then the chemicals seemed
to work their way through the rubber, and my hands still paled.

Meanwhile, the blackened asbestos dust from the brake pads was 11
just plain hazardous. It was caked onto the calipers and the whole of
the brake assembly. Cleaning it out demanded a screwdriver and a rag
and copious amounts of Brakleen. It was close-up work, so that however careful I was, I still inhaled the dust.

12   You take all the precautions you can in a repair shop. You keep as many doors and windows open as possible. You keep fans going. You back out cars and bikes to start them up, or if you have to start them inside, you attach a hose to the exhaust pipe and run the fumes outside. You could, of course, wear a mask, but few mechanics do. Most know they should, but the masks are hot and stuffy and they get in the way. And besides, the truth is that most mechanics do not worry about fumes. They have bigger things to worry about: a jack or a hoist giving way, a fire, a loose part spinning off. Auto mechanics is not a safe profession.

13   Despite all the protestations of writers and researchers that intellectual work is hard and exhausting, physical work is harder. Like anyone who's done it day in and day out, I now know this in my bones.

14   For years, I argued that intellectual work was exhausting, as indeed it can be. After a few hours at the typewriter, there is little I can do for a while. All my energy has been consumed, poured onto the page. Sometimes I do some physical work for a change—scythe an overgrown garden, for instance, or clean the oven. In such circumstances, physical work seems a pleasure and a relief, something that produces a healthy kind of exhaustion instead of the enervating overload of the mind that I am escaping.

15   This kind of short-term excursion into physical work can indeed make it seem attractive. But when you do it for a living, it exacts a heavy toll. The long-term effects of fumes and asbestos dust working their way into the body's cells are one thing, but the short term can be riskier still. With all due respect to the physical strain on hands, eyes, back, and brain from working at a keyboard all day, in physical work you can literally break your back.

16   I was lucky. I only sprained mine.

17   The culprit was a Datsun 240Z. It arrived on a truck with a note that read, "It went to Woodstock, and while there, the gears went." Just that, and a signature.

18   It hadn't been cruising the idyllic scenery of Woodstock. It had been drag racing. The owners had put a six-cylinder 260 engine into it, with triple carbs and a psi gauge. There'd been a big pop, it seemed, and then—nothing. No motion.

19   "We'll have to pull out the transmission and replace it," said Carl.

20   I was delighted. The heavier the work—the more it got down to the basics, into the actual drive mechanisms—the happier I was because the more I'd learn. Better still, if we had to replace the transmission, I could take the broken one apart. I already knew from the exploded diagrams in my textbook that there's nothing like taking things apart to understand how they work. Putting them back together again, I had still to discover, is yet another level of understanding.

The Z-car rode so low to the ground that we had to jack it up just to get the arms of the hydraulic lift underneath it. Harvey removed the bolt at the bottom of the transmission case so we could drain the transmission fluid—foul-smelling stuff—and found a small chunk of metal sitting on top of the bolt. "Bad sign," he said. "Something's come loose and ripped through the gears." 21

The next stage was to get the exhaust system off. That should have been simple enough, but there was so much gunk and rust that even after we'd loosened all the bolts, nothing moved. So Harvey stood up front and yanked, and I stood toward the back, pulling and yanking at the pipe above my head. 22

I felt something go inside me. Somewhere in my abdomen, it seemed. But I was focused on that exhaust pipe, eyes half-closed against flecks of grit and rust, and paid no attention. Harvey finally managed to loosen the front end, then we swapped places, me steadying as he pulled, and finally, lo and behold, the pipe slid off. We disconnected the fuel and oil lines, and then faced the really tough part. 23

When you're deeply involved in hard work, you simply don't notice pain. By the time we got the transmission case down from its mountings and into the yard, and then dismantled the clutch, it was late afternoon, and it was clear that this was going to be a long, drawn-out job. The drive plate and flywheel were so badly worn that they too would have to be replaced. 24

I went home that night exhausted. That was nothing unusual. Most evenings I'd flop down in an armchair with a beer in one hand, and find myself unable to move. It was the kind of deep exhaustion that comes only from hard physical work, the kind that you can feel in every muscle of your body, that seems to reach into your bones and sit there, making them feel both incredibly heavy and weightless at the same time. There is a strange kind of floating feeling to this exhaustion, yet at the same time you are convinced that you must weigh twice what you usually weigh. 25

If someone had shouted "Fire!" right then, I'd have nodded, said "Fine," and not moved an inch. 26

This stage of exhaustion would usually last a good half-hour or so, and in that half hour, I'd hold my hands up in front of my face and wonder where all those cuts and burns and scrapes had come from. From the repair shop, obviously, but what car, what movement, what moment? I never knew. Cuts and burns and scrapes and other minor injuries were just part of the job, so much so that I never noticed them at the time. Only later, in another place and time, in a comfortable armchair as the sun was setting, did they begin to seem remarkable. And then I'd feel an odd pride in them. They were proof of my work, small badges of my apprenticeship. 27

28   That Z-car had been a tougher job than most. We'd been working on it nearly the whole of the ten-hour day, and now, as I sat still, I realized my abdomen was really hurting, and that the pain was spreading to my back. A pulled muscle, I thought. We had three days off now for the Fourth of July weekend, and I was glad: my body needed it.

29   The next morning, I picked up a loaded wheelbarrow of split wood, turned it to the right, and could almost swear that I heard something go pop in my lower back, just like the gears of that Z-car. For the first time in my life, I understood what crippling pain was. By the time I got to a chiropractor in Barre, the only one around who'd see me on a holiday weekend, I couldn't walk without a crutch.

30   Half an hour later, I walked out carrying the crutch—still in pain, but mobile. The chiro, young and gentle, merely smiled tolerantly when I compared him to Christ.

31   "This back has forty-eight hours to heal," I told him.

32   "It will probably take four or five weeks," he said.

33   I shook my head. "It can't," I said. "I've got to go to work."

34   He studied my face. "Come on in tomorrow and the next day," he said, "and we'll see what we can do."

35   That included the Fourth of July itself. Rob Borowske became more and more Christ-like in my mind. Forty-eight hours of cold compresses, gentle stretching, electrical stimulation, aspirin, and chiropractic adjustments did not make for the happiest of weekends, but on the morning of July 5, I was there at Just Imports, a compress strapped to my lower back, cautiously mobile.

36   It wasn't macho that made me so determined. Partly it was the awareness that if I lay in bed and played invalid, my back would "freeze" and take far longer to heal. But more than that, it was the knowledge that Harvey and Bud would have to literally break their backs before they'd stay away from work. A mere "subluxation" simply did not rank. Not alongside what Harvey had been through.

37   The back healed quickly. Between Rob's four or five weeks and my forty-eight hours, it compromised on two weeks, although by the middle of the first week I was working as I had been. Being on my feet all day helped. Besides, I had to take apart that transmission case, discovering in the process that Harvey had been right: ball bearings had come loose and torn through the gears. No wonder nothing would move.

38   Harvey asked after the back a couple of times, but after that it was business as usual. Neither he nor Bud nor Carl thought it at all odd that I should turn up for work. Injuries were just part of the job. My back, the left foot I bruised badly when I moved a motorcycle the wrong way, the concussion I'd get of couple of weeks later when I'd stand up and hit my head on the strut of the hydraulic lift ("Every apprentice has to do it at least once," said Harvey)—these were just par for the course. As

one injury healed and another replaced it, I began to think of them as rites of passage: stages in my evolution as an apprentice.

✧ Evaluating the Text

1. Describe the tasks Hazleton confronted in her everyday work as an auto mechanic.

2. What explains her unwillingness to let her back injury incapacitate her?

3. In your opinion, what does being an apprentice in an auto repair shop mean to her? What satisfactions does she seem to be getting from it?

✧ Exploring Different Perspectives

1. Compare the satisfactions that Hazleton and Louise Rafkin (see "A Yen for Cleaning") derive from their unconventional attitudes toward the unusual work they do.

2. To what extent did Lesley Hazleton feel she had to prove herself to her peers in a way that is comparable to Jackie Chan's (see "A Dirty Job") experiences?

✧ Extending Viewpoints through Writing

1. Compare the demands of hard physical work with the stresses of hard intellectual work. Which did you find more exhausting and why?

2. Have you ever had a job where you performed work traditionally associated with the opposite gender? Did you find it to be a pleasant or unpleasant experience?

3. Have you ever had the experience of trying to get a job and thinking that your gender, ethnicity, or race was a factor in your prospective employer's decision whether to hire you?

Kon Krailet

In the Mirror

◆————————

Kon Krailet is the pen name of Pakon Phongwarapha, who was born to an immigrant Chinese family in Thailand in 1947. His first published story appeared when he was sixteen. He moved to Bangkok to pursue a literary career, worked as a proofreader, and then with his wife, the writer Khwan Phiangphuthai, published Youth *magazine. Four short story collections of Krailet's have been published in Thailand:* Fire of Life, Golden Flowers, Report from the Pung Clan, *and most recently,* We Are Not Flowers, We Are Life. *"In the Mirror," translated by Benedict R. O'G. Anderson and Ruchira Chinnapongse Mendiones, was first published in* Waves of the Chao Praya, *an anthology edited by Sujit Wong Thet (1978). This story depicts a poignant conflict generated by a clash between new urban and traditional cultural values.*

The kingdom of Thailand (formerly Siam) is a constitutional monarchy in Southeast Asia bordered by Burma to the west and northwest, Laos to the north and east, Cambodia to the southeast, and Malaysia and the Gulf of Siam to the south. Although there are large Chinese, Malay, Khmer, and Vietnamese minorities, Thais, who are ethnically related to the Shan of Burma and the Lao of Laos, constitute 75 percent of the population. Migrating to the area from China in the thirteenth century, the Thais established kingdoms at Sukhothai in 1238 and Ayutthaya in 1350. The arrival of Portuguese traders in the sixteenth century marked the beginning of Siam's relations with the West. During the Vietnam War Thailand strongly supported the United States and was the site of American air bases until 1976. The influx of tens of thousands of Vietnamese and Cambodian refugees in the 1970s and 1980s severely strained the Thai economy. The present king, Bhumibol Adulyadej, known as Rama IX, has ruled since 1946, has few executive responsibilities but is highly respected. The sex show industry described by Kon Krailet in his story "In the Mirror" reflects in part the role Thailand has played as a rest and recreation (R & R) stop for American G.I.s during the Vietnam War and Japanese businessmen since then. As a result Thailand has the highest rate of HIV infection in Southeast Asia.

1   Chiwin[1] sits quietly in a dark corner, waiting for his moment to come....

---

[1]The name Chiwin, hardly chosen at random, also means "life."

Tonight the place is packed, since it's the beginning of the month 2
and people still have enough cash to go out and enjoy themselves. Chiwin lights up a cigarette and inhales listlessly. It's very strange, but this
evening he feels lonely, moody, not himself. He's got a lot of complicated problems on his mind, among them a letter from his mother. *"Win,
my dear son, your father isn't very well. The rice planting season's already
here, but there's no one at home. How are things going for you in Bangkok?
Have you found a job yet or not? We haven't heard from you at all...."* Parts
of the letters Mother wrote usually went like this. In fact, of course, she
hadn't written them at all. She was illiterate, so she must have asked
someone in the neighborhood to write them for her.

Actually, it's only now that Chiwin takes cognizance of how long 3
it's been since he left home. Days turned into years before he was aware
of it. In this city, where he now lives, night and day are unlike night and
day anywhere else.... They rush by so rapidly that he doesn't have time
to think about things as they happen.... If he does think about them, it's
only cursorily, for a moment or so.... like a brief gust of wind which
merely rustles the leaves and then vanishes without a trace....

His mother's letter brings to his mind images of various people, 4
but heaped up on one another in such confusion that he feels dizzy and
disoriented. And Chiwin inhales cigarette smoke, puff after puff, one
after the other....

It's so dark in that corner that people can't see each other's faces. 5
The customers sitting at the tables loom up only as obscure silhouettes.
The waitresses move back and forth, some holding flashlights to guide
new arrivals in search of empty tables. On the tiny stage a naked girl is
dancing to the pounding rhythm of a song. Her name is Latda. She has
two children, plus a do-nothing husband drunk day in day out. So
she's had to come and work as a go-go girl, stripping her body for people to have a look. She'd told him all about it one day, not long after
they'd got to know each other.... The Tale of Latda...cracked in pieces
like the lives of all the women in this place, full of knots and problems.
If one had a good and happy life, who would ever want to bare every
inch of one's body for any Tom, Dick, or Harry to stare at? Chiwin reflects, like someone who thinks he understands pretty well how the
people working here tick.

The last strains of the song die away. Latda steps down from the 6
stage. There's some halfhearted clapping from a few of the customers,
none of whom know why they clap. Utter silence for a second, as
though the spectators sense that the moment they've been waiting for
has finally arrived. The lights on the stage turn pale pink. A slow, soft
melody...láa-laa-láa-laa-laa-laa-laa...strikes up.... Another girl, dressed
in black underwear, takes her turn on the stage. She makes her appearance slowly and silently.

7   And now they're playing Chiwin's musical cue. He stubs out his cigarette and pushes himself to his feet. He steps out of the dark corner into the pink glow, with the lithe movements of a young man of twenty-four. Some of the male spectators who remember him stare at him now, half in scorn, half wanting to do it themselves.

8   "You know, it's not easy at all," Chiwin had once told one of those who spoke to him in this tone. "It's only when you're on stage that you realize it's really no piece of cake."

9   No one has much of an idea about the music that's now being played, and it seems as if no one has the slightest interest in finding out. Most of the spectators simply know that when it's played it's time for the house's "special program" to begin. The words, accompanied by rhythmic sighs, most likely describe the mood of a young woman on a lonely night. The girl on the stage stretches out on her back and begins to writhe and quiver as though her flesh were burning with desire. Then she slowly removes the two little bits of clothing from her body.

10   Her name is Wanphen....

11   Chiwin has now stepped up onto the stage. The play of spotlight moves back and forth between purple, blue, and red. Wanphen's act is so well done that it makes some of the young men close by the stage almost forget to breathe. Chiwin slowly unbuttons his shirt, then shakes his head two or three times. His eyes are getting used to the lights, which keep changing color like a magic show.

12   A moment later and Chiwin has nothing left to himself but his bared body. It's a handsome, well-proportioned body, full of young flesh and blood. He throws his clothes in a heap in one corner. Everything takes place with the utmost slowness, as if in this piece of life time has ceased to exist. At this moment no one can think of anything else—even if the country should meanwhile collapse in ruins.

13   Chiwin stretches his body out alongside Wanphen and embraces her, while caressing her naked flesh with his hands. He kisses her once, and she kisses him in turn, then turns her face away and snuggles it into the hollow of his neck.

14   "How many times have I told you, Elder Brother Win!" he hears her whisper. "Please don't smoke before doing the show with me. It smells horrible. I can't stand the stink, and I lose the mood...."

15   "I'm sorry," he whispers back, as he rolls his body back and forth over hers. "Something's been bothering me. I've been in a bad mood, so I forgot...."

16   How many times now had he partnered this woman!... Chiwin thinks about the man with the unremarkable face who comes to wait for her every night when the bar closes. He can't imagine what the man's real feelings are. He comes to wait here in silence, and he goes home in silence. He must feel something. How could one man not understand another? But the two of us don't even know each other. And

we both suffer. At least the man had once stared at Chiwin with a strange, cold gleam in his eye.

"He's my husband," Wanphen had once explained, "a real hus-   17
band, you know; we're properly registered and all."

"How can he stand having you come here and do this kind of show   18
with me?" He couldn't put the gleam in the man's eye out of his mind.

"What can you do?" she'd answered seriously. "It's a job. It's a way   19
to make a living. If you live with a woman like me, you have to be able
to take it."

She's right. That's what it is, a job. O.K. At least it's a job for me too   20
right now. Chiwin has the feeling that he won't be able to perform well
tonight. He doesn't feel prepared at all. The young man rolls over and
down. Wanphen knows the signs very well, so she presses her body
tightly to him. Deploying all her skills, using everything she has, she
begins, with intense concentration, to arouse his desire. The play of the
lights halts for a moment at pink, bathing the bodies of the couple and
bringing out their beauty.

Chiwin stretches out full length and closes his eyes. The whole   21
world darkens before his vision. The air-conditioning makes the air cold
and moist, but he feels the sweat beginning to ooze from some of his
pores. His ears catch the soft music…when the song comes to an end, it
starts up again, in an endless, indolent cycle, making his thoughts drift
far away, to the past, to broad rice fields and to days and nights long
gone.

…By now the rains must have started back home…. Sometimes   22
one could see the gray-white rain pouring down, moving in over the
rice fields from the horizon, blurring everything in sight. The nights
would be chilly and damp, and filled with the loud croaking of big and
little frogs. And mornings, if the sun shone at all, its beams would be
soft and tender, soon to vanish as the thick rain clouds piled up once
more. In the rainy season, the earth would be turned over once again
with the plow. And it wouldn't be long before the rice plants came up
green, ripening later to a brilliant yellow throughout the paddies. But
this isn't his work anymore. He abandoned it a long time ago. It's hard
work, backbreakingly hard. Worse still, the harder you work, the poor-
er you get. He'd been so utterly, indescribably tired of that way of life
that he'd struggled to get a better education, and with every ounce of
will turned his face and headed toward Bangkok to find a new life….

…And my little brother Wang…. I wonder if he's out of the   23
monkhood yet? Mother doesn't mention him in her letter. He's been in
since last Lent.[2] Does he really want to study in the temple to become a

---

[2]The Buddhist "Lent," which runs from mid-July to mid-October, is a time designated for religious retreat and for the ordination of new monks.

Maha?[3] Doesn't he know these days there's no road to Nirvana any-more? And what about my little sister Wan? She must be buckling down to look after the kids she produces year in year out, giving her almost no breathing space for anything else. She got married to a boy from another subdistrict before she was even eighteen. Everyone's left the family home. Only Father and Mother still remain, and how much can they do on their own? And now Father's sick too....

24   Last night he'd had a terrible dream. It seemed that Father was in it somehow, but he couldn't arrange the images of the dream properly. All he knew was that it was so horrible that when he woke up his heart was pounding with fear. And then he remembered that it was a long time since he'd dreamed at all. Every night he fell into a deep sleep, as though his body'd been picked up and laid casually down on the bed, feeling nothing, till a new day dawned and the time came for him to get up once again. And when the next night fell, he'd be picked up and laid down once again in the same old place. Dreams are the travels of one's soul. It's no good if one lives without dreams. It shows that there's no soul left inside. So it's a good thing he dreamed last night, even if the dream was a nightmare....

25   Chiwin feels Wanphen's body arching up and pressing tightly to him almost all over. As she rains kisses over his chest and in the hollow of his neck, she whispers....

26   "What's the matter with you tonight...huh?"

27   "I told you, I'm really feeling down...." Chiwin embraces her in turn, mechanically. "I keep thinking about my father...."

28   "You crazy? This is no time to think about your father.... If you go on like this, how can we do the show? In no time at all, the crowd'll be booing us!"

29   Chiwin shakes his head once. Some sort of realization makes him push his body up from hers on outstretched arms. If only this night were over! The spectators are dead quiet, each pair of eyes glued to the stage. He puts everything out of his mind, draws Wanphen's body onto his, and begins to go through all the acts he usually performs on this stage.

30   Many of the people up front move closer and closer. Some of them even poke their faces in, right close up—as though this were the single most extraordinary thing in life, something they'd never seen from the day they were born. Some of the customers who have girls sitting with them begin to grope them obscenely. His gaze meets their eyes and in a flash he senses that in some things men may not understand other men at all. In their eyes glitter a thousand and one things—pleasure and de-

---

[3]Maha is a title awarded to any monk who has passed at least the lowest of the seven grades of the ecclesiastical examination system for the study of Pali texts.

KRAILET ◆ In the Mirror

sire. Some of the men pretend to be unaffected by the scene, though in fact their souls are seething through every vein.

"What have I become?" Chiwin asks himself. He feels like a male   31 animal in the rutting season, brutishly copulating with a female animal, right before the eyes of a group of studmasters. The more powerfully he performs, and the more varied the couplings, the more they're satisfied.

He glances down at Wanphen for a moment. He is now fully   32 astride her body. She is sighing and groaning, twisting and writhing her body as if she's being aroused to the limit, even though actually she experiences nothing from what she's doing. This is the first time that Chiwin understands her life clearly, and he feels a heartrending pity for her. He wants to ask her just one question: how much does she suffer from living this way? Having intercourse with a man she doesn't love in front of a crowd. Pretending to experience so much pleasure to arouse all these people…in exchange for no more than a hundred baht a night. Do her children back home know what's going on? Isn't there a night when she goes back home, lies down, and cries? After all, she still has feelings, doesn't she?

Chiwin lifts his head and stares once again at the audience, as if   33 searching for even one person with some understanding of the things that go on in the stories of the people working here. But he sees nothing but faces burning more hotly than ever with satisfaction and excitement. In fact, it looks like some of them have even reached a climax.

Chiwin begins to see the truth….   34

All of us here are simply victims…Latda…Wanphen…me…even   35 those people sitting there watching with such satisfied expressions. All of them feel the pressure of society outside. So they come here for emotional compensation, to build up a superiority complex. They come to eat and drink. They come to sit and watch others expose their genitals and perform every variety of sexual intercourse. This allows them to feel contempt for people they can then regard as lower than themselves. Man has a deep abiding instinct to shove his way up over his fellow men. The truth is that we're all animals of the city, who live lives of pain and suffering in the midst of a demented society. The only difference between us is that those who have greater advantages stand on top of those who have less, and so on down the line.

"Give it to her! All the way, kid…!" comes a roaring cheer from a   36 table to the left, mixed with delighted laughter from a group of friends. Wanphen clutches him still more tightly to her body. I wonder what she's thinking about now. Chiwin stares at her, but can't see her clearly. In her eyes there's an expression of entreaty. He grits his teeth, swallows his saliva down his dry throat, and gasps for breath. The sweat oozes from his forehead, back, and shoulders. A stinging drop trickles down into one eye, blurring his vision. Feeling a numb rage, Chiwin is almost at the point of jumping up and kicking out in the direction of those voices. But in fact he doesn't dare do anything, not even respond with words.

37   Wanphen's hands, still clasped around his back, give him a stealthy pinch. "Take it easy, Elder Brother Win." Her voice is barely audible. "Don't listen to those crazy people. I'm not a cow or a water buffalo, you know...."

38   So that's it! He's turned Wanphen herself into a victim of his own oppression. He comes to himself at the nip of her nails and the sound of her voice. Suddenly the tears well up in his eyes, mixed with drops of sweat. He pushes his body up, leaning on his outstretched arms, and stares Wanphen full in the eyes. When he bends over and gives her a kiss, she's surprised by a touch she's never felt from him before. Just then the song ends and the stage lights dim to darkness.

39   Chiwin goes into the bathroom, his shirt still unbuttoned. He turns on the tap, washes his hands, and scoops up some water to rub in the hollow of his neck. As he lifts his head, he encounters his own face reflected in the little mirror above the basin.

40   Indeed man encounters his real self when he stands before a mirror....

41   In the bare, empty bathroom the faint sound of music filters in. He leans on his hands, gripping the basin's edge, and stares at that face for a long time, in silent questioning.

42   He thinks back to his mother's letter. *"How are things going for you in Bangkok? Have you found a job yet?"* How can he possibly tell his mother about the kind of work that he has found? She would faint dead away. And he himself can't really say why he's struggled so hard to make a living this way. The easy answer is probably because he was hungry and had reached a dead end.

43   When he'd set off for Bangkok, carrying his teacher's certificate with him, who could have known that for months he'd be clutching at straws, trying to compete with tens of thousands, hundreds of thousands, of others, taking test after test? And then go home, waiting to learn the results of his applications, place after place, day after day. At first his hopes had still been bright and clear. But, as time passed, they'd faded, like a candle that melts itself completely away, dimming down to his last baht. Then a friend of his, who worked as a bartender in a go-go club, had invited him along to try this line of work.

44   "Don't worry...at first you feel a bit shy.... But you get used to it after a while.... A good-looking guy with a nice build like yours is just what these people are looking for. You get a hundred a night, two or three thousand a month. It's far better than being a teacher. You talk yourself blue in the face for nothing but a few pennies a month." His friend had patted him on the shoulder and said, "OK? Give it a go, to tide you over while you wait to hear about your job applications. You want to starve?

You don't have to worry about getting picked up. The police don't make any trouble, the people there have got connections high up."

Is this the true image of a man who's studied to become a teacher? 45
Chiwin stares at his reflection with a feeling of nausea. His hair's a mess, his eyes dry and lifeless, with a sad, evasive look. The skin on his face and lips is parched and wan with strain. Not a shred of dignity left, though he's still young and strong. How did a man with clear, firm hopes and goals end up as someone who doesn't have the courage to confront even his own face?

Suddenly he feels a terrible churning deep in his abdomen. It 46
surges up through his insides to his throat. Chiwin clings tightly to the washbasin, hiccups once, and then, before being conscious of it, doubles over, arches his neck, and vomits in a torrent. All the different foods he ate earlier in the evening, accumulated in his belly, spout out in streams, splattering the washbasin. Once, twice, three times. Sounds of retching follow quickly, one after the other. Each time, he spits out what he'd swallowed earlier, till he's gasping with exhaustion. Snot and tears join together in a dirty stream. Chiwin lifts one forearm to wipe his mouth, and smells the sour stink pervading everything.

The reflection in the mirror is now a murky blur, because of the 47
tears which well up and fill the sockets of his eyes. He feels so dizzy that he almost cannot stay on his feet. Chiwin swallows his viscous saliva and hiccups once again. This time what he vomits up is a thick, clear liquid. It spouts out so violently that it seems to carry with it his liver, kidneys, and intestines.

✧ Evaluating the Text

1. What can you infer about the differences in values between rural Thailand and main urban areas like Bangkok in terms of the kinds of work Chiwin would be performing at home as opposed to what he now does?

2. How would you characterize Chiwin? How do his feelings about his co-workers' lives help explain how he feels about what he does?

3. How do Wanphen's comments to Chiwin during the course of their performance emphasize the fact that it is a staged performance? How do their real feelings contrast with what they are doing on the stage?

✧ Exploring Different Perspectives

1. Compare the attitude toward work in Lesley Hazleton's "Confessions of a Fast Woman" with that of Krailet's main character.

2. How do both the account by R. K. Narayan in "Misguided 'Guide'" and Krailet's story deal with the creation of a theatrical illusion?

✧ Extending Viewpoints through Writing

1. What is the most unpleasant job you ever had to do to make money? Describe your experiences.

2. Did you ever have a job that appeared enviable to others that you knew was not what it appeared to be? Describe the job and why it looked appealing to others but was not to you.

Victor Villaseñor

Rain of Gold

◆

Victor Villaseñor was born in 1940 in the barrio of Carlsbad, California, to immigrant parents. He attended the University of San Diego and Santa Clara University. Villaseñor was a construction worker in California from 1965–1970 and has attained recognition as an authentic voice of the Chicano community. Although he flunked English in college (because of his fifth grade reading ability), later trips to Mexico and introduction to art, history, and works of literature by Homer, F. Scott Fitzgerald, and James Joyce crystallized his decision to become a writer. Completely self-taught, Villaseñor wrote for ten years, completing nine novels and sixty-five short stories, and he received more than 260 rejections before he sold his first book Macho! *in 1973. He since has written an acclaimed work of nonfiction,* Rain of Gold *(1992), from which the following excerpt is drawn, and its sequel,* Wild Steps of Heaven *(1995), which is a saga of the Villaseñor family.*

Mexico was inhabited as far back as 20,000 B.C. Before the arrival of the Spanish in the early sixteenth century, great Indian civilizations, such as the Aztecs and Mayas, flourished. A wave of Spanish explorers, including Hernán Cortés, arrived in the 1500s, overthrew the Aztec empire, and turned Mexico into a colony of Spain, until Mexico achieved its independence in 1821. Although recently Mexico's economy has been on the rebound, previous cycles of economic instability and the earthquake that devastated Mexico City (one of the largest cities in the world with a population of nearly 17 million) in 1985, have led many to cross the border into the United States in hope of finding work.

In 1988, Carlos Salinas de Gortari was elected president, promising to bring democratic reforms. Legislative elections in 1991 endorsed Gortari's efforts. Mexico, along with Canada and the United States, negotiated the North American Free Trade Agreement (NAFTA), which is intended to reduce tariffs and increase trade between these countries. A new government was formed in 1994 under the leadership of Ernesto Zedillo of the Institutional Revolutionary Party (PRI). Following the devaluation of the peso in December 1994, an emergency economic plan was introduced to reduce inflation and stimulate investment, and it appears to have been successful. In 1998, PRI candidates won a majority of regional governor's races, a sign of the democratization of the Mexican political process.

1   The weeks passed and Doña Margarita prayed to God, asking him to heal her son's wounds. God heard her prayers and the bandages came off. Juan could see in the broken bathroom mirror that he had a long, swollen scar, thick as a worm, across his chin and all the way to his left ear. Turning his head side to side, he discovered that if he lowered his chin and kept his head slightly turned to the left, the scar wasn't quite as noticeable.

2   He decided to grow a beard and keep it until the red ridge of swollen flesh went down. In some ways he'd been very lucky. It had been such a clean, razor-sharp knife, the wound would eventually disappear.

3   A couple of days later, Juan went to town to look for work. He was broke. The two bastards had stolen all of his money. He had to get some tortillas on the table before he went searching for those two sons-of-bitches to kill them.

4   In town, Juan found out that they were hiring at a local rock quarry, so he walked out to the quarry while the sun was still low. Getting there, Juan could see that there were at least fifty other Mexicans waiting to be hired ahead of him. The tall, lanky Anglo who was doing the hiring dropped the clipboard to his side. "Well, that's it for today," he said. "But you guys just all come on out tomorrow and maybe you'll get lucky."

5   Hearing the word, "lucky," Juan became suspicious. As a professional gambler, he never liked to leave anything to chance. He glanced around at his fellow countrymen, wondering what they were going to do about this. But he could see that they weren't going to do anything.

6   Juan took up ground. "Excuse me," he said. "But I'm new in town, so I'd like to know how you do your hiring. Should I give you my name for tomorrow, or do you only hire the same men every day?"

7   The tall Anglo smiled at him as if he'd said something ridiculous. "What's your name?" asked the Anglo.

8   "Juan Villa*señor*," said Juan, pronouncing the double "l's" of his name like a "y" and giving his name a dignified, natural sound.

9   "Well, Juan Vilee-senoreee," said the foreman, twisting his name into something ugly, "you just come on out here tomorrow if you want a job. That's all you gotta do. You ain't got to know no more. Catch my lingo, *amigo?*" And saying this, the man rocked back and forth on his feet and spit on the ground. Juan could see that the man was so mad that his jaw was twitching. But Juan said nothing. He simply lowered his eyes and turned to go. His heart was pounding. Why, this bastard had twisted his name into a piece of dog shit.

10   The other workmen moved aside, letting Juan pass by. Juan could feel the foreman's eyes burning into his back. But he already knew that he was never going to return. This bastard could take his job and stick it up his ass, as far as Juan was concerned.

11   But Juan had gone no more than a few yards when another Anglo came out of the office. "Doug!" he yelled at the man with the clipboard. "We need another powder man! Ask them if any of 'em has a license!"

"Hell, Jim, they ain't nothing but Mexicans," he said. 12

"Ask 'em," repeated the big, beefy man named Jim. 13

"¡*Oye*! ¡*Espérense*!" called Doug in perfectly good Spanish. "Do any 14
of you have a powder license?"

Juan had a license to handle dynamite from the Copper Queen in 15
Montana, but he glanced around to see if anyone had priority over him.
No one raised his hand.

"I got one," said Juan. 16

"Where'd you get your license?" asked Doug. 17

"From the Copper Queen Mining Company," said Juan. 18

"Oh, in Arizona," said Jim. 19

"No, from Montana," said Juan. 20

The two Anglos glanced at each other. They were a long way from 21
Montana.

"Let's see your license," said Doug. 22

Calmly, deliberately, Juan walked back to the two Anglos. They 23
both towered over him. But Juan's mammoth neck and thick shoulders
were wider than either of theirs.

He brought out his wallet and carefully took the paper out of his 24
billfold that said he was licensed to do dynamite work. He handed it to
Doug, who unfolded it, glanced it over, then handed it to Jim.

Reading it, Jim said, "Looks good to me," and he handed the paper 25
back to Doug. "Hire him."

"All right, Juan Villas*eñor*-eee," said Doug, pronouncing Juan's last 26
name with less of a mean twist this time, "you got a job for the day. But
just one little screw-up and you're out! Now go over to that shed and
ask for Kenny. Show him your license and he'll fix you up."

"Sure," said Juan, taking back his license and going across the 27
yard.

Everywhere were Mexicans bent over shovels and picks. It was a 28
huge rock quarry. They looked like ants crawling about the great slab
of rock that had been cut away from the mountain. Teams of horses and
mules were moving the loads of rock, and the Mexicans drove these
teams, too.

At the toolshed, Juan asked for Kenny. An old Anglo came up. He 29
was chewing tobacco. He was short and thick and his eyes sparkled
with humor. Juan liked him immediately. He didn't have that dried-
out, sour-mean look of Doug's. He handed him his license.

"So how long you been a powder man, eh?" asked Kenny, looking 30
over the license.

"Oh, three or four years," said Juan. 31

"All in Montana?" asked Kenny, walking over to the sledge ham- 32
mers and bars.

Juan froze, but only for a moment. He'd originally learned his 33
trade in prison at Turkey Flat, but he saw no reason for this man to
know that. So he lied. "Yes," he said, "all in Montana."

34   "I see," said Kenny, coming forward with a sledge and a fistful of bars. He looked into Juan's eyes, but Juan didn't shy away. "Well," said the old man, handing Juan the tools, "where or how a man learned his trade ain't my concern." He spat a long stream of brown juice. "What interests me is the result," he added.

35   Walking around the shed, they headed for the cliff of cut rock in the distance. Climbing halfway up the face of the cliff, Kenny showed Juan where he wanted him to drill his holes to set the charges. Juan set his tools down and slipped off his jacket. The other dynamite men were already hard at work, drilling their holes. They were all Anglos.

36   Juan glanced up at the sun and saw that it was already beginning to get hot. He slipped his shirt out of his pants so it would hang loose and the sweat could drip off him freely. He'd learned this trick from an old Greek when he'd worked in Montana. A big, loose shirt could work like an air conditioner. Once the sweat started coming fast, the garment would hold it and let the sun evaporate the sweat like a cooling unit.

37   Juan could feel the other powder men watching him. A couple of them had already stripped down to their waists and they were bare-chested to the sun. They were all huge, well-muscled men and towered over Juan. But Juan felt no need to hurry or show off. He'd worked with the best of them up in Montana before he'd gone to work for Duel. He knew his trade.

38   Spitting into the palms of his thick hands, Juan set his feet and picked up his short bar with his left hand and his sledge hammer with his right. He centered the point of the bar on the rock in front of him and he raised the sledge over his head, coming down real soft and easy on the head of the bar. He did this again and again, turning the bar each time with his left hand. He knew that Kenny and the other powder men were watching him, but he never let on. He just kept up a soft, steady, easy pace. He wasn't about to push the sledge. He would let the weight of the big hammer do the work for him all day long. Only a stupid, young fool pushed the iron. An experienced man let the iron do the work for him.

39   Kenny brought out his chew, cut off a piece, put it in his mouth and continued watching, but Juan still felt no nervousness. He'd worked at his trade for three months at Turkey Flat, and in Montana he'd done it for nearly three years, so he knew that he was good at his job. He wasn't one of these men who rushed in the morning to show off to the boss and then had nothing left to give in the afternoon. No, he could work all day long, from sunup until sundown, without ever slowing down. In fact, he was so steady and sure at his job that he'd won many a bet in Montana by placing a dime on the head of the bar and hitting it so smoothly that the dime wouldn't fall off, even after a hundred hits. An old Greek had also taught him this trick. Why, he could make the sledge and the bar sing, once he got going.

It was noon, and the sunlight was blinding hot on the great slab of   40
rock. Juan had gone past all the Anglo powder men except one. This
Anglo was huge. His name was Jack, and he wasn't just big, he was extremely well-muscled. But Juan wasn't impressed by this. He'd seen
many big, strong men collapse under the hot, noon sun. And Jack had
been one of the first to strip to the waist to show off his muscles, so he
was now sweating fast and Juan knew that he wouldn't be able to keep
up his pace all afternoon.

Juan decided to slow down and not push the man. He'd already   41
proven himself. All he had to do now was give an honest day's work.

Then the horn blew, and it was time to eat lunch. The powder men   42
all took their tools and put them in the shade so they wouldn't get too
hot to handle when they came back to work.

Jack, the big man, came walking up close to Juan. It looked like he   43
was going to say hello to him and shake his hand; but he didn't. He just
laughed and turned away, joking with the other powder men. Juan
didn't take offense, figuring that he was just having fun. He walked
alongside Jack, hoping that maybe he and the big man could quit the
competition that had started up between them and they could become
friends. After all, he'd become friends with many Greeks and Anglos in
Montana. But walking across the yard, the powder men acted as if Juan
didn't exist.

Then, when they got in line to wash up before they ate, and it was   44
Juan's turn to wash, the man in front of Juan didn't hand him the tin cup.
No, he dropped it, instead. At first, Juan thought it was an accident, but
then, when he bent over to pick up the cup, the man kicked it away.

Juan stood up and saw that all the powder men were sneering at   45
him, especially Jack, who was grinning ear-to-ear. Quickly, Juan lowered his eyes so none of them would see what he was thinking. And he
turned and walked away, tall and slow and with all the dignity he could
muster. These smart-ass *gringos* had just made up his mind for him. This
afternoon they were going to see a Greek-trained drilling machine.

He never once turned to glance back at them. No, he just kept go-   46
ing across the yard as slowly and proudly as he could. Getting to the
Mexicans under the shade of a tree, he was given a cup when it was his
turn to drink and wash up. But he had no lunch to eat, so he just sat
down to rest.

Oh, it was a good thing that he hadn't brought his gun to work, or   47
he would have been tempted to kill Jack and the seven other powder
men. No one ridiculed him. Not even in prison when he'd been a child
and they'd tried to rape him. He was his father's son when it came to
having a terrible temper. He was truly of the crazy Villaseñors. Why,
he'd once seen his father grab a mule's leg that had kicked him and
yank it up to bite it, dislocating the mule's hip. Then his father had
beaten the mule to death with his bare fists.

48   Juan was sitting there, seething with rage, when a thick-necked Mexican named Julio called him over.

49   "*Amigo*," he said, "come and eat with us."

50   Julio and several other Mexican men were sitting under a tree, heating their tacos on a shovel that they'd washed.

51   "No, *gracias*," said Juan, "you go ahead and eat…to your health, my blessings." And saying this, Juan moved his hand, palm up, welcoming the man to fulfill himself. It was a very Mexican gesture, one especially common in the mountainous area of Jalisco.

52   "So you're from Jalisco, eh?" said Julio, turning over the bean tacos with a stick on the shovel.

53   "Why, yes, how did you know?" asked Juan.

54   Julio laughed. "Oh, I'm just a visionary from Guanajuato," he said, "who's seen that gesture of the hand too many times not to know a *tapatío*." A *tapatío* was what the people from Jalisco were called.

55   "Come on, don't be so proud," said another Mexican named Rodolfo. "You got nothing to eat and you got to be strong for this afternoon." Rodolfo was tall and slender and had pockmarks all over his face, but he wasn't hard to look at. His eyes had a twinkle of mischief, and he had that confident air of a man who'd seen many battles. "We all saw that little movement of the cup across the yard. Those powder men, they're all *cabrones!*"[1]

56   "You saw it, eh?" said Juan, glancing across the yard to the powder men who were all sitting together and eating.

57   "Of course," said Rodolfo, "and we knew it was coming the moment we learned that one of our people had gotten a job so elevated."

58   "Go ahead," said Julio to Juan, taking the shovel off the little fire, "take a taco before this son-of-a-bitch schoolteacher from Monterrey eats all our lunches again." Saying this, Julio picked up one of the tacos with his fingertips from the hot shovel and tossed it to Juan, who reflexively caught it. "Eat, *hombre*," he said to Juan good-naturedly, "so you can fart like a burro and screw those *gringo* sons-of-bitches this afternoon!"

59   "Which leads us to a very important question," said Rodolfo, the tall schoolteacher from Monterrey, "just how'd you ever get up there, anyway?"

60   "I have a powder license," said Juan, starting to eat.

61   "Oh, and how did you manage that miracle?" asked Rodolfo. "Hell, we got men here who know how to drill and set dynamite with the best of them, but none of them has been able to get a license." He ate his taco in two huge bites, working his big, lean jaws like a wolf.

62   "In Montana," said Juan, eating in small, courteous bites to show that he wasn't starving—but he was. "The Greeks up there, they'd

---

[1]*Cabrones* is a derogatory term that slanders masculinity.

never seen a Mexican, and so they'd thought I was Chinese and they made me a driller, thinking all Chinese know powder."

The Mexicans burst out laughing. But Rodolfo laughed the hardest of all. 63

"So that's how it's done, eh?" said Rodolfo. "We *Mejicanos* got to be Chinese!" 64

"It worked for me," said Juan, laughing, too. 65

"I'll be damned," said the teacher, reaching for another taco. "Next you'll tell me that we'd be better off if we were Negroes, too." 66

"Shit, yes!" said Julio, who was very dark-skinned. "The blacker the better!" 67

They all laughed and ate together and Juan felt good to be back among his people. The jokes, the gestures, and the way they laughed with their heads thrown back and their mouths open, it was all so familiar. 68

Then the horn blew, and it was time to get back to work. The pock-faced man came close to Juan. "Be careful, my friend," he said. "That scar you wear may only be a small token compared to what awaits you this afternoon." 69

Juan nodded, having thought that no one could see his scar with his five-day-old beard. "*Gracias*," he said, "but I haven't gotten this far in life without being as wary as the chick with the coyote." 70

The tall man laughed, offering Juan his hand. "Rodolfo Rochin." 71

Juan took the schoolteacher's hand. "Juan Villase*ñor*," he said. 72

"He's right," said Julio, coming up. "They're going to try and kill you. Hell, if they don't, soon we'll have all their jobs." 73

Juan nodded. "I'll be careful," he said. 74

"Good," said the thick man. "Julio Sanchez." 75

"Juan Villase*ñor*," said Juan once again. 76

Then Juan turned and started across the open yard, and all the Mexicans watched after him. Not one of their people had ever worked up on the cliff before. 77

Picking up his tools, Juan walked by the powder men and climbed up the cliff. Jack came up and took his place alongside Juan, grinning at him. But Juan paid him no attention and went to work, iron singing at a good, steady pace. 78

Jack picked up his sledge and tore at the rock. He was still half a hole ahead of Juan and wanted to keep it like that. The big man pounded at the rock, arms pumping, iron pounding, and he tried to pull farther ahead of Juan. But Juan only smiled, glancing up at the hot sun, his ally. 79

The sun was going down, and it was the last hour of the day when Juan came up even with Jack. The other powder men stopped their work and watched. Jack grinned, still feeling confident, and began his new hole. He was huge and rippling with muscle, but Juan could see that he was all used up because he just didn't have the rhythm of the hammer down to a steady song. 80

81   Juan grinned back at Jack, spat into his hands, and began his new hole, too. But at a much slower pace. And the big man pulled ahead of him and the other powder men laughed, truly enjoying it. But Rodolfo and Julio and the other Mexicans down below knew what was coming. So they stopped their work and looked up at the two men pounding the iron up on the tall cliff.

82   The muscles were standing on the big man's back, and his forearms were corded up into huge ropes. But still, Juan kept going at a slow, steady, easy pace, fully realizing that the boiling white sun was on his side and the *gringo* wouldn't be able to keep up his reckless pace for long.

83   Kenny saw what was going on, and he started for the cliff to bring the senseless competition to a stop when Doug came up behind him.

84   "Don't, Shorty," he said to Kenny. "Let that little bastard kill himself, trying to keep up with Big Jack."

85   Kenny never even smiled. Juan was his own size, so he just spat out a stream of tobacco, already knowing who was going to win. "Whatever you say, Doug," he said.

86   And Kenny and Doug took up watch, too.

87   Jack was pounding on, tearing into his bar with his big sledge, but he could see that Juan was keeping up with him at a much slower rhythm. It seemed like magic. Juan was going so easy and, yet, his iron was still drilling into the stone at a good pace.

88   Jack began to tire but he was tough, so he just forced his body to go harder. His lungs screamed for air, his huge muscles began to cramp, but he'd die before he gave up and let a Mexican beat him.

89   But then here came Juan, coming in for the kill, and he now picked up the pace, too. Juan was catching up to Jack, closing fast, and then going past him with good, steady power when, suddenly, a bunch of bars came sliding down the face of the cliff from above them.

90   "Watch out!" yelled Kenny.

91   Juan just managed to leap out of the way before the bars struck him.

92   Kenny turned to Doug and saw that he was grinning ear-to-ear. "All right!" barked Kenny. "No more of this horseshit! Now all of you, get back to work! You got thirty minutes to quitting time, damn it!"

93   Turning in their tools that afternoon, Kenny took Juan aside. "*Amigo*," he said, "you and me, we're short, so we don't got to always go around being the big man. Jack, he's not so bad, believe me. I know him. It's just that a lot is expected of him." He cut a new chew with his pocket knife, offering Juan some, but Juan refused. "I like your work," he added, putting the new cut in his mouth, "you ease off *mañana* and I promise you that you got a job here as long as I'm powder foreman."

94   Juan looked into the old man's bright, blue eyes, blue like his own father's. "You got a deal," he said.

95   "Good," said Kenny, and he put his knife away and stuck out his hand and Juan took it.

This was the first time that Juan had ever met a man who had even 96
bigger, thicker hands than his own. Why, Kenny's hands were monstrous, just like his own father's.

That day, Juan Salvador was paid two dollars, twice as much as the 97
regular laborers. Walking back to town that afternoon with his people,
Juan was a hero. He was the Mexican who screwed the *cabrón gringo!*

✧ Evaluating the Text

1. How do the initial reactions to Juan's request for work reveal the racial
   prejudice against Mexicans that existed in his father's time?

2. How does the encounter between Juan and Jack dramatize the separa-
   tion of Anglos from Mexicans and the antagonism between them that
   was quite typical in the work gangs?

3. What means does Villaseñor use to structure the account in a sus-
   penseful way?

✧ Exploring Different Perspectives

1. How do the accounts by Villaseñor and Jackie Chan (see "A Dirty
   Job") involve proving oneself?

2. Discuss the respective struggle against the ongoing stereotypes based
   on sex or ethnicity in the accounts by Villaseñor and Lesley Hazelton
   (see "Confessions of a Fast Woman").

✧ Extending Viewpoints through Writing

1. Did you ever have to prove yourself against prevailing stereotypes?
   What were they? Describe what happened?

2. In several places in Villaseñor's account, he makes a point of com-
   menting on the more efficient way of working that his father had developed, which enabled him to outperform seemingly more powerful
   men. What techniques have you developed to make your work, including study habits, more efficient? Describe them and tell how you
   developed them.

Tomoyuki Iwashita

Why I Quit the Company

◆

Tomoyuki Iwashita signed on to work for a prominent Japanese corpora-
tion just after graduating from college. The life of the typical "salaryman"
did not appeal to him for reasons he explains in "Why I Quit the Compa-
ny," which originally appeared in The New Internationalist, *May 1992.*
He is currently a journalist based in Tokyo.

1   When I tell people that I quit working for the company after only a
year, most of them think I'm crazy. They can't understand why I would
want to give up a prestigious and secure job. But I think I'd have been
crazy to stay, and I'll try to explain why.

2   I started working for the company immediately after graduating
from university. It's a big, well-known trading company with about 6,000
employees all over the world. There's a lot of competition to get into this
and other similar companies, which promise young people a wealthy
and successful future. I was set on course to be a Japanese "yuppie."

3   I'd been used to living independently as a student, looking after
myself and organizing my own schedule. As soon as I started working
all that changed. I was given a room in the company dormitory, which
is like a fancy hotel, with a twenty-four-hour hot bath service and all
meals laid on. Most single company employees live in a dormitory like
this, and many married employees live in company apartments. The
dorm system is actually a great help because living in Tokyo costs more
than young people earn—but I found it stifling.

4   My life rapidly became reduced to a shuttle between the dorm and
the office. The working day is officially eight hours, but you can never
leave the office on time. I used to work from nine in the morning until
eight or nine at night, and often until midnight. Drinking with colleagues after work is part of the job; you can't say no. The company
building contained cafeterias, shops, a bank, a post office, a doctor's office, a barber's…. I never needed to leave the building. Working, drinking, sleeping, and standing on a horribly crowded commuter train for
an hour and a half each way: This was my life. I spent all my time with

*For information in Japan, see p. 79.

the same colleagues; when I wasn't involved in entertaining clients on the weekend, I was expected to play golf with my colleagues. I soon lost sight of the world outside the company.

This isolation is part of the brainwashing process. A personnel manager said: "We want excellent students who are active, clever, and tough. Three months is enough to train them to be devoted businessmen." I would hear my colleagues saying: "I'm not making any profit for the company, so I'm not contributing." Very few employees claim all the overtime pay due to them. Keeping an employee costs the company 50 million yen ($400,000) a year, or so the company claims. Many employees put the company's profits before their own mental and physical well-being.

Overtiredness and overwork leave you little energy to analyze or criticize your situation. There are shops full of "health drinks," cocktails of caffeine and other drugs, which will keep you going even when you're exhausted. *Karoshi* (death from overwork) is increasingly common and is always being discussed in the newspapers. I myself collapsed from working too hard. My boss told me: "You should control your health; it's your own fault if you get sick." There is no paid sick leave; I used up half of my fourteen days' annual leave because of sickness.

We had a labor union, but it seemed to have an odd relationship with the management. A couple of times a year I was told to go home at five o'clock. The union representatives were coming around to investigate working hours; everyone knew in advance. If it was "discovered" that we were all working overtime in excess of fifty hours a month our boss might have had some problem being promoted; and our prospects would have been affected. So we all pretended to work normal hours that day.

The company also controls its employees' private lives. Many company employees under thirty are single. They are expected to devote all their time to the company and become good workers; they don't have time to find a girlfriend. The company offers scholarships to the most promising young employees to enable them to study abroad for a year or two. But unmarried people who are on these courses are not allowed to get married until they have completed the course! Married employees who are sent to train abroad have to leave their families in Japan for the first year.

In fact, the quality of married life is often determined by the husband's work. Men who have just gotten married try to go home early for a while, but soon have to revert to the norm of late-night work. They have little time to spend with their wives and even on the weekend are expected to play golf with colleagues. Fathers cannot find time to communicate with their children and child rearing is largely left to mothers. Married men posted abroad will often leave their family behind in

Japan; they fear that their children will fall behind in the fiercely competitive Japanese education system.

Why do people put up with this? They believe this to be a normal   10
working life or just cannot see an alternative. Many think that such personal sacrifices are necessary to keep Japan economically successful. Perhaps, saddest of all, Japan's education and socialization processes do not equip people with the intellectual and spiritual resources to question and challenge the status quo. They stamp out even the desire for a different kind of life.

11   However, there are some signs that things are changing. Although many new employees in my company were quickly brainwashed, many others, like myself, complained about life in the company and seriously considered leaving. But most of them were already in fetters— of debt. Pleased with themselves for getting into the company and anticipating a life of executive luxury, these new employees throw their money around. Every night they are out drinking. They buy smart clothes and take a taxi back to the dormitory after the last train has gone. They start borrowing money from the bank and soon they have a debt growing like a snowball rolling down a slope. The banks demand no security for loans; it's enough to be working for a well-known company. Some borrow as much as a year's salary in the first few months. They can't leave the company while they have such debts to pay off.

12   I was one of the few people in my intake of employees who didn't get into debt. I left the company dormitory after three months to share an apartment with a friend. I left the company exactly one year after I entered it. It took me a while to find a new job, but I'm working as a journalist now. My life is still busy, but it's a lot better than it was, I'm lucky because nearly all big Japanese companies are like the one I worked for, and conditions in many small companies are even worse.

13   It's not easy to opt out of a life-style that is generally considered to be prestigious and desirable, but more and more young people in Japan are thinking about doing it. You have to give up a lot of superficially attractive material benefits in order to preserve the quality of your life and your sanity. I don't think I was crazy to leave the company. I think I would have gone crazy if I'd stayed.

✧ Evaluating the Text

1. What features of Iwashita's account address the crucial issue of his company's attempt to totally control the lives of employees?

2. What psychological effects led him to actually quit his secure job?

3. In what important respects do Japanese corporate employees differ from their American counterparts? In what ways are they similar?

✧ Exploring Different Perspectives

1. Compare the very different perspectives of Iwashita and Louise Rafkin (see "A Yen for Cleaning"). Describe any underlying cultural commonalities that you can find in these very different accounts of Japanese life.

2. How do the issues of brainwashing and exploitation occur in Iwashita's article and in Kon Krailet's story "In the Mirror"?

✧ Extending Viewpoints through Writing

1. Drawing on work experiences you have had, discuss any similarities and differences you found on the question of conformity and subservience to the company. Analyze the different motivations that drive Japanese and American workers.

2. If you were in Iwashita's situation, would you have made the same decision he did? Why or why not?

Louise Rafkin

A Yen for Cleaning

———————◆———————

*Louise Rafkin found the time while cleaning houses for a living to get a B.A.
in English from Lewis and Clark College in Oregon and a M.A. in Compar-
ative Literature from the University of California, Santa Cruz, in 1981. Her
work has appeared in numerous magazines and journals, including* The
New York Times Magazine, Whole Earth Review, *and* Poets and
Writers. *"A Yen for Cleaning," from* Other People's Dirt: A Housecleaner's Curious Adventures *(1998), recounts her unusual spiritual
quest to Japan, where she was a participant in a cleaning commune.*

> *Who is the foe for whom they attack*
> *With rag a brush and pail?*
> *'Tis, dust—but not seen dirt alone:*
> *The heart's dust they assail.*
>
> —Rokumangyogan, *"The Army of Peace"*

1   Some people vacation in Yellowstone, Aruba, or New Orleans.
Others go to Bali to lie on white beaches, or to the Himalayas to climb
steep mountains. I went to Japan to clean toilets.

2   I heard about a group of cleaning people in Japan through a friend,
who connected me with Sho Ishikawa. Sho, about forty, now lives in
Manhattan but had been raised in Japan as a member of a cleaning commune. His parents, who had spent most of their lives in the commune,
still live there, and his father is one of the present spiritual leaders.

3   "It is difficult to imagine cleaning for your whole life," Sho said in
the first of several phone conversations. "Growing up, I felt like there
was a dark cloud over my head." Sho always knew he would leave the
commune, and as soon as he finished school he took off for New York
to become a Buddhist monk. After a number of years he left the Zen
community, and he's now working in the world of public accounting.
Sho became the gatekeeper to my exotic experience. He tried to explain
the history of the group.

4   *Ittoen* ("One Light" or "One Lamp Garden") is rooted in the spiritual awakening, teachings, and life example of Tenko Nishida (1872–
1968). Followers worship Nishida's Oneness of Light philosophy while
embracing all spiritualities based in the desire for peace and grounded
in the ideal of humble service. (Both Buddha and Christ lived the life of
the homeless, I was reminded later, and both washed the feet of others.)

Sho sketched out the life of Tenko-san, as he is referred to by most. In the late 1800s, Tenko-san, a failing land developer, became dissatisfied by the corruption of capitalism. Unwilling to struggle against others for his own survival, he challenged the accepted assumption that one worked in order to live. Tenko-san's awakening occurred after three days of meditation and an insight about the deep, natural bonding between mothers and children. This relationship became the metaphor he used to explain the pure interdependence people could have, both with each other and with "the light," or God. Life was given freely to all and was not something that had to be worked for; work was therefore a way of offering thanksgiving for the gift of life.

Renouncing his family, status, and all possessions, Tenko-san began to serve others. He lived a simple life, scrubbing, mopping, chopping wood, and cleaning what were then rudimentary privies. In return, he was offered food and shelter, even money. Declining all but the bare necessities, giving service became the way he connected with others. For him, this was enlightenment.

Over the next ten years, Tenko-san attracted followers, and together they lived what he called the life of the "homeless." In 1928, some land outside of Kyoto was donated for the establishment of a community. In the fifties and sixties, the commune had hundreds of members; now, nearly thirty years after Tenko-san's death, only about 150 disciples remain.

I don't think Sho quite knew why I wanted to travel ten thousand miles to scrub toilets with a bunch of people I couldn't even communicate with, and I wasn't quite sure myself. Nevertheless, after a succession of phone calls to Japan, a weeklong visit was arranged that would culminate on the national Day of Labor, a day the entire community went cleaning. Sho's own English teacher, a woman close to seventy who had lived over forty years in the commune, would be my official host.

In preparation for this adventure, I attempted to learn a handful of the many Japanese words for *dirty*. In addition to the basic word for *dirty, kitanai,* the Japanese language offered a plethora of delightfully onomatopoeic names, each detailing the various kinds and ways things could be soiled. *Gicho-gicho,* dripping with grease, sounded much more disgusting than *gucho-gucho,* messed up or jumbled. My favorite, which I chanted one day while wiping sludge from behind a toilet, was *nuru-nuru,* "slimy." Hopeless at languages, out of my unwieldly mouth the word *shimikomu,* the specific term for ground-in grime, sounded like a whale at an amusement park.

Japan itself was astoundingly clean. Before my week with the cleaners, I spent some time in Tokyo, during which I became thoroughly convinced that I lived in the wrong country. Litter? No. Graffiti? No. Clean people. Clean cars, buses, and streets. Trains were not only spotless, on time, and pleasant smelling, they were carpeted and *upholstered*. (Imagine, if you can, a New York subway carpet after a day of commuters.) People with colds considerately donned face masks, and poop-scooping for pet dogs was fastidiously executed with tiny shovels and rakes.

11   But all this cleanliness seemed occasionally to lead to excess. The first time I entered a department store bathroom I was shocked to hear the sound of a flushing toilet as I sat down, *before* I went. I jumped, alarmed at the possibility of being doused from underneath, but there was no whirlpool below, only calm waters. I sat down again, warily, and the phantom flushing resumed.

12   The next toilet I sat upon sang like a babbling brook. The next, at the contemporary museum simulated the flow of running tap water. Finally, with difficulty and slightly obscene charades, I learned that many Japanese women were embarrassed by the sound of peeing, and had become accustomed to flushing on the way into the toilet in order to shroud evidence of their bodily functions. This doubled water usage, and officials, fearing shortages, joined engineers in developing the camouflaging toilets. Extreme, yes, but I would graciously accept the trade-off. Sweet-smelling taxis with soft, plush seats, lace doilies on the headrests, and complimentary Kleenex?

13   I could live with babbling toilets.

14   By the time I had made my way to the cleaning compound, I had begun to recognize Japan's contradictory nature. Sure, everything was squeaky-clean, yet you can buy dirty underpants, supposedly soiled by genuine schoolgirls, from streetside vending machines. And, though nobody seemed able or willing to speak English, English was absolutely everywhere, albeit oddly configured. "Let's Wedding" announced a bridal shop advertisement, while my brand of coffee was called Blendy. The powdered creamer? Creap. A popular beverage slung the off-putting slogan "Sweat drink!" and the cigarette billboards proclaimed "Today I Smoke." I bought a thermos so I could brew up my own Blendy and Creap (the four-dollar coffee was busting me). The thermos was named Twinkleheart and the tag promised "Fall in love with twinkleheart and she becomes charming happiness for awhile."

15   I hoped so. I was starting to feel lonely.

16   The day I was due at Ittoen, I was riddled with apprehension. I still knew little of where I was going or what I'd be doing. At a Kyoto marketplace, a fishmonger asked me where I was staying. I told him and he made gestures as if he were sweeping with a broom. I nodded. He bowed, low, then gathered up sellers from the neighboring stalls. A volley of Japanese nods ensued. Soon I was surrounded by a half-circle of bobbing bowers. One woman gave me a strange green Japanese pastry, and another forced upon me what seemed like a package of

dried fish fins. Bowing while shuffling backward, I tripped and nearly landed in a box of spiky sea urchins. The hoopla made me a little nervous. I wondered what kind of cult I was staying with.

I pondered how to spend the few short hours I had left before I needed to board the commuter train that would take me from Kyoto to Ittoen. Meditation at one of Kyoto's famous temples? Quiet contemplation over a cup of green tea?

Hardly. I had read all my books, and suddenly, the thought of a week without reading matter made me panic. Map in hand, I struggled to find a bookstore that sold used English titles. The one shop I found had slim pickings, which forced me to buy several volumes I'd be embarrassed to carry stateside. The most promising one was *Best American Sports Stories,* several years out of date.

I still had two full packs of sugar-free bubble gum I'd brought from home. Provisions intact, I was ready. At the last minute I bought a bag of M&M's at the train station's Let's Kiosk; chocolate might console me if things went badly.

Ittoen was tucked into the hills east of Kyoto; gorgeously kept grounds hugged a mishmash of buildings. A brand-new high-tech semi-high-rise sidled up next to a cluster of traditional Japanese bungalows with thatched roofs and curling corners. I entered the compound feeling renewed confidence. I was quite relieved to find that the place actually existed.

Outside the office, which resembled a typical bank office—faxes, copiers, computers, and phones—I met Sho's teacher, Ayako Isayama, a slight, short-haired woman, in a black karate like *gi.* She politely invited me to follow her to my room, taking off at such a clip that in order to keep up I was forced into a gallop. If I hadn't known her age, I'd have guessed about half. Who said that cleaning aged a person quickly? Even her hands were youthful.

The grounds we passed through were impeccably groomed; maples and mossy rolling hills, a small brook snaking through the center of the many buildings. Several older women, similarly dressed, swept leaves with traditional bamboo brooms and exchanged words with Ayako as we made our way up a forest path. I was introduced as Sho's friend, though I hadn't even met him yet. Nevertheless, I nodded and said, "Good!" each time I was asked, "Sho, good?"

I was taken aback by the largeness of the whole place. From Sho's description, I had imagined a small group of dedicated toilet cleaners living in spartan quarters, buckets and sponges always at hand. Instead, I found a highly organized group that ran what was essentially a small town with its own complicated economy. I would soon learn that the commune supported itself by operating various businesses, including a school for every age group (available to those on "the outside" as well to members), a printing press, an agricultural program, a theater and performance group, as well as a "theme park" located in a southern province. The park, dedicated to the theme of peace, featured replicas of Easter Island statuettes and a huge "Peace Bell," which, according to Ayako, resonated with a beautifully calming tone.

24   The group also facilitated training sessions for young factory workers and business people, and as we approached the building in which I was to stay, we encountered a single-file line of *gi*-clad men and women who looked, as they jogged past, to be in their early twenties. Though it was late afternoon and the fall air was crisp and chilling, they wore their flip-flops barefooted, without *tabi*, the split-toed Japanese socks.

25   "Mr. Donut workers," Ayako explained, "returned from *gyogan*, humble toilet cleaning."

26   I loved Mr. Donut. Not only was it the only place in Japan that offered free refills on coffee, but the employees would greet each customer with a bow and a phrase something like: "I am your servant. How may I humbly serve you?" Even in the overly polite, ever-gracious world of Japanese commerce (where I had the best Big Mac I've ever had served to me *at my table* by the nicest, cleanest, most pleasant McDonald's worker I have ever met), an average Mr. Donut employee stood head-and-shoulders above the others. I had once passed a Mr. Donut shop just before it opened and saw the whole group of workers, heads bowed, chanting what seemed to be a prayer of thankfulness.

27   "Four days' training. Humble toilet cleaning, door-to-door service," Ayako explained.

28   More inquiry revealed that four thousand Mr. Donut workers spent time at Ittoen each year; the training was aimed to promote humility and facilitate group dynamics. For toilet cleaning they were assigned specific houses in nearby towns. And they would seek out a variety of other tasks—washing clothes, babysitting, weeding—wherever they were needed, undertaking such service in the tradition of *takuhatsu*, "road-side service," like the "begging-bowl rounds" practiced by Zen monks, who still visit households to recite religious chants. In the afternoons they worked at Ittoen, gathering wood, clearing fields, and tending the gardens. The last day was spent reflecting on their training.

29   I marveled as the group passed. It's a stretch for me to imagine a group of American workers, say from Dunkin' Donuts or Burger King, jogging door-to-door, heads bowed, begging to clean toilets.

30   The building in which I was to stay was old, one of the original ones donated in the thirties by a "Friend of Light," one of the many people who lived elsewhere in Japan and supported the group financially and materially. I settled into my room, a sparse square covered in *tatami* mats and centered with a *kotatsu*—a table with a heater attached underneath. The *kotatsu* was the only furniture in the room, as well as the sole source of heat. By now, late afternoon, the room was already frigid. Ay-

ako switched on the table and demonstrated how to sit tucked under its overhanging blankets. Over the next week I spent many hours squeezing as much of myself as far under the table as possible, bending and twisting like a yogi so that more of me might glean a little warmth.

That night Ayako made dinner in the quiet, dark kitchen in our   31
huge and, except for us, empty dormitory. We chatted in simple English. Ayako's skills were more than adequate; however, our cultural differences made the conversation stilted. I asked if I might be able to clean with the Mr. Donut trainees.

Ayako, considering my request, looked away from me. "Difficult,   32
with no Japanese," she shorthanded. "May not be possible."

She rose and began to wash the dishes. I noticed how dirty the   33
kitchen was, the walls spotted with oil and grease, not at all how I had imagined it would be.

"Saturday," she said. "You clean Saturday, with the group."   34

It was Monday.   35

"Morning service at five-thirty," she announced and disappeared   36
behind the sliding door to her room. That first night I set the *kotatsu* over my futon, although it was surely a fire risk. At least my toes wouldn't freeze.

If somewhere there is a record for speed-changing shoes, Ayako   37
must hold it. As at every Japanese house, each time we entered our building, we left our street shoes at the front door and put on what were essentially bedroom slippers. Slippers came off before entering tatami rooms, where socks were the appropriate footwear. Hundreds of these changes happened every day, and Ayako made each as smoothly as if she were an Olympian passing a baton. I stumbled and fumbled, often catching myself with a socked toe on the foyer—a definite no-no. (But because my feet were so often aired, I was pleased to have packed many pairs of clean, fresh-smelling socks.)

At dawn's light I followed Ayako down the dusky corridor of our   38
ancient building, where after my first shoe mishap of the day (still sleepy, I nearly toppled over while making the change), she sped off toward the Spirit Hall. I loped to catch up.

Inside the bare wood hall, both Buddhist and Christian images   39
flanked the altar. At center position was a round window overlooking a view of the forest. Ittoen elders and Mr. Donut people lined up on both sides of the room, settled in *seiza* (kneeling, heels under buttocks) on *tatami* platforms, men on one side and women on the other. I took a seat behind Ayako. Everyone looked more comfortable than me. My ankles and joints started to ache after only a few minutes. With some relief, I noticed, several of the Mr. Donut youngsters began to fidget after a while, though the women in front of me, a few who had to have

been over eighty, looked like they could sit folded up origami-wise for hours.

40   Orchestrated by the current leader—Tenko-san's grandson, a tall, pleasant-looking man of about fifty—the service was both calming and invigorating. We began with a song recounting Ittoen history, and then chanted a semiobscure Buddhist *sutra,* the gist of which is nonattachment to worldly goods. Morning stretches were performed to the accompaniment of a resounding *"ooomm,"* which grew even louder with each repetition.

41   After the service I raced behind Ayako back to our place, where she offered me a choice of toilet brush or broom. I chose the brush and was handed a bucket and rag. Both the squat toilet and the two standard toilets were fairly clean, but I did the job well, as I had the notion that I would be judged as a person on the quality of my cleaning. By the end of the week I realized this was stupid, but that first day I practically took the finish off the porcelain and wiped every inch of the wooden stalls and floors.

42   Ayako set off to mop the entire building and was, of course, finished before me. Experience and a lifetime of cleaning, I told myself consolingly.

43   Breakfast—miso soup, rice, warmed bits of various vegetables, dried indistinguishable fruit, and green tea—seemed at first frighteningly unrelated to my usual fare (coffee and toast), but the warm food in the unheated building actually tasted good. Emulating Ayako, who cites the hundreds starving in Rwanda as one reason she never wastes even a morsel of food, I ate everything on my plate. I marveled at the tastiness of the rice, finding the speckled gruel unusually savory. Upon inspection, however, I discovered tiny fish heads, half the size of a grain of rice. I swallowed deliberately, eyes and all. That week I put many things in my mouth I wished I hadn't. Only by the third day did I find myself seriously daydreaming about pizza.

44   After breakfast I was free till morning teatime.

45   "What should I clean?" I asked, as I finished drying the breakfast dishes.

46   Ayako seemed puzzled by my request and gave me a book about Ittoen, in English, before retreating into her room to tackle stacks of correspondence and translations.

47   I set upon the kitchen, tackling the counters and scouring the walls with a wire brush and Look!, a Japanese cleanser (which for some reason is pronounced *Rooku*), until I thought they might crumble. Apparently some foreign boarders had recently lived in the building, Ayako reported, and they cooked with gallons of oil and were not into cleaning. Four hours later I had only finished half the area.

48   "Very nice, much better now," Ayako said, pouring us glasses of thin, sweet yogurt. "Funny American who likes to clean!"

✧ Evaluating the Text

1. What prompted Rafkin to go to Japan to join a cleaning commune? As far as you can infer, why did this particular path to spiritual enlightenment appeal to her?

2. When Rafkin arrived, what did she discover about the Japanese cultural attitudes toward cleaning and the idea of cleanliness, in general, and at the commune in Ittoen, specifically?

3. In Rafkin's view, why would it have been highly unlikely for her to imagine an equivalent group of American workers "from Dunkin' Donuts or Burger King, jogging door-to-door, heads bowed, begging to clean toilets"?

✧ Exploring Different Perspectives

1. Compare Rafkin's experiences with Lesley Hazleton's (see "Confessions of a Fast Woman") in terms of the personal fulfillment that each derived from what for most people would be onerous tasks.

2. How is the idea of fitting into the commune of cleaners for Rafkin as important for her, in its own way, as it is for Jackie Chan (see "A Dirty Job") to earn the respect of his fellow stuntmen?

✧ Extending Viewpoints through Writing

1. Have you ever derived personal satisfaction from a task that others found either socially unacceptable or distasteful? What was it? Describe your experiences.

2. Rafkin's experiences at the Japanese McDonald's and Dunkin' Donuts were very unusual. In fact, her appreciation of the value the Japanese attach to cleanliness was reconfirmed. What comparable or contrasting experiences have you had, if any, with the American counterparts of these franchises?

Jackie Chan

A Dirty Job

◆

*Jackie Chan (whose given name is Chan Kong Sang) was born in Hong
Kong in 1954. At the age of seven, he was sold by his parents to the Beijing
Opera School in Hong Kong, where he learned kung fu and singing and
was a teen-age member of the famous troup called* The Seven Little Fortunes. *Chan started in movies at seventeen as a stuntman (as he describes
in the following account from his book* I Am Jackie Chan: My Life in Action, *1998) and developed his own unique style, incorporating physical
comedy with dangerous stunts and nonstop action. He has directed and
starred in numerous films, which feature his trademark comic emphasis and
life-endangering stunts, which he always performs without doubles.*

*Hong Kong is a former British crown colony that was restored, in
1997, to Chinese sovereignty. It is situated at the mouth of China's Pearl
River on the southern coast of Guangdong Province. Hong Kong's population of 6.3 million (of whom 98 percent are Chinese) is one of the most
densely populated regions in the world. Its magnificent natural harbor
(Victoria Harbor) was the reason it was first acquired by Britain, and it
has become one of the most successful manufacturing and export centers
in the world. It is an open question whether Hong Kong's laissez faire
economy and society will be allowed to continue to develop without Chinese interference. Yet, for China, Hong Kong remains a vital source of foreign exchange and a key commercial link with the West. It is one of the
greatest trading, shopping, and banking centers in the Far East. Only
about one-seventh of the land is arable and food and water must be imported, much of it from China.*

1   In my short career in the movies, I'd already met a lot of famous actors and directors. I was never very impressed; they were pretty, or
handsome, or (in the case of the directors) loud and domineering. But
none of them could do what I could do: fight, and fly, and fall, and get
up and do it again—even if I was broken or hurt. I couldn't really understand what made them so great.

2   But the senior stuntmen were something else. They were a wild
and rugged bunch, living one minute at a time because they knew that
every day they spent in their profession could be their last. They
smoked, drank, and gambled, spending every penny of each evening's
pay by the time the sun rose the next day. Words didn't mean anything

to them; if you wanted to make a statement, you did it with your body—jumping higher, tumbling faster, falling farther. With Oh Chang out of my life, I began to hang out with the senior guys after shooting wrapped. Every night, we'd brush off the dust of the day's work and find ways of laughing at the injuries that we or our brothers had suffered—"we get paid in scars and bruises," one older stuntman told me, only half joking. Of course, every small injury was just a reminder that the next one around the corner could be the big one that might cripple or kill; and so we drank, and we smoked, and we played, partly to celebrate surviving one more day, partly to forget that when the sun rose again we'd be facing the same giant risks for the same small rewards.

The senior stuntmen had a phrase that described their philosophy,   3
as well as the men who were fearless and crazy enough to follow it: *lung fu mo shi*. It literally meant "dragon tiger"—power on top of power, strength on top of strength, bravery on top of bravery. If you were *lung fu mo shi* you laughed at life, before swallowing it whole. One way of being *lung fu mo shi* was to do an amazing stunt, earning shouts and applause from the sidelines. An even better way was to try an amazing stunt, fail, and get up smiling, ready to try it again. *"Wah! Lung fu mo shi!"* they'd shout, and you'd know that your drinks would be paid for all night.

For us, especially us junior guys, to be *lung fu mo shi* was the highest   4
compliment we could imagine. And so I threw myself into my work, putting every last bit of energy into proving that I had the spirit of dragons and tigers—impressing stunt coordinators with my willingness to do anything, no matter how boring or how crazy. I'd get to the studio early, and leave with the very last group. I'd volunteer to test difficult stunts for free, to prove that they could be done—and sometimes they could, sometimes they couldn't. I never let anyone see me scream or cry, waiting until I got back home to release all of my pent-up pain. My neighbors would pound on the walls in annoyance as I howled in my apartment alone early in the morning; they never bothered me in person, because they probably thought I was a dangerous lunatic.

One day, we were working on a scene in which the hero of the film   5
was to tumble over a balcony railing backward, spin in midair, and land on his feet, alert and ready to fight. The actor playing the hero was, of course, sitting in the shade, flirting with one of the supporting actresses and drinking tea. It was our job to take the fall.

Most falls of this type were done with the assistance of a thin steel   6
wire, attached to a cloth harness that went underneath the stuntman's clothing. The wire would be run through a pulley tied to a solid anchor—in this case, the railing of the balcony—then fastened to a stout rope, which two or three stuntmen not in the scene would hold on to, their feet planted firmly. This would prevent disaster in case the

fall went wrong, allowing them to yank on the wire and stop an out-of-control plummet to the ground.

7   Today, we were working with a director whom we stuntmen universally considered an idiot. He was a no-talent hack—which didn't make him any worse than a lot of the directors working at the time; the problem was that he was a no-talent hack with pretensions toward art.

8   We'd learned pretty quickly that that was a combination that could get stuntmen killed.

9   "No wires," shouted the director, his puffy, bearded face turning red. The stunt coordinator, a lean, hollow-cheeked man in his mid-forties, crossed his arms in quiet defiance. My fellow juniors and I thought the coordinator was just about the coolest guy in the world, partly because he never treated us like kids, and partly because he'd stood up time and time again to directors with unrealistic expectations. The night after one epic argument, he treated us to drinks all night at our usual bar.

10   "Even if I wanted to direct, they would never let me, because I have made too many enemies," he confided to us. "But I will give you a word of advice, in case any of you should find yourself in the big chair. If you want the respect of your stunt people, and that is the only way you will make good movies, never ask them to do a stunt that you can't or won't do yourself. If you learn nothing else from me, remember this rule." And then he shouted, *"Kam pai,"* which means, "Empty cup," and so of course, we did.

11   I still follow that rule today.

12   I know that some people call me a crazy director, saying I demand the impossible—but I know they're wrong, because every risk I ask my stuntmen to take is one that I've taken before. Somehow, it didn't kill me, and so they understand that—with the luck that stuntmen depend on to survive—it won't kill them.

13   The director we were working with that day was so fat he could barely walk, much less do stunts. He had no idea how dangerous a fifteen-foot fall could be, even for a trained professional.

14   "Do you realize that one of my men could be killed doing this stunt?" asked our coordinator, showing remarkable restraint

15   "That's what they're paid for," retorted the director. "If you use wires in this scene, the fall will look like a puppet dropping to the ground. Unacceptable!"

16   The director even refused to lay out a padded mat or a stack of cardboard boxes to cushion the fall, wanting to shoot the scene from a wide angle in a single cut.

17   "Ridiculous," said our coordinator. "You want this stunt done that way, you do it yourself. None of my men will volunteer to take that kind of risk."

18   Throughout this dialogue, I was considering the setup for the stunt. The main problem with the fall was that it took place backward.

You couldn't see where you would land, or figure out how far you were, from the ground. But it was all a matter of timing—counting out the moments in your head before twisting your body to avoid a messy impact.

I could do this stunt, I decided. I could, and I would.   19

"Excuse me," I blurted. "I'd like to try the fall."   20

The stunt coordinator looked at me with a stony expression, then   21
pulled me aside.

"Are you trying to make me look foolish?" he said angrily.   22

"No," I said, sticking out my chin. "You're right. The director is an   23
idiot. You don't want to risk any of your experienced people on this
stunt, because you need them. But I'm nobody, and if I don't do something like this, I'll always be nobody. If I fail, then the director knows
you were right. If I succeed, I'll say that it was because you told me exactly what to do—and he'll know better than to challenge you again."

The stunt coordinator looked at me with narrowed eyes. "Yuen   24
Lo," he said, "you're a clever boy. Don't make the mistake of trying to
be too clever for your own good."

Then he turned back to the director and threw up his hands. "All   25
right," he said. "There's actually someone stupid enough to try this
stunt your way. I've just done my best to tell him how to do it without
killing himself. Maybe if he's lucky, he'll just be crippled for life."

And then he walked up to the director until his face was just inches   26
away, close enough to feel the heat of his breath. "And you," he said,
his voice flat and dangerous. "You cross me up again, and all of us walk
off this set. I don't give a damn about your reputation, your big ideas,
or your ego. We risk our lives because we are stuntmen, and that is
what we do. Not because you piss in our direction."

The director turned purple, and then pale. Not a single stuntman   27
moved or made a noise. Finally, he nodded, and waved his flabby hand
at the cameraman.

I felt the coordinator's touch on my shoulder. "Good luck," he said.   28
"Keep your body loose, be ready to roll as soon as you hit the ground.
And whatever you do, don't land on your head or back. I don't mind
taking you to the hospital, but I don't want to take you to the cemetery."

And then I was pulling on my costume, while a makeup girl   29
dabbed rouge on my cheeks and streaks of fake blood across my brow.
I climbed the stairs to the balcony and looked down at the crowd below. Every eye was on me, and the camera was ready to roll. But at that
moment, the only eyes I cared about were the eyes of my fellow stuntmen, watching me do something foolish and fantastic.

Lung fu mo shi, I thought. It was time to prove myself. The actor   30
playing the villain who would knock me over the railing joined me,
staring at me and shaking his head in disbelief. I shrugged and smiled
at him, then raised my hand to show I was ready.

31   "Action!" shouted the director.

32   "Rolling!" answered the cameraman.

33   And then, as the fake kick from the villain nearly brushed my nose, I vaulted backward over the railing, counted quickly in my head and arched my back, twisting my body smoothly through the air. I saw a flash of ground as my head came up and I got my legs underneath me, just in time to catch the ground with my feel I stumbled a bit, giving a small stutter step as I pulled myself upright

34   *Success!* The director cut the camera and actually pulled himself up and out of his chair. The stunt coordinator trotted over to where I was standing, as my brothers shouted my name. He slapped me on the back, grinning broadly. "You'll be a stuntman yet," he said.

35   Maybe it was cocky, but cocky was what being a stuntman was all about. "I almost lost my footing on the landing," I said. "Let me try it again—I'll get it perfect this time."

36   He laughed, squeezing my arms until they ached. "Try it again?" he bellowed. "Did you hear that, men? Once is not enough for the boy. *Lung fu mo shi!*"

37   And my stunt brothers echoed the phrase: *"Lung fu mo shi!"*

38   That night, the stuntmen gave me a new nickname: Double Boy. "Once ain't enough for Double! Better try again!" they laughed.

39   "He wants to work twice as hard, he has to drink twice as much, right?" said the stunt coordinator. "One more round, Double. *Kam pai!*"

40   That night, for the first time since I left the school, and the first time since I'd lost Oh Chang, I felt like I'd found a place where I belonged. I was with family.

41   I was home.

✧ Evaluating the Text

1. What kind of career had Jackie Chan had in the movies before the incident described in this account? Why was it important for him to distinguish himself before his fellow stuntmen?

2. What criticism does Chan make about the prevailing class system that determines who is valued among the cast and crew?

3. Why was the stunt he performed so dangerous and what does it show about him that he was ready to do it again?

✧ Exploring Different Perspectives

1. Discuss how Chan's account and R. K. Narayan's narrative (see "Misguided 'Guide'") give you a behind the scenes glimpse of filmmaking

in Hong Kong and in Bombay. In what sense are the effects that are so popular with audiences really carefully constructed illusions?

2. In what way is earning the respect of his fellow stuntmen both similar to and different from Juan's in Victor Villaseñor's "Rain of Gold"? In what sense is one personal and the other cultural?

✧ Extending Viewpoints through Writing

1. How did Chan's account alter your perspective on kung-fu acrobatics, which have become so much a part of action films?

2. What is the riskiest "stunt" you have ever performed? How much forethought and preparation went into it? What happened? Would you do it again? Why or why not?

R. K. Narayan

Misguided "Guide"

◆

*R. K. Narayan was born in 1906 in Madras, in southern India, and edu-
cated there and at Maharaja's College in Mysore. His first novel,* Swami
and Friends *(1935), and its successor,* The Bachelor of Arts *(1937), are
set in the fictional village of Malgudi, which Narayan created as a microcosm for all of life in India. His other "Malgudi" novels include* A Tiger for
Malgudi *(1983) and* Talkative Man *(1986). His novel* The Guide *(1958)
received the National Prize of the Indian Literary Academy, his country's
highest literary honor, and was adapted for the stage and produced as an off-
Broadway show in New York City in 1968. He has also published numerous
collections of short stories and two travel books, as well as collections of essays and a volume of memoirs. "Misguided 'Guide'" is drawn from* A
Writer's Nightmare: Selected Essays *(1958–1988).*

1   The letter came by airmail from Los Angeles. "I am a producer and
actor from Bombay," it read. "I don't know if my name is familiar to you."

2   He was too modest. Millions of young men copied his screen image, walking as he did, slinging a folded coat over the shoulder carelessly, buffing up a lock of hair over the right temple, and assuming
that the total effect would make the girls sigh with hopeless longing.
My young nephews at home were thrilled at the sight of the handwriting of Dev Anand.

3   The Letter went on to say, "I was in London and came across your
novel *The Guide*. I am anxious to make it into a film. I can promise you
that I will keep to the spirit and quality of your writing. My plans are to
make both a Hindi and an English film of this story." He explained how
he had arranged with an American film producer for collaboration. He
also described how he had flown from London to New York in search
of me, since someone had told him I lived there, and then across the
whole continent before he could discover my address. He was ready to
come to Mysore if I should indicate the slightest willingness to consider
his proposal.

4   I cabled him an invitation, already catching the fever of hurry characteristic of the film world. He flew from Los Angeles to Bombay to Bangalore, and motored down a hundred miles without losing a moment.

*For more information on India, see p. 34.

A small crowd of autograph-hunters had gathered at the gate of   5
my house in Yadava Giri. He expertly eluded the inquisitive crowd,
and we were soon closeted in the dining room, breakfasting on *idli, dosai,* and other South Indian delicacies, my nephews attending on the
star in a state of elation. The talk was all about *The Guide* and its cine-
matic merits. Within an hour we had become so friendly that he could
ask without embarrassment, "What price will you demand for your
story?" The checkbook was out and the pen poised over it. I had the
impression that if I had suggested that the entire face of the check be
covered with closely knit figures, he would have obliged me. But I
hemmed and hawed, suggested a slight advance, and told him to go
ahead. I was sure that if the picture turned out to be a success he would
share with me the glory and the profits. "Oh, certainly," he affirmed, "if
the picture, by God's grace, turns out to be a success, we will be on top
of the world, and the sky will be the limit!"

The following months were filled with a sense of importance: Long   6
Distance Calls, Urgent Telegrams, Express Letters, sudden arrivals and
departures by plane and car. I received constant summonses to be
present here or there. "PLEASE COME TO DELHI. SUIT RESERVED
AT IMPERIALL HOTEL. URGENTLY NEED YOUR PRESENCE."

Locking away my novel-in-progress, I fly to Delhi. There is the   7
press conference, with introductions, speeches and overflowing con-
viviality. The American director explains the unique nature of their
present effort: for the first time in the history of Indian movie-making,
they are going to bring out a hundred-percent-Indian story, with a hundred-percent-Indian cast, and a hundred-percent-Indian setting, for an
international audience. And mark this: actually in colour-and-wide-
screen-first-time-in-the-history-of-this-country.

A distinguished group of Americans, headed by the Nobel Prize   8
winner Pearl Buck, would produce the film. Again and again I heard
the phrase: "Sky is the limit," and the repeated assurances: "We will
make the picture just as Narayan has written it, with his co-operation at
every stage." Reporters pressed me for a statement. It was impossible
to say anything but the pleasantest things in such an atmosphere of
overwhelming optimism and good fellowship.

Soon we were assembled in Mysore. They wanted to see the exact   9
spots which had inspired me to write *The Guide*. Could I show them the
locations? A photographer, and some others whose business with us I
never quite understood, were in the party. We started out in two cars.
The American director, Tad Danielewski, explained that he would direct
the English version first. He kept discussing with me the finer points of
my novel. "I guess your hero is a man of impulsive plans? Self-made,
given to daydreaming?" he would ask, and add, before I could muster
an answer, "Am I not right?" Of course he had to be right. Once or twice
when I attempted to mitigate his impressions, he brushed aside my

comments and went on with his own explanation as to what I must have had in mind when I created such-and-such a character.

10   I began to realize that monologue is the privilege of the film maker, and that it was futile to try butting in with my own observations. But for some obscure reason, they seemed to need my presence, though not my voice. I must be seen and not heard.

11   We drove about 300 miles that day, during the course of which I showed them the river steps and a little shrine overshadowed by a banyan on the banks of Kaveri, which was the actual spot around which I wrote *The Guide*. As I had recalled, nothing more needed to be done than put the actors there and start the camera. They uttered little cries of joy at finding a "set" so readily available. In the summer, when the river dried up, they could shoot the drought scenes with equal ease. Then I took them to the tiny town of Nanjangud, with its little streets, its shops selling sweets and toys and ribbons, and a pilgrim crowd bathing in the holy waters of the Kabini, which flowed through the town. The crowd was colourful and lively around the temple, and in a few weeks it would increase a hundredfold when people from the surrounding villages arrived to participate in the annual festival—the sort of crowd described in the last pages of my novel. If the film makers made a note of the date and sent down a cameraman at that time, they could secure the last scene of my novel in an authentic manner and absolutely free of cost.

12   The producer at once passed an order to his assistant to arrange for an outdoor unit to arrive here at the right time. Then we all posed at the portals of the ancient temple, with arms encircling each other's necks and smiling. This was but the first of innumerable similar scenes in which I found myself posing with the starry folk, crushed in the friendliest embrace.

13   From Nanjangud we drove up mountains and the forests and photographed our radiant smiles against every possible background. It was a fatiguing business on the whole, but the American director claimed that it was nothing to what he was used to. He generally went 5,000 miles in search of locations, exposing hundreds of rolls of film on the way.

14   After inspecting jungles, mountains, village streets, hamlets and huts, we reached the base of Gopalaswami Hill in the afternoon, and drove up the five-mile mud track; the cars had to be pushed up the steep hill after encroaching vegetation had been cleared from the path. This was a part of the forest country where at any bend of the road one could anticipate a tiger or a herd of elephants; but, luckily for us, they were out of view today.

15   At the summit I showed them the original of the "Peak House" in my novel, a bungalow built 50 years ago, with glassed in verandas affording a view of wildlife at night, and a 2,000-foot drop to a valley

beyond. A hundred yards off, a foot-track wound through the under-
growth, leading on to an ancient temple whose walls were crumbling
and whose immense timber doors moved on rusty hinges with a groan.
Once again I felt that here everything was ready-made for the film.
They could shoot in the bright sunlight, and for the indoor scenes they
assured me that it would be a simple matter to haul up a generator and
lights.

Sitting under a banyan tree and consuming sandwiches and lem-   16
onade, we discussed and settled the practical aspects of the expedition:
where to locate the base camp and where the advance units consisting
of engineers, mechanics, and truck drivers, in charge of the generator
and lights. All through the journey back the talk involved schedules
and arrangements for shooting the scenes in this part of the country. I
was impressed with the ease they displayed in accepting such mighty
logistical tasks. Film executives, it seemed to me, could solve man-
kind's problems on a global scale with the casual confidence of demi-
gods, if only they could take time off their illusory pursuits and notice
the serious aspects of existence.

Then came total silence, for many weeks. Finally I discovered that   17
they were busy searching for their locations in Northern India.

This was a shock. I had never visualized my story in that part of In-   18
dia, where costumes, human types and details of daily life are different.
They had settled upon Jaipur and Udaipur in Rajaputana, a thousand
miles away from my location for the story.

Our next meeting was in Bombay, and I wasted no time in speaking   19
of this problem. "My story takes place in south India, in Malgudi, an
imaginary town known to thousands of my readers all over the world,"
I explained. "It is South India in costume, tone and contents. Although
the whole country is one, there are diversities, and one has to be faithful
in delineating them. You have to stick to my geography and sociology.
Although it is a world of fiction there are certain inner veracities."

One of them replied: "We feel it a privilege to be doing your story."   20
This sounded irrelevant as an answer to my statement.

We were sitting under a gaudy umbrella beside a blue swimming   21
pool on Juhu Beach, where the American party was housed in princely
suites in a modern hotel. It was hard to believe that we were in India.
Most of our discussions took place somewhat amphibiously, on the
edge of the swimming pool, in which the director spent a great deal of
his time.

This particular discussion was interrupted as a bulky European   22
tourist in swimming briefs fell off the diving plank, hit the bottom and
had to be hauled out and rendered first aid. After the atmosphere had
cleared, I resumed my speech. They listened with a mixture of respect
and condescension, evidently willing to make allowances for an author's whims.

23   "Please remember," one of them tried to explain, "that we are shooting, for the first time in India, in wide screen and Eastman Colour, and we must shoot where there is spectacle. Hence Jaipur."

24   "In that case," I had to ask, "Why all that strenuous motoring near my home? Why my story at all, if what you need is a picturesque spectacle?"

25   I was taken aback when their reply came! "How do you know that Malgudi is where you think it is?"

26   Somewhat bewildered, I said, with what I hoped was proper humility, "I suppose I know because I have imagined it, created it and have been writing novel after novel set in the area for the last 30 years."

27   "We are out to expand the notion of Malgudi", one of them explained. "Malgudi will be where we place it, in Kashmir, Rajasthan, Bombay, Delhi, even Ceylon."

28   I could not share the flexibility of their outlook or the expanse of their vision. It seemed to me that for their purpose a focal point was unnecessary. They appeared to be striving to achieve mere optical effects.

29   I recalled a talk with Satyajit Ray, the great director, some years earlier, when I met him in Calcutta. He expressed his admiration for *The Guide* but also his doubts as to whether he could ever capture the tone and atmosphere of its background. He had said, "Its roots are so deep in the soil of your part of our country that I doubt if I could do justice to your book, being unfamiliar with its milieu...." Such misgivings did not bother the American director. I noticed that though he was visiting India for the first time, he never paused to ask what was what in this bewildering country.

30   Finally he solved the whole problem by declaring, "Why should we mention where the story takes place? We will avoid the name 'Malgudi.'" Thereafter the director not only avoided the word Malgudi but fell foul of anyone who uttered that sound.

31   My brother, an artist who has illustrated my stories for 25 years, tried to expound his view. At a dinner in his home in Bombay, he mentioned the forbidden word to the director. Malgudi, he explained, meant a little town, not so picturesque as Jaipur, of a neutral shade, with characters wearing dhoti and jibba when they were not barebodied. The Guide himself was a man of charm, creating history and archaeology out of thin air for his clients, and to provide him with solid, concrete monuments to talk about would go against the grain of the tale. The director listened and firmly said, "There is no Malgudi, and that is all there is to it."

32   But my brother persisted. I became concerned that the controversy threatened to spoil our dinner. The director replied, in a sad tone, that they could as well have planned a picture for black and white and narrow screen if all one wanted was what he contemptuously termed a "Festival Film," while he was planning a million-dollar spectacle to

open simultaneously in 2,000 theaters in America. I was getting used to arguments everyday over details. My story is about a dancer in a small town, an exponent of the strictly classical tradition of South Indian *Bharat Natyam*. The film makers felt this was inadequate. They therefore engaged an expensive, popular dance director with a troupe of a hundred or more dancers, and converted my heroine's performances into an extravaganza in delirious, fruity colours and costumes. Their dancer was constantly traveling hither and thither in an Air India Boeing no matter how short the distance to be covered. The moviegoer, too, I began to realize, would be whisked all over India. Although he would see none of the countryside in which the novel was set, he would see the latest U.S. Embassy building in New Delhi, Parliament House, the Ashoka Hotel, the Lake Palace, Elephant Caves and whatnot. Unity of place seemed an unknown concept for a film maker. (Later Mrs. Indira Gandhi, whom I met after she had seen a special showing of the film, asked, "Why should they have dragged the story all over as if it were a travelogue, instead of confining themselves to the simple background of your book?" She added as an afterthought, and in what seemed to me an understatement: "Perhaps they have other considerations.")

The co-operation of many persons was needed in the course of the film making, and anyone whose help was requested had to be given a copy of *The Guide*. Thus there occurred a shortage, and an inevitable black market, in copies of the book. A production executive searched the bookshops in Bombay, and cornered all the available copies at any price. He could usually be seen going about like a scholar with a bundle of books under his arm. I was also intrigued by the intense study and pencil-marking that the director was making on his copy of the book; it was as if he were studying it for a doctoral thesis. Not until I had a chance to read his "treatment" did I understand what all his penciling meant: he had been marking off passages and portions that were to be avoided in the film. 33

When the script came, I read through it with mixed feelings. The director answered my complaints with "I have only exteriorized what you have expressed. It is all in your book." 34

"In which part of my book" I would ask without any hope of an answer. 35

Or he would say, "I could give you two hundred reasons why this change should be so." I did not feel up to hearing them all. If I still proved truculent he would explain away "This is only a first draft. We could make any change you want in the final screenplay." 36

The screenplay was finally presented to me with a great flourish and expressions of fraternal sentiments at a hotel in Bangalore. But I learned at this time that they had already started shooting and had even completed a number of scenes. Whenever I expressed my views, the answer would be either, "Oh, it will all be rectified in the editing," 37 or, "We will deal with it when we decide about the retakes. But please wait until we have a chance to see the rushes." By now a bewildering number of hands were behind the scenes, at laboratories, workshops, carpentries, editing rooms and so forth. It was impossible to keep track of what was going on, or get hold of anyone with a final say. Soon I trained myself to give up all attempts to connect the film with the book of which I happened to be the author.

38   But I was not sufficiently braced for the shock that came the day when the director insisted upon the production of two tigers to fight and destroy each other over a spotted deer. He wished to establish the destructive animality of two men clashing over one woman: my heroine's husband and lover fighting over her. The director intended a tiger fight to portray depths of symbolism. It struck me as obvious. Moreover it was not in the story. But he asserted that it was; evidently I had intended the scene without realizing it.

39   The Indian producer, who was financing the project, groaned at the thought of the tigers. He begged me privately, "Please do something about it. We have no time for tigers; and it will cost a hell of a lot to hire them, just for a passing fancy." I spoke to the director again, but he was insistent. No tiger, no film, and two tigers or none.

40   Scouts were sent out through the length and breadth of India to explore the tiger possibilities. They returned to report that only one tiger was available. It belonged to a circus and the circus owner would under no circumstance consent to have the tiger injured or killed. The director decreed, "I want the beast to die, otherwise the scene will have no meaning." They finally found a man in Madras, living in the heart of the city with a full-grown Bengal tiger which he occasionally lent for jungle pictures, after sewing its lips and pulling out its claws.

41   The director examined a photograph of the tiger, in order to satisfy himself that they were not trying to palm off a pi-dog in tiger clothing, and signed it up. Since a second tiger was not available, he had to settle for its fighting a leopard. It was an easier matter to find a deer for the sacrifice. What they termed a "second unit" was dispatched to Madras to shoot the sequence. Ten days later the unit returned, looking forlorn.

42   The tiger had shrunk at the sight of the leopard, and the leopard had shown no inclination to maul the deer, whose cries of fright had been so heart-rending that they had paralyzed the technicians. By prodding, kicking and irritating the animals, they had succeeded in producing a spectacle gory enough to make them retch. "The deer was actually lifted and fed into the jaws of the other two," said an assistant cameraman. (This shot passes on the screen, in the finished film, in the winking of an eye as a bloody smudge, to the accompaniment of a lot of wild uproar.)

43   Presently another crisis developed. The director wanted the hero to kiss the heroine, who of course rejected the suggestion as unbecoming

an Indian woman. The director was distraught. The hero, for his part, was willing to obey the director, but he was helpless, since kissing is a co-operative effort. The American director realized that it is against Indian custom to kiss in public; but he insisted that the public in his country would boo if they missed the kiss. I am told that the heroine replied: "There is enough kissing in your country at all times and places, off and on the screen, and your public, I am sure, will flock to a picture where, for a change, no kissing is shown." She stood firm. Finally, the required situation was apparently faked by tricky editing.

Next: trouble at the governmental level. A representation was made to the Ministry dealing with films, by an influential group, that *The Guide* glorified adultery, and hence was not fit to be presented as a film, since it might degrade Indian womanhood. The dancer in my story, to hear their arguments, has no justification for preferring Raju the Guide to her legally wedded husband. The Ministry summoned the movie principals to Delhi and asked them to explain how they proposed to meet the situation. They promised to revise the film script to the Ministry's satisfaction. 44

In my story the dancer's husband is a preoccupied archaeologist who has no time or inclination for marital life and is not interested in her artistic aspirations. Raju the Guide exploits the situation and weans her away from her husband. That is all there is to it—in my story. But now a justification had to be found for adultery. 45

So the archaeological husband was converted into a drunkard and womanizer who kicks out his wife when he discovers that another man has watched her dance in her room and has spoken encouragingly to her. I knew nothing about this drastic change of my characters until I saw the "rushes" some months later. This was the point at which I lamented most over my naivete: the contract that I had signed in blind faith, in the intoxication of cheques bonhomie, and backslapping, empowered them to do whatever they pleased with my story, and I had no recourse. 46

Near the end of the project I made another discovery: the extent to which movie producers will go to publicize a film. The excessive affability to pressmen, the entertaining of V.I.P.s, the button-holding of ministers and officials in authority, the extravagant advertising campaigns, seem to me to drain off money, energy and ingenuity that might be reserved for the creation of an honest and sensible product. 47

On one occasion Lord Mountbatten was passing through India, and someone was seized with the sudden idea that he could help make a success of the picture. A banquet was held at Raj Bhavan in his honor, and the Governor of Bombay, Mrs. Vijayalaxmi Pandit, was kind enough to invite us to it. I was home in Mysore as Operation Mountbatten was launched, so telegrams and long-distance telephone calls poured in on me to urge me to come to Bombay at once. I flew in just in time to dress and reach Raj Bhavan. It was red-carpeted, crowded and 48 gorgeous. When dinner was over, leaving the guests aside, our hostess managed to isolate his Lordship and the "Guide"-makers on a side veranda of this noble building. His Lordship sat on a sofa surrounded by us; close to him sat Pearl Buck, who was one of the producers and who, by virtue of her seniority and standing, was to speak for us. As she opened the theme with a brief explanation of the epoch-making effort that was being made in India, in colour and wide-screen, with a hundred-percent-Indian cast, story and background, his Lordship displayed no special emotion. Then came the practical demand: in order that this grand, stupendous achievement might bear fruit, would Lord Mountbatten influence Queen Elizabeth to preside at the world premiere of the film in London in due course?

49 Lord Mountbatten responded promptly, "I don't think it is possible. Anyway what is the story?"

50 There was dead silence for a moment, as each looked at the other wondering who was to begin. I was fully aware that they ruled me out; they feared that I might take 80,000 words to narrate the story, as I had in the book. The obvious alternative was Pearl Buck, who was supposed to have written the screenplay.

51 Time was running out and his Lordship had others to talk to. Pearl Buck began.

52 "It is the story of a man called Raju. He was a tourist guide...."

53 "Where does it take place?"

54 I wanted to shout, "Malgudi, of course." But they were explaining, "We have taken the story through many interesting locations—Jaipur, Udaipur."

55 "Let me hear the story."

56 "Raju was a guide," began Pearl Buck again.

57 "In Jaipur?" asked his Lordship.

58 "Well, no. Anyway he did not remain a guide because when Rosie came..."

59 "Who is Rosie?"

60 "A dancer...but she changed her name when she became a...a... dancer...."

61 "But the guide? What happened to him?"

62 "I am coming to it. Rosie's husband..."

63 "Rosie is the dancer?"

64 "Yes, of course...." Pearl Buck struggled on, but I was in no mood to extricate her.

65 Within several minutes Lord Mountbatten said, "Most interesting." His deep bass voice was a delight to the ear, but it also had a ring of finality and discouraged further talk. "Elizabeth's appointments are complicated these days. Anyway her private secretary Lord—must know more about it than I do. I am rather out of touch now. Anyway, perhaps I could ask Philip." He summoned an aide and said, "William,

please remind me when we get to London...." Our Producers went home feeling that a definite step had been taken to establish the film in proper quarters. As for myself, I was not so sure.

Elaborate efforts were made to shoot the last scene of the story, in which the saint fasts on the dry river's edge, in hopes of bringing rain, and a huge crowd turns up to witness the spectacle. For this scene the director selected a site at a village called Okla, outside Delhi on the bank of the Jamuna river, which was dry and provided enormous stretches of sand. He had, of course, ruled out the spot we had visited near Mysore, explaining that two coconut trees were visible a mile away on the horizon and might spoil the appearance of unrelieved desert which he wanted. Thirty truckloads of property, carpenters, lumber, painters, artisans and art department personnel arrived at Okla to erect a two-dimensional temple beside a dry river, at a cost of 80,000 rupees. As the director kept demanding, "I must have 100,000 people for a helicopter shot," I thought of the cost: five rupees per head for extras, while both the festival crowd at Nanjangud and the little temple on the river would cost nothing. ₆₆

The crowd had been mobilized, the sets readied and lights mounted, and all other preparations completed for shooting the scene next morning when, at midnight, news was brought to the chiefs relaxing at the Ashoka Hotel that the Jamuna was rising dangerously as a result of unexpected rains in Simla. All hands were mobilized and they rushed desperately to the location to save the equipment. Wading in knee-deep water, they salvaged a few things. But I believe the two-dimensional temple was carried off in the floods. ₆₇

Like a colony of ants laboriously building up again, the carpenters and artisans rebuilt, this time at a place in Western India called Limdi, which was reputed to have an annual rainfall of a few droplets. Within one week the last scene was completed, the hero collapsing in harrowing fashion as a result of his penance. The director and technicians paid off the huge crowd and packed up their cameras and sound equipment, and were just leaving the scene when a storm broke—an unknown phenomenon in that part of the country—uprooting and tearing off everything that stood. Those who had lingered had to make their exit with dispatch. ₆₈

This seemed to me an appropriate conclusion for my story, which, after all, was concerned with the subject of rain, and in which Nature, rather than film makers, acted in consonance with the subject. I remembered that years ago when I was in New York City on my way to sign the contract, before writing *The Guide,* a sudden downpour caught me on Madison Avenue and I entered the Viking Press offices dripping wet. I still treasure a letter from Keith Jennison, who was then my editor. "Somehow I will always, from now on," he wrote, "associate the rainiest days in New York with you. The afternoon we officially became your publishers was wet enough to have made me feel like a fish ever since." ₆₉

✧ Evaluating the Text

1. What change in attitude did Narayan experience between the beginning and the end of the "project"? What key steps or incidents can you discover en route to his change of perspective?

2. What features of "Bollywood" (that is, the Bombay version of Hollywood, where hundreds of films are made each week) does Narayan satirize in his account?

3. In what way would an authentic film made from Narayan's novel differ from the one actually made? Based on your answer, evaluate whether the film producers were correct in their decisions concerning locations, story line, and other aspects of the project.

✧ Exploring Different Perspectives

1. What contrasting attitudes toward the public display of sexuality can you discover between Narayan's account and Kon Krailet's story "In the Mirror"? What differences in cultural values between India and Thailand emerge?

2. Compare Narayan's and Jackie Chan's attitudes (in "A Dirty Job") toward the treatment of film stars.

✧ Extending Viewpoints through Writing

1. In a short essay, discuss some of the ways in which an Indian movie differs from a Hollywood picture in terms of the cultural values of each society.

2. Have you ever counted on something as a sure thing, only to have it subsequently never materialize—an event, a trip, a material possession, a relationship? How is counting on something that never came about more dispiriting than never having believed it could happen at all? How did this experience help you understand R. K. Narayan's feelings in "Misguided 'Guide'"?

Machado de Assis

A Canary's Ideas

◆——————————◆

Joaquim María Machado de Assis (1839–1908) was born in Rio de Janiero where he lived most of his life. His father, a house painter, was a mulatto Brazilian, the son of former slaves; his mother was a white Portuguese immigrant from the Azores. Machado attended only five years of elementary school. Beyond that, he educated himself and became fluent in several languages, including French, Spanish, and English. He began supporting himself at age fifteen, working at a variety of jobs, including typesetting, proofreading, and editing. In 1874 he entered the civil service in the Ministry of Agriculture and for the last thirty-four years of his life led the quiet, unturbulent life of a happily married, but childless, government bureaucrat. He used the financial security of his civil service position to carry on an astonishingly prolific career as a writer. Machado's early love was the theater, and by the time he was thirty he had written nineteen plays and opera librettos, most of them produced by theater companies in the city. He was also a skilled poet and regular newspaper columnist. After 1870, he turned his attention primarily to short stories and novels. His first great success was Epitaph of a Small Winner *(1881), written from a startlingly original point of view, namely the posthumous memoirs of the narrator, Braz Cubas—a tongue-in-cheek account of his life.*

Machado's second novel, Philosopher or Dog? *(1891), and his acknowledged masterpiece,* Dom Casmurro *(1900), both feature protagonists who are reflective skeptics tinged with madness. These unreliable narrators are a feature of his work. His close attention to the protagonist's stream of consciousness, his cool irony, unexpected juxtaposition of times, characters, and value systems conveyed in a forceful, unique style anticipate many features of the twentieth-century novel. He is now acknowledged by critics to be a master of the early modern novel, equal to Gustave Flaubert and Henry James. His complete works fill thirty-one volumes, and he is the author of over one hundred short stories, of which "A Canary's Ideas," translated by Jack Schmitt and Lorie Ishimatsu (1976), is typical. In this story, an egocentric, reasoning canary forms his impression of the universe by what surrounds him at the moment.*

The largest South American country, Brazil occupies almost half of the continent and is the only country in South America whose culture, history, and language were shaped by Portugal, whose first permanent settlement in what is present-day São Paulo occurred in 1532. Since the

Europeans landed in 1500, the population of native tribes has been re-
duced from an estimated 6 million to 200,000 today. Brazil's population is
an amalgam of Indian, black, and European strains.

1   A man by the name of Macedo, who had a fancy for ornithology, related to some friends an incident so extraordinary that no one took him seriously. Some came to believe he had lost his mind. Here is a summary of his narration.

2   At the beginning of last month, as I was walking down the street, a carriage darted past me and nearly knocked me to the ground. I escaped by quickly side-stepping into a secondhand shop. Neither the racket of the horse and carriage nor my entrance stirred the proprietor, dozing in a folding chair at the back of the shop. He was a man of shabby appearance: his beard was the color of dirty straw, and his head was covered by a tattered cap which probably had not found a buyer. One could not guess that there was any story behind him, as there could have been behind some of the objects he sold, nor could one sense in him that austere, disillusioned sadness inherent in the objects which were remnants of past lives.

3   The shop was dark and crowded with the sort of old, bent, broken, tarnished, rusted articles ordinarily found in secondhand shops, and everything was in that state of semidisorder befitting such an establishment. This assortment of articles, though banal, was interesting. Pots without lids, lids without pots, buttons, shoes, locks, a black shirt, straw hats, fur hats, picture frames, binoculars, dress coats, a fencing foil, a stuffed dog, a pair of slippers, gloves, nondescript vases, epaulets, a velvet satchel, two hatracks, a slingshot, a thermometer, chairs, a lithographed portrait by the late Sisson, a backgammon board, two wire masks for some future Carnival—all this and more, which I either did not see or do not remember, filled the shop in the area around the door, propped up, hung, or displayed in glass cases as old as the objects inside them. Further inside the shop were many objects of similar appearance. Predominant were the large objects—chests of drawers, chairs, and beds—some of which were stacked on top of others which were lost in the darkness.

4   I was about to leave, when I saw a cage hanging in the doorway. It was as old as everything else in the shop, and I expected it to be empty so it would fit in with the general appearance of desolation. However, it wasn't empty. Inside, a canary was hopping about. The bird's color, liveliness, and charm added a note of life and youth to that heap of wreckage. It was the last passenger of some wrecked ship, who had arrived in the shop as complete and happy as it had originally been. As

soon as I looked at the bird, it began to hop up and down, from perch to perch, as if it meant to tell me that a ray of sunshine was frolicking in the midst of that cemetery. I'm using this image to describe the canary only because I'm speaking to rhetorical people, but the truth is that the canary thought about neither cemetery nor sun, according to what it told me later. Along with the pleasure the sight of the bird brought me, I felt indignation regarding its destiny and softly murmured these bitter words:

"What detestable owner had the nerve to rid himself of this bird for   5
a few cents? Or what indifferent soul, not wishing to keep his late master's pet, gave it away to some child, who sold it so he could make a bet on a soccer game?"

The canary, sitting on top of its perch, trilled this reply: 6

"Whoever you may be, you're certainly not in your right mind. I   7
had no detestable owner, nor was I given to any child to sell. Those are the delusions of a sick person. Go and get yourself cured, my friend...."

"What?" I interrupted, not having had time to become astonished.   8
"So your master didn't sell you to this shop? It wasn't misery or laziness that brought you, like a ray of sunshine, to this cemetery?"

"I don't know what you mean by 'sunshine' or 'cemetery.' If the ca-   9
naries you've seen use the first of those names, so much the better, because it sounds pretty, but really, I'm sure you're confused."

"Excuse me, but you couldn't have come here by chance, all alone.   10
Has your master always been that man sitting over there?"

"What master? That man over there is my servant. He gives me   11
food and water every day, so regularly that if I were to pay him for his services, it would be no small sum, but canaries don't pay their servants. In fact, since the world belongs to canaries, it would be extravagant for them to pay for what is already in the world."

Astonished by these answers, I didn't know what to marvel at   12
more—the language or the ideas. The language, even though it entered my ears as human speech, was uttered by the bird in the form of charming trills. I looked all around me so I could determine if I were awake and saw that the street was the same, and the shop was the same dark, sad, musty place. The canary, moving from side, was waiting for me to speak. I then asked if it were lonely for the infinite blue space....

"But, my dear man," trilled the canary, "what does 'infinite blue   13
space' mean?"

"But, pardon me, what do you think of this world? What is the   14
world to you?"

"The world," retorted the canary, with a certain professorial air, "is   15
a secondhand shop with a small rectangular bamboo cage hanging from a nail. The canary is lord of the cage it lives in and the shop that surrounds it. Beyond that, everything is illusion and deception."

16   With this, the old man woke up and approached me, dragging his feet. He asked me if I wanted to buy the canary. I asked if he had acquired it in the same way he had acquired the rest of the objects he sold and learned that he had bought it from a barber, along with a set of razors.

17   "The razors are in very good condition," he said.

18   "I only want the canary."

19   I paid for it, ordered a huge, circular cage of wood and wire, and had it placed on the veranda of my house so the bird could see the garden, the fountain, and a bit of blue sky.

20   It was my intention to do a lengthy study of this phenomenon, without saying anything to anyone until I could astound the world with my extraordinary discovery. I began by alphabetizing the canary's language in order to study its structure, its relation to music, the bird's appreciation of aesthetics, its ideas and recollections. When this philological and psychological analysis was done, I entered specifically into the study of canaries: their origin, their early history, the geology and flora of the Canary Islands, the bird's knowledge of navigation, and so forth. We conversed for hours while I took notes, and it waited, hopped about, and trilled.

21   As I have no family other than two servants, I ordered them not to interrupt me, even to deliver a letter or an urgent telegram or to inform me of an important visitor. Since they both knew about my scientific pursuits, they found my orders perfectly natural and did not suspect that the canary and I understood each other.

22   Needless to say, I slept little, woke up two or three times each night, wandered about aimlessly, and felt feverish. Finally, I returned to my work in order to reread, add, and emend. I corrected more than one observation, either because I had misunderstood something or because the bird had not expressed it clearly. The definition of the world was one of these. Three weeks after the canary's entrance into my home, I asked it to repeat to me its definition of the world.

23   "The world," it answered, "is a sufficiently broad garden with a fountain in the middle, flowers, shrubbery, some grass, clear air, and a bit of blue up above. The canary, lord of the world, lives in a spacious cage, white and circular, from which it looks out on the rest of the world. Everything else is illusion and deception."

24   The language of my treatise also suffered some modifications, and I saw that certain conclusions which had seemed simple were actually presumptuous. I still could not write the paper I was to send to the National Museum, the Historical Institute, and the German universities, not due to a lack of material but because I first had to put together all my observations and test their validity. During the last few days, I neither left the house, answered letters, nor wanted to hear from friends or relatives. The canary was everything to me. One of the servants had the

job of cleaning the bird's cage and giving it food and water every morning. The bird said nothing to him, as if it knew the man was completely lacking in scientific background. Besides, the service was no more than cursory, as the servant was not a bird lover.

One Saturday I awoke ill, my head and back aching. The doctor ordered complete rest. I was suffering from an excess of studying and was not to read or even think, nor was I even to know what was going on in the city or the rest of the outside world. I remained in this condition for five days. On the sixth day I got up, and only then did I find out that the canary, while under the servant's care, had flown out of its cage. My first impulse was to strangle the servant—I was choking with indignation and collapsed into my chair, speechless and bewildered. The guilty man defended himself, swearing he had been careful, but the wily bird had nevertheless managed to escape.

"But didn't you search for it?"

"Yes, I did, sir. First it flew up to the roof, and I followed it. It flew to a tree, and then who knows where it hid itself? I've been asking around since yesterday. I asked the neighbors and the local farmers, but no one has seen the bird."

I suffered immensely. Fortunately, the fatigue left me within a few hours, and I was soon able to go out to the veranda and the garden. There was no sign of the canary. I ran everywhere, making inquiries and posting announcements, all to no avail. I had already gathered my notes together to write my paper, even though it would be disjointed and incomplete, when I happened to visit a friend who had one of the largest and most beautiful estates on the outskirts of town. We were taking a stroll before dinner when this question was trilled to me:

"Greetings, Senhor Macedo, where have you been since you disappeared?"

It was the canary, perched on the branch of a tree. You can imagine how I reacted and what I said to the bird. My friend presumed I was mad, but the opinions of friends are of no importance to me. I spoke tenderly to the canary and asked it to come home and continue our conversations in that world of ours, composed of a garden, a fountain, a veranda, and a white circular cage.

"What garden? What fountain?"

"The world, my dear bird."

"What world? I see you haven't lost any of your annoying professorial habits. The world," it solemnly concluded, "is an infinite blue space, with the sun up above."

Indignant, I replied that if I were to believe what it said, the world could be anything—it had even been a secondhand shop....

"A secondhand shop?" it trilled to its heart's content. "But is there really such a thing as a secondhand shop?"

✦ Evaluating the Text

1. How is the narrator characterized? In what way is he defined by his zealous amateur interest in ornithology?

2. In what different circumstances does the narrator encounter the canary? How does the canary redefine its conception of the world to suit each new environment in which it finds itself?

3. In what ways are the canary and the narrator similar to each other? Keep in mind the circumstances in which the canary is first encountered and what the narrator hopes to achieve through his research.

✦ Exploring Different Perspectives

1. Compare the psychological profiles of the narrator in "A Canary's Ideas" with that of Tomoyuki Iwashita in "Why I Quit the Company."

2. In your opinion, is it really any crazier for Jackie Chan to risk breaking his neck in his desire to prove himself as a stuntman than it is for the obsessed ornthithologist to devote his life to his "talking" canary? Why or why not?

✦ Extending Viewpoints through Writing

1. Marlon Brando once defined an actor as "a guy who, if you ain't talking about him, ain't listening." Describe the most egocentric person you have ever known or someone whose hobby or work took over his or her life.

2. How do pet's often reflect submerged aspects of their owners' personalities? What actions did a pet of yours ever take that led you to believe it possessed intelligence and was able to communicate its feelings and intentions to you?

Connecting Cultures

Lesley Hazleton, "Confessions of a Fast Woman"

In what respects is becoming an apprentice auto mechanic a rite of passage similar to those described by Tepilit Ole Saitoti (see "The Initiation of a Maasai Warrior" in Chapter 2)?

Kon Krailet, "In the Mirror"

How is the commercialization of sexuality a feature of both Kim Chernin's account (see "The Flesh and the Devil" in Chapter 3) and Krailet's story?

Victor Villaseñor, "Rain of Gold"

Discuss the theme of powerlessness versus overcoming odds in Victor Villaseñor's narrative and Gloria Anzaldúa's story "Cervicide" in Chapter 7.

Tomoyuki Iwashita, "Why I Quit the Company"

How is the concept of the "job" that Iwashita describes similar to Kyoko Mori's "job description" for the Japanese wife in "Polite Lies" in Chapter 3?

Louise Rafkin, "A Yen for Cleaning"

How do the spiritual overtones of cleaning enter into the narratives of Rafkin and Pat Mora (see "Remembering Lobo" in Chapter 1)?

Jackie Chan, "A Dirty Job"

Compare Chan's account with Douchan Gersi's (see "Initiated into an Iban Tribe of Headhunters" in Chapter 2) as perilous initiations into desired groups.

R. K. Narayan, "Misguided 'Guide'"

What role does the concept of cultural authenticity (and inauthenticity) play in films in the accounts by Narayan and Jesse W. Nash ("Confucius and the VCR" in Chapter 7)?

Machado de Assis, "A Canary's Ideas"

Compare the solipsism of the inhabitants in H. G. Wells's story "The Country of the Blind" in Chapter 7 with that of the canary in this story. What similarities can you discover?

5

Class and Caste

◆

Every society can be characterized in terms of social class. Although the principles by which class is identified vary widely from culture to culture, from the amount of money you earn in the United States to what kind of accent you speak with in England to what religious caste you are born into in India, class sets boundaries around individuals in terms of opportunities and possibilities. The concept of class in its present form has been in force for only a few hundred years in Western cultures. In prior times, for example, in medieval Europe, your position and chances in life were determined at birth by the *estate* into which you were born, whether that of peasant, clergy, or noble.

Conflicts based on inequalities of social class are often intertwined with those of race, because minorities usually receive the least education, have the least political clout, earn the least income, and find work in occupations considered menial without the possibility of advancement. In some societies, such as in India, for example, an oppressive caste system based on tradition has, until recently, been responsible for burdening the "untouchables" with the most onerous tasks.

Class conditions our entire lives by setting limitations that determine, more than we might like to admit, who we can be friends with, what our goals are, and even who we can marry.

Class reflects the access one has to important resources, social privileges, choices, and a sense of control over one's life. Whereas caste in India is something one cannot change, social stratification in the United States is less rigid, and upward mobility is possible through a variety of means, such as work, financial success, marriage, and education. More frequently, however, a de facto class system can be said to exist in terms of health care, salaries, housing, and opportunities for education, which vary greatly for the rich and the poor.

The writers in this chapter explore many of the less obvious connections between social class and the control that people exercise over their lives. In "What Is Poverty?" Jo Goodwin Parker brings home the day to day consequences of being poverty stricken in the southern United States. Mahdokht Kashkuli, in "The Button," describes the circumstances of a family in modern-day Iran that force them to place one of their children in an orphanage. Alonso Salazar, in "The Lords of Creation," provides a first-hand account of a teen-age contract killer's life in the underworld of Colombia's drug capital, Medellín. Mary Crow Dog and Richard Erdoes, in "Civilize Them with a Stick," recount the racism experienced by Native Americans attending a government-run boarding school. Although officially outlawed, the caste known as untouchables lead lives similar to that described by Viramma in her autobiographical account "Pariah." Lee Stringer, who as a homeless person was one of America's "untouchables," describes, in "Life on the Street," his day to day struggle to survive. The Argentinian writer Liliana Heker creates, in her story "The Stolen Party," a poignant tableau of a young girl's first awareness of the cruelties of class differences.

Jo Goodwin Parker

What Is Poverty?

◆

Jo Goodwin Parker's poignant and realistic account of the shame, humiliation, and outrage of being poor was first given as a speech in Deland, Florida, on December 27, 1965, and was published in America's Other Children: Public Schools Outside Suburbia, *edited by George Henderson (1971). Parker reveals in graphic detail the hard choices she was forced to make in an ever-losing battle to preserve the health of her three children.*

1   You ask me what is poverty? Listen to me. Here I am, dirty, smelly, and with no "proper" underwear on and with the stench of my rotting teeth near you. I will tell you. Listen to me. Listen without pity. I cannot use your pity. Listen with understanding. Put yourself in my dirty, worn out, ill-fitting shoes, and hear me.

2   Poverty is getting up every morning from a dirt- and illness-stained mattress. The sheets have long since been used for diapers. Poverty is living in a smell that never leaves. This is a smell of urine, sour milk, and spoiling food sometimes joined with the strong smell of long-cooked onions. Onions are cheap. If you have smelled this smell, you did not know how it came. It is the smell of the outdoor privy. It is the smell of young children who cannot walk the long dark way in the night. It is the smell of the mattresses where years of "accidents" have happened. It is the smell of the milk which has gone sour because the refrigerator long has not worked, and it costs money to get it fixed. It is the smell of rotting garbage. I could bury it, but where is the shovel? Shovels cost money.

3   Poverty is being tired. I have always been tired. They told me at the hospital when the last baby came that I had chronic anemia caused from poor diet, a bad case of worms, and that I needed a corrective operation. I listened politely—the poor are always polite. The poor always listen. They don't say that there is no money for iron pills, or better food, or worm medicine. The idea of an operation is frightening and costs so much that, if I had dared, I would have laughed. Who takes care of my children? Recovery from an operation takes a long time. I have three children. When I left them with "Granny" the last time I had a job, I came home to find the baby covered with fly specks, and a diaper that had not been changed since I left. When the dried diaper came off, bits of my baby's flesh came with it. My other child was playing with a sharp bit of

288

broken glass, and my oldest was playing alone at the edge of a lake. I made twenty-two dollars a week, and a good nursery school costs twenty dollars a week for three children. I quit my job.

Poverty is dirt. You say in your clean clothes coming from your clean house, "Anybody can be clean." Let me explain about housekeeping with no money. For breakfast I give my children grits with no oleo or cornbread without eggs and oleo. This does not use up many dishes. What dishes there are, I wash in cold water and with no soap. Even the cheapest soap has to be saved for the baby's diapers. Look at my hands, so cracked and red. Once I saved for two months to buy a jar of Vaseline for my hands and the baby's diaper rash. When I had saved enough, I went to buy it and the price had gone up two cents. The baby and I suffered on. I have to decide every day if I can bear to put my cracked, sore hands into the cold water and strong soap. But you ask, why not hot water? Fuel costs money. If you have a wood fire it costs money. If you burn electricity, it costs money. Hot water is a luxury. I do not have luxuries. I know you will be surprised when I tell you how young I am. I look so much older. My back has been bent over the wash tubs every day for so long, I cannot remember when I ever did anything else. Every night I wash every stitch my school age child has on and just hope her clothes will be dry by morning.

Poverty is staying up all night on cold nights to watch the fire, knowing one spark on the newspaper covering the walls means your sleeping children die in flames. In summer poverty is watching gnats and flies devour your baby's tears when he cries. The screens are torn and you pay so little rent you know they will never be fixed. Poverty means insects in your food, in your nose, in your eyes, and crawling over you when you sleep. Poverty is hoping it never rains because diapers won't dry when it rains and soon you are using newspapers. Poverty is seeing your children forever with runny noses. Paper handkerchiefs cost money and all your rags you need for other things. Even more costly are antihistamines. Poverty is cooking without food and cleaning without soap.

Poverty is asking for help. Have you ever had to ask for help, knowing your children will suffer unless you get it? Think about asking for a loan from a relative, if this is the only way you can imagine asking for help. I will tell you how it feels. You find out where the office is that you are supposed to visit. You circle that block four or five times. Thinking of your children, you go in. Everyone is very busy. Finally, someone comes out and you tell her that you need help. That never is the person you need to see. You go see another person, and after spilling the whole shame of your poverty all over the desk between you, you find that this isn't the right office after all—you must repeat the whole process, and it never is any easier at the next place.

7   You have asked for help, and after all it has a cost. You are again told to wait. You are told why, but you don't really hear because of the red cloud of shame and the rising black cloud of despair.

8   Poverty is remembering. It is remembering quitting school in junior high because "nice" children had been so cruel about my clothes and my smell. The attendance officer came. My mother told him I was pregnant. I wasn't, but she thought that I could get a job and help out. I had jobs off and on, but never long enough to learn anything. Mostly I remember being married. I was so young then. I am still young. For a time, we had all the things you have. There was a little house in another town, with hot water and everything. Then my husband lost his job. There was unemployment insurance for a while and what few jobs I could get. Soon, all our nice things were repossessed and we moved back here. I was pregnant then. This house didn't look so bad when we first moved in. Every week it gets worse. Nothing is ever fixed. We now had no money. There were a few odd jobs for my husband, but everything went for food then, as it does now. I don't know how we lived through three years and three babies, but we did. I'll tell you something, after the last baby I destroyed my marriage. It had been a good one, but could you keep on bringing children in this dirt? Did you ever think how much it costs for any kind of birth control? I knew my husband was leaving the day he left, but there were no good-bys between us. I hope he has been able to climb out of this mess somewhere. He never could hope with us to drag him down.

9   That's when I asked for help. When I got it, you know how much it was? It was, and is, seventy-eight dollars a month for the four of us; that is all I ever can get. Now you know why there is no soap, no needles and thread, no hot water, no aspirin, no worm medicine, no hand cream, no shampoo. None of these things forever and ever and ever. So that you can see clearly, I pay twenty dollars a month rent, and most of the rest goes for food. For grits and cornmeal, and rice and milk and beans. I try my best to use only the minimum electricity. If I use more, there is that much less for food.

10   Poverty is looking into a black future. Your children won't play with my boys. They will turn to other boys who steal to get what they want. I can already see them behind the bars of their prison instead of behind the bars of my poverty. Or they will turn to the freedom of alcohol or drugs, and find themselves enslaved. And my daughter? At best, there is for her a life like mine.

11   But you say to me, there are schools. Yes, there are schools. My children have no extra books, no magazines, no extra pencils, or crayons, or paper and the most important of all, they do not have health. They have worms, they have infections, they have pink-eye all summer. They do not sleep well on the floor, or with me in my one bed. They do not suffer from hunger, my seventy-eight dollars keeps us alive, but

they do suffer from malnutrition. Oh yes, I do remember what I was taught about health in school. It doesn't do much good. In some places there is a surplus commodities program. Not here. The county said it cost too much. There is a school lunch program. But I have two children who will already be damaged by the time they get to school.

But, you say to me, there are health clinics. Yes, there are health clinics and they are in the towns. I live out here eight miles from town. I can walk that far (even if it is sixteen miles both ways), but can my little children? My neighbor will take me when he goes; but he expects to get paid, *one way or another.* I bet you know my neighbor. He is that large man who spends his time at the gas station, the barbershop, and the corner store complaining about the government spending money on the immoral mothers of illegitimate children.

Poverty is an acid that drips on pride until all pride is worn away. Poverty is a chisel that chips on honor until honor is worn away. Some of you say that you would do *something* in my situation, and maybe you would, for the first week or the first month, but for year after year after year?

Even the poor can dream. A dream of a time when there is money. Money for the right kinds of food, for worm medicine, for iron pills, for toothbrushes, for hand cream, for a hammer and nails and a bit of screening, for a shovel, for a bit of paint, for some sheeting, for needles and thread. Money to pay *in money* for a trip to town. And, oh, money for hot water and money for soap. A dream of when asking for help does not eat away the last bit of pride. When the office you visit is as nice as the offices of other governmental agencies, when there are enough workers to help you quickly, when workers do not quit in defeat and despair. When you have to tell your story to only one person, and that person can send you for other help and you don't have to prove your poverty over and over again.

I have come out of my despair to tell you this. Remember I did not come from another place or another time. Others like me are all around you. Look at us with an angry heart, anger that will help you help me. Anger that will let you tell of me. The poor are always silent. Can you be silent too?

✧ Evaluating the Text

1. What hard choices confront Parker when she tries to decide whether she should work and send her three children to nursery school or leave them with her mother?

2. What are the obstacles Parker faces in simply trying to keep her three children clean and fed? What trade-offs is she constantly forced to consider because she does not have enough money?

3. Explain why being poor and knowing your children will suffer if you do not get help from state or government agencies is a source of shame and humiliation. What does Parker mean when she says the poor are very polite and good listeners? Why is this so?

4. How does Parker answer critics who suggest how she might improve her situation? For example, what does she reveal about the amount of money she receives from public relief, what it will buy, the opportunities offered by public schools, food give-away programs, school-lunch programs, and health clinics? How, in each case, does she answer the objections that well-meaning people might raise? What damaging consequences for her children does Parker foresee because of her inability to help them in the present?

✧ Exploring Different Perspectives

1. Compare the circumstances Parker is in with those of the family in Mahdokht Kashkuli's "The Button." How are their circumstances very similar but their reactions quite different?

2. What different set of cultural dynamics might explain the choices made by Antonio in "The Lords of Creation" when compared with those facing Parker?

✧ Extending Viewpoints through Writing

1. How did reading this article change preconceptions you may have had about the poor?

2. To discover what you really value, consider the following hypothetical situation. You can save only one inanimate item from a raging fire. What would you save and why?

Mahdokht Kashkuli

The Button

◆

Mahdokht Kashkuli was born in 1950 in Teheran, Iran. She was married at age fourteen and, unlike similar marriages, hers did not prevent her from pursuing an education. She succeeded in obtaining her bachelor of arts in performing literature from Teheran University. By 1982 she had completed two master's degrees, one in library science and one in linguistics, and a doctorate in the language, culture, and religion of ancient Iran from the same university. She started her career first as a researcher for Iranian Educational Television from 1975 to 1985 and then as a professor of performing literature at Teheran University. Her short stories, including "The Fable of Rain in Iran," "The Fable of Creation in Iran," "Our Customs, Our Share," "The Pearl and the Moon," and "Tears and Water," have won her national recognition. She is presently working on a novel. "The Button," translated by Soraya Sullivan, was first published in the summer of 1978 in the periodical Arash. *This short story explores the heartbreaking consequences of a family's poverty in contemporary Iran.*

Iran, known as Persia until 1935, is an Islamic republic south of Russia and northeast of Saudi Arabia. Shiite Islam has been the state religion since the 1500s. Iran has the largest population of Shiite Moslems in the world. The Qur'an (Koran), the scripture of the Moslems, is made up of revelations delivered to Mohammed by the Angel Gabriel and also includes revelations to other prophets (Adam, Noah, Abraham, Isaac, Jacob, Joseph, Moses, and Jesus). The discovery of oil in Iran in the early 1900s made the country the object of British and Russian attempts at domination. Between 1925 and 1979, Iran was ruled by the Shahs (father and son), whose regime was supported by the United States, until Muhammad Reza Shah Pahlevi was ousted by popular opposition and replaced by the aged Moslem leader Ayatollah Ruhollah Khomeini. Since this time, the clergy (Mullahs) have carried out a conservative and fundamentalist interpretation of Islam. In 1979, Iranian militants seized the U.S. embassy in Teheran and held the occupants hostage until a negotiated agreement freed them in 1981. Concurrently, a full-scale border war with Iraq began in 1980 and ended eight years later, with casualties estimated at 1 million. In June 1989, Khomeini died, four months after exhorting the Moslem world to assassinate British author Salman Rushdie for writing The Satanic Verses *(1988), a novel perceived as blasphemous to Islam. Hashemi Rafsanjani first came to power as president in 1989 and, despite opposition from fundamentalist*

293

clerics, was reelected in June 1993. In May, 1997, a moderate cleric, Mo-
hammad Khatami, won Iran's first free presidential election and called for
establishing better relations with the West. Pro-Khatami reform candidates
won 73 percent of the parliamentary seats in February 2000.

1   My sister was perched in the doorway, sobbing bitterly; her curly, russet hair was stuck to her sweaty forehead. My mother was doing her wash by the pond, paying no attention to my sister's sobs or my father's shouts, "Hurry up Reza! Move it!" I was holding on to the edge of the mantle shelf tightly, wishing that my hand would remain glued there permanently. It was only a few nights ago that I had heard, with my own ears, my father's voice whispering to my mother, "Woman, stop grumbling! God knows that my heart is aching too, but we don't have a choice. I can't even provide them with bread. What else can I do? This way, we'll have one less mouth to feed." I had cocked my ears to hear who that "one less mouth to feed" was. I remained frozen, holding my breath for a few minutes; then I heard my father say, "Reza is the naughtiest of all; the most restless. Akbar and Asghar are more tame, and we can't send the girls away. It's not wise." Suddenly a dry cough erupted from my mouth. My father called out, "Reza! Reza! Are you awake?" I did not answer him. He fell silent, and then my mother's snorts followed the awkward silence. My father went on, "Woman, who said the orphanage is a bad place? They teach the kids, they feed them, they clothe them. At least this one will have a chance to live a good life." My mother's snorts stopped. She groaned, "I don't know. I don't know anything. Just do what you think is best." And then there was silence.

2   Why are they going to make me the "one less mouth to feed"? What is an orphanage? I wish I hadn't nibbled the bread on my way home from the bakery; I wish I hadn't quarreled with Asghar; I wish I hadn't messed around with my mother's yarn, as if it were a ball; I wish I hadn't pulled the bottle out of Kobra's mouth, and drunk her milk; I wish I could stay still, like the mannequin in the clothing store at the corner. Then they wouldn't make me the "one less mouth to feed." My pillow was soaked with tears.

3   I ran outside with puffy eyes the next morning. Ahmad was standing at the other end of the alley, keeping watch for Husain so he could pick a fight with him. I yelled, "Ahmad, Ahmad! What's an orphanage?" Keeping his eyes still on the door to Husain's house, Ahmad said, "It's a place where they put up poor people's children." "Have you been there?" I asked. He shouted indignantly, "Listen to this goddamn wretch! You can't be nice to anyone these days!" I ran back to the house, scared. If Ahmad hadn't been waiting for Husain, he surely would have beaten me up.

4   My father's screams shot up again, "Are you deaf? Hurry up, it's late!" I released my grip on the shelf and went down the stairs. The salt-

iness of my tears burned my face. My father said, "What's wrong? Why are you crying? Come, my boy! Come wash your face!" Then he took my hand and led me to the pond and splashed a handful of the murky water on my face. He wiped my face with his coat lining. I became uneasy. My father seldom showed signs of affection; I suspected that he was being affectionate because he had decided to make me the "one less mouth to feed." We walked towards the door. He pulled aside the old cotton rug hanging before the door with his bony hands. Then he said, in a tone as if he were talking to himself, "One thousand…God knows, I had to pull a thousand strings before they agreed to admit you."

I asked, while I kept my head down, "Why?" My father screamed   5
angrily, "He asks why again! Because!" I lowered my head. My eyes met his shoes. They were strangely crooked and worn out; maybe he had them on wrong…. The lower part of his long underwear showed from beneath his pants. He was wearing a belt to hold his loose pants up, and they creased like my mother's skirt. "I'm telling you, Reza, a thousand strings," he repeated. "You must behave when you get there." I didn't look at him but said grudgingly, "I don't want to behave!"

He threw a darting glance at me and raved, his hand rising to cuff   6
me on the back of the neck but he changed his mind and said instead, "They'll teach you how to behave yourself." Indignantly I said, "I don't want to go to an orphanage, and if you take me there, I'll run away." I pulled my hand out of his quickly and ran ahead, knowing that he'd hit me this time. But he didn't. He only said, "You think they admit everyone? I've been running around for a year, resorting to everyone I know." I said, "Dad, I don't want to go to the orphanage. They keep poor children there." "What do you think you are, rich?" my father said. "Listen to him use words bigger than his mouth!" And he broke out laughing. When he laughed I saw his gold teeth. There were two of them. I thought to myself, "What does it take to be rich? My father has gold teeth, my mother has gold teeth, and my brother has a fountain pen." I looked at his face. He wasn't laughing anymore; his face had turned gray. I said spontaneously, "Dad, is the landlord rich?" He didn't hear me, or it seemed he didn't, and said absentmindedly, "What?" I said, "Nothing."

I thought about the landlord. He sends his oldest son or his young   7
daughter to collect the rent two weeks before the rent is due. His oldest son enters my father's shop and stands in the front of the mirror, scrutinizing himself, resting one hand on his waist. My father rushes to him and says, "Do you want a haircut?" The landlord's son responds, "No. You just gave me one on Thursday." My father says politely, "What can I do for you, then?" The landlord's son says, "Is the rent ready?" My father answers, "Give me a few more days. Tell Haji Agha I'll pay before the due date." And the next day his young daughter shows up in the shop. She is so small that she can hardly see herself in the mirror. She holds her veil tightly under her chin with those tiny, delicate hands, and says, "Hel-

lo!" My father smiles and says, "Hello, cutie pie! What can I do for you?" The girl laughs cheerfully and says, "My father sent me after the rent. If it's ready, give it to me." My father picks a sugar cube out of the sugar bowl, puts it gently in her palm, and says, "Tell Haji Agha, fine!"

8   We reached the intersection. My father held my hand in his tightly and stopped to look around. We then crossed the street. He was mumbling to himself, "The damn thing is so far away...."

9   I felt sick. I said, "Wait a minute!" He eyed me curiously and said, "Why, what's wrong?" I said, "I'm tired; I don't want to go to the orphanage." He mimicked me, pursing his lips, and said, "You don't understand! You were always dumb, dense!"

10   I remembered that my father was always unhappy with me, although I swept the shop every day and watered the China roses he had planted in front of the shop. I would take my shirt off on hot summer afternoons and jump in the brook with my underpants. The elastic of my pants was always loose and I always tried to tie it into a knot, never succeeding to make it tight enough to stay. In the brook, I held my pants with one hand while I watered the China roses with a small bowl. It felt nice and cool there. Flies would gather around my shoulders and arms. Grandmother used to say, "God made flies out of wax." But I didn't understand why they didn't melt in the hot sun; they flew off my body and landed on the China rose flowers and I shook the branches with my bowl to disperse them. The flowers were my father's and no fly was allowed to sit on them. In spite of all my efforts, my father was always unhappy with me; he was unhappy with my mother, with my sisters and brothers, with the landlord, and with the neighbors. But he was happy with one person: God. He would sigh, tap himself hard on the forehead, and say, "Thank God!"

11   I said to him one day, "Why are you thanking God, Dad?" Suddenly, he hit me in the mouth with the back of his hand. My upper lip swelled and my mouth tasted bloody. I was used to the taste of blood because whenever I bled in the nose, I tasted blood in my mouth. I covered my mouth, walked to the garden and spat in the dirt. I looked at the bubbles on my spittle, tapped myself on the forehead and said, "Thank God!" Then I picked up a piece of watermelon skin lying on the brook and smacked it on the head of a yellow dog that always used to nap by the electric post. The yellow dog only opened its eyes, looked at me indifferently, and shut its eyes again, thanking God, perhaps.

12   We passed another street before we got to the bus station. A few people were waiting in line; one of them was sitting at the edge of the brook. My father took my hand and led me to the front of the bus line. Someone said, "This is not the end of the line, old man!" I only looked at my father.

13   He said to me, "Ignore him. Just stay right here!" The bus came and my father pushed me towards it. I tore my feet off the ground and

jumped on the coach-stop, feeling as if I were floating in the air. Some-one said, "Old man, the end of the line is on the other side! Look how people give you a headache on a Monday morning!" My father didn't hear him; he pushed me forward. I was stuck between a seat and the handle bar.... So, today is Monday.... Every week on Monday my mother does her wash. The clothesline spread around the entire yard. I liked the smell of damp clothes. In spite of my mother's curses, I liked cupping my hands underneath the dripping clothes so that the water that dripped could tickle my palms. Every Monday we had yogurt soup for lunch. My brother and I would take a bowl to the neighbor-hood dairy store to buy yogurt. On the way back, we took turns licking the surface of the yogurt. When we handed the bowl to my mother, she would scream at us and beat the first one of us she could get her hands on.... I felt depressed. I wished I could jump out the window.

The bus stopped at a station and we got off. My father walked ahead of me while I dragged my feet along behind him. 14

He waited for me to catch up, then he said, "Move it! He walks like a corpse. Hurry up, it's late!" I stopped momentarily and said, "Dad, I don't want to go. I don't want to go to the orphanage." My father froze in his spot. He said incredulously, "What did you say? You think you know what's good for you? Don't you want to become a decent human being some day? They have rooms, there. They have food, and they'll teach you everything you need to learn to get a decent job." I sobbed, "To hell with anyone who has a decent job. To hell with decent jobs. I don't want one! I like staying home. I like playing with Asghar and Ak-bar. I want to sell roasted corn with the kids from the neighborhood in the summer. I want to help you out in the shop. I don't want to go." 15

My father sprang towards me, but suddenly retreated and became affectionate. He said, "Let's go, good boy! We're almost there." I felt sorry for him because every time he was kind he looked miserable. My father was walking ahead of me and I was following him, dragging my feet on the street like that yellow dog. On the next street, we stopped in front of a big metal door. A chair was placed inside the door to keep it ajar. A man was sitting on the chair, playing with a ring of prayer beads. He had on a navy blue coat with metal buttons. His eyes were half-closed and his mouth was open. His cheeks were puffy, as if he had a toothache. My father greeted him and said, "Mr. Guard!" The man opened his eyes. Strands of blood ran through the white of his eyes. He said with a gloomy voice, "What is it, what do you want?" My father thrust his hand in both his pockets, took out an envelope and ex-tended it toward the guard with both hands. The man looked at my fa-ther, then threw a threatening glance at me. He yawned, stared at the envelope for a while (I didn't believe he could read), shook his head, coughed, and said, "They won't leave you alone; one leaves, another 16 comes!" Then he pushed the door with the tip of his shoes. The door opened just enough to let me in.

17   After my father walked through the doorway behind me, the guard gave him the envelope and said, "The first door!" My father was walking fast, and when he opened the hallway door, my heart started beating violently and I started to cry. He said, "My boy, my sweet Reza, this is a nice place. The people here are nice, the kids are all your own age...."

18   He didn't finish his sentence. He pushed on the door. The door opened and I saw a woman inside the room. I wished she were my mother, but she was heavier than my mother, with a deep vertical wrinkle between her eyebrows. She wore a blue uniform and her hair was a bleached blonde.

19   My father pushed me further in and said, "Greet her, Reza! Greet her!" I didn't feel like greeting anyone.

20   My father handed the woman the envelope. She opened it, pulled the letter out halfway, and started reading it. Then she turned to my father and said, "Go to the office so they can complete his file."

21   My father leaped and ran out the door. Then, as though he had remembered something, he returned and stood in front of the door, rubbing his hand on the wood frame of the door. He raised one hand to tap on his forehead and say, "Thank God," but stopped, rubbed his forehead gently and sighed. His eyes were as moist and shiny as the eyes of the yellow dog hanging around his shop. Her head still lowered on the letter, the woman said, "Go, old man! What are you waiting for? Go to the office!" Father took a few steps backwards, then tore himself from the door and disappeared into the corridor.

22   The woman looked at me, then turned her gaze toward the window and fixed it there. While she had her back to me, she said, "Don't cry, boy! Please don't, I'm not in the mood!" Then she turned around and put her hands on my shoulders. Her hands were as heavy as my mother's but not as warm. She took my hand and walked me toward the door. We passed one corridor, and entered another. Then we entered a room, then another corridor and another room. There were a few people in the room. One was sitting in the doorway, whistling; one was leaning against the desk; one was sitting in a chair writing something. Although the room was furnished with chairs and desks, it was not warm. The woman said, "Say hello to these people!" I looked at her but didn't say anything. I didn't feel like talking to them. I didn't hear what they said to each other, either. I only wanted to sit still and look at them. We left that room and went into another. There was another woman there. I wished she were my mother. She was wearing a blue uniform and had a red scarf around her neck. I think she had a cold because she sniffled constantly. As soon as she saw me, she checked me out thoroughly and spoke with a nasal voice, "Is he new here? I don't know where we're going to put him." She then opened a closet, took out a uniform and said

to me, "Take your jacket off and wear this!" Then she continued, "Take your shirt off, too. How long has it been since your last shower?" I didn't answer. Her words hit my ears and bounced right off. She went toward the closet again and asked, "Are you done?" I looked around and then looked at myself, my eyes becoming fixed on my jacket. It had only one button. The button had belonged to my mother's jacket before she used it to replace my missing button. The woman's voice went on, "Quit stalling, boy! Hurry up, I have tons of work to do!"

I put my hand on the button and pulled it out, then hid it in my palm. The woman said, "Are you done?" I said, "Yes!"   23

I thrust the button in my uniform pocket and wiped my tears with the back of my hand.   24

✧ Evaluating the Text

1. Of what imagined crimes does the narrator accuse himself that might explain why he is the one to be sent to an orphanage instead of one of his three siblings?

2. How would you characterize the boy's relationship with his father? In your view, what has caused the father to choose him to be the one out of his four children to be sent to an orphanage?

3. How does Reza's attitude toward the button reveal his feelings and emotions?

✧ Exploring Different Perspectives

1. Discuss this story in terms of how parents who live in poverty (see "What Is Poverty?") have to face hard choices, find themselves in "no-win" situations, and are forced to make sacrifices.

2. How do both Kashkuli's "The Button" and Mary Crow Dog's "Civilize Them with a Stick" deal with the issue of what happens to children who are raised by the state?

✧ Extending Viewpoints through Writing

1. What insight does this story provide into the prevailing economic and social conditions in modern Iranian society?

2. Write about one of your grandparents or parents through an object you connect with him or her. Under what circumstances did you first come across this object? What associations connect this object with your parent or grandparent?

Alonso Salazar

The Lords of Creation

◆

Alonso Salazar is a leading Colombian journalist and social scientist. Salazar journeyed into the jails, hospitals, and shantytowns of Medellín, Colombia's second largest city and drug capital, to interview teenage con-tract killers, their families, priests, and self-defense vigilantes. His book, Born to Die in Medellín (1990), *provides a graphic exploration of one of the most violent societies in the world. "The Lords of Creation," trans-lated by Nick Caistor, taken from this book, provides riveting insight into the world of Medellín's youth gangs.*

The only South American country with both Pacific and Caribbean coastlines, the republic of Colombia is bordered by Panama to the northwest, Venezuela to the northeast, Ecuador and Peru to the south, and Brazil to the southeast. After being conquered by the Spanish in the 1530s, Colombia's struggle for independence from Spain began in 1810, lasted nine years, and ended with the victory of Simón Bolívar in 1819. From its inception, the re-public of New Granada, as it was then called (which originally included Venezuela, Ecuador, and Panama) was torn by the opposition between fed-eralist liberals and centralist conservatives. As many as 100,000 people were killed in a civil war that raged from 1899 to 1903. Civil war again erupted in 1948, and orderly government was restored as a result of com-promise between liberals and conservatives in 1958. Widespread poverty and a political climate destabilized by guerilla warfare in urban areas led to a precarious economy ostensibly dependent on coffee, its major legal crop, but even more dependent on the illegal growth and trafficking in marijuana and cocaine. After several rounds of elections, Ernesto Samper was elected president in August 1994 for a four-year term. In 1998, the Conservative Party challenger, Andres Pastrana, won a run-off election.

1   Silhouetted against the full moon, the shape of a headless cat strung up by its paws. Its blood has been collected in a bowl on the floor. Only a few drops continue to fall. As each one hits the bowl it makes tiny ripples, which grow until the whole surface seems full of tossing waves. Waves that shake to the noise of heavy rock being played at full blast. The cat's head is in the corner, its luminous green eyes staring sightlessly. Fifteen people are taking part in the silent rit-ual. The city is spread below them.

2   Warm blood is mixed with wine in a glass. The blood of a cat that climbs walls, leaps nonchalantly from fence to fence, walks on the si-

lent pads of its paws across rooftops, vanishes effortlessly into the shadows of night. Cat's blood, full of the urge to pounce unerringly on its prey. Blood that conjures up strange energies, that speeds the brain.

Antonio recalls in a jumble of images the moment of his own initi-   3
ation into one of the teenage gangs in a neighbourhood on the hills of north-east Medellín. In his feverish dreams as he fights for life, he sees himself on the streets again. Strange shapes appear in the sea of city lights. They raise the cup to seal their pact. There is no need for words, they all know what they are committing themselves to, what the laws are, the rewards and the punishment. From now on they will be all for one and one for all, they will be as one. They'll be the lords of creation.

But now Antonio is in the San Rafael Ward of the Saint Vincent de   4
Paul hospital. A military ward, full of the wounded and the dying, the victims of an unequal war waged day and night along undefined fronts on the streets of Medellín. One Tuesday, three months earlier, Antonio was blasted with a shotgun as he boarded a bus in his neighbourhood. The shot perforated his stomach, leaving him hovering between life and death. Although only twenty, Antonio has often faced death, but has never felt it so close to him. He knows, even though he won't admit it, that he's not going to make it. He has a skinny body, a face drained of colour, dark eyes sunk in huge sockets. He begins to tell me his life story in a calm voice, searching inside himself, as if taking stock for reasons of his own.

ANTONIO

When I was a kid I used to get a bit of money using a home-made   5
pistol. Then Lunar and Papucho—they're both dead now—let me have proper guns, so I started to steal and kill for real. You get violent because there are a lot of guys who want to tell you what to do, to take you over, just because you're a kid. You've got to keep your wits about you, to spread your own wings. That's what I did, and off I flew; anybody who got in my way paid for it.

I learned that lesson from my family. From the old woman, who's   6
tough as nails. She's with me whatever I do. She might not look much, but she's always on my side. The only regret I have in quitting this earth is leaving her on her own. To know she might be all alone in her old age. She's fought hard all her life, and she doesn't deserve that.

My old man died about 14 years ago. He was a hard case too, and   7
taught me a lot, but he was always at the bottle, and left us in the lurch. That was why I had to fend for myself, to help my ma and my brothers and sisters. That's how I started in a gang—but also because it was something inside me, I was born with this violent streak.

Lunar, the leader of the gang, was only a teenager but he was   8
tough all right. He'd been in the business for years already. He lived in

Bello for a while and knew the people from Los Monjes. He learned a lot from them, so when he came to live here he started up his own gang. He had a birthmark or *lunar* on his cheek, that's how he got the nickname. It was thanks to him and Papucho, the other leader, that I learned how to do things properly.

9   I'll never forget the first time I had to kill someone. I had already shot a few people, but I'd never seen death close up. It was in Copacabana, a small place near Medellín. We were breaking into a farmhouse one morning when the watchman suddenly appeared out of nowhere. I was behind a wall, he ran in front of me, I looked up and was so startled I emptied my revolver into him. He was stone dead. That was tough, I won't lie, it was tough for me to take. For two weeks I couldn't eat a thing because I saw his face even in my food…but after that it got easy. You learn to kill without it disturbing your sleep.

10   Now it's me who's the gang leader. Papucho was killed by the guys up on the hill there. They set a trap for him and he fell for it. They asked him to do a job for them, then shot him to pieces. A friend of his was behind it, who'd sold out. Lunar made me second-in-command because we understood each other almost without speaking—we didn't need words.

11   Lunar didn't last much longer; he was never one to back down from a fight, never a chicken. He really enjoyed life; he always said we were all playing extra time anyway. And he was enjoying himself when he died: he was at a dance about three blocks down the hill when they shot him three times in the back. He was on his own because he reckoned there were no skunks down there. The kid who shot him died almost before he could blink. We tracked him down that same night, and sent him on his trip to the stars.

12   After Lunar's death another wise guy thought he'd take over the gang. I had to get tough and show him who was boss. For being such a smart ass now he's pushing up the dirt as well. It's me who gives the orders round here, I say what we do and don't do. There were about fifty of us to begin with, but a lot of them have been killed or put inside, and others have grassed. There's only twenty of us real hard cases left. They're all teenagers, between 15 and 18. I'm the oldest. A lot get killed or caught, but more always want to join, to get some action.

13   Whenever anyone wants to join I ask around: "Who is this kid? Can I trust him?" Then I decide if he can join or not. They're all kids who see things as they are; they know they won't get anywhere by working or studying, but if they join us they'll have ready money. They join because they want to, not because we force them. We don't tell anybody they have to. Not all of them are really poor, some do it for their families, others because they want to live in style.

14   Before we finally choose someone we give him a test: to take something somewhere, to carry guns and to keep them hidden. Then finally

we give them a job to do. If the kid shows he can do it, then he's one of us. But if he ever grasses on us, if he shoots his mouth off, if he gets out of line, then he's dead meat. Everyone understands that. Then again, we support each other all we can; "If you haven't got something and I have, take it, friend—as a gift, not a loan." We also help if someone's in trouble. We look after each other, but nobody can double-cross us.

We take good care of our guns, because they're hard to come by.   15
The last kid I shot died because of that.

"Antonio, help me out will you brother? Lend me a gun for a job I   16
have to do," he said to me.

"I'll let you have this .38, but be sure you give it back tomorrow;   17
you know the rules."

I lent it to him because the kid had always been straight with us,   18
but this time he wasn't. So I went to talk to him, and he came up with a really strange excuse. He said the law had taken it from him. I gave him another two days, and when he didn't show up I passed the death sentence. He knew he was a marked man, so he didn't make any attempt to hide. It was easy for me.

The thing is, it's hard to find guns. You either have to shoot a guy   19
to get his, or buy them, and a good weapon costs. We nearly always buy them from the police, and they sell us the ammo too. I've also bought grenades from a retired army guy. We've had T-55s, 32-shot mini-Uzis, 9mm Ingrands, but we usually use sawn-off shotguns, pistols and revolvers. We're all good shots.

We practise late at night, two, three in the morning, in some woods   20
over at Rionegro. We set up a line of bottles and fire at them. I smash the lot. You have to keep a steady hand when you're on a job, you only have one chance to kill someone, you can't afford to miss. You only have a few seconds so you have to know what you're doing: if the dummy doesn't die, you could. You have to know how to handle your weapon, to shoot straight, and how to make your get-away. We learn a lot from films. We get videos of people like Chuck Norris, Black Cobra, Commando, or Stallone, and watch how they handle their weapons, how they cover each other, how they get away. We watch the films and discuss tactics.

We learn to ride motor bikes on the hills round here. They're all   21
souped up, really quick. Most of them are stolen; we buy papers for them for 20,000 pesos[1] down at the traffic police. Our territory is from the bus terminal down to the school. People who don't mess with us have no problems, but anyone who tries to muscle in either gets out or dies. We help the people in our neighbourhood, they come to us and say: "we've got nothing to eat," so we help them and keep them happy. And when we've done a job that pays well, we make sure they get

---

[1]£1 = 545 pesos (1990).

some. We look after them so that they're on our side. Whenever someone tries to move in on our territory, I personally go and kneecap them as a warning they should never come back.

22   Lots of kids in the neighbourhood want to be in a gang. All I tell them is if that's what they want to do they have to be serious about it, but I don't force them to join. Most of them start by stealing cars, then they save up to buy a shotgun, which is the cheapest weapon around. We give them cartridges so they can get started.

23   I reckon I've killed 13 people. That's 13 I've killed personally, I don't count those we've shot when we're out as a gang. If I die now, I'll die happy. Killing is our business really, we do other jobs, but mostly we're hired to kill people.

24   People from all sorts of places contract us: from Bellavista jail, from El Poblado, from Itagüí. People who don't want to show their faces, and take you on to get rid of their problem for them. I try to work out whether our client means business, if he can pay us. We charge according to who we have to hit: if he's important, we charge more. We're putting our lives, our freedom, our guns on the line. If we have to leave the city to deal with some big shot, our price is anything up to three million. Here in Medellín the lowest we go is half a million.

25   We don't care who we have to give it to, we know it has to be done, that's all there is to it. Whoever it may be: I have no allegiances. I'll drive the bike and gun anyone down myself, no problem. Sometimes we don't even know who it is we have to kill. You hear later who the hit was, from the news on the radio. It's all the same to us, we've done our job, that's all.

26   Whenever I have to kill someone, all I think is: too bad for him he crossed my path. If their back is towards me, I call out, so I can make sure I've got the right guy, and when he turns round, I give it to him. I don't worry about it, I don't worry about running into the law, or that things will go wrong, nothing like that. I only hope I don't kill a woman or a child in a shoot-out. If I'm going to kill, there has to be a reason for it.

27   Once we went out to a small town to deal with a local councillor. We don't usually know who is giving us the contract, but in this case it was more or less direct contact, and we realised that the guy who wanted him dead was the leader of a political party. We kept well away from him after that, because you can be the ones who end up paying. They can easily have you rubbed out as well to get rid of witnesses. We made a million on that job.

28   The week before, we went to the town to see the lie of the land. We were shown the client, we took a look at where the police were, worked out how to get out afterwards. On the Saturday, I went back with a girlfriend. She was carrying the weapon—a submachine gun—in her bag. We took a room in the best hotel, pretending we were a honeymoon couple. We took our time checking out the town, making sure nothing could go wrong.

On the Sunday, two of the gang stole a car in Medellín, and kept   29
the owner in a room in Guayaquil until the job was done. One of them
drove to the town and parked where we'd agreed, right on time. The
councillor always liked to have a coffee in a corner bar after his meetings. My girlfriend showed up with the gun around two in the afternoon. I took it and waited for the action. Waiting like that really gets
you down. You get real nervous. I've found a trick which always helps
me: I get a bullet, take out the lead, and pour the gunpowder into a hot
black coffee. I drink the lot, and that steadies my nerves.

At ten to six I left the hotel and sat waiting in the bar. It was a hot   30
evening, and there were a lot of people on the street. I saw our car arrive and park a few metres away. The target came in a couple of minutes later. On the dot as promised.

It was beginning to get dark, which is always useful. I took another   31
good look round to make sure there was nothing unusual going on,
then paid for my drink. When the waiter was giving me my change, I
pulled out the submachine gun and started firing. Everybody hit the
floor. When something like that happens in a small town, they all stay
well out of it, no one is expecting it. I went over and put a final bullet in
him, because some of these guys are really tough and you have to make
sure of your money. It was all over in seconds. While I had been firing,
they had started the car, so I walked to it as calm as could be, and got
in. We made sure we didn't drive too fast out of town. We made as if
we were going out on the main highway, but then headed off down a
side road. We drove for about a quarter of an hour, then left the car by
the roadside. We walked for an hour, until we came to a safe house on
a farm owned by a friend of the politician who had hired us. We caught
a bus back to Medellín about five o'clock the next morning. They sent
the gun back to us a few days later. Everything had been well planned
and worked like clockwork.

That night we had a huge party. We'd already had the pay-off, so as   32
the saying goes: "the dead to their graves, the living to the dance." It
was like Christmas. We bought a pig, crates of beer and liquor, set up a
sound system in the street, and gave it all we'd got 'til morning.

The bus struggles up the hill, along narrow twisting streets full of   33
people and shops. From this main road you have to walk another two
blocks up a narrow alley-way, then climb a gully before you reach the
Montoya family's house. The roof is made of corrugated iron and cardboard; the walls are not plastered, just painted with a blue wash. Red
geraniums flower outside. The house is three tiny rooms. Posters of
movie stars and rock musicians cover the walls. Lost in one corner under a layer of cobwebs is a small picture of the Virgin of El Carmen. A
horseshoe and a piece of aloe vera hang over the front door to bring
good luck.

34   Doña Azucena, Antonio's mother, is a small, thin woman. Her face shows the marks of all she has been through in her life. Two children, aged four and six, whom she had by her second husband, cling to her legs. She works in a cafe in the centre of Medellín. A few years ago, when she still had legs worth showing off, she worked in the Porteño bar in Guayaquil. The kind of bar where men go to drink liquor and pick up women. Doña Azucena takes some photos out of an old album which show her in high heels, a mini skirt, and wearing bright scarlet lipstick. She would never dream of showing them to her children. It was in that bar, to the sound of music from Olimpo Cárdenas and Julio Jaramillo, that her second husband fell in love with her. A much older man, she lived with him for four years until one weekend, she never knew why, he walked out and didn't come back. She didn't miss him, because her older children had never got on with him, and because she herself had lost all her affection for him.

DOÑA AZUCENA

35   In the bar there's a big picture of a man hanging from a branch. A tiger is trying to climb the tree, there's a rattlesnake in the tree-top, and under the branch is a pool full of crocodiles. I used to look at that picture and think my life was exactly like that. Wherever I've been, I've lost out.

36   I can remember it like it was yesterday. I was at a rural school in Liborina, a beautiful part of the country. It was May, the month of the Holy Virgin, and we were preparing to celebrate. Our teacher, who was called Petronilla, asked me to pick some roses for the altar, and said I should make sure to cut all the thorns off. I went down a path below the school where there were some lovely rose bushes. I picked them and sat down to snip the thorns off. Then I went back to the school and gave them to the teacher. She took them, but a splinter got caught in her finger, so suddenly she drew back her hand and slapped me across the face. Without even thinking about it, I slashed at her with the knife, the one I'd used to cut the roses. She was badly wounded, but they managed to save her life. That was the end of school for me.

37   I've always had a quick temper, I've never let anyone put anything over on me. That's how my family was, that's how my children are. I was born in Urrao, but we had to leave there when I was still little because of the political violence. My father, whose name was Antonio too, was a die-hard Liberal, every weekend he'd go into town, get drunk, and start shouting "Up with the Liberals!" for everyone to hear. As soon as the violence started, we began to get death threats.

38   Once my father and his brothers had to take on a bunch of Conservative thugs who were terrorising the area. We knew they'd come up after us. So the men borrowed some shotguns and took up their posi-

tions on a bit of a hill just below the house. When they saw the Conservatives arrive, they fired at them and they ran off.

That same evening Don Aquileo, a neighbour who was a Conservative too, but who got on well with us, came up to see us. He told us   39
that down in town everyone was saying they'd get together and come up and finish us off. There'd already been other tremendous massacres in the countryside, so we decided to get out that same night and go to Liborina, where we had family. Later some Liberal guerrillas got organised in Urrao, led by Captain Franco. But that was after we left. We had a dreadful time there, I can remember passing lots of mutilated bodies by the roadsides, those are things you never forget.

A few years later, I was a teenager by then, we moved on to Chig-   40
orodó, in Urabá, because they said the land was fertile there. We began to clear a farm in the jungle, about two hours from the nearest town. That was where my mother María died. The climate killed her. The weather was impossible. Up there the heat is hellish, and it can rain the whole day long. It was a struggle to clear the jungle, but eventually we were able to plant bananas and maize.

The good times didn't last long. We'd just begun to harvest our   41
crops, when the violence began there too. Not between Conservatives and Liberals, but just between people for no reason at all. There was a store where we all used to go at weekends to talk and drink. But soon people began to fight with machetes. The men got drunk and killed each other without ever knowing why, or rather, at the slightest excuse.

My brothers have always been difficult, they've fought with almost   42
everyone. But above all they got into trouble with a family called García, who came from Dabeiba. There were about ten of them, all dangerous men. It was when they started threatening us that we decided to sell up and come to Medellín.

We settled in the Barrio Popular. We built a place up on this hill,   43
just when people had started moving in. Soon everywhere was full of shacks. People who had lost their land in the country because of the violence, and had come to the city to escape.

I can remember the day when Don Polo was out laying the floor for   44
his place. He'd come from Andes with his family. The police on horseback turned up, and wanted to take him away. We all used to help each other, to protect ourselves, so I went out and started to shout at them.

"You can't take him if you haven't got an arrest warrant."   45

"You're not the law, you bitch, we are, and we know what we're   46
doing," one of them shouted back, pointing his rifle at me.

I was really angry by then, and I thought well, if I'm going to die   47
then so be it, may God forgive me all my sins but this injustice shouldn't be allowed to happen. Other people began pouring out of their houses. Then a police car arrived. We were still arguing, and one of the police hit me with the butt of his rifle.

48   "Come on, it's you we're going to arrest for causing an obstruction," he said, pushing me into the car.

49   I began to kick out, and my neighbours all closed round the car, saying: "You've no right to take Doña Azucena."

50   "Drive off," the captain told his driver.

51   "Which way? D'you want me to kill all these people?"

52   They all crowded closer and closer round the car, and finally pulled me out. The other policemen on horseback were shouting insults all the time. Then a young fellow hit one of them with a stick, and they all fired at him. The rest of us ran off. They picked up his body and left. They took him to the hospital, but he died. Things like that happened all the time, the police would come up to destroy our houses, but we'd all stand firm. A lot of lives were lost. That's why we've never liked the law, it seems they're always out to get the poor.

53   It was around that time that I married Diego Montoya. He was a young man who had just moved to Medellín from Puerto Berrío. I went with him against my family's wishes; they didn't like him because he was black. We went to live with one of his sisters over in Santa Cruz. For a few years it was good, he looked after me and remembered all the little details—everything was fine. We had five children, almost one after the other: Claudia, Diego, Antonio, Orlando, and Nelly.

54   But gradually Diego went downhill. He became a tremendous drinker and would give me almost nothing for the kids, so I had to go and find work, first of all in houses over in Laureles, then in a bar in Guayaquil. One day when I came back from work I found my eldest daughter Claudia with her leg all bloody. Diego's sister's eldest son had sliced her with a saw because she had picked up something he was working with. I took my belt off, went to find the boy, and gave him a good thrashing. His mother tried to defend him, so I started on her too. When Diego came back later that night, I told him what had happened. His sister went whining to him, and told him he should teach me a lesson.

55   "He's not going to teach me any lesson, you do it if you want to," I told her.

56   "But he's your husband," she replied.

57   "That he may be, but if I have to show him what's what, I will."

58   Diego got really angry and left. By the time he returned I was in bed, reading a magazine by candlelight.

59   "I'm leaving, thanks for everything. All your things are on the table," I told him.

60   I'd put his revolver and some money he'd given me on the table by the bed. He didn't say a word, but got into bed. At about five in the morning, he got up again. He stood there for a minute staring at me, then went over to our daughter's bed, stroked her hair, gave her a kiss, and began to cry.

"Wake up sweetheart, wake up so we can talk about it," he said to me, shaking me gently by the shoulder. 61

"There's nothing for us to talk about. I've already given you back all your things, what more do I owe you?" 62

"Can't you wait 'til Saturday so I can sort things out?" 63

"When did you ever sort things out? All you do is make one promise after another, then spend every cent you earn on whores and booze." 64

"Just wait, in the next few days I'm expecting a big note, I promise I'll hand it over to you," he begged, and my heart softened. 65

"OK, let's see; if you love your children and want to stay with them, then buy us somewhere to live, that's the only condition. I'll give you all day today to think about it, if you don't come up with something by tonight, I'm off." 66

He didn't come back to sleep that night, but the next day, Saturday, he arrived very early. He took me and the children to look at a plot of land in the Barrio Popular. We did the deal there and then, and the following week had already built a place. We've been living in this gully ever since. 67

This is where I brought up my children. Diego died 14 years ago, a few months after he had an accident that crippled him. While he was at home sick he told people's fortunes for them. He knew a lot. Just by looking at the palm of someone's hand he could tell what was wrong, what their illness was, if they had been smoking too much dope, if a woman had the evil eye on them. Then he'd give them a cure or take the spell off them. He learned from his father, who practised these things down in Puerto Berrío. I asked him to teach me, but he always said: "You're too black-hearted, if you learned this, you'd use it to harm people." 68

It's true that in some ways I can be hard. I wouldn't harm a soul, but if anyone crosses me, they're for it. That's what I've always taught my children, that they've got to make people respect them. They've got it in their blood, they were born as rebellious as me. My eldest worked for a while in the building trade, but then he fell in with some friends and began to go wrong. At first they dealt in marijuana, then they started with robberies. At the moment he's doing three years in Acacías, Meta, for assault. 69

Ever since he was little, Antonio's been the wildest of the lot. The same thing happened to him at school as me, although I've never told them my story. In his third year at primary school they had a teacher who used to punish them terribly, so one day Antonio and a friend waited for him outside the school and stabbed him with a knife. Since then, Antonio's been on the streets. 70

It was Diego, his older brother, who got him started in crime. Antonio was only eleven when he was sent to a remand home, in Floresta. He'd had a fight with a neighbour's boy, Doña Blanca's son, a kid's 71 quarrel. But then Alberto, her older son, threatened to give him a hiding. I spoke to them and said that if anyone was going to give him a hiding it would be me. In return they insulted me, and that drove my kids wild. Without my knowing it, Diego gave Antonio a gun.

72   "If you let that Alberto lay a finger on you, I'll give you another hiding myself. You have to show you're a Montoya," Diego told him.

73   One day soon after, I was making lunch when I heard some shots and a terrific row outside. I ran out and saw Alberto lying on the pavement. Antonio had shot him five times. Fortunately he didn't die, but since then it's been war between our two families. Two of them have died, and my sons have been wounded several times.

74   After Antonio got out of the remand home he studied plumbing and electrics at the San José school. But that didn't last long, he was soon back on the streets. A few days later I saw him with a couple of boys who were a good bit older than him, Papucho and Lunar, both of them dead now. They were the ones who sealed his fate. People began to be afraid of them, grassed on them to the police, and they came looking for them.

75   All I can say is that he's been a good son to me. I've had to work in bars all these years to earn enough to keep my family. It's hard for a woman on her own. Antonio is the one who's helped me the most. He's never drunk a lot, and whenever he's done a job he always brings something back for the house.

76   I've been with him through thick and thin. Whenever he's inside I always go and visit him. I've often had to struggle with the police, but I've made sure they respect me as a woman. I've made a vow to the Fallen Christ of Girardota to make sure my boy gets well quickly. That's what I want, I want him to get well and go and find the coward who shot him, things can't stay like this. None of my family is going to feel safe with that fellow around.

77   Antonio knew they wanted to kill him, that's why he left home. That Tuesday, he came up here in the morning and was chatting with the girls, playing with the dog. I went down to the main street to buy things for lunch. As I was coming back I saw two of the Capucho gang on the corner. That scared me, but I walked past them calmly, as if I hadn't even seen them.

78   "Antonio, get away from here, they're out to get you," I told him when I reached home.

79   "Don't worry, ma, the day I die I'll have my bags packed and ready, but today isn't the day," he said laughing, lying back on the bed.

80   In the afternoon he went round to his girlfriend Claudia's house next door. He was still joking about, listening to music as if nothing was wrong. At six I saw the others again, they were at the bottom of the gully. They had their hands in their pockets, and were staring up our way. The worst of it was that Antonio didn't have any protection. I went and found him and told him what was going on.

"It looks bad out there, I think you should find some way to get away."　81

"Cool it, ma, I'll be off in a minute. Go round to Gitano's place and tell him to bring a couple of guns up here, that there's going to be some action."　82

I sneaked out the back way and went to find Gitano.　83

"Doña Azucena, he's not back from town, and anyway he hasn't got any guns either," they told me.　84

When I told Antonio that Gitano wasn't around, he looked worried, but pretended everything was all right.　85

"I'm going over the wall at the back here," he said. "You two go out the front and act normal, while I get away."　86

We went out and sat on the front porch to chat. The Capucho boys were still down at the bottom of the gully, so I relaxed a bit. But then 15 minutes later I got a call from the hospital.　87

"We have your boy Antonio Montoya here, he's in a bad way."　88

In the three months since then I've been down there every afternoon between two and five, when you can visit them. Every week the hospital is full of wounded kids, they come and go, new ones take the place of those who get better, but Antonio is still there. I don't know how all this is going to end.　89

The priest went to give him confession yesterday, I've no idea what Antonio told him about his life. When the priest came out he greeted me very formally. "Don't worry, he has repented and is at peace with God," he told me. And that did bring me peace of mind. Even though I'm not much of a believer it's always better to know you're at peace with God.　90

ANTONIO

I'd like to be out on the streets of my neighbourhood again, that's my territory. I love walking down them. I've always got my wits about me of course, my eyes wide open and my gun in my pocket, because I've got as many enemies as friends. You never know where you might get shot from. A lot of people are after me, I've got a lot of admirers in other gangs. The law is also on my tail. If I get out of here, I'm going to be real careful.　91

There've always been gangs in our neighbourhood: the Nachos, the Montañeros, Loco Uribe's gang, the Calvos…and as the song says: "this bed ain't big enough for everyone." You have to be on the lookout, if you're not careful one of the other gangs muscles in and people start leaving you. You have to make sure of your territory, that's the main thing. The biggest war we ever had was with the Nachos, who were hired killers like us. When they first showed up we did nothing, but then they started throwing their weight around, upsetting people. Until one day Martín, one of our gang, told them where to get off, and　92 they shot him. That same night we went up to their place and taught them a lesson. Six of us went up there in groups of two: we met up on the street corner where they hung out, and took them completely by surprise. We shot two of them. They thought they were such tough guys they never even imagined anyone would come for them.

93 A few days later they came for us. We were waiting for them. I put a handkerchief over my face, put on a baseball cap, and went out with my submachine gun. Others from the gang were covering me, watching what would happen.

94 "We want peace, not war," one of the Nachos shouted.

95 "We don't want peace, what we want is war," Lunar shouted back, and fired off a volley into the air.

96 Of course they didn't really want peace, what they were trying to do was to see all our faces so they could pick us off. In the end they retreated back up the gully. "Get them to start making your coffins," they shouted from up top.

97 From then on it was war. They would come down into the gully, we'd go and raid them, both sides would try to ambush each other...it was a real shootin' war that left a lot of people dead.

98 The Nachos went to pieces after the police got their leader in a raid. Even I have to admit that the guy was a real man: he and this other guy were fighting it out with the pigs for hours. They say that when Nacho had only one bullet left he shut himself in the bathroom of the house they were holed up in and shot himself in the head. After that his gang was nothing, they had no stomach for a fight. A few days later the law arrested about twenty of them, and now they're all in Bellavista for a good long while.

99 The gang wars have been tough: whole families have been wiped out in vendettas. What happens is if one of the gang or one of your relatives gets killed, you go out and get the bastard who did it, or one of his family; but we never touch women. If you don't react, they walk all over you.

100 We also fight police, but it's easier with them. They're shit scared when they come up here, and we know our own territory. Of course they've caught me twice, and I ended up in Bellavista as well.

101 The first time was the hardest. I'd been holed up in a house in a nearby neighbourhood. About midnight I woke up to hear them knocking the door down.

102 "Open up, this is the police," they shouted.

103 I tried to escape out the back, but the place was surrounded. Before I could do a thing, the police were everywhere. They put me into the patrol car without even letting me get dressed, and took me off to the F-2 headquarters. All they found in the house were three guns we had stashed there.

104 At the station they put me in a tub with water up to my neck. They left me there all night freezing my balls off, and ran electric current

through me too. They kept asking me about the others in the gang, who the leaders were, but I didn't say a word.

"Think you're a real tough guy, don't you, you fairy," they shouted, 105 kicking me as hard as they could in the stomach.

I didn't think I was tough at all, but to grass on people is the lowest 106 you can go. They asked me about enemies of mine, but I didn't even give them away, although I knew where they hung out. It's like Cruz Medina sings in the tango: "Don't anyone ask who wounded me so, you're wasting your time, you'll never know. Let me die here in peace, and don't be surprised at that, when a man is a man, he won't squeal like a rat."

I was sent to Bellavista prison for illegal possession of firearms. I 107 didn't have a record, and they couldn't get anything out of me, so they got mad. They even tried to get people from the neighbourhood to testify against me, but nobody would. There may be people who hate your guts, but they know that if they start blabbing, they're signing their own death warrants. Either you get them once you're out, or one of the gang does it for you.

I was three months in the slammer. That was only about long 108 enough to get over the beating the pigs had given me. I met several of the gang in the jail. I was lucky that the boss man on our block was an old guy I'd done a job for, who liked me. If you end up in Bellavista with no one to look after you, you're done for. You get kicked from block to block until you end up in the worst hole, where they steal everything you've got, even your sex.

That's why I was lucky, because I had someone to look out for me. 109 Of course I met up with a few of my old enemies too, some of the Nachos and others. But the worst was a guy called Pepe, whose brother I had shot. I told the boss man about him, and he said: "Tell him to get out of here, and if he cuts up rough about it, send him to the funeral parlour."

I sent the message to Pepe, and a few days later he changed blocks. 110 Whatever the boss man says goes. Nobody in there can do anything without his permission.

Once I got into a fight. I had some air-cushion Nike running shoes, 111 the ones that cost 20,000 pesos. Two guys came up to me: "Listen, sweetheart, get those shoes off, they've been sold," one of them said, a switchblade in his hand.

"You listen. Tell whoever bought them to come and take them off, 112 I'm too tired," I said, pulling out a metal bar I had hidden in my jacket.

Three of my gang appeared out of nowhere, and we set on them. I 113 ended up stabbing one right in the heart. He died on the way to the infirmary. The other one got away. One of us was wounded too, but nothing serious. In Bellavista they don't even bother to make any enquiries, they know no one will say a word. Anyone who's been hit gets his own back if he can, if not, he chokes on it.

I paid my way out of Bellavista. There are people who act as go- 114 betweens with the judges. My case was easy, because it wasn't a serious charge and nobody came forward to accuse me of anything else. I paid around 250,000 pesos. Or rather, some associates of the gang who'd just done a job paid it for me.

115   After that I went back to my patch, to my normal life. Half the time I'm happy, the other half I'm worked up. When I haven't got anything to do, I get up late, it's almost dark by the time I hit the streets. I hang around the street corners listening to rock music with the gang or I go to a bar with my girl to listen to love songs or country music.

116   My girl is called Claudia. I know I can trust her, she knows what I do, and backs me up, but she doesn't want to get involved at all. She works in a dress factory and comes home early every day. She's got expensive tastes: she likes new clothes, jewels, all the fancy stuff, and I give her everything she wants. At the weekend either we go out to bars in Bello, or dance salsa, or go down into Manrique to listen to some smoochy music. She's a good-looker, but what I most like about her is that she's serious. Because there's a lot of girls who make your eyes pop, but most of them are just good for a quick lay, a one night stand. Sometimes we like to party at the houses we hide up in, and we get girls in. Fabulous women, but they're only out for what they can get from you. The only real girlfriend I've had is Claudia.

117   Things have got very difficult. This gang's appeared called the Capuchos, they're killing people all over the place. It was them who shot me. I knew they were after me, that's why I split from home. But then I got it into my head to go up and say hello to the old woman and Claudia. I thought everything was quiet because the police were snooping around the neighbourhood a lot at the time. I didn't want any trouble, so I went up there without a weapon. Ma soon told me that they were out looking for me. I wasn't worried, I knew they wouldn't dare come up to the house. It's in a narrow gully, so long as you're under cover you can take on anyone.

118   I was waiting for some of the gang to arrive with the guns so we could get rid of those guys. By the time night fell and they hadn't arrived, I realised things were getting serious. So I climbed out of the back of the house and made for the road up top. I walked about a block, and saw a bus coming down, so I waved it to stop. Just as I was getting on, I saw a kid about two metres from me with a shotgun. Then I felt this heat spreading all through my body, and that was the last I knew. I was out for four days before I came round. What got me most was that a lot of people in the neighbourhood knew what was going on but didn't warn me. The Capuchos had every exit staked. I guess it's everyone's turn sometime, and that day it was mine.

119   What I wish is that they had killed me there and then, without time for me to let out a sigh or feel any pain, or even to say "they've got me." I'd have preferred that to this feeling that my body and my mind are

being torn apart. Having to stare death in the face all day long, grinning and beckoning at me, but not daring to come any closer. Better to die straight off, so you don't get to see how all your so-called friends abandon you. In here you realise that people are only with you in the good times. As Don Olimpo sings: "When you're on top of the world, you can have friends galore, but when fate trips you up, you'll see it's all lies, they won't want you any more." I don't care about dying, we were all born to die. But I want to die quickly, without all this pain and loneliness.

Last night Antonio had his final dream. He dreamt he was up   120
again on the flat roof of the house in the gully where he'd been happiest, blowing his mind with all his gang to the music of drums and electric guitars.

ANTONIO

The city at night is fabulous, it's all light and darkness. I feel just   121
like one of those dots, lost in a sea of light. That's what we are, a tiny light, or maybe a patch of darkness. In the end, we're all or nothing. We can do great things, but we're all mortal. Look closely at the yellow lights, and they turn into all colours, they spread upwards until they make a rainbow in the night. Then they're like a huge cascade of white water that is falling and falling into a deep, invisible well. Then the water gushes out again, this time like a giant flame, making a great bonfire that devours everything. Afterwards there are only red embers and ashes, which are blown everywhere. Now everything is a desert, nothing grows, nothing blooms. The city at night is a screen, a lot of images that flash in front of your eyes. Take a good look at the buildings in the centre. They're pointed-headed monsters. You can see their long arms stretching out, trying to catch something. It's us they're trying to grab. But we're as high and as far away as a cloud. We're on the heights where we can look down on everything, where nothing can touch us. We're the lords of all creation.

✧ *Evaluating the Text*

1. What picture do you get of Antonio, his relationship with other gang members, and the reasons for his life of violence? What insight does this interview give you into the values of being a member of a gang?

2. Describe the circumstances that surround recruitment, weapons used, training, role models, and the nature of the jobs performed.

3. What insight do you get from learning about Antonio's mother, Doña Azucena, that sheds light on the direction his life has taken?

❖ Exploring Different Perspectives

1. How do the different cultural factors explain the reactions of Antonio's mother in this account and the reactions of the mother in Jo Goodwin Parker's "What Is Poverty?"

2. What insight do the accounts by Salazar and Mary Crow Dog (see "Civilize Them with a Stick") provide into rebellion against mainstream society?

❖ Extending Viewpoints through Writing

1. Have you ever belonged to a gang or club? Describe your experiences, emphasizing the advantages and disadvantages you found in being a member.

2. Describe the role popular music and films play in Antonio's life. Are there songs or movies that you have seen that have had as strong an effect in shaping your outlook as those mentioned by Antonio?

Mary Crow Dog
and Richard Erdoes

Civilize Them with a Stick

◆

Mary Crow Dog (who later took the name Mary Brave Bird) was born in 1956 and grew up on a South Dakota reservation in a one-room cabin without running water or electricity. She joined the new movement of tribal pride sweeping Native American communities in the 1960s and 1970s and was at the siege of Wounded Knee, South Dakota, in 1973. She married the American Indian Movement (AIM) leader Leonard Crow Dog, the movement's chief medicine man. Her powerful autobiography Lakota Woman, *written with Richard Erdoes, one of America's leading writers on Native American affairs and the author of eleven books, became a national bestseller and won the American Book Award for 1991. In it she describes what it was like to grow up a Sioux in a white-dominated society. Her second book,* Ohitka Woman *(1993), also written with Richard Erdoes, continues the story of a woman whose struggle for a sense of self and freedom is a testament to her will and spirit. In "Civilize Them with a Stick," from* Lakota Woman, *the author recounts her personal struggle as a young student at a boarding school run by the Bureau of Indian Affairs.*

> *...Gathered from the cabin, the wickiup, and the tepee,*
> *partly by cajolery and partly by threats;*
> *partly by bribery and partly by force,*
> *they are induced to leave their kindred*
> *to enter these schools and take upon themselves*
> *the outward appearance of civilized life.*
>
> —Annual report of the Department of Interior, 1901

It is almost impossible to explain to a sympathetic white person   1
what a typical old Indian boarding school was like; how it affected the
Indian child suddenly dumped into it like a small creature from another
world, helpless, defenseless, bewildered, trying desperately and instinctively to survive and sometimes not surviving at all. I think such children were like the victims of Nazi concentration camps trying to tell
average, middle-class Americans what their experience had been like.
Even now, when these schools are much improved, when the buildings
are new, all gleaming steel and glass, the food tolerable, the teachers
well trained and well intentioned, even trained in child psychology—
unfortunately the psychology of white children, which is different from

ours—the shock to the child upon arrival is still tremendous. Some just seem to shrivel up, don't speak for days on end, and have an empty look in their eyes. I know of an eleven-year-old on another reservation who hanged herself, and in our school, while I was there, a girl jumped out of the window, trying to kill herself to escape an unbearable situation. That first shock is always there....

2   The mission school at St. Francis was a curse for our family for generations. My grandmother went there, then my mother, then my sisters and I. At one time or other every one of us tried to run away. Grandma told me once about the bad times she had experienced at St. Francis. In those days they let students go home only for one week every year. Two days were used up for transportation, which meant spending just five days out of three hundred and sixty-five with her family. And that was an improvement. Before grandma's time, on many reservations they did not let the students go home at all until they had finished school. Anybody who disobeyed the nuns was severely punished. The building in which my grandmother stayed had three floors, for girls only. Way up in the attic were little cells, about five by five by ten feet. One time she was in church and instead of praying she was playing jacks. As punishment they took her to one of those little cubicles where she stayed in darkness because the windows had been boarded up. They left her there for a whole week with only bread and water for nourishment. After she came out she promptly ran away, together with three other girls. They were found and brought back. The nuns stripped them naked and whipped them. They used a horse buggy whip on my grandmother. Then she was put back into the attic—for two weeks.

3   My mother had much the same experiences but never wanted to talk about them, and then there I was, in the same place. The school is now run by the BIA—the Bureau of Indian Affairs—but only since about fifteen years ago. When I was there, during the 1960s, it was still run by the Church. The Jesuit fathers ran the boys' wing and the Sisters of the Sacred Heart ran us—with the help of the strap. Nothing had changed since my grandmother's days. I have been told recently that even in the '70s they were still beating children at that school. All I got out of school was being taught how to pray. I learned quickly that I would be beaten if I failed in my devotions or, God forbid, prayed the wrong way, especially prayed in Indian to Wakan Tanka, the Indian Creator.

4   The girls' wing was built like an F and was run like a penal institution. Every morning at five o'clock the sisters would come into our large dormitory to wake us up, and immediately we had to kneel down at the sides of our beds and recite the prayers. At six o'clock we were herded into the church for more of the same. I did not take kindly to the discipline and to marching by the clock, left-right, left-right. I was never one to like being forced to do something. I do something because I feel like doing it. I felt this way always, as far as I can remember, and my sister

Barbara felt the same way. An old medicine man once told me: "Us La-kotas are not like dogs who can be trained, who can be beaten and keep on wagging their tails, licking the hand that whipped them. We are like cats, little cats, big cats, wildcats, bobcats, mountain lions. It doesn't matter what kind, but cats who can't be tamed, who scratch if you step on their tails." But I was only a kitten and my claws were still small.

Barbara was still in the school when I arrived and during my first year or two she could still protect me a little bit. When Barb was a seventh-grader she ran away together with five other girls, early in the morning before sunrise. They brought them back in the evening. The girls had to wait for two hours in front of the mother superior's office. They were hungry and cold, frozen through. It was wintertime and they had been running the whole day without food, trying to make good their escape. The mother superior asked each girl, "Would you do this again?" She told them that as punishment they would not be allowed to visit home for a month and that she'd keep them busy on work details until the skin on their knees and elbows had worn off. At the end of her speech she told each girl, "Get up from this chair and lean over it." She then lifted the girls' skirts and pulled down their underpants. Not little girls either, but teenagers. She had a leather strap about a foot long and four inches wide fastened to a stick, and beat the girls, one after another, until they cried. Barb did not give her that satisfaction but just clenched her teeth. There was one girl, Barb told me, the nun kept on beating and beating until her arm got tired.

I did not escape my share of the strap. Once, when I was thirteen years old, I refused to go to Mass. I did not want to go to church because I did not feel well. A nun grabbed me by the hair, dragged me upstairs, made me stoop over, pulled my dress up (we were not allowed at the time to wear jeans), pulled my panties down, and gave me what they called "swats"—twenty-five swats with a board around which Scotch tape had been wound. She hurt me badly.

My classroom was right next to the principal's office and almost every day I could hear him swatting the boys. Beating was the common punishment for not doing one's homework, or for being late to school. It had such a bad effect upon me that I hated and mistrusted every white person on sight, because I met only one kind. It was not until much later that I met sincere white people I could relate to and be friends with. Racism breeds racism in reverse.

The routine at St. Francis was dreary. Six A.M., kneeling in church for an hour or so; seven o'clock, breakfast; eight o'clock, scrub the floor, peel spuds, make classes. We had to mop the dining room twice every day and scrub the tables. If you were caught taking a rest, doodling on the bench with a fingernail or knife, or just rapping, the nun would come up with a dish towel and just slap it across your face, saying, "You're not supposed to be talking, you're supposed to be working!" Monday mornings we had cornmeal mush, Tuesday oatmeal, Wednesday rice and raisins, Thursday cornflakes, and Friday all the leftovers mixed together or sometimes fish. Frequently the food had bugs or rocks in it. We were eating hot dogs that were weeks old, while the nuns were dining on ham, whipped potatoes, sweet peas, and cranberry sauce. In winter our dorm was icy cold while the nuns' rooms were always warm.

9   I have seen little girls arrive at the school, first-graders, just fresh from home and totally unprepared for what awaited them, little girls with pretty braids, and the first thing the nuns did was chop their hair off and tie up what was left behind their ears. Next they would dump the children into tubs of alcohol, a sort of rubbing alcohol, "to get the germs off." Many of the nuns were German immigrants, some from Bavaria, so that we sometimes speculated whether Bavaria was some sort of Dracula country inhabited by monsters. For the sake of objectivity I ought to mention that two of the German fathers were great linguists and that the only Lakota–English dictionaries and grammars which are worth anything were put together by them.

10   At night some of the girls would huddle in bed together for comfort and reassurance. Then the nun in charge of the dorm would come in and say, "What are the two of you doing in bed together? I smell evil in this room. You girls are evil incarnate. You are sinning. You are going to hell and burn forever. You can act that way in the devil's frying pan." She would get them out of bed in the middle of the night, making them kneel and pray until morning. We had not the slightest idea what it was all about. At home we slept two and three in a bed for animal warmth and a feeling of security.

11   The nuns and the girls in the two top grades were constantly battling it out physically with fists, nails, and hair-pulling. I myself was growing from a kitten into an undersized cat. My claws were getting bigger and were itching for action. About 1969 or 1970 a strange young white girl appeared on the reservation. She looked about eighteen or twenty years old. She was pretty and had long, blond hair down to her waist, patched jeans, boots, and a backpack. She was different from any other white person we had met before. I think her name was Wise. I do not know how she managed to overcome our reluctance and distrust, getting us into a corner, making us listen to her, asking us how we were treated. She told us that she was from New York. She was the first real hippie or Yippie we had come across. She told us of people called the Black Panthers, Young Lords, and Weathermen. She said, "Black people are getting it on. Indians are getting it on in St. Paul and California. How about you?" She also said, "Why don't you put out an underground paper, mimeograph it. It's easy. Tell it like it is. Let it all hang out." She spoke a strange lingo but we caught on fast.

12   Charlene Left Hand Bull and Gina One Star were two full-blood girls I used to hang out with. We did everything together. They were

willing to join me in a Sioux uprising. We put together a newspaper which we called the *Red Panther.* In it we wrote how bad the school was, what kind of slop we had to eat—slimy, rotten, blackened potatoes for two weeks—the way we were beaten. I think I was the one who wrote the worst article about our principal of the moment, Father Keeler. I put all my anger and venom into it. I called him a goddam wasičun son of a bitch. I wrote that he knew nothing about Indians and should go back to where he came from, teaching white children whom he could relate to. I wrote that we knew which priests slept with which nuns and that all they ever could think about was filling their bellies and buying a new car. It was the kind of writing which foamed at the mouth, but which also lifted a great deal of weight from one's soul.

On Saint Patrick's Day, when everybody was at the big powwow, we distributed our newspapers. We put them on windshields and bulletin boards, in desks and pews, in dorms and toilets. But someone saw us and snitched on us. The shit hit the fan. The three of us were taken before a board meeting. Our parents, in my case my mother, had to come. They were told that ours was a most serious matter, the worst thing that had ever happened in the school's long history. One of the nuns told my mother, "Your daughter really needs to be talked to." "What's wrong with my daughter?" my mother asked. She was given one of our *Red Panther* newspapers. The nun pointed out its name to her and then my piece, waiting for mom's reaction. After a while she asked, "Well, what have you got to say to this? What do you think?" 13

My mother said, "Well, when I went to school here, some years back, I was treated a lot worse than these kids are. I really can't see how they can have any complaints, because we was treated a lot stricter. We could not even wear skirts halfway up our knees. These girls have it made. But you should forgive them because they are young. And it's supposed to be a free country, free speech and all that. I don't believe what they done is wrong." So all I got out of it was scrubbing six flights of stairs on my hands and knees, every day. And no boy-side privileges. 14

The boys and girls were still pretty much separated. The only time one could meet a member of the opposite sex was during free time, between four and five-thirty, in the study hall or on benches or the volleyball court outside, and that was strictly supervised. One day Charlene and I went over to the boys' side. We were on the ball team and they had to let us practice. We played three extra minutes, only three minutes more than we were supposed to. Here was the nuns' opportunity for revenge. We got twenty-five swats. I told Charlene, "We are getting too old to have our bare asses whipped that way. We are old enough to have babies. Enough of this shit. Next time we fight back." Charlene only said, "Hoka-hay!" 15

We had to take showers every evening. One little girl did not want to take her panties off and one of the nuns told her, "You take those 16 underpants off—or else!" But the child was ashamed to do it. The nun was getting her swat to threaten the girl. I went up to the sister, pushed her veil off, and knocked her down. I told her that if she wanted to hit a little girl she should pick on me, pick one her own size. She got herself transferred out of the dorm a week later.

17   In a school like this there is always a lot of favoritism. At St. Francis it was strongly tinged with racism. Girls who were near-white, who came from what the nuns called "nice families," got preferential treatment. They waited on the faculty and got to eat ham or eggs and bacon in the morning. They got the easy jobs while the skins, who did not have the right kind of background—myself among them—always wound up in the laundry room sorting out ten bushel baskets of dirty boys' socks every day. Or we wound up scrubbing the floors and doing all the dishes. The school therefore fostered fights and antagonism between whites and breeds, and between breeds and skins. At one time Charlene and I had to iron all the robes and vestments the priests wore when saying Mass. We had to fold them up and put them into a chest in the back of the church. In a corner, looking over our shoulders, was a statue of the crucified Savior, all bloody and beaten up. Charlene looked up and said, "Look at that poor Indian. The pigs sure worked him over." That was the closest I ever came to seeing Jesus.

18   I was held up as a bad example and didn't mind. I was old enough to have a boyfriend and promptly got one. At the school we had an hour and a half for ourselves. Between the boys' and the girls' wings were some benches where one could sit. My boyfriend and I used to go there just to hold hands and talk. The nuns were very uptight about any boy-girl stuff. They had an exaggerated fear of anything having even the faintest connection with sex. One day in religion class, an all-girl class, Sister Bernard singled me out for some remarks, pointing me out as a bad example, an example that should be shown. She said that I was too free with my body. That I was holding hands which meant that I was not a good example to follow. She also said that I wore unchaste dresses, skirts which were too short, too suggestive, shorter than regulations permitted, and for that I would be punished. She dressed me down before the whole class, carrying on and on about my unchastity.

19   I stood up and told her, "You shouldn't say any of those things, miss. You people are a lot worse than us Indians. I know all about you, because my grandmother and my aunt told me about you. Maybe twelve, thirteen years ago you had a water stoppage here in St. Francis. No water could get through the pipes. There are water lines right under the mission, underground tunnels and passages where in my grandmother's time only the nuns and priests could go, which were off-limits to everybody else. When the water backed up they had to go through all the water lines and clean them out. And in those huge pipes they found the bodies of newborn babies. And they were white babies. They weren't In-

dian babies. At least when our girls have babies, they don't do away with them that way, like flushing them down the toilet, almost.

"And that priest they sent here from Holy Rosary in Pine Ridge be-   20 cause he molested a little girl. You couldn't think of anything better than dump him on us. All he does is watch young women and girls with that funny smile on his face. Why don't you point him out for an example?"

Charlene and I worked on the school newspaper. After all we had   21 some practice. Every day we went down to Publications. One of the priests acted as the photographer, doing the enlarging and developing. He smelled of chemicals which had stained his hands yellow. One day he invited Charlene into the darkroom. He was going to teach her developing. She was developed already. She was a big girl compared to him, taller too. Charlene was nicely built, not fat, just rounded. No sharp edges anywhere. All of a sudden she rushed out of the darkroom, yelling to me, "Let's get out of here! He's trying to feel me up. That priest is nasty." So there was this too to contend with—sexual harassment. We complained to the student body. The nuns said we just had a dirty mind.

We got a new priest in English. During one of his first classes he   22 asked one of the boys a certain question. The boy was shy. He spoke poor English, but he had the right answer. The priest told him, "You did not say it right. Correct yourself. Say it over again." The boy got flustered and stammered. He could hardly get out a word. But the priest kept after him: "Didn't you hear? I told you to do the whole thing over. Get it right this time." He kept on and on.

I stood up and said, "Father, don't be doing that. If you go into an   23 Indian's home and try to talk Indian, they might laugh at you and say, 'Do it over correctly. Get it right this time!'"

He shouted at me, "Mary, you stay after class. Sit down right now!"   24

I stayed after class, until after the bell. He told me, "Get over here!"   25

He grabbed me by the arm, pushing me against the blackboard,   26 shouting, "Why are you always mocking us? You have no reason to do this."

I said, "Sure I do. You were making fun of him. You embarrassed   27 him. He needs strengthening, not weakening. You hurt him. I did not hurt you."

He twisted my arm and pushed real hard. I turned around and hit   28 him in the face, giving him a bloody nose. After that I ran out of the room, slamming the door behind me. He and I went to Sister Bernard's office. I told her, "Today I quit school. I'm not taking any more of this, none of this shit anymore. None of this treatment. Better give me my diploma. I can't waste any more time on you people."

Sister Bernard looked at me for a long, long time. She said, "All   29 right, Mary Ellen, go home today. Come back in a few days and get your diploma." And that was that. Oddly enough, that priest turned out okay. He taught a class in grammar, orthography, composition, things like that. I think he wanted more respect in class. He was still young and unsure of himself. But I was in there too long. I didn't feel like hearing it. Later he became a good friend of the Indians, a personal friend of myself and my husband. He stood up for us during Wounded Knee and after. He stood up to his superiors, stuck his neck way out, became a real people's priest. He even learned our language. He died prematurely of cancer. It is not only the good Indians who die young, but the good whites, too. It is the timid ones who know how to take care of themselves who grow old. I am still grateful to that priest for what he did for us later and for the quarrel he picked with me—or did I pick it with him?—because it ended a situation which had become unendurable for me. The day of my fight with him was my last day in school.

✧ Evaluating the Text

1. What aspects of life at the government boarding school most clearly illustrate the government's desire to transform Native Americans? How did Mary Crow Dog react to the experiences to which she was subjected at the government-run school?

2. What historical insight did the experiences of Mary Crow Dog's mother and grandmother provide into those of Mary Crow Dog herself?

3. Why was the incident of the underground newspaper a crucial one for Mary Crow Dog?

✧ Exploring Different Perspectives

1. How do both Mary Crow Dog's account and Mahdokht Kashkuli's story "The Button" dramatize the effects of being raised by the state?

2. In what sense are Native Americans the untouchables or outcasts in the United States in ways that are comparable to Viramma as recounted in "Pariah"? What explains the very different reactions both have in their respective situations?

✧ Extending Viewpoints through Writing

1. What experiences have you had that made you aware of institutionalized racism?

2. How did this essay give you insight into the vast difference between the traditional culture of Native Americans and their lives in the present?

Viramma

Pariah

———————◆———————

Viramma is an agricultural worker and midwife in Karani, a village in southeast India. She is a member of the caste known as untouchable. She has told her life story over a period of ten years to Josiane and Jean-Luc Racine. She communicates an impression of great strength and fatalism (of her twelve children, only three survive) and her account, translated by Will Hobson, which first appeared in GRANTA, Spring 1997, is a vivid portrait of one at the margin of society.

I am the midwife here. I was born in the village of Velpakkam in   1
Tamil Nadu, and when I married, I came to Karani, my husband's village. I was still a child then. I am a farm worker and, like all my family, I am a serf, bonded to Karani's richest landowner. We are Pariahs. We live apart from the other castes; we eat beef, we play the drums at funerals and weddings because only we can touch cow hide; we work the land. My son Anbin corrects me when I say "Pariah"; he says we should use the word "Harijan."[1] Every day people from the political parties come to the village and tell us to demand higher wages, to fight the caste system. And they mean well. But how would we survive? We have no land, not even a field.

We midwives help women during labour and are paid twenty ru-   2
pees a month by the state. When a woman goes into labour, her relatives come and find me: "Eldest sister-in-law! The woman's in pain at home!" So I drop everything; I go and see her, examine her, turn her round one way, then the other; I pester her a bit and then tell her more or less when the child is going to be born. And it always turns out as I said it would. When the child is born, I cut the cord with a knife and tell one of the other women attending to find a hoe and a crowbar and to dig a hole in the channel near the house. I wait for the placenta to come out and go and bury it immediately. Then I take care of the mother. I stretch her out on a mat, propped up with pillows, wash the baby with soap and hot water and lay it down next to its mother. Then I put a sickle and some margosa leaves at the head of the mat, so spirits don't come near them—those rogue spirits love to prowl around the lanes in

---

*For information on India, see p. 34.
[1]*Harijan* means "loved ones of God." The name change was suggested by Mahatma Gandhi.

the evening or at night, eating any food left lying on the ground and trying to possess people.

3   It's well known that they follow us everywhere we go, when we're hoeing or planting out; when we're changing our sanitary towels; when we're washing our hair. They sense that we're going to visit a woman in labour and then they possess us. That's why we put down the sickle and the margosa leaves. After the birth I'll visit the mother quite often, to make sure everything's going all right. If impurities have stayed in the womb, I'll cook the leaves of the "cow's itch" plant, extract the juice and make the mother drink it three times.

4   That's how a birth happens here. We Pariahs prefer to have babies at home. I tell the nurse if the newborns are boys or girls, and she goes and enters them in the registers at Pondicherry hospital. In the past, we'd take women to hospital only in emergencies. We went there in an ox-cart or a rickshaw, and often the woman died on the way. Nowadays doctors visit the villages and give medicines and tonics to women when they become pregnant. In the sixth or seventh month they're meant to go to the dispensary for a check-up. A nurse also comes to the village. Yes, everything has changed now.

5   I had my twelve children alone; I didn't let anyone near me. "Leave me in peace," I always said to the nurses. "It will come out on its own! Why do you want to rummage around in there?" I always give birth very gently—like stroking a rose. It never lasts long: I'm not one of those women whose labours drag on all night, for days even.

6   When I'm giving birth I first make a point of preparing a tray for Ettiyan—the god of death's assistant—and his huge men, with their thick moustaches and muscly shoulders. On the tray I put green mangoes, coconuts and other fruit as well as some tools: a hoe, a crowbar, a basket, so that they can set to work as soon as the child comes out of the sack in our womb. Yes! I've seen enough to know what I'm talking about. I've had a full bushel of children! Everything we eat goes into that sack: that's how the child grows. Just think what a mystery it is. With the blood he collects over ten months, Isvaran [the god Siva] moulds a baby in our womb. Only he can do that. Otherwise how could a sperm become a child?

7   I've always had plenty of milk. It used to flow so much that the front of my sari was all stiff. It's well known that we breastfeed our children for a long time. That prevents us from having another child immediately. If we were always pregnant, how could we work and eat? Rich women can stretch their legs and take a rest. But to get my rice, I have to work: planting out, hoeing, grazing the cows, collecting wood. When we've got a little one in our arms, it's the same: we take it everywhere, and we worry, because while we're working we don't really know what it's doing, where it is. That's why we try to wait at least

three years, until the child grows up, walks and can say, "Dad," "Mum," "That's our cow." That's what we take as a sign. Then we can start "talking" again, "doing it." If we time it like this, the child will be strong and chubby.

But Isvaran has given me a baby a year. Luckily my blood has   8 stayed the same; it hasn't turned, and my children have never been really emaciated. Of course that also depends on the way you look after them. For me, that used to be my great worry! I managed to feed them well. As soon as I had a little money, I'd buy them sweets. I'd make them rice whenever I could, some *dosai*, some *idli*. I'd put a little sugar in cow's milk…. That's how I took care of them. There are some women who just let their children be without giving them regular meals. Human beings can only live if you put at least a little milk in their mouths when they're hungry! It happens with us that some women skip their children's mealtimes when they're working. But how do you expect them to grow that way?

Isvaran has done his work well; he's put plenty of children in my   9 womb: beautiful children, born in perfect health. It's only afterwards that some have died. One of diarrhoea, another of apoplexy. All of them have walked! Two of my children even came to the peanut harvest. I pierced their noses to put a jewel in. I plaited their hair and put flowers in it and pretty *potteu* on their foreheads, made with paste. I took good care of my little ones. I never neglected them. I dressed them neatly. If high-caste people saw them running in the street, they'd talk to them kindly, thinking that they were high-caste children.

How many children have I had? Wait…I've had twelve. The first   10 was a girl, Muttamma. Then a boy, Ganesan. After that, a girl, Arayi. *Ayo!* After that I don't remember any more. But I've definitely had twelve: we registered them at the registry office. Yes, when there's a birth, you have to go there and declare it. "Here Sir, I've had a boy or a girl and I name it Manivelu, Nataraja or Perambata." Down there they enter all that into a big ledger. *Ayo!* If we went to that office, perhaps they could tell us how many children I've had and their names as well. *Ayo!* Look at that, I don't remember any more. They're born; they die. I've haven't got all my children's names in my head: all I have left are Miniyamma, my fourth child; Anbin, my eighth; and Sundari, my eleventh.

A pregnant woman is prey to everything that roams around her: 11 ghosts, ghouls, demons, the evil spirits of people who have committed suicide or died violent deaths. She has to be very careful, especially if she is a Pariah. We Pariah women have to go all over the place, grazing the cattle, collecting wood. We're outside the whole time, even when the sun's at its height. Those spirits take advantage of this: they grab us and possess us so we fall ill, or have miscarriages. Something like that happened to me when I was pregnant with my second child.

12   One of my nephews died suddenly, the day after his engagement. One night when I was asleep I saw him sitting on me—I felt him! My husband told me that I had squeezed him very tight in my arms, that I'd been delirious and mumbling something. The following day we decided that the boy needed something, and that's why he'd come. My husband went to get bottles of arrack and palm wine. I arranged the offerings in the middle of the house: betel, areca nuts, lime, a big banana leaf with a mountain of rice, some salt fish, some toast, a cigar, bottles of alcohol, a jar of water and a beautiful oil lamp. In the meantime my husband went to find the priest from the temple of Perumal [Vishnu]—he's the one responsible for funerals. The priest asked us to spread river sand next to the offerings. He called on Yama, the god of death, and drew the sign of Yama in the sand. We ate that evening as usual and went to sleep in a corner. You must never sleep opposite the door, because a spirit might slap you when it comes in if it finds you in its way. You have to be brave when a spirit arrives! In fact you won't see it; you only hear its footsteps, like the sound of little bells, *djang, djang,* when an ox-cart goes by. It goes *han! han! han!* as if it's craving something. It always comes with its messengers, all tied to each other with big ropes. You hear them walking with rhythmic, heavy steps: *ahum! ahum! ahum!*

13   We were very afraid. As soon as the spirit came in, the lamp went out in a flash, even though it was full of oil. We heard it walking about and eating its fill and then suddenly it fled. We heard it running away very fast. When day broke soon after it had gone, we rushed to see what had happened. The rice was scattered, everywhere. On the sand we found a cat's paw-print, and part of Yama's sign had been rubbed out. The spirit had come in the form of a cat! While we were waiting for the priest to come, we collected the offerings in a big wicker basket. The priest himself was very satisfied and said that the spirit wouldn't come back. But I fell ill soon after and had a miscarriage.

14   There are worse spirits, though: the *katteri,* for example, who spy on women when they are pregnant. You have to be very careful with them. There are several sorts of *katteri*: Rana Katteri, who has bleeding wounds and drinks blood; or Irsi Katteri, the foetus eater—she's the one who causes miscarriages. As soon as she catches the smell of a foetus in a woman's womb, she's there, spying, waiting for her chance. We can tell immediately that it's that bitch at work if there are black clots when a baby aborts: she sucks up the good blood and leaves only the bad.

15   My first three children were born at my mother's house. Their births went well, and they died in good shape. It was the spirit living in that house who devoured them. My grandfather knew about sorcery. People came to see him; they used to say that he called up the spirit, talked to it and asked it to go along with him when he went out. It lived with him, basically. When my grandfather died, we tried to drive it away but it was no use; it used to come back in the form of my grand-

father; it joined in conversations, calling my grandmother by her name like her dead husband used to. And my grandmother used to answer back, "Ah! The only answer I'll give you is with my broom, you dog! I recognize you! I know who you are! Get out of here!" It would just throw tamarind seeds at her face. When a sorcerer came from Ossur to try and get rid of it, it turned vicious. The sorcerer told us he couldn't do anything against it. The spirit had taken root in that ground. It was old and cunning: we were the ones who had to go. It destroyed everything! Everything! A garlic clove couldn't even grow! My father had to sell his paddy field. I gave birth three times there: none of those children survived. The spirit ate them as and when they were born. Nothing prospered. That's how it is with the spirits.

All my children have been buried where they died: the first ones at Velpakkam, the others at Karani. My mother insisted we burn the first-born and throw her ashes in the river so a sorcerer didn't come and get them. The ashes or bones of first-borns are coveted by magicians. A tiny bit of ash or hair is enough for them. You see them with a hoe on their shoulder prowling around where a first-born has been burnt or buried. We made sure that everything disappeared. We have a saying that if you dissolve the ashes completely in water, you'll immediately have another child.   16

Until they grow up, we mothers always have a fire in our belly for our children: we must feed them, keep them from sickness, raise them to become men or women who can work. One of my three sisters died of a kind of tuberculosis. She had been married and she left a son. I brought him up after her death, but like his mother, he was often ill. Before she died, my sister had prayed that he would become strong, so I took up her prayers. I went into three houses and in each one I asked for a cubit of fabric. I put the three bits of fabric on the ground and laid the child on them. Then I went into three other houses and exchanged the child for three measures of barley, saying, "The child is yours; the barley is mine." Of course afterwards I would get the child back. Then I went to three other houses to collect handfuls of dirt. I mixed the three handfuls, spread them out and rolled the baby in them, saying, "Your name will be Kuppa! You are Kuppa! You have been born of dirt!" Then I pierced his nostril with a silver thread which I twisted into a ring. That worked very well for him! He's still alive and he still wears that ring in his nose today.   17

What is more important for us women than children? If we don't draw anything out of our womb, what's the use of being a woman? A woman who has no son to put a handful of rice in her mouth, no daughter to close her eyes, is an unhappy woman. She or her parents must have failed in their dharma. I have been blessed in that way: Isvaran has filled my womb. Ah, if all my children were alive, they'd do all the trades in the world! One would be a labourer, another a carpenter. I   18 would have made one of them study. We could have given two daughters away in marriage and enjoyed our grandchildren. I would be able to go and rest for a month with each of my sons. Yes, we would have been proud of our children.

✧ Evaluating the Text

1. In what specific ways does the caste into which Viramma was born determine every aspect of her life?

2. Folk beliefs and superstitions play a very important role in Viramma's world. What are some of these and how does her belief in them provide an explanation for the things that have happened to her?

3. From a western perspective, Viramma's attitude toward child-bearing is unusual. However, she earns her living as a midwife and has become reconciled to the death of most of her own children. What cultural values unique to India does she embody?

✧ Exploring Different Perspectives

1. Compare and contrast the everyday lives and attitudes, as social outcasts, of Viramma and Jo Goodwin Parker (see "What Is Poverty?").

2. In your opinion, would Viramma, despite great poverty, have ever considered placing one of her children in an orphanage as the parents did in Kashkuli's story "The Button"? Why or why not?

✧ Extending Viewpoints through Writing

1. Have you ever known anyone whose explanation for events was rooted in superstition? What were the events and what were the superstitions that explained them?

2. What is your own attitude toward having large families? Do you think people should have as many children as they want? Why or why not? As a research project, you might investigate the one-child policy in China.

Lee Stringer

Life on the Street

———————◆———————

Lee Stringer is an African American self-educated writer who survived stretches of homelessness in New York City and an addiction to crack. His accounts of life among New York City's outcasts, collecting cans for a nickel a piece, sleeping in Grand Central Station, being run off subway platforms for distributing the Street News *(a weekly paper he put together for those in the same situation), are compelling and devoid of self-pity. This narrative is taken from his book* Grand Central Winter: Stories from the Street *(1998) with a foreword by Kurt Vonnegut, who played an instrumental role in getting Stringer's work noticed by the public.*

The Streets of New York City, 1985. As far as I was concerned, liv- 1
ing on the streets was not an insurmountable inconvenience. There were
some rough days, before I learned the ins and outs of soup kitchens and
such. But once I hooked into picking up cans at a nickel a pop, I couldn't
even be bothered with that cattle-call ordeal. And what a pleasure it was
to sleep rent- and worry-free under the stars of Central Park.

Then one day the heels of my twenty-four-ninety-five-on-special 2
Fayva shoes caved in. Soon after that the soles sprang open as well, and
I couldn't imagine how I would get up the cash to replace them while
going barefoot. So I asked around on the street where I might come by
a pair of freebies, and was steered toward the Bowery.

"That's where they got all them missions," I was told. 3

Surprisingly no one on the subway seemed to notice my bare feet 4
when I made the fifty-block trip from midtown to the Lower East Side.
I stumbled around down there until I came upon a ragtag queue of
Bowery bums in front of a white two-story stucco building. It turned
out this was the well-known Bowery Mission. And their nine-to-five
was helping down-on-their-luck types like me.

"You can get clothes in here?" I asked the weathered grapehead 5
teetering on his feet at the end of the line, too-big clothes hanging off
his bones. He must have been well into his third bottle of the day. I
could barely decipher what he said. But I seemed to hear something of
the affirmative in his din. So I joined him on line.

We were each issued a ticket at the door, assembled in the day 6
room, then dispatched, ten at a time, to a modest dining room in the
back. It was a makeshift meal, cadged together from many sources, but
it was filling and satisfying.

7   After everyone was fed, they opened up the storeroom where they kept a supply of donated clothes. But I was out of luck. Size thirteen-and-a-half wide are not easy to come by. I spent the afternoon in their day room, slouched in a chair, drifting in and out of sleep. At one point I opened my eyes to see a pair of young slicksters straddling some old geezer who was off somewhere in dreamland. Curious, I watched them through the lashes of one half-opened eye.

8   Evidently whatever they were up to required much preliminary bickering. They stood there, one on either side of their quarry, scowling and hissing at each other, until whatever was their bother got itself resolved. Then the guy on the right reached out and, holding taut the fabric of their mark's trousers with one hand and wielding a single-edge razor like a surgeon with the other, neatly laid the pocket open.

9   I would have thought it a fruitless business; thievery in a place like this. But lo and behold, they came up with a fistful of random coins and crumpled bills. They scurried out the door after that like they had just knocked over a Brink's truck.

10   A man across the room, long face, drooping mustache, cap drawn over his eyes, looked my way, shaking his head solemnly from side to side.

11   "That's the trouble with us black folk," he said. "Always victimizing our own. Why don't they steal from the white man? White man got all the money!"

12   Growing up, whenever I mentioned a new schoolmate, my mother would ask, "What flavor? Chocolate or vanilla?" If I answered vanilla, she would raise her eyebrows. "I'll bet you *they* have money," she'd exclaim. I never did like what that implied about my own prospects. And I liked it a lot less sitting barefoot in the day room of the Bowery Mission. I might have called Longface on it, but looking around me, I couldn't see anything that might contradict his assumptions.

13   Instead I asked him where I could get some shoes.

14   "Just down the street," he told me. "City-run shelter on East Third Street. Anything you need."

15   The Bowery Intake Center on East Third was typical of the Depressingly Utilitarian school of urban municipal architecture. And through its ugly, turd-colored doors trudged a noticeably more desolate and desperate breed, it seemed, than I had seen at any of the privately run places. Those who couldn't—or wouldn't—enter its hallowed halls had set up a cardboard squatters' shantytown between the Dumpsters parked along the outside walls; a tableau that had *discarded* written all over it.

16   Inside, a limp-lidded security guard pointed the way into a large dim, spiritless box of a room, distressed, fifties-vintage vinyl-aluminum chairs scattered ad hoc, listless human forms slumped in them. Lethargy pervaded the room like a fog. People stood twenty deep, numb,

impatient, before a bank of lead-glass windows at the front of the room, the workers behind them indifferently plodding through the rigors of state-sanctioned, pro-forma Samaritanism.

I walked over to the only vacant window—the one with a hand- 17 written sign designating it number one—tapped on the glass, and was greeted by a scowl that said, *Don't do that!* Then a form slid through a slot at the base of the window. I was told to fill it out—which I did promptly—and was just as promptly told to wait until I was called.

This turned out to be a matter of several long hours, during which 18 I sat on the floor, slumped against the wall, being jostled rudely awake by the guard and told "No sleeping" whenever I drifted off. When I finally heard my name blasted over the speakers, I resolved to keep things as simple as possible.

"All I need is a pair of shoes," I told the lady behind Window 2. 19 "They don't even have to be fresh out of the box."

A bemused twinkle came to her eyes. "It don' work this way," she 20 said, a hint of the islands in her voice as she announced with some pride, "We have a system here. Intake. Meal ticket. Shelter voucher. You want us to help you, you do the whole ting."

By three o'clock I had been hooked up with the works and bussed 21 up to Ward's Island—right across the East River from my former Ninety-sixth Street apartment ironically—accompanied by a hairy, spike-thin white guy who wasn't even on the same planet and a talky, blubberous, Jheri-curled brother of ambiguous sexuality. We were each subjected to a pat-down search, followed by a grave quickie lecture on the prohibitions of bringing contraband into the shelter, and were then told someone would be out to get us. The big queen chirped away as we waited on a bench just inside the complex, taking a certain pride in his extensive knowledge of the workings of the shelter system. He was obviously a regular.

"You are about to enter the *Waldorf* of city shelters," he informed 22 me. "This here's as good as it gets."

"And who are you?" I asked him, "the Zagat of the down-and-out?" 23

He found that one doggone funny. Slapped me on my thigh and 24 yucked it up. When a worker came out to fetch the white kid, it was "Would you follow me, please, Mr. Williams?" But when he came back later to fetch one of us, it was "Yo cuz, wanna come this way?"

Both Zagat and I thought that was a scream. 25

I was the last one in; ushered into a large, prison-style shower 26 room, issued soap, a towel, delousing agent, and told to strip and shower. I was immensely grateful for the shower. I stepped from it feeling human again.

I was then given a handwritten ticket and sent upstairs, where I was 27 issued underwear, a shirt, slacks, socks, and, at last, a pair of shoes. Secondhand, Oxford-brown penny loafers to be exact—minus the pennies. I was also assigned a bed number and told to be in by nine o'clock or my bed would go to someone else.

28   "And remember," they added. "If you go out, you can't come back in for an hour. Same thing once you come in. Can't go out for an hour. Got it?"

29   I got it.

30   Up in the dorm I was offered a bargain on a bologna and cheese on white by an enterprising Puerto Rican fellow, running what seemed to be a lucrative trade selling cut-rate sandwiches out of his locker. I was hungry but I declined. Thoughts of jockstraps and old Nikes commingling with the food kept insinuating themselves.

31   A little later a purveyor's truck rolled up to the back of the building and off-loaded an awesome shitload of food, huge bags of rice, sacks of potatoes, whole hams, turkeys, and roasts, industrial-size cans of fruit and vegetables, two-gallon jugs of milk. *That's the end of Slick's sandwich trade*, I thought to myself.

32   Only, in the four meals I had there, none of that stuff ever showed up on our plates. Breakfast was composed of a minibox of cereal, a half pint of milk, and a piece of fruit. Lunch and dinner were the same—a large serving spoon's worth of three-bean salad, three slices of fried salami, and two slices of bread.

33   "We won't see none of that," declared Zagat when I told him about the truck. (And let's face it, if he was an authority on anything, it would be food.) "Most of that stuff is going out the other door."

34   "No way," I said. "The Volunteers of America run this place for the city. A nonprofit."

35   "Nonprofit, huh?" Zagat said with a sigh. "Look. They make money on us. The city pays them for every swinging dick that comes through the door. Pays for all them goodies you saw coming in too. Probably selling the shit, for all I know."

36   I nodded, but I was having a hard time buying it.

37   "Don't believe me," Zagat said. "Tell you what. Go into the kitchen and tell them you want you a pork chop. Go ahead. Boy, they'll look at you like you're out your mind. 'A pork what? Nigger, you better *get* outta here and get your black ass a job!'"

38   The way he said it, I cracked up.

39   "It's all a hustle, brother," Zagat went on. "Without us all these people wouldn't have their jobs. They *need* folks like us. Me, I hustle 'em right back. I *get* mines. Already got three digits going under different names"—*Digits* being welfare benefits—"I were you, I'd get it now, brother. While you can. 'Cause I'll tell you. Pretty soon? This shit?"—he said this, taking in the universe in one expansive sweep of his arm—"Gonna be dead. These new people coming in? Uh-uh, honey. They're fixin' to *kill* all this welfare shit."

40   Later that day I discovered my locker had been gone through. I didn't have all that much of anything. All the same, I slept with my

stuff tucked underneath the mattress that night. I didn't stay another night. I didn't like the karma of the place, for want of a better way to put it—the guards, the pat-downs, the food lines, the whole, watch-your-back, watch-your-mouth, watch-out-for-number-one, jailhouse mentality. I figured I'd just as well take my chances on the street. But my day and a half of sheltered life did confirm what had been hinted at in the pocket incident at the Bowery Mission. That even at the very bottom of existence it's still all about money.

The next day I donned my original clothes, which they had laundered for me, and the secondhand, Oxford-brown penny loafers minus their eponymous coins, and left behind my voucher, my meal ticket, my clothing issue, and everything else they had given me.   41

✧ Evaluating the Text

1. How would you characterize the life circumstances in which Stringer finds himself?

2. What incongruity can you discover between Stringer's predicament and the kind of person he seems to be based on his use of language and seeming sophistication?

3. Once he enters the universe of the welfare shelter, what features of life there make it impossible for him to stay? How is the shelter run? Who really benefits from the shelter's existence?

✧ Exploring Different Perspectives

1. What aspects of Viramma's (see "Pariah") philosophy make it possible for her to accept her life circumstances as compared with Stringer? Is being homeless and poor in America worse than being poor in India? Explain your answer.

2. Discuss how the center of one's universe comes down to items as simple as soap or shoes and the hard choices one has to make in Stringer's and in Jo Goodwin Parker's accounts.

✧ Extending Viewpoints through Writing

1. How did Stringer's narrative change your perception of people you may have passed on the street who were homeless?

2. At the center of Stringer's account is an indictment of the social service system in New York City. Do you find his appraisal fair? Why or why not?

Liliana Heker

The Stolen Party

---◆---

The Argentine writer Liliana Heker was born in Buenos Aires in 1943. As editor-in-chief of two literary magazines, the Escarahajo de Oro, *and the* Ornitorrinco *("The Platypus"), Heker provided an invaluable forum for writers and critics over twenty-five years. This period coincided with Argentina's descent into chaos under military dictatorships. Her influential published works include* Those That Saw the Bramble *(1966),* Zona de Clivage *(1988),* The Edges of the Real Thing *(1991), and* The Aim of History *(1996). Heker's short story, "The Stolen Party," translated by Alberto Manguel for his anthology* Other Fires *(1985), is a work of great social insight and literary power. It has since become the title story of Heker's collection of short stories in English (1994).*

Argentina, the second largest nation in South America after Brazil, won independence from Spain in 1819 and quickly became a favored destination for European immigrants, who today make up a sizeable majority of the population. Repeated coups and military dictatorships have marked Argentina's history in the twentieth century. General Juan Perón came to power in 1944, established a dictatorship and ruled with the aid of his wife Eva Perón ("Evita") until he was overthrown by a military coup in 1955. He returned to power in 1973, died in 1974, and was succeeded by his third wife, Isabel, who was overthrown by a military coup in March 1976. The junta made up of commanders of the military was led by General Jorge Videla. Under his rule, tens of thousands of political opponents who had supported Péron were siezed, often never to be seen again. In 1982, Argentina's unsuccessful war against Great Britain over the Falkland Islands (Islas Malvinas) *led to the fall of General Leopoldo Galtieri, who had replaced Videla the year before, and to democratic elections in 1983, which returned the country to civilian rule. In 1989, a Peronist, Carlos Raúl Menem, was elected president as Argentina faced devastating inflation and a deteriorating economy. Peronists lost their majority in the 1997 legislative elections.*

1   As soon as she arrived she went straight to the kitchen to see if the monkey was there. It was: What a relief! She wouldn't have liked to admit that her mother had been right. *Monkeys at a birthday?* her mother had sneered. *Get away with you, believing any nonsense you're told!* She was cross, but not because of the monkey, the girl thought; it's just because of the party.

2   "I don't like you going," she told her. "It's a rich people's party."

"Rich people go to Heaven too," said the girl, who studied religion at school.   3

"Get away with Heaven," said the mother. "The problem with you, young lady, is that you like to fart higher than your ass."   4

The girl didn't approve of the way her mother spoke. She was barely nine, and one of the best in her class.   5

"I'm going because I've been invited," she said. "And I've been invited because Luciana is my friend. So there."   6

"Ah yes, your friend," her mother grumbled. She paused. "Listen, Rosaura," she said at last. "That one's not your friend. You know what you are to them? The maid's daughter, that's what."   7

Rosaura blinked hard: She wasn't going to cry. Then she yelled: "Shut up! You know nothing about being friends!"   8

Every afternoon she used to go to Luciana's house and they would both finish their homework while Rosaura's mother did the cleaning. They had their tea in the kitchen and they told each other secrets. Rosaura loved everything in the big house, and she also loved the people who lived there.   9

"I'm going because it will be the most lovely party in the whole world, Luciana told me it would. There will be a magician, and he will bring a monkey and everything."   10

The mother swung around to take a good look at her child, and pompously put her hands on her hips.   11

"Monkeys at a birthday?" she said. "Get away with you, believing any nonsense you're told!"   12

Rosaura was deeply offended. She thought it unfair of her mother to accuse other people of being liars simply because they were rich. Rosaura too wanted to be rich, of course. If one day she managed to live in a beautiful palace, would her mother stop loving her? She felt very sad. She wanted to go to that party more than anything else in the world.   13

"I'll die if I don't go," she whispered, almost without moving her lips.   14

And she wasn't sure whether she had been heard, but on the morning of the party she discovered that her mother had starched her Christmas dress. And in the afternoon, after washing her hair, her mother rinsed it in apple vinegar so that it would be all nice and shiny. Before going out, Rosaura admired herself in the mirror, with her white dress and glossy hair, and thought she looked terribly pretty.   15

Señora Ines also seemed to notice. As soon as she saw her, she said: 16

"How lovely you look today, Rosaura."   17

Rosaura gave her starched skirt a slight toss with her hands and walked into the party with a firm step. She said hello to Luciana and asked about the monkey. Luciana put on a secretive look and whispered into Rosaura's ear: "He's in the kitchen. But don't tell anyone, because it's a surprise."   18

19   Rosaura wanted to make sure. Carefully she entered the kitchen and there she saw it: deep in thought, inside its cage. It looked so funny that the girl stood there for a while, watching it, and later, every so often, she would slip out of the party unseen and go and admire it. Rosaura was the only one allowed into the kitchen. Señora Ines had said: "You yes, but not the others, they're much too boisterous, they might break something." Rosaura had never broken anything. She even managed the jug of orange juice, carrying it from the kitchen into the dining room. She held it carefully and didn't spill a single drop. And Señora Ines had said: "Are you sure you can manage a jug as big as that?" Of course she could manage. She wasn't a butterfingers, like the others. Like that blonde girl with the bow in her hair. As soon as she saw Rosaura, the girl with the bow had said:

20   "And you? Who are you?"

21   "I'm a friend of Luciana," said Rosaura.

22   "No," said the girl with the bow, "you are not a friend of Luciana because I'm her cousin and I know all her friends. And I don't know you."

23   "So what," said Rosaura. "I come here every afternoon with my mother and we do our homework together."

24   "You and your mother do your homework together?" asked the girl, laughing.

25   "I and Luciana do our homework together," said Rosaura, very seriously.

26   The girl with the bow shrugged her shoulders.

27   "That's not being friends," she said. "Do you go to school together?"

28   "No."

29   "So where do you know her from?" said the girl, getting impatient.

30   Rosaura remembered her mother's words perfectly. She took a deep breath.

31   "I'm the daughter of the employee," she said.

32   Her mother had said very clearly: "If someone asks, you say you're the daughter of the employee; that's all." She also told her to add: "And proud of it." But Rosaura thought that never in her life would she dare say something of the sort.

33   "What employee?" said the girl with the bow. "Employee in a shop?"

34   "No," said Rosaura angrily. "My mother doesn't sell anything in any shop, so there."

35   "So how come she's an employee?" said the girl with the bow.

36   Just then Señora Ines arrived saying *shh shh,* and asked Rosaura if she wouldn't mind helping serve out the hotdogs, as she knew the house so much better than the others.

37   "See?" said Rosaura to the girl with the bow, and when no one was looking she kicked her in the shin.

38   Apart from the girl with the bow, all the others were delightful. The one she liked best was Luciana, with her golden birthday crown; and

then the boys. Rosaura won the sack race, and nobody managed to catch her when they played tag. When they split into two teams to play charades, all the boys wanted her for their side. Rosaura felt she had never been so happy in all her life.

But the best was still to come. The best came after Luciana blew out the candles. First the cake. Señora Ines had asked her to help pass the cake around, and Rosaura had enjoyed the task immensely, because everyone called out to her, shouting "Me, me!" Rosaura remembered a story in which there was a queen who had the power of life or death over her subjects. She had always loved that, having the power of life or death. To Luciana and the boys she gave the largest pieces, and to the girl with the bow she gave a slice so thin one could see through it. 39

After the cake came the magician, tall and bony, with a fine red cape. A true magician: He could untie handkerchiefs by blowing on them and make a chain with links that had no openings. He could guess what cards were pulled out from a pack, and the monkey was his assistant. He called the monkey "partner." "Let's see here, partner," he would say, "turn over a card." And, "Don't run away, partner: Time to work now." 40

The final trick was wonderful. One of the children had to hold the monkey in his arms and the magician said he would make him disappear. 41

"What, the boy?" they all shouted. 42

"No, the monkey!" shouted back the magician. 43

Rosaura thought that this was truly the most amusing party in the whole world. 44

The magician asked a small fat boy to come and help, but the small fat boy got frightened almost at once and dropped the monkey on the floor. The magician picked him him up carefully, whispered something in his ear, and the monkey nodded almost as if he understood. 45

"You mustn't be so unmanly, my friend," the magician said to the fat boy. 46

"What's unmanly?" said the fat boy. 47

The magician turned around as if to look for spies. 48

"A sissy," said the magician. "Go sit down." 49

Then he stared at all the faces, one by one. Rosaura felt her heart tremble. 50

"You, with the Spanish eyes," said the magician. And everyone saw that he was pointing at her. 51

She wasn't afraid. Neither holding the monkey, nor when the magician made him vanish; not even when, at the end, the magician flung his red cape over Rosaura's head and uttered a few magic words...and the monkey reappeared, chattering happily, in her arms. The children clapped furiously. And before Rosaura returned to her seat, the magician said: 52

"Thank you very much, my little countess." 53

54   She was so pleased with the compliment that a while later, when her mother came to fetch her, that was the first thing she told her.

55   "I helped the magician and he said to me, "Thank you very much, my little countess.'"

56   It was strange because up to then Rosaura had thought that she was angry with her mother. All along Rosaura had imagined that she would say to her: "See that the monkey wasn't a lie?" But instead she was so thrilled that she told her mother all about the wonderful magician.

57   Her mother tapped her on the head and said: "So now we're a countess!"

58   But one could see that she was beaming.

59   And now they both stood in the entrance, because a moment ago Señora Ines, smiling, had said: "Please wait here a second."

60   Her mother suddenly seemed worried.

61   "What is it?" she asked Rosaura.

62   "What is what?" said Rosaura. "It's nothing; she just wants to get the presents for those who are leaving, see?"

63   She pointed at the fat boy and at a girl with pigtails who were also waiting there, next to their mothers. And she explained about the presents. She knew, because she had been watching those who left before her. When one of the girls was about to leave, Señora Ines would give her a bracelet. When a boy left, Señora Ines gave him a yo-yo. Rosaura preferred the yo-yo because it sparkled, but she didn't mention that to her mother. Her mother might have said: "So why don't you ask for one, you blockhead?" That's what her mother was like. Rosaura didn't feel like explaining that she'd be horribly ashamed to be the odd one out. Instead she said:

64   "I was the best-behaved at the party."

65   And she said no more because Señora Ines came out into the hall with two bags, one pink and one blue.

66   First she went up to the fat boy, gave him a yo-yo out of the blue bag, and the fat boy left with his mother. Then she went up to the girl and gave her a bracelet out of the pink bag, and the girl with the pigtails left as well.

67   Finally she came up to Rosaura and her mother. She had a big smile on her face and Rosaura liked that. Señora Ines looked down at her, then looked up at her mother, and then said something that made Rosaura proud:

68   "What a marvelous daughter you have, Herminia."

69   For an instant, Rosaura thought that she'd give her two presents: the bracelet and the yo-yo. Señora Ines bent down as if about to look for something. Rosaura also leaned forward, stretching out her arm. But she never completed the movement.

70   Señora Ines didn't look in the pink bag. Nor did she look in the blue bag. Instead she rummaged in her purse. In her hand appeared two bills.

"You really and truly earned this," she said handing them over. 71
"Thank you for all your help, my pet."

Rosaura felt her arms stiffen, stick close to her body, and then she 72
noticed her mother's hand on her shoulder. Instinctively she pressed
herself against her mother's body. That was all. Except her eyes. Rosaura's eyes had a cold, clear look that fixed itself on Señora Ines's face.

Señora Ines, motionless, stood there with her hand outstretched. 73
As if she didn't dare draw it back. As if the slightest change might shat-
ter an infinitely delicate balance.

✦ Evaluating the Text

1. How do all the events at the party coupled with Rosaura's expectations lead her to believe that she was an invited guest?

2. Implicit in the title is the concept that the party has been "stolen."
   There are many different ways to interpret this title. For example, Rosaura behaves as if she is a guest when in fact she is not. How do you
   understand the title?

3. Examine carefully Rosaura's responses to her mother, her feelings when
   she is chosen to distribute the birthday cake and is allowed to hold the
   monkey, and how she understands Señora Ines's comment that she is "a
   marvelous daughter." Collectively, do these suggest she is repressing
   her real position as a social inferior and is simply not "getting it?" Why
   or why not?

✦ Exploring Different Perspectives

1. Compare the mother–daughter relationship in Heker's story with that
   of Mary Crow Dog and her mother in "Civilize Them with a Stick."

2. Compare caste and class as they set limits on one's life in Heker's story
   and in Viramma's account, "Pariah."

✦ Extending Viewpoints through Writing

1. Rosaura suffers when she discovers her real social position is not what
   she had believed. Have you ever felt that a sense of belonging was stolen from you because of class limitations? Describe your experience.

2. The display of wealth is an important feature of Heker's story. Have
   you ever attended a party where the purpose was to impress others
   with an extravagant display? Describe in detail the setting and events
   at this party and the extent to which your view of yourself changed in
   this environment.

Connecting Cultures

---◆---

Jo Goodwin Parker, "What Is Poverty?"

Discuss the devastating effects of poverty on the human spirit, drawing on the accounts by Parker and Luis Alberto Urrea (see "Border Story" in Chapter 7).

Mahdokht Kashkuli, "The Button"

Compare the treatment of children who are perceived as burdensome in Kashkuli's story and Christy Brown's account in "The Letter 'A'" in Chapter 2.

Alonso Salazar, "The Lords of Creation"

What similarities and differences can you discover in the dehumanizing effects of violence as depicted in Salazar's account and Jerzy Kosinski's "The Miller's Tale" in Chapter 2?

Mary Crow Dog and Richard Erdoes, "Civilize Them with a Stick"

How does the phenomenon of diminished self-esteem as a result of propaganda by those in power enter into the accounts by Mary Crow Dog and Ngũgĩ wa Thiong'o (see "Decolonising the Mind" in Chapter 6)?

Viramma, "Pariah"

Compare and contrast the superstitions and cultural beliefs in Viramma's account with those in Bessie Head's story "Looking for a Rain God" in Chapter 8.

Lee Stringer, "Life on the Street"

Discuss the similarities between trying to survive in New York City as described by Stringer with surviving in Tijuana as portrayed by Luis Alberto Urrea in "Border Story" in Chapter 7.

Liliana Heker, "The Stolen Party"

How does the theme of depending on the charity of others play a role in Heker's story and Milorad Pavić's story "The Wedgwood Tea Set" in Chapter 6?

6

The Individual in Society

◆

No conflicts between different points of view are more dramatic than those between individual citizens and the nation-states to which they relinquish a certain degree of freedom in exchange for the benefits that can be achieved only through collective political and social institutions, such as the military and the legal, health care, and educational systems. The allegiance that individuals owe their governments and the protection of individual rights that citizens expect in return have been the subject of intense analysis through the ages by such figures as Socrates in Plato's *Apology* and *Crito,* Henry David Thoreau in "Civil Disobedience," and Martin Luther King, Jr., in "A Letter from Birmingham Jail." The readings that follow continue this debate by providing accounts drawn from many different societies and revealing assumptions and expectations that are very different, in many cases, from those that characterize our own democratic form of government.

The concept of the state includes the political processes and organizations that serve as the means through which individuals and groups obtain and employ power. Political organization in different cultures may take a variety of forms, whether that of a chieftain in a tribal culture or more complex distributions of power and authority in societies like that of the United States, with two parties, an electoral college, judges, courts, prisons, armed forces, a state department, and other institutions designed to maintain and regulate order.

In theory, the legal processes of a society exist to enforce that society's concept of justice and its accompanying norms, laws, and customs. In practice, however, penalties and fines, imprisonment, torture, ostracism, and even death are meted out in many cultures in far more arbitrary ways.

In the former Yugoslavia, for example, the use of the phrase *ethnic cleansing* has served to conceal a genocidal policy in which state power was employed to destroy entire groups of people on grounds of presumed ethnicity.

A politicized environment within a state has an intensely corrosive effect in personal relationships when individual loyalties clash with officially decreed allegiances. Authors in many countries and cultures describe the seductive and persuasive powers that the state can mobilize through propaganda and the threat of force to manipulate its citizens. Regimes also remain in power by channeling the frustrations of one group against another. Many of the following selections explore the predicaments of ordinary citizens trying to survive oppression.

The Italian writer Natalia Ginzburg, in "The Son of Man," describes the material and spiritual desolation her country experienced during World War II. A story, "The Wedgwood Tea Set," whose form may remind you of an allegory or parable, by the Serbian writer Milorad Pavić, probes the deceptive nature of geopolitical realities. Speaking from a postcolonial perspective in Kenya, Ngũgĩ wa Thiong'o, in "Decolonising the Mind," analyzes the damaging psychological consequences of having been forbidden by the British rulers to write or speak his native language while in school. With unusual honesty, Rae Yang, in "At the Center of the Storm," tells how she and the other Red Guards tyrannized school teachers and those who had been authority figures before Mao Zedong's Cultural Revolution. The Chilean author, Luis Sepulveda, in "Daisy," displays an unusual ironic detachment in his account of having to cope with the literary pretensions of the guard when he was imprisoned. A public flogging in modern-day Pakistan provokes Anwar Iqbal's indignation in "Fifteen Lashes." Based on a true incident in Cyprus, Panos Ioannides's story, "Gregory," explores the question of conscience during wartime.

Natalia Ginzburg

The Son of Man

◆━━━━━━━◆

Natalia Ginzburg (1916–1991) was born in Palermo, Italy, and is one of the most notable postwar Italian writers. Her keen sense for the details of everyday family life underlie the appeal that her work has for readers around the world. A prolific novelist, short story writer, dramatist, and essayist, she was a political activist and was elected to the Italian Parliament in 1983. Below the surface of her novels, such as Family Sayings *(1967), are the devastating losses produced by war and social upheaval, which Ginzburg discusses in the following essay, "The Son of Man." This essay first appeared in English in* A Map of Hope: Women's Writing on Human Rights—An International Literary Anthology, *edited by Marjorie Agosin (1999). Ginzburg's other works published in English include the novels* A Light for Fools *(1956) and* Voices in the Evening *(1963). Her award-winning play,* The Advertisement *(1969), was produced at the Old Vic Theater in London.*

*Italy is a republic in southern Europe, extending into the Mediterranean Sea as a boot-shaped peninsula, bordered to the northwest by France, to the north by Switzerland and Austria, and to the northeast by Slovenia. From the fourth century B.C. to the fifth century A.D., the history of Italy is for the most part that of the Roman Empire. The Italian Renaissance, in the fourteenth century, awakened Europe from the Middle Ages and bequeathed countless great works of art and culture to the world. Reacting to Austria's domination in the mid-1800s, Italian nationalism (*Risorgimento, *or "resurgence") ultimately united different political elements under a parliament and a king. In 1922, Italy came under the Fascist leadership of Benito Mussolini, who later joined Germany and Japan (as the Axis Powers) in World War II until Fascism was overthrown in 1943. In 1946, Italy became a republic and joined NATO (North Atlantic Treaty Organization) in 1949. The postwar era has been a turbulent one politically with a succession of short-lived coalition governments. Recent huge budget deficits have curtailed economic growth and forced the government to cut spending in health and education, moves that have resulted in strikes and social unrest. An April 1993 referendum to replace the proportional system of voting by a majority system was approved by over 80 percent of the voters. The prevailing system had led to weak coalition governments coming into power and a breakdown in government services. A new prime minister, Carlo Azeglio Ciampi, committed the government to implementing political reform. He*

*was succeeded as prime minister by Silvio Berlusconi in May 1994 and
Lamberto Dini in January 1995.*

1   There has been a war and people have seen so many houses reduced to rubble that they no longer feel safe in their own homes which
once seemed so quiet and secure. This is something that is incurable
and will never be cured no matter how many years go by. True, we
have a lamp on the table again, and a little vase of flowers, and pictures
of our loved ones, but we can no longer trust any of these things because once, suddenly, we had to leave them behind, or because we
have searched through the rubble for them in vain.

2   It is useless to believe that we could recover from twenty years like
those we have been through. Those of us who have been fugitives will
never be at peace. A ring at the door-bell in the middle of the night can
only mean the word "police" to us. And it is useless for us to tell ourselves over and over again that behind the word "police" there are now
friendly faces from whom we can ask for help and protection. This
word always fills us with fear and suspicion. When I look at my sleeping children I think with relief that I will not have to wake them and
run off into the night. But it is not a deep, lasting relief. It always seems
to me that some day or other we shall once again have to get up and
run off in the middle of the night, and leave everything—the quiet
rooms, our letters, mementoes, clothes—behind us.

3   Once the experience of evil has been endured it is never forgotten.
Someone who has seen a house collapse knows only too clearly what
frail things little vases of flowers and pictures and white walls are. He
knows only too well what a house is made of. A house is made of
bricks and mortar and can collapse. A house is not particularly solid. It
can collapse from one moment to the next. Behind the peaceful little
vases of flowers, behind the teapots and carpets and waxed floors there
is the other true face of a house—the hideous face of a house that has
been reduced to rubble.

4   We shall not get over this war. It is useless to try. We shall never be
people who go peacefully about their business, who think and study
and manage their lives quietly. Something has happened to our houses.
Something has happened to us. We shall never be at peace again.

5   We have seen reality's darkest face, and it no longer horrifies us.
And there are still those who complain that writers use bitter, violent
language, that they write about cruel, distressing things, that they
present reality in the worst possible light.

6   We cannot lie in our books and we cannot lie in any of the things
we do. And perhaps this is the one good thing that has come out of the
war. Not to lie, and not to allow others to lie to us. Such is the nature of
the young now, of our generation. Those who are older than us are still
too fond of falsehoods, of the veils and masks with which they hide re-

ality. Our language saddens and offends them. They do not understand our attitude to reality. We are close to the truth of things. This is the only good the war has given us, but it has given it only to the young. It has given nothing but fear and a sense of insecurity to the old. And we who are young are also afraid, we also feel insecure in our homes, but we are not made defenceless by this fear. We have a toughness and strength which those who are older than us have never known.

For some the war started only with the war, with houses reduced 7 to rubble and with the Germans, but for others it started as long ago as the first years of Fascism, and consequently for them the feeling of insecurity and constant danger is far greater. Danger, the feeling that you must hide, the feeling that—without warning—you will have to leave the warmth of your bed and your house, for many of us all this started many years ago. It crept into our childish games, followed us to our desks at school and taught us to see enemies everywhere. This is how it was for many of us in Italy, and elsewhere, and we believed that one day we would be able to walk without anxiety down the streets of our own cities, but now that we can perhaps walk there without anxiety we realize that we shall never be cured of this sickness. And so we are constantly forced to seek out a new strength, a new toughness with which to face whatever reality may confront us. We have been driven to look for an inward peace which is not the product of carpets and little vases of flowers.

There is no peace for the son of man. The foxes and the wolves 8 have their holes, but the son of man hath not where to lay his head. Our generation is a generation of men. It is not a generation of foxes and wolves. Each of us would dearly like to rest his head somewhere, to have a little warm, dry nest. But there is no peace for the son of man. Each of us at some time in his life has had the illusion that he could sleep somewhere safely, that he could take possession of some certainty, some faith, and there rest his limbs. But all the certainties of the past have been snatched away from us, and faith has never after all been a place for sleeping in.

And we are a people without tears. The things that moved our par- 9 ents do not move us at all. Our parents and those older than us disapprove of the way we bring up our children. They would like us to lie to our children as they lied to us. They would like our children to play with woolly toys in pretty pink rooms with little trees and rabbits painted on the walls. They would like us to surround their infancy with veils and lies, and carefully hide the truth of things from them. But we cannot do this. We cannot do this to children whom we have woken in the middle of the night and tremblingly dressed in the darkness so that we could flee with them or hide them, or simply because the air-raid sirens were lacerating the skies. We cannot do this to children who have seen terror and horror in our faces. We cannot bring ourselves to tell these children that we found them under cabbages, or that when a person dies he goes on a long journey.

10   There is an unbridgeable abyss between us and the previous generation. The dangers they lived through were trivial and their houses were rarely reduced to rubble. Earthquakes and fires were not phenomena that happened constantly and to everyone. The women did their knitting and told the cook what to make for lunch and invited their friends to houses that did not collapse. Everyone thought and studied and managed his life quietly. It was a different time and probably very fine in its way. But we are tied to our suffering, and at heart we are glad of our destiny as men.

✧ Evaluating the Text

1. In what fundamental ways has the author been changed by the experience of war?

2. Throughout her essay, Ginzburg uses the idea of "houses reduced to rubble" many times. What does this phrase symbolize for her?

3. In what way has the experience that Ginzburg survived made it impossible to raise her children the way she would have otherwise?

✧ Exploring Different Perspectives

1. In what way has witnessing the violence of which people are capable during revolutions and war produced similar psychological effects, despite the very different societies depicted by Ginzburg and by Rae Yang as portrayed in "At the Center of the Storm"?

2. Compare the theme of civilization's fragile veneer in Ginzburg's essay and in Milorad Pavić's story "The Wedgwood Tea Set."

✧ Extending Viewpoints through Writing

1. Ginzburg has the experience of never again being able to believe that "behind the word 'police' there are now friendly faces from whom we can ask for help and protection." Have you or a friend ever been involved in an incident with the police that fundamentally altered your perceptions either positively or negatively? Describe your experience.

2. As a Jew in Italy during World War II, Ginzburg was constantly aware of her precarious situation. This made her more self-reliant. How does the 1998 Academy Award–winning film *Life Is Beautiful* illustrate many aspects of Ginzburg's account?

Milorad Pavić

The Wedgwood Tea Set

◆

Milorad Pavić, one of the best known contemporary Serbian prose writers, was born in 1929 in Belgrade. He has been credited with the invention of a kind of fiction that gives the impression of an inexhaustible text through the blending of the fantastic into realistic narratives. This "hyperfiction," as it is known, is well illustrated by the following story, "The Wedgwood Tea Set," translated by Darka Topali, which originally appeared in The Prince of Fire: An Anthology of Contemporary Serbian Short Stories, *edited by Radmila J. Gorup and Madezda Obradovic (1998). Notable among Pavić's works are* Landscape Painted with Tea *(1988),* Dictionary of the Khazars *(1988), and* The Inner Side of the Wind *(1993).*

The Balkans (Balkan means "forested mountain" in Turkish) to which Milorad Pavić, who himself is Serbian, refers at the end of his story are the states that occupy the mountainous Balkan Peninsula of southeastern Europe, an area that was part of the Ottoman Empire. It is usually considered to include Albania, Bulgaria, Greece, Romania, European Turkey, and the states that were formerly part of Yugoslavia (Bosnia, Hercegovina, Croatia, Macedonia, and Slovenia) and present-day Yugoslavia (Serbia and Montenegro). The peninsula was at times part of ancient Greece and the Roman and Byzantine Empires and was ruled by Turks as part of the Ottoman Empire from the late fifteenth century to the end of the Balkan Wars in 1913. The term Balkanization *has entered common usage as referring to the disintegration of a geographic area into politically contentious groups. A war in 1999 between NATO forces and Serbia was followed by a period of enforced peace under NATO occupation. NATO's intervention came in response to Serbian aggression against ethnic Albanians (about 14 percent of the population of Serbia), most of whom were living in the province of Kosovo.*

In the story you are about to read, the protagonists' names will be given at the end instead of the beginning. 1

At the capital's mathematics faculty, my younger brother, who was 2
a student of philology and military science, introduced us to each other. Since she was searching for a companion with whom to prepare for Mathematics I, we began studying together, and as she did not come from another town as I did, we studied in her parents' big house. Quite early each morning, I passed by the shining Layland-Buffalo car, which

belonged to her. In front of the door I would stoop down and look for a stone, put it in my pocket, ring the doorbell, and go upstairs. I carried no books, notebooks, or instruments; everything stayed at her place and was always ready for work. We studied from seven to nine, then we were served breakfast and would continue till ten; from ten to eleven we would usually go over the material already covered. All that time, I would be holding the stone in my hand. In case I should doze off, it would fall on the floor and wake me up before anyone noticed. After eleven she would continue to study, but not I. So we prepared for the mathematics exam every day except Sunday, when she studied alone. She very quickly realized that I could not keep up with her and that my knowledge lagged more and more behind hers. She thought that I went home to catch up on the lessons I had missed, but she never said a thing. "Let everyone like an earthworm eat his own way through," she thought, aware that by teaching another she wasn't teaching herself.

3   When the September term came, we agreed to meet on the day of the examination and take the exam together. Excited as she was, she didn't have time to be especially surprised that I didn't show up and that I did not take the exam, either. Only after she had passed the exam did she ask herself what had happened to me. But I didn't appear till winter. "Why should every bee gather honey, anyway?" she concluded, but still asked herself sometimes, "What's he up to? He is probably one of those smile-carriers, who buys his merchandise in the East, and sells it in the West, or vice versa...."

4   When Mathematics II was on the agenda, she suddenly met me one morning, noticing with interest the new patches on my elbows and the newly grown hair, which she had not seen before. It was again the same. Each morning I would come at a certain hour, and she would descend through the green and layered air, as if through water full of cool and warm currents, open the door for me, sleepy, but with that mirror-breaking look of hers. She would watch for one moment how I squeezed out my beard into the cap and how I took off my gloves. Bringing together the middle finger and the thumb, with a decisive gesture I would simultaneously turn them inside out, thus taking them both off with the same movement. When that was over, she would immediately go to work. She made up her mind to study with all her strength, which happened daily. With untiring will and regularity, she delved into all details of the subject, no matter if it was morning, when we started out fresh, after breakfast, or toward the end, when she worked a bit more slowly but not skipping a single thing. I would still quit at eleven, and she would soon notice again that I couldn't concentrate on what I was doing, that my looks grew old in an hour, and that I was behind her again. She would look at my feet, one of which was always ready to step out, while the other was completely still. Then they would change positions.

When the January term arrived, she had the feeling that I could not pass the exam, but she was silent, feeling a trifle guilty herself. "Anyway," she concluded, "should I kiss his elbow to make him learn? If he cuts bread on his head, that's his own affair...."

When I didn't show up then either, she was nevertheless surprised, and after finishing the exam looked for the list of candidates to check whether I was perhaps scheduled for the afternoon or some other day. To her great surprise, my name wasn't on the list for that day at all—or any other day, for that matter. It was quite obvious: I hadn't even signed up for that term.

When we saw each other again in May, she was preparing Concrete. When she asked me if I was studying for the exams I had not taken before, I told her that I, too, was preparing Concrete, and we continued to study together as in the old times, as if nothing had happened. We spent the whole spring studying, and when the June term came, she had already realized that I would not appear this time, either, and that she wouldn't be seeing me till fall. She watched me pensively with beautiful eyes so far apart that there was space between them for an entire mouth. And naturally, things were the same once again. She took and passed the Concrete exam, and I didn't even bother to come. Returning home satisfied with her success, but totally puzzled as far as my position was concerned, she noticed that, in the hurry of the previous day, I had forgotten my notebooks. Among them she caught sight of my student's booklet. She opened it and discovered with astonishment that I was not a student of mathematics at all, but of something else, and that I had been passing my exams regularly. She recalled the interminable hours of our joint study, which for me must have been a great strain without purpose, a big waste of time, and she asked the inevitable question: what for? Why did I spend all that time with her studying subjects that had nothing to do with my interests and the exams that I had to pass? She started thinking and came to one conclusion: one should always be aware of what is passed over in silence. The reason for all that was not the exam but she herself. Who would have thought that I would be so shy and unable to express my feelings for her? She immediately went to the rented room where I lived with a couple of people my age from Asia and Africa, was surprised by the poverty she saw, and received the information that I had gone home. When they also gave her the address of a small town near Salonica, she took her Buffalo without hesitation and started off toward the Aegean coast in search of me, having made up her mind to act as if she had discovered nothing unusual. So it was.

She arrived at sunset and found the house she had been told about wide open, with a great white bull tied to a nail, upon which fresh bread was impaled. Inside she noticed a bed, on the wall an icon, below the icon a red tassel, a pierced stone tied to a string, a top, a mirror, and an apple. A young naked person with long hair was lying on the bed, tanned by the sun, back turned to the window and resting on one elbow. The long ridge of the spine, which went all the way down the back and ended between the hips, curving slightly, vanished beneath a rough army blanket. She had the impression that the girl would turn any moment and that she would also see her breasts, deep, strong, and glowing in the warm evening. When that really took place, she saw that it was not a woman at all lying on the bed. Leaning on one arm I was chewing my moustache full of honey, which substituted for dinner. When she was noticed and brought into the house, she could still not help thinking of that first impression of finding a female person in my bed. But that impression, as well as the fatigue from a long drive, were soon forgotten. From a mirror-bottomed plate she received a double dinner: for herself and her soul in the mirror: some beans, a nut, and fish, and before the meal a small silver coin, which she held, as did I, under the tongue while eating. So one supper fed all four of us: the two of us and our two souls in the mirrors. After dinner she approached the icon and asked me what it represented.

9   "A television set," I told her. In other words, it is the window to another world which uses mathematics quite different from yours.

10   "How so?" she asked.

11   "Quite simple," I answered. "Machines, space crafts, and vehicles built on the basis of your quantitative mathematical evaluations are founded upon three elements, which are completely lacking in quantity. These are: singularity, the point, and the present moment. Only a sum of singularities constitutes a quantity; singularity itself is deprived of any quantitative measurement. As far as the point is concerned, since it doesn't have a single dimension, not width or height or length or depth, it can undergo neither measurement nor computation. The smallest components of time, however, always have one common denominator: that is the present moment, and it, too, is devoid of quantity and is immeasureable. Thus, the basic elements of your quantitative science represent something to whose very nature every quantitative approach is alien. How then should I believe in such a science? Why are machines made according to these quantitative misconceptions of such a short lifespan, three, four or more times shorter than the human ones? Look, I also have a white 'buffalo' like you. Only, he is made differently from yours, which was manufactured at Layland. Try him out and you will see that in a way he is better than the one you own."

12   "Is he tame?" she asked, smiling.

13   "Certainly," I answered. "Go ahead and try."

14   In front of the door she stroked the big white bull and slowly climbed onto his back. When I also mounted him, turning my back to the horns and facing her, I drove him by the sea, so that he had two feet

in the water and the other two feet on the sand. She was surprised at first when I started to undress her. Piece by piece of her clothing fell into the water; then she started unbuttoning me. At one moment she stopped riding on the bull and started riding on me, feeling that I was growing heavier and heavier inside her. The bull beneath us did everything that we would otherwise have had to do ourselves, and she could tell no longer who was driving her pleasure, the bull or I. Sitting upon the double lover, she saw through the night how we passed by a forest of white cypresses, by people who were gathering dew and pierced stones on the seashore, by people who were building fires inside their own shadows and burning them up, by two women bleeding light, by a garden two hours long, where birds sang in the first hour and evening came in the second, where fruit bloomed in the first and there was a blizzard behind the winds. Then she felt that all the weight from me had passed into her and that the spurred bull had suddenly turned and taken her into the sea, leaving us finally to the waves that would separate us....

However, she never told me a word about her discovery. In the fall, when she was getting ready to graduate and when I offered to study with her again, she was not the least bit surprised. As before, we studied every day from seven until breakfast and then until half past ten; only now she did not try to help me master the subject I was doing and also stayed after ten-thirty for half an hour, which separated us from the books. When she graduated in September, she wasn't surprised at all when I didn't take the examination with her.   15

She was really surprised when she did not see me any more after that. Not that day, nor the following days, weeks, or examination terms. Never again. Astonished, she came to the conclusion that her assessment of my feelings for her was obviously wrong. Confused at not being able to tell what it was all about, she sat one morning in the same room in which we had studied together for years; then she caught sight of the Wedgwood tea set, which had been on the table since breakfast. Then she realized. For months, day after day, with tremendous effort and an immeasurable loss of time and energy, I had worked with her only in order to get a warm breakfast every morning, the only meal I was able to eat during those years. Having realized that, she asked herself another thing. Was it possible that in fact I hated her?   16

At the end, there is one more obligation left: to name the protagonists of this story. If the reader has not thought of it already, here is the answer. My name is the Balkans. Hers, Europe.   17

✧ Evaluating the Text

1. How does the narrator in the story present himself? What unusual details suggest things may not be as they appear?

2. What course of events does the narrator's relationship follow with the girl with whom he is studying?

3. After discovering who the protagonists really are, what new perspective did you gain on the events in the story? Specifically, what does the title mean?

✧ Exploring Different Perspectives

1. What insight do both Milorad Pavić's story and Ngũgĩ wa Thiong'o's narrative, "Decolonising the Mind," offer into the methods and consequences of colonization?

2. Compare Pavić's story with Luis Sepulveda's account, "Daisy," as narratives of attempted accommodation with the ruling powers.

✧ Extending Viewpoints through Writing

1. Milorad Pavić uses the framework of students preparing for exams as a microcosm for larger issues of politics and power. How have your own experiences as a student made you more sensitive to disparities in the gap between those with power and the powerless?

2. Try to compose your own parable or allegory using individuals as countries, as Pavić does, to represent social conditions and power relationships.

Ngũgĩ wa Thiong'o

Decolonising the Mind

◆

Ngũgĩ wa Thiong'o is regarded as one of the most important contempo-
rary writers on the African continent. He wrote his first novels, Weep
Not, Child *(1964) and* The River Between *(1965), in English, and* Cai-
taani Mūtharava-Ini *(translated as* Devil on the Cross, *1982) in his*
native language, Gĩkũyũ. He was chairman of the department of literature
at the University of Nairobi until his detention without trial by the Ken-
yan authorities in 1977, an account of which appeared under the title Detained: A Writer's Prison Diary *(1981). The international outcry over*
his imprisonment eventually produced his release. This selection comes
from Decolonising the Mind: The Politics of Language in African
Literature *(1986), a work that constitutes, says Ngũgĩ, "my farewell to*
English as a vehicle for any of my writings." Subsequently, he has written
novels and plays in Gĩkũyũ.

Kenya is a republic in East Africa. Discoveries by anthropologists
and archaeologists in the Great Rift Valley in Kenya have unearthed re-
mains of what may be the earliest known humans, believed to be some 2
million years old. German missionaries were the first Europeans to make
their way into Kenya in 1844, making contact with the then-ruling Maa-
sai (for more background on the Maasai, see p. 114) and Kĩkũyũ tribes.
The Imperial British East Africa Company wrested political control from
Germany, and Kenya became a British protectorate in 1890 and a Crown
Colony in 1920. Increasingly violent confrontations between European
settlers and the Kĩkũyũs reached a crisis in the 1950s during the terror
campaign of the Mau Mau rebellion. In response, the British declared a
state of emergency, which was not lifted until 1960.

Originally a leader of the Mau Mau uprising, Jomo Kenyatta became
Kenya's first president in 1964, on the first anniversary of Kenya's inde-
pendence, and served until his death in 1978. Continuing opposition and
unrest prompted Kenyatta's government to imprison political dissidents,
including Ngũgĩ wa Thiong'o. Kenyatta's successor, Daniel T. arap Moi,
has yielded to pressure to open the country to an open-party democracy.
National elections were held in December 1992, which returned Moi to
power amid tensions threatening the democratization process. Moi was
reelected as president on January 5, 1998.

Black Africans of forty different ethnic groups make up 97 percent of the
population. The official languages are Swahili and English. The situation
described by Thiong'o has changed to the extent that children are now taught

in their native languages for the first three years of school, after which instruction is exclusively in English.

1   I was born into a large peasant family: father, four wives and about twenty-eight children. I also belonged, as we all did in those days, to a wider extended family and to the community as a whole.

2   We spoke Gĩkũyũ as we worked in the fields. We spoke Gĩkũyũ in and outside the home. I can vividly recall those evenings of story-telling around the fireside. It was mostly the grown-ups telling the children but everybody was interested and involved. We children would re-tell the stories the following day to other children who worked in the fields picking the pyrethrum flowers, tea-leaves or coffee beans of our European and African landlords.

3   The stories, with mostly animals as the main characters, were all told in Gĩkũyũ. Hare, being small, weak but full of innovative wit and cunning, was our hero. We identified with him as he struggled against the brutes of prey like lion, leopard, hyena. His victories were our victories and we learnt that the apparently weak can outwit the strong. We followed the animals in their struggle against hostile nature—drought, rain, sun, wind—a confrontation often forcing them to search for forms of co-operation. But we were also interested in their struggles amongst themselves, and particularly between the beasts and the victims of prey. These twin struggles, against nature and other animals, reflected real-life struggles in the human world.

4   Not that we neglected stories with human beings as the main characters. There were two types of characters in such human-centred narratives: the species of truly human beings with qualities of courage, kindness, mercy, hatred of evil, concern for others; and a man-eat-man two-mouthed species with qualities of greed, selfishness, individualism and hatred of what was good for the larger co-operative community. Co-operation as the ultimate good in a community was a constant theme. It could unite human beings with animals against ogres and beasts of prey, as in the story of how dove, after being fed with castor-oil seeds, was sent to fetch a smith working far away from home and whose pregnant wife was being threatened by these man-eating two-mouthed ogres.

5   There were good and bad story-tellers. A good one could tell the same story over and over again, and it would always be fresh to us, the listeners. He or she could tell a story told by someone else and make it more alive and dramatic. The differences really were in the use of words and images and the inflexion of voices to effect different tones.

6   We therefore learnt to value words for their meaning and nuances. Language was not a mere string of words. It had a suggestive power well beyond the immediate and lexical meaning. Our appreciation of the suggestive magical power of language was reinforced by the games we played with words through riddles, proverbs, transpositions of syl-

lables, or through nonsensical but musically arranged words.[1] So we learnt the music of our language on top of the content. The language, through images and symbols, gave us a view of the world, but it had a beauty of its own. The home and the field were then our pre-primary school but what is important, for this discussion, is that the language of our evening teach-ins, and the language of our immediate and wider community, and the language of our work in the fields were one.

And then I went to school, a colonial school, and this harmony was   7
broken. The language of my education was no longer the language of my culture. I first went to Kamaandura, missionary run, and then to another called Maanguuū run by nationalists grouped around the Gĩkũyũ Independent and Karinga Schools Association. Our language of education was still Gĩkũyũ. The very first time I was ever given an ovation for my writing was over a composition in Gĩkũyũ. So for my first four years there was still harmony between the language of my formal education and that of the Limuru peasant community.

It was after the declaration of a state of emergency over Kenya in   8
1952 that all the schools run by patriotic nationalists were taken over by the colonial regime and were placed under District Education Boards chaired by Englishmen. English became the language of my formal ed-ucation. In Kenya, English became more than a language: it was *the* lan-guage, and all the others had to bow before it in deference.

Thus one of the most humiliating experiences was to be caught   9
speaking Gĩkũyũ in the vicinity of the school. The culprit was given cor-poral punishment—three to five strokes of the cane on bare buttocks—or was made to carry a metal plate around the neck with inscriptions such as I AM STUPID or I AM A DONKEY. Sometimes the culprits were fined money they could hardly afford. And how did the teachers catch the culprits? A button was initially given to one pupil who was supposed to hand it over to whoever was caught speaking his mother tongue. Whoever had the button at the end of the day would sing who had given it to him and the ensuing process would bring out all the culprits of the day. Thus children were turned into witch-hunters and in the process were being taught the lucrative value of being a traitor to one's immediate community.

The attitude to English was the exact opposite: any achievement in   10
spoken or written English was highly rewarded; prizes, prestige, applause; the ticket to higher realms. English became the measure of in-telligence and ability in the arts, the sciences, and all the other branches

---

[1]Example from a tongue twister: "Kaana ka Nikoora koona koora: na ko koora koona kaana ka Nikoora koora koora." I'm indebted to Wangui wa Goro for this ex-ample. 'Nichola's child saw a baby frog and ran away: and when the baby frog saw Nichola's child it also ran away.' A Gĩkũyũ-speaking child has to get the correct tone and length of vowel and pauses to get it right. Otherwise it becomes a jumble of *k*'s and *r*'s and *na*'s [Author's note].

of learning. English became *the* main determinant of a child's progress up the ladder of formal education.

11   As you may know, the colonial system of education in addition to its apartheid racial demarcation had the structure of a pyramid: a broad primary base, a narrowing secondary middle, and an even narrower university apex. Selections from primary into secondary were through an examination, in my time called Kenya African Preliminary Examination, in which one had to pass six subjects ranging from Maths to Nature Study and Kiswahili. All the papers were written in English. Nobody could pass the exam who failed the English language paper no matter how brilliantly he had done in the other subjects. I remember one boy in my class of 1954 who had distinctions in all subjects except English, which he had failed. He was made to fail the entire exam. He went on to become a turn boy in a bus company. I who had only passes but a credit in English got a place at the Alliance High School, one of the most elitist institutions for Africans in colonial Kenya. The requirements for a place at the University, Makerere University College, were broadly the same: nobody could go on to wear the undergraduate red gown, no matter how brilliantly they had performed in all the other subjects unless they had a credit—not even a simple pass!—in English. Thus the most coveted place in the pyramid and in the system was only available to the holder of an English language credit card. English was the official vehicle and the magic formula to colonial elitedom.

12   Literary education was now determined by the dominant language while also reinforcing that dominance. Orature (oral literature) in Kenyan languages stopped. In primary school I now read simplified Dickens and Stevenson alongside Rider Haggard. Jim Hawkins, Oliver Twist, Tom Brown—not Hare, Leopard, and Lion—were now my daily companions in the world of imagination. In secondary school, Scott and G. B. Shaw vied with more Rider Haggard, John Buchan, Alan Paton, Captain W. E. Johns. At Makerere I read English: from Chaucer to T. S. Eliot with a touch of Graham Greene.

13   Thus language and literature were taking us further and further from ourselves to other selves, from our world to other worlds.

14   What was the colonial system doing to us Kenyan children? What were the consequences of, on the one hand, this systematic suppression of our languages and the literature they carried, and on the other the elevation of English and the literature it carried? To answer those questions, let me first examine the relationship of language to human experience, human culture, and the human perception of reality.

15   Language, any language, has a dual character: it is both a means of communication and a carrier of culture. Take English. It is spoken in Britain and in Sweden and Denmark. But for Swedish and Danish people English is only a means of communication with non-Scandinavians. It is not a carrier of their culture. For the British, and particularly the English, it is

additionally, and inseparably from its use as a tool of communication, a carrier of their culture and history. Or take Swahili in East and Central Africa. It is widely used as a means of communication across many nationalities. But it is not the carrier of a culture and history of many of those nationalities. However in parts of Kenya and Tanzania, and particularly in Zanzibar, Swahili is inseparably both a means of communication and a carrier of the culture of those people to whom it is a mother-tongue.

Culture transmits or imparts those images of the world and reality   16
through the spoken and the written language, that is through a specific language. In other words, the capacity to speak, the capacity to order sounds in a manner that makes for mutual comprehension between human beings is universal. This is the universality of language, a quality specific to human beings. It corresponds to the universality of the struggle against nature and that between human beings. But the particularity of the sounds, the words, the word order into phrases and sentences, and the specific manner, or laws, of their ordering is what distinguishes one language from another. Thus a specific culture is not transmitted through language in its universality but in its particularity as the language of a specific community with a specific history. Written literature and orature are the main means by which a particular language transmits the images of the world contained in the culture it carries.

Language as communication and as culture are then products of   17
each other. Communication creates culture: culture is a means of communication. Language carries culture, and culture carries, particularly through orature and literature, the entire body of values by which we come to perceive ourselves and our place in the world. How people perceive themselves affects how they look at their culture, at their politics and at the social production of wealth, at their entire relationship to nature and to other beings. Language is thus inseparable from ourselves as a community of human beings with a specific form and character, a specific history, a specific relationship to the world.

So what was the colonialist imposition of a foreign language doing   18
to us children?

The real aim of colonialism was to control the people's wealth: what   19
they produced, how they produced it, and how it was distributed; to control, in other words, the entire realm of the language of real life. Colonialism imposed its control of the social production of wealth through military conquest and subsequent political dictatorship. But its most important area of domination was the mental universe of the colonised, the control, through culture, of how people perceived themselves and their relationship to the world. Economic and political control can never be complete or effective without mental control. To control a people's culture is to control their tools of self-definition in relationship to others.

For colonialism this involved two aspects of the same process: the   20
destruction or the deliberate undervaluing of a people's culture, their art,

dances, religions, history, geography, education, orature and literature, and the conscious elevation of the language of the coloniser. The domination of a people's language by the languages of the colonising nations was crucial to the domination of the mental universe of the colonised.

21   Take language as communication. Imposing a foreign language, and suppressing the native languages as spoken and written, were already breaking the harmony previously existing between the African child and the three aspects of language. Since the new language as a means of communication was a product of and was reflecting the 'real language of life' elsewhere, it could never as spoken or written properly reflect or imitate the real life of that community. This may in part explain why technology always appears to us as slightly external, *their* product and not *ours*. The word "missile" used to hold an alien faraway sound until I recently learnt its equivalent in Gĩkũyũ, *ngurukuhĩ*, and it made me apprehend it differently. Learning, for a colonial child, became a cerebral activity and not an emotionally felt experience.

22   But since the new, imposed languages could never completely break the native languages as spoken, their most effective area of domination was the third aspect of language as communication, the written. The language of an African child's formal education was foreign. The language of the books he read was foreign. The language of his conceptualisation was foreign. Thought, in him, took the visible form of a foreign language. So the written language of a child's upbringing in the school (even his spoken language within the school compound) became divorced from his spoken language at home. There was often not the slightest relationship between the child's written world, which was also the language of his schooling, and the world of his immediate environment in the family and the community. For a colonial child, the harmony existing between the three aspects of language as communication was irrevocably broken. This resulted in the disassociation of the sensibility of that child from his natural and social environment, what we might call colonial alienation. The alienation became reinforced in the teaching of history, geography, music, where bourgeois Europe was always the centre of the universe.

23   This disassociation, divorce, or alienation from the immediate environment becomes clearer when you look at colonial language as a carrier of culture.

24   Since culture is a product of the history of a people which it in turn reflects, the child was now being exposed exclusively to a culture that was a product of a world external to himself. He was being made to stand outside himself to look at himself. *Catching Them Young* is the title of a book on racism, class, sex, and politics in children's literature by Bob Dixon. "Catching them young" as an aim was even more true of a colonial child. The images of this world and his place in it implanted in a child take years to eradicate, if they ever can be.

25   Since culture does not just reflect the world in images but actually, through those very images, conditions a child to see that world in a cer-

tain way, the colonial child was made to see the world and where he stands in it as seen and defined by or reflected in the culture of the language of imposition.

And since those images are mostly passed on through orature and literature it meant the child would now only see the world as seen in the literature of his language of adoption. From the point of view of alienation, that is of seeing oneself from outside oneself as if one was another self, it does not matter that the imported literature carried the great humanist tradition of the best in Shakespeare, Goethe, Balzac, Tolstoy, Gorky, Brecht, Sholokhov, Dickens. The location of this great mirror of imagination was necessarily Europe and its history and culture and the rest of the universe was seen from the centre.   26

But obviously it was worse when the colonial child was exposed to images of his world as mirrored in the written languages of his coloniser. Where his own native languages were associated in his impressionable mind with low status, humiliation, corporal punishment, slow-footed intelligence and ability or downright stupidity, non-intelligibility and barbarism, this was reinforced by the world he met in the works of such geniuses of racism as a Rider Haggard or a Nicholas Monsarrat; not to mention the pronouncement of some of the giants of western intellectual and political establishment, such as Hume ("...the negro is naturally inferior to the whites..."),[2] Thomas Jefferson ("...the blacks ...are inferior to the whites on the endowments of both body and mind..."),[3] or Hegel with his Africa comparable to a land of childhood still enveloped in the dark mantle of the night as far as the development of self-conscious history was concerned. Hegel's statement that there was nothing harmonious with humanity to be found in the African character is representative of the racist images of Africans and Africa such a colonial child was bound to encounter in the literature of the colonial languages.[4] The results could be disastrous.   27

---

[2]Quoted in Eric Williams, *A History of the People of Trinidad and Tobago,* London 1964, p. 32 [Author's note].

[3]Ibid, p. 31 [Author's note].

[4]In references to Africa in the introduction to his lectures in *The Philosophy of History,* Hegel gives historical, philosophical, rational expression and legitimacy to every conceivable European racist myth about Africa. Africa is even denied her own geography where it does not correspond to myth. Thus Egypt is not part of Africa; and North Africa is part of Europe. Africa proper is the especial home of ravenous beasts, snakes of all kinds. The African is not part of humanity. Only slavery to Europe can raise him, possibly, to the lower ranks of humanity. Slavery is good for the African. "Slavery is in and for itself *injustice,* for the essence of humanity is *freedom;* but for this man must be matured. The gradual abolition of slavery is therefore wiser and more equitable than its sudden removal." (Hegel, *The Philosophy of History,* Dover edition, New York: 1956, pp. 91–9.) Hegel clearly reveals himself as the nineteenth-century Hitler of the intellect [Author's note].

28   In her paper read to the conference on the teaching of African literature in schools held in Nairobi in 1973,[5] entitled "Written Literature and Black Images," the Kenyan writer and scholar Professor Mĩcere Mũgo related how a reading of the description of Gagool as an old African woman in Rider Haggard's *King Solomon's Mines* had for a long time made her feel mortal terror whenever she encountered old African women. In his autobiography *This Life,* Sydney Poitier describes how, as a result of the literature he had read, he had come to associate Africa with snakes. So on arrival in Africa and being put up in a modern hotel in a modern city, he could not sleep because he kept on looking for snakes everywhere, even under the bed. These two have been able to pinpoint the origins of their fears. But for most others the negative image becomes internalised and it affects their cultural and even political choices in ordinary living.

✧ Evaluating the Text

1. In what way would stories involving animals as heroes be especially important to the children to whom they were told? How might the nature of the conflicts in the animal stories better prepare children to deal with conflicts in real life? To what extent do these stories transmit cultural values by stressing the importance of resourcefulness, high self-esteem, a connection to the past, and a pride in one's culture?

2. In addition to transmitting cultural values, how did hearing these stories, along with riddles and proverbs, imbue the children with a love of the language of Gĩkũyũ and enhance their responsiveness to and skill with features of narrative, imagery, inflection, and tone? How did hearing different people tell the same stories contribute to their development of critical abilities in distinguishing whether a given story was told well or poorly?

3. Describe the disruption Thiong'o experienced when he first attended a colonial school, where he was forbidden to speak the language of the community from which he came. How do the kinds of punishments meted out for speaking Gĩkũyũ give you some insight into how psychologically damaging such an experience could be for a child? Which of the examples Thiong'o gives, in your opinion, most clearly reveals the extent to which speaking English was rewarded? In what way was the knowledge of English the single most important determinant of advancement?

4. Explain how the British as colonizers of Kenya sought to achieve dominance by (1) devaluing native speech, dance, art, and traditions and

[5]The paper is now in Akivaga and Gachukiah's *The Teaching of African Literature in Schools,* published by Kenya Literature Bureau [Author's note].

(2) promoting the worth of everything British, including the speaking of English. How does changing the language a people are allowed to speak change the way they perceive themselves and their relationship to those around them? Why did the British try to make it impossible for Kenyans to draw on the cultural values and traditions embodied in their language, Gĩkũyũ? Why was it also in the British interest to encourage and even compel Kenyans to look at themselves only through a British perspective? How was this view reinforced by teaching Kenyans British literature?

✦ Exploring Different Perspectives

1. Compare the accounts by Thiong'o and Rae Yang (see "At the Center of the Storm") in terms of reprogramming citizens to accept a "correct" ideology, whether that of British colonialism or Mao Zedong's Cultural Revolution.

2. Compare how the effects of British colonialism, according to Thiong'o, create a relationship between the dominating powers and those they dominate to that depicted in Milorad Pavić's story "The Wedgwood Tea Set"?

✦ Extending Viewpoints through Writing

1. For a research project, you might compare Thiong'o's discussion of the stories he heard as a child with Bruno Bettleheim's study *The Uses of Enchantment: The Meaning and Importance of Fairy Tales* (1976). Bettleheim suggests that these traditional forms of storytelling help children build inner strength by acknowledging that real evil exists and can be dangerous while offering hope that those who are resourceful can overcome the evil.

2. Discuss the extent to which Thiong'o's argument expresses a rationale similar to that advanced by proponents of bilingualism. You might also wish to consider the similarities and differences in political terms between the situation Thiong'o describes and that of a Hispanic or Chinese child in the United States. If you come from a culture where English was not your first language, to what extent did your experiences match Thiong'o's when you entered a school where English was the required language?

Rae Yang

At the Center of the Storm

◆

Rae Yang, who teaches East Asian Studies at Dickinson College, offers an unusual perspective of one who grew up in China and, at the age of fifteen, joined the Red Guards in Beijing. Her account of her life working on a pig farm and the political and moral crises that she experienced as a result of the Cultural Revolution offers a unique portrait of someone who was a committed, and even fanatic, revolutionary, who only later had misgivings about what the Red Guards had done. The following chapter is drawn from Spider Eaters *(1997).*

China's modern history has been characterized by cycles of liberalization followed by violent oppression. In 1957, reaction against the so-called "let a hundred flowers bloom" period led to a crackdown against intellectuals. In 1966, Mao launched the Cultural Revolution to purge the government and society of liberal elements. Revolutionary Red Guards composed of ideologically motivated young men and women acted with the army to attack so-called bourgeois elements in the government and in the culture at large. After Mao's death in 1976, a backlash led to the imprisoning of Mao's wife, Jiang Qing, and three colleagues (the "Gang of Four").

1   From May to December 1966, the first seven months of the Cultural Revolution left me with experiences I will never forget. Yet I forgot things almost overnight in that period. So many things were happening around me. The situation was changing so fast. I was too excited, too jubilant, too busy, too exhausted, too confused, too uncomfortable.... The forgotten things, however, did not all go away. Later some of them sneaked back into my memory, causing me unspeakable pain and shame. So I would say that those seven months were the most terrible in my life. Yet they were also the most wonderful! I had never felt so good about myself before, nor have I ever since.

2   In the beginning, the Cultural Revolution exhilarated me because suddenly I felt that I was allowed to think with my own head and say what was on my mind. In the past, the teachers at 101 had worked hard to make us intelligent, using the most difficult questions in mathematics, geometry, chemistry, and physics to challenge us. But the mental

*For information on China, see p. 57.

abilities we gained, we were not supposed to apply elsewhere. For instance, we were not allowed to question the teachers' conclusions. Students who did so would be criticized as "disrespectful and conceited," even if their opinions made perfect sense. Worse still was to disagree with the leaders. Leaders at various levels represented the Communist Party. Disagreeing with them could be interpreted as being against the Party, a crime punishable by labor reform, imprisonment, even death.

Thus the teachers created a contradiction. On the one hand, they wanted us to be smart, rational, and analytical. On the other hand, they forced us to be stupid, to be "the teachers' little lambs" and "the Party's obedient tools." By so doing, I think, they planted a sick tree; the bitter fruit would soon fall into their own mouths. 3

When the Cultural Revolution broke out in late May 1966, I felt like the legendary monkey Sun Wukong, freed from the dungeon that had held him under a huge mountain for five hundred years. It was Chairman Mao who set us free by allowing us to rebel against authorities. As a student, the first authority I wanted to rebel against was Teacher Lin, our homeroom teacher—in Chinese, *banzhuren*. As *banzhuren*, she was in charge of our class. A big part of her duty was to make sure that we behaved and thought correctly. 4

Other students in my class might have thought that I was Teacher Lin's favorite. As our Chinese teacher, she read my papers in front of the class once in a while. That was true. (Only she and I knew that the grades I got for those papers rarely went above 85. I could only imagine what miserable grades she gave to others in our class.) She also chose me to be the class representative for Chinese, which meant if others had difficulties with the subject, I was to help them. In spite of all these, I did not like Teacher Lin! She had done me a great wrong in the past. I would never forget it. 5

In my opinion, Lin was exactly the kind of teacher who, in Chairman Mao's words, "treated the students as their enemies." In 1965, we went to Capital Steel and Iron Company in the far suburb of Beijing to do physical labor. One night there was an earthquake warning. We were made to stay outdoors to wait for it. By midnight, no earthquake had come. Two o'clock, still all quiet. Three o'clock, four o'clock, five.... The night was endless. Sitting on the cold concrete pavement for so many hours, I was sleepy. I was exhausted. My only wish at the moment was to be allowed to go into the shack and literally "hit the hay." Without thinking I grumbled: "Ai! How come there is still no earthquake?" 6

Who should have thought that this remark was overheard by Teacher Lin? All of a sudden she started criticizing me in a loud voice. 7

"The workers and the poor and lower-middle peasants would never say such a thing! Think of all the property that will be damaged by an earthquake. Think of all the lives that may be lost! Now you are 8 looking forward to an earthquake! Only class enemies look forward to earthquakes! Where did your class feelings go? Do you have any proletarian feelings at all?..."

9   She went on and on. Her shrill voice woke up everybody, my classmates as well as students in the other five parallel classes. All were sitting outside at the moment. Everybody turned to watch us. Three hundred pairs of eyes! It was such a shame! I felt my cheeks burning. I wanted to defend myself. I wanted to tell Teacher Lin that although there might be some truth in what she said, I had never been in an earthquake. I was merely tired and wished the whole thing over. Besides, I was only half awake when I said that. I was not looking forward to an earthquake!

10   In fact, what I really wanted to tell her was that I knew why she was making such a fuss about my remark, which if she had not seized would have drifted away and scattered in the morning breeze like a puff of vapor: she was using this as an opportunity to show off her political correctness in front of all these teachers and students. At my cost! Later she might be able to cash in on it, using it as her political capital....

11   But of course I knew it would be crazy for me to talk back like that. Contradicting the teacher would only lead me into more trouble. So I swallowed the words that were rolling on the tip of my tongue and lowered my head. Hot tears assaulted my eyes. Tears of anger. Tears of shame. I bit my lips to force them back. *Let's wait and see, Teacher Lin. Someday I will have my revenge. On you!*

12   Now the time had come for the underdogs to speak up, to seek justice! Immediately I took up a brush pen, dipped it in black ink and wrote a long *dazibao* (criticism in big characters). Using some of the rhetorical devices Teacher Lin had taught us, I accused her of lacking proletarian feelings toward her students, of treating them as her enemies, of being high-handed, and suppressing different opinions. When I finished and showed it to my classmates, they supported me by signing their names to it. Next, we took the *dazibao* to Teacher Lin's home nearby and pasted it on the wall of her bedroom for her to read carefully day and night. This, of course, was not personal revenge. It was answering Chairman Mao's call to combat the revisionist educational line. If in the meantime it caused Teacher Lin a few sleepless nights, so be it! This revolution was meant to "touch the soul" of people, an unpopular teacher in particular.

13   Teacher Lin, although she was not a good teacher in my opinion, was not yet the worst. Teacher Qian was even worse. He was the political teacher who had implemented the Exposing Third Layer of Thoughts campaign. In the past many students believed that he could read people's minds. Now a *dazibao* by a student gave us a clue as to how he acquired this eerie ability. Something I would not have guessed in a thousand years! He had been reading students' diaries in class

breaks, while we were doing physical exercise on the sports ground. The student who wrote the *dazibao* felt sick one day and returned to his classroom earlier than expected. There he had actually seen Qian sneak a diary from a student's desk and read it. The student kept his silence until the Cultural Revolution, for Qian was his *banzhuren.*

So this was Qian's so-called "political and thought work"! What could it teach us but dishonesty and hypocrisy? Such a "glorious" example the school had set for us, and in the past we had revered him so much! Thinking of the nightmare he gave me, I was outraged. "Take up a pen, use it as a gun." I wrote another *dazibao* to denounce Teacher Qian. 14

Within a few days *dazibao* were popping up everywhere like bamboo shoots after a spring rain, written by students, teachers, administrators, workers, and librarians. Secrets dark and dirty were exposed. Everyday we made shocking discoveries. The sacred halo around the teachers' heads that dated back two thousand five hundred years to the time of Confucius disappeared. Now teachers must drop their pretentious airs and learn a few things from their students. Parents would be taught by their kids instead of vice versa, as Chairman Mao pointed out. Government officials would have to wash their ears to listen to the ordinary people. Heaven and earth were turned upside down. The rebellious monkey with enormous power had gotten out. A revolution was underway. 15

Looking back on it, I should say that I felt good about the Cultural Revolution when it started. It gave me a feeling of superiority and confidence that I had never experienced before. Yet amidst the new freedom and excitement, I ran into things that made me very uncomfortable. 16

I remember one day in July, I went to have lunch at the student dining hall. On the way I saw a crowd gathering around the fountain. I went over to take a look. The fountain had been a pleasant sight in the past. Sparkling water swaying in the wind among green willow twigs, making the air fresh and clean. In Beijing it was a luxury ordinary middle schools did not enjoy. When the Cultural Revolution broke out, the water was turned off. Now the bottom of the fountain was muddy, littered with wastepaper and broken glass. 17

On this day I saw a teacher in the fountain, a middle-aged man. His clothes were muddy. Blood was streaming down his head, as a number of students were throwing bricks at him. He tried to dodge the bricks. While he did so, without noticing it, he crawled in the fountain, round and round, like an animal in the zoo. Witnessing such a scene, I suddenly felt sick to my stomach. I would have vomited, if I had not quickly turned round and walked away. Forget about lunch. My appetite was gone. 18

Sitting in an empty classroom, I wondered why this incident upset me so much: *This is the first time I've seen someone beaten. Moreover this person isn't a stranger. He's a teacher at 101. Do I pity him? Maybe a little? Maybe not. After all I don't know anything about him. He might be a counterrevolutionary or a bad element. He might have done something very bad; thus* 19 *he deserved the punishment. Something else bothers me, then—not the teacher. What is it?*

20   Then it dawned on me that I was shocked by the ugliness of the scene. *Yes. That's it! In the past when I read about torture in revolutionary novels, saw it in movies, and daydreamed about it, it was always so heroic, so noble; therefore it was romantic and beautiful. But now, in real life, it happened in front of me. It's so sordid! I wish I'd seen none of it! I don't want the memory to destroy my hero's dream.*

21   This teacher survived; another was not so fortunate. Teacher Chen, our art teacher, was said to resemble a spy in the movies. He was a tall, thin man with sallow skin and long hair, which was a sign of decadence. Moreover, he seemed gloomy and he smoked a lot. "If a person weren't scheming or if he didn't feel very unhappy in the new society, why would he smoke like that?" a classmate asked me, expecting nothing but heartfelt consent from me. "Not to say that in the past he had asked students to draw naked female bodies in front of plaster statues to corrupt them!" For these "crimes," he was beaten to death by a group of senior students.

22   When I heard this, I felt very uncomfortable again. The whole thing seemed a bad joke to me. Yet it was real! Teacher Chen had taught us the year before and unlike Teacher Lin and Teacher Qian, he had never treated students as his enemies. He was polite and tolerant. If a student showed talent in painting, he would be delighted. On the other hand, he would not embarrass a student who "had no art cells." I had never heard complaints about him before. Yet somehow he became the first person I knew who was killed in the Cultural Revolution.

23   Living next door to Teacher Chen was Teacher Jiang, our geography teacher. While Teacher Chen was tall and lean, Teacher Jiang was short and stout. Both were old bachelors, who taught auxiliary courses. Before the Cultural Revolution Teacher Jiang was known for two things. One was his unkempt clothes. The other was the fact that he never brought anything but a piece of chalk to class. Yet many students said that he was the most learned teacher at 101. He had many maps and books stored in his funny big head.

24   If Teacher Jiang had been admired by students before, he became even more popular after the revolution started and Teacher Chen was killed. Since August 1966 Red Guards were allowed to travel free of charge to places all over China. Before we set off, everybody wanted to get a few tips from him, and afterwards we'd love to tell him a few stories in return. It was our chance to show off what we had learned from the trips. Thus from August to December, Teacher Jiang had many visitors. Happy voices and laughter were heard from across the lotus pond in front of his dorm house. At night lights shone through his windows often into the small hours. Geography turned out a true blessing for Teacher Jiang, while art doomed Teacher Chen.

25   In contrast to the teachers who lost control over their lives in 1966, we students suddenly found power in our hands. Entrance examinations for senior middle school and college were canceled. Now it was entirely up to us to decide what we would do with our time. This was a big change. In the past, decisions had always been made for us by our parents, teachers, and leaders. At school, all courses were required and we took them according to a fixed schedule, six classes a day, six days a week. College was the same as middle schools. After college, the state would assign everybody a job, an iron rice bowl. Like it or not, it would be yours for life.

Now those who had made decisions for us—teachers, parents, 26 administrators—were swept aside by the storm. We were in charge. We could do things on our own initiative. We made plans. We carried them out. So what did we do? Instead of routine classes, we organized meetings at which we shared our family history. (People who spoke up at such meetings were of course revolutionary cadres' children. Others could only listen.) I remember Wu, a girl from a high-ranking cadre's family, told a story that left a deep impression on me.

In 1942 Japanese troops raided the Communist base in the north. 27 At this time Wu's older brother was only several months old. He was a beautiful baby boy, with a chubby face and the mother's large brown eyes. The mother gave him the name Precious. Day and night she longed for the father to come back from the front to meet his firstborn.

But before the father returned, the Japanese invaders came. Wu's 28 mother took the baby and fled to the mountains. She and many others hid in a cavern. The enemy soldiers came near, searching for them. At this moment the baby woke up and was about to cry. Her mother had no choice but to cover his mouth with her own hand. Or else all would have been found and killed by the Japanese.

The baby was in agony. He struggled with all his might for his life. 29 His lovely little face turned red and then blue. His tiny hands grabbed at his mother's, desperately trying to push it away so that he could breathe. His plump little feet kicked helplessly. The mother's heart was pierced by ten thousand arrows, but she did not dare loosen her grip. Finally the Japanese went away. By then the baby had turned cold in her arms.

Wu burst into tears and we all cried with her. 30

Why does she cry like that? Yes. I understand. The brother! Because he 31 *died so tragically, he will always be loved most by the parents. The perfect child. The most "precious" one, the one they sacrificed for the revolution. Wu and her other siblings cannot rival him, no matter how good they are....*

But of course that was not why she cried or why we cried with her 32 on that day. We cried because we were deeply moved by the heroic struggle and tremendous sacrifice made by our parents and older brothers and sisters. The stories we told at such meetings convinced us that our lives were on the line: if we should allow the revolution to deteriorate, the evil imperialists and beastly Nationalists would come back. As a slogan of the thirties went, "Cut the grass and eliminate the roots"—if we did not act, they would kill our parents who were revolutionary cadres and make sure that none of us would survive to seek revenge on them.

33   Suddenly I felt that these classmates of mine were dearer to me than my own brothers and sisters. I loved them! They loved me! Today we shed tears in the same room. Tomorrow we would shed blood in the same ditch. I was willing to sacrifice my life for any of them, while before the Cultural Revolution I mistrusted them, seeing them as nothing but my rivals.

34   In fact, it was not fear for our lives but pride and a sense of responsibility that fired us up. Chairman Mao had said that we were the morning sun. We were the hope. The future of China and the fate of humankind depended on us. The Soviet Union and East European countries had changed colors. Only China and Albania remained true to Marxism and Leninism. By saving the revolution in China, we were making history. We must uproot bureaucracy and corruption in China, abolish privileges enjoyed by government officials and the intelligentsia, reform education, reform art and literature, reform government organizations.... In short, we must purify China and make it a shining example. Someday the whole world would follow us onto this new path.

35   Aside from sharing family history, we biked to universities and middle schools all over Beijing to read *dazibao* and attend mass rallies where Lin Biao, Zhou Enlai, and Mao's wife, Jiang Qing, showed up to give speeches. I first heard the term "Red Guard" in late June at Middle School attached to Qinghua University, two months before most Chinese would hear of it. It was an exciting idea. On our way back, my schoolmates and I were so preoccupied with the notion that our bikes stopped on a riverbank. Next thing I remember, we were tearing up our red scarves, which only a month before had been the sacred symbol of the Young Pioneers. Now they represented the revisionist educational line and to tear them up was a gesture of rebellion. We tied the strips of red cloth around our left arms in the style of workers' pickets of the 1920s. When we rode away from the spot, we had turned ourselves into Red Guards.

36   People in the street noticed our new costume: faded army uniforms that had been worn by our parents, red armbands, wide canvas army belts, army caps, the peaks pulled down low by girls in the style of the boys.... Some people smiled at us. Some waved their hands. Their eyes showed surprise, curiosity, excitement, admiration. I don't think I saw fear. Not yet.

37   When people smiled at us, we smiled back, proud of ourselves. Our eyes were clear and bright. Our cheeks rosy and radiant. Red armbands fluttered in the wind. We pedaled hard. We pedaled fast. All of

us had shiny new bikes, a luxury most Chinese could not afford at the time. (In my case, Father had bought me a new bike so as to show his support for the Cultural Revolution. Being a dreamer himself, he believed, or at least hoped, that the Cultural Revolution would purify the Communist Party and save the revolution.)

When we rang the bells, we rang them in unison, for a long time. It was not to warn people to get out of our way. It was to attract their attention. Or maybe we just wanted to listen to the sound. The sound flew up, crystal clear and full of joy, like a flock of white doves circling in the blue sky. At the time, little did I know that this was the first stir of a great storm that would soon engulf the entire country. 38

On August 18, 1966, I saw Chairman Mao for the first time. The night before, we set off from 101 on foot a little after midnight and arrived at Tian'anmen Square before daybreak. In the dark we waited anxiously. Will Chairman Mao come? was the question in everybody's mind. Under a starry sky, we sang. 39

"Lifting our heads we see the stars of Beidou [the Big Dipper], lowering our heads we are longing for Mao Zedong, longing for Mao Zedong...." 40

We poured our emotions into the song. Chairman Mao who loved the people would surely hear it, for it came from the bottom of our hearts. 41

Perhaps he did. At five o'clock, before sunrise, like a miracle he walked out of Tian'anmen onto the square and shook hands with people around him. The square turned into a jubilant ocean. Everybody was shouting "Long live Chairman Mao!" Around me girls were crying; boys were crying too. With hot tears streaming down my face, I could not see Chairman Mao clearly. He had ascended the rostrum. He was too high, or rather, the stands for Red Guard representatives were too low. 42

Earnestly we chanted: "We-want-to-see-Chair-man-Mao!" He heard us! He walked over to the corner of Tian'anmen and waved at us. Now I could see him clearly. He was wearing a green army uniform and a red armband, just like all of us. My blood was boiling inside me. I jumped and shouted and cried in unison with a million people in the square. At that moment, I forgot myself; all barriers that existed between me and others broke down. I felt like a drop of water that finally joined the mighty raging ocean. I would never be lonely again. 43

The night after, we celebrated the event at 101. Everybody joined the folk dance called *yangge* around bonfires. No one was shy. No one was self-conscious. By then, we had been up and awake for more than forty hours, but somehow I was still bursting with energy. Others seemed that way too. After dancing a couple of hours, I biked all the way home to share the happiness with my parents. By this time, they no longer minded that I woke them up at three o'clock in the morning. In fact, they had urged me to wake them up whenever I got home so that they could hear the latest news from me about the revolution. 44

Seeing Chairman Mao added new fuel to the flame of our revolu-   45
tionary zeal. The next day, my fellow Red Guards and I held a meeting
to discuss our next move. Obviously if we loved Chairman Mao, just
shouting slogans was not enough. We must do something. But what
could we do? By mid-August the teachers at 101 had been criticized
and some were detained in "cow sheds." Even the old school principal,
Wang Yizhi, had been "pulled down from the horse" because of her
connection with Liu Shaoqi, the biggest capitalist-roader in the Party.
On campus, little was left for us to rebel against. Therefore, many Red
Guards had walked out of schools to break "four olds" (old ideas, old
culture, old customs and old habits) in the city.

46   This was what we should do. Only first we had to pinpoint some
"four olds." I suggested that we go to a nearby restaurant to get rid of
some old practices. Everybody said: "Good! Let's do it!" So we jumped
onto our bikes and rushed out like a gust of wind.

47   Seeing a group of Red Guards swarming in, everybody in the restaurant tensed up. In August, people began to fear Red Guards who
summoned the wind, raised the storm, and spread terror all over
China. Small talk ceased. All eyes were fastened on us.

48   I stepped forward and began ritualistically: "Our great leader
Chairman Mao teaches us, 'Corruption and waste are very great
crimes.'" After that, I improvised: "Comrades! In today's world there
are still many people who live in poverty and have nothing to eat. So
we should not waste food. Nor should we behave like bourgeois ladies
and gentlemen who expect to be waited on by others in a restaurant.
From now on, people who want to eat in this restaurant must follow
new rules: One, go to the window to get your own food. Two, carry it to
the table yourselves. Three, wash your own dishes. Four, you must finish the food you ordered. Otherwise you may not leave the restaurant!"

49   While I said this, I saw some people change color and sweat broke
out on their foreheads. They had ordered too much food. Now they had
to finish it under the watchful eyes of a group of Red Guards. This was
not an enviable situation. But nobody in the restaurant protested. Contradicting a Red Guard was asking for big trouble. It was like playing
with thunderbolts and dynamite. So people just lowered their heads
and swallowed the food as fast as they could. Some of them might develop indigestion afterwards, but I believed it was their own fault. By
showing off their wealth at a restaurant, they wasted the blood and
sweat of the peasants. Now they got caught and lost face. This should
teach them a lesson!

50   While my comrades and I were breaking "four olds" at restaurants,
other Red Guards were raiding people's homes all over the city. News of
victory poured in: Red Guards discovered guns, bullets, old deeds, gold
bars, foreign currency, yellow books and magazines (pornography)....
Hearing this, people in my group became restless. But somehow I was

not eager to raid homes, and I did not ask myself why. "We are busy making revolution at restaurants, aren't we?"

Then one day an old woman stopped us in the street and insisted   51
that we go with her to break some "four olds" in the home of a big capitalist. None of us could say No to this request. So she led us to the home of a prominent overseas Chinese, where the "four olds" turned out to be flowers.

The courtyard we entered was spacious. A green oasis of cool   52
shade, drifting fragrance, and delicate beauty: tree peonies and bamboo were planted next to Tai Lake rocks. Orchids and chrysanthemums grew along a winding path inlaid with cobblestones. A trellis of wisteria stood next to a corridor. Goldfish swam under water lilies in antique vats....

Strange! Why does this place look familiar? I am sure I've never been here   53
before. Could it be I've seen it in a dream?...

Suddenly the answer dawned on me: *this place looks just like Nainai's*   54
home. Nainai's home must have been raided. Maybe several times by now. Is
she still there? Did they kick her out? Is she all right? And what happened to
the beautiful flowers she and Third Aunt planted?... No use thinking about
such things! I can't help her anyway. She is a capitalist. I am a Red Guard. I
have nothing to do with her!

The question in front of me now is what to do with these flowers. Smash   55
them! Uproot them! Trample them to the ground! Flowers, plants, goldfish,
birds, these are all bourgeois stuff. The new world has no place for them. My
fellow Red Guards have already started. I mustn't fall behind.

So I lifted up a flowerpot and dropped it against a Tai Lake rock.   56
Bang! The sound was startling. *Don't be afraid. The first step is always the*
most difficult. Bang! Bang! *Actually it isn't so terrible. Now I've started, I*
can go on and on. To tell the truth, I even begin to enjoy breaking flowerpots!
Who would have thought of that?...

After a while, we were all out of breath. So we ordered the family   57
to get rid of the remaining flowers in three days, pledging that we'd come back to check on them. Then we left. Behind us was a world of broken pots, spilled soil, fallen petals, and bare roots. Another victory of Mao Zedong thought.

On my way home, surprise caught up with me. I was stopped by a   58
group of Red Guards whom I did not know. They told me that my long braids were also bourgeois stuff. Hearing this, I looked around and saw Red Guards stand on both sides of the street with scissors in their hands. Anyone who had long or curly hair would be stopped by them, their hair cut off on the spot in front of jeering kids. Suddenly I felt my cheeks burning. To have my hair cut off in the street was to lose face. So I pleaded with them, vowing that I would cut my braids as soon as I got home. They let me go. For the time being, I coiled my braids on top of my head and covered them with my army cap.

Fearing that other surprises might be in store for me in the street, I   59
went straight home. There I found Aunty in dismay. It turned out that
she too had seen Red Guards cutting long hair in the street. So she did
not dare leave home these couple of days and we were about to run out
of groceries.

60   "What shall I do?" she asked me. "If I cut my hair, won't I look like
an old devil, with short white hair sticking up all over my head?" Her
troubled look reminded me that since her childhood, Aunty always
had long hair. Before she was married, it was a thick, long braid. Then
a bun, for a married woman, which looked so elegant on the back of
her head. Even in Switzerland, she had never changed her hairstyle.
But now neither she nor I had any choice. If we did not want to lose
face in the street, we'd better do it ourselves at home.

61   While Aunty and I were cutting each other's hair, my parents were
burning things in the bathroom. The idea was the same: to save face
and avoid trouble, better destroy all the "four olds" we had before others found them out. So they picked out a number of Chinese books,
burned them together with all the letters they had kept and some old
photographs. The ash was flushed down the toilet. Repair the house
before it rains. That was wise. No one could tell whose home would be
raided next. Better be prepared for the worst.

62   Now suddenly it seemed everybody in my family had trouble, including Lian, who was eleven. His problem was our cat, Little Tiger. Lian
found him three years ago playing hide and seek in a lumber yard. Then
he was a newborn kitten. So little that he did not even know how to
drink milk. Aunty taught us how to feed him. Put milk in a soupspoon.
Tilt it to make the milk flow slowly through the depression in the middle
of the handle. Put the tip of the handle into the kitten's tiny mouth. He
tasted the milk. He liked it. He began to drink it. By and by the kitten
grew into a big yellow cat with black stripes. On his forehead, three hor-
izontal lines formed the Chinese character *wang*, which means king. We
called him Little Tiger because in China the tiger is king of all animals.

63   Little Tiger's life was in danger now, for pets were considered
bourgeois too. This morning Lian had received an ultimatum from kids
who were our neighbors. It said we had to get rid of Little Tiger in three
days or else they would come and take revolutionary action. This time
we could not solve the problem by doing it ourselves. Little Tiger was a
member of our family. We had to think of a way to save his life.

64   Aunty suggested that we hide him in a bag, take him out to a faraway place, and let him go. He would become a wild cat. Good idea.
Only I did not want to do this. What would people say if they found
that I, a Red Guard, was hiding a cat in my bag? So I told Lian to do it
and went back to school. Since the Cultural Revolution started, I had a
bed in the student dormitory and spent most of the nights there.

65   A few days later when I came back home, Aunty told me what had
happened to Little Tiger. (Lian himself wouldn't talk about it.) When

Lian took him out, he was spotted by the boys who had given him the ultimatum. Noticing something was moving in his bag, they guessed it was the cat. They grabbed the bag, swung it round, and hit it hard against a brick wall. "Miao!" Little Tiger mewed wildly. The boys laughed. It was fun. They continued to hit him against the wall. Lian started to cry and he begged them to stop. Nobody listened to him. Little Tiger's blood stained the canvas bag, leaving dark marks on the brick wall. But he was still alive. Only his mewing became weak and pitiable. Too bad a cat had nine lives! It only prolonged his suffering and gave the boys more pleasure. Bang! Bang! Little Tiger was silent. Dead at last. Lian ran back and cried in Aunty's arms for a long time.

A week after our cat was killed by the boys, a neighbor whom I   66
called Guma killed herself. On that day, I happened to be home. I heard a commotion outside and looked. Many people were standing in front of our building. When I went out, I saw clearly that Guma was hanging from a pipe in the bathroom. Another gruesome sight I could not wipe from my memory.

Why did she kill herself? Nobody knew the answer. Before she   67
died, she was a typist at the college. A quiet little woman. She had no enemies; no historical problems. Nobody had struggled against her. So people assumed that she killed herself for her husband's sake.

The love story between her and her husband must have been quite   68
dramatic. Mother said a writer had interviewed them because he wanted to write a book about it. Guma's husband, whom I called Guzhang, was a professor in the French department. I used to like him a lot because of his refined, gentle manner and the many interesting books he owned. Recently, however, it became known that Guzhang had serious historical problems. In his youth he had studied in France and joined the Communist Party there. Later somehow he dropped out of the Party and turned away from politics. Because of this, he was accused of being a renegade. A renegade he seemed to me, like one who was a coward in revolutionary novels and movies. The following story would prove my point.

After Guma killed herself, Guzhang wanted to commit suicide too.   69
He went to the nearby Summer Palace and jumped into the lake. But the place he jumped was too shallow. After a while he climbed out, saying the water was too cold. When people at the college heard this story, he became a laughingstock. Even Aunty remarked: "You may know people for a long time and still you don't know their hearts. Who should have thought that Guma, a woman so gentle and quiet, was so resolute, while Guzhang, a big man, did not have half her courage."

These words seemed sinister. To tell the truth, I was alarmed by   70
them. Just a couple of days before a nanny had killed herself at the nearby University of Agriculture. The old woman was a proletarian pure and simple. So why did she kill herself?

Her death was caused by a new chapter in the breaking "four olds"   71
campaign. The idea was actually similar to mine: in the past bourgeois

ladies and gentlemen were waited on hand and foot by the working people. In the new society such practices should be abolished. The working people would no longer serve and be exploited by bourgeois ladies and gentlemen. Thus the new rule said those who were labeled bourgeois ladies and gentlemen were not allowed to use nannies. As for those who were not labeled bourgeois ladies and gentlemen, they were not allowed to use nannies either. Because if they used nannies, it was proof enough that they were bourgeois ladies and gentlemen, and bourgeois ladies and gentlemen were not allowed to use nannies. Thus according to the new rule, no family was allowed to use nannies.

72   As a result, the old woman killed herself, because she lost her job and had no children to support her. Though she had saved some money for her old age, another new rule had it all frozen in the bank.

73   Aunty was in exactly the same situation. When she first came to work for us, she was forty-six. Then her son died. Now she was sixty-two, an old woman by traditional standards. Right now all her savings were frozen in the bank. Whether someday she might get them back or not, and if yes when, was anybody's guess. Now the deadline set by the Red Guards of the college for all the nannies to leave was drawing near. Recently Aunty made me uneasy. I was frightened by her eyes. They were so remote, as if they were in a different world. I could not get in touch with them. Then she made that strange comment about being resolute. Could she mean…?

74   On the evening before Aunty left (fortunately she had kept her old home in the city, to which now she could return), Father gathered our whole family together. Solemnly he made a pledge to her. He said that he would continue to support her financially for as long as she lived. Although for the time being she had to leave, she would always be a member of our family. She needn't worry about her old age.

75   That was, in my opinion, the exact right thing to say at the right moment. Even today when I look back on it, I am proud of Father for what he said on that hot summer evening thirty years ago. By then tens of thousands of nannies were being driven out of their employers' homes in Beijing, and who knows how many in the whole country. But few people had the kindness and generosity to say what Father said.

76   Aunty said nothing in return. But she was moved. From then on, she took our family to be her own. Instead of a burden, she became a pillar for our family through one storm after another. She did not quit until all her strength was used up.

✦ Evaluating the Text

1. As a result of the Cultural Revolution, how did personal animosities, jealousies, and the need for revenge become legitimized in the new political environment?

2. What principles motivated the Red Guards? What different areas of society were touched by them? Why were most of their activities involved with destruction of every kind—even including cutting off Yang's braids?

3. As her narrative proceeds, Yang has several experiences that lead her to question her initial zeal. What are some of these and how do they change her attitude?

✧ Exploring Different Perspectives

1. Compare Yang's account with Panos Ioannides's story, "Gregory," in terms of conscience or remorse for actions taken that turned out to be totally unnecessary.

2. Compare Yang's narrative with Anwar Iqbal's account, "Fifteen Lashes," in terms of the way governments manipulate and terrorize the populace through scapegoating.

✧ Extending Viewpoints through Writing

1. Yang is completely honest in admitting the excesses in which she participated and about which she was very enthusiastic. Did you ever have a change of heart about something about which you were at one time zealous? Describe your experience. What caused you to change your attitude?

2. Yang presents a comprehensive picture of the topsy-turvy effect the Cultural Revolution had on Chinese society when it imbued the Red Guards with power over teachers, parents, administrators, and others who once had power over them. What scenario can you imagine would occur in American society if a comparable table-turning revolution took place?

Luis Sepulveda

Daisy

◆

The Chilean expatriot novelist Luis Sepulveda takes us inside the prison where he was confined and reveals, with surprising good humor, one of his experiences. This chapter, translated by Chris Andrews and drawn from Full Circle: A South American Journey, *reveals Sepulveda's ironic sensibility as he tries to evade torture and remain an honest critic of his jailor's literary efforts. His works include his acclaimed detective novel* The Old Man Who Read Love Stories *(1992) and* The Name of the Bullfighter *(1996).*

Chile, whose name comes from an Indian word Tchil *meaning "the deepest point of the earth," is located on the west coast of South America, bordered by Peru, Bolivia, Argentina, and the Pacific Ocean. It stretches like a ribbon 2,800 miles from north to south and is only 265 miles at its widest point. It is composed of three distinct climatic and geographic regions. The range of Andes mountains reaching more than 22,000 feet above sea level separate it from Argentina. Spain conquered northern Chile from the native Incas in the mid 1500s, but met continued resistance from the tribal Indians who lived in the south. The struggle for independence from Spanish rule was achieved in 1818. Chile was democratic until the overthrow of President Salvador Allende in 1973 under a United States-supported military coup. A repressive military junta headed by General Augusto Pinochet gained control until 1990, when he stepped down. His elected successors have gained a measure of confidence with the population over the last decade. Probably due to the free and compulsory system of education, Chile has one of the highest literacy rates in Latin America.*

1   The military had rather inflated ideas of our destructive capacity. They questioned us about plans to assassinate all the officers in American military history, to blow up bridges and seal off tunnels, and to prepare for the landing of a terrible foreign enemy whom they could not identify.

2   Temuco is a sad, grey, rainy city. No-one would call it a tourist attraction, and yet the barracks of the Tucapel regiment came to house a sort of permanent international convention of sadists. The Chileans, who were the hosts, after all, were assisted in the interrogations by primates from Brazilian military intelligence—they were the worst—North Americans from the State Department, Argentinian paramilitary personnel, Italian neo-fascists and even some agents of Mossad.

I remember Rudi Weismann, a Chilean with a passion for the South   3
and sailing, who was tortured and interrogated in the gentle language
of the synagogues. This infamy was too much for Rudi, who had
thrown in his lot with Israel: he had worked on a kibbutz, but in the
end his nostalgia for Tierra del Fuego had brought him back to Chile.
He simply could not understand how Israel could support such a gang
of criminals, and though till then he had always been a model of good
humour, he dried up like a neglected plant. One morning we found
him dead in his sleeping bag. No need for an autopsy, his face made it
clear: Rudi Weismann had died of sadness.

The commander of the Tucapel regiment—a basic respect for paper   4
prevents me from writing his name—was a fanatical admirer of Field
Marshal Rommel. When he found a prisoner he liked, he would invite
him to recover from the interrogations in his office. After assuring the
prisoner that everything that happened in the barracks was in the best
interests of our great nation, the commander would offer him a glass of
Korn—somebody used to send him this insipid, wheat-based liquor
from Germany—and make him sit through a lecture on the Afrika
Korps. The guy's parents or grandparents were German, but he couldn't
have looked more Chilean: chubby, short-legged, dark untidy hair. You
could have mistaken him for a truck driver or a fruit vendor, but when
he talked about Rommel he became the caricature of a Nazi guard.

At the end of the lecture he would dramatise Rommel's suicide,   5
clicking his heels, raising his right hand to his forehead to salute an invisible flag, muttering "Adieu geliebtes Vaterland," and pretending to
shoot himself in the mouth. We all hoped that one day he would do it
for real.

There was another curious officer in the regiment: a lieutenant   6
struggling to contain a homosexuality that kept popping out all over
the place. The soldiers had nicknamed him Daisy, and he knew it.

We could all tell that it was a torment for Daisy not to be able to   7
adorn his body with truly beautiful objects, and the poor guy had to
make do with the regulation paraphernalia. He wore a .45 pistol, two
cartridge clips, a commando's curved dagger, two hand grenades, a
torch, a walkie-talkie, the insignia of his rank and the silver wings of the
parachute corps. The prisoners and the soldiers thought he looked like a
Christmas tree.

This individual sometimes surprised us with generous and appar-   8
ently disinterested acts—we didn't know that the Stockholm syndrome
could be a military perversion. For example, after the interrogations he
would suddenly fill our pockets with cigarettes or the highly prized aspirin tablets with vitamin C. One afternoon he invited me to his room.

"So you're a man of letters," he said, offering me a can of Coca-Cola.   9
"I've written a couple of stories. That's all," I replied.   10

11   "You're not here for an interrogation. I'm very sorry about what's happening, but that's what war is like. I want us to talk as one writer to another. Are you surprised? The army has produced some great men of letters. Think of Don Alonso de Ercilla y Zúñiga, for example."

12   "Or Cervantes," I added.

13   Daisy included himself among the greats. That was his problem. If he wanted adulation, he could have it. I drank the Coca-Cola and thought about Garcés, or rather, about his chicken, because, incredible as it seems, the cook had a chicken called Dulcinea, the name of Don Quixote's mistress.

14   One morning it jumped the wall which separated the common-law prisoners from the POWs, and it must have been a chicken with deep political convictions, because it decided to stay with us. Garcés caressed it and sighed, saying: "If I had a pinch of pepper and a pinch of cumin, I'd make you a chicken marinade like you've never tasted."

15   "I want you to read my poems and give me your opinion, your honest opinion," said Daisy, handing me a notebook.

16   I left that room with my pockets full of cigarettes, caramel sweets, tea bags and a tin of US Army marmalade. That afternoon I started to believe in the brotherhood of writers.

17   They transported us from the prison to the barracks and back in a cattle truck. The soldiers made sure there was plenty of cow shit on the floor of the truck before ordering us to lie face down with our hands behind our necks. We were guarded by four of them, with North American machine guns, one in each corner of the truck. They were almost all young guys brought down from northern garrisons, and the harsh climate of the South kept them flu-ridden and in a perpetually filthy mood. They had orders to fire on the bundles—us—at the slightest suspect movement, or on any civilian who tried to approach the truck. But as time wore on, the discipline gradually relaxed and they turned a blind eye to the packet of cigarettes or piece of fruit thrown from a window, or the pretty and daring girl who ran beside the truck blowing us kisses and shouting: "Don't give up, comrades! We'll win!"

18   Back in prison, as always, we were met by the welcoming committee organised by Doctor "Skinny" Pragnan, now an eminent psychiatrist in Belgium. First he examined those who couldn't walk and those who had heart problems, then those who had come back with a dislocation or with ribs out of place. Pragnan was expert at estimating how much electricity had been put into us on the grill, and patiently determined who would be able to absorb liquids in the next few hours. Then finally it was time to take communion: we were given the aspirin with vitamin C and an anticoagulant to prevent internal haematomas.

19   "Dulcinea's days are numbered," I said to Garcés, and looked for a corner in which to read Daisy's notebook.

20   The elegantly inscribed pages were redolent of love, honey, sublime suffering and forgotten flowers. By the third page I knew that Daisy

hadn't even gone to the trouble of reusing the ideas of the Mexican poet Amado Nervo—he'd simply copied out his poems word for word.

I called out to Peyuco Gálvez, a Spanish teacher, and read him a couple of lines.   21

"What do you think, Peyuco?"   22

"Amado Nervo. The book is called *The Interior Gardens.*"   23

I had got myself into a real jam. If Daisy found out that I knew the work of this sugary poet Nervo, then it wasn't Garcés's chicken whose days were numbered, but mine. It was a serious problem, so that night I presented it to the Council of Elders.   24

"Now, Daisy, would he be the passive or the active type?" enquired Iriarte.   25

"Stop it, will you. My skin's at risk here," I replied.   26

"I'm serious. Maybe our friend wants to have an affair with you, and giving you the notebook was like dropping a silk handkerchief. And like a fool you picked it up. Perhaps he copied out the poems for you to find a message in them. I've known queens who seduced boys by lending them *Demian* by Hermann Hesse. If Daisy is the passive type, this business with Amado Nervo means he wants to test your nerve, so to speak. And if he's the active type, well, it would have to hurt less than a kick in the balls."   27

"Message my arse. He gave you the poems as his own, and you should say you liked them a lot. If he was trying to send a message, he should have given the notebook to Garcés; he's the only one who has an interior garden. Or maybe Daisy doesn't know about the pot plant," remarked Andrés Müller.   28

"Let's be serious about this. You have to say something to him, and Daisy mustn't even suspect that you know Nervo's poems," declared Pragnan.   29

"Tell him you liked the poems, but that the adjectives strike you as a bit excessive. Quote Huidobro: when an adjective doesn't give life, it kills. That way you'll show him that you read his poems carefully and that you are criticising his work as a colleague," suggested Gálvez.   30

The Council of Elders approved of Gálvez's idea, but I spent two weeks on tenterhooks. I couldn't sleep. I wished they would come and take me to be kicked and electrocuted so I could give the damned notebook back. In those two weeks I came to hate good old Garcés: 31

"Listen, mate, if everything goes well, and you get a little jar of capers as well as the cumin and the pepper, we'll have such a feast with that chicken."   32

After a fortnight, I found myself at last stretched out face down on the mattress of cowpats with my hands behind my neck. I thought I was going mad: I was happy to be heading towards a session of the activity known as torture.   33

Tucapel barracks. Service Corps. In the background, the perpetual green of Cerro Ñielol, sacred to the Mapuche Indians. There was a   34 waiting room outside the interrogation cell, like at the doctor's. There they made us sit on a bench with our hands tied behind our backs and black hoods over our heads. I never understood what the hoods were for, because once we got inside they took them off, and we could see the interrogators—the toy soldiers who, with panic-stricken faces, turned the handle of the generator, and the health officers who attached the electrodes to our anuses, testicles, gums and tongue, and then listened with stethoscopes to see who was faking and who had really passed out on the grill.

35   Lagos, a deacon of the Emmaus International ragmen, was the first to be interrogated that day. For a year they had been working him over to find out how the organisation had come by a couple of dozen old military uniforms which had been found in their warehouses. A trader who sold army surplus gear had donated them. Lagos screamed in pain and repeated over and over what the soldiers wanted to hear: the uniforms belonged to an invading army which was preparing to land on the Chilean coast.

36   I was waiting for my turn when someone took off the hood. It was Lieutenant Daisy.

37   "Follow me," he ordered.

38   We went into an office. On the desk I saw a tin of cocoa and a carton of cigarettes which were obviously there to reward my comments on his literary work.

39   "Did you read my poesy?" he asked, offering me a seat.

40   Poesy. Daisy said poesy, not poetry. A man covered with pistols and grenades can't say "poesy" without sounding ridiculous and effete. At that moment he revolted me, and I decided that even if it meant pissing blood, hissing when I spoke and being able to charge batteries just by touching them, I wasn't going to lower myself to flattering a plagiarising faggot in uniform.

41   "You have pretty handwriting, Lieutenant. But you know these poems aren't yours," I said, giving him back the notebook.

42   I saw him begin to shake. He was carrying enough arms to kill me several times over, and if he didn't want to stain his uniform, he could order someone else to do it. Trembling with anger he stood up, threw what was on the desk onto the floor and shouted:

43   "Three weeks in the cube. But first, you're going to visit the chiropodist, you piece of subversive shit!"

44   The chiropodist was a civilian, a landholder who had lost several thousand hectares in the land reform, and who was getting his revenge by participating in the interrogations as a volunteer. His speciality was peeling back toenails, which led to terrible infections.

45   I knew the cube. I had spent my first six months of prison there in solitary confinement: it was an underground cell, one and a half metres wide by one and a half metres long by one and a half metres high. In

the old days there had been a tannery in the Temuco jail, and the cube was used to store fat. The walls still stank of fat, but after a week your excrement fixed that, making the cube very much a place of your own.

You could only stretch out across the diagonal, but the low tempera-   46
tures of southern Chile, the rainwater and the soldiers' urine made you want to curl up hugging your legs and stay like that wishing yourself smaller and smaller, so that eventually you could live on one of the islands of floating shit, which conjured up images of dream holidays. I was there for three weeks, running through Laurel and Hardy films, remembering the books of Salgari, Stevenson and London word by word, playing long games of chess, licking my toes to protect them from infection. In the cube I swore over and over again never to become a literary critic.

✧ Evaluating the Text

1. To what paradoxical aspects of prison life does Sepulveda have to adapt himself in order to survive?

2. What unusual mixture of character traits and aspirations does Daisy display, given his role as prison guard and torturer? What kind of relationship does Sepulveda have with Daisy?

3. In what ways is Sepulveda's style unusual, in view of his predicament? In what sense might his style itself be a way of coping with the dangerous circumstances with which he was confronted?

✧ Exploring Different Perspectives

1. Compare the accounts of Sepulveda and Anwar Iqbal (see "Fifteen Lashes") in terms of the ironic narrative style that both authors adopt.

2. To what extent do the accounts by Sepulveda and Ngũgĩ wa Thiong'o ("Decolonising the Mind") reveal the psychological value placed on authenticity in language and literature as a strategy of rebellion?

✧ Extending Viewpoints through Writing

1. If you had been in the same situation as Sepulveda, would you have been as honest? Why or why not?

2. Plagiarism is a moral problem with which students are often confronted. What experiences have you had either directly or indirectly? Tell what happened.

Anwar Iqbal

Fifteen Lashes

———————— ◆ ————————

Anwar Iqbal is a journalist living in Pakistan. In "Fifteen Lashes" (GRANTA, Autumn 1998) he provides a forthright and disquieting account of the practice, common in modern-day Pakistan, of public flogging as punishment for various crimes, including solicitation of prostitutes.

With India's independence in 1947, the nation of Pakistan was established as a separate Muslim state comprising two regions on either side of India separated by a thousand miles, with East Pakistan sharing a border with Burma. The creation of the Indo-Pakistani border was followed by an exodus of 7 million Hindus to India and an equal number of Muslims to Pakistan. In 1971, East Pakistan declared its independence and took the name Bangladesh. Pakistan's precarious economic conditions worsened in the 1980s, when million of refugees fleeing the Soviet invasion of Afghanistan poured into Pakistan. In 1988, Benazir Bhutto became the first woman to govern a Muslim country, a position she held for two years, until she was ousted by a no-confidence vote in the National Assembly because of accusations of nepotism and corruption. She was replaced by Nawaz Sharif in 1990.

1   I was an apprentice newspaper reporter when General Zia ul-Haq came to power in Pakistan in the military coup of 1977. That was more than twenty years ago; but there are scenes from his reign that I shall always remember. The general was keen on Islamic law and Islamic punishment, but, though stonings and amputations of the hands were often talked of, the general came down in favour of flogging, a form of punishment which in Pakistan owes as much to an inherited British colonial tradition as to the penal code of Islam. Floggings were always a part of prison life in Pakistan. The general's innovation was to make them public, *pour encourager les autres.*

2   Soon after he took over, the general arranged a big public flogging-show and I, as a reporter, was sent to watch. The victims were lined up in white pyjamas, loose white shirts and white caps. They looked like circus animals waiting for the crack of the trainer's whip. All were men, most of them middle-aged. They looked pale, and they shook with fear. Some even wet their trousers when the flogging began, but it had little effect on their captors or the doctor whose job it was to exam-

ine each victim and declare him fit to be flogged. The stage was built in a big open space between the old city of Rawalpindi and the new capital Islamabad; the two places adjoin each other. Normally, children played football, cricket and hockey there. It was an open platform, about fifteen feet high, and could be viewed from every corner of the huge ground. A wooden frame was fixed in the middle of the platform where every victim was to be tied, his hands and feet separately as on a cross. His face would be turned towards the stage where the policemen, the magistrate, and other important people were sitting; the press had special seats so that they could watch the flogging closely and report every detail. His hips, which would receive the whip, were to face the audience. A microphone was fixed on the frame, near where the victim's mouth was to be, so that everybody could hear him scream. Centre stage stood a tall and well-built man wearing only a loincloth. He was rubbing oil all over his body. Then he did some push-ups to show his muscles. When he finished, he picked up a big stick, soaked in oil, from a corner where about half a dozen such sticks were kept for him to choose from. He picked one and tried it in the air. The whip made a horrible hissing noise every time he cut the air with it. The whipper, who was a convict himself, had been brought specially from the prison to perform the job, which earned him privileges inside. He received superior food and spent most of his time exercising. He was in great demand and toured Pakistan from city to city to flog whenever the government thought it needed to scare people. He looked very intimidating. He was now ready to flog. All his muscles tightened and bulged like the feathers of a rooster ready to fight. As those on the stage prepared for the flogging, thousands of people had already gathered to watch it. The ground was full to capacity. So were the neighbouring roads and side streets. There were people on the rooftops of nearby buildings. Some even clung to the trees and electricity poles around the ground. The poor watched with a cautious nonchalance; they have learned not to appear too interested in such things because they tend to supply the victims whenever their rulers need to demonstrate their strength. The rich behaved differently. They had come by car and on their motorbikes and were cruising around, waiting for the spectacle to begin. The young among them were dressed in tight jeans and bright shirts and some of them had brought their girlfriends with them. Some might have committed the same sin for which the fifteen victims were to be flogged: drinking alcohol and having sex with women other than their wives. But they did not seem bothered. They were safe in doing whatever they did because they belonged to the so-called "VIP" class where no law, religious or secular, applies. They also had better, safer places in which to drink or screw and did not have to frequent cheap hotels which the police would raid whenever their bosses felt the need

to impress the public with activity. All the victims were arrested from a
hotel in a lower-middle-class neighbourhood of the old city. The raiding party, so it was said, had found more than fifty people drinking alcohol and having sex. All of them were convicted in a trial completed
in three days. Most of them were over fifty and so found unfit for flogging. The women involved in this crime were also convicted but were
spared the whip. Those men found fit were brought for flogging.

3   Now the flogging was to start. The man with the stick indicated
that he was ready. An official came on to the stage, detached the microphone from the wooden frame and announced the name of the first
man who was to be whipped. He then read out the allegations against
him and signalled the guards to bring him on to the platform. Two constables brought the convict on to the stage. He looked utterly helpless.
He was not trembling. He did not even look afraid. He looked more
like an animal about to be slaughtered and unable to understand what
was happening to him. He could not follow verbal commands. So to
make him move, one of the constables had to give him a little push. He
moved, and then kept walking so that he would have fallen off the opposite end of the stage if the other constable had not stopped him. It
was as if his mind had stopped functioning. There seemed to be no co-
ordination between his thoughts and his actions. Each of his hands and
feet appeared to be moving separately. The constables led him to the
frame. Then the doctor came, examined him, listened to his heart with
a stethoscope, and declared him fit for flogging. The man listened to
the pronouncement with indifference, as if it did not concern him. He
even nodded his head twice, as if endorsing the doctor's decision. By
now the crowd was completely silent. Even the hawkers, selling ice
cream and fresh fruits to the crowd, were quiet. The constables lifted
the man up on to the frame, and tied his hands and feet to the scaffolding: his face was turned towards the stage and his buttocks exposed to
the crowd. They tied another piece of cloth above his hips to mark the
target. Then they moved aside. Now all eyes were fixed on the whip-
man who was fiercely slashing the air with his whip. The crowd was so
quiet that the microphone picked up the slashing of the whip and carried it everywhere. The man on the scaffolding also heard the sound.
So far he had been very quiet but the slashing sound changed him. He
started trembling and then cried, very loudly. The loudspeakers carried
his voice to the crowd and beyond, but nobody spoke a word. Now a
magistrate, also sitting on the stage, asked the whip-man to begin. He
tested the whip for the last time, slowly hitting his left palm and then
came running, stopped a foot or two from the scaffolding and hit the
victim with full force. The whip touched his skin, went into his flesh
and came out again. The man shrieked in agony. Those sitting on the
stage could see blood oozing from the wound. *One,* said the official
counting the whips. The man was sobbing now which could be heard

on the loudspeakers. The whipper went back to his mark and came running again when the magistrate signalled him to resume. The whip hit the flesh, the man shouted for help, the flogger withdrew, came back again, hit him and withdrew. Once this sequence was broken when the doctor came to examine the victim. After his examination, he invited the whip-man to continue. The constable untied the man after the fifteenth lash and he fell on to the stage. They removed him on a stretcher and brought the next man.

This was my first public flogging. Several months later I went to a *maidan*, a public space, in Rawalpindi where a blind woman was to be flogged for sexual misbehaviour. An audience of hundreds of men surrounded the stage where she was to be whipped. They displayed neither sorrow nor passion. They chatted about politics and sport as they waited for the flogging to begin. Then a police officer came and asked them to go home because a higher court had suspended the flogging. Soon the *maidan* rang with voices of disapproval. The men wanted to watch the *tamasha*, the hullabaloo. They were there to watch the woman's helplessness and to enjoy it. But the policemen were ready with their batons, so they had to disperse. And the truth was that I shared their disappointment. Although I had been writing against public flogging ever since it began, I wanted to watch it. I might go back to my typewriter and condemn it, but I did not want to miss the spectacle. 4

This was an unpleasant discovery to make about myself. A sorrowful, angry disgust—with myself and the country I lived in—thus became a feature of my life. 5

✧ *Evaluating the Text*

1. What purpose is public flogging designed to serve in Pakistan? For what kinds of offenses is it decreed? Is the law as Iqbal understands it justly enforced? Why or why not?

2. What kinds of hoopla accompany public floggings? To what extent does the way that the event is staged suggest that it is a form of entertainment as well as an object lesson?

3. How do you understand Iqbal's reaction to witnessing a public flogging?

✧ *Exploring Different Perspectives*

1. Making an unpleasant discovery about oneself is a theme in both "Fifteen Lashes" and in Panos Ioannides's story, "Gregory." To what extent do the narrators discover that they have directly or indirectly collaborated with their governments?

2. Discuss the ritualized nature of punishment as a theme in both Iqbal's account and in Luis Sepulveda's narrative.

✧ Extending Viewpoints through Writing

1. What kinds of objectives is imprisonment supposed to achieve in Western culture? Given a choice, would you rather be subjected to a few minutes of intense pain and public humiliation, as Iqbal describes, or be locked away for a couple of years in an American prison? Discuss the reasons for your choice.

2. Is it likely that the West would consider copying the practices of Islamic nations and institute punishments such as flogging? Why or why not? Do you think it would be a good idea? Explain your answer.

Panos Ioannides

Gregory

◆————————◆

Panos Ioannides was born in Cyprus in 1935 and was educated in Cyprus, the United States, and Canada. He has been the head of TV programs at Cyprus Broadcasting Corporation. Ioannides is the author of many plays, which have been staged or telecast internationally, and has written novels, short stories, and radio scripts. "Gregory" was written in 1963 and first appeared in The Charioteer, a Review of Modern Greek Literature *(1965). The English translation is by Marion Byron and Catherine Raisiz. This compelling story is based on a true incident that took place during the Cypriot Liberation struggle against the British in the late 1950s. Ioannides takes the unusual approach of letting the reader experience the torments of a soldier ordered to shoot a prisoner, Gregory, who had saved his life and was his friend.*

Cyprus is an island republic with a population of nearly 700,000 situated in the eastern Mediterranean south of Turkey and west of Syria and has been inhabited since 6500 B.C. Seventy-seven percent of the people are of Greek origin, living mainly in the south, and the remaining population, situated in the north, is of Turkish descent. Cyprus came under British administration in 1878 and was annexed by Britain in 1914. The quest among Greek Cypriots for self-rule and union with Greece has been a source of continuous civil discord, erupting in 1955 into a civil war. The conflict was aggravated by Turkish support of Turkish Cypriot demands for partition of the island. A settlement was reached in 1959 including provisions for both union with Greece and partition. In 1960, Makarios III, leader of the Greek Cypriot Nationalists, was elected president, a development that did not prevent continued fighting. A United Nations peacekeeping force was sent to Cyprus in 1965. In 1974, in response to the overthrow by Greek Army officers of the Makarios regime, Turkey invaded Cyprus. Since then, Cyprus has remained a divided state, and little progress has been made toward reunification. The Greek sector is led by President Glafcos Ierides who was reelected in 1998.

My hand was sweating as I held the pistol. The curve of the trigger was biting against my finger. 1

Facing me, Gregory trembled. 2

His whole being was beseeching me, "Don't!" 3

Only his mouth did not make a sound. His lips were squeezed tight. If it had been me, I would have screamed, shouted, cursed. 4

5   The soldiers were watching....

6   The day before, during a brief meeting, they had each given their opinions: "It's tough luck, but it has to be done. We've got no choice."

7   The order from Headquarters was clear: "As soon as Lieutenant Rafel's execution is announced, the hostage Gregory is to be shot and his body must be hanged from a telegraph pole in the main street as an exemplary punishment."

8   It was not the first time that I had to execute a hostage in this war. I had acquired experience, thanks to Headquarters which had kept entrusting me with these delicate assignments. Gregory's case was precisely the sixth.

9   The first time, I remember, I vomited. The second time I got sick and had a headache for days. The third time I drank a bottle of rum. The fourth, just two glasses of beer. The fifth time I joked about it, "This little guy, with the big pop-eyes, won't be much of a ghost!"

10   But why, dammit, when the day came did I have to start thinking that I'm not so tough, after all? The thought had come at exactly the wrong time and spoiled all my disposition to do my duty.

11   You see, this Gregory was such a miserable little creature, such a puny thing, such a nobody, damn him.

12   That very morning, although he had heard over the loudspeakers that Rafel had been executed, he believed that we would spare his life because we had been eating together so long.

13   "Those who eat from the same mess tins and drink from the same water canteen," he said, "remain good friends no matter what."

14   And a lot more of the same sort of nonsense.

15   He was a silly fool—we had smelled that out the very first day Headquarters gave him to us. The sentry guarding him had got dead drunk and had dozed off. The rest of us with exit permits had gone from the barracks. When we came back, there was Gregory sitting by the sleeping sentry and thumbing through a magazine.

16   "Why didn't you run away, Gregory?" we asked, laughing at him, several days later.

17   And he answered, "Where would I go in this freezing weather? I'm O.K. here."

18   So we started teasing him.

19   "You're dead right. The accommodations here are splendid...."

20   "It's not so bad here," he replied. "The barracks where I used to be are like a sieve. The wind blows in from every side...."

21   We asked him about his girl. He smiled.

22   "Maria is a wonderful person," he told us. "Before I met her she was engaged to a no-good fellow, a pig. He gave her up for another girl. Then nobody in the village wanted to marry Maria. I didn't miss my chance. So what if she is second-hand. Nonsense. Peasant ideas, my friend. She's beautiful and good-hearted. What more could I want?

And didn't she load me with watermelons and cucumbers every time I passed by her vegetable garden? Well, one day I stole some cucumbers and melons and watermelons and I took them to her. 'Maria,' I said, 'from now on I'm going to take care of you.' She started crying and then me, too. But ever since that day she has given me lots of trouble—jealousy. She wouldn't let me go even to my mother's. Until the day I was recruited, she wouldn't let me go far from her apron strings. But that was just what I wanted…."

He used to tell this story over and over, always with the same words, the same commonplace gestures. At the end he would have a good laugh and start gulping from his water jug.   23

His tongue was always wagging! When he started talking, nothing could stop him. We used to listen and nod our heads, not saying a word. But sometimes, as he was telling us about his mother and family problems, we couldn't help wondering, "Eh, well, these people have the same headaches in their country as we've got."   24

Strange, isn't it!   25

Except for his talking too much, Gregory wasn't a bad fellow. He was a marvelous cook. Once he made us some apple tarts, so delicious we licked the platter clean. And he could sew, too. He used to sew on all our buttons, patch our clothes, darn our socks, iron our ties, wash our clothes….   26

How the devil could you kill such a friend?   27

Even though his name was Gregory and some people on his side had killed one of ours, even though we had left wives and children to go to war against him and his kind—but how can I explain? He was our friend. He actually liked us! A few days before, hadn't he killed with his own bare hands a scorpion that was climbing up my leg? He could have let it send me to hell!   28

"Thanks, Gregory!" I said then, "Thank God who made you…."   29

When the order came, it was like a thunderbolt. Gregory was to be shot, it said, and hanged from a telegraph pole as an exemplary punishment.   30

We got together inside the barracks. We sent Gregory to wash some underwear for us.   31

"It ain't right."   32

"What is right?"   33

"Our duty!"   34

"Shit!"   35

"If you dare, don't do it! They'll drag you to court-martial and then bang-bang…."   36

Well, of course. The right thing is to save your skin. That's only logical. It's either your skin or his. His, of course, even if it was Gregory, the fellow you've been sharing the same plate with, eating with your fingers, and who was washing your clothes that very minute.   37

38   What could I do? That's war. We had seen worse things.

39   So we set the hour.

40   We didn't tell him anything when he came back from the washing. He slept peacefully. He snored for the last time. In the morning, he heard the news over the loudspeaker and he saw that we looked gloomy and he began to suspect that something was up. He tried talking to us, but he got no answers and then he stopped talking.

41   He just stood there and looked at us, stunned and lost....

Now, I'll squeeze the trigger. A tiny bullet will rip through his chest. Maybe I'll lose my sleep tonight but in the morning I'll wake up alive.

Gregory seems to guess my thoughts. He puts out his hand and asks, "You're kidding, friend! Aren't you kidding?"

What a jackass! Doesn't he deserve to be cut to pieces? What a thing to ask at such a time. Your heart is about to burst and he's asking if you're kidding. How can a body be kidding about such a thing? Idiot! This is no time for jokes. And you, if you're such a fine friend, why don't you make things easier for us? Help us kill you with fewer qualms? If you would get angry—curse our Virgin, our God—if you'd try to escape it would be much easier for us and for you.

So it is *now*.

Now, Mr. Gregory, you are going to pay for your stupidities wholesale. Because you didn't escape the day the sentry fell asleep; because you didn't escape yesterday when we sent you all alone to the laundry—we did it on purpose, you idiot! Why didn't you let me die from the sting of the scorpion?

So now don't complain. It's all your fault, nitwit.

Eh? What's happening to him now?

Gregory is crying. Tears flood his eyes and trickle down over his cleanshaven cheeks. He is turning his face and pressing his forehead against the wall. His back is shaking as he sobs. His hands cling, rigid and helpless, to the wall.

Now is my best chance, now that he knows there is no other solution and turns his face from us.

I squeeze the trigger.

Gregory jerks. His back stops shaking up and down.

I think I've finished him! How easy it is.... But suddenly he starts crying out loud, his hands claw at the wall and try to pull it down. He screams, "No, no...."

I turn to the others. I expect them to nod, "That's enough."

They nod, "What are you waiting for?"

I squeeze the trigger again.

The bullet smashed into his neck. A thick spray of blood spurts out.

Gregory turns. His eyes are all red. He lunges at me and starts punching me with his fists.

"I hate you, hate you...," he screams.

I emptied the barrel. He fell and grabbed my leg as if he wanted to hold on.

He died with a terrible spasm. His mouth was full of blood and so were my boots and socks.   42

We stood quietly, looking at him.   43

When we came to, we stooped and picked him up. His hands were frozen and wouldn't let my legs go.   44

I still have their imprints, red and deep, as if made by a hot knife.   45

"We will hang him tonight," the men said.   46

"Tonight or now?" they said.   47

I turned and looked at them one by one.   48

"Is that what you all want?" I asked.   49

They gave me no answer.   50

"Dig a grave," I said.   51

Headquarters did not ask for a report the next day or the day after.   52
The top brass were sure that we had obeyed them and had left him swinging from a pole.

They didn't care to know what happened to that Gregory, alive or   53
dead.

✦ Evaluating the Text

1. Much of the story's action takes place during the few seconds when the narrator must decide whether to pull the trigger. Why do you think Ioannides chooses to tell the story from the executioner's point of view rather than from Gregory's? What in the narrator's past leads his superiors (and the narrator himself) to conclude that he is the one best-suited to kill Gregory?

2. What details illustrate that Gregory has become a friend to the narrator and other soldiers? In what way does he embody the qualities of humanity, decency, and domestic life that the soldiers were forced to leave behind? Why is his innocence a source of both admiration and irritation? How does Gregory's decision to marry Maria suggest the kind of person he is and answer the question as to why he doesn't try to escape when he is told he is going to be killed? What explains why he doesn't perceive the threat to his life even at the moment the narrator points a gun at his head?

3. Discuss the psychological process that allows the narrator to convert his anguish at having to shoot Gregory into a justification for doing so.

4. When the narrator fires the first shot, why does he hope the other soldiers will stop him from firing again? Why don't they stop him? At the end, how does the narrator's order not to hang Gregory's body reveal his distress after shooting Gregory? Why is it ironic that the higher-ups never inquire whether their orders have been carried out? What does this imply and why does it make the narrator feel even worse?

✧ Exploring Different Perspectives

1. Compare and contrast the moral dilemma that faces the narrator in "Gregory" with that faced by Rae Yang as a Red Guard in her memoir "At the Center of the Storm."

2. How does the theme of public punishment as an object lesson provided by governments enter into Ioannides's story and in Anwar Iqbal's account, "Fifteen Lashes"?

✧ Extending Viewpoints through Writing

1. In your opinion, is Gregory a good person or just a fool who is stupid enough to get killed when he does not have to die?

2. If you were in the narrator's shoes, what would you have done? Do you think you would have made yourself hate Gregory, as the narrator did, in order to be able to kill him?

Connecting Cultures

Natalia Ginzburg, The Son of Man

Compare Ginzburg's account with Saida Hagi-Dirie Herzi's story, "Against the Pleasure Principle," in Chapter 2, in terms of the anxiety that the betrayal of trust engenders.

Milorad Pavić, The Wedgwood Tea Set

Compare Pavić's story with David R. Counts's narrative, "Too Many Bananas" in Chapter 7, in terms of a network of social relationships that springs from something necessary and basic, that is, food.

Ngũgĩ wa Thiong'o, Decolonising the Mind

In what ways do both Thiong'o and Mary Crow Dog (see "Civilize Them with a Stick" in Chapter 5) add to your understanding of what life is like for native people living under the domination of a different culture?

Rae Yang, At the Center of the Storm

Discuss the theme of revenge as it is presented in Yang's narrative and in Nabil Gorgy's story, "Cairo Is a Small City" in Chapter 8.

Luis Sepulveda, Daisy

Discuss the surreal environments in which Sepulveda and Lee Stringer (see "Life on the Street" in Chapter 5) find themselves and their encounters with incongruous characters who inhabit these environments.

Anwar Iqbal, Fifteen Lashes

Discuss the means Islamic cultures have evolved to manage sexuality as expressed in both Iqbal's account and Saida Haagi-Dirie Herzi's story, "Against the Pleasure Principle," in Chapter 2.

Panos Ioannides, Gregory

In what sense are the protagonists in the stories by Ioannides and Gloria Anzaldúa (see "Cervicide" in Chapter 7) coerced into killing someone or something they care about because of the political circumstances in which they find themselves?

7

Strangers in a Strange Land

◆

In some ways, our age—the age of the refugee, of the displaced person, and of mass emigration—is defined by the condition of exile. Being brought up in one world and then emigrating to a different culture inevitably produces feelings of alienation. Moving to another country involves living among people who dress differently, eat different foods, have different customs, and speak a different language. Understandably, forming relationships with people whose cultural frame of reference is often radically different from one's own invariably leads to "culture shock," to a greater or lesser degree. Without insight into the norms that govern behavior in a new environment, it is often difficult for immigrants to interpret the actions of others: to know what particular facial expressions and gestures might mean, what assumptions govern physical contact, how people express and resolve conflicts, or what topics of conversation are deemed appropriate.

The jarring, intense, and often painful emotional experience of having to redefine oneself in a strange land, of trying to reconcile conflicting cultural values, forces immigrants to surrender all ideas of safety, the comfort of familiar surroundings, and a common language. Ironically, the condition of *not* belonging, of being caught between two cultures, at home in neither, gives the exile the chance to develop a tolerance for conflicting messages and the ability to see things from outside the controlling frame of reference of a single culture.

The works in this chapter explore the need of those who have left home, whether as refugees, emigrants, or travelers, to make sense of their lives in a new place. These selections offer many perspectives on the experience of learning a new language and the void created by the failure to communicate, the intolerance of the dominant culture toward minorities, and the chance to create a new life for oneself.

In "Ethnicity and Identity: Creating a Sense of Self," Claire Chow records the observations of three Asian American women who have struggled to redefine themselves in a new country. The survival of the human spirit in the harrowing conditions in Tijuana, on the United States–Mexican border, is graphically portrayed by Luis Alberto Urrea in "Border Story." The Chicana writer Gloria Anzaldúa, in "Cervicide," tells a poignant story of a Mexican American family living on the Texas border. For Vietnamese immigrants, says Jesse W. Nash, in his essay "Confucius and the VCR," Asian films are the only real link to the culture they left behind. Palden Gyatso, a Tibetan monk living in India, describes in "Autobiography of a Tibetan Monk," his happiness at meeting the Dalai Lama coupled with his sadness at seeing his fellow Tibetan exiles. David R. Counts, in "Too Many Bananas," reveals the many lessons about reciprocity he learned while doing fieldwork in New Guinea. H. G. Wells, a pioneer of the science fiction genre, creates in his story, "The Country of the Blind," a profound parable that probes assumptions about cultural superiority.

Claire S. Chow

Ethnicity and Identity: Creating a Sense of Self

◆

Claire Chow was born in 1952 in New Brunswick, New Jersey. She received her B.A. from Occidental College in 1974, a M.A. in English literature from the University of Chicago in 1975, and a second M.A. in counseling from the University of San Francisco in 1979. She is currently in private practice as a psychotherapist in San Ramon, California. Chow's writing is strongly influenced by the work she does as a therapist, and in the following account drawn from Leaving Deep Water *(1998), we see three Asian American women struggling to come to terms with their identity in a new land.*

1   Who can say how ethnic identity is formed? Is it nurtured like the seed in the soil by parents who cultivate ways of thinking, values, preferences? Does it develop in response to the external world, a reaction to the stereotypes and perceptions promulgated "out there"? Is the simple fact of distinctive physical appearance enough to form the core of an identity, around which other influences solidify, the grain of sand that eventually becomes the pearl?

2   This is not a question that can be answered with certainty. But I believe there are a number of factors that influence the extent to which a person identifies with one or both cultures. First are the demographic characteristics: age, generational status, date of personal or family immigration. Also significant is the availability of extended family and ethnic community (especially as a child), peer influences, relationships with parents, sociopolitical events such as the internment, and exposure to political ideology, for example, the movement to ensure civil rights for Asian Americans. But perhaps the single most important factor is simply individual preference, which itself is based on life experience and temperament. Thus, two children growing up in the same house could come to maturity with different ideas about their ethnicity.

3   I believe that by the time an Asian American woman reaches adulthood, she chooses how to identify herself. That choice may be largely unconscious, but it is still a manifestation of individual will. After all, isn't this the grand and glorious thing about the American experience: the opportunity to define yourself, to forge your own image? Living here, the notion of the frontier, with its promise of transformation, beckons to us all.

In this chapter are stories of women who have worked, sometimes   4
against tremendous odds, to resolve this question of ethnicity and
identity.

Doreen, who lives in a small town in North Carolina, talks about   5
her struggle to hold on to the Asian half of her heritage.

"Today began as all others with a quick shower and a look in the   6
mirror asking myself, 'Who am I?' Then, off to work I went. It is early
fall and my skin is beginning to fade back to a natural yellow-ivory col-
or. This is one of those minor features of mine that always provokes a
question in the minds of curious people. In the course of this day, a co-
worker placed his arm next to mine and asked, 'Are you one of *those?*'
'Yes,' I answered quietly. 'My father was Chinese.'

"Ever since I can remember, I have felt different, I have had this   7
sense inside that I was not like the people who surrounded me. Everyone in my family is tall, red-haired, green-eyed. I'm short and on the
stocky side. Doing good at five five and a half. No legs. Eyes slanted
just a little too much. Face just a little too round. In the fourth grade, the
teacher had us project our profiles on an overhead. My nose was so flat,
the kids all started laughing. And when my beautiful tall white mother,
who is of Welsh-Scottish descent, got mad at me, which she did frequently, she'd scream, 'You have such a *fat, flat, ugly* nose.'

"My mother put her maiden name on my birth certificate. No father.   8
Virgin birth, of course. When I was twelve, she admitted that the man she
was married to was not my father. But she refused to tell me who my real
father was. One Christmas she asked what I wanted. 'The name of my father,' I said, not missing a beat. No answer. So I continued to feel different,
to look at myself in the mirror and try to figure it out. I used to cut that
long blond hair off my Barbies; it made me mad that I was never given a
doll who looked like me. For a long time, I was bitter about the Miss
America pageant, never a dark-skinned or dark-haired beauty queen.

"Two years ago, I got my hair cut very short, almost a bob. I had a   9
picture taken of myself and gave a copy to my mother. She was furious.
She hated that photograph. Finally, my husband said to me, 'You've got
to pursue this. You need to confront her.' So I did. And in her anger, my
mother told me the one true thing, one of the very few things I could
ever believe. She told me that my father was Chinese. That statement
helped put things in place, gave me an explanation that made sense.
But at a deeper level, I didn't really need to hear her say those words
out loud, because I *knew* it was true. I have always known, it has just
never been articulated before.

"Learning about my parentage explains a lot. Like why, as a small   10
child, I always treasured Oriental things. Like why I feel more
comfortable around Chinese people than whites. Not even Japanese so

much, but Chinese. Like why, at eighteen years of age, I left the South, took a bus to New York City determined to live in Chinatown. I remember arriving at Port Authority, sitting in a coffee shop for a few hours and then telling myself, 'OK, this is why you came here, to live among Chinese people. Now go do it!' I had a wonderful experience. The Chinese would confirm stuff about me. Look behind my glasses at my eyes. They knew. I learned to speak Cantonese, a little Mandarin. They didn't treat me like a whole Chinese, but that's OK because I didn't expect them to. But at least they didn't treat me like I was white. I've never really felt white.

11   "Perhaps if my mother hadn't treated me the way she did, my need to know my father wouldn't be so great. Perhaps if I didn't have this feeling that I made my mother uncomfortable, that she doesn't like to look at me, doesn't want to be reminded of my Chinese father, I might not have quite this drive to pursue my heritage. But that's not what has happened.

12   "My husband and I now live in North Carolina. I'd love to be somewhere where there are more Chinese people. For example, Hong Kong. I'd love to have been there in '97, watching the clock tick off the minutes until the country reverted back to China. But we're here now because of my husband's job. When we bought our house a few years ago, one of the neighbors stopped in to say hello. She also asked, 'What is your nationality?' When I told her, she said, 'I knew you weren't pure white.' Now I want to ask you, what the heck is 'pure white'? *Who* is 'pure white'? All these white people came here from somewhere else. So I call myself a mutt.

13   "I would like to know more about my father. But I'm afraid that I may never be able to trace him. The only thing I have to go on is what a relative once told me, that a Chinese doctor from Manchuria brought over a group of his friends to live here when the Japanese were invading. Perhaps my father is one of those men. But my mom will not give me his name or his identity. In the meantime, it just helps to be able to look in the mirror and have a better sense of who that person really is. What I want is this: More than anything else, I want my Chinese heritage."

14   The adoption of an Asian child by white parents adds another level of complexity to the question of developing an ethnic identity. Renée is thirty-two years old, lives in Oregon, and works with battered women.

15   "A few years ago, I hired a good attorney, got a restraining order, and after eight years of marriage, left my abusive husband. Now, maybe for the first time in my life, I feel free to find out who I really am: as a woman, as a Korean American, as a person worthy of dignity and respect.

16   "My Korean mother abandoned me as an infant. I was adopted by white parents through an agency when I was twenty-four months old and moved to Salem, Oregon. I'm not too keen on the agency these

days. Their philosophy, at least back then, was that the little Korean children should be grateful to be raised by white Christian families. I still have a letter from the woman who ran the agency saying that 'since an orphan has no place in Korean society, you were a nobody and now you are a person.'

"My mother is religious in a Bible-beating sort of way, and she also   17
bought these notions of gratitude and Christian service, which she has tried to impose on me. She wanted me to go to a Bible college, but when I went to an academic school instead and majored in social science, she was convinced I would be doomed. Now I have this nice purple candle in my living room. It has a sun, star, and a moon on it, sits in a simple brass holder. She asks me what I need that for. I tell my mom that it's my way to honor witches and lesbians. My ex-husband also thought I should be grateful. He loved to introduce me as his Korean wife who should be 'serving him,' and frequently pointed out that if I had stayed back in Korea, I would be 'eating dogs and worms.'

"I grew up thinking I was white. After all, I was raised in an all-   18
American family, with all-white relatives, on hamburgers. In fact, sometimes I blame all those cow hormones for my overdeveloped bust, which was a source of constant discomfort for me as a teenager. I used to think, 'If these things keep growing, one of these days I'm just going to fall over and die.' My uncle and aunt, whom I call the 'King and Queen of the Right Wing,' also would treat me as if I was white. In their eyes, I *was* white. So the fact that I'm a woman of color, that I do oppression training in my work, completely eludes them. They love to talk about how the Mexicans in our town are always the ones getting picked up for DUIs, etc., right in front of me. Usually, I just let it go, but once in a while if I do decide to speak up, I feel like one of my relatives is thinking, 'We better cool it, the race police is here.'

"I was never pushed to excel academically, but I became an over-   19
achiever all on my own. I worked hard for good grades, joined all kinds of clubs, etc. I even got elected to be on the homecoming court. But even so, I always felt unattractive. In high school, I got into this big thing about eye surgery. My mother had a cousin who was a plastic surgeon and I went to see him when I was fifteen. He refused to do the surgery and tried to convince me that my eyes were in fact pretty. That didn't stop me from trying to curl my lashes with one of those curler things, which always caught my eyelid instead of my lashes anyhow. And my nose was too flat. So flat, in fact, that at the time of the *Roots* thing, kids were calling me Kunta Kinte. And my breasts were too large, especially for an Asian, who should be petite. And my hair was wrong too. It was black, not blond. My hair stylist had to break the news to me that my hair just would not feather like Farrah Fawcett's.

"After high school, I suddenly started getting asked out a lot. There   20
was this whole 'all Asian women are beautiful and sexy' thing going

on. White guys would come up to me and start gibbering, then tell me, 'In Cantonese, that means you're beautiful.' I bought it. I was only attracted to white men and there were plenty available, so that was a period of my life marked by a lot of oversexualized behavior. I also used to go to the library and check out books in the Asian section and look up the chapters on women's roles. I read about geishas, I learned that we should be compliant and passive along with being sexually enticing. In fact, I have to admit that I used my 'Asianness' to attract my ex-husband. The stereotypes allowed me to project an image of myself that was exciting to me, one that made me stand out a little from the crowd. Besides, at that period of my life, I was screwed up in so many ways that this gave me at least *some* kind of an identity.

21   "The main reason I was screwed up is that I hadn't resolved the sexual abuse I suffered as a child. When I was nine years old, a Chinese pastor came to live with us. He was married to this nutso woman whom my mother had fostered. One day, when I was eleven, I was asked to pour him some tea at dinner. I was so mad that I deliberately spilled hot tea on his leg. My mother asked me why, and I started screaming, told her that he had been touching me for two years and I wanted him *out* of the house. What really got to me was that no one said anything after that. They just wanted to get on with dinner. Later, I repeated my message to my mother. She tried to tell me that he was a pastor, sometimes men do something they're sorry about, etc., etc. But finally, she did kick him out. After that, I never wanted anything to do with Asian men again. I was afraid they'd all be like this guy, who preyed on me because of my ethnicity. Who was also, I realize now, the perfect pedophile in the most insidious way.

22   "Marrying a white guy unfortunately did not spare me further abuse. During those terrible years of marriage—the name-calling, threats, the jokes about taking nude pictures of me to send to Asian porno magazines, and the rape (my ex claimed there was no such thing since he 'owned me')—my mother's only response was to 'pray about it.' Well, I don't know about prayer, but I do know that divorce has made a fundamental difference in my life. At my divorce party (where I gave away wedding presents from his family, who hated me anyhow for being Korean, as door prizes), I realized I had all these friends who really supported me. They clapped and cheered for me and I knew that this was my real family, the place where I could really be myself. A Korean American woman and proud of it!"

23   Sarah, like Renée, was adopted by white parents. Unlike Renée, however, Sarah was encouraged by her family to pursue her cultural roots. But even with this support, she describes a lifetime of grappling with the question, "What makes me Asian?"

"When I was twenty-five, I went to Hawaii to meet my birth 24
mother for the first time in my life. The day before I was due to leave
was very hard. I cried a lot and she held me. As I curled up in her arms,
I could hear her heart beat and I said to myself, I *know* this. I can't describe the feeling any better. It was amazing to see her, to touch her, to
know it was her. I look a lot like my birth mother and I realized that for
the first time in my life, I had a *match*.

"All my life, I have been searching for my Asian heritage. I was 25
adopted by white parents who tried hard to give my sister (also
adopted, and Filipina) and me a connection to our culture. My mother
took lessons in Chinese cooking, brought us along to her Asian studies
classes, bought us books about Asian women. But still, somehow, it
wasn't enough. I'm not sure I could say what exactly I needed, all I
know is that something was missing.

"In third grade I decided to try to copy my Asian friends' behavior. 26
They were quiet, reserved, polite. They knew how to make themselves
invisible. I learned to imitate them, but it never felt right. Rubbed
against the grain. Still, to this day, I sometimes fall back on that behavior. I'm quieter in groups, more polite than a lot of people I know. I'm
sure what I felt was that if I could be more Asian, I could find my identity. And if I could be more Asian, I could be more like my birth mother.

"At the same time that I was trying to figure out what it meant to 27
be Asian, my teachers would take one look at me and know what it
meant to *them*. It was naturally assumed that I should be in the gifted
and talented program even though my test scores didn't quite justify it.
Also, I could do no wrong. I looked so innocent. Who would suspect
that I was the one responsible for those paper airplanes sailing across
the classroom? I loved it! I played it for all it was worth. And yet, I always had the sense that 'I'm Asian, but I'm not.' I had a lot of Asian
friends, but my home life wasn't nearly as restrictive as theirs. Unlike
them, I had the freedom to follow my heart's desires. And I'm grateful
for that.

"My grandmother also treated me on the basis of how I looked. I 28
used to get so mad because she could never tell me and my sister apart.
We don't look that much alike aside from both being Asian. She'd ask,
'Now, which one are you?' and every year would give us identical presents. Two red sweaters. Two white bears. As a result of all this, I felt
that I didn't really fit in anywhere. I had a bunch of friends, but I
floated from group to group. A true chameleon.

"I had another chance to experiment with my ethnic identity in col- 29
lege. I went to Humboldt State, where I was one of a very few Asians. I
cultivated the 'long-haired exotic Polynesian' look and dated anyone I
set my sights on. I got what I wanted. In this guise, I could get away
with things my friends wouldn't dare to try. For example, I was able to

date three different men and one woman at the same time, be perfectly open about it, and not have to justify my behavior to anyone. That's 'just Sarah,' my friends would say. A package deal.

30   Then, I cut my hair very short. My whole life changed. I was no longer the enticing Asian. No one asked me out. I was now the 'dyke,' even if I was dating men. I knew when I cut my hair this might happen, but it was still disappointing. Two and a half feet of hair does not a person make. I wished they could see beyond that. The whole question of my identity was up for grabs again.

31   "I also had the experience, at Humboldt, of feeling for the first time in my life that I wished I was not Asian. One evening, my friends and I went out to a bar. Somewhere along the line, I noticed this scruffy-looking guy in the corner just staring at me. He gave me the creeps. But it was more than just being a woman and feeling vulnerable to the power of a man. I had this sense that he was one of those white supremacist types who wanted to hurt me because I was Asian, and I was reminded of nightmares where men in white hoods would hunt me down, of hanging from a tree. I realized that, in this town, I had *nowhere to hide.* I could not blend in, I would always be identifiable.

32   "Today, I call myself an Asian woman. I don't like the term 'American,' because to me, American means 'white male.' I still may not know exactly who I am, but at least I know who I'm *not.*"

✧ Evaluating the Text

1. The reader hears the voices of Doreen, Renée, Sarah, and Claire Chow herself. Collectively, what impression do they convey about how Asian American women choose to define themselves?

2. With what kind of stereotypes have the women that Chow interviewed had to contend and to what extent did they play along or go against the stereotypes?

3. To what extent do the interviews presented by Chow answer the questions she poses in her introduction?

✧ Exploring Different Perspectives

1. How are the experiences of the women Chow interviews unexpectedly very similar to those of Nunez in H. G. Wells's story, "The Country of the Blind"?

2. Discuss how the experiences of Renée and Sarah, who were adopted by white parents, are similar to those of Prieta in Gloria Anzaldúa's story "Cervicide"?

✧ *Extending Viewpoints through Writing*

1. Although Doreen, Renée, and Sarah have had to cope with being stereotyped because of their "Asianness," we have all had the experience of being stereotyped to some degree. Discuss your experiences along these lines and tell what you did to either challenge or accommodate yourself to the stereotype.

2. The women in this account must choose how to define themselves, that is, with which racial or ethnic group to identify as being most like them. If you could choose any group with which to identify, which would you choose and what does this tell you about yourself? If you could choose to live in a heterogeneous society or a homogeneous one, which would you choose and why?

Luis Alberto Urrea

Border Story

◆

Luis Alberto Urrea was born in Tijuana to an American mother and a Mexican father. He was raised in San Diego and graduated from the University of California in 1977. After working as a film extra, he worked as a volunteer from 1978 to 1982 with Spectrum Ministries, a Protestant organization with headquarters in San Diego that provided food, clothing, and medicine to the poor on the Mexican side of the border. In 1982, he went to Massachusetts, where he taught expository writing at Harvard. Among Urrea's many published works are By the Lake of Sleeping Children: The Secret Life of the Mexican Border *(1996),* Ghost Sickness *(1997),* Nobody's Son: Notes from an American Life *(1998), and* Wandering Time: Western Notebooks *(1999).* Across the Wire: Life and Hard Times on the Mexican Border *(1993), from which "Border Story" is taken, offers a compassionate and unprecedented account of what life is like for those refugees living on the Mexican side of the border.*

1   When I was younger, I went to war. The Mexican border was the battlefield. There are many Mexicos; there are also many Mexican borders, any one of which could fill its own book. I, and the people with me, fought on a specific front. We sustained injuries and witnessed deaths. There were machine guns pointed at us, knives, pistols, clubs, even skyrockets. I caught a street-gang member trying to stuff a lit cherry bomb into our gas tank. On the same night, a drunk mariachi opened fire on the missionaries through the wall of his house.

2   We drove five beat-up vans. We were armed with water, medicine, shampoo, food, clothes, milk, and doughnuts. At the end of a day, like returning veterans from other battles, we carried secrets in our hearts that kept some of us awake at night, gave others dreams and fits of crying. Our faith sustained us—if not in God or "good," then in our work.

3   Others of us had no room for or interest in such drama, and came away unscathed—and unmoved. Some of us sank into the mindless joy of fundamentalism, some of us drank, some of us married impoverished Mexicans. Most of us took it personally. Poverty *is* personal: it smells and it shocks and it invades your space. You come home dirty when you get too close to the poor. Sometimes you bring back vermin: they hide in

*For information on Mexico, see p. 241.

your hair, in your underpants, in your intestines. These unpleasant possibilities are a given. They are the price you occasionally have to pay.

In Tijuana and environs, we met the many ambassadors of poverty: 4
lice, scabies, tapeworm, pinworm, ringworm, fleas, crab lice. We met diphtheria, meningitis, typhoid, polio, *turista* (diarrhea), tuberculosis, hepatitis, VD, impetigo, measles, chronic hernia, malaria, whooping cough. We met madness and "demon possession."

These were the products of dirt and disregard—bad things afflicting   5
good people. Their world was far from our world. Still, it would take you only about twenty minutes to get there from the center of San Diego.

For me, the worst part was the lack of a specific enemy. We were   6
fighting a nebulous, all-pervasive *It*. Call it hunger. Call it despair. Call it the Devil, the System, Capitalism, the Cycle of Poverty, the Fruits of the Mexican Malaise. It was a seemingly endless circle of disasters. Long after I'd left, the wheel kept on grinding.

At night, the Border Patrol helicopters swoop and churn in the air   7
all along the line. You can sit in the Mexican hills and watch them herd humans on the dusty slopes across the valley. They look like science fiction crafts, their hard-focused lights raking the ground as they fly.

Borderlands locals are so jaded by the sight of nightly people-hunt-   8
ing that it doesn't even register in their minds. But take a stranger to the border, and she will *see* the spectacle: monstrous Dodge trucks speeding into and out of the landscape; uniformed men patrolling with flashlights, guns, and dogs; spotlights; running figures; lines of people hurried onto buses by armed guards; and the endless clatter of the helicopters with their harsh white beams. A Dutch woman once told me it seemed altogether "un-American."

But the Mexicans keep on coming—and the Guatemalans, the Sal-   9
vadorans, the Panamanians, the Colombians. The seven-mile stretch of Interstate 5 nearest the Mexican border is, at times, so congested with Latin American pedestrians that it resembles a town square.

They stick to the center island. Running down the length of the is-   10
land is a cement wall. If the "illegals" (currently, "undocumented workers"; formerly, "wetbacks") are walking north and a Border Patrol vehicle happens along, they simply hop over the wall and trot south. The officer will have to drive up to the 805 interchange, or Dairy Mart Road, swing over the overpasses, then drive south. Depending on where this pursuit begins, his detour could entail five to ten miles of driving. When the officer finally reaches the group, they hop over the wall and trot north. Furthermore, because freeway arrests would endanger traffic, the Border Patrol has effectively thrown up its hands in surrender.

It seems jolly on the page. But imagine poverty, violence, natural   11
disasters, or political fear driving you away from everything you know. Imagine how bad things get to make you leave behind your family,

your friends, your lovers; your home, as humble as it might be; your church, say. Let's take it further—you've said good-bye to the graveyard, the dog, the goat, the mountains where you first hunted, your grade school, your state, your favorite spot on the river where you fished and took time to think.

12   Then you come hundred—or thousands—of miles across territory utterly unknown to you. (Chances are, you have never traveled farther than a hundred miles in your life.) You have walked, run, hidden in the backs of trucks, spent part of your precious money on bus fare. There is no AAA or Travelers Aid Society available to you. Various features of your journey north might include police corruption; violence in the forms of beatings, rape, murder, torture, road accidents; theft; incarceration. Additionally, you might experience loneliness, fear, exhaustion, sorrow, cold, heat, diarrhea, thirst, hunger. There is no medical attention available to you. There isn't even Kotex.

13   Weeks or months later, you arrive in Tijuana. Along with other immigrants, you gravitate to the bad parts of town because there is nowhere for you to go in the glittery sections where the *gringos* flock. You stay in a run-down little hotel in the red-light district, or behind the bus terminal. Or you find your way to the garbage dumps, where you throw together a small cardboard nest and claim a few feet of dirt for yourself. The garbage-pickers working this dump might allow you to squat, or they might come and rob you or burn you out for breaking some local rule you cannot possibly know beforehand. Sometimes the dump is controlled by a syndicate, and goon squads might come to you within a day. They want money, and if you can't pay, you must leave or suffer the consequences.

14   In town, you face endless victimization if you aren't streetwise. The police come after you, street thugs come after you, petty criminals come after you; strangers try your door at night as you sleep. Many shady men offer to guide you across the border, and each one wants all your money now, and promises to meet you at a prearranged spot. Some of your fellow travelers end their journeys right here—relieved of their savings and left to wait on a dark corner until they realize they are going nowhere.

15   If you are not Mexican, and can't pass as *tijuanense*, a local, the tough guys find you out. Salvadorans and Guatemalans are routinely beaten up and robbed. Sometimes they are disfigured. Indian—Chinantecas, Mixtecas, Guasaves, Zapotecas, Mayas—are insulted and pushed around; often they are lucky—they are merely ignored. They use this to their advantage. Often they don't dream of crossing into the United States: a Mexican tribal person would never be able to blend in, and they know it. To them, the garbage dumps and street vending and begging in Tijuana are a vast improvement over their former lives. As Doña Paula, a Chinanteca friend of mine who lives at the Tijuana garbage dump, told me, "This is the garbage dump. Take all you need. There's plenty here for *everyone!*"

If you are a woman, the men come after you. You lock yourself in   16
your room, and when you must leave it to use the pestilential public
bathroom at the end of your floor, you hurry, and you check every corner. Sometimes the lights are out in the toilet room. Sometimes men
listen at the door. They call you "good-looking" and "bitch" and "*mama-
cita*," and they make kissing sounds at you when you pass.

You're in the worst part of town, but you can comfort yourself—at   17
least there are no death squads here. There are no torturers here, or
bandit land barons riding into your house. This is the last barrier, you
think, between you and the United States—*los Yunaites Estaites*.

You still face police corruption, violence, jail. You now also have a   18
wide variety of new options available to you: drugs, prostitution, white
slavery, crime. Tijuana is not easy on newcomers. It is a city that has always thrived on taking advantage of a sucker. And the innocent are the
ultimate suckers in the Borderlands.

If you have saved up enough money, you go to one of the *coyotes*   19
(people-smugglers), who guide travelers through the violent canyons
immediately north of the border. Lately, these men are also called *polleros*, or "chicken-wranglers." Some of them are straight, some are land
pirates. Negotiations are tense and strange: *polleros* speak a Spanish
you don't quite understand—like the word *polleros*. Linguists call the
new border-speak "Spanglish," but in Tijuana, Spanglish is mixed with
slang and *pochismos* (the polyglot hip talk of Mexicans infected with
gringoismo; the *cholos* in Mexico, or Chicanos on the American side).

Suddenly, the word for "yes," *sí*, can be *simón* or *siról*. "No" is *chale*.   20
"Bike" (*bicicleta*) is *baica*. "Wife" (*esposa*) is *wafia*. "The police" (*la policía*)
are *la chota*. "Women" are *rucas* or *morras*. You don't know what they're
talking about.

You pay them all your money—sometimes it's your family's life-   21
long savings. Five hundred dollars should do it. "*Orale*," the dude tells
you, which means "right on." You must wait in Colonia Libertad, the
most notorious *barrio* in town, ironically named "Liberty."

The scene here is baffling. Music blares from radios. Jolly women at   22
smoky taco stands cook food for the journeys, sell jugs of water. You
can see the Border Patrol agents cruising the other side of the fence;
they trade insults with the locals.

When the appointed hour comes, you join a group of *pollos* (chick-   23
ens) who scuttle along behind the *coyote*. You crawl under the wires, or,
if you go a mile east, you might be amazed to find that the famous
American Border Fence simply stops. To enter the United States, you
merely step around the end of it. And you follow your guide into the
canyons. You might be startled to find groups of individuals crossing
the line without *coyotes* leading them at all. You might wonder how
they have mastered the canyons, and you might begin to regret the loss
of your money.

24   If you have your daughters or mothers or wives with you—or if you are a woman—you become watchful and tense, because rape and gang rape are so common in this darkness as to be utterly unremarkable. If you have any valuables left after your various negotiations, you try to find a sly place to hide them in case you meet *pandilleros* (gang members) or *rateros* (thieves—ratmen). But, really, where can you put anything? Thousands have come before you, and the hiding places are pathetically obvious to robbers: in shoulder bags or clothing rolls, pinned inside clothes, hidden in underwear, inserted in body orifices.

25   If the *coyote* does not turn on you suddenly with a gun and take everything from you himself, you might still be attacked by the *rateros*. If the *rateros* don't get you, there are roving zombies that you can smell from fifty yards downwind—these are the junkies who hunt in shambling packs. If the junkies somehow miss you, there are the *pandilleros*— gang-bangers from either side of the border who are looking for some bloody fun. They adore "taking off" illegals because it's the perfect crime: there is no way they can ever be caught. They are Tijuana *cholos*, or Chicano *vatos*, or Anglo head-bangers.

26   Their sense of fun relies heavily on violence. Gang beatings are their preferred sport, though rape in all its forms is common, as always. Often the *coyote* will turn tail and run at the first sight of *pandilleros*. What's another load of desperate chickens to him? He's just making a living, taking care of business.

27   If he doesn't run, there is a good chance he will be the first to be assaulted. The most basic punishment these young toughs mete out is a good beating, but they might kill him in front of the *pollos* if they feel the immigrants need a lesson in obedience. For good measure, these boys—they are mostly *boys*, aged twelve to nineteen, bored with Super Nintendo and MTV—beat people and slash people and thrash the women they have just finished raping.

28   Their most memorable tactic is to hamstring the *coyote* or anyone who dares speak out against them. This entails slicing the muscles in the victim's legs and leaving him to flop around in the dirt, crippled. If you are in a group of *pollos* that happens to be visited by these furies, you are learning border etiquette.

29   Now, say you are lucky enough to evade all these dangers on your journey. Hazards still await you and your family. You might meet white racists, complimenting themselves with the tag "Aryans"; they "patrol" the scrub in combat gear, carrying radios, high-powered flashlights, rifles, and bats. Rattlesnakes hide in bushes—you didn't count on that complication. Scorpions, tarantulas, black widows. And, of course, there is the Border Patrol (*la migra*).

30   They come over the hills on motorcycles, on horses, in huge Dodge Ramcharger four-wheel drives. They yell, wear frightening goggles,

have guns. Sometimes they are surprisingly decent; sometimes they are too tired or too bored to put much effort into dealing with you. They collect you in a large group of fellow *pollos,* and a guard (a Mexican Border Patrol agent!) jokes with your group in Spanish. Some cry, some sulk, most laugh. Mexicans hate to be rude. You don't know what to think—some of your fellow travelers take their arrest with aplomb. Sometimes the officers know their names. But you have been told repeatedly that the Border Patrol sometimes beats or kills people. Everyone talks about the Mexican girl molested inside its building.

The Border Patrol puts you into trucks that take you to buses that take you to compounds that load you onto other buses that transport you back to Tijuana and put you out. Your *coyote* isn't bothered in the least. Some of the regulars who were with you go across and get brought back a couple of times a night. But for you, things are different. You have been brought back with no place to sleep. You have already spent all your money. You might have been robbed, so you have only your clothes—maybe not all of them. The robbers may have taken your shoes. You might be bloodied from a beating by *pandilleros,* or an "accident" in the Immigration and Naturalization Service compound. You can't get proper medical attention. You can't eat, or afford to feed your family. Some of your compatriots have been separated from their wives or their children. Now their loved ones are in the hands of strangers, in the vast and unknown United States. The Salvadorans are put on planes and flown back to the waiting arms of the military. As you walk through the cyclone fence, back into Tijuana, the locals taunt you and laugh at your misfortune. 31

If you were killed, you have nothing to worry about. 32

Now what? 33

Perhaps you'll join one of the other groups that break through the Tortilla Curtain every night. The road-runners. They amass at dusk along the cement canal that separates the United States from Mexico. This wide alley is supposedly the Tijuana River, but it's usually dry, or running with sewage that Tijuana pumps toward the U.S. with great gusto. 34

As soon as everybody feels like it—there are no *coyotes* needed here—you join the groups passing through the gaping holes in the fence. Houses and alleys and cantinas back up against it, and in some spots, people have driven stolen cars into the poles to provide a wider passage. You rush across the canal and up the opposite slope, timing your dash between passing *migra* trucks and the overflights of helicopters. Following the others, you begin your jog toward the freeway. Here, there are mostly just Border Patrol officers to outrun—not that hard if you're in good shape. There are still some white-supremacist types bobbling around, but the cops will get them if they do anything serious. No, here the problem is the many lanes of I-5. 35

36   You stand at the edge of the road and wonder how you're going to cut across five lanes of traffic going sixty miles an hour. Then, there is the problem of the next five lanes. The freeway itself is constructed to run parallel to the border, then swing north. Its underpasses and storm-drain pipes offer another subterranean world, but you don't know about them. All you know is you have to get across at some point, and get far from the hunters who would take you back.

37   If you hang around the shoulder of I-5 long enough, you will find that many of your companions don't make it. So many have been killed and injured that the *gringos* have put up warning signs to motorists to watch for running people. The orange signs show a man, a woman, and a child charging across. Some *gringos* are so crazy with hate for you that they speed up, or aim for you as you run.

38   The vague blood of over a hundred slain runners shadows the concrete.

39   On either side of the border, clustered near the gates, there are dapper-looking men, dressed in nice cowboy clothes, and they speak without looking anyone in the eye. They are saying, "Los Angeles, San Bernardino, San Francisco."

40   They have a going concern: business is good.

41   Once you've gotten across the line, there will always be the ques-tion of *Where do I go now?* "Illegal aliens" have to eat, sleep, find work. Once across, you must begin another journey.

42   Not everyone has the energy to go on. Even faith—in Jesus, the Vir-gin Mary, or the Streets of Gold—breaks down sooner or later. Many of these immigrants founder at the border. There is a sad swirl of human-ity in Tijuana. Outsiders eddy there who have simply run out of strength. If North America does not want them, Tijuana wants them even less. They become the outcasts of an outcast region. We could all see them if we looked hard enough: they sell chewing gum. Their chil-dren sing in traffic. In bars downtown, the women will show us a breast for a quarter. They wash our windshields at every stoplight. But mostly, they are invisible. To see them, we have to climb up the little canyons all around the city, where the cardboard shacks and mud and smoke look like a lost triptych by Hieronymus Bosch. We have to wade into the garbage dumps and the orphanages, sit in the little churches and the hospitals, or go out into the back country, where they raise their goats and bake red bricks and try to live decent lives.

43   They are not welcome in Tijuana. And, for the most part, Tijuana it-self is not welcome in the Motherland. Tijuana is Mexico's cast-off child. She brings in money and *gringos,* but nobody would dare claim

her. As a Mexican diplomat once confided to me, "We both know Tijuana is not Mexico. The border is nowhere. It's a no-man's-land."

I was born there.   44

MY STORY

I was born in Tijuana, to a Mexican father and an American mother.   45
I was registered with the U.S. government as an American Citizen, Born Abroad. Raised in San Diego, I crossed the border all through my boyhood with abandon, utterly bilingual and bicultural. In 1977, my father died on the border, violently. (The story is told in detail in a chapter entitled "Father's Day.")

In the Borderlands, anything can happen. And if you're in Tijuana   46
long enough, anything *will* happen. Whole neighborhoods appear and disappear seemingly overnight. For example, when I was a boy, you got into Tijuana by driving through the Tijuana River itself. It was a muddy floodplain bustling with animals and belching old cars. A slum that spread across the riverbed was known as "Cartolandia." In borderspeak, this meant "Land of Cardboard."

Suddenly, it was time for Tijuana to spruce up its image to attract   47
more American dollars, and Cartolandia was swept away by a flash flood of tractors. The big machines swept down the length of the river, crushing shacks and toppling fences. It was like magic. One week, there were choked multitudes of sheds; the next, a clear, flat space awaiting the blank concrete of a flood channel. Town—no town.

The inhabitants of Cartolandia fled to the outskirts, where they   48
were better suited to Tijuana's new image as Shopping Mecca. They had effectively vanished. Many of them homesteaded the Tijuana municipal garbage dump. The city's varied orphanages consumed many of their children.

Tijuana's characteristic buzz can be traced directly to a mixture of   49
dread and expectation: there's always something coming.

I never intended to be a missionary. I didn't go to church, and I had   50
no reason to believe I'd be involved with a bunch of Baptists. But in 1978, I had occasion to meet a remarkable preacher known as Pastor Von (Erhardt George von Trutzschler III, no less): as well as being a minister, he was a veteran of the Korean War, a graphic artist, a puppeteer, a German baron, an adventurer, and a practical joker. Von got me involved in the hardships and discipline he calls "Christian Boot Camp."

After working as a youth pastor in San Diego for many years, he   51
had discovered Mexico in the late sixties. His work there began with the typical church do-good activities that everyone has experienced at least once: a bag of blankets for the orphans, a few Christmas toys, alms for

the poor. As Protestantism spread in Mexico, however, interest in Von's preaching grew. Small churches and Protestant orphanages and Protestant *barrios,* lacking ministers of their own, began asking Von to teach. Preaching and pastoring led to more work; work led to more needs; more needs pulled in more workers. On it went until Von had put in thirty or so years slogging through the Borderlands mud, and his little team of die-hard renegades and border rats had grown to a nonprofit corporation (Spectrum Ministries, Inc.), where you'll find him today.

52   Von's religious ethic is similar in scope to Teresa of Calcutta's. Von favors actual works over heavy evangelism. Spectrum is based on a belief Christians call "living the gospel." This doctrine is increasingly rare in America, since it involves little lip service, hard work, and no glory.

53   Von often reminds his workers that they are "ambassadors of Christ" and should comport themselves accordingly. Visitors are indelicately stripped of their misconceptions and prejudices when they discover that the crust on Von and his crew is a mile thick: the sight of teenybopper Bible School girls enduring Von's lurid pretrip briefing is priceless. Insouciantly, he offers up his litany: lice, worms, pus, blood; diarrhea, rattletrap outhouses, no toilet paper; dangerous water and food; diseased animals that will leave you with scabies; rats, maggots, flies; *odor.* Then he confuses them by demanding love and respect for the poor. He caps his talk with: "Remember—you are not going to the zoo. These are people. Don't run around snapping pictures of them like they're animals. Don't rush into their shacks saying, 'Ooh, gross!' They live there. Those are their homes."

54   Because border guards often "confiscate" chocolate milk, the cartons must be smuggled into Mexico under bags of clothes. Because the floors of the vans get so hot, the milk will curdle, so the crew must first freeze it. The endless variations of challenge in the Borderlands keep Von constantly alert—problems come three at a time and must be solved on the run.

55   Like the time a shipment of tennis shoes was donated to Spectrum. They were new, white, handsome shoes. The only problem was that no two shoes in the entire shipment matched. Von knew there was no way the Mexican kids could use *one* shoe, and they—like teens everywhere— were fashion-conscious and wouldn't be caught dead in unmatching sneakers.

56   Von's solution was practical and witty. He donned unmatched shoes and made his crew members wear unmatched shoes. Then he announced that it was the latest California surfer rage; kids in California weren't considered hip unless they wore unmatched shoes. The shipment was distributed, and shoeless boys were shod in the *faux* fashion craze begun by Chez Von.

57   Von has suffered for his beliefs. In the ever more conservative atmosphere of American Christianity (read: Protestantism), the efforts of

Spectrum have come under fire on several occasions. He was once denounced because he refused to use the King James Bible in his sermons—clearly the sign of a heretic.

Von's terse reply to criticism: "It's hard to 'save' people when they're dead."   58

Von has a Monday night ministerial run into Tijuana, and in his   59
heyday, he was hitting three or four orphanages a night. I was curious, unaware of the severity of the poverty in Tijuana. I knew it was there, but it didn't really mean anything to me. One night, in late October 1978, my curiosity got the better of me. I didn't believe Von could show me anything about my hometown that I didn't know. I was wrong. I quickly began to learn just how little I really knew.

He managed to get me involved on the first night. Actually, it was   60
Von and a little girl named América. América lived in one of the orphanages barely five miles from my grandmother's house in the hills above Tijuana.

She had light hair and blue eyes like mine—she could have been   61
my cousin. When she realized I spoke Spanish, she clutched my fingers and chattered for an hour without a break. She hung on harder when Von announced it was time to go. She begged me not to leave. América resorted to a tactic many orphanage children master to keep visitors from leaving—she wrapped her legs around my calf and sat on my foot. As I peeled her off, I promised to return on Von's next trip.

He was waiting for me in the alley behind the orphanage.   62

"What did you say to that girl?" he asked.   63

"I told her I'd come back next week."   64

He glared at me. "Don't *ever* tell one of my kids you're coming   65
back," he snapped. "Don't you know she'll wait all week for you? Then she'll wait for months. Don't say it if you don't mean it."

"I mean it!" I said.   66

I went back the next time to see her. Then again. And, of course,   67
there were other places to go before we got to América's orphanage, and there were other people to talk to after we left. Each location had people waiting with messages and questions to translate. It didn't take long for Von to approach me with a proposition. It seemed he had managed the impressive feat of spending a lifetime in Mexico without picking up any Spanish at all. Within two months, I was Von's personal translator.

It is important to note that translation is often more delicate an art   68
than people assume. For example, Mexicans are regularly amused to read *TV Guide* listings for Spanish-language TV stations. If one were to leave the tilde (~) off the word años, or "years," the word becomes the plural for "anus." Many cheap laughs are had when "The Lost Years" becomes "The Lost Butt Holes."

69   It was clear that Von needed reliable translating. Once, when he had arranged a summer camping trip for *barrio* children, he'd written a list of items the children needed to take. A well-meaning woman on the team translated the list for Von, and they Xeroxed fifty or sixty copies.

70   The word for "comb" in Spanish is *peine,* but leave out a letter, and the word takes on a whole new meaning. Von's note, distributed to every child and all their families, read:

> You must bring CLEAN CLOTHES
> TOOTH PASTE
> SOAP
> TOOTHBRUSH
> SLEEPING BAG
> and BOYS—You Must Remember
> to BRING YOUR PENIS!

71   Von estimates that in a ten-year period his crew drove several *million* miles in Mexico without serious incident. Over five-hundred people came and went as crew members. They transported more than sixty thousand visitors across the border.

72   In my time with him, I saw floods and three hundred-mile-wide prairie fires, car wrecks and gang fights, monkeys and blood and shit. I saw human intestines and burned flesh. I saw human fat through deep red cuts. I saw people copulating. I saw animals tortured. I saw birthday parties in the saddest sagging shacks. I looked down throats and up wombs with flashlights. I saw lice, rats, dying dogs, rivers black with pollywogs, and a mound of maggots three feet wide and two feet high. One little boy in the back country cooked himself with an overturned pot of boiling *frijoles;* when I asked him if it hurt, he sneered like Pancho Villa and said, "Nah." A maddened Pentecostal tried to heal our broken-down van by laying hands on the engine block. One girl who lived in a brickyard accidentally soaked her dress in diesel fuel and lit herself on fire. When I went in the shed, she was standing there, naked, her entire front burned dark brown and red. The only part of her not burned was her vulva; it was a startling cleft, a triangular island of white in a sea of burns.

73   I saw miracles, too. A boy named Chispi, deep in a coma induced by spinal meningitis, suffered a complete shutdown of one lobe of his brain. The doctors in the intensive care unit, looking down at his naked little body hard-wired to banks of machinery and pumps, just shook their heads. He was doomed to be a vegetable, at best. His mother, fished out of the cantinas in Tijuana's red-light district, spent several nights sitting in the hospital cafeteria sipping vending-machine coffee and telling me she hoped there were miracles left for people like her.

Chispi woke up. The machines were blipping and pinging, and he   74
sat up and asked for Von. His brain had regenerated itself. They un-
hitched him, pulled out the catheters, and pulled the steel shunt out of
his skull. He went home. There was no way anybody could explain it.
Sometimes there were happy endings, and you spent as much time
wondering about them as grieving over the tragedies.

God help me—it was fun. It was exciting and nasty. I strode, fearless,   75
through the Tijuana garbage dumps and the Barrio of Shallow Graves. I
was doing good deeds, and the goodness thrilled me. But the squalor,
too, thrilled me. Each stinking gray *barrio* gave me a wicked charge. I was
arrested one night by Tijuana cops; I was so terrified that my knees wob-
bled like Jell-O. After they let me go, I was happy for a week. Mexican
soldiers pointed machine guns at my testicles. I thought I was going to
die. Later, I was so relieved, I laughed about it for days. Over the years, I
was cut, punctured, sliced: I love my scars. I had girlfriends in every village, in every orphanage, at each garbage dump. For a time, I was a hero.
And at night, when we returned, caked in dried mud, smelly, exhausted,
and the good Baptists of Von's church looked askance at us, we felt dangerous. The housewives, grandmothers, fundamentalists, rock singers,
bikers, former drug dealers, schoolgirls, leftists, republicans, jarheads,
and I were all transformed into *The Wild Bunch.*

It added a certain flair to my dating life as well. It was not uncom-   76
mon for a Mexican crisis to track me down in the most unlikely places.
I am reminded of the night I was sitting down to a fancy supper at a
woman's apartment when the phone rang. A busload of kids from one
of our orphanages had flipped over, killing the American daughter of
the youth minister in charge of the trip. All the *gringos* had been arrested. The next hour was spent calling Tijuana cops, Mexican lawyers,
cousins in Tijuana, and Von. I had to leave early to get across the border.

Incredibly, in the wake of this tragedy, the orphanage kids were   77
taken to the beach by yet another *gringo* church group, and one of the
boys was hit by a car and killed.

My date was fascinated by all this, no doubt.   78

Slowly, it became obvious that nobody outside the experience un-   79
derstood it. Only among ourselves was hunting for lice in each other's
hair considered a nice thing. Nobody but us found humor in the ap-
palling things we saw. No one else wanted to discuss the particulars of
our bowel movements. By firsthand experience, we had become diag-
nosticians in the area of gastrointestinal affliction. Color and content
spoke volumes to us: pale, mucus-heavy ropes of diarrhea suggested
amoebas. Etc.

One of Von's pep talks revolved around the unconscionable wealth   80
in the United States. "Well," he'd say to some unsuspecting *gringo*,
"you're probably not rich. You probably don't even have a television.
Oh, you *do?* You have three televisions? One in each room? Wow. But

surely you don't have furniture? You do? Living room furniture and beds in the bedrooms? Imagine that!

81   "But you don't have a floor, do you? Do you have carpets? Four walls? A roof! What do you use for light—candles? *Lamps!* No way. Lamps.

82   "How about your kitchen—do you have a stove?"

83   He'd pick his way through the kitchen: the food, the plates and pots and pans, the refrigerator, the ice. Ice cream. Soda. Booze. The closets, the clothes in the closets. Then to the bathroom and the miracle of indoor plumbing. Whoever lived in that house suddenly felt obscenely rich.

84   I was never able to reach Von's level of commitment. The time he caught scabies, he allowed it to flourish in order to grasp the suffering of those from whom it originated. He slept on the floor because the majority of the world's population could not afford a bed.

✧ Evaluating the Text

1. What impression do you get of the narrator's personal involvement in the conditions he describes? Why was he there, and what did he hope to accomplish?

2. How does Urrea's description of what it feels like to be in the situation of those he describes make it possible to empathize with them? What details did you find especially effective in communicating this experience?

3. What are some of the dangers one faces that might be encountered when crossing the border? What future awaits those who turn back?

✧ Exploring Different Perspectives

1. The role that religion plays in ministering to those in exile is a theme in both Urrea's account and Palden Gyatso's memoir. What differences and similarities can you discover between these two narratives?

2. Urrea and Gloria Anzaldúa (see "Cervicide") take very different approaches in dramatizing the plight of Mexican immigrants. What does fiction do that nonfiction cannot, and vice versa?

✧ Extending Viewpoints through Writing

1. Have you or a member of your family ever had to relocate from one country to another? Was the situation physically or psychologically similar to the one Urrea describes?

2. Putting yourself in the same situation, after reading Urrea's description of the dangers that might befall one trying to cross the border, would you take the chance if you already knew what might await you? Why or why not?

Gloria Anzaldúa

Cervicide

---◆---

Gloria Anzaldúa is a Chicana poet and fiction writer who grew up in south Texas. She has edited several highly praised anthologies. This Bridge Called My Back: Writings by Radical Women of Color *won the 1986 Before Columbus Foundation American Book Award.* Borderlands—La Frontera, the New Mestiza *was selected as one of the best books of 1987 by* Library Journal. *Her recent work includes* Making Face, Making Soul *(1990),* La Prieta *(1991), and a children's book,* Friends from the Other Side *(1993). She has been a contributing editor for* Sinister Wisdom *since 1984 and has taught Chicano studies, feminist studies, and creative writing at the University of Texas at Austin, San Francisco State University, and the University of California, Santa Cruz. "Cervicide" first appeared in* Labyris *(vol. 4, no. 11, Winter 1983). In it, Anzaldúa tells the poignant story of a Mexican American family living on the Texas border who are forced to kill a pet deer whose detection by the game warden would result in an unaffordable fine or the father's imprisonment.*

1   *La venadita.* The small fawn. They had to kill their pet, the fawn. The game warden was on the way with his hounds. The penalty for being caught in possession of a deer was $250 or jail. The game warden would put *su papí en la cárcel.*

2   How could they get rid of the fawn? Hide it? No, *la guardia's* hounds would sniff Venadita out. Let Venadita loose in the *monte?* They had tried that before. The fawn would leap away and seconds later return. Should they kill Venadita? The mother and Prieta looked toward *las carabinas* propped against the wall behind the kitchen door—the shiny barrel of the .22, the heavy metal steel of the 40-40. No, if *they* could hear his pickup a mile and a half down the road, he would hear the shot.

3   Quick, they had to do something. Cut Venadita's throat? Club her to death? The mother couldn't do it. She, Prieta, would have to be the

---

Cervicide—the killing of a deer. In archetypal symbology the Self appears as a deer for women.

su papí en la cárcel—her father in jail.

monte—the woods.

Prieta—literally one who is dark-skinned, a nickname.

one. The game warden and his *perros* were a mile down the road. Prieta loved her *papí*.

In the shed behind the corral, where they'd hidden the fawn, Prieta found the hammer. She had to grasp it with both hands. She swung it up. The weight folded her body backwards. A thud reverberated on Venadita's skull, a wave undulated down her back. Again, a blow behind the ear. Though Venadita's long lashes quivered, her eyes never left Prieta's face. Another thud, another tremor. *La guardia* and his hounds were driving up the front yard. The *venadita* looked up at her, the hammer rose and fell. Neither made a sound. The tawny, spotted fur was the most beautiful thing Prieta had ever seen. She remembered when they had found the fawn. She had been a few hours old. A hunter had shot her mother. The fawn had been shaking so hard, her long thin legs were on the edge of buckling. Prieta and her sister and brothers had bottle-fed Venadita, with a damp cloth had wiped her skin, had watched her tiny, perfectly formed hooves harden and grow.

Prieta dug a hole in the shed, a makeshift hole. She could hear the warden talking to her mother. Her mother's English had suddenly gotten bad—she was trying to stall *la guardia*. Prieta rolled the fawn into the hole, threw in the empty bottle. With her fingers raked in the dirt. Dust caked on her arms and face where tears had fallen. She patted the ground flat with her hands and swept it with a dead branch. The game warden was strutting toward her. His hounds sniffing, sniffing, sniffing the ground in the shed. The hounds pawing pawing the ground. The game warden, straining on the leashes *les dio un tirón, sacó los perros*. He inspected the corrals, the edge of the woods, then drove away in his pickup.

✦ Evaluating the Text

1. To what pressures is the family subject because they are illegal immigrants?

2. Discuss the consequences for the narrator of having to make such a choice and perform such an action. In your opinion, how will she be different from then on? In what sense might the deer symbolize the self that can no longer exist?

3. How does being forced to choose between a deer she loves and her loyalty to her father, whom she loves, illustrate the kind of predicament in which those without power find themselves?

perros—dogs
les dio un tirón, sacó los perros—jerked the dogs out

❖ Exploring Different Perspectives

1. How does Luis Alberto Urrea's description in "Border Story" of what life is like on the United States–Mexican border help to explain why the protagonist in "Cervicide" faces such a terrible choice?

2. In what ways is the protagonist, Prieta, in Anzaldúa's story at the mercy of the powers that be in a strange land in much the same way as is Nunez in "The Country of the Blind"? Compare the sacrifices required of both.

❖ Extending Viewpoints through Writing

1. What actions did a pet of yours take that led you to believe it showed evidence of consciousness, motivation, and intelligence? What could your pet say about you that no human being knows?

2. Describe your search for a name for your pet. What character traits important to you or your family does this name reveal?

Jesse W. Nash

Confucius and the VCR

◆——————

*Jesse W. Nash currently teaches religious studies at Loyola University,
New Orleans. He is the author of* Vietnamese Catholicism *(1992) and*
Romance, Gender, and Religion in a Vietnamese-American Community *(1995). Nash has also studied the important role that videotaped
films, imported from Taiwan and Hong Kong and dubbed into Vietnamese,
play in the lives of Vietnamese immigrants in the United States. "Confucius and the VCR" originally appeared in* Natural History, *May 1988.*

    *Bordered by Cambodia and Laos to the west, China to the north, and
the South China Sea to the east and south, Vietnam was first visited by European traders in the early sixteenth century. After the French captured
Saigon in 1859, Vietnam was under the control of France until World
War II, when the Viet Minh, a coalition of nationalists and communists,
established a republic headed by Ho Chi Minh. France's attempts to reas-
sert control resulted in the French Indochina War (1946–1954), in which
the French were defeated. In the Geneva Conference of 1954, Vietnam was
divided, pending nationwide free elections, into North Vietnam, controlled
by communists, and South Vietnam, controlled by nationalists. Ngo Dinh
Diem's refusal to hold these elections, out of fear of a communist victory,
precipitated the Vietnam War of 1954–1975, in which South Vietnam,
aided by the United States, fought communist insurgents, who were supported by North Vietnam. United States troops were withdrawn in 1973,
after a cease-fire, and in 1975 the communists overran the south. The
country was reunified as the Socialist Republic of Vietnam in 1976. In
1978, Vietnam invaded Cambodia, deposed the genocidal Pol Pot regime,
and installed a government that remained until the Vietnamese withdrew
in 1989. Since 1989, Vietnam has been committed to a policy of* doi moi
*(renovation), which includes private enterprise and trade, an interest in
tourism, and better relations with the United States. Some economic sanc-
tions have been lifted since 1993 and the United States has opened a diplomatic office in Hanoi. Nash offers insight into the lives of great numbers of
Vietnamese who fled the country during and after the war.*

    *The unification of North and South Vietnam into the Socialist Re-
public of Vietnam took place formally in July 1976. Between 1975 and
1984, approximately 550,000 "boat people" found refuge abroad. By
1989, 57,000 in Hong Kong would be forcibly repatriated following agreements reached in 1992 between the Communist Party of Vietnam and the*

United Kingdom. Market-oriented reforms in recent years have begun a process of shifting the economy to one based on free-enterprise principles.

1   Vietnamese immigrants in the United States are intensely curious about almost all movies or television shows, aptly referring to themselves as "movie addicts." The TV set and videocassette recorder have become common features of their homes and are the focus of much conversation concerning what it means to be an American and what it means to be Vietnamese in the United States.

2   American television and movies worry many Vietnamese, especially parents and elders, who see them as glorifying the individual and his or her war with the family, social institutions, the community, and even the state. Reflecting the individualism of American culture, conflict resolution typically occurs at the expense of the family or community (except in situation comedies usually panned as being "saccharine" or "unrealistic" by television critics). American movies and television, many Vietnamese assert, are most effective in imagining worlds of mistrust, promoting self-righteous rebellion, and legitimizing the desires of the individual.

3   The antiauthorianism of much of American television and movies disturbs Vietnamese, but there are also offerings they commend, such as "The Cosby Show," which explores and promotes values they themselves prize: familial loyalty, togetherness, and a resolution of conflicts within the established social structures. Such shows, I've been told, remind the Vietnamese of their Confucian education and heritage.

4   Because the language of the immigrant community is still primarily Vietnamese, movies on videotapes imported from Taiwan and Hong Kong and dubbed in Vietnamese form a significant portion of the entertainment diet. The movies most favored are long, multitape epics that run from five to more than twenty hours. These include contemporary crime stories, soap operas, and romantic comedies, but the clear favorites are the medieval-military-romance cum kung fu extravaganzas.

5   There is a steady stream of customers at the various local shops that rent imported videotapes. Neighbors, friends, and relatives compare notes on favorite films and stars. Posters and pocket photos of heroes and heroines are eagerly bought. Entire families will sit through the night eating up the latest kung fu romance, their reddened eyes a testimony of devotion to the genre and quality of the film.

6   Atop nearly every TV set in the community rests a tape. While babysitting, grandmothers and aunts will place toddlers in front of the tube and play a Chinese film. (Depending on the time of day, little boys will cut in to watch "The Transformers," "Thundercats," or "G.I. Joe.") Young women confess that they would like to visit Hong Kong, where their favorite movies are made and their favorite stars live. Young men with a definite tendency to hesitancy and the doldrums are not so much

reacting to a harsh social and familial atmosphere as modeling their behavior on the beloved melancholic hero of the Chinese movie. Older, more mature men are not immune to the wiles of the films either. I have observed formerly impassive faces creased with emotion and dampened by tears during the viewing of a particularly sad movie, the dialogue of which is punctuated by sniffling sounds and a periodic blowing of noses.

The plots of these films are complicated and try the patience of out- 7
side audiences to whom I have introduced these films. Their broad outline can best be described as a series of concentric circles of conflict. At the outer edge, there is a general global conflict, such as a war between the Chinese and the Mongols (the latter sure to bring heated boos from the audience). Moving toward the center, the scope of the conflict—but not its intensity—narrows to two families or two different kung fu schools. Judging either side is a difficult endeavor; the conflict is not merely a matter of an obvious good versus an obvious evil, as in American movies. Conflict is inherent in the human desire to form groups, whether the group is a family unit or a kung fu school. And beneath this umbrella of intergroup conflict, there is intragroup conflict. This kind of conflict is generally romantically induced when someone falls in love with a member of an opposing family or school.

While Western media are filled with conflict, they have nothing 8
over the conflict-fraught Chinese film. Take, for example, *The Mighty Sword* (Than Chau Kiem Khach). Bac Phi, the hero, is a promising kung fu artist, whose master has high hopes of elevating him to take his own place upon retirement. To belong to a kung fu school is to belong to a family, with all that that entails in Oriental culture. The master is the father, and the other members are brothers and sisters. The school's members generally marry members of other schools to form alliances. As in any real family, there is considerable conflict and dissent, but the ideal of remaining faithful and obedient to the master is stressed.

Bac Phi's troubles begin when he helps a damsel, Lady Tuyet, who 9
is being besieged by ruffians. She herself is an incredibly gifted kung fu fighter and, as fate would have it, perhaps the most beautiful woman in the world. They immediately fall in love—love at first sight being the rule in the world of Chinese film.

In the film one gets a feel for the Chinese and, by derivation, the 10
Vietnamese way of romance. The hero and heroine do not touch; most certainly, they do not fondle or kiss. With a particularly sad melody in the background, they look into each other's eyes. The viewers all sigh and point; they know that the two are in love by "reading their eyes." Traditionally in Vietnam, lovers communicated with their eyes. Folklore, proverbs, and songs all depict a romance of the eyes: "Like a knife cutting the yellow betel leaf,/His eyes glance, her eyes dart back and forth." The stage is set for what appears to be a romance made in Heaven. Our two lovers vow to marry and to love each other forever.

11   After this moment, the meaning of the sad melody becomes apparent. The hero and heroine have pledged their love in ignorance of certain facts ruling the social reality around them. The lovers learn that their two schools are mortal enemies. Bac Phi's school and master are held to be responsible for the murder of Tuyet's father, and neither Bac Phi's master nor Tuyet's mother will countenance the marriage. The intragroup relationships of both lovers are strained. Tuyet and her mother are at odds and come to blows. Bac Phi's relationship with his best friend is strained, and he learns that his master is planning to have him marry another girl.

12   At this point in American television and movies, we would expect an easy solution to the problem. (To the dismay of the audience, I counseled "Elope!") The Chinese and Vietnamese solution is much more complicated. To decide between Tuyet and his school is not a simple matter, and characteristically for the Chinese hero, Bac Phi is paralyzed by the situation, torn between his lover and his quasi family, his desire and his duty. He becomes lovesick and pines away for Tuyet but never decides once and for all to choose her over his school.

13   To make matters worse, there are forces behind the scenes manipulating all involved as if they were puppets. Unseen powers are seeking to deepen the rift between Bac Phi's school and that of Tuyet. These powers attempt to undermine Bac Phi's love for and trust in Tuyet by posing one of their own as Tuyet and having him/her murder one of Bac Phi's schoolmates. An already impossible situation is raised to the nth degree. Bac Phi, because of his position in his school, must now avenge the death.

14   The conflict and its resolution are characteristic of the Vietnamese community. When I asked why the couple simply didn't run away and elope, the Vietnamese audience laughed. "That is the American way," I was told. "But we have a Confucian tradition." The Vietnamese were trained in Confucian values at school and at home. Confucianism, in a Vietnamese context, is a tradition of loyalty to one's family, superiors, and prior obligations. "We were always taught to love our parents more than life itself," one woman observed. "Parents were more important than the man or woman you loved."

15   The conflict would not actually be resolved by Bac Phi and Tuyet eloping and abandoning the social units to which they belong. As the Vietnamese themselves ask, "Could Tuyet trust Bac Phi if he were to fudge on his obligations to his school?" If Bac Phi will sever the bonds of previously established relationships, such as those with friends and superiors, what guarantee does Tuyet have that, when she has lost her figure and taken on wrinkles, he won't abandon her and chase after a younger, more nubile woman? There is a logic of trust in the films and the community that forbids them to take advantage of a simplistic formula, namely, "If you want it, go for it." The Vietnamese, ever moralistic, will ask, "Is it right for you to want it?"

16   The conflict, in the case of *The Mighty Sword,* is eventually resolved by the defeat of the powers behind the scenes, by a change of heart and

character on the part of Tuyet's mother and Bac Phi's master, and by the two lovers working to break the endless cycle of revenge and misunderstanding. The conflict is resolved within the social structures, not by their destruction. Despite the mazelike layers of deceit, fear, and manipulation, the movie ends affirming the ultimate worthwhileness of living in society, of being a social animal and not merely a lover.

Unlike most American television shows and movies, the Chinese hero does not always get the girl. A happy ending cannot be predicted. Although most Vietnamese I have talked to prefer a happy ending to their Chinese films, they appreciate and approve of the ethical message of a melancholic ending. "Love doesn't conquer all," one viewer told me, tears in his eyes. "Sometimes we have to pay for our mistakes. Sometimes we don't get what we want just because we want it." One woman recommended a particularly touching Chinese soap opera to me. "It has a very sad ending. It is very beautiful. It is very Confucian." She explained that the movie, which I later watched with a lump in my jaded throat, tried to teach that romance must be accompanied by ethics. One cannot simply be a lover. One also has to be a good son or daughter and citizen.   17

In America, where films and television shows tend to glorify the individual and romance, the Chinese films the Vietnamese adore reaffirm traditional values and help educate their children in the art of being Confucian. Traditional Vietnamese Confucianism has sneaked in through the back door, so to speak, through the VCR. American pluralism and technology have made this possible. They also may have let in a Trojan horse that promises to offer a venerable critique of certain American values. The Vietnamese may do American culture a favor by offering a counter-vision of what it means to be a social animal, and not merely an animal.   18

✧ Evaluating the Text

1. Beyond providing entertainment, what function do the foreign videos serve for the Vietnamese immigrant community?

2. Nash analyzes a Chinese film, *The Mighty Sword,* to illustrate the ways in which the values, mores, and expectations of these Chinese-made films differ from their American counterparts. What are some of these differences and what do they reveal about each culture?

3. How does the title suggest the distinctive contribution that Asian culture can offer to America?

✧ Exploring Different Perspectives

1. Compare the idealization of Chinese culture depicted by Nash with the reality of life in China from the perspective of a Tibetan exile (see Palden Gyatso, "Autobiography of a Tibetan Monk").

2. Compare perspectives on Asian American identity in Nash's account with Claire Chow's interviews in "Ethnicity and Identity: Creating a Sense of Self."

✧ *Extending Viewpoints through Writing*

1. Nash makes the point that some Chinese-made films offer "a counter-vision of what it means to be a social animal." Have you ever seen a movie that offered you a window into another culture? In what way was its perspective different from that presented in American films?

2. Nash observes that videos provide a portable means for preserving a cultural enclave for immigrants. When you watch movies in a foreign language, do you prefer them to be subtitled or dubbed into English? Explain your preference.

Palden Gyatso

Autobiography of a Tibetan Monk

◆───────◆

Palden Gyatso was born in 1933 into a well-off Tibetan family. He joined a rural Buddhist monastery at the age of ten. In 1960, he was arrested by the Chinese and spent the next thirty-three years in prison, where he was beaten and starved, but refused to cooperate with his torturers. Because he was skillful at Tibetan carpet weaving, his life was spared; but it was not until 1992 that he was released from prison, at which point he fled to India. Speaking as one of the many Tibetan Buddhist monks who suffered in Chinese prisons, Gyatso writes in this Prologue to Fire Under the Snow: The Autobiography of a Tibetan Monk *(1997) of his happiness at meeting the Dalai Lama.*

    Since 1965, Tibet has been an autonomous region in southwest China, bordered by Myanmar, Nepal, India, Bhutan, and Pakistan. Tibet is a high, arid plateau surrounded by mountain ranges, including the renowned Himalayas in the south. The economy is primarily pastoral, based on raising livestock, particularly yaks, and barley. The harsh environment and its physical isolation kept Tibet independent for much of its history. Tibetans are of Mongolian descent and follow an indigenous form of Buddhism, the chief figure of which is the Dalai Lama, who is believed to be the reincarnation of the ancestor of all Tibetans. The events behind Palden Gyatso's narrative begin when the Chinese, in 1969, forcibly tried to assimilate the Tibetans. Religious worship was prohibited, and monasteries and religious sites were destroyed. Since then, the Chinese government has tolerated Tibetan Buddhism (except during the imposition of martial law in the capital city of Lhasa from 1989 to 1992). The Chinese have recently brought in great numbers of Han Chinese (now 14 percent of the population) in an effort to assert control over the Tibetans. The effort on the part of the Chinese government to eradicate the Tibetan identity has led many Tibetans to flee into exile in neighboring Nepal and India.

It seemed that I had been preparing for this meeting all my life. After waiting outside a gate guarded by an Indian soldier in a khaki uniform, shivering in the monsoon wind and carrying an old Lee Enfield rifle at his side, I was body-searched by a young Tibetan in a blue suit. Then, a minute later, I was in the presence of the Dalai Lama. I had a strange feeling of both joy and sadness. I knew that had it not been for the tragedy that had befallen my country I could never have dreamed of such a meeting with the man we Tibetans call Kyabgon, the Saviour. The shabby guards, the simple bungalow shrouded in a murky mist, made the Dalai Lama's palace in exile a sad contrast to the vision of splendour that my country still conjures up in my mind.

2   Ever since leaving Lhasa, I had been thinking hard about what to tell the Dalai Lama. Should I begin with an account of my arrest? Should I tell him about all the people who had died from hunger, about the prisoners who had chosen to end their lives? Or should I tell him about the Tibetans who dutifully carried out the orders of the Chinese to curry favour and ensure a comfortable life? Perhaps I should tell him about the younger generation of Tibetans who now hold defiant demonstrations in prison, or about the Tibetan torturers who brutalise the bodies of their compatriots with blows and electric prods. After all, these torturers are Tibetans too, and were nourished by the same Land of Snows.

3   When I finally found myself in front of His Holiness, however, my mind became empty. At the sight of his maroon-robes and his friendly, grinning countenance I lowered my head, looking up only when he asked me a series of questions. "How did you escape? When were you first arrested? Which prison were you in?" he began. I should have realised that I was not the first prisoner to stand before him. For the last thirty-five years a steady stream of Tibetans have made their arduous escape across the Himalayas and found themselves standing before the Dalai Lama. They all do so in the hope of seeing him and whispering in his ear words they have rehearsed in their minds countless times. Every Tibetan who escapes over the mountains ends his or her journey with a short walk across the tarmac path to the audience room in Dharamsala and has the opportunity to utter the words that are carved on their hearts.

4   After I had been speaking for twenty minutes, the Dalai Lama stopped me. "You should write your story," he said. At the time I did not realise the significance of his advice. I decided I would write an account of my sufferings, including the names of all the people who had perished in the prison. The document would go to the Dalai Lama, so that these deaths should not go unrecorded. At the time, it never crossed my mind that I would write *a book*.

5   In Tibet we have a long tradition of writing biographies of great lamas and figures who attain a high degree of spirituality. These books are known as *Namthar*. They are never merely good stories, but are intended to impart spiritual teachings and are read as guides to life. The power of these books is recognised by all. "When we read the *Namthar* of the great warrior King Gesar," the Tibetan saying goes, "even a beggar would be moved to pick up a sword; when we read the biography of the great hermit Milarepa, even a prince would wish to renounce the world."

6   When the suggestion was made that I should write my story, I was embarrassed and puzzled by people's interest. It was not that I had no

desire to tell my story; on the contrary, one of the main reasons for my escape from Tibet was to be able to speak to the world. I had spent thirty years in prison and during that time I had experienced and witnessed unimaginable horrors. Every prisoner lives with the hope that somehow, once the world learns of their suffering, there will be a rush to help those who have fallen into the pit of hell.

In my prison, we used to sing, "one day the sun will shine through the dark clouds." The vision of the sun dispelling the dark clouds and our unbroken spirits kept us alive. It was not only prisoners who were resilient; so were ordinary men and women who lived their daily lives in the shadow of the Chinese Communist Party. Even today, young boys and girls who knew nothing of feudal Tibet and who are said to be the sons and daughters of the Party are crying out for freedom. Our collective will to resist what is unjust is like a fire that cannot be put out. Looking back, I can see that man's love of freedom is like a smouldering fire under snow.   7

Several days after my first visit to the Dalai Lama, I stood in the open yard of the new temple which faces His Holiness's palace. The Tibetans had named it Jokhang, after the holiest of all the temples in Lhasa. It had been rebuilt on a knoll and housed some of the religious images that had been rescued by devotees and smuggled across the Himalayas. In the Jokhang in Lhasa there is a bronze statue of the Buddha which was brought to Tibet in the seventh century A.D. as a gift from the Chinese princess who married the great Tibetan king, Srongsten Gampo. This historical event was regarded as of great significance by the Chinese. I remember being told the story again and again in prison, with the emphasis on how the betrothal of Princess Wenchen had brought culture to Tibet and unified the country with the motherland. In the beginning we used to ask, "Does this mean that Tibet also belongs to Nepal, because Srongsten Gampo was also married to a Nepalese princess?" Soon this sort of questioning came to be regarded as counterrevolutionary and was likely to earn you a term in prison.   8

The temple in Dharamsala was bursting with activity. Dozens of old people were circling the shrine and turning the prayer wheels, recreating that familiar music which in my childhood had mingled with the mumbling voices of elderly pilgrims reciting the six-syllable mantra, "Om mani pad me om." The mist that shrouded the temple slowly dissolved and the plains of India appeared through the clouds. This incongruous sight of Tibetans in a foreign land finally convinced me that I should tell my story in writing, not to advertise my suffering but as a testimony to my country's torment. In this way I could show that while I might be free, my country was still occupied.   9

As I gazed towards the dusty plains of India, I was overwhelmed by sadness. I vividly recalled the routine of prison life, the regularity of study sessions, the confession meetings and the reward and punishment   10 meetings, which had defined my life for the past thirty years. The scars of prison life remained painfully in my mind.

11   Dharamsala, with its lush green forests and rain, so different from Tibet, has become the resting place for so many of us. Every day, I meet fellow prisoners who have made the arduous journey to the foothills of the Himalayas. Their delight in being free is combined with a recognition of the past suffering of others. We congratulate each other on the sheer luck of surviving.

12   I am free in a foreign land, but lingering images of horror still haunt me. I am now living in a small hut nailed together from bits of tin and wood. The room is no bigger than the isolation unit in the prison. The torrents of monsoon rain beating on the tin roof keep me awake all night and the musty odour of damp clings to the walls and floor, although everyone says it will be better when the monsoon is over. In the next hut a group of youths who also made their way over the treacherous mountains listen to Lhasa Radio and cheerfully join in with the latest pop songs. It is strange how people still hanker for news of a place they have fled, and how they long to hear familiar sounds from home, as if to reassure themselves that they are alive.

13   Dharamsala is special not because it has become home for so many of us, but because it is the spiritual refuge of the Dalai Lama, the Buddha of Compassion. In prison we had uttered the name Dharamsala in hushed tones, developing a sense of reverence and awe for the place. Shortly after my arrival, I was given the task of interviewing other new arrivals to record their testimonies. I could not believe how many of us had the same story to tell. There was not a single individual without a story of horror and brutality, and I realised that all subjugated people share the common experience of bruised bodies, scattered lives and broken families.

14   Most of those who escape across the snowy peaks are young children. Some are sent away from home by their parents at the age of seven or eight in the hope that they will have a future in a foreign land. These are not the children of rich landlords or wealthy traders; they are the children of the same poor peasants whom the Communists claim to have liberated from servitude.

15   Dharamsala has a cosmopolitan character, with people from Japan, America, Israel and Europe mingling in the two narrow, muddy streets which form the main market of McLeod Ganj. I befriended many foreigners from countries I never knew existed, including a young English woman called Emily and a Dutch woman called Francisca, who regularly visited my hut to talk to me. It was during the course of those conversations that the story of my life began to unfold. I realised that because I had been lucky enough to survive, I was also duty bound to bear witness to the suffering of others.

16   Perhaps through the story of my life I can tell the story of my country and give expression to the pain felt by every Tibetan.

✦ Evaluating the Text

1. In light of his past experiences, what did Gyatso's meeting with the Dalai Lama represent to him? How did the advice he received change Gyatso's preconceptions about writing his autobiography?

2. Gyatso was clearly experiencing mixed emotions in his new home in Dharamsala, India. How would you characterize his conflict?

3. In what sense does Gyatso intend his memoir to be a voice for all those who wished to escape the oppressive Chinese Communist Party?

✦ Exploring Different Perspectives

1. In what way were Gyatso's experiences, before fleeing to Dharamsala, similar to those of Nunez in H. G. Wells's story "The Country of the Blind"?

2. Compare the role played by radios and VCRs in permitting exiles to maintain a tenuous link with cultures left behind, as developed in Gyatso's memoir and Jesse W. Nash's account in "Confucius and the VCR."

✦ Extending Viewpoints through Writing

1. Is there a belief you hold so strongly that you would be willing to undergo imprisonment and possibly torture to defend it? What is it and why does it mean so much to you?

2. Tibet has always held a certain mystique for the West and has been the subject of a number of films (for example, *Shangri-La* [1953] and more recently in 1997 *Seven Days in Tibet,* starring Brad Pitt). Rent a video of such a film and discuss the values connected with Tibet. Present your opinion as to why it holds the allure it does.

David R. Counts

Too Many Bananas

◆

David R. Counts teaches in the anthropology department at McMaster University in Ontario, Canada. Together with his wife, Dorothy A. Counts, he has edited a number of works, including Coping with the Final Tragedy: Dying and Grieving in Cross-Cultural Perspective *(1991) and* Aging and Its Transformations: Moving Toward Death in Pacific Societies *(1992). This selection is drawn from his book* The Humbled Anthropologist: Tales from the Pacific *(1990). The Counts are currently doing extensive research on the phenomena of the RV (recreation vehicle) community as a kind of "other" in American culture.*

New Guinea, the world's second-largest island after Greenland, is located in the Southwestern Pacific Ocean north of Australia. The western half of the island, known as Irian Jaya, is administered by Indonesia. Papua, which occupies the eastern half of New Guinea, was formerly a territory of Australia. It became the independent nation of Papua New Guinea in 1975. As one might gather from David R. Counts's article, the chief food crops are bananas, taro roots, and yams. The economy of New Guinea is one of the least developed of any area in the world. Most of the people farm land and grow their own food.

NO WATERMELON AT ALL

1   The woman came all the way through the village, walking between the two rows of houses facing each other between the beach and the bush, to the very last house standing on a little spit of land at the mouth of the Kaini River. She was carrying a watermelon on her head, and the house she came to was the government "rest house," maintained by the villagers for the occasional use of visiting officials. Though my wife and I were graduate students, not officials, and had asked for permission to stay in the village for the coming year, we were living in the rest house while the debate went on about where a house would be built for us. When the woman offered to sell us the watermelon for two shillings, we happily agreed, and the kids were delighted at the prospect of watermelon after yet another meal of rice and bully beef. The money changed hands and the seller left to return to her village, a couple of miles along the coast to the east.

2   It seemed only seconds later that the woman was back, reluctantly accompanying Kolia, the man who had already made it clear to us that

he was the leader of the village. Kolia had no English, and at that time, three or four days into our first stay in Kandoka Village on the island of New Britain in Papua New Guinea, we had very little Tok Pisin. Language difficulties notwithstanding, Kolia managed to make his message clear: The woman had been outrageously wrong to sell us the watermelon for two shillings and we were to return it to her and reclaim our money immediately. When we tried to explain that we thought the price to be fair and were happy with the bargain, Kolia explained again and finally made it clear that we had missed the point. The problem wasn't that we had paid too much; it was that we had paid at all. Here he was, a leader, responsible for us while we were living in his village, and we had shamed him. How would it look if he let guests in his village *buy* food? If we wanted watermelons, or bananas, or anything else, all that was necessary was to let him know. He told us that it would be all right for us to give little gifts to people who brought food to us (and they surely would), but *no one* was to sell food to us. If anyone were to try—like this woman from Lauvore—then we should refuse. There would be plenty of watermelons without us buying them.

The woman left with her watermelon, disgruntled, and we were   3
left with our two shillings. But we had learned the first lesson of many about living in Kandoka. We didn't pay money for food again that whole year, and we did get lots of food brought to us...but we never got another watermelon. That one was the last of the season.

LESSON 1: *In a society where food is shared or gifted as part of social life, you may not buy it with money.*

TOO MANY BANANAS

In the couple of months that followed the watermelon incident, we   4
managed to become at least marginally competent in Tok Pisin, to negotiate the construction of a house on what we hoped was neutral ground, and to settle into the routine of our fieldwork. As our village leader had predicted, plenty of food was brought to us. Indeed, seldom did a day pass without something coming in—some sweet potatoes, a few taro, a papaya, the occasional pineapple, or some bananas—lots of bananas.

We had learned our lesson about the money, though, so we never   5
even offered to buy the things that were brought, but instead made gifts, usually of tobacco to the adults or chewing gum to the children. Nor were we so gauche as to haggle with a giver over how much of a return gift was appropriate, though the two of us sometimes conferred as to whether what had been brought was a "two-stick" or a "three-stick" stalk, bundle, or whatever. A "stick" of tobacco was a single large leaf, soaked in rum and then twisted into a ropelike form. This, wrapped in half a sheet of newsprint (torn for use as cigarette paper),

sold in the local trade stores for a shilling. Nearly all of the adults in the village smoked a great deal, and they seldom had much cash, so our stocks of twist tobacco and stacks of the Sydney *Morning Herald* (all, unfortunately, the same day's issue) were seen as a real boon to those who preferred "stick" to the locally grown product.

6   We had established a pattern with respect to the gifts of food. When a donor appeared at our veranda we would offer our thanks and talk with them for a few minutes (usually about our children, who seemed to hold a real fascination for the villagers and for whom most of the gifts were intended) and then we would inquire whether they could use some tobacco. It was almost never refused, though occasionally a small bottle of kerosene, a box of matches, some laundry soap, a cup of rice, or a tin of meat would be requested instead of (or even in addition to) the tobacco. Everyone, even Kolia, seemed to think this arrangement had worked out well.

7   Now, what must be kept in mind is that while we were following their rules—or seemed to be—we were *really still buying food.* In fact we kept a running account of what came in and what we "paid" for it. Tobacco as currency got a little complicated, but since the exchange rate was one stick to one shilling, it was not too much trouble as long as everyone was happy, and meanwhile we could account for the expenditure of "informant fees" and "household expenses." Another thing to keep in mind is that not only did we continue to think in terms of our buying the food that was brought, we thought of them as *selling it.* While it was true they never quoted us a price, they also never asked us if we needed or wanted whatever they had brought. It seemed clear to us that when an adult needed a stick of tobacco, or a child wanted some chewing gum (we had enormous quantities of small packets of Wrigley's for just such eventualities) they would find something surplus to their own needs and bring it along to our "store" and get what they wanted.

8   By late November 1966, just before the rainy season set in, the bananas were coming into flush, and whereas earlier we had received banana gifts by the "hand" (six or eight bananas in a cluster cut from the stalk), donors now began to bring bananas, "for the children," by the *stalk!* The Kaliai among whom we were living are not exactly specialists in banana cultivation—they only recognize about thirty varieties, while some of their neighbors have more than twice that many—but the kinds they produce differ considerably from each other in size, shape, and taste, so we were not dismayed when we had more than one stalk hanging on our veranda. The stalks ripen a bit at the time, and having some variety was nice. Still, by the time our accumulation had reached *four* complete stalks, the delights of variety had begun to pale a bit. The fruits were ripening progressively and it was clear that even if we and the kids ate nothing but bananas for the next week, some would still fall from the stalk onto the floor in a state of gross

overripeness. This was the situation as, late one afternoon, a woman came bringing yet another stalk of bananas up the steps of the house.

Several factors determined our reaction to her approach: one was that there was literally no way we could possibly use the bananas. We hadn't quite reached the point of being crowded off our veranda by the stalks of fruit, but it was close. Another factor was that we were tired of playing the gift game. We had acquiesced in playing it—no one was permitted to sell us anything, and in turn we only gave things away, refusing under any circumstances to sell tobacco (or anything else) for money. But there had to be a limit. From our perspective what was at issue was that the woman wanted something and she had come to trade for it. Further, what she had brought to trade was something we neither wanted nor could use, and it should have been obvious to her. So we decided to bite the bullet. 9

The woman, Rogi, climbed the stairs to the veranda, took the stalk from where it was balanced on top of her head, and laid it on the floor with the word, "Here are some bananas for the children." Dorothy and I sat near her on the floor and thanked her for her thought but explained, "You know, we really have too many bananas—we can't use these; maybe you ought to give them to someone else...." The woman looked mystified, then brightened and explained that she didn't want anything for them, she wasn't short of tobacco or anything. They were just a gift for the kids. Then she just sat there, and we sat there, and the bananas sat there, and we tried again. "Look," I said, pointing up to them and counting, "we've got four stalks already hanging here on the veranda—there are too many for us to eat now. Some are rotting already. Even if we eat only bananas, we can't keep up with what's here!" 10

Rogi's only response was to insist that these were a gift, and that she didn't want anything for them, so we tried yet another tack: "Don't *your* children like bananas?" When she admitted that they did, and that she had none at her house, we suggested that she should take them there. Finally, still puzzled, but convinced we weren't going to keep the bananas, she replaced them on her head, went down the stairs, and made her way back through the village toward her house. 11

As before, it seemed only moments before Kolia was making his way up the stairs, but this time he hadn't brought the woman in tow. "What was wrong with those bananas? Were they no good?" he demanded. We explained that there was nothing wrong with the bananas at all, but that we simply couldn't use them and it seemed foolish to take them when we had so many and Rogi's own children had none. We obviously didn't make ourselves clear because Kolia then took up the same refrain that Rogi had—he insisted that we shouldn't be worried about taking the bananas, because they were a gift for the children and Rogi hadn't wanted anything for them. There was no reason, he added, to send her away with them—she would be ashamed. I'm 12 afraid we must have seemed as if we were hard of hearing or thought he was, for our only response was to repeat our reasons. We went through it again—there they hung, one, two, three, *four* stalks of bananas, rapidly ripening and already far beyond our capacity to eat—we just weren't ready to accept any more and let them rot (and, we added to ourselves, pay for them with tobacco, to boot).

13   Kolia finally realized that we were neither hard of hearing nor intentionally offensive, but merely ignorant. He stared at us for a few minutes, thinking, and then asked: "Don't you frequently have visitors during the day and evening?" We nodded. Then he asked, "Don't you usually offer them cigarettes and coffee or milo?" Again, we nodded. "Did it ever occur to you to suppose," he said, "that your visitors might be hungry?" It was at this point in the conversation, as we recall, that we began to see the depth of the pit we had dug for ourselves. We nodded, hesitantly. His last words to us before he went down the stairs and stalked away were just what we were by that time afraid they might be. "When your guests are hungry, *feed them bananas!*"

LESSON 2: *Never refuse a gift, and never fail to return a gift. If you cannot use it, you can always give it away to someone else—there is no such thing as too much—there are never too many bananas.*

NOT ENOUGH PINEAPPLES

14   During the fifteen years between that first visit in 1966 and our residence there in 1981 we had returned to live in Kandoka village twice during the 1970s, and though there were a great many changes in the village, and indeed for all of Papua New Guinea during that time, we continued to live according to the lessons of reciprocity learned during those first months in the field. We bought no food for money and refused no gifts, but shared our surplus. As our family grew, we continued to be accompanied by our younger children. Our place in the village came to be something like that of educated Kaliai who worked far away in New Guinea. Our friends expected us to come "home" when we had leave, but knew that our work kept us away for long periods of time. They also credited us with knowing much more about the rules of their way of life than was our due. And we sometimes shared the delusion that we understood life in the village, but even fifteen years was not long enough to relieve the need for lessons in learning to live within the rules of gift exchange.

15   In the last paragraph I used the word *friends* to describe the villagers intentionally, but of course they were not all our friends. Over the years some really had become friends, others were acquaintances, others remained consultants or informants to whom we turned when we needed information. Still others, unfortunately, we did not like at all.

We tried never to make an issue of these distinctions, of course, and to be evenhanded and generous to all, as they were to us. Although we almost never actually refused requests that were made of us, over the long term our reciprocity in the village was balanced. More was given to those who helped us the most, while we gave assistance or donations of small items even to those who were not close or helpful.

One elderly woman in particular was a trial for us. Sara was the eldest of a group of siblings and her younger brother and sister were both generous, informative, and delightful persons. Her younger sister, Makila, was a particularly close friend and consultant, and in deference to that friendship we felt awkward in dealing with the elder sister.   16

Sara was neither a friend nor an informant, but she had been, since she returned to live in the village at the time of our second trip in 1971, a constant (if minor) drain on our resources. She never asked for much at a time. A bar of soap, a box of matches, a bottle of kerosene, a cup of rice, some onions, a stick or two of tobacco, or some other small item was usually all that was at issue, but whenever she came around it was always to ask for something—or to let us know that when we left, we should give her some of the furnishings from the house. Too, unlike almost everyone else in the village, when she came, she was always empty-handed. We ate no taro from her gardens, and the kids chewed none of her sugarcane. In short, she was, as far as we could tell, a really grasping, selfish old woman—and we were not the only victims of her greed.   17

Having long before learned the lesson of the bananas, one day we had a stalk that was ripening so fast we couldn't keep up with it, so I pulled a few for our own use (we only had one stalk at the time) and walked down through the village to Ben's house, where his five children were playing. I sat down on his steps to talk, telling him that I intended to give the fruit to his kids. They never got them. Sara saw us from across the open plaza of the village and came rushing over, shouting, "My bananas!" Then she grabbed the stalk and went off gorging herself with them. Ben and I just looked at each other.   18

Finally it got to the point where it seemed to us that we had to do something. Ten years of being used was long enough. So there came the afternoon when Sara showed up to get some tobacco—again. But this time, when we gave her the two sticks she had demanded, we confronted her.   19

First, we noted the many times she had come to get things. We didn't mind sharing things, we explained. After all, we had plenty of tobacco and soap and rice and such, and most of it was there so that we could help our friends as they helped us, with folktales, information, or even gifts of food. The problem was that she kept coming to get things, but never came to talk, or to tell stories, or to bring some little something that the kids might like. Sara didn't argue—she agreed. "Look," we suggested, "it doesn't have to be much, and we don't mind giving you   20 things—but you can help us. The kids like pineapples, and we don't have any—the next time you need something, bring something—like maybe a pineapple." Obviously somewhat embarrassed, she took her tobacco and left, saying that she would bring something soon. We were really pleased with ourselves. It had been a very difficult thing to do, but it was done, and we were convinced that either she would start bringing things or not come. It was as if a burden had lifted from our shoulders.

21   It worked. Only a couple of days passed before Sara was back, bringing her bottle to get it filled with kerosene. But this time, she came carrying the biggest, most beautiful pineapple we had seen the entire time we had been there. We had a friendly talk, filled her kerosene container, and hung the pineapple up on the veranda to ripen just a little further. A few days later we cut and ate it, and whether the satisfaction it gave came from the fruit or from its source would be hard to say, but it was delicious. That, we assumed, was the end of that irritant.

22   We were wrong, of course. The next afternoon, Mary, one of our best friends for years (and no relation to Sara), dropped by for a visit. As we talked, her eyes scanned the veranda. Finally she asked whether we hadn't had a pineapple there yesterday. We said we had, but that we had already eaten it. She commented that it had been a really nice-looking one, and we told her that it had been the best we had eaten in months. Then, after a pause, she asked, "Who brought it to you?" We smiled as we said, "Sara!" because Mary would appreciate our coup— she had commented many times in the past on the fact that Sara only *got* from us and never gave. She was silent for a moment, and then she said, "Well, I'm glad you enjoyed it—my father was waiting until it was fully ripe to harvest it for you, but when it went missing I thought maybe it was the one you had here. I'm glad to see you got it. I thought maybe a thief had eaten it in the bush."

LESSON 3: *Where reciprocity is the rule and gifts are the idiom, you cannot demand a gift, just as you cannot refuse a request.*

23   It says a great deal about the kindness and patience of the Kaliai people that they have been willing to be our hosts for all these years despite our blunders and lack of good manners. They have taught us a lot, and these three lessons are certainly not the least important things we learned.

✧ Evaluating the Text

1. How does Counts's initial experience of offering money for watermelon teach him his first important lesson about the culture of New Guinea?

2. How does the idea of "too many bananas" sum up the important principle of reciprocity that Counts learns? In your own words, describe the principle involved.

3. How does the experience Counts has with Sara lead to his ironic realization of the third lesson about the culture of New Guinea?

✧ Exploring Different Perspectives

1. Compare Counts's essay with H. G. Wells's story "The Country of the Blind" as narratives of acculturation. What shifts in perspective are required of Counts and Nunez?

2. In what ways do the simplest of material goods take on paramount importance in Counts's narrative and in Luis Alberto Urrea's "Border Story"?

✧ Extending Viewpoints through Writing

1. What experiences have you had that involved the principle of reciprocity in your relationship with another? Discuss one incident and the lesson you learned.

2. If you were a "stranger in a strange land," would you feel more comfortable if you had many of your material possessions with you? Why or why not?

H. G. Wells

The Country of the Blind

◆

H. G. (Herbert George) Wells (1866–1946) is generally acknowledged as having shaped the genre of literature we now call science fiction with his novel The Time Machine *(1895). Born into a poor family and afflicted with tuberculosis, Wells was a student of the biologist Thomas Henry Huxley (whose grandson Aldous Huxley wrote* Brave New World *in 1932), who opened Wells's mind to Charles Darwin's theories and the belief that humanity is an evolving species. Wells joined the Fabian Society of Sociologists in 1903 and was strongly influenced by their concept of a utopian political state. His brilliant novels include* The Island of Dr. Moreau *(1896),* The Invisible Man *(1897), and* The War of the Worlds *(1898), which was the basis of Orson Wells's famous 1938 radio play (which caused a panic throughout the United States). "The Country of the Blind" (1911) is perhaps Wells's finest short story and will evoke, for many, Plato's "Allegory of the Cave."*

1   Three hundred miles and more from Chimborazo, one hundred from the snows of Cotopaxi, in the wildest wastes of Ecuador's Andes, there lies that mysterious mountain valley, cut off from the world of men, the Country of the Blind. Long years ago that valley lay so far open to the world that men might come at last through frightful gorges and over an icy pass into its equable meadows; and thither indeed men came, a family or so of Peruvian half-breeds fleeing from the lust and tyranny of an evil Spanish ruler. Then came the stupendous outbreak of Mindo bamba, when it was night in Quito for seventeen days, and the water was boiling at Yaguachi and all the fish floating dying even as far as Guayaquil; everywhere along the Pacific slopes there were landslips and swift thawings and sudden floods, and one whole side of the Arauca crest slipped and came down in thunder, and cut off the Country of the Blind for ever from the exploring feet of men. But one of these early settlers had chanced to be on the hither side of the gorges when the world had so terribly shaken itself, and he perforce had to forget his wife and his child and all the friends and possessions he had left up there, and start life over again in the lower world. He started it again but ill, blindness overtook him, and he died of punishment in the mines; but the story he told begot a legend that lingers along the length of the Cordilleras of the Andes to this day.

He told of his reason for venturing back from that vastness, into   2
which he had first been carried lashed to a llama, beside a vast bale of
gear, when he was a child. The valley, he said, had in it all that the heart
of man could desire—sweet water, pasture, and even climate, slopes of
rich brown soil with tangles of a shrub that bore an excellent fruit, and
on one side great hanging forests of pine that held the avalanches high.
Far overhead, on three sides, vast cliffs of grey-green rock were capped
by cliffs of ice; but the glacier stream came not to them but flowed away
by the farther slopes, and only now and then huge ice masses fell on
the valley side. In this valley it neither rained nor snowed, but the
abundant springs gave a rich green pasture, that irrigation would
spread over all the valley space. The settlers did well indeed there.
Their beasts did well and multiplied, and but one thing marred their
happiness. Yet it was enough to mar it greatly. A strange disease had
come upon them, and had made all the children born to them there—
and indeed, several older children also—blind. It was to seek some
charm or antidote against this plague of blindness that he had with fatigue and danger and difficulty returned down the gorge. In those
days, in such cases, men did not think of germs and infections but of
sins; and it seemed to him that the reason of this affliction must lie in
the negligence of these priestless immigrants to set up a shrine as soon
as they entered the valley. He wanted a shrine—a handsome, cheap, ef-
fectual shrine—to be erected in the valley; he wanted relics and such-
like potent things of faith, blessed objects and mysterious medals and
prayers. In his wallet he had a bar of native silver for which he would
not account; he insisted there was none in the valley with something of
the insistence of an inexpert liar. They had all clubbed their money and
ornaments together, having little need for such treasure up there, he
said, to buy them holy help against their ill. I figure this dim-eyed
young mountaineer, sunburnt, gaunt, and anxious, hat-brim clutched
feverishly, a man all unused to the ways of the lower world, telling this
story to some keen-eyed, attentive priest before the great convulsion; I
can picture him presently seeking to return with pious and infallible
remedies against that trouble, and the infinite dismay with which he
must have faced the tumbled vastness where the gorge had once come
out. But the rest of his story of mischances is lost to me, save that I
know of his evil death after several years. Poor stray from that remote-
ness! The stream that had once made the gorge now bursts from the
mouth of a rocky cave, and the legend his poor, ill-told story set going
developed into the legend of a race of blind men somewhere "over
there" one may still hear today.

And amidst the little population of that now isolated and forgotten   3
valley the disease ran its course. The old became groping and purblind,
the young saw but dimly, and the children that were born to them saw

never at all. But life was very easy in that snow-rimmed basin, lost to all
the world, with neither thorns nor briars, with no evil insects nor any
beasts save the gentle breed of llamas they had lugged and thrust and
followed up the beds of the shrunken rivers in the gorges up which they
had come. The seeing had become purblind so gradually that they
scarcely noted their loss. They guided the sightless youngsters hither
and thither until they knew the whole valley marvellously, and when at
last sight died out among them the race lived on. They had even time to
adapt themselves to the blind control of fire, which they made carefully
in stoves of stone. They were a simple strain of people at the first, unlet-
tered, only slightly touched with the Spanish civilisation, but with something of a tradition of the arts of old Peru and of its lost philosophy.
Generation followed generation. They forgot many things; they devised
many things. Their tradition of the greater world they came from became
mythical in colour and uncertain. In all things save sight they were
strong and able; and presently the chance of birth and heredity sent one
who had an original mind and who could talk and persuade among
them, and then afterwards another. These two passed, leaving their effects, and the little community grew in numbers and in understanding,
and met and settled social and economic problems that arose. Generation followed generation. Generation followed generation. There came a
time when a child was born who was fifteen generations from that ancestor who went out of the valley with a bar of silver to seek God's aid, and
who never returned. Thereabouts it chanced that a man came into this
community from the outer world. And this is the story of that man.

4   He was a mountaineer from the country near Quito, a man who
had been down to the sea and had seen the world, a reader of books in
an original way, an acute and enterprising man, and he was taken on
by a party of Englishmen who had come out to Ecuador to climb
mountains, to replace one of their three Swiss guides who had fallen ill.
He climbed here and he climbed there, and then came the attempt on
Parascotopetl, the Matterhorn of the Andes, in which he was lost to the
outer world. The story of the accident has been written a dozen times.
Pointer's narrative is the best. He tells how the party worked their difficult and almost vertical way up to the very foot of the last and greatest precipice, and how they built a night shelter amidst the snow upon
a little shelf of rock, and, with a touch of real dramatic power, how
presently they found Nunez had gone from them. They shouted, and
there was no reply, shouted and whistled, and for the rest of that night
they slept no more.

5   As the morning broke they saw the traces of his fall. It seems impossible he could have uttered a sound. He had slipped eastward towards
the unknown side of the mountain; far below he had struck a steep slope
of snow, and ploughed his way down it in the midst of a snow ava-
lanche. His track went straight to the edge of a frightful precipice, and

beyond that everything was hidden. Far, far below, and hazy with distance, they could see trees rising out of a narrow, shut-in valley—the lost Country of the Blind. But they did not know it was the lost Country of the Blind, nor distinguish it in any way from any other narrow streak of upland valley. Unnerved by this disaster, they abandoned their attempt in the afternoon, and Pointer was called away to the war before he could make another attack. To this day Parascotopetl lifts an unconquered crest, and Pointer's shelter crumbles unvisited amidst the snows.

And the man who fell survived.   6

At the end of the slope he fell a thousand feet, and came down in   7
the midst of a cloud of snow upon a snow slope even steeper than the one above. Down this he was whirled, stunned and insensible, but without a bone broken in his body; and then at last came to gentler slopes, and at last rolled out and lay still, buried amidst a softening heap of the white masses that had accompanied and saved him. He came to himself with a dim fancy that he was ill in bed; then realised his position with a mountaineer's intelligence, and worked himself loose and, after a rest or so, out until he saw the stars. He rested flat upon his chest for a space, wondering where he was and what had happened to him. He explored his limbs, and discovered that several of his buttons were gone and his coat turned over his head. His knife had gone from his pocket and his hat was lost, though he had tied it under his chin. He recalled that he had been looking for loose stones to raise his piece of the shelter wall. His ice-axe had disappeared.

He decided he must have fallen, and looked up to see, exaggerated   8
by the ghastly light of the rising moon, the tremendous flight he had taken. For a while he lay, gazing blankly at that vast pale cliff towering above, rising moment by moment out of a subsiding tide of darkness. Its phantasmal, mysterious beauty held him for a space, and then he was seized with a paroxysm of sobbing laughter. . . .

After a great interval of time he became aware that he was near the   9
lower edge of the snow. Below, down what was now a moonlit and practicable slope, he saw the dark and broken appearance of rock-strewn turf. He struggled to his feet, aching in every joint and limb, got down painfully from the heaped loose snow about him, went downward until he was on the turf, and there dropped rather than lay beside a boulder, drank deep from the flask in his inner pocket, and instantly fell asleep.

He was awakened by the singing of birds in the trees far below.   10

He sat up and perceived he was on a little alp at the foot of a vast   11
precipice, that was grooved by the gully down which he and his snow had come. Over against him another wall of rock reared itself against the sky. The gorge between these precipices ran east and west and was full of the morning sunlight, which lit to the westward the mass of fallen mountain that closed the descending gorge. Below him it seemed there was a precipice equally steep, but behind the snow in the gully he found

a sort of chimney-cleft dripping with snow-water down which a desperate man might venture. He found it easier than it seemed, and came at last to another desolate alp, and then after a rock climb of no particular difficulty to a steep slope of trees. He took his bearings and turned his face up the gorge, for he saw it opened out above upon green meadows, among which he now glimpsed quite distinctly a cluster of stone huts of unfamiliar fashion. At times his progress was like clambering along the face of a wall, and after a time the rising sun ceased to strike along the gorge, the voices of the singing birds died away, and the air grew cold and dark about him. But the distant valley with its houses was all the brighter for that. He came presently to talus, and among the rocks he noted—for he was an observant man—an unfamiliar fern that seemed to clutch out of the crevices with intense green hands. He picked a frond or so and gnawed its stalk and found it helpful.

12   About midday he came at last out of the throat of the gorge into the plain and the sunlight. He was stiff and weary; he sat down in the shadow of a rock, filled up his flask with water from a spring and drank it down, and remained for a time resting before he went on to the houses.

13   They were very strange to his eyes, and indeed the whole aspect of that valley became, as he regarded it, queerer and more unfamiliar. The greater part of its surface was lush green meadow, starred with many beautiful flowers, irrigated with extraordinary care, and bearing evidence of systematic cropping piece by piece. High up and ringing the valley about was a wall, and what appeared to be a circumferential water-channel, from which the little trickles of water that fed the meadow, plants came, and on the higher slopes above this flocks of llamas cropped the scanty herbage. Sheds, apparently shelters or feeding-places for the llamas, stood against the boundary wall here and there. The irrigation streams ran together into a main channel down the centre of the valley, and this was enclosed on either side by a wall breast high. This gave a singularly urban quality to this secluded place, a quality that was greatly enhanced by the fact that a number of paths paved with black and white stones, and each with a curious little kerb at the side, ran hither and thither in an orderly manner. The houses of the central village were quite unlike the casual and higgledy-piggledy agglomeration of the mountain villages he knew; they stood in a continuous row on either side of a central street of astonishing cleanness; here and there their parti-coloured façade was pierced by a door, and not a solitary window broke their even frontage. They were parti-coloured with extraordinary irregularity; smeared with a sort of plaster that was sometimes grey, sometimes drab, sometimes slate-coloured or dark brown; and it was the sight of this wild plastering first brought the word "blind" into the thoughts of the explorer. "The good man who did that," he thought, "must have been as blind as a bat."

He descended a steep place, and so came to the wall and channel   14
that ran about the valley, near where the latter spouted out its surplus
contents into the deeps of the gorge in a thin and wavering thread of
cascade. He could now see a number of men and women resting on
piled heaps of grass, as if taking a siesta, in the remoter part of the
meadow, and nearer the village a number of recumbent children, and
then nearer at hand three men carrying pails on yokes along a little
path that ran from the encircling wall towards the houses. These latter
were clad in garments of llama cloth and boots and belts of leather, and
they wore caps of cloth with back and ear flaps. They followed one another in single file, walking slowly and yawning as they walked, like
men who have been up all night. There was something so reassuringly
prosperous and respectable in their bearing that after a moment's hesitation Nunez stood forward as conspicuously as possible upon his
rock, and gave vent to a mighty shout that echoed round the valley.

The three men stopped, and moved their heads as though they   15
were looking about them. They turned their faces this way and that,
and Nunez gesticulated with freedom. But they did not appear to see
him for all his gestures, and after a time, directing themselves towards
the mountains far away to the right, they shouted as if in answer.
Nunez bawled again, and then once more, and as he gestured ineffec-
tually the word "blind" came up to the top of his thoughts. "The fools
must be blind," he said.

When at last, after much shouting and wrath, Nunez crossed the   16
stream by a little bridge, came through a gate in the wall, and approached them, he was sure that they were blind. He was sure that this
was the Country of the Blind of which the legends told. Conviction had
sprung upon him, and a sense of great and rather enviable adventure.
The three stood side by side, not looking at him, but with their ears directed towards him, judging him by his unfamiliar steps. They stood
close together like men a little afraid, and he could see their eyelids
closed and sunken, as though the very balls beneath had shrunk away.
There was an expression near awe on their faces.

"A man," one said, in hardly recognisable Spanish—"a man it is—   17
a man or a spirit—coming down from the rocks."

But Nunez advanced with the confident steps of a youth who en-   18
ters upon life. All the old stories of the lost valley and the Country of
the Blind had come back to his mind, and through his thoughts ran this
old proverb, as if it were a refrain—

"In the Country of the Blind the One-eyed Man is King."   19

"In the Country of the Blind the One-eyed Man is King."   20

And very civilly he gave them greeting. He talked to them and   21
used his eyes.

"Where does he come from, brother Pedro?" asked one.   22

23   "Down out of the rocks."

24   "Over the mountains I come," said Nunez, "out of the country beyond there—where men can see. From near Bogota, where there are a
hundred thousands of people, and where the city passes out of sight."

25   "Sight?" muttered Pedro. "Sight?"

26   "He comes," said the second blind man, "out of the rocks."

27   The cloth of their coats Nunez saw was curiously fashioned, each
with a different sort of stitching.

28   They startled him by a simultaneous movement towards him, each
with a hand outstretched. He stepped back from the advance of these
spread fingers.

29   "Come hither," said the third blind man, following his motion and
clutching him neatly.

30   And they held Nunez and felt him over, saying no word further
until they had done so.

31   "Carefully," he cried, with a finger in his eye, and found they
thought that organ, with its fluttering lids, a queer thing in him. They
went over it again.

32   "A strange creature, Correa," said the one called Pedro. "Feel the
coarseness of his hair. Like a llama's hair."

33   "Rough he is as the rocks that begot him," said Correa, investigating Nunez's unshaven chin with a soft and slightly moist hand.
"Perhaps he will grow finer." Nunez struggled a little under their examination, but they gripped him firm.

34   "Carefully," he said again.

35   "He speaks," said the third man. "Certainly he is a man."

36   "Ugh!" said Pedro, at the roughness of his coat.

37   "And you have come into the world?" asked Pedro.

38   "Out of the world. Over mountains and glaciers; right over above
there, half-way to the sun. Out of the great big world that goes down,
twelve days' journey to the sea."

39   They scarcely seemed to heed him. "Our fathers have told us men
may be made by the forces of Nature," said Correa. "It is the warmth of
things and moisture, and rottenness—rottenness."

40   "Let us lead him to the elders," said Pedro.

41   "Shout first," said Correa, "lest the children be afraid. This is a
marvelous occasion."

42   So they shouted, and Pedro went first and took Nunez by the hand
to lead him to the houses.

43   He drew his hand away. "I can see," he said.

44   "See?" said Correa.

45   "Yes, see," said Nunez, turning towards him, and stumbled against
Pedro's pail.

46   "His senses are still imperfect," said the third blind man. "He
stumbles, and talks unmeaning words. Lead him by the hand."

"As you will," said Nunez, and was led along, laughing.   47

It seemed they knew nothing of sight.   48

Well, all in good time, he would teach them.   49

He heard people shouting, and saw a number of figures gathering   50
together in the middle roadway of the village.

He found it taxed his nerve and patience more than he had antici-   51
pated, that first encounter with the population of the Country of the
Blind. The place seemed larger as he drew near to it, and the smeared
plasterings queerer, and a crowd of children and men and women (the
women and girls, he was pleased to note, had some of them quite
sweet faces, for all that their eyes were shut and sunken) came about
him, holding on to him, touching him with soft, sensitive hands, smelling at him, and listening at every word he spoke. Some of the maidens
and children, however, kept aloof as if afraid, and indeed his voice
seemed coarse and rude beside their softer notes. They mobbed him.
His three guides kept close to him with an effect of proprietorship, and
said again and again, "A wild man out of the rocks."

"Bogota," he said. "Bogota. Over the mountain crests."   52

"A wild man—using wild words," said Pedro. "Did you hear   53
that—*Bogota?* His mind is hardly formed yet. He has only the begin-
nings of speech."

A little boy nipped his hand. "Bogota!" he said mockingly.   54

"Ay! A city to your village. I come from the great world—where   55
men have eyes and see."

"His name's Bogota," they said.   56

"He stumbled," said Correa, "stumbled twice as we came hither."   57

"Bring him to the elders."   58

And they thrust him suddenly through a doorway into a room as   59
black as pitch, save at the end there faintly glowed a fire. The crowd
closed in behind him and shut out all but the faintest glimmer of day,
and before he could arrest himself he had fallen headlong over the feet
of a seated man. His arm, outflung, struck the face of someone else as
he went down; he felt the soft impact of features and heard a cry of anger, and for a moment he struggled against a number of hands that
clutched him. It was a one-sided fight. An inkling of the situation came
to him, and he lay quiet.

"I fell down," he said; "I couldn't see in this pitchy darkness."   60

There was a pause as if the unseen persons about him tried to un-   61
derstand his words. Then the voice of Correa said: "He is but newly
formed. He stumbles as he walks and mingles words that mean nothing with his speech."

Others also said things about him that he heard or understood im-   62
perfectly.

"May I sit up?" he asked, in a pause. "I will not struggle against   63
you again."

64   They consulted and let him rise.

65   The voice of an older man began to question him, and Nunez found himself trying to explain the great world out of which he had fallen, and the sky and mountains and sight and such-like marvels, to these elders who sat in darkness in the Country of the Blind. And they would believe and understand nothing whatever he told them, a thing quite outside his expectation. They would not even understand many of his words. For fourteen generations these people had been blind and cut off from all the seeing world; the names for all the things of sight had faded and changed; the story of the outer world was faded and changed to a child's story; and they had ceased to concern themselves with anything beyond the rocky slopes above their circling wall. Blind men of genius had arisen among them and questioned the shreds of belief and tradition they had brought with them from their seeing days, and had dismissed all these things as idle fancies, and replaced them with new and saner explanations. Much of their imagination had shrivelled with their eyes, and they had made for themselves new imaginations with their ever more sensitive ears and finger-tips. Slowly Nunez realised this; that his expectation of wonder and reverence at his origin and his gifts was not to be borne out; and after his poor attempt to explain sight to them had been set aside as the confused version of a new-made being describing the marvels of his incoherent sensations, he subsided, a little dashed, into listening to their instruction. And the eldest of the blind men explained to him life and philosophy and religion, how that the world (meaning their valley) had been first an empty hollow in the rocks, and then had come, first, inanimate things without the gift of touch, and llamas and a few other creatures that had little sense, and then men, and at last angels, whom one could hear singing and making fluttering sounds, but whom no one could touch at all, which puzzled Nunez greatly until he thought of the birds.

66   He went on to tell Nunez how this time had been divided into the warm and the cold, which are the blind equivalents of day and night, and how it was good to sleep in the warm and work during the cold, so that now, but for his advent, the whole town of the blind would have been asleep. He said Nunez must have been specially created to learn and serve the wisdom they had acquired, and for that all his mental incoherency and stumbling behavior he must have courage, and do his best to learn, and at that all the people in the doorway murmured encouragingly. He said the night—for the blind call their day night—was now far gone, and it behooved every one to go back to sleep. He asked Nunez if he knew how to sleep, and Nunez said he did, but that before sleep he wanted food.

67   They brought him food—llama's milk in a bowl, and rough salted bread—and led him into a lonely place to eat out of their hearing, and

afterwards to slumber until the chill of the mountain evening roused them to begin their day again. But Nunez slumbered not at all.

Instead, he sat up in the place where they had left him, resting his   68
limbs and turning the unanticipated circumstances of his arrival over and over in his mind.

Every now and then he laughed, sometimes with amusement, and   69
sometimes with indignation.

"Unformed mind!" he said. "Got no senses yet! They little know   70
they've been insulting their heaven-sent king and master. I see I must bring them to reason. Let me think—let me think."

He was still thinking when the sun set.   71

Nunez had an eye for all beautiful things, and it seemed to him   72
that the glow upon the snowfields and glaciers that rose about the valley on every side was the most beautiful thing he had ever seen. His eyes went from that inaccessible glory to the village and irrigated fields, fast sinking into the twilight, and suddenly a wave of emotion took him, and he thanked God from the bottom of his heart that the power of sight had been given him.

He heard a voice calling to him from out of the village.   73

"Ya ho there, Bogota! Come hither!"   74

At that he stood up smiling. He would show these people once and   75
for all what sight would do for a man. They would seek him, but not find him.

"You move not, Bogota," said the voice.   76

He laughed noiselessly, and made two stealthy steps aside from   77
the path.

"Trample not on the grass, Bogota; that is not allowed."   78

Nunez had scarcely heard the sound he made himself. He stopped   79
amazed.

The owner of the voice came running up the piebald path towards   80
him.

He stepped back into the pathway. "Here I am," he said.   81

"Why did you not come when I called you?" said the blind man.   82
"Must you be led like a child? Cannot you hear the path as you walk?"

Nunez laughed. "I can see it," he said.   83

"There is no such word as *see*," said the blind man, after a pause.   84
"Cease this folly, and follow the sound of my feet."

Nunez followed, a little annoyed.   85

"My time will come," he said.   86

"You'll learn," the blind man answered. "There is much to learn in   87
the world. "

"Has no one told you, 'In the Country of the Blind the One-eyed   88
Man is King'?"

"What is blind?" asked the blind man carelessly over his shoulder.   89

90   Four days passed, and the fifth found the King of the Blind still incognito, as a clumsy and useless stranger among his subjects.

91   It was, he found, much more difficult to proclaim himself than he had supposed, and in the meantime, while he meditated his *coup d'état*, he did what he was told and learned the manners and customs of the Country of the Blind. He found working and going about at night a particularly irksome thing, and he decided that that should be the first thing he would change.

92   They led a simple, laborious life, these people, with all the elements of virtue and happiness, as these things can be understood by men. They toiled, but not oppressively; they had food and clothing sufficient for their needs; they had days and seasons of rest; they made much of music and singing, and there was love among them, and little children.

93   It was marvellous with what confidence and precision they went about their ordered world. Everything, you see, had been made to fit their needs; each of the radiating paths of the valley area had a constant angle to the others, and was distinguished by a special notch upon its kerbing; all obstacles and irregularities of path or meadow had long since been cleared away; all their methods and procedure arose naturally from their special needs. Their senses had become marvellously acute; they could hear and judge the slightest gesture of a man a dozen paces away—could hear the very beating of his heart. Intonation had long replaced expression with them, and touches gesture, and their work with hoe and spade and fork was as free and confident as garden work can be. Their sense of smell was extraordinarily fine; they could distinguish individual differences as readily as a dog can, and they went about the tending of the llamas, who lived among the rocks above and came to the wall for food and shelter, with ease and confidence. It was only when at last Nunez sought to assert himself that he found how easy and confident their movements could be.

94   He rebelled only after he had tried persuasion.

95   He tried at first on several occasions to tell them of sight. "Look you here, you people," he said. "There are things you do not understand in me."

96   Once or twice one or two of them attended to him; they sat with faces downcast and ears turned intelligently towards him, and he did his best to tell them what it was to see. Among his hearers was a girl, with eyelids less red and sunken than the others, so that one could almost fancy she was hiding eyes, whom especially he hoped to persuade. He spoke of the beauties of sight, of watching the mountains, of the sky and the sunrise, and they heard him with amused incredulity that presently became condemnatory. They told him there were indeed no mountains at all, but that the end of the rocks where the llamas grazed was indeed the end of the world; thence sprang a cavernous roof of the universe, from which the dew and the avalanches fell; and

when he maintained stoutly the world had neither end nor roof such as they supposed, they said his thoughts were wicked. So far as he could describe sky and clouds and stars to them it seemed to them a hideous void, a terrible blankness in the place of the smooth roof to things in which they believed—it was an article of faith with them that the cavern roof was exquisitely smooth to the touch. He saw that in some manner he shocked them, and gave up that aspect of the matter altogether, and tried to show them the practical value of sight. One morning he saw Pedro in the path called Seventeen and coming towards the central houses, but still too far off for hearing or scent, and he told them as much. "In a little while," he prophesied, "Pedro will be here." An old man remarked that Pedro had no business on Path Seventeen, and then, as if in confirmation, that individual as he drew near turned and went transversely into Path Ten, and so back with nimble paces towards the outer wall. They mocked Nunez when Pedro did not arrive, and afterwards, when he asked Pedro questions to clear his character, Pedro denied and outfaced him, and was afterwards hostile to him.

Then he induced them to let him go a long way up the sloping   97
meadows towards the wall with one complacent individual, and to him he promised to describe all that happened among the houses. He noted certain goings and comings, but the things that really seemed to signify to these people happened inside of or behind the windowless houses—the only things they took note of to test him by—and of these he could see or tell nothing; and it was after the failure of this attempt, and the ridicule they could not repress, that he resorted to force. He thought of seizing a spade and suddenly smiting one or two of them to earth, and so in fair combat showing the advantage of eyes. He went so far with that resolution as to seize his spade, and then he discovered a new thing about himself, and that was that it was impossible for him to hit a blind man in cold blood.

He hesitated, and found them all aware that he snatched up the   98
spade. They stood alert, with their heads on one side, and bent ears towards him for what he would do next.

"Put that spade down," said one, and he felt a sort of helpless hor-   99
ror. He came near obedience.

Then he thrust one backwards against a house wall, and fled past   100
him and out of the village.

He went athwart one of their meadows, leaving a track of trampled   101
grass behind his feet, and presently sat down by the side of one of their ways. He felt something of the buoyancy that comes to all men in the beginning of a fight, but more perplexity. He began to realise that you cannot even fight happily with creatures who stand upon a different mental basis to yourself. Far away he saw a number of men carrying spades and sticks come out of the street of houses, and advance in a spreading line along the several paths towards him. They advanced

slowly, speaking frequently to one another, and ever and again the whole cordon would halt and sniff the air and listen.

102   The first time they did this Nunez laughed. But afterwards he did not laugh.

103   One struck his trail in the meadow grass, and came stooping and feeling his way along it.

104   For five minutes he watched the slow extension of the cordon, and then his vague disposition to do something forthwith became frantic. He stood up, went a pace or so towards the circumferential wall, turned, and went back a little way. There they all stood in a crescent, still and listening.

105   He also stood still, gripping his spade very tightly in both hands. Should he charge them?

106   The pulse in his ears ran into the rhythm of "In the Country of the Blind the One-eyed Man is King!"

107   Should he charge them?

108   He looked back at the high and unclimbable wall behind— unclimbable because of its smooth plastering, but withal pierced with many little doors, and at the approaching line of seekers. Behind these, others were now coming out of the street of houses.

109   Should he charge them?

110   "Bogota!" called one. "Bogota! where are you?"

111   He gripped his spade still tighter, and advanced down the meadows towards the place of habitations, and directly he moved they converged upon him. "I'll hit them if they touch me," he swore; "by Heaven, I will. I'll hit." He called aloud, "Look here, I'm going to do what I like in this valley. Do you hear? I'm going to do what I like and go where I like!"

112   They were moving in upon him quickly, groping, yet moving rapidly. It was like playing blind man's buff, with everyone blindfolded except one. "Get hold of him!" cried one. He found himself in the arc of a loose curve of pursuers. He felt suddenly he must be active and resolute.

113   "You don't understand," he cried in a voice that was meant to be great and resolute, and which broke. "You are blind, and I can see. Leave me alone!"

114   "Bogota! Put down that spade, and come off the grass!"

115   The last order, grotesque in its urban familiarity, produced a gust of anger.

116   "I'll hurt you," he said, sobbing with emotion. "By Heaven, I'll hurt you. Leave me alone!"

117   He began to run, not knowing clearly where to run. He ran from the nearest blind man, because it was a horror to hit him. He stopped, and then made a dash to escape from their closing ranks. He made for where a gap was wide, and the men on either side, with a quick percep-

tion of the approach of his paces, rushed in on one another. He sprang forward, and then saw he must be caught, and *swish!* the spade had struck. He felt the soft thud of hand and arm, and the man was down with a yell of pain, and he was through.

Through! And then he was close to the street of houses again, and blind men, whirling spades and stakes, were running with a sort of reasoned swiftness hither and thither.   118

He heard steps behind him just in time, and found a tall man rushing forward and swiping at the sound of him. He lost his nerve, hurled his spade a yard wide at his antagonist, and whirled about and fled, fairly yelling as he dodged another.   119

He was panic-stricken. He ran furiously to and fro, dodging when there was no need to dodge, and in his anxiety to see on every side of him at once, stumbling. For a moment he was down and they heard his fall. Far away in the circumferential wall a little doorway looked like heaven, and he set off in a wild rush for it. He did not even look round at his pursuers until it was gained, and he had stumbled across the bridge, clambered a little way among the rocks, to the surprise and dismay of a young llama, who went leaping out of sight, and lay down sobbing for breath.   120

And so his *coup d'état* came to an end.   121

He stayed outside the wall of the valley of the Blind for two nights   122
and days without food or shelter, and meditated upon the unexpected. During these meditations he repeated very frequently and always with a profounder note of derision the exploded proverb: "In the Country of the Blind the One-eyed Man is King." He thought chiefly of ways of fighting and conquering these people, and it grew clear that for him no practicable way was possible. He had no weapons, and now it would be hard to get one.

The canker of civilisation had got to him even in Bogota, and he   123
could not find it in himself to go down and assassinate a blind man. Of course, if he did that, he might then dictate terms on the threat of assassinating them all. But—sooner or later he must sleep!…

He tried also to find food among the pine trees, to be comfortable un- 124
der pine boughs while the frost fell at night, and—with less confidence— to catch a llama by artifice in order to try to kill it—perhaps by hammering it with a stone—and so finally, perhaps, to eat some of it. But the llamas had a doubt of him and regarded him with distrustful brown eyes, and spat when he drew near. Fear came on him the second day and fits of shivering. Finally he crawled down to the wall of the Country of the Blind and tried to make terms. He crawled along by the stream, shouting, until two blind men came out to the gate and talked to him.

"I was mad," he said. "But I was only newly made."   125

They said that was better.   126

127   He told them he was wiser now, and repented of all he had done.

128   Then he wept without intention, for he was very weak and ill now, and they took that as a favourable sign.

129   They asked him if he still thought he could "*see.*"

130   "No," he said."That was folly. The word means nothing—less than nothing!"

131   They asked him what was overhead.

132   "About ten times ten the height of a man there is a roof above the world of—of rock—and very, very smooth."... He burst again into hysterical tears. "Before you ask me any more, give me some food or I shall die."

133   He expected dire punishments, but these blind people were capable of toleration. They regarded his rebellion as but one more proof of his general idiocy and inferiority; and after they had whipped him they appointed him to do the simplest and heaviest work they had for anyone to do, and he, seeing no other way of living, did submissively what he was told.

134   He was ill for some days, and they nursed him kindly. That refined his submission. But they insisted on his lying in the dark, and that was a great misery. And blind philosophers came and talked to him of the wicked levity of his mind, and reproved him so impressively for his doubts about the lid of rock that covered their cosmic casserole that he almost doubted whether indeed he was not the victim of hallucination in not seeing it overhead.

135   So Nunez became a citizen of the Country of the Blind, and these people ceased to be a generalised people and became individualities and familiar to him, while the world beyond the mountains became more and more remote and unreal. There was Yacob, his master, a kindly man when not annoyed; there was Pedro, Yacob's nephew; and there was Medina-saroté, who was the youngest daughter of Yacob. She was little esteemed in the world of the blind, because she had a clear-cut face, and lacked that satisfying, glossy smoothness that is the blind man's ideal of feminine beauty; but Nunez thought her beautiful at first, and presently the most beautiful thing in the whole creation. Her closed eyelids were not sunken and red after the common way of the valley, but lay as though they might open again at any moment; and she had long eyelashes, which were considered a grave disfigurement. And her voice was strong, and did not satisfy the acute hearing of the valley swains. So that she had no lover.

136   There came a time when Nunez thought that, could he win her, he would be resigned to live in the valley for all the rest of his days.

137   He watched her; he sought opportunities of doing her little services, and presently he found that she observed him. Once at a rest-day gathering they sat side by side in the dim starlight, and the music was sweet. His hand came upon hers and he dared to clasp it. Then very

tenderly she returned his pressure. And one day, as they were at their meal in the darkness, he felt her hand very softly seeking him, and as it chanced the fire leaped then and he saw the tenderness of her face.

He sought to speak to her.   138

He went to her one day when she was sitting in the summer moon-   139
light spinning. The light made her a thing of silver and mystery. He sat down at her feet and told her he loved her, and told her how beautiful she seemed to him. He had a lover's voice, he spoke with a tender reverence that came near to awe, and she had never before been touched by adoration. She made him no definite answer, but it was clear his words pleased her.

After that he talked to her whenever he could make an opportu-   140
nity. The valley became the world for him, and the world beyond the mountains where men lived in sunlight seemed no more than a fairy tale he would some day pour into her ears. Very tentatively and timidly he spoke to her of sight.

Sight seemed to her the most poetical of fancies, and she listened to   141
his description of the stars and the mountains and her own sweet white-lit beauty as though it was a guilty indulgence. She did not believe, she could only half understand, but she was mysteriously delighted, and it seemed to him that she completely understood.

His love lost its awe and took courage. Presently he was for de-   142
manding her of Yacob and the elders in marriage, but she became fearful and delayed. And it was one of her elder sisters who first told Yacob that Medina-saroté and Nunez were in love.

There was from the first very great opposition to the marriage of   143
Nunez and Medina-saroté; not so much because they valued her as because they held him as a being apart, an idiot, an incompetent thing below the permissible level of a man. Her sisters opposed it bitterly as bringing discredit on them all; and old Yacob, though he had formed a sort of liking for his clumsy, obedient serf, shook his head and said the thing could not be. The young men were all angry at the idea of corrupting the race, and one went so far as to revile and strike Nunez. He struck back. Then for the first time he found an advantage in seeing, even by twilight, and after that fight was over no one was disposed to raise a hand against him. But they still found his marriage impossible.

Old Yacob had a tenderness for his last little daughter, and was   144
grieved to have her weep upon his shoulder.

"You see, my dear, he's an idiot. He has delusions; he can't do any-   145
thing right. "

"I know," wept Medina-saroté. "But he's better than he was. He's   146
getting better. And he's strong, dear father, and kind—stronger and kinder than any other man in the world. And he loves me—and, father, I love him."

147   Old Yacob was greatly distressed to find her inconsolable, and, besides—what made it more distressing—he liked Nunez for many things. So he went and sat in the windowless council-chamber with the other elders and watched the trend of the talk, and said, at the proper time, "He's better than he was. Very likely, some day, we shall find him as sane as ourselves."

148   Then afterwards one of the elders, who thought deeply, had an idea. He was the great doctor among these people, their medicine-man, and he had a very philosophical and inventive mind, and the idea of curing Nunez of his peculiarities appealed to him. One day when Yacob was present he returned to the topic of Nunez.

149   "I have examined Bogota," he said, "and the case is clearer to me. I think very probably he might be cured."

150   "That is what I have always hoped," said old Yacob.

151   "His brain is affected," said the blind doctor.

152   The elders murmured assent.

153   "Now, *what* affects it?"

154   "Ah!" said old Yacob.

155   "*This,*" said the doctor, answering his own question. "Those queer things that are called the eyes, and which exist to make an agreeable soft depression in the face, are diseased, in the case of Bogota, in such a way as to affect his brain. They are greatly distended, he has eyelashes, and his eyelids move, and consequently his brain is in a state of constant irritation and distraction."

156   "Yes?" said old Yacob. "Yes?"

157   "And I think I may say with reasonable certainty that, in order to cure him completely, all that we need do is a simple and easy surgical operation—namely, to remove these irritant bodies."

158   "And then he will be sane?"

159   "Then he will be perfectly sane, and a quite admirable citizen."

160   "Thank Heaven for science!" said old Yacob, and went forth at once to tell Nunez of his happy hopes.

161   But Nunez's manner of receiving the good news struck him as being cold and disappointing.

162   "One might think," he said, "from the tone you take, that you did not care for my daughter."

163   It was Medina-saroté who persuaded Nunez to face the blind surgeons.

164   "*You* do not want me," he said, "to lose my gift of sight?"

165   She shook her head.

166   "My world is sight."

167   Her head drooped lower.

168   "There are the beautiful things, the beautiful little things—the flowers, the lichens among the rocks, the lightness and softness on a

piece of fur, the far sky with its drifting down of clouds, the sunsets and the stars. And there is *you*. For you alone it is good to have sight, to see your sweet, serene face, your kindly lips, your dear, beautiful hands folded together.... It is these eyes of mine you won, these eyes that hold me to you, that these idiots seek. Instead, I must touch you, hear you, and never see you again. I must come under that roof of rock and stone and darkness, that horrible roof under which your imagination stoops.... No; you would not have me do that?"

A disagreeable doubt had risen in him. He stopped, and left the thing a question.   169

"I wish," she said, "sometimes—" She paused.   170

"Yes?" said he, a little apprehensively.   171

"I wish sometimes—you would not talk like that."   172

"Like what?"   173

"I know it's pretty—it's your imagination. I love it, but *now*—"   174

He felt cold. *"Now?"* he said faintly.   175

She sat quite still.   176

"You mean—you think—I should be better, better perhaps—"   177

He was realising things very swiftly. He felt anger, indeed, anger at the dull course of fate, but also sympathy for her lack of understanding—a sympathy near akin to pity.   178

"Dear," he said, and he could see by her whiteness how intensely her spirit pressed against the things she could not say. He put his arms about her, he kissed her ear, and they sat for a time in silence.   179

"If I were to consent to this?" he said at last, in a voice that was very gentle.   180

She flung her arms about him, weeping wildly. "Oh, if you would," she sobbed, "if only you would!"   181

For a week before the operation that was to raise him from the servitude and inferiority to the level of a blind citizen, Nunez knew nothing of sleep, and all through the warm sunlit hours, while the others slumbered happily, he sat brooding or wandered aimlessly, trying to bring his mind to bear on his dilemma. He had given his answer, he had given his consent, and still he was not sure. And at last work-time was over, the sun rose in splendour over the golden crests, and his last day of vision began for him. He had a few minutes with Medina-saroté before she went apart to sleep.   182

"Tomorrow," he said, "I shall see no more."   183

"Dear heart!" she answered, and pressed his hands with all her strength.   184

"They will hurt you but little," she said; "and you are going through this pain—you are going through it, dear lover, for *me*.... Dear, if a woman's heart and life can do it, I will repay you. My dearest one, my dearest with the tender voice, I will repay."   185

186   He was drenched in pity for himself and her.

187   He held her in his arms, and pressed his lips to hers, and looked on her sweet face for the last time. "Good-bye!" he whispered at that dear sight, "good-bye!"

188   And then in silence he turned away from her.

189   She could hear his slow retreating footsteps, and something in the rhythm of them threw her into a passion of weeping.

190   He had fully meant to go to a lonely place where the meadows were beautiful with white narcissus, and there remain until the hour of his sacrifice should come, but as he went he lifted up his eyes and saw the morning, the morning like an angel in golden armour, marching down the steeps....

191   It seemed to him that before this splendour he, and this blind world in the valley, and his love, and all, were no more than a pit of sin.

192   He did not turn aside as he had meant to do, but went on, and passed through the wall of the circumference and out upon the rocks, and his eyes were always upon the sunlit ice and snow.

193   He saw their infinite beauty, and his imagination soared over them to the things beyond he was now to resign for ever.

194   He thought of that great free world he was parted from, the world that was his own, and he had a vision of those further slopes, distance beyond distance, with Bogota, a place of multitudinous stirring beauty, a glory by day, a luminous mystery by night, a place of palaces and fountains and statues and white houses, lying beautifully in the middle distance. He thought how for a day or so one might come down through passes, drawing ever nearer and nearer to its busy streets and ways. He thought of the river journey, day by day, from great Bogota to the still vaster world beyond, through towns and villages, forest and desert places, the rushing river day by day, until its banks receded and the big steamers came splashing by, and one had reached the sea—the limitless sea, with its thousand islands, its thousands of islands, and its ships seen dimly far away in their incessant journeyings round and about that greater world. And there, unpent by mountains, one saw the sky—the sky, not such a disc as one saw it here, but an arch of immeasurable blue, a deep of deeps in which the circling stars were floating....

195   His eyes scrutinised the great curtain of the mountains with a keener inquiry.

196   For example, if one went so, up that gully and to that chimney there, then one might come out high among those stunted pines that ran round in a sort of shelf and rose still higher and higher as it passed above the gorge. And then? That talus might be managed. Thence perhaps a climb might be found to take him up to the precipice that came below the snow; and if that chimney failed, then another farther to the east might serve his purpose better. And then? Then one would be out upon the amber-lit snow there, and halfway up to the crest of those beautiful desolations.

He glanced back at the village, then turned right round and re-   197
garded it steadfastly.

He thought of Medina-saroté, and she had become small and   198
remote.

He turned again towards the mountain wall, down which the day   199
had come to him.

Then very circumspectly he began to climb.   200

When sunset came he was no longer climbing, but he was far and   201
high. He had been higher, but he was still very high. His clothes were
torn, his limbs were blood-stained, he was bruised in many places, but
he lay as if he were at his ease, and there was a smile on his face.

From where he rested the valley seemed as if it were in a pit and   202
nearly a mile below. Already it was dim with haze and shadow, though
the mountain summits around him were things of light and fire. The little details of the rocks near at hand were drenched with subtle beauty—
a vein of green mineral piercing the grey, the flash of crystal faces here
and there, a minute, minutely beautiful orange lichen close beside his
face. There were deep mysterious shadows in the gorge, blue deepening into purple, and purple into a luminous darkness, and overhead
was the illimitable vastness of the sky. But he heeded these things no
longer, but lay quite inactive there, smiling as if he were satisfied
merely to have escaped from the valley of the Blind in which he had
thought to be King.

The glow of the sunset passed, and the night came, and still he lay   203
peacefully contented under the cold stars.

✧ *Evaluating the Text*

1. Nunez and the community he has come upon perceive each other in
   diametrically opposite ways. What expectations shape the view each
   has of the other?

2. The choice Nunez ultimately confronts is one that requires him to decide what is most important to him. In your opinion, what explains his
   final decision?

3. In what ways has Wells followed through on the premise of this story in
   almost every conceivable detail of the environment? Discuss the values
   and beliefs of the inhabitants as they have evolved over generations.

✧ *Exploring Different Perspectives*

1. In what sense do Nunez and David R. Counts (in "Too Many Bananas") have to rethink their basic assumptions about what is normal?

2. Part of the poignancy of this story is due to the situation of the main character, Nunez, who is faced with a no-win situation. Compare this to the similar no-win predicament portrayed by Gloria Anzaldúa in her story "Cervicide."

✧ Extending Viewpoints through Writing

1. Nunez's situation is analogous to predicaments confronting those who find themselves in coercive political or social environments. Describe an example of this from your own experiences, where it would have been unwise to attempt to convince others of the opposite of what they believed. How is this premise used as a basis for Plato's classic "The Allegory of the Cave"?

2. If you were faced with the choice Nunez confronts, what would you have done? Which of your senses, if any, would you be willing to give up to ensure being with the person you loved?

Connecting Cultures

---◆---

Claire S. Chow, "Ethnicity and Identity: Creating a Sense of Self"

Compare the ways in which Judith Ortiz Cofer (in "The Myth of the Latin Woman" in Chapter 3) and any of the women interviewed by Chow have learned to cope with being stereotyped.

Luis Alberto Urrea, "Border Story"

Compare and contrast the reactions of the protagonists to the horrifying conditions in Tijuana and Medellín (see Alonso Salazar's "The Lords of Creations" in Chapter 5).

Gloria Anzaldúa, "Cervicide"

How do the stories by Anzaldúa and Mahdokht Kashkuli (see "The Button" in Chapter 5) dramatize the predicament of families faced with dehumanizing choices?

Jesse W. Nash, "Confucius and the VCR"

How is the conflict between the Asian emphasis on respect for parents and the American desire for independence an important theme in Nash's article and in Kazuo Ishiguro's story "Family Supper" in Chapter 1?

Palden Gyatso, "Autobiography of a Tibetan Monk"

Compare the overlapping perspectives of Gyatso and of Rae Yang (see "At the Center of the Storm" in Chapter 6) on Chinese Communism.

David R. Counts, "Too Many Bananas"

In what sense is the way that the bureaucracy operates shelters for the homeless, as described by Lee Stringer in "Life on the Street" in Chapter 5, similar to the way things operate in New Guinea, according to Counts?

H. G. Wells, "The Country of the Blind"

In what way is Ngũgĩ wa Thiong'o's experiences with the repression of language in Kenya (see "Decolonising the Mind" in Chapter 6) similar to the character Nunez's fictional situation in H. G. Wells's story?

8

Customs, Rituals, and Sports

◆

In the customs, rituals, and sports that a society embraces, we can see most clearly the hidden cultural logic and unconscious assumptions that people in the society rely on to interpret everything that goes on in their world. Customs, rituals, and even sports that may seem bizarre or strange to an outsider appear entirely normal and natural to those within the culture. Unfortunately, the potential for conflict exists as soon as people from different cultures whose "natural" ways do not coincide make contact with each other.

As communications, emigration, and travel make the world smaller, the potential for cross-cultural misunderstanding accelerates. Correspondingly, the need grows to become aware of the extent to which our own and other people's conclusions about the world are guided by different cultural presuppositions. Analysis of the customs of cultures other than our own allows us to temporarily put aside our taken-for-granted ways of seeing the world, even if we are normally unaware of the extent to which we rely on these implicit premises—to understand that the meanings we give to events, actions, and statements are not their only possible meanings.

The range and diversity of the selections in this chapter allow you to temporarily replace your own way of perceiving the world and become aware, perhaps for the first time, of the cultural assumptions that govern your interpretations of the world.

What to some would be a shocking and callous attitude toward animals is, explains Guanlong Cao, in "The Culture of Killing," an integral and much desired feature of cooking in China. The cultural value placed on having good teeth in America provided Slavenka Drakulić (as told in "On Bad Teeth") with the means to understand crucial differences between Americans and her fellow East Europeans. Based on real events, "Looking for a Rain God" by Bessie Head tells how a family in drought-plagued Botswana came to sacrifice their children in exchange for rain. Gino Del Guercio's "The Secrets of Haiti's Living Dead" reveals that, in contrast to its stereotyped image, voodoo is part of a cohesive system of social control in Haiti. The Egyptian writer Nabil Gorgy, in "Cairo Is a Small City," tells how a ruthless engineer is held accountable to the traditional Bedouin concept of justice in modern-day Egypt. Octavio Paz, in "Fiesta," explores the important role that fiestas play in Mexican culture and their relationship to the Mexican national character. Finally, the unusual sport of stone lifting provides a window into the self-sufficient, rugged way of life that defines Basque culture in the essay by Tad Friend.

Guanlong Cao

The Culture of Killing

———————◆———————

Guanlong Cao was born in Shanghai Province, China. Under communist rule, his family lost all their possessions and all six of them were forced to live in a small attic over a button factory in Shanghai. Cao's thinly fictionalized account of his life from the 1950s through the 1970s is told in his award-winning book The Attic: Memoirs of a Chinese Landlord's Son, *translated by Cao and Nancy Moskin (1996), from which the following chapter is drawn. Cao emigrated to the United States in 1987, attended Middlebury College as a 42-year-old undergraduate, and obtained a Master of Fine Arts degree from the School of the Museum of Fine Arts at Tufts University. His artwork includes sculpture, photographs, paintings, and prints. In "The Culture of Killing," Cao appears to be regaling the reader with a shocking series of recipes, but the subtext alludes to the repression and pain he and his family experienced.*

1   Ever since I was quite young, I have heard and seen a colorful panoply of killing. Compared with the rich and profound techniques developed for killing *Homo sapiens* in ancient and contemporary China, my experiences are trivial and insignificant. But I still want to record them in this small book to make my humble contribution to the brilliance of Chinese civilization.

2   There are two methods of preparing eels for cooking. If the eels are thick, they are usually deboned alive. Eels are very slimy, so the amateur has difficulty with the job. But in the hands of the expert they meet a quick end.

3   The eel is clamped by the left hand, with the middle finger above and the index and ring fingers below. An awl pins the eel's head to the board below. A long stroke of the right hand smoothes the writhing eel. Simultaneously, a razor held between thumb and index finger of the right hand cleanly fillets the left side from neck to tail. Another slash of the razor, and the eel is left a whip of white bones. The mouth still gently spills bloody foam.

4   The meat from eels that are butchered alive is tender. In most cases, however, eels are given a hot shower before they are prepared. The eel vendor does not provide his own boiling water. Hot water shops are

---

*For information on China, see p. 57.

commonly built adjacent to a marketplace. The vendor carries a half-bucket of eels to the hot water shop and places it under the tap.

"Is the water ready?" he asks.   5

The operator of the boiler nods his head.   6

With a yank, the vendor opens the tap and a thick column of   7
steaming water pours into the bucket.

All the eels get excited.   8

The wooden bucket is well designed, with a wide bottom and a   9
small mouth—no eel is able to jump out. The eel carnival lasts only a
few seconds; then the commotion subsides. A mound of foam lingers
on the rim like the head on draft beer.

There are also two ways to terminate rabbits. For the common rab-   10
bit, simply grab its hind legs and, with a quick swing, hit its head on a
cement floor. But the long-haired rabbit requires special treatment.

Long-haired rabbits are used for fur. The furrier usually checks the   11
quality of the pelt by grasping the hairs between his fingers and comb-
ing through them. The fewer hairs that are shed, the better the fur. The
following procedure is specifically designed to strengthen the adher-
ence of the hair to the skin.

A steel bar, one inch thick, a foot and a half long, is prepared. One   12
end is filed smooth and round, the other end is fixed in a wooden handle. The bar is heated on a stove. When it glows red, the rabbit is taken
out of its cage and put on the table. The furrier caresses the rabbit's
back. Feeling soothed and comfortable, the rabbit lifts its tail. At the
split second the anus is exposed, the bar is plunged in. The rabbit's
mouth opens. Before a sound can escape, the poker protrudes from between its teeth. The unique stimulation makes every pore contract,
clutching each hair in a death grip.

I never saw with my own eyes a banquet where they served White   13
Jade of the Golden Monkey. I read about it in a musty antique recipe at
the book flea market near the Temple of Letters. Under the title there
was a line drawing, in characteristically warped perspective, depicting
the construction of a special table.

The table was built in two halves with a hole in the middle. The head 14
of the monkey emerged through the hole, with its neck clamped by the
two sides. It could breathe, but it could not retract its head. A couple of
bars were installed beneath the table, as a perch for the sacrifice.

It was the exotic illustration that held me. Confronting the brain-   15
wrenching classical Chinese, I squatted at the stall. Retrieving all the
rusty vocabulary that my mother had stuffed into my head from the
"Imperial Essays," I eventually deciphered the recipe.

First, the book instructed, the guests must bathe in water infused   16
with jasmine petals. The tableware and utensils had to be fashioned of
pure silver. I remember a line of the recipe that read:

Only with clear mind, only with pure silver, can the soul of the monkey be adopted into thy heart.

17   When the monkey was in position, a ladleful of hot oil was sprinkled on its head. The hair was thereby loosened and easy to pull out. Care had to be taken when pouring the oil so as not to burn the ears and eyes of the monkey. The book decreed:

The ears and eyes of the golden monkey are portals. The spirit of heaven and earth enter through them, and in the brain foregather. No damage should be done.

18   The dehairing could be assigned to an assistant, but the breaking of the skull had to be performed by an expert. The monkey's head was struck with a silver hammer. The force had to be precise. If the blow was too gentle, the skull would remain intact. If it was too strong, the monkey would be knocked out, or even worse, the "white jade" under the scalp might be smashed.

19   When the skull was broken, the shards were carefully picked out with silver tweezers. Then the membrane had to be peeled off. Extreme caution had to be taken—the membrane was tightly wrapped around the brain. If the brain was accidentally broken, the juices would escape. That was called "leaking the heavenly secret" and meant the dish was ruined. When the membrane had been removed, the "white jade" was presented to the distinguished guests.

20   At this point, the monkey was still conscious. Its eyes glittered, looking around at all the guests. The diners, in contrast, closed their eyes in meditation, waiting for the most sacred moment—"jade breaking." (I believe the term had been appropriated from classical novels where it suggested the taking of a maiden's virginity.)

21   Breaking the "jade" was a great honor, and the ritual was performed by the oldest or highest-ranking guest. The spoon designed for jade breaking was very small, only the size of a peanut shell, but the handle was twice as long as a regular spoon's.

22   The honored guest slowly extended the spoon toward the "jade." A slight tap, and the brain oozed out.

23   He scooped a half spoonful of "jade" and solemnly brought it to his lips. Closing his eyes, he savored the taste from the tip of his tongue to the back of his palate. Then he emitted a long sigh. He opened his eyes, his pupils shining. He looked around at everyone gathered at the table.

24   A hubbub arose.

25   Starting from the jade-breaker and moving around the table from east to west, the guests tasted the delicacy, one by one. The sequence from east to west was crucial. If the direction of rotation was incorrect, the energy of the universe would turn into evil fire, driving the diners insane. Weird as it sounds, modern medicine recognizes a similar

pathological condition in New Guinea called laughing disease, or kuru. It results from eating raw, infected brains.

Small world.   26

Live Fish Feast is a famous dish in Nanjing, the former capital of   27
the Nationalist government. The only people who can afford to consume it are senior leaders or foreign guests. It is not that the fish is rare;
any freshwater fish such as carp or trout is good enough. Rather, it is
the involved cooking process that makes the feast a lofty endeavor. In
all of Nanjing, only two or three chefs are qualified to prepare the dish.

In February 1972 President Nixon visited China. At a press confer-   28
ence in Shanghai, a reporter in his entourage abruptly asked an out-of-
the-blue question:

"Is Live Fish Feast considered a remnant of the old society?"   29

Perhaps he was just trying to show off the knowledge he had   30
gleaned from a dust-covered book the night before he left for his assignment. But the Chinese government took it very seriously. The Foreign Ministry dispatched a chef by helicopter from Nanjing to
Shanghai. In the Foreign Guest House restaurant, the chef demonstrated Live Fish Feast.

The Central Documentary Movie Company shot the whole proce-   31
dure in color. The film was distributed worldwide to prove that, in the
midst of the Cultural Revolution, China still took good care of its cultural traditions.

The movie began with a close-up of a fish tank. A few plump carp   32
swam gracefully in the water. Then the lens tilted up and a chef approached the tank. With a big smile, he stuck his hand into the water
and pulled out a carp.

Close-up: the fish flapped its tail, splashing drops of water.   33

Fade-in: the kitchen. A smoking pot of oil on the stove. The chef   ?4
swiftly scaled and gutted the fish. Inserting two fingers into the gills, he
dipped the body of the fish into the hot oil. The whole movie theater vi-
brated with the sound of sizzling oil, 120 decibels, fully expressing the
intensity of the heat. The fish's head remained suspended by the chef,
one inch above the surface of the oil. The gills still pulsed in the smoke.

The deep frying took only two or three seconds. Then with a flour-   35
ish, the fish was flung onto a white, oval platter.

The complicated sauce was prepared well in advance: dried lilly   36
flower, wood ear fungus, wild mushrooms, shrimp extract, sesame oil,
coriander, ginger, garlic, and more. One flash of the ladle and the whole
fish was colorfully dressed.

A long pan shot brought the carp to the table.   37

A round of cheers was followed by an air raid of chopsticks.   38

Close-up: the body of the fish had already become a skeleton, but   39
the head remained fresh. The eyes still sparkled. The mouth still
murmured....

40   There are virtually no taboos in the gamut of Chinese food. Almost anything can be turned into a delicacy. Of things with two wings, airplanes are the only exception. Of things with four legs, only benches are pardoned. Not only do we eat anything, but we eat it with a unique twist. The consumption of two kinds of birds provides examples.

41   Deep-fried sparrow is a popular game dish. It's not difficult to catch sparrows. In the evening, when the sparrows have gone to roost in the shrubs, large nets are hung in front of the bushes. Then, behind the nests, a gong is suddenly beaten. The startled sparrows fly out and crash into the net. With their wings entangled in the threads, they can easily be picked out, one by one.

42   The tricky part is getting rid of the feathers.

43   Sparrows have fragile skin. If the bird is plucked after it is dead, the skin will come off with the feathers. Sparrows are small to begin with; if you lose the skin how much is left? So sparrows are usually plucked alive.

44   Defeathering live sparrows is labor intensive. But at least their cheeping and the constant fluttering of their wings in your hands relieve some of the monotony.

45   I remember when I was a sixth grader, one of the third-place winners of the annual Grammar School Invention Contest was a classmate of mine. I no longer can recall his proper name, but everyone called him Black Skin. Black Skin's invention was the Easy Pigeon Terminator.

46   It was a citywide contest, so winning third place was a big honor. Proudly, the school officials called a grand assembly for Black Skin to lecture on his invention.

47   Black Skin said his father was a chef in a game restaurant, and red-cooked (stewed in soy sauce) pigeon was one of his specialties. Black Skin told us that his father had once asked him to help kill pigeons. Black Skin Sr. told Black Skin Jr., and Black Skin Jr. told us, that the pigeons were not supposed to be killed with a knife. If the blood drained out, the meat would taste dry and tough.

48   Black Skin took a live pigeon from a bamboo cage under the podium and started his demonstration. First he showed us the traditional method. He held the bird in his left hand. With his right thumb and index finger, he tightly covered the two breathing holes above the beak. The pigeon began to struggle. The spasms gradually subsided. Black Skin released his fingers, and the pigeon revived.

49   Black Skin said you had to cut off the bird's air supply for at least five minutes to finish it. The day he worked for his father, Black Skin killed twenty pigeons in a row. His fingers became flattened and trembled for two days. The tedious work inspired his invention.

50   Then Black Skin showed us his award-winning machine. The Easy Pigeon Terminator was definitely easy to use. It consisted of two clips linked together. One clip held the beak from above and below. The

other clamped the air holes from left and right. The ends of the clips were rubber-tipped to better seal out the air.

Black Skin plugged the pigeon into his device and tossed it onto the stage. Flapping its wings, the pigeon tried to take off, but the clips were attached to a cast-iron block. So, dragging its head, the bird performed a bizarre dance on the stage.   51

Finally it calmed down.   52

This time Black Skin did not let it revive.   53

There is a famous dish in Yunnan Province called Baby Mice.   54

Keep a cage full of female mice, mate them to a male mouse, and a   55
continuous supply of baby mice is guaranteed. A baby mouse is only as big as the last segment of your little finger. Pink. No hair.

One serving of Baby Mice consists of four infants. The squirming ba- 56
bies are put in a small gilded-porcelain dish and brought to the table. Simultaneously, a dish of sauce is served: mustard, wild pepper, soy sauce, sesame oil, white vinegar, brown sugar, and so on. The list of ingredients is complex, and every restaurant has its own secret recipe. But eating the baby mice is always simple. You just pick one up with pointed, ivory chopsticks and drop it in the sauce. It rolls and wiggles, coating its body with all the spices. Then you pick it up again, and pop it in your mouth.

Chew and chew.   57

While Baby Mice describes one dish's contents, the meaning of   58
Purple Strips is difficult to guess. Purple Strips was a therapeutic food in Guangxi Province, which borders Vietnam. The primary ingredient was a young cow, around one year old, having just reached puberty but not yet been mated.

The young cow was led to the edge of a pond. The pond appeared   59
quite ordinary, just a regular fish pond. But there were no fish in it. Instead, in the mud under the water, millions of leeches lay in ambush.

Instinctually the cow felt that something was wrong. She kicked   60
her hind legs and tried to retreat. But she could not withstand the whips laid across her buttocks for long, and gradually she waded into the water. The army of leeches that had been waiting impatiently in the mud swarmed out and latched onto every part of the cow.

In five or six minutes, the owner dragged the cow back out of the   61
water. Her whole body was covered with leeches. With a thin, bamboo blade, he scraped the already engorged leeches into a wooden bucket.

Though he did not wear a watch, the owner had to have a good   62
sense of timing. If the session was too short, the leeches would not have siphoned enough blood. If it was too long, they would have sucked their fill and contentedly fallen off into the water.

After the first leech harvest was complete, the owner drove the   63
cow back into the pond. The process was repeated again and again.

As the volume of leeches in the bucket increased, the cow's blood   64
was being draining away. Eventually, the owner led the withered cow

to the butcher shop where she was slaughtered. The womb was saved for later use.

65   The leeches had enjoyed their warm blood banquet for some time; now it was their turn to contribute. When a cauldron of water reached a rolling boil, the leeches were dumped in. They were instantly scooped out and chilled in cold water. Once removed from their cold bath, they were spread on a wide bamboo sieve to drain. Women sitting around the sieve slit each leech lengthwise with sharp, pointed blades and turned it inside out. Then they picked out a coagulated cow's blood strip with the tip of their knife and dropped it into an iced jar where it was reserved.

66   Traditional Chinese medical theory assumes that a woman's infertility is the result of low *chi*, or energy, in the blood. Cow's blood can aid the *chi*, but it is too hot. Taken directly, the heat can linger in the woman's body for many months, leading to prolonged bleeding after she gives birth. Leeches, residing in mud at the bottom of brooks or ponds, have a *yin*, or cool, nature. Once the cow's blood is sucked by the leeches, the *yang* of the blood is instantly balanced by the *yin* of the leeches. The heat is significantly quenched, yet the energy remains. Hence, the miraculous, therapeutic effect of Purple Strips, which enhances the blood energy in a cool fashion.

67   Even better, the spirit of the leeches can contribute their unique elasticity to the woman and help her withstand intense expansions and contractions during her long labor.

68   Yet a dose of Purple Strips was extremely expensive. Ordinary women from farmers' families dared not even think of it. Only a few ladies from aristocratic families could afford the cure.

69   To prepare a proper dose, the cow's womb was thinly sliced. Accompanied by wild ginseng, yellow angelica, black longans, red dates, shark fins, and swallows' nests, the womb soup was simmered all night. The Purple Strips were not removed from the iced jar until the moment of serving. They were submerged in the simmering broth, and almost immediately the pot was removed from the stove. Never overcook the Purple Strips. Even a few seconds' delay will totally ruin the treasure—the active energy, stored in the blood, will shrivel and die out.

70   While surveying or studying primitive cultures of the past and present, it is not unusual for archaeologists or anthropologists to bump into isolated achievements so advanced that no satisfactory explanation can be made for their origins. The Red Petals described below serves as an example.

71   Like many Asian ethnic groups, villagers living in the cloud-shrouded Daliang Mountains in the deep south of Sichuan Province were fond of dog meat. It was their unique slaughtering process, however, that earned the esteemed reputation of their Red Petals dog meat.

As with Purple Strips, Red Petals derived its name from blood—in   72
this case, dog's blood. Dog's blood is even hotter than cow's blood;
consuming it will give the eater an instant nosebleed. The only use for
dog's blood was to splash it on an enemy's statue in a ritual curse before a tribal fight—to burn the evil to death. Since such rituals were not
a frequent practice, most of the blood had to be discarded.

But blood is the stream that carries nutrition, and it is a shame to   73
throw out the baby with the bath water. Some researchers have therefore assumed that the unique slaughtering process used to produce
Red Petals dog meat was developed to save the nutrition while dispos-
ing of the waste.

Two sticks were employed in the procedure. One stick stretched   74
the dog's forelegs wide open; the other stretched the hindlegs. In this
cruciform position, the dog was skinned alive. Then the dog was released from the sticks and allowed to roam freely in the enclosed pit of
the slaughterhouse.

The naked dog wouldn't bark. Like a drunk, he slowly and quietly   75
walked around the pit, one circle after another. His staring white eyeballs never blinked—there was nothing to blink with. Blood was seep-
ing out from his exposed muscles, dripping along his staggering legs.
Red petals were blooming under his paws. It took at least ten minutes
before the dog finally collapsed.

There is a significant difference between the conventional throat-   76
slashing slaughtering and the flaying-alive process. In the first practice,
all the nutrition is flushed away with the blood through the cut artery.
But in the latter method, the blood is forced to sieve through all the
capillaries while the nutrition carried by the warm liquid is filtered and
reserved by the billions of cells of the dog's flesh.

✧ Evaluating the Text

1. According to Cao, Chinese culture has evolved an unusual philosophy,
   and a number of accompanying techniques, regarding what can be
   eaten and how it should be cooked. What is this philosophy and what
   objectives underlie the variety of preparations?

2. What is Cao's attitude toward the cultural practices he describes? Do
   you get a sense that he is drawing an equivalence between culinary rituals and politics? Explain your answer.

3. Part of the unique effect of this piece is directly due to the tone Cao
   adopts. How would you characterize the voice you hear, his attitude
   toward the subject, and the impression he wishes to leave with the
   reader?

✧ *Exploring Different Perspectives*

1. Discuss how the pursuit of magical objectives leads to a trangression of normal boundaries in both Cao's account and in Bessie Head's story "Looking for a Rain God."

2. Compare the unusual dishes with strange ingredients designed to have magical effects described by Cao and Gino Del Guercio in "The Secrets of Haiti's Living Dead."

✧ *Extending Viewpoints through Writing*

1. The Chinese attitude toward what can be eaten and how it should be prepared differs markedly from American culinary norms. In an essay, discuss the paradox of a highly civilized culture that views such practices as the epitome of sophisticated dining.

2. What cultural values, folk superstitions and beliefs (such as the existence of energy, or *chi,* and the balance of yin and yang) might help explain the emphasis on eating animals that are as close to being alive as possible?

Slavenka Drakulić

On Bad Teeth

---◆---

Slavenka Drakulić is a leading Croatian journalist and novelist. Her insightful commentary on East European affairs first appeared in her columns in the magazine Danas, *published in Zagreb. She is a regular contributor to* The Nation, The New Republic, *and* The New York Times Magazine. *Her novel,* Holograms of Fear *(1992) received the Independent Foreign Fiction Award. Her nonfiction works include* How We Survived Communism and Even Laughed *(1992) and* Balkan Express: Fragments from the Other Side of War *(1993) and have been translated into eleven languages. "On Bad Teeth" is drawn from her chronicle of obvious and less obvious aspects of daily life under communism in the country formerly known as Yugoslavia. This essay first appeared in* Cafe Europa: Life After Communism *(1996).*

Croatia is about the size of West Virginia and is situated along the eastern coast of the Adriatic Sea, extending inland to the slopes of the Julian Alps in Slovenia and into the Pannonian Valley to the banks of the Drava and Danube rivers. The capital, Zagreb, lies on the Sava River, and many famous cities, including the medieval port of Dubrovnik, are found along the extended coastline. Although Slavs began settling the Balkan peninsula as early as the sixth century A.D., Croatians were first united into a single state by King Tomislav in 925. The Croats accepted Roman Catholicism in the eleventh century, and by the 1500s, Croatia and Hungary became part of the Hapsburg Empire. In 1914 the assassination of Austria's crown prince in Sarajevo (Bosnia) embroiled the entire Balkans into World War I. For decades, Croatia was part of Yugoslavia under the socialist federation led by Josip Broz Tito. When Tito died in 1980, his authority was transferred to a collective state presidency, which had a rotating chairman. With the fall of communism and the weakening of the federation, Yugoslavia declared its independence in June 1991 and was recognized by the international community in January 1992. Opposition from the Yugoslav Army and the Serbian government, which strongly opposed independence, led to fierce fighting and the destruction of entire cities, which created a serious refugee problem. Various cease-fires brokered by the United Nations produced an uneasy peace that did not last long, as fighting between the Croats, Serbs, and Muslims broke out again in 1993. Additionally, Croatian irregulars became involved in the more serious civil war in Bosnia–Hercegovina. The most recent president of Croatia was Franjo Tudjman. United Nations peacekeeping forces played an active role in creating circumstances under which elections could take place in 1996. In 1997 Tudjman was reelected to a second five-year term. Tudjman died in December 1999.

1   In a way, I was initiated into capitalism through toothpaste.

2   When I first visited the States in 1983, I loved to watch TV commercials. This is when I noticed that Americans were obsessed by their teeth. Every second commercial seemed to be for a toothpaste. Where I come from, toothpaste is toothpaste. I couldn't believe there were so many different kinds. What were they all *for*? After all the purpose of it is just to clean your teeth. In my childhood there were two kinds, mint flavour and strawberry flavour, and both of them had the same brand name, Kalodont. For a long time I was convinced that Kalodont was the word for toothpaste, because nobody at home used the generic word. We never said, "Do you have toothpaste?" we said, "Do you have Kalodont?" It is hardly surprising, then, that such a person would react with nothing short of disbelief when faced with the American cosmetic (or is it pharmaceutical?) industry and its endless production line. Toothpaste with or without sugar, with or without flour, with or without baking soda, calcium, vitamins....

3   Over the years, on subsequent visits I continued to be fascinated by this American obsession with toothpaste, from the common varieties all the way up to Rembrandt, the most snobbish brand, if there could be such a thing as snobbishness about toothpaste. I soon learned that there could: in one women's magazine I saw it recommended as a Christmas present! Needless to say, in every commercial for toothpaste at least one bright, impressively beautiful set of teeth flashes across the screen, but this image is not confined to selling toothpaste. As we all know, beautiful teeth are used to advertise beer, hair shampoo, cars, anything. Indeed, they are an indispensable feature of any American advertisement. The foreigner soon learns that they stand not only as a symbol for both good looks and good health, but for something else as well.

4   If you think that such advertising might be part of the Americans' national obsession with health in general, you are not far from the truth. Americans seem to be passionate about their health and their looks, which appear to be interchangeable qualities. Health and good looks are essential badges of status among the middle classes. Nothing but narcissism, you could retort, but it is more than that. This connection between teeth and social status is not so evident to an Eastern European. I personally had some doubts about those TV teeth, I thought that they must be artificial, some kind of prosthesis made out of plastic or porcelain. They were just too good to be true. How could people have such fine teeth? Intrigued, I decided to take a good look around me.

I noticed that the people I met, that is mostly middle-class urban 5
professionals, generally, do have a set of bright, white teeth of their
own, not unlike the TV teeth. It was even more surprising to me that I
could detect no cavities, no missing teeth, no imperfections. I was astonished. The secret was revealed to me when a friend took her son to
the dentist. When they returned, the little boy's upper teeth were fixed
with a dreadful-looking kind of iron muzzle: a brace, I learned. It was
obviously painful for him. "Poor little thing!" I exclaimed, but his
mother showed no mercy. Moreover, she was proud that she could afford this torture device. I was puzzled. When she explained to me that
the brace cost between $2,000 and $3,000, her attitude seemed even
more sinister. I eventually realised that the mystery of beautiful teeth is
not only about hygiene, but about money. She had money enough to get
her son's teeth fixed, and the little boy was brave enough to stand the
pain, because somehow he understood that this was a requirement of
his social status. All the other boys from his private school had braces,
too. He was going to grow up being well aware of the fact that his
healthy, beautiful teeth were expensive and, therefore, an indication of
prestige. Moreover, his mother could count on him to brush them three
times a day, with an electric toothbrush and the latest toothpaste promising even healthier and more beautiful teeth, as if that were possible. In
the long run, all the discomfort would be worth it.

Seeing the boy's brace, the connection between health and wealth 6
in America became a bit clearer to me. Clean, healthy teeth feature so
much in advertising because Americans have no free dental care, and
neither is it covered by any medical insurance. Therefore, if you invest
money and educate your child early enough (a bit of suffering is
needed, too), you will save a lot later. But how much money did this
take? I got my answer when I had to visit a dentist myself. On one of
my last visits my filling fell out, and just to have it refilled with some
temporary white stuff, whatever it was, I had to pay $100. This would
be a minor financial catastrophe for any Eastern European citizen used
to free dental care in his own country; it was expensive even by American standards. Only then did I become fully aware of what it means
not to have free dental care.

Predictably enough, I was outraged. How was it possible for dental 7
work to be so expensive in this country? For $100 back home I could
have coated my tooth in pure gold! And why was it that such an affluent country did not provide its citizens with basic services like free
dental work? This was one of the very few areas in which we from
former communist countries had some advantage over Americans—
and we would like to keep it.

On my way home, I thought what a blessing it was that we did not 8
have to worry about our teeth, or about whether we could afford to look

after them—or at least, we did not have to worry yet, in my country, anyway. However, immediately upon my arrival in Zagreb, I realized that I could allow myself such rose-tinted thoughts only as long as I was on the other side of the Atlantic, from where everything at home looked a bit blurred, especially the general state of people's teeth. Back at home, I was forced to adjust my view. It was as if I had been myopic before and now I had got the right pair of glasses and could finally see properly. And what I saw did not please me at all.

9   On the bus from the airport I met one of my acquaintances, a young television reporter. For the first time I noticed that half of his teeth were missing and that those which remained looked like the ruins of a decayed medieval town. I had known this guy for years, but I had never thought about the state of the inside of his mouth before, or if I had, I'd considered it totally unimportant. Now I also noticed that, in order to hide his bad teeth, he had grown a moustache and developed a way of laughing which didn't involve him opening his mouth too wide. Even so, his bad teeth were still obvious.

10   This encounter did not cheer me up. Sitting next to the young reporter, I wondered how he managed to speak in front of a TV camera without making a mistake that would reveal his terrible secret. Without smiling, perhaps? This would be perfectly acceptable, because he reports on the war, but wasn't he tired of this uncomfortable game of hide-and-seek? Wouldn't it be much more professional and make life easier if he visited a good dentist and got it all over with? But this is not something we are supposed to talk about. How do you say such a thing to a person if he is not your intimate friend? You can't just say, "Listen, why don't you do something about your teeth?" Perhaps I should have pulled out my toothpaste and handed it to him, or casually dropped the name of my dentist, something like what my friend did last summer. A woman standing next to her in a streetcar emanated an extremely unpleasant odour from her hairy armpits. My friend could not stand it. She pulled her own deodorant stick out of her handbag and gave it to the woman. The funny thing is that the woman accepted it without taking offence. I, on the other hand, could not risk offending my acquaintance.

11   I continued my investigations at home. Yes, I admit that I looked into the mouths of friends, relatives, acquaintances, neighbours—I could not help it. I discovered that the whole nation had bad teeth, it was just that I had not been able to see it before. I concluded that the guy on the bus was only a part of the general landscape, that he was no exception, and that therefore his failure to attend to his teeth was perfectly normal. I tried to explain this attitude to myself: perhaps people were afraid of drilling? Of course. Who isn't? But if nothing else, there must be an aesthetic drive in every human being, or one would at least think so. Yet, for some reason, aesthetics and communism don't go well

together and though we might call our current state post-communism, we still have a communist attitude in such matters.

You could also argue that dentists, being employed by the state, are   12
not well paid. Consequently, they don't put much effort into their job. You can claim as well that the materials they use are not of good quality. That is all probably true. But, I still believe that having your teeth repaired to a mediocre standard is preferable to treasuring the medieval ruins in your mouth or being toothless altogether.

There is no excuse that sounds reasonable enough for such negli-   13
gence. The problem is that the condition of your teeth in Eastern Europe is regarded as a highly personal matter, not a sign of your standard of living or a question for public discussion. Having good teeth is simply a matter of being civilised and well mannered. Strangely enough, however, dirty shoes, dirty fingernails or dandruff are no longer tolerated: these are considered impolite, even offensive. Yet like such matters of personal hygiene, good teeth are not only a question of money. Dental work has been free for the last forty years. At present there co-exists a mixture of both state-run general medical care, which includes dental care, and private dentists. If you want, you can have excellent dental work done. I know people who travel from Vienna to Bratislava, Budapest, Ljubljana or Zagreb to have their teeth repaired more cheaply. But if you asked people in Eastern Europe who can afford it why they don't go to a private dentist for a better service, they would probably tell you that this is not their priority at the moment. Instead they want to fix their car, or buy a new carpet.

It is clear that leaders and intellectuals here certainly don't care   14
about such a minor aspect of their image. They are preoccupied with the destiny of their respective nations, they do not have time for such trivial matters. The American idea that it is not very polite for a public figure to appear with bad teeth, just as it would be inappropriate to make a speech in your pyjamas, is not understood here. You can meet exquisitely dressed politicians or businessmen, but wait until they open their mouths! If these public figures are not worried about this aspect of their looks, why should ordinary people be concerned about theirs? They too have more important things to do, for example surviving. There is also that new breed, the *nouveau riche* of post-communism. Previously everything was valued by one's participation in politics; now it is slowly replaced by money. The arrogance of these people originates there. Unfortunately, money does not guarantee good manners, or a regular visit to the dentist for that matter.

I can only try to imagine the horrors when free dental work is re-   15
placed by private dentists whose prices nobody can afford. How many decades will we have to wait until our teeth look like American ones? It is a question of perception. In order to improve your looks, you have to

be convinced that it is worth the trouble. In other words, we are dealing with a problem of self-esteem, with a way of thinking, rather than a superficial question. Bad teeth are the result of bad dentists and bad food, but also of a specific culture of thinking, of not seeing yourself as an individual. What we need here is a revolution of self-perception. Not only will that not come automatically with the new political changes, but I am afraid that it will also take longer than any political or economic developments. We need to accept our responsibilities towards both others and ourselves. This is not only a wise sort of investment in the future, as we can see in the case of Americans, it also gives you the feeling that you have done what you can to improve yourself, be it your teeth, your health, your career, education, environment or society in general.

16   Individual responsibility, including the responsibility for oneself, is an entirely new concept here, as I have stated many times elsewhere. This is why the revolution of self-perception has a long way to go. As absurd as it may sound, in the old days one could blame the Communist Party even for one's bad teeth. Now there is no one to blame, but it takes time to understand that. If you have never had it, self-respect has to be learned. Maybe our own teeth would be a good place to start.

17   But I can see signs of coming changes. Recently a good friend borrowed some money from me in order to repair her apartment. When the time came to give it back, she told me that I would have to wait, because she needed the money for something very urgent. She had finally decided to have her teeth fixed by a private dentist. No wonder she was left without a penny. But what could I have said to that? I said the only thing I could say: "I understand you, this must come first."

18   Finally, I guess it is only fair that I should declare the state of my own teeth. I am one of those who much too often used the free dental work so generously provided by the communist state for the benefit of its people. I was afraid of the dentist, all right, but also brave enough to stand the pain because I had overcome the psychological barrier at an early age.

19   When I was in the third grade a teacher showed us a cartoon depicting a fortress—a tooth—attacked by bad guys—bacteria. They looked terribly dangerous, digging tunnels and ditches with their small axes until the fortress almost fell into their hands. Then the army of good guys, the white blood cells, arrived and saved it at the last moment. The teacher explained to us how we could fight the bad guys by brushing our teeth regularly with Kalodont and by visiting a dentist every time we spotted a little hole or felt pain. I took her advice literally—I was obviously very impressed by the cartoon, just as I was impressed by the American TV commercials thirty years later. The result is that today I can say that I have good teeth, although six of them are missing. How did that happen? Well, when I spotted a little cavity, I would immediately go to the dentist all by myself. This was mistake number one. You could not choose your own dentist at that time, and my family had to go

to a military hospital. A dentist there would usually fill the cavity, but for some reason the filling would soon fall out. Then he would make an even bigger hole and fill it again, until eventually there was not much tooth left.

Those "dentists" were in fact young students of dentistry drafted   20
into the army. For them, this was probably an excellent chance to improve their knowledge by practising on patients. When they'd finished practising on me a more experienced dentist would suggest I had the tooth out. What could I, a child, do but agree? This was mistake number two, of course. I had to learn to live with one gap in my jaw, then another, and another. Much later I had two bridges made by a private dentist. He didn't even ask me why I was missing six of my teeth; he knew how things had worked in those days. My only consolation was that I did not have to pay much for my bridgework.

Like everyone else in the post-communist world, I had to learn the   21
meaning of the American proverb "There is no such thing as a free lunch." The Americans are right. You don't get anything properly done if you don't pay for it sooner or later.

✧ Evaluating the Text

1. What connection did Drakulić discover between the importance placed on impressive teeth in American culture and social status? As she became further acquainted with American society, how did this feature provide a key to unlock many aspects of the culture for her?

2. Once sensitized to what, in America, is so pervasive and important, how did Drakulić react upon her return to Zagreb? What did she conclude about the role that bad teeth play in East European culture?

3. How does Drakulić tie together her discussion of teeth with life in a postcommunist society?

✧ Exploring Different Perspectives

1. Communism, as Drakulić experienced it in East Europe and as Guanlong Cao experienced it in China (see "The Culture of Killing"), gave each author insights into the relationships between individuals and the cultural values and customs of their respective societies. Compare several of these.

2. In what sense do fiestas in Mexico, as described by Octavio Paz in "Fiesta," convey some of the same values that having good teeth do in America, as seen by Drakulić?

✧ *Extending Viewpoints through Writing*

1. If you were faced with a choice of fixing your car, buying a new carpet, or fixing your teeth (a choice mentioned by Drakulić), which would you choose and why?

2. When Drakulić returned to East Europe, she was appalled by the pervasiveness of bad teeth, something she had not previously noticed. To what extent do you let your assessment of other people depend on the state of their teeth?

Bessie Head

Looking for a Rain God

◆

*Bessie Head (1937–1986) was born in Pietermaritzburg, South Africa,
the daughter of a black father and a white mother. She suffered the childhood trauma of being "reclassified"; she was taken from her mother at
birth and brought up by foster parents as a Coloured. Her mother was
treated as insane because of her relationship with a black man. Head was
raised by her foster parents until she was thirteen, when she was placed in
a mission orphanage. The emotional scars of her childhood are powerfully
recorded in the widely acclaimed* A Question of Power *(1973), a fictional study of madness produced by the violence of the apartheid system.
After completing her education, she taught grammar school and wrote fiction for a local newspaper. In 1963, Head moved to a farm commune in
Serowe, Botswana, with her son. She lived there, working as a teacher and
a gardener in a local village until her death.*

*Head's writing grows directly out of her experience of village life. Her
first novel,* When Rain Clouds Gather *(1968), presents the epic struggle of a village trying to survive a devastating drought. Her next two novels,* Maru *(1971) and* A Question of Power *(1973), depict women
struggling to overcome oppression in their societies and earned her the
distinction of being one of Africa's major female writers. As a chronicler of
village life, Head wrote two histories,* Serowe: Village of the Rain Wind
(1981) and A Bewitched Crossroad *(1985). "Looking for a Rain God,"
from* The Collector of Treasures and Other Botswana Tales *(1977), is
based on a shocking local incident revealing how an ancient tribal ritual
resurfaced after years of drought in modern-day Botswana.*

*The conditions of drought so graphically described by Bessie Head in
this 1977 story were again confronted by the country during six successive years of drought between 1981 and 1987.*

It is lonely at the lands where the people go to plough. These lands   1
are vast clearings in the bush, and the wild bush is lonely too. Nearly all
the lands are within walking distance from the village. In some parts of
the bush where the underground water is very near the surface, people
made little rest camps for themselves and dug shallow wells to quench
their thirst while on their journey to their own lands. They experienced

*For information on Botswana, see p. 179.

all kinds of things once they left the village. They could rest at shady watering places full of lush, tangled trees with delicate pale-gold and purple wildflowers springing up between soft green moss and the children could hunt around for wild figs and any berries that might be in season. But from 1958, a seven-year drought fell upon the land and even the watering places began to look as dismal as the dry open thornbush country; the leaves of the trees curled up and withered; the moss became dry and hard and, under the shade of the tangled trees, the ground turned a powdery black and white, because there was no rain. People said rather humorously that if you tried to catch the rain in a cup it would only fill a teaspoon. Toward the beginning of the seventh year of drought, the summer had become an anguish to live through. The air was so dry and moisture-free that it burned the skin. No one knew what to do to escape the heat and tragedy was in the air. At the beginning of that summer, a number of men just went out of their homes and hung themselves to death from trees. The majority of the people had lived off crops, but for two years past they had all returned from the lands with only their rolled-up skin blankets and cooking utensils. Only the charlatans, incanters, and witch doctors made a pile of money during this time because people were always turning to them in desperation for little talismans and herbs to rub on the plough for the crops to grow and the rain to fall.

2   The rains were late that year. They came in early November, with a promise of good rain. It wasn't the full, steady downpour of the years of good rain but thin, scanty, misty rain. It softened the earth and a rich growth of green things sprang up everywhere for the animals to eat. People were called to the center of the village to hear the proclamation of the beginning of the ploughing season; they stirred themselves and whole families began to move off to the lands to plough.

3   The family of the old man, Mokgobja, were among those who left early for the lands. They had a donkey cart and piled everything onto it, Mokgobja—who was over seventy years old; two girls, Neo and Boseyong; their mother Tiro and an unmarried sister, Nesta; and the father and supporter of the family, Ramadi, who drove the donkey cart. In the rush of the first hope of rain, the man, Ramadi, and the two women, cleared the land of thornbush and then hedged their vast ploughing area with this same thornbush to protect the future crop from the goats they had brought along for milk. They cleared out and deepened the old well with its pool of muddy water and still in this light, misty rain, Ramadi inspanned two oxen and turned the earth over with a hand plough.

4   The land was ready and ploughed, waiting for the crops. At night, the earth was alive with insects singing and rustling about in search of food. But suddenly, by mid-November, the rain flew away; the rain clouds fled away and left the sky bare. The sun danced dizzily in the sky, with a strange cruelty. Each day the land was covered in a haze of

mist as the sun sucked up the last drop of moisture out of the earth. The family sat down in despair, waiting and waiting. Their hopes had run so high; the goats had started producing milk, which they had eagerly poured on their porridge, now they ate plain porridge with no milk. It was impossible to plant the corn, maize, pumpkin, and watermelon seeds in the dry earth. They sat the whole day in the shadow of the huts and even stopped thinking, for the rain had fled away. Only the children, Neo and Boseyong, were quite happy in their little-girl world. They carried on with their game of making house like their mother and chattered to each other in light, soft tones. They made children from sticks around which they tied rags, and scolded them severely in an exact imitation of their own mother. Their voices could be heard scolding the day long: "You stupid thing, when I send you to draw water, why do you spill half of it out of the bucket!" "You stupid thing! Can't you mind the porridge pot without letting the porridge burn!" And then they would beat the rag dolls on their bottoms with severe expressions.

The adults paid no attention to this; they did not even hear the funny   5
chatter; they sat waiting for rain; their nerves were stretched to breaking-point willing the rain to fall out of the sky. Nothing was important, beyond that. All their animals had been sold during the bad years to purchase food, and of all their herd only two goats were left. It was the women of the family who finally broke down under the strain of waiting for rain. It was really the two women who caused the death of the little girls. Each night they started a weird, high-pitched wailing that began on a low, mournful note and whipped up to a frenzy. Then they would stamp their feet and shout as though they had lost their heads. The men sat quiet and self-controlled; it was important for men to maintain their self control at all times but their nerve was breaking too. They knew the women were haunted by the starvation of the coming year.

Finally, an ancient memory stirred in the old man, Mokgobja. When   6
he was very young and the customs of the ancestors still ruled the land, he had been witness to a rain-making ceremony. And he came alive a little, struggling to recall the details which had been buried by years and years of prayer in a Christian church. As soon as the mists cleared a little, he began consulting in whispers with his youngest son, Ramadi. There was, he said, a certain rain god who accepted only the sacrifice of the bodies of children. Then the rain would fall; then the crops would grow, he said. He explained the ritual and as he talked, his memory became a conviction and he began to talk with unshakable authority. Ramadi's nerves were smashed by the nightly wailing of the women and soon the two men began whispering with the two women. The children continued their game: "You stupid thing! How could you have lost the money on the way to the shop! You must have been playing again!"

After it was all over and the bodies of the two little girls had been   7
spread across the land, the rain did not fall. Instead, there was a

deathly silence at night and the devouring heat of the sun by day. A terror, extreme and deep, overwhelmed the whole family. They packed, rolling up their skin blankets and pots, and fled back to the village.

8   People in the village soon noted the absence of the two little girls. They had died at the lands and were buried there, the family said. But people noted their ashen, terror-stricken faces and a murmur arose. What had killed the children, they wanted to know? And the family replied that they had just died. And people said amongst themselves that it was strange that the two deaths had occurred at the same time. And there was a feeling of great unease at the unnatural looks of the family. Soon the police came around. The family told them the same story of death and burial at the lands. They did not know what the children had died of. So the police asked to see the graves. At this, the mother of the children broke down and told everything.

9   Throughout that terrible summer the story of the children hung like a dark cloud of sorrow over the village, and the sorrow was not assuaged when the old man and Ramadi were sentenced to death for ritual murder. All they had on the statute books was that ritual murder was against the law and must be stamped out with the death penalty. The subtle story of strain and starvation and breakdown was inadmissible evidence at court; but all the people who lived off crops knew in their hearts that only a hair's breadth had saved them from sharing a fate similar to that of the Mokgobja family. They could have killed something to make the rain fall.

✧ Evaluating the Text

1. How does the author lay the psychological groundwork for what otherwise would come as a shock—the choice of the two young girls in the family as sacrificial victims? Look carefully at how the girls must appear to everyone else in the family, especially in a culture where everyone, to survive, must contribute to the welfare of all. Looked at in this way, how do details such as their sloppiness (spilling food or water) and disobedience contribute to the family's decision to kill them in exchange for rain? How do the games Neo and Boseyong play provide further insight into how they are already being treated by the adults?

2. How does overwhelming stress reactivate a belief in rituals that lie just below the surface of collective tribal memory? From the details concerning the slaughter and dismemberment of the girls, how, in your opinion, was this ritual supposed to have worked?

3. Even though the police respond, as representatives of the social order, and execute Mokgobja and Ramadi for killing their children, why is it significant that Head ends the story with the statement that the other

villagers "could have killed something to make the rain fall"? What does this tell you about Head's attitude toward the events in the story?

✦ Exploring Different Perspectives

1. In both this story set in Botswana and in Gino Del Guercio's account of voodoo in Haiti (see "The Secrets of Haiti's Living Dead"), how are officially unsanctioned rituals resorted to in times of extreme political, environmental, and psychological stress?

2. How is the theme of ritual murder used in Head's story and in Nabil Gorgy's story "Cairo Is a Small City"?

✦ Extending Viewpoints through Writing

1. To what extent does this story give you insight into the lives of people who live in colonized nations where Western Christian values are superimposed on tribal customs and beliefs? As a follow-up research project you might wish to investigate the practice of Santéria, a religion originating in Africa, brought to the United States by Cuban émigrées. See Joseph M. Murphy's *Santéria: An African Religion in America* (1988), Judith Gleason's *Santéria, Bronx* (1975), Migene Gonzalez-Wippler's *The Santéria Experience* (1982), and *Rituals and Spells of Santéria* (1984).

2. Did your family have a secret that they kept either from someone in the family or from the outside world? If it can now be revealed, tell what it was. Does the secret seem as significant as it did at the time?

Gino Del Guercio

The Secrets of
Haiti's Living Dead

◆───────────

Gino Del Guercio is a national science writer for United Press International and was a MACY fellow at Boston's television station WGBH. He is currently a documentary filmmaker, specializing in scientific and medical subjects, for Boston Science Communications, Inc. "The Secrets of Haiti's Living Dead" was first published in Harvard Magazine *(January/February 1986). In 1982, Wade Davis, a Harvard-trained ethnobotanist, whose exploits formed the basis for this article, traveled into the Haitian countryside to investigate accounts of Zombies—the infamous living dead of Haitian folklore. Davis's research led him to obtain the poison associated with the process. His findings were first presented in* The Serpent and the Rainbow *(1988), a work that served as the basis for the movie of the same name, directed by Wes Craven, and later in* Passage of Darkness *(1988). Davis is currently research associate in ethnobotany at the New York Botanical Garden.*

The republic of Haiti in the West Indies occupies the western third of the island of Hispaniola, which it shares with the Dominican Republic. French rule of Haiti lasted from 1697 until Toussaint l'Ouverture, a former slave, led Haiti to become the second independent nation in the Americas, in 1804. For the most part, Haiti's history has been fraught with intrigue and violence. In 1957, François "Papa Doc" Duvalier established a dictatorship and was succeeded by his son Jean Claude ("Baby Doc"), who fled the country in 1986. In December 1990, the Reverend Jean Bertrand Aristide, a champion of the poor, was elected head of the government in Haiti's first democratic elections. Aristide was subsequently forced into exile, and the government was placed under military control. After the expulsion of the United Nations and the Organization of American States (OAS) missions by a military junta in July 1994, fifteen thousand American troops moved into Haiti in September. President Aristide briefly returned to office in October of 1994. Del Guercio's report reveals the extent to which Haitian life is controlled by voodoo, a religious belief, West African in origin, that is characterized by induced trances and magical rituals. Until this century, Voodoo was the state religion and continues to flourish despite opposition from Roman Catholicism, the other major religion in Haiti.

Five years ago, a man walked into l'Estére, a village in central   1
Haiti, approached a peasant woman named Angelina Narcisse, and
identified himself as her brother Clairvius. If he had not introduced
himself using a boyhood nickname and mentioned facts only intimate
family members knew, she would not have believed him. Because,
eighteen years earlier, Angelina had stood in a small cemetery north of
her village and watched as her brother Clairvius was buried.

The man told Angelina he remembered that night well. He knew   2
when he was lowered into his grave, because he was fully conscious,
although he could not speak or move. As the earth was thrown over his
coffin, he felt as if he were floating over the grave. The scar on his right
cheek, he said, was caused by a nail driven through his casket.

The night he was buried, he told Angelina, a voodoo priest raised   3
him from the grave. He was beaten with a sisal whip and carried off to
a sugar plantation in northern Haiti where, with other zombies, he was
forced to work as a slave. Only with the death of the zombie master
were they able to escape, and Narcisse eventually returned home.

Legend has it that zombies are the living dead, raised from their   4
graves and animated by malevolent voodoo sorcerers, usually for some
evil purpose. Most Haitians believe in zombies, and Narcisse's claim is
not unique. At about the time he reappeared, in 1980, two women
turned up in other villages saying they were zombies. In the same year,
in northern Haiti, the local peasants claimed to have found a group of
zombies wandering aimlessly in the fields.

But Narcisse's case was different in one crucial respect; it was doc-   5
umented. His death had been recorded by doctors at the American-
directed Schweitzer Hospital in Deschapelles. On April 30, 1962, hospital records show, Narcisse walked into the hospital's emergency room
spitting up blood. He was feverish and full of aches. His doctors could
not diagnose his illness, and his symptoms grew steadily worse. Three
days after he entered the hospital, according to the records, he died.
The attending physicians, an American among them, signed his death
certificate. His body was placed in cold storage for twenty hours, and
then he was buried. He said he remembered hearing his doctors pro-
nounce him dead while his sister wept at his bedside.

At the Centre de Psychiatrie et Neurologie in Port-au-Prince, Dr.   6
Lamarque Douyon, a Haitian-born, Canadian-trained psychiatrist, has
been systematically investigating all reports of zombies since 1961.
Though convinced zombies were real, he had been unable to find a scientific explanation for the phenomenon. He did not believe zombies were
people raised from the dead, but that did not make them any less interesting. He speculated that victims were only made to *look* dead, probably
by means of a drug that dramatically slowed metabolism. The victim
was buried, dug up within a few hours, and somehow reawakened.

7   The Narcisse case provided Douyon with evidence strong enough to warrant a request for assistance from colleagues in New York. Douyon wanted to find an ethnobotanist, a traditional-medicines expert, who could track down the zombie potion he was sure existed. Aware of the medical potential of a drug that could dramatically lower metabolism, a group organized by the late Dr. Nathan Kline—a New York psychiatrist and pioneer in the field of psychopharmacology—raised the funds necessary to send someone to investigate.

8   The search for that someone led to the Harvard Botanical Museum, one of the world's foremost institutes of ethnobiology. Its director, Richard Evans Schultes, Jeffrey professor of biology, had spent thirteen years in the tropics studying native medicines. Some of his best-known work is the investigation of curare, the substance used by the nomadic people of the Amazon to poison their darts. Refined into a powerful muscle relaxant called D-tubocurarine, it is now an essential component of the anesthesia used during almost all surgery.

9   Schultes would have been a natural for the Haitian investigation, but he was too busy. He recommended another Harvard ethnobotanist for the assignment, Wade Davis, a 28-year-old Canadian pursuing a doctorate in biology.

10   Davis grew up in the tall pine forests of British Columbia and entered Harvard in 1971, influenced by a *Life* magazine story on the student strike of 1969. Before Harvard, the only Americans he had known were draft dodgers, who seemed very exotic. "I used to fight forest fires with them," Davis says. "Like everybody else, I thought America was where it was at. And I wanted to go to Harvard because of that *Life* article. When I got there, I realized it wasn't quite what I had in mind."

11   Davis took a course from Schultes, and when he decided to go to South America to study plants, he approached his professor for guidance. "He was an extraordinary figure," Davis remembers. "He was a man who had done it all. He had lived alone for years in the Amazon." Schultes sent Davis to the rain forest with two letters of introduction and two pieces of advice: wear a pith helmet and try ayahuasca, a powerful hallucinogenic vine. During that expedition and others, Davis proved himself an "outstanding field man," says his mentor. Now, in early 1982, Schultes called him into his office and asked if he had plans for spring break.

12   "I always took to Schultes's assignments like a plant takes to water," says Davis, tall and blond, with inquisitive blue eyes. "Whatever Schultes told me to do, I did. His letters of introduction opened up a whole world." This time the world was Haiti.

13   Davis knew nothing about the Caribbean island—and nothing about African traditions, which serve as Haiti's cultural basis. He certainly did not believe in zombies. "I thought it was a lark," he says now.

Davis landed in Haiti a week after his conversation with Schultes,   14
armed with a hypothesis about how the zombie drug—if it existed—
might be made. Setting out to explore, he discovered a country materially impoverished, but rich in culture and mystery. He was impressed
by the cohesion of Haitian society; he found none of the crime, social
disorder, and rampant drug and alcohol abuse so common in many of
the other Caribbean islands. The cultural wealth and cohesion, he believes, spring from the country's turbulent history.

During the French occupation of the late eighteenth century,   15
370,000 African-born slaves were imported to Haiti between 1780 and
1790. In 1791, the black population launched one of the few successful
slave revolts in history, forming secret societies and overcoming first
the French plantation owners and then a detachment of troops from
Napoleon's army, sent to quell the revolt. For the next hundred years
Haiti was the only independent black republic in the Caribbean, populated by people who did not forget their African heritage. "You can almost argue that Haiti is more African than Africa," Davis says. "When
the west coast of Africa was being disrupted by colonialism and the
slave trade, Haiti was essentially left alone. The amalgam of beliefs in
Haiti is unique, but it's very, very African."

Davis discovered that the vast majority of Haitian peasants practice   16
voodoo, a sophisticated religion with African roots. Says Davis, "It was
immediately obvious that the stereotypes of voodoo weren't true. Going
around the countryside, I found clues to a whole complex social world."
Vodounists believe they communicate directly with, indeed are often
possessed by, the many spirits who populate the everyday world.
Vodoun society is a system of education, law, and medicine; it embodies
a code of ethics that regulates social behavior. In rural areas, secret
vodoun societies, much like those found on the west coast of Africa, are
as much or more in control of everyday life as the Haitian government.

Although most outsiders dismissed the zombie phenomenon as   17
folklore, some early investigators, convinced of its reality, tried to find a
scientific explanation. The few who sought a zombie drug failed. Nathan
Kline, who helped finance Davis's expedition, had searched unsuccess-
fully, as had Lamarque Douyon, the Haitian psychiatrist. Zora Neale
Hurston, an American black woman, may have come closest. An anthropological pioneer, she went to Haiti in the Thirties, studied vodoun society, and wrote a book on the subject, *Tell My Horse,* first published in
1938. She knew about the secret societies and was convinced zombies
were real, but if a powder existed, she too failed to obtain it.

Davis obtained a sample in a few weeks.   18

He arrived in Haiti with the names of several contacts. A BBC re-   19
porter familiar with the Narcisse case had suggested he talk with Marcel
Pierre. Pierre owned the Eagle Bar, a bordello in the city of Saint Marc.

He was also a voodoo sorcerer and had supplied the BBC with a physiologically active powder of unknown ingredients. Davis found him willing to negotiate. He told Pierre he was a representative of "powerful but anonymous interests in New York," willing to pay generously for the priest's services, provided no questions were asked. Pierre agreed to be helpful for what Davis will only say was a "sizable sum." Davis spent a day watching Pierre gather the ingredients—including human bones—and grind them together with mortar and pestle. However, from his knowledge of poison, Davis knew immediately that nothing in the formula could produce the powerful effects of zombification.

20   Three weeks later, Davis went back to the Eagle Bar, where he found Pierre sitting with three associates. Davis challenged him. He called him a charlatan. Enraged, the priest gave him a second vial, claiming that this was the real poison. Davis pretended to pour the powder into his palm and rub it into his skin. "You're a dead man," Pierre told him, and he might have been, because this powder proved to be genuine. But, as the substance had not actually touched him, Davis was able to maintain his bravado, and Pierre was impressed. He agreed to make the poison and show Davis how it was done.

21   The powder, which Davis keeps in a small vial, looks like dry black dirt. It contains parts of toads, sea worms, lizards, tarantulas, and human bones. (To obtain the last ingredient, he and Pierre unearthed a child's grave on a nocturnal trip to the cemetery.) The poison is rubbed into the victim's skin. Within hours he begins to feel nauseated and has difficulty breathing. A pins-and-needles sensation afflicts his arms and legs, then progresses to the whole body. The subject becomes paralyzed; his lips turn blue for lack of oxygen. Quickly—sometimes within six hours—his metabolism is lowered to a level almost indistinguishable from death.

22   As Davis discovered, making the poison is an inexact science. Ingredients varied in the five samples he eventually acquired, although the active agents were always the same. And the poison came with no guarantee. Davis speculates that sometimes instead of merely paralyzing the victim, the compound kills him. Sometimes the victim suffocates in the coffin before he can be resurrected. But clearly the potion works well enough often enough to make zombies more than a figment of Haitian imagination.

23   Analysis of the powder produced another surprise. "When I went down to Haiti originally," says Davis, "my hypothesis was that the formula would contain concombre zombi, the 'zombie's cucumber,' which is a Datura plant. I thought somehow Datura was used in putting people down." Datura is a powerful psychoactive plant, found in West Africa as well as other tropical areas and used there in ritual as well as criminal activities. Davis had found Datura growing in Haiti. Its popular name suggested the plant was used in creating zombies.

But, says Davis, "there were a lot of problems with the *Datura* hy-   24
pothesis. Partly it was a question of how the drug was administered.
Datura would create a stupor in huge doses, but it just wouldn't produce the kind of immobility that was key. These people had to appear
dead, and there aren't many drugs that will do that."

One of the ingredients Pierre included in the second formula was a   25
dried fish, a species of puffer or blowfish, common to most parts of the
world. It gets its name from its ability to fill itself with water and swell
to several times its normal size when threatened by predators. Many of
these fish contain a powerful poison known as tetrodotoxin. One of the
most powerful nonprotein poisons known to man, tetradotoxin turned
up in every sample of zombie powder that Davis acquired.

Numerous well-documented accounts of puffer fish poisoning ex-   26
ist, but the most famous accounts come from the Orient, where *fugu* fish,
a species of puffer, is considered a delicacy. In Japan, special chefs are licensed to prepare *fugu*. The chef removes enough poison to make the
fish nonlethal, yet enough remains to create exhilarating physiological
effects—tingles up and down the spine, mild prickling of the tongue
and lips, euphoria. Several dozen Japanese die each year, having bitten
off more than they should have.

"When I got hold of the formula and saw it was the *fugu* fish, that   27
suddenly threw open the whole Japanese literature," says Davis. Case
histories of *fugu* poisoning read like accounts of zombification. Victims
remain conscious but unable to speak or move. A man who had "died"
after eating *fugu* recovered seven days later in the morgue. Several
summers ago, another Japanese poisoned by *fugu* revived after he was
nailed into his coffin. "Almost all of Narcisse's symptoms correlated.
Even strange things such as the fact that he said he was conscious and
could hear himself pronounced dead. Stuff that I thought had to be
magic, that seemed crazy. But, in fact, that is what people who get *fugu*-
fish poisoning experience."

Davis was certain he had solved the mystery. But far from being   28
the end of his investigation, identifying the poison was, in fact, its starting point. "The drug alone didn't make zombies," he explains. "Japanese victims of puffer-fish poisoning don't become zombies, they
become poison victims. All the drug could do was set someone up for a
whole series of psychological pressures that would be rooted in the culture. I wanted to know why zombification was going on," he says.

He sought a cultural answer, an explanation rooted in the structure   29
and beliefs of Haitian society. Was zombification simply a random
criminal activity? He thought not. He had discovered that Clairvius
Narcisse and "Ti Femme," a second victim he interviewed, were village
pariahs. Ti Femme was regarded as a thief. Narcisse had abandoned his
children and deprived his brother of land that was rightfully his.
Equally suggestive, Narcisse claimed that his aggrieved brother had

sold him to a *bokor,* a voodoo priest who dealt in black magic; he made cryptic reference to having been tried and found guilty by the "masters of the land."

30   Gathering poisons from various parts of the country, Davis had come into direct contact with the vodoun secret societies. Returning to the anthropological literature on Haiti and pursuing his contacts with informants, Davis came to understand the social matrix within which zombies were created.

31   Davis's investigations uncovered the importance of the secret societies. These groups trace their origins to the bands of escaped slaves that organized the revolt against the French in the late eighteenth century. Open to both men and women, the societies control specific territories of the country. Their meetings take place at night, and in many rural parts of Haiti the drums and wild celebrations that characterize the gatherings can be heard for miles.

32   Davis believes the secret societies are responsible for policing their communities, and the threat of zombification is one way they maintain order. Says Davis, "Zombification has a material basis, but it also has a societal logic." To the uninitiated, the practice may appear a random criminal activity, but in rural vodoun society, it is exactly the opposite—a sanction imposed by recognized authorities, a form of capital punishment. For rural Haitians, zombification is an even more severe punishment than death, because it deprives the subject of his most valued possessions: his free will and independence.

33   The vodounists believe that when a person dies, his spirit splits into several different parts. If a priest is powerful enough, the spiritual aspect that controls a person's character and individuality, known as *ti bon ange,* the "good little angel," can be captured and the corporeal aspect, deprived of its will, held as a slave.

34   From studying the medical literature on tetrodotoxin poisoning, Davis discovered that if a victim survives the first few hours of the poisoning, he is likely to recover fully from the ordeal. The subject simply revives spontaneously. But zombies remain without will, in a trance-like state, a condition vodounists attribute to the power of the priest. Davis thinks it possible that the psychological trauma of zombification may be augmented by *Datura* or some other drug; he thinks zombies may be fed a *Datura* paste that accentuates their disorientation. Still, he puts the material basis of zombification in perspective: "Tetrodotoxin and *Datura* are only templates on which cultural forces and beliefs may be amplified a thousand times."

35   Davis has not been able to discover how prevalent zombification is in Haiti. "How many zombies there are is not the question," he says. He compares it to capital punishment in the United States: "It doesn't really matter how many people are electrocuted, as long as it's a possibility." As a sanction in Haiti, the fear is not of zombies, it's of becoming one.

Davis attributes his success in solving the zombie mystery to his   36
approach. He went to Haiti with an open mind and immersed himself
in the culture. "My intuition unhindered by biases served me well," he
says. "I didn't make any judgments." He combined this attitude with
what he had learned earlier from his experiences in the Amazon.
"Schultes's lesson is to go and live with the Indians as an Indian."
Davis was able to participate in the vodoun society to a surprising degree, eventually even penetrating one of the Bizango societies and
dancing in their nocturnal rituals. His appreciation of Haitian culture is
apparent. "Everybody asks me how did a white person get this information? To ask the question means you don't understand Haitians—
they don't judge you by the color of your skin."

As a result of the exotic nature of his discoveries, Davis has gained   37
a certain notoriety. He plans to complete his dissertation soon, but he
has already finished writing a popular account of his adventures. To be
published in January by Simon and Schuster, it is called *The Serpent and
the Rainbow,* after the serpent that vodounists believe created the earth
and the rainbow spirit it married. Film rights have already been op-
tioned; in October Davis went back to Haiti with a screenwriter. But
Davis takes the notoriety in stride. "All this attention is funny," he says.
"For years, not just me, but all Schultes's students have had extraordinary adventures in the line of work. The adventure is not the end point,
it's just along the way of getting the data. At the Botanical Museum,
Schultes created a world unto itself. We didn't think we were doing
anything above the ordinary. I still don't think we do. And you know,"
he adds, "the Haiti episode does not begin to compare to what others
have accomplished—particularly Schultes himself."

✧ *Evaluating the Text*

1. To what extent does Del Guercio's account gain credibility because he
   begins with the mysterious case of Clairvius Narcisse? How is Narcisse's identification by his sister intended to put the case beyond all
   doubt and leave the process of zombification as the only possible explanation for his otherwise inexplicable "death"?

2. Why is it important to Guercio's account that he mentions physicians
   from the United States as well as Haitian doctors who certified the
   "death" of Clairvius Narcisse? What is Del Guercio's attitude toward
   this phenomenon? How is this attitude revealed in the way he con-
   structs his report?

3. How does the threat of zombification serve as a preventative measure
   that ensures social control in deterring crimes against the community?
   How did it operate in the cases of Clairvius Narcisse and "Ti Femme"?

In what way is the reality of the social mechanism of zombification quite different from how it has been presented in movies and popular culture?

4. What kind of independent confirmation of the effects of tetrodotoxin, a potent neurotoxin that drastically reduces metabolism and produces paralysis, did Davis discover in his research on the effects of Japanese victims of *fugu* fish poisoning?

✧ *Exploring Different Perspectives*

1. How does the concept of death and resurrection enter into the account by Del Guercio and in Bessie Head's story, "Looking for a Rain God"?

2. In what sense is the Haitian concept of the separable soul similar to the Chinese concept of *chi* or vital force? Compare the rituals each culture has developed around this concept (see "The Culture of Killing")?

✧ *Extending Viewpoints through Writing*

1. If you are familiar with or interested in the processes by which various religious cults enlist and program their members, you might compare their methods to those of the vodoun priests in terms of positive and negative reinforcement of psychological, sociological, and physiological conditioning.

2. If you have had the opportunity to see the movie *The Serpent and the Rainbow* (1988), directed by Wes Craven, you might wish to compare its representation of the events described in this article with Wade Davis's book *The Serpent and the Rainbow* (1985). For further research on this subject, you might consult Wade Davis, *Passage of Darkness: The Ethnobiology of the Haitian Zombie* (1988), an in-depth study of the political, social, and botanical mechanisms of zombification.

Nabil Gorgy

Cairo Is a Small City

◆

Nabil Gorgy was born in Cairo in 1944 and studied civil engineering at Cairo University. After working as an engineer in New York City, he returned to Cairo, where he now runs his own art gallery. His interests in mysticism, Egyptology, and Sufi traditions are reflected in his novel The Door *(1981). His most recent collection of short stories is* The Slave's Dream and Other Stories *(1991). In "Cairo Is a Small City," translated by Denys Johnson-Davies (1983), an upper-class Egyptian engineer falls victim to an age-old Bedouin tradition.*

Egypt is an Arab republic in northeastern Africa, bordered by the Mediterranean in the north, Israel and the Red Sea to the east, the Sudan to the south, and Libya to the west. Egypt was the site of one of the earliest civilizations that developed in the Nile valley over 5,000 years ago and flourished until it became part of the Roman Empire in 30 B.C. As always, Egypt depends on the Nile River for maintaining arable lands, and its economy, although weakened in the 1980s by earlier Arab–Israeli wars, remains primarily agricultural. Under the leadership of Anwar Sadat, in 1979 Egypt became the first Arab nation to sign a peace treaty with Israel. In 1981, Sadat was assassinated by Muslim fundamentalists, and his successor, Hosni Mubarak, has faced the difficult task of dealing with the resurgence of Islamic fundamentalism while moving Egypt into a position of leadership in the Arab world. Egypt joined the United States and other nations in sending troops to Saudi Arabia after the August 1990 invasion of Kuwait by Iraq. Saadawi's analysis reveals the extent to which women's lives in the Middle East are constrained by age-old Islamic laws and customs. In October 1993, Hosni Mubarak was sworn in for a third six-year term as president. Since 1997, the government instituted a policy designed to promote more efficient farming methods.

On the balcony of his luxury flat Engineer Adil Salim stood watching some workmen putting up a new building across the wide street along the centre of which was a spacious garden. The building was at the foundations stage, only the concrete foundations and some of the first-floor columns having been completed. A young ironworker with long hair was engaged in bending iron rods of various dimensions. Adil noticed that the young man had carefully leant his Jawa motorcycle against a giant crane that crouched at rest awaiting its future tasks. "How the scene has changed!" Adil could still remember the picture of

1

old-time master craftsmen, and of the workers who used to carry large
bowls of mixed cement on their calloused shoulders.

2   The sun was about to set and the concrete columns of a number of
new constructions showed up as dark frameworks against the light in
this quiet district at the end of Heliopolis.

3   As on every day at this time there came down into the garden di-
viding the street a flock of sheep and goats that grazed on its grass, and
behind them two bedouin women, one of whom rode a donkey, while
the younger one walked beside her. As was his habit each day, Adil
fixed his gaze on the woman walking in her black gown that not so
much hid as emphasized the attractions of her body, her waist being
tied round with a red band. It could be seen that she wore green plastic
slippers on her feet. He wished that she would catch sight of him on the
balcony of his luxurious flat; even if she did so, Adil was thinking,
those bedouin had a special code of behaviour that differed greatly
from what he was used to and rendered it difficult to make contact
with them. What, then, was the reason, the motive, for wanting to think
up some way of talking to her? It was thus that he was thinking, following her with his gaze as she occasionally chased after a lamb that
was going to be run over by a car or a goat left far behind the flock.

4   Adil, who was experienced in attracting society women, was
aware of his spirit being enthralled: days would pass with him on the
balcony, sunset after sunset, as he watched her without her even knowing of his existence.

5   Had it not been for that day on which he had been buying some
fruit and vegetables from one of the shopkeepers on Metro Street, and
had not the shopkeeper seen another bedouin woman walking behind
another flock, and had he not called out to her by name, and had she
not come, and had he not thrown her a huge bundle of waste from the
shop, after having flirted with her and fondled her body—had it not
been for that day, Adil's mind would not have given birth to the plan
he was determined, whatever the cost, to put through, because of that
woman who had bewitched his heart.

6   As every man, according to Adil's philosophy of life, had within him
a devil, it was sometimes better to follow this devil in order to placate
him and avoid his tyranny. Therefore Engineer Adil Salim finally decided to embark upon the terrible, the unthinkable. He remembered from
his personal history during the past forty years that such a temporary alliance with this devil of his had gained him a courage that had set him
apart from the rest of his colleagues, and through it he had succeeded in
attaining this social position that had enabled him to become the owner
of this flat whose value had reached a figure which he avoided mentioning even in front of his family lest they might be upset or feel envy.

7   Thus, from his balcony on the second floor in Tirmidhi Street, Engineer Adil Salim called out in a loud voice "Hey, girl!" as he summoned

the one who was walking at the rear of the convoy. When the flock continued on its way without paying any attention, he shouted again: "Hey, girl—you who sell sheep," and before the girl moved far away he repeated the word "sheep." Adil paid no attention to the astonishment of the doorman, who had risen from the place where he had been sitting at the entrance, thinking that he was being called. In fact he quietly told him to run after the two bedouin women and to let them know that he had some bread left over which he wanted to give them for their sheep.

From the balcony Adil listened to the doorman calling to the two   8
women in his authoritative Upper Egyptian accent, at which they came to a stop and the one who was riding the donkey looked back at him. Very quickly Adil was able to make out her face as she looked towards him, seeking to discover what the matter was. As for the young girl, she continued on behind the flock. The woman was no longer young and had a corpulent body and a commanding look which she did not seek to hide from him. Turning her donkey round, she crossed the street separating the garden from his building and waited in front of the gate for some new development. Adil collected up all the bread in the house and hurried down with it on a brass tray. Having descended to the street, he went straight up to the woman and looked at her. When she opened a saddlebag close by her leg, he emptied all the bread into it.

"Thanks," said the woman as she made off without turning to-   9
wards him. He, though, raising his voice so that she would hear, called out, "And tomorrow too."

During a period that extended to a month Adil began to buy bread   10
which he did not eat. Even on those days when he had to travel away or to spend the whole day far from the house, he would leave a large paper parcel with the doorman for him to give to the bedouin woman who rode the donkey and behind whom walked she for whom the engineer's heart craved.

Because Adil had a special sense of the expected and the probable,   11
and after the passing of one lunar month, and in his place in front of the building, with the bread on the brass tray, there occurred that which he had been wishing would happen, for the woman riding the donkey had continued on her way and he saw the other, looking around her carefully before crossing the road, ahead of him, walking towards him. She was the most beautiful thing he had set eyes on. The speed of his pulse almost brought his heart to a stop. How was it that such beauty was to be found without it feeling embarrassed at ugliness, for after it any and every thing must needs be so described? When she was directly in front of him, and her kohl-painted eyes were scrutinizing him, he sensed a danger which he attributed to her age, which was no more than twenty. How was it that she was so tall, her waist so slim, her breasts so full, and how was it that her buttocks swayed so enticingly

as she turned away and went off with the bread, having thanked him? His imagination became frozen even though she was still close to him: her pretty face with the high cheekbones, the fine nose and delicate lips, the silver, crescent-shaped earrings, and the necklace that graced her bosom? Because such beauty was "beyond the permissible," Adil went on thinking about Salma—for he had got to know her name, her mother having called her by it in order to hurry her back lest the meeting between the lovers be prolonged.

12   Adil no longer troubled about the whistles of the workers who had now risen floor by floor in the building opposite him, being in a state of infatuation, his heart captured by this moonlike creature. After the affair, in relation to himself, having been one of boldness, to end in seeing or greeting her, it now became a matter of necessity that she turn up before sunset at the house so that he might not be deprived of the chance of seeing her. So it was that Engineer Adil Salim fell in love with the beautiful bedouin girl Salma. And just as history is written by historians, so it was that Adil and his engineering work determined the history of this passion in the form of a building each of whose columns represented a day and each of whose floors was a month. He noted that, at the completion of twenty-eight days and exactly at full moon, Salma would come to him in place of her mother to take the bread. And so, being a structural engineer, he began to observe the moon, his yearning increasing when it was in eclipse and his spirits sparkling as its fullness drew near till, at full moon, the happiness of the lover was completed by seeing the beloved's face.

13   During seven months he saw her seven times, each time seeing in her the same look she had given him the first time: his heart would melt, all resolution would be squeezed out of him and that fear for which he knew no reason would be awakened. She alone was now capable of granting him his antidote. After the seventh month Salma, without any preamble, had talked to him at length, informing him that she lived with her parents around a spring at a distance of an hour's walk to the north of the airport, and that it consisted of a brackish spring alongside which was a sweet one, so that she would bathe in the first and rinse herself clean in the other, and that there were date palms around the two springs, also grass and pasturage. Her father, the owner of the springs and the land around them, had decided to invite him and so tomorrow "he'll pass by you and invite you to our place, for tomorrow we attend to the shearing of the sheep."

14   Adil gave the lie to what he was hearing, for it was more than any stretch of the imagination could conceive might happen.

15   The following day Adil arrived at a number of beautifully made tents, where a vast area of sand was spread out below date palms that

stretched to the edge of a spring. Around the spring was gathered a large herd of camels, sheep and goats that spoke of the great wealth of the father. It was difficult to believe that such a place existed so close to the city of Cairo. If Adil's astonishment was great when Salma's father passed by him driving a new Peugeot, he was yet further amazed at the beauty of the area surrounding this spring."It's the land of the future," thought Adil to himself. If he were able to buy a few *feddans* now he'd become a millionaire in a flash, for this was the Cairo of the future. "This is the deal of a lifetime," he told himself.

On the way the father asked a lot of questions about Adil's work   16
and where he had previously lived and about his knowledge of the desert and its people. Though Adil noticed in the father's tone something more than curiosity, he attributed this to the nature of the Bedouin and their traditions.

As the car approached the tents Adil noticed that a number of men   17
were gathered under a tent whose sides were open, and as the father and his guest got out of the car the men turned round, seated in the form of a horse-shoe. With the father sitting down and seating Engineer Adil Salim alongside him, one of the sides of the horse-shoe was completed. In front of them sat three men on whose faces could be seen the marks of time in the form of interlaced wrinkles.

The situation so held Adil's attention that he was unaware of   18
Salma except when she passed from one tent to another in the direction he was looking and he caught sight of her gazing towards him.

The man who was sitting in a squatting position among the three   19
others spoke. Adil heard him talking about the desert, water and sheep, about the roads that went between the oases and the *wadi*, the towns and the springs of water, about the bedouin tribes and blood ties; he heard him talking about the importance of protecting these roads and springs, and the palm trees and the dates, the goats and the milk upon which the suckling child would be fed; he also heard him talk about how small the *wadi* was in comparison to this desert that stretched out endlessly.

In the same way as Adil had previously built the seven-storey   20
building that represented the seven months, each month containing twenty-eight days, till he would see Salma's face whenever it was full moon, he likewise sensed that this was the tribunal which had been set up to make an enquiry with him into the killing of the man whom he had one day come across on the tracks between the oases of Kharga and Farshout. It had been shortly after sunset when he and a friend, having visited the iron ore mines in the oases of Kharga had, instead of taking the asphalt road to Assiout, proceeded along a rough track that took them down towards Farshout near to Kena, as his friend had to make a report about the possibility of repairing the road and of extending the railway line to the oases. Going down from the high land towards the

wadi, the land at a distance showing up green, two armed men had appeared before them. Adil remembered how, in a spasm of fear and astonishment, of belief and disbelief, and with a speed that at the time he thought was imposed upon him, a shot had been fired as he pressed his finger on the trigger of the revolver which he was using for the first time. A man had fallen to the ground in front of him and, as happens in films, the other had fled. As for him and his friend, they had rushed off to their car in order to put an end to the memory of the incident by reaching the *wadi.* It was perhaps because Adil had once killed a man that he had found the courage to accept Salma's father's invitation.

21   "That day," Adil heard the man address him, "with a friend in a car, you killed Mubarak bin Rabia when he went out to you, Ziyad al-Mihrab being with him."

22   This was the manner in which Engineer Adil Salim was executed in the desert north-west of the city of Cairo: one of the men held back his head across a marble-like piece of stone, then another man plunged the point of a tapered dagger into the spot that lies at the bottom of the neck between the two bones of the clavicle.

✧ Evaluating the Text

1. How is the engineer, Adil Salim, characterized? What incidents reveal these character traits most clearly? How does he see himself? To what does he attribute his success and affluence?

2. Under what circumstances does the engineer first meet the Bedouin girl? What is his attitude toward her?

3. After reading the story, discuss the significance of the title, especially as it sheds light on the surprising consequences for the engineer. To what extent does the title suggest that the Cairo of the Bedouins and the Cairo of the engineer, although seemingly very different, are basically the same?

✧ Exploring Different Perspectives

1. In both Gorgy's story and Gino Del Guercio's account (see "The Secrets of Haiti's Living Dead"), the protagonists living in modern times come into contact with much older ways of perceiving the world. How does this operate as a theme in both works?

2. How does the psychology of sacrifice enter into both Gorgy's and Bessie Head's stories (see "Looking for a Rain God")? In what sense are both titles ironic?

✧ *Extending Viewpoints through Writing*

1. In a short essay, discuss Gorgy's attitude toward ancient cultural traditions as they emerge in the story.

2. Adil's actions and reactions indicate that he is in love. What actions and reactions of your own or someone you know serve as sure-fire signs of being in love?

Octavio Paz

Fiesta

◆

Octavio Paz (1914–1998), born in Mexico City, was a poet, essayist, and unequalled observer of Mexican society. He served as a Mexican diplomat in France and Japan and as Ambassador to India before resigning from the diplomatic service to protest the Tlatelolco Massacre (government massacre of 300 students in Mexico City) in 1968. His many volumes of poetry include Sun Stone *(1958), a new reading of the Aztec myths;* Marcel Duchamp *(1968);* The Children of the Mire *(1974); and* The Monkey Grammarian *(1981). In 1990, Paz was awarded the Nobel Prize for Literature. As an essayist whose works have helped redefine the concept of Latin American culture, Paz wrote* The Other Mexico *(1972) and* The Labyrinth of Solitude, *translated by Lysander Kemp (1961), from which "Fiesta" is taken. In the following essay, Paz offers insight, conveyed with his typical stylistic grace and erudition, into the deep psychological needs met by fiestas in Mexican culture.*

1   The solitary Mexican loves fiestas and public gatherings. Any occasion for getting together will serve, any pretext to stop the flow of time and commemorate men and events with festivals and ceremonies. We are a ritual people, and this characteristic enriches both our imaginations and our sensibilities, which are equally sharp and alert. The art of the fiesta has been debased almost everywhere else, but not in Mexico. There are few places in the world where it is possible to take part in a spectacle like our great religious fiestas with their violent primary colors, their bizarre costumes and dances, their fireworks and ceremonies and their inexhaustible welter of surprises: the fruit, candy, toys and other objects sold on these days in the plazas and open-air markets.

2   Our calendar is crowded with fiestas. There are certain days when the whole country, from the most remote villages to the largest cities, prays, shouts, feasts, gets drunk and kills, in honor of the Virgin of Guadalupe or Benito Juaréz. Each year on the fifteenth of September, at eleven o'clock at night, we celebrate the fiesta of the *Grito*[1] in all the plazas of the Republic, and the excited crowds actually shout for a whole hour...the better, perhaps, to remain silent for the rest of the year. Dur-

---

*For information on Mexico, see p. 241.
[1]Padre Hildalgo's call-to-arms against Spain, 1810.—*Tr.*
[2]Fiesta of the Virgin of Guadalupe.—*Tr.*

ing the days before and after the twelfth of December,[2] time comes to a full stop, and instead of pushing us toward a deceptive tomorrow that is always beyond our reach, offers us a complete and perfect today of dancing and revelry, of communion with the most ancient and secret Mexico. Time is no longer succession, and becomes what it originally was and is: the present, in which past and future are reconciled.

But the fiestas which the Church and State provide for the country as a whole are not enough. The life of every city and village is ruled by a patron saint whose blessing is celebrated with devout regularity. Neighborhoods and trades also have their annual fiestas, their ceremonies and fairs. And each one of us—atheist, Catholic, or merely indifferent—has his own saint's day, which he observes every year. It is impossible to calculate how many fiestas we have and how much time and money we spend on them. I remember asking the mayor of a village near Mitla, several years ago, "What is the income of the village government?" "About 3,000 pesos a year. We are very poor. But the Governor and the Federal Government always help us to meet our expenses." "And how are the 3,000 pesos spent?" "Mostly on fiestas, señor. We are a small village, but we have two patron saints." 3

This reply is not surprising. Our poverty can be measured by the frequency and luxuriousness of our holidays. Wealthy countries have very few: there is neither the time nor the desire for them, and they are not necessary. The people have other things to do, and when they amuse themselves they do so in small groups. The modern masses are agglomerations of solitary individuals. On great occasions in Paris or New York, when the populace gathers in the squares or stadiums, the absence of people, in the sense of *a* people, is remarkable: there are couples and small groups, but they never form a living community in which the individual is at once dissolved and redeemed. But how could a poor Mexican live without the two or three annual fiestas that make up for his poverty and misery? Fiestas are our only luxury. They replace, and are perhaps better than, the theater and vacations, Anglo-Saxon weekends and cocktail parties, the bourgeois reception, the Mediterranean café. 4

In all of these ceremonies—national or local, trade or family—the Mexican opens out. They all give him a chance to reveal himself and to converse with God, country, friends or relations. During these days the silent Mexican whistles, shouts, sings, shoots off fireworks, discharges his pistol into the air. He discharges his soul. And his shout, like the rockets we love so much, ascends to the heavens, explodes into green, red, blue, and white lights, and falls dizzily to earth with a trail of golden sparks. This is the night when friends who have not exchanged more than the prescribed courtesies for months get drunk together, trade confidences, weep over the same troubles, discover that they are brothers, and sometimes, to prove it, kill each other. The night is full of songs and loud cries. The lover wakes up his sweetheart with an 5 orchestra. There are jokes and conversations from balcony to balcony, sidewalk to sidewalk. Nobody talks quietly. Hats fly in the air. Laughter and curses ring like silver pesos. Guitars are brought out. Now and then, it is true, the happiness ends badly, in quarrels, insults, pistol shots, stabbings. But these too are part of the fiesta, for the Mexican does not seek amusement: he seeks to escape from himself, to leap over the wall of solitude that confines him during the rest of the year. All are possessed by violence and frenzy. Their souls explode like the colors and voices and emotions. Do they forget themselves and show their true faces? Nobody knows. The important thing is to go out, open a way, get drunk on noise, people, colors. Mexico is celebrating a fiesta. And this fiesta, shot through with lightning and delirium, is the brilliant reverse to our silence and apathy, our reticence and gloom.

6   According to the interpretation of French sociologists, the fiesta is an excess, an expense. By means of this squandering the community protects itself against the envy of the gods or of men. Sacrifices and offerings placate or buy off the gods and the patron saints. Wasting money and expending energy affirms the community's wealth in both. This luxury is a proof of health, a show of abundance and power. Or a magic trap. For squandering is an effort to attract abundance by contagion. Money calls to money. When life is thrown away it increases; the orgy, which is sexual expenditure, is also a ceremony of regeneration; waste gives strength. New Year celebrations, in every culture, signify something beyond the mere observance of a date on the calendar. The day is a pause: time is stopped, is actually annihilated. The rites that celebrate its death are intended to provoke its rebirth, because they mark not only the end of an old year but also the beginning of a new. Everything attracts its opposite. The fiesta's function, then, is more utilitarian than we think: waste attracts or promotes wealth, and is an investment like any other, except that the returns on it cannot be measured or counted. What is sought is potency, life, health. In this sense the fiesta, like the gift and the offering, is one of the most ancient of economic forms.

7   This interpretation has always seemed to me to be incomplete. The fiesta is by nature sacred, literally or figuratively, and above all it is the advent of the unusual. It is governed by its own special rules, that set it apart from other days, and it has a logic, an ethic and even an economy that are often in conflict with everyday norms. It all occurs in an enchanted world: time is transformed to a mythical past or a total present; space, the scene of the fiesta, is turned into a gaily decorated world of its own; and the persons taking part cast off all human or social rank and become, for the moment, living images. And everything takes place as if it were not so, as if it were a dream. But whatever happens, our actions have a greater lightness, a different gravity. They take on other meanings and with them we contract new obligations. We throw down our burdens of time and reason.

8   In certain fiestas the very notion of order disappears. Chaos comes back and license rules. Anything is permitted: the customary hierarchies vanish, along with all social, sex, caste, and trade distinctions. Men disguise themselves as women, gentlemen as slaves, the poor as the rich. The army, the clergy, and the law are ridiculed. Obligatory sacrilege, ritual profanation is committed. Love becomes promiscuity. Sometimes the fiesta becomes a Black Mass. Regulations, habits and customs are violated. Respectable people put away the dignified expressions and conservative clothes that isolate them, dress up in gaudy colors, hide behind a mask, and escape from themselves.

Therefore the fiesta is not only an excess, a ritual squandering of the goods painfully accumulated during the rest of the year; it is also a revolt, a sudden immersion in the formless, in pure being. By means of the fiesta society frees itself from the norms it has established. It ridicules its gods, its principles, and its laws: it denies its own self.   9

The fiesta is a revolution in the most literal sense of the word. In the confusion that it generates, society is dissolved, is drowned, insofar as it is an organism ruled according to certain laws and principles. But it drowns in itself, in its own original chaos or liberty. Everything is united: good and evil, day and night, the sacred and the profane. Everything merges, loses shape and individuality and returns to the primordial mass. The fiesta is a cosmic experiment, an experiment in disorder, reuniting contradictory elements and principles in order to bring about a renascence of life. Ritual death promotes a rebirth; vomiting increases the appetite; the orgy, sterile in itself, renews the fertility of the mother or of the earth. The fiesta is a return to a remote and undifferentiated state, prenatal or presocial. It is a return that is also a beginning, in accordance with the dialectic that is inherent in social processes.   10

The group emerges purified and strengthened from this plunge into chaos. It has immersed itself in its own origins, in the womb from which it came. To express it in another way, the fiesta denies society as an organic system of differentiated forms and principles, but affirms it as a source of creative energy. It is a true "re-creation," the opposite of the "recreation" characterizing modern vacations, which do not entail any rites or ceremonies whatever and are as individualistic and sterile as the world that invented them.   11

Society communes with itself during the fiesta. Its members return to original chaos and freedom. Social structures break down and new relationships, unexpected rules, capricious hierarchies are created. In the general disorder everybody forgets himself and enters into otherwise forbidden situations and places. The bounds between audience and actors, officials and servants, are erased. Everybody takes part in the fiesta, everybody is caught up in its whirlwind. Whatever its mood, its character, its meaning, the fiesta is participation, and this trait distinguishes it from all other ceremonies and social phenomena. Lay or reli-   12 gious, orgy or saturnalia, the fiesta is a social act based on the full participation of all its celebrants.

13   Thanks to the fiesta the Mexican opens out, participates, communes with his fellows and with the values that give meaning to his religious or political existence. And it is significant that a country as sorrowful as ours should have so many and such joyous fiestas. Their frequency, their brilliance and excitement, the enthusiasm with which we take part, all suggest that without them we would explode. They free us, if only momentarily, from the thwarted impulses, the inflammable desires that we carry within us. But the Mexican fiesta is not merely a return to an original state of formless and normless liberty: the Mexican is not seeking to return, but to escape from himself, to exceed himself. Our fiestas are explosions. Life and death, joy and sorrow, music and mere noise are united, not to re-create or recognize themselves, but to swallow each other up. There is nothing so joyous as a Mexican fiesta, but there is also nothing so sorrowful. Fiesta night is also a night of mourning.

14   If we hide within ourselves in our daily lives, we discharge ourselves in the whirlwind of the fiesta. It is more than an opening out: we rend ourselves open. Everything—music, love, friendship—ends in tumult and violence. The frenzy of our festivals shows the extent to which our solitude closes us off from communication with the world. We are familiar with delirium, with songs and shouts, with the monologue …but not with the dialogue. Our fiestas, like our confidences, our loves, our attempts to reorder our society, are violent breaks with the old or the established. Each time we try to express ourselves we have to break with ourselves. And the fiesta is only one example, perhaps the most typical, of this violent break. It is not difficult to name others, equally revealing: our games, which are always a going to extremes, often mortal; our profligate spending, the reverse of our timid investments and business enterprises; our confessions. The somber Mexican, closed up in himself, suddenly explodes, tears open his breast and reveals himself, though not without a certain complacency, and not without a stopping place in the shameful or terrible mazes of his intimacy. We are not frank, but our sincerity can reach extremes that horrify a European. The explosive, dramatic, sometimes even suicidal manner in which we strip ourselves, surrender ourselves, is evidence that something inhibits and suffocates us. Something impedes us from being. And since we cannot or dare not confront our own selves, we resort to the fiesta. It fires us into the void; it is a drunken rapture that burns itself out, a pistol shot in the air, a skyrocket.

✧ Evaluating the Text

1. What factors contribute to the popularity of fiestas in Mexico, especially in relationship to the Mexican national character, as described by

Paz? In what way are people's experiences of time during the fiesta period qualitatively different from their experience of time during the rest of the year?

2. How does Paz's use of economic information as to the cost and frequency of fiestas help explain the extraordinary importance they play in Mexican life?

3. In what sense does a fiesta provide an opportunity for the solitary individual to be "at once resolved and redeemed"? What do you think Paz means by this?

4. How do Paz's comparisons between Mexican attitudes toward celebrations, life, and death with those of Europeans and North Americans make it easier for his readers to understand his analysis?

✧ Exploring Different Perspectives

1. Discuss the psychology of sacrificing what normally would be conserved to placate the gods and attract abundance, as revealed in Paz's essay and Bessie Head's story "Looking for a Rain God."

2. Discuss the theme of expenditure of material possessions for a desired purpose as explored by Paz and Slavenka Drakulić in "On Bad Teeth."

✧ Extending Viewpoints through Writing

1. Have you ever been at a party that came close in spirit to the Mexican fiesta, when people use the occasion to renew friendships, get drunk together, and discover kinships? If so, describe your experiences and discuss the similarities and differences in terms of the emotional transformation that such celebrations encourage.

2. To what extent do celebrations such as weddings, baptisms, bar mitzvahs, Mardi Gras in New Orleans, and vacations serve much the same function in the United States as fiestas do in Mexico?

Tad Friend

"Uno . . . Dos . . . Tres Urrrrnggghhh!"

◆───────────

Tad Friend lives in New York City and is a frequent contributor to The New Yorker, Vogue, Gentlemen's Quarterly, *and numerous other popular magazines. His range of interests is enormous and covers such subjects as traveling in Mongolia, profiling the actress Emma Thompson, covering Gary Shandling's lawsuits against his manager, and the esoteric sport of stone lifting in the Basque region, the subject of the following essay that he wrote for* Outside *(1997). This article was selected to be included in* The Best American Sports Writing, *edited by Bill Littlefield and series editor Glenn Stout (1998).*

The Basque region, bordering northern Spain and southwest France, is inhabited by approximately 2.5 million people who are probably the oldest ethnic group in Europe and are genetically and culturally unique. Their ancient language is unrelated to any Indo-European language and predates the Roman conquest. Under the Franco regime, the use of the Basque language in Spain was outlawed. Although in appearance they resemble their French and Spanish neighbors, their blood type has the lowest frequency of Type B and the highest occurrence of Types O and Rh-negative of any other ethnic group in Europe. Traditionally, the Basques make a living by working the land and fishing. There has always been a strong separatist movement in Basque culture. They were granted home rule by Spain in 1980. Because of the Basque tradition of inheritance known as primogeniture, under which the eldest son inherits the family farm, younger sons have migrated to North and South America. Christianity came to the Basque region in the fourth and fifth centuries and produced such famous figures as St. Ignatius of Loyola. The population is mainly Roman Catholic to this day. The culture is distinguished by unique forms of games, music, folklore, and competitive sports, such as jai alai and stone lifting.

1   In a dusty pelota court in the old Basque village of Arcangues, Migueltxo Saralegi squares his shoulders and throws his hands to the sky. Wearing blue shorts with white thigh pads, a leather waistcoat, and two black tummy belts, he cuts a heraldic figure. Saralegi's reach is actually to expand his lungs, but his aspect makes one imagine he's summoning ancient gods.

510

Now the stone lifter bends over a lead-filled block of granite. 2
Grasping handholds on its far side, he bucks the awkward object onto
his padded thighs, his face crimsoning as his lungs explode in a
whoosh. The stone weighs 250 kilograms—550 pounds. Saralegi slides
his hands to the stone's base and then jumps back while levering it end
over end to his chest. For the third combination in this dance of balanced force—Saralegi should be the hero of every mover who ever
schlepped a grand piano—he drives his torso back again and boosts
the stone to his left shoulder. He cradles it there, then removes his
hands and pirouettes before shrugging the stone onto a foam hassock.

Two hundred tourists give Saralegi a polite golf clap. Rich Ger- 3
mans and Brits sprung from four gleaming buses, they are kitted out in
red "Basque" berets and cloth belts, and everyone carries a glass of rum
punch. After witnessing dances, a pelota match, and woodcutting, they
are in a folkways frame of mind—curious to see more Basque exotica,
but emotionally disengaged. Saralegi has a parallel view: he drove two
hours into France from Pamplona solely for the money. He gets about
four hundred dollars; the tourists get a show. No harm done.

Yet the 29-year-old actually holds the world's stone-lifting record 4
of 326 kilos, or 717 pounds, and in three days he'll attempt a new mark
of 327 before an entirely different audience: knowledgeable Basques
primed by a daylong "festival of hunting and fishing." To the Basques,
these *herri kilorak*—"rural sports," derived from clearing the land and
from farming—epitomize their manly culture. Such contests include
log-chopping, scything, handling oxen and donkeys in stone-dragging
races, running with 200-pound sacks on one's shoulder, tossing hay
bales over an elevated rope, and most impressively, the *harrijasotzaile*,
or stone lifting. Stone lifting is "no longer a folkloric exhibition, or for
circus strongmen," the local *Diario de Navarra* proudly editorializes. "It
requires much more strenuous training than a weight lifter['s]." In November and December, when Saralegi bulks up for the following summer's record attempts, he lifts 88,000 pounds *per day*.

To put it in terms that every American can understand, Saralegi's 5
record of 326 kilos is equivalent to hoisting seven supermodels. Indeed,
Saralegi calls the record stone La Gorda—the Fat One—as if it were a
fleshy but fickle mistress. In cold weather he wraps her in a blanket,
and if she refuses to come to his shoulder he mutters, "She didn't want
love today." If she balks repeatedly he calls her *culebra!* (snake) and
puta! (whore).

Now Saralegi rolls out a granite ball that weighs only 220 pounds, 6
and the announcer invites the audience to give it a try. Three men come
and strain at the sphere, then slink off to general giggling. No tourist
has ever lifted it above the instep of an Italian loafer. Saralegi, who's
maintained a fixed expression throughout these indignities, whisks the
ball to his shoulder in one pull and whips it around his neck six times.

The applause is much more appreciative; their representatives' humbling has given the audience a connection to the feat.

7   Afterward, as the tourists are herded off to a ghastly "Basque" feast, I try the granite ball myself. By straining till my eyeballs fill with blood I nudge it perhaps six microns. "How much does he think I could lift?" I ask Edurne Percaz, the voluble brunette who works at a Pamplona gym with Saralegi and who is serving as my translator. (Saralegi, who suffers interviews warily and whose Spanish has an elementary-school flavor, is happiest conversing in Euskara, the k-, x-, and z-riddled tongue spoken by one-fourth of the 2.5 million Basques.) His surprisingly gentle hand envelops my biceps; next to his 290-pound Clydesdale frame I feel like Ichabod Crane. 'Fifty kilos," he says in Spanish, "but tell him seventy to make him happy.

8   "I'm sorry," he adds pityingly, "but we are just stronger. It's the race." The Basques believe they are Europe's oldest people, having inhabited the land straddling the Pyrenees since at least 4000 B.C. They have the world's highest percentage of Rh-negative blood and claim to be bigger and stronger and braver than any arriviste Aryans, Franks, and Normans, claim to be the world's toughest soldiers—claim, in fact, to have landed in America before Columbus. "We do our tasks," Saralegi says. "We have a history with the stones. An Italian man with the same muscles can't pick up our stones—because he has no reason to."

9   And with that Saralegi picks up his stones, slides them onto a handcart, and dollies them up wooden planks into the back of his beat-up Peugeot van. Then the world's greatest stone lifter takes a push broom and sweeps up the woodcutter's sawdust, working steadily with workmanlike strokes until everything is tidy, until the job is done.

10   The streets of this Pamplona neighborhood are full of Basques who are sweaty and cheerful and rather drunk on *kalimotxo*, their dignifying name for red wine mixed with Coca-Cola. I am equally sweaty and cheerful, and just possibly more drunk. A spontaneous festival has broken out here in Milagrosa: Teenagers thread in and out on stilts; dancers click fingers and shake leg bells as they sing "Azuri Beltza"; children parade in pointed hats crowned with feathers, wearing twin cowbells attached to the backs of their wool doublets. When they hop in unison the streets ring. A man inside a mechanical bull's body that shoots out sparks chases the children about in a cloud of smoke and happy screams.

11   At midnight we pause for dinner at the Sorgintze bar. We've already hit the Sorgintze four times, acquiring new friends with each pass. I am surrounded by grinning Saralegi supporters gobbling up trenchers of greasy cod and toothsome asparagus. Meanwhile Saralegi, preparing for the record attempt in two days, has already been asleep for three hours at his mother's house in nearby Leitza. In his home vil-

lage Saralegi can ramble with the dogs and feed the cows and never answer the phone. He can dream tidy dreams. If he raises the stone, he will reward himself only with a gigantic ham sandwich.

"Migueltxo is a champion, a monster," says Josu, shaking his head   12
at such self-denial. "But all Basques can lift 100 kilos—how much can you lift?"

"One hundred kilos at least," I say, made rash by *kalimotxo.*   13

"I can lift 150 kilos," says Zube. I am astonished: Zube works at the   14
Volkswagen factory, but he is as soft and mild as a tub of sweet butter. "But just now I have a bad back," he admits, having caught my eye.

"Men are always boasting about these sports because they have   15
nothing to do, really," Percaz whispers to me before addressing the table: "Women are the kings of the Basque household, and men are the kings of nothing." All the men groan and roll their eyes.

About 2 A.M. the kings of nothing lead us down the street to an out-   16
door concert for Basque independence. The black eagle of freedom flutters on yellow pennants, and the square is thronged with *jarrai,* the radical young separatists who last year rampaged through the city of Bilbao, burning banks and buses. The women have brightly hennaed hair, the men a punk look: shaved heads with rattails, piratical earrings, and Che and *Amnistía!* T-shirts.

Some 500 of the older colleagues of the *jarrai,* the Marxist–Leninist   17
Euskadi Ta Askatasuna, are in prison. A terrorist group whose name means "Basque Homeland and Liberty," the ETA has killed more than 800 people since it was founded in 1959 to battle Franco, who seemed intent upon genocidal revenge for the Basques' having opposed him in the Spanish Civil War. First Franco's German allies bombed defenseless Guernica in 1937; later Franco exiled 200,000 Basques, put 100,000 in prison, and outlawed the Basque language.

But when I ask about the ETA, everyone frowns. Their extremism is   18
out of favor now that their pressure has led to limited self-determination: today the Basques have their own schools, television, and police force. Zube gestures to the crowd, as if to say that tonight everyone just wants to drink and throb around. "That is the stereotype Americans have," says Percaz, "that we all shoot people. And your other stupidity is about running the bulls at San Fermin."

Pamplona's eight-day Fiesta de San Fermin, beginning every July 6,   19
was first made traveler's legend by Ernest Hemingway in *The Sun Also Rises.* Hemingway described an unlucky runner being gored to death, and nearly every year nowadays, as the men flee the rampaging bulls in the daily race through the streets, a drunk American stumbles, forgets to hurl his rolled-up newspaper aside—bulls charge at movement—and gets himself ripped a new one.

Handing me another scarlet drink, Percaz explains that for the   20
Basques, this chase down slick flagstones is a way to triumph over

death, to feel life coursing through your veins. "You have to grow up watching it to truly understand. That man trains all year long to run the bulls," she says, pointing to a slight, potbellied gentleman, whose training protocol seems to be chugging *patxaran* liqueur until it dribbles down his chin.

21   "I could run the bulls as well as that guy," I say. "And next year I will." This is the *kalimotxo* working its ruination, yet my brainstorm seems fiendishly plausible. I will run every morning of the fiesta, hoping to survive till the somewhat easier *encierro*, the *encierro de la villavesa*: all the bulls are dead, so the proud warriors lope in front of a bus.

22   "*You* can't run the bulls," Percaz says, tossing her hair. "Not really."

23   "Anyone can *run*," I say.

24   "You don't understand anything," she says. "Nothing. And tell me this while we are speaking of Americans who have no good ideas in their head: why don't you have topless bathing?"

25   I mumble something about our Puritan forebears. "Here I can kiss my friends on the lips in public," she interrupts.

26   "But not with the tongue," I counter.

27   "Yes," she says. "Sure, why not? You are 150 years behind us sexually."

28   "Maybe in public," I say, hazily trying to mount a defense of American debauchery. "But in private we are tremendous bedroom athletes."

29   "No," Percaz says decidedly. "No, I have been to America."

30   The next afternoon we drive to Lumbier for a village sports festival. Beside the road an occasional red-tile-roofed village shoots up from the swaths of green wheat and then is gone. They are somehow dustier and more insular than other Spanish villages, and more helter-skelter than French Basque villages. Poplars line the river course and hills crowd in, unsettling the eye like a bunched-up quilt on an unmade bed.

31   In Lumbier we are nearly bowled over by a parade of 15-foot-high papier-mâché "giants," including Ferdinand and Isabella. We follow a huge, sad Don Quixote through the stone valleys to the square. (Quixote was far too inept to be a Basque, but he makes a splendid costume.) Every Basque town has an annual festival, seizing any reason to party: honoring the Virgin Mary, celebrating fishwives, or simply seeing who can pull the head off of a greased goose. Lumbier's festival, for instance, is to celebrate expatriates from the Navarra province, none of whom seem to be here.

32   Yet in the square the presentation of rural sports has attracted perhaps five hundred people. First is the *sokatira*, the tug of war, which the Basques claim to have invented. Then comes the *aizkolaris*, in which two men race to chop through a succession of wide beech logs, teetering atop them with their axes flashing in the hot sun.

Then a special exhibition: Nartxi Saralegi, Migueltxo's 37-year-old brother, places his 6-year-old son, Ruben, atop a small log and hands him a George-Washington-and-the-cherry-tree-size ax. Nartxi points to a spot on the log, and the boy makes the first cut. Nartxi touches another spot, lower down. And so it continues for hundreds of tiny blows, including one that narrowly misses Ruben's toes as he slips off the log. When the beech finally splits, the applause is warm and generous.

Finally the announcer introduces Iñaki Perurena, a butcher from the Saralegis' home village of Leitza and a legendary stone lifter: he raised the single-lift record from 250 kilos all the way to 318 and still holds records for lifting 267 kilos with one hand and for revolving the 100-kilo stone around his neck 36 times in a minute. Perurena is 40 now, his gingery hair and beard thinning. He is a little chubby, perhaps, and his brow shines with sweat. But he takes the microphone eagerly: "Friends, thanks for gathering to see our countrymen's work made sport. I am happy to see so many of you here, because it means we will never lose the traditions. And it is our traditions, special to us alone, that make us who we are." He stretches his hands to the sky, pauses dramatically, and then runs to the 200-kilo stone with the quick steps of a lover.

As he lifts it four times to gathering applause, I talk with Nartxi Saralegi, who holds his son tenderly but looks a trifle grim. The Basques love Perurena's gusto and still consider him the sport's eminence, though Migueltxo topped his single-lift record four years ago and has raised it six times since. "Perurena is a showman," Nartxi says, "grabbing the microphone though there is already an announcer. I only wish they were the same age, just once, so everyone would see that Migueltxo is *better*. Still," he acknowledges, "Migueltxo would never be able to make that speech." Migueltxo is like Ferdinand the Bull, possessing none of the I'm-the-man braggadocio required to cross over from athlete to cultural (and advertising) phenomenon. "I try and try to get him to talk, to gesture to the crowd," Nartxi says, "but I cannot even get him to tell *me* about his feelings."

Ten years ago Nartxi, a Navarra champion in woodcutting but never world-class, saw his youngest brother's career languishing in Leitza. Migueltxo's only training was lifting the stone, as it had been since age 11, when he spied a 65-kilo stone around the house and found it "a temptation." At 18 he was stuck on the 280-kilo stone. So Nartxi installed Migueltxo in his house in Pamplona, had his wife cook him special fat- and sugar-free lunches and dinners, and built him a training area in his garage, where he would lift stones regularly with Nartxi when he wasn't lifting weights with his trainer. Nartxi became almost a father to Migueltxo, even more so since their father died last year.

"I control everything," Nartxi says simply. "I am sharper, more open-minded, and I have more concentration—many times I have made Migueltxo lift when he is not feeling like it." Nartxi's frustration is evident: to make ends meet, both men must work at the Gymnasio Jolaskide, Migueltxo as a fitness trainer, Nartxi as a receptionist. Nartxi believes he could go much farther in the sport, for he has the mind and passion of a great lifter—but it is Migueltxo who has the body.

38   That body has been reinforced like a missile silo. I later ask Saralegi's trainer, a slim, bullet-headed man named Jose Luis Tovias, what I would need to do to become a stone lifter. He laughed for a while. "Go to Lourdes," he said at last, ashing a cigarette. "Seriously? Well, first get your weight up to 130 kilos," he suggested, plumping me up 50 kilos, "but by eating only proteins. No hamburgers, no lamb. No alcohol. Then the basic exercise is the squat, because the most important muscles are the quadriceps and the back. Migueltxo does 500 kilos"—1,100 pounds—"five times in a row." Saralegi also bench-presses 450 pounds and curls 200 pounds. Eight years ago he totaled his car but emerged unscathed. The doctor told him, "Your body was ready for a big shock."

39   "Migueltxo doesn't have the quick strength in the wrists and the knees to be an Olympic weight lifter," Tovias said. "He has a slower force. But it's mentally more difficult. He has time to think between the three movements, time to feel his body falling apart." Saralegi knows he has only a few more years to make records and hopes to reach at least 330 kilos before his knees give way.

40   Here in Lumbier comes the hope of the future: Perurena's 13-year-old son, Inaxio, will lift a 90-kilo stone four times. His father hovers nervously as Inaxio makes the sign of the cross and tips the stone back on shaky, coltish legs. Perurena can't resist helping a little on the final lift, so the referee requests a relift. Inaxio staggers under the weight but ultimately raises it, to sustained cheering. Then Perurena lifts 250 kilos four times, huffing and clutching his lower back in between reps so that the audience bends and jerks with him in silent unison, willing the stone up. After the last hoist he spreads his arms in happy exhaustion. "I want to be like my father," Inaxio tells me, his face reverent.

41   Perurena then comes over to talk, crowding me cheerfully with his elbows and stalking the conversation like a boxer, his blue singlet soaked with sweat: "We are not force men only—we have feelings," he says. "The stone gives me everything. The view of my life always has the stone in the middle of it." He folds Inaxio in a sideways hug. "When he was three I let him start touching the stones—and it's important that he's listening to this interview. It's not just the lifting; it's the life. Lifting and teaching Inaxio to lift are different pages of the same book."

42   And Saralegi, I ask? "We are very different," he says. "My son should learn from Migueltxo how to train, which I never did so much. But Migueltxo's focus is to hold the record stone—that is his only goal, his only interest in this task of ours. For me, I will do this the rest of my life. Even when I have no hair, when I am as bald as the stone, I will be

lifting with pride in my job. And the people will come see me to encourage, and to relish the effort."

Migueltxo Saralegi eyes La Gorda nervously, as if his mistress had   43
picked a fight. Two days ago he added a kilo to it and spray-painted the
new number in red: "327 K" He also lifted it in practice. But now he
stands on a small platform in the Salburua fields outside Victoria at
5:30 on a hot, still Sunday afternoon with several thousand people
watching. It is a strange, jerry-built venue, removed from the rest of the
festival happenings. Basque television broadcasts all of Saralegi's
record attempts, so the stage bustles with cameras and technicians and
is further checkered by five sponsors' banners, including Volkswagen
and Kaiku Milk. For the record attempt he'll be paid about $12,000—
enough to buy a new van.

Saralegi rosins the stone's edges as if he were dusting it with dia-   44
monds. Incongruous *trikitixa*, Basque accordion ditties, play on the loudspeakers. "We have to be very quiet for the moment of the great deed,"
the emcee bellows, "quiet like we are in church." Saralegi grimaces—all
that silent expectation only increases the pressure. His best friend, a
plumber named Ibon, towels Saralegi's red, sweating face.

Nartxi fixes his brother with his fierce green eyes. "You are going to   45
do it," he commands. Migueltxo scuffs at the floor with his special red
and white shoes, and Nartxi, who misses nothing, insists, "The floor is
not as bad as we thought—you are 100 percent!" In fact the stage is
much too bouncy, and its planks are dangerously far apart. After
Nartxi checked out the footing yesterday he told Ibon privately,
"Migueltxo won't do it."

"It is too hot, and the floor is very bad," the TV announcer intones,   46
and Nartxi whips around, glaring. But Migueltxo's concentration is
such that he hears none of this. He turns to stare out the back of the
stage into an empty green field, taking huge breaths that echo through
the microphone. Two black eagles rise above the field, circling on the
convection currents. He mimes the lift to himself, picturing where the
stone will touch his body. Beside him Nartxi shadows the movements
in tandem, leaning in as if to merge his strength with his brother's.

Then Saralegi turns and begins. He hoicks the weight to his thighs,   47
his eyelids closing over with the effort. The huge stone seems to be
squeezing him. After a steadying pause, he jumps back and pulls it to
his chest. This is the lift's crucial maneuver—akin to balancing a plate
on a stick with your nose and jumping back to steady it, only the plate
is top-heavy and weighs 719 pounds. But Saralegi's heel catches in a
crack and his body shivers sideways. Nartxi, miming alongside, has his
notional stone shoulder-high, but Migueltxo's stone hovers just out of
control in midair. Ibon and Nartxi leap forward, but Migueltxo has already thumped the stone onto the tuffet.

48   The applause is generous and encouraging, and he gives a scrunchy-faced wave. But he stares angrily at the stone, measuring its edges with his hands. As Ibon wipes his face again, he murmurs, "The floor is a whore." Only once has he nabbed a record on the second try— the first effort saps 20 percent of his energy—but Nartxi doggedly psyches him up: "Breathe, breathe!" Migueltxo braces and heaves, but the stone makes it only halfway off his thighs. He waves again but looks crestfallen.

49   Nartxi tries to spin the failure. "In a way it's good," he says afterward, "because the people need to see that this is not easy to do, that he requires good conditions." Meanwhile, a Viscayan stone lifter named Zelia is metronomically hoisting a 150-kilo stone, aiming at his own record of 52 lifts in 10 minutes. Zelia has asthma, and by the time he has broken the record with 56 lifts he is utterly out of air and topples sideways into his handlers' arms. The crowd loves it, the drama as much as the record.

50   But Migueltxo, who hasn't much use for Zelia, remarks that "that record is easier, because the man can always lift the stone. In my record, sometimes the winner is the man, sometimes the stone." Rendered smaller and more loquacious by defeat, he now sits readily for an interview with *Diario de Navarra*. "The first problem is that the stone was very heavy," he explains—a funny line, were his intent not so methodical.

51   Almost drowning out Migueltxo's plain talk are the hugely amplified announcements of Tom Knapp, an American trapshooter in the neighboring field. Knapp throws two clay targets into the air, shoots one, ejects the cartridge, shoots it, and then shoots the other target. His buttery voice rides over the cheering, announcing "A *muy rápidas* Berelli! And so easy-loading!" It becomes clear that the exhibition is purely an ad for the Berelli rifle. Knapp mentions Berelli thirty times in a minute— "It's like having two Berellis in one—a semiautomatic Berelli and a pump Berelli!"—as he blows balloons and vegetables to smithereens.

52   Nartxi listens to all this odious persuasion—"I have a new product from Berelli for the ladies of the house only!"—with surprising care, sifting, within his manager's role, for promotional tips. "If Migueltxo were an American it would be the best," he says at last. "He would understand...." He gestures delphically, a glyph of love and frustration. "He would understand that part of the job is to sell himself." But Migueltxo pays it no mind at all, only rolling his eyes and waving good-bye as he's ushered off for his urine test.

✧ Evaluating the Text

1. Compare the very different perspectives on what stone lifting means to the Basques and to the tourists who witness Saralegi's performance.

2. In what sense is stone lifting a way of life with its own values, regimen, and mythology for the Basques?

3. From the Basque perspective, in what sense is stone lifting a more authentic reflection of Basque culture than the better known running of the bulls at Pamplona, popularized by Ernest Hemingway? In what other ways do Basques wish to define themselves as a distinct ethnic group, although they live on the border between France and Spain?

✧ Exploring Different Perspectives

1. Compare the significance of stone lifting for the Basques with what the fiesta means for Mexicans (see Octavio Paz's "Fiesta").

2. Discuss stone lifting as an object of cultural pride for the Basques in the same way that culinary practices exemplify the pride of the Chinese, according to Guanlong Cao (see "The Culture of Killing").

✧ Extending Viewpoints through Writing

1. What is the most amazing feat of physical strength you have ever witnessed? Describe it. You might watch broadcasts of the world's strongest man competitions on ESPN. How do you explain the appeal of these spectacles? Is lifting an immensely heavy (500+ pounds) stone a more authentic display of strength than any of the other ingenious feats (for example, dragging three stretch limousines over a certain distance) that comprise these contests? Why or why not?

2. Select another sport and analyze in an essay the ways it reveals significant aspects of a national culture (for example, cricket in the West Indies, hurling in Ireland, kendo in Japan, lacrosse in Canada, jai alai in the Basque region, polo in Argentina, soccer in Brazil, or cock fighting in Bali).

Connecting Cultures

◆

Guanlong Cao, *The Culture of Killing*

Discuss the similarities and differences in Chinese cuisine as described by Cao and the preparation of *fugu* fish in Japanese culture, as portrayed in Kazuo Ishiguro's story "A Family Supper" in Chapter 1.

Slavenka Drakulić, *On Bad Teeth*

Discuss the level of tolerance extended by Americans toward those who look different as revealed in Drakulić's article and in Sucheng Chan's "You're Short, Besides!" in Chapter 2.

Bessie Head, *"Looking for a Rain God"*

How do Head's story and Ngũgĩ wa Thiong'o's account (see "Decolonising the Mind" in Chapter 6) reveal the dual nature of tribal society in Botswana and Kenya? What attitude do both works reveal toward the recently imposed layer of colonial "civilization"?

Gino Del Guercio, *"The Secrets of Haiti's Living Dead"*

Explore the similarities in social conditioning that results in the concept of a pariah (see Viramma's "Pariah" in Chapter 5) with the methods that Voodoun priests in Haiti use to control their victims.

Nabil Gorgy, *"Cairo Is a Small City"*

What is the significance of the very different ways that revenge is pursued in Gorgy's story and in "The Miller's Tale" by Jerzy Kosinski in Chapter 2?

Octavio Paz, *"Fiesta"*

Discuss the role that excess and violence play in producing public catharsis in such forms of ritualized public theater as described by Paz and Anwar Iqbal in "Fifteen Lashes" in Chapter 6.

Tad Friend, *"Uno…Dos…Tres…Urrrrnggghhh!"*

In its own way, the self-imposed discipline of a stone lifter shares similarities with the unlikely profession of cleaning toilets in Japan, as described by Louise Rafkin in "A Yen for Cleaning" in Chapter 4. In an essay, discuss the symbolic nature of both avocations.

Rhetorical Index

◆

DESCRIPTION

Patricia Hampl   "Grandmother's Sunday Dinner"
Gayatri Devi   "A Princess Remembers"
Fatima Mernissi   "Moonlit Nights of Laughter"
Douchan Gersi   "Initiated into an Iban Tribe of Headhunters"
Tepilit Ole Saitoti   "The Initiation of a Maasai Warrior"
Lesley Hazleton   "Confessions of a Fast Woman"
Louise Rafkin   "A Yen for Cleaning"
Luis Alberto Urrea   "Border Story"
Octavio Paz   "Fiesta"

NARRATION (PERSONAL)

Patricia Hampl   "Grandmother's Sunday Dinner"
Gayle Pemberton   "Antidisestablishmentarianism"
Pat Mora   "Remembering Lobo"
Gayatri Devi   "A Princess Remembers"
Serena Nanda   "Arranging a Marriage in India"
Fatima Mernissi   "Moonlit Nights of Laughter"
Christy Brown   "The Letter 'A'"
Sucheng Chan   "You're Short, Besides"
Tepilit Ole Saitoti   "The Initiation of a Maasai Warrior"
Helen Fremont   "After Long Silence"
Paul Monette   "Borrowed Time: An AIDS Memoir"
Lesley Hazleton   "Confessions of a Fast Woman"
Victor Villaseñor   "Rain of Gold"
Tomoyuki Iwashita   "Why I Quit the Company"
Jackie Chan   "A Dirty Job"
Alonso Salazar   "The Lords of Creation"
Mary Crow Dog   "Civilize Them with a Stick"
Viramma   "Pariah"
Lee Stringer   "Life on the Street"
Rae Yang   "At the Center of the Storm"
Luis Sepulveda   "Daisy"
Palden Gyatso   "Autobiography of a Tibetan Monk"

NARRATION (OBSERVATION AND REPORTING)

Daniela Deane   "The Little Emperors"
Kim Chernin   "The Flesh and the Devil"
Judith Ortiz Cofer   "The Myth of the Latin Woman"
Marjorie Shostak   "Memories of a !Kung Girlhood"
Natalia Ginzburg   "The Son of Man"

JOURNALS AND DIARIES

SPEECHES

FICTION

Geographical Index

$\blacklozenge$

Acknowledgments

◆

Mary Crow Dog and Richard Erdoes, "Civilize Them with a Stick" from *Lakota Woman*. Copyright © 1990 by Mary Crow Dog and Richard Erdoes. Reprinted with the permission of Grove/Atlantic, Inc.

Lennard J. Davis, "Visualizing the Disabled Body" (editors' title, originally titled and excerpted from "Visualizing the Disabled Body: The Classical Nude and the Fragmented Torso") from *Enforcing Normalcy: Disability, Deafness, and the Body*. Copyright © 1995 by Leonard J. Davis. Reprinted with the permission of Verso.

Daniela Deane, "The Little Emperors" from *The Los Angeles Times Magazine* (July 26, 1992). Copyright © 1992 by the *Los Angeles Times*. Reprinted by permission.

Gino Del Guercio, "The Secrets of Haiti's Living Dead" from *Harvard Magazine* (January/February 1986). Copyright © 1986 by Gino Del Guercio. Reprinted with the permission of the author.

Gayatari Devi and Santha Rama Rau, "A Visit to Baroda" from *A Princess Remembers: The Memories of the Maharani of Jaipur*. Copyright © 1976 by Gayatari Devi and Santha Rama Rau. Reprinted with the permission of the William Morris Agency, Inc. on behalf of the author.

Mahasweta Devi, "Giribala" from *Of Women, Outcasts, Peasants, and Rebels: A Selection of Bengali Short Stories*, edited by Kalpana Bardhan. Copyright © 1990 by the Regents of the University of California. Reprinted with the permission of the University of California Press.

Slavenka Drakulic, "On Bad Teeth" from *Cafe Europa: Life After Communism*. Copyright © 1996 by Slavenka Drakulic. Reprinted with the permission of W. W. Norton & Company, Inc.

Helen Fremont, excerpt from *After Long Silence*. Copyright © 1999 by Helen Fremont. Reprinted with the permission of Delacorte Press, a division of Random House, Inc.

Tad Friend, "Uno…Dos…Tres…Urrrrnggghhh!" from *Outside Magazine* (1997). Reprinted with the permission of the author.

Douchan Gersi, "Initiated Into an Iban Tribe" from *Explorer* (New York: Jeremy P. Tarcher/St. Martin's Press, 1987), pp. 272–276. Copyright © 1987 by Douchan Gersi. Reprinted by permission.

Natalia Ginzburg, "The Son of Man" from *A Map of Hope: Women's Writing on Human Rights—An International Literary Anthology*, edited by Marjorie Agosin, 1999. Reprinted with the permission of Giulio Einaudi Editore.

Nabil Gorgy, "Cairo Is a Small City" from *Modern Arabic Short Stories*, translated by Denys Johnson-Davies (Washington, DC: Three Continents Press, 1988). Copyright © 1988 by Denys Johnson-Davies. Reprinted with the permission of the translator.

Palden Gyatso, "Prologue" from *The Autobiography of a Tibetan Monk*, translated by Palden Gyatso and Taering Shakya. Copyright © 1997 by Palden Gyatso and Taering Shakya. Reprinted with the permission of Grove/Atlantic, Inc.

Patricia Hampl, "Grandmother's Sunday Dinner" from *A Romantic Education*. Copyright © 1981, 1997 by Patricia Hampl. Reprinted with the permission of W. W. Norton & Company, Inc.

Leslie Hazleton, "Confessions of a Fast Woman" from *Confessions of a Fast Woman.* Copyright © 1992 by Leslie Hazleton. Reprinted with the permission of Addison-Wesley Publishing Company.

Liliana Heker, "The Stolen Party" from *Other Fires: Short Fiction by Latin-American Women,* edited by Alberto Manguel. Copyright © 1982 by Lillian Heker. Copyright © 1986 by Alberto Manguel. Reprinted with the permission of Clarkson Potter/Publishers, a division of Random House, Inc.

Saida Hagi-Dirie Herzi, "Against the Pleasure Principle" from *A Map of Hope: Women's Writing on Human Rights,* edited by Marjorie Agosin. Copyright © 1999 by Rutgers, the State University. Reprinted with the permission of Rutgers University Press.

Panos Ionnides, "Gregory," translated by Marion Byron and Catherine Raizis, from *The Charioteer: A Review of Modern Greek Literature.* Copyright © 1989 by Panos Ioannides. English translation copyright © 1989 by Marion Byron and Catherine Raizis. Reprinted with the permission of Pella Publishing, New York, NY.

Anwar Iqbal, "Fifteen Lashes" from *Granta* 63 (Autumn 1998). Reprinted with the permission of the author.

Kazuo Ishiguro, "Family Supper" from *Firebird 2* (London: Penguin, 1982). Reprinted with the permission of the Estate of Kazuo Ishiguro c/o Rogers Coleridge & White Ltd.

Tomoyuki Iwashita, "Why I Quit the Company" from *The New Internationalist* (May 1992). Copyright © 1992. Reprinted with the permission of the publishers.

Mahdokht Kashkuli, "The Button" from *Stories by Iranian Women Since the Revolution,* translated by Sorayua Sullivan (Austin: Center for Middle Eastern Studies, University of Texas at Austin, 1991). Reprinted with the permission of Center for Middle Eastern Studies, The University of Texas at Austin.

Kon Krailet, "In the Mirror" from Trevor Carolan, ed., *The Colors of Heaven: Short Stories from the Pacific Rim* (New York: Random House, 1991). Reprinted by permission.

Fatima Mernissi, "Moonlit Nights of Laughter" from *Dreams of Trespass: Tales of a Harem Girlhood.* Copyright © 1994 by Fatima Mernissi. Reprinted with the permission of Perseus Books Publishers, a member of Perseus Books L.L.C.

Paul Monette, "Borrowed Time" from *Borrowed Time: An AIDS Memoir.* Copyright © 1988 by Paul Monette. Reprinted with the permission of Harcourt, Inc.

Pat Mora, "Remembering Lobo" from *Nepantla.* Copyright © 1993 by The University of New Mexico. Reprinted with the permission of The University of New Mexico Press.

Kyoko Mori, excerpt from "Bodies" from *Polite Lies: On Being a Woman Caught Between Cultures.* Copyright © 1997 by Kyoko Mori. Reprinted with the permission of Henry Holt and Company, LLC.

Serena Nanda, "Arranging a Marriage in India" from *The Naked Anthropologist: Tales from Around the World,* edited by Philip R. deVita, 1992. Reprinted with the permission of the author.

R. N. Narayan, "Misguided 'Guide'" from *A Writer's Nightmare: Selected Essays 1958-1988* (New York: Penguin Books, 1988). Copyright© 1988 by R. N. Narayan. Reprinted by permission of The Wallace Literary Agency.

Jesse W. Nash, "Confucius and the VCR" from *Natural History* (May 1988). Copyright © 1988 by The American Museum of Natural History. Reprinted with permission.

Jo Goodwin Parker, "What Is Poverty?" from *America's Other Children,* edited by George Henderson. Copyright © 1971 by University of Oklahoma Press. Reprinted with the permission of the publishers.

Milorad Pavić, "The Wedgwood Tea Set," translated by Darka Topali, from *The Prince of Fire: An Anthology of Contemporary Serbian Short Stories,* edited by Radmila J. Gorup and Madezda Obradovic. Copyright © 1998 by the University of Pittsburgh Press. Reprinted with the permission of the publishers.

Octavio Paz, "The Day of the Dead" from *The Labyrinth of Solitude,* translated by Lysander Kemp. Copyright © 1961 by Grove Press, Inc. Reprinted with the permission of Grove/Atlantic, Inc.

Gayle Pemberton, "Antidisestablishmentarianism" from *The Hottest Water in Chicago* (Boston: Faber and Faber, 1992). Copyright © 1992 by Gayle Pemberton. Reprinted with the permission of the author.

Louise Rafkin, "A Yen for Cleaning" from *Other People's Dirt: A Housecleaner's Curious Adventures.* Copyright © 1998 by Louise Rafkin. Reprinted with the permission of Algonquin Books of Chapel Hill, a division of Workman Publishing.

Shirley Saad, "Amina" from *Opening the Gates: A Century of Arab Feminist Writing,* Margot Badran and Miriam Cooke, eds. Copyright © 1990. Reprinted with the permission of Indiana University Press.

Tepilit Ole Saitoti, "The Initiation of a Maasai Warrior" from *The Worlds of a Maasai Warrior.* Copyright © 1986 by Tepilit Ole Saitoti. Reprinted with the permission of Random House, Inc.

Alonso Salazar, "The Lords of Creation" from *Born to Die in Medellín,* translated by Nick Caistor. Copyright © 1990 by CINEP. Reprinted with the permission of Latin America Bureau, London.

Luis Sepulveda, excerpt from *Full Circle: A South American Journey,* translated by Chris Andrews. Copyright © 1996. Reprinted with the permission of Lonely Planet Publications.

Lee Stringer, excerpt from *Grand Central Winter: Stories from the Street.* Copyright © 1998 by Lee Stringer. Reprinted with the permission of Seven Stories Press, New York, NY.

Ngugi wa Thiong'o, "Decolonising the Mind" from *Decolonising the Mind: The Politics of Language in African Literature.* Copyright © 1985 by Ngugi wa Thiong'o. Reprinted with the permission of East African Educational Publishers, Nairobi, Kenya.

Pronunciation Key

The pronunciation of each of the following names is shown in parentheses according to the following pronunciation key.

1. A heavy accent ' is placed after a syllable with the primary accent.
2. A lighter accent ´ is placed after a syllable with the secondary accent.
3. The letters and symbols used to represent given sounds are pronounced as in the examples below.

a	bat, nap		o	box, hot
ā	way, cape		ō	boat, go
â	dare, air		ô	ought, order
ä	art, far		oi	voice, joy
			oo	ooze, rule
b	cabin, back		ou	loud, out
ch	beach, child			
d	do, red		p	pot, paper
			r	read, run
e	bet, merry		s	see, miss
ē	equal, beet		sh	show, push
ė	learn, fern			
			t	tell, ten
f	fit, puff		th	thin, path
g	give, go		t∦	that, smooth
h	how, him			
			u	up, butter
i	pin, big		u̇	put, burn
ī	deny, ice		ü	rule, ooze
j	jam, fudge			
k	keep, kind		v	river, save
			w	west, will
l	love, all		y	yes, yet
m	my, am		z	zeal, lazy
n	in, now		zh	vision, measure
ng	sing, long			

ə occurs only in unaccented syllables and indicates the sound of

a	in alone
e	in taken
i	in pencil
o	in gallop
u	in circus

FOREIGN SOUNDS

a   as in French *ami*
Y   as in French *do;* or as in German *über*
œ   as in French *feu;* or as in German *schön*
N   as in French *bon*
H   as in German *ach;* or as in Scottish *loch*
R   as in Spanish *pero;* or as in German *mare*

EXAMPLES

Gayatri Devi	(gā a´ trē de´ vē)
Kazuo Ishiguro	(kä zü´ ō ish i gür´ ö)
Tepilit Ole Saitoti	(te´ pə lit ō´ lē sī tō´ tē)
Saida Hagi-Dirie Herzi	(sä ē´ də hagē di´ rē hėr´ zē)
Mahasweta Devi	(mä´ hə swe´ tə de´ vē)
Shirley Saad	(shúr´ lē säd)
Tomoyuki Iwashita	(tō mō yü´ kē i wä shē´ tä)
Kon Krailet	(kon krā´ let)
Mahdokht Kashkuli	(mə dōkt´ käsh kü´ lē)
Milorad Pavić	(mil´ ôr əd pä´ vich)
Ngũgĩ wa Thiong'o	(nə gōō´ gē wä tē ong´ ō)
Luis Alberto Urrea	(loo ēs´ al bâr´ tō oo Rē´ ə)
Guanlong Cao	(gwon´ long chou)
Slavenka Drakulić	(slə ven´ kə dra kül´ ich)

Index of Authors and Titles

◆

535

(U.S.)

Canada

United States

Atlantic Ocean

Mexico

Puerto Rico

Haiti

Colombia

Pacific Ocean

Brazil

Chile

Only countries mentioned in
selections are labeled on this map.

Argentina